Giving Beyond the Gift

Giving Beyond the Gift

Apophasis and Overcoming Theomania

ELLIOT R. WOLFSON

FORDHAM UNIVERSITY PRESS   *New York* 2014

Library of Congress Cataloging-in-Publication Data

Wolfson, Elliot R.
    Giving beyond the gift : apophasis and overcoming theomania / Elliot R.
Wolfson. — First edition.
        pages cm
    Includes bibliographical references and index.
    ISBN 978-0-8232-5570-2 (cloth : alk. paper) —
    ISBN 978-0-8232-5571-9 (pbk. : alk. paper)
    1. Jewish philosophy—20th century.   I. Title.
    B5800.W65 2014
    181'.06—dc23   2013034990

Printed in the United States of America

16 15 14   5 4 3 2 1

First edition

To the blessed memory
of Michael A. Signer

Altissima quaeque flumina minimo sono labi

Even as the egomaniac does not live anything directly, whether it be a perception or an affection, but reflects on his perceiving or affectionate I and thus misses the truth of the process, thus the theomaniac . . . will not let the gift take full effect but reflects instead on that which gives, and misses both.
—Martin Buber, *I and Thou*

But where does the opening come from and how is it given? What speaks in the "It gives"?
—Martin Heidegger, "The End of Philosophy and the Task of Thinking"

CONTENTS

ACKNOWLEDGMENTS

First and foremost, I want to thank Helen Tartar for her abiding support over these many years. Since working with Helen on *Language, Eros, Being: Kabbalistic Hermeneutics and Poetic Imagination*, published by Fordham University Press in 2005, I have found her to be a steadfast friend and devoted editor. Beyond her commitment to my scholarship in particular, her deep aesthetic passion for the printed book more generally is an enduring source of inspiration and hope.

Second, I would like to acknowledge the sage advice for revision of the manuscript offered by Karmen MacKendrick and Aaron Hughes. I am appreciative of their willingness to sacrifice some of their valuable time to engage my work critically and to help improve the final version.

Finally, I express my heartfelt gratitude to Virginia Burrus, who repeatedly reminds me of the wisdom conveyed in the *Gospel of Philip*, "And whatever cannot receive certainly cannot give." More than any other human being I have encountered on the path of my life's journey, Virginia has taught me by example that receiving is indeed the most profound sense of giving. For the gift of her time I am eternally grateful.

Truths are illusions of which we have forgotten that they are illusions.

—Friedrich Nietzsche, *On Truth and Lying in a Non-Moral Sense*

In this book, I offer a philosophical examination of the themes of apophasis, transcendence, and immanence in a number of twentieth-century Jewish thinkers. The implications, however, go well beyond the specificity of this cultural formation. Consistent with all my work, in this study I delve deeply into one tradition out of the conviction that the particular is indexical of what we are still compelled to call the universal. Mindful of, and in some measure beholden to, the postmodern critique of foundationalism, let me be clear that there is no crypto-transcendentalism at work here, no appeal to what Lyotard called *les grand récits*, the "great stories" or "metanarratives," no recourse to an essentializing or totalizing truth, no positing an infinite transcendence or metaphysical absolute. Although inviolably committed to the truth that there is no inviolable truth, I nonetheless acknowledge the inherently contradictory and subversive repercussions of the relativist position: if meaning is always to be determined from context, in line with the historicizing hermeneutic that prevails in academic discourse, then the veracity of this assertion and the methodological presumption that ensues therefrom cannot be sufficiently generalized to justify the argument for contextualization. Simply put, without the ability to step out of context, we could not cultivate the cognitive apparatus necessary to detect the parameters of any context. Every statement avowing the relativity of truth can be true only if it is false.

My upholding of the universal is certainly not meant to efface the particular; indeed, the universal I envision is one continuously shaped by the particular, the *universal singularity*, to borrow the language of Alain Badiou,[1] and in that sense, the concrete is what is most abstract, the contingent the most unconditional, the exception the most inclusive. Operating with a tetralemmic logic informed by the middle way (*madhyamaka*) of the Mahāyāna tradition—A is A; A is not-A; A is both A and not-A; A is neither A nor not-A—the path of my thinking leads to the dialectical overcoming of the dialectical resolution of these binary oppositions,[2] and thus I resist (à la Hegel) both the universalization of the particular and the particularization of the universal. Closer to the cadence of our experience, in my opinion, is the recognition that the determinacy of the universal is always in the process of being determined by the indeterminacy that is the particular and that the indeterminacy of the particular is always in the process of being determined by the determinacy that is the universal. Following this line of reasoning, and in consonance with a relational rather than a substantialist notion of self, I assume that in the domain of intersubjectivity, too, we must say that one is veritably the singularity of oneself insofar as one is otherwise than oneself, that the exteriority of the interior—the homelessness that alights the way back home in the foreboding night of our solitude—is gauged by the interiority of the exterior, that individuality consists of embracing an alterity that is, at least qua potential, universalizable: the difference between us is what invariably makes us the same and therefore categorically not subject to the categorical.

The investigation that informs the inquiry to unfold in this book is impelled by the belief that a theolatrous impulse lingers in the very heart of monotheism, even when the latter is explicated in the apophatic idiom of philosophical theology, a trend that has become quite fashionable in the academy these last few decades. The extent to which the scriptural foundation of the monotheistic faiths may itself be considered idolatrous is a line of inquiry that has been explored by other scholars. To cite one relatively recent example: in his *Saving God: Religion after Idolatry*, Mark Johnston suggests that the "anthropocentric accretions" of the first verses of the Decalogue (Exodus 20:3–6) "may have already obscured the real nature of the Highest One, so that the original ban on idolatry is itself refracted through an idolatrous prism."[3] Striking a similar note in another passage, Johnston observes that the representations of Yahweh as vengeful and punitive appear to be "an idolatrous projection onto the Highest One of the insecurities associated with the patriarchal psychological structure of ancient Near Eastern tribal life."[4] This backsliding is not limited to Judaism. In Christianity and Islam, too, we can discern the "historical sediments of our collective resistance to True Divinity. The sacred scriptures often exhibit a self-incriminating character, in that they serve also to expose the idolatrous potential of even the ostensible true believers."[5]

Idolatry, in the most rudimentary sense, is the worship of graven images, but more expansively, the term connotes the spiritual materialism[6] that turns one's attention away from the supreme being, who is demarcated as the "wholly other," the "numinous One" that transcends all images, "toward supposed deities whose embodiment is under the influence or control of human beings."[7] Johnston's own desire to purge monotheism of this erroneous supernaturalism[8] is predicated on theological assumptions that are not only imposed on the scriptural portraits of God but also entangle him in the very web whence he wishes to escape.[9] Thus, in the beginning of the book he states the belief that colors the whole of his exposition: "God is transcendent; that is, God can come into view, if he comes into view at all, only as a result of his self-presentation."[10] For Johnston, there appears to be no contradiction in linking transcendence and self-presentation. But what is the nature of this "self" that presents itself as an essential feature of divine transcendence? Addressing the possibility of a clash between religion and science, or the appropriate worship of the divine and nature, Johnston asserts, "But that seems impossible, since the Highest One cannot require that we believe or act on falsehoods."[11] It is reasonable to hope that this is correct, but to assume that it is so either textually or philosophically implicates one in attributing a moral sense to God that reflects what we presume to be the standard of goodness.[12] As laudable as this might be, to say that "the Highest One is not indifferent to justice, and is not a perpetrator of evil"[13] is itself a form of anthropomorphizing that, strictly speaking, compromises the impenetrability of the supreme being.

Johnston argues that the legitimacy of the call of the "Most High" on us "does not derive from an awesome power to punish or reward us," but rather "only from the fact that the Most High is the true object of our ownmost wills, the very thing we obscurely desire in everything that we desire . . . In demanding that we be guided by his will, the Most High has to be calling us to express our own most enlightened and authentic willing. . . . The idolaters are *slaves* to their gods, while the worship of the Most High is the embrace of our own truest natures."[14] But are we any less enslaved to God if we believe that the worship of that God is the worship of our truest nature? To be sure, from Johnston's perspective, the ban on idolatry and the representational imaging of the divine occasion the "idea of the Most High as the one whose transcendence is just the other side of his immanence in this world. This world, properly seen, is the outpouring and self-disclosure that is the Highest One."[15]

I note, parenthetically, that I am not convinced of the accuracy of Johnston's presentation of the biblical views on divine transcendence and immanence. The tenor of the Hebrew Bible regarding these technical theological taxonomies is better captured by Yochanan Muffs:

> The use of the terms *immanent* and *transcendent* often serve to obfuscate the problem: God is not as much of this world as the term *immanent* would suggest, nor is He as out of the world as the term *transcendent* might indicate. God is both close and far. Even though He is not close in the sense that He is identified with the world, derived from it, or subject to it, He is intensely concerned with the people who live in the world, specifically with Israel. There is no doubt that God appears in the Bible as a person possessed with a wide range of emotions: concern, joy, sadness, regret, and chagrin, among many others.[16]

The problematic feature about idolatry is not the personification of the divine with multiple facets—the pagan belief in a plurality of deities is converted over time in ancient Israel to the point that YHWH becomes, as it were, "a whole pantheon in Himself"[17]—but rather the assumption that there is a sphere of reality above the divine and to which it is subject against its own volition.[18]

Notwithstanding my reservations regarding Johnston's manner of construing the distinction between transcendence and immanence, I will accept it for the sake of the discussion. The shortcoming of his argument is that to think or to speak of a transcendence that exceeds natural phenomena augments the imaginative representation of that transcendence as an aspect of immanence. To view the world as the kenosis of a transempirical absolute Being—all that we experience in the cosmos allegedly is what God is not, inasmuch as the divine being is other than worldly being and thus can only be present as absent, appearing as what cannot appear except by not appearing—confirms the ascription of an unassimilable alterity to the transcendence. However, the plausibility of this claim is severely challenged by the conjecture that divine transcendence is imagined as the *other side* of divine immanence in the world. At best, therefore, the transcendent can assume the status of a relative other, that is, an other in relation to the same, indeed, the mirror opposite or shadow phantom of the same, the exteriorization of the interior that can be ascertained phenomenally only as the interiorization of the exterior; immanence, we might say, assumes the status of convexity vis-à-vis the concavity of transcendence. Even agnostic claims that all we can know is that we cannot know and apophatic utterances that all we can speak is that we cannot speak are, in the last analysis, self-refuting human fabrications—they are true only if untrue and untrue only if true.

Here it is apposite to recall the observation of Jean-Luc Nancy that the enduring legacy of monotheism is "the fact that divine unicity is the correlate of a presence that can no longer be given in this world but rather must be sought beyond it (the presence in this world being that of an 'idol,' the rejection of which is no doubt the great generation and federating motif of the threefold Abrahamic traditions)."[19] If one attends to Nancy's words carefully, one is led to the unsettling realization that "monotheism is in truth atheism," which is to say, the aniconic ramification of the monotheistic creed is the undoing and demythologization of theism.[20] As Nancy puts it elsewhere:

> the unique *thēos*, deprived of appearance [*figure*] and name, really represents an invention, even the invention, of "god" in general. There is neither "the god" nor "the divine," nor even perhaps "the gods": these do not come first or, again, they do not quite exist so long as there are the people or the species of immortal figures. . . . We must therefore suppose that the invention of "atheism" is contemporaneous and correlative with the invention of "theism." Both terms, in effect, have their unity in the principal paradigm or premise [*paradigme principiel*].[21]

In another work, Nancy went so far as to say that post-ontotheological attempts to locate the divine in the "difference" between beings, as opposed to in the "fullness of metaphysical being," fail because "far from being rediscovered, God disappears even more surely and definitively through bearing all the names of a generalized and multiplied difference. Monotheism dissolves into polyatheism, and it is no good asserting that this polyatheism is the true word and the true presence of God in his distance from the supreme Being of metaphysics. For the infinitely absent god, or the god infinitely distended by the infinite distance of god, should no longer be termed 'God,' nor be presented in any way as 'God' or as divine."[22]

Counterintuitively, monotheism is not correlated antithetically to polytheism as multiplicity is to unity. The unique God is not simply the "reunion," "subsumption," or "spiritualization" of multiple gods under one unifying principle. The pairing of monotheism ideationally with polyatheism stems from the fact that both terms signify the "absenting of presence,"[23] which is not to say an absence that is "the negative of a presence" but rather an absence that is "the *nihil* that opens and that disposes itself as the space of all presence,"[24] that is, the withdrawal that fosters the engendering of the nothing that is the substrate of being, the nihility that makes creation possible.[25] In Nancy's own terms:

> Mono-theism or a-theism is thus a complete metamorphosis of divinity and origin. Nothing is given any longer, except that alone which is still given . . . . It is the gift offered by the unique God, but if this gift is still given from one side . . . it cannot be reduced to that state: it is more properly giving, it is the very act of gift and in this act the singular history according to which the human being—and with it all "creatures"—is a partner more than a simple recipient of divine action (for to receive the gift is part of the gift itself) is engaged. . . . Creation forms, then, a nodal point in a "deconstruction of monotheism," insofar as such a deconstruction proceeds from monotheism itself, and perhaps is its most active resource. The unique God, whose unicity is the correlate of the creating act, cannot precede its creation any more than it can subsist above it or apart from it in some way. It merges with it: merging with it, it withdraws in it, and withdrawing there it empties itself there, emptying itself it is nothing other than the opening of the void. Only the opening is divine, but the divine is nothing more than the opening.[26]

The ensuing chapters will grapple with the extent to which the discernment that the final iconoclastic achievement of monotheism calls for destroying the idol of the very God personified as the deity that must be worshipped without being idolized. As Henri Atlan deftly expressed the paradox, "the ultimate idol is the personal God of theology . . . the only discourse about God that is not idolatrous is necessarily an atheistic discourse. Alternatively, whatever the discourse, the only God who is not an idol is a God who is not a God."[27] Several of the twentieth-century Jewish thinkers to be discussed, to wit, Hermann Cohen, Martin Buber, Franz Rosenzweig, and Emmanuel Levinas, were all keenly aware of the pitfalls of scriptural theism and the penchant of the human imagination to conjure false representations of transcendence, and yet, in differing degrees, they each gave in to the temptation of personifying that transcendence, even as they tried either to circumvent or to restrain it by apophatically purging the kataphatic descriptions of the deity. By contrast, Jacques Derrida and Edith Wyschogrod, the other two Jewish thinkers treated at length in this book, were able to carry the project of dénégation one step further. Despite their many differences, they both embarked on a path that culminated in the aporetic suspension of belief. Unlike Cohen, Buber, Rosenzweig, and Levinas, Derrida and Wyschogrod were prepared to thrust aside the authority of tradition, and, as a consequence, they accepted the fate of social dislocation and political estrangement, occupying a place that is no place, nomadically adrift without any discernible lifeline to be reanchored in a specific liturgical community.

Derrida and Wyschogrod well understood that the removal of all images from God, if maintained unfailingly, seriously compromises the viability of devotional piety. To deplete God of the anthropomorphic and anthropopathic embellishments decisively curtails the imagination's ability to concoct the deity in personalist terms. If we retain the use of theological terms, they should be viewed, according to the formulation of Carl Raschke, as "pure *semiotic formalisms*." In a manner comparable to mathematical postulates or scientific models, religious concepts form an ensemble of signs that contribute to the structuring of a virtual as opposed to an actual reality. The experience of a theistic God, therefore, can be delineated as a "particular *event horizon*," which is perceived as "eminently real," but it can never materialize with the sensual concreteness of observable data. Indeed, the horizon established by this eventality—as vividly as it may present itself to human imagination—is best depicted as a territory that is peculiarly not a territory, a territory beyond all territorialization, the margin to which we are propelled by attunement to the surpassing of language through language.[28] Lest there be any misunderstanding, let me emphasize that the metalinguistic nonphenomenon of which I speak does not imply the positing of an ineffable alterity but rather the denial thereof; words beget words in an endlessly extending chain of signifiers that is not bound by any transcendental signified at either termini, an endless succession of metonymic replacements and metaphoric substitutions.

The undercurrent of this book is the recognition of the codependency of religion and idolatry. Contrary to what is commonly held to be the theological import of monotheism and the greatest contribution of ancient Israel and later Judaism to the history of religion, the turning toward God is not a turning away from idol images. The following portrayal of Judaism from the *Dialectic of Enlightenment* by Max Horkheimer and Theodor Adorno can be taken as exemplary of this sentiment: "It places all hope in the prohibition on invoking falsity as God, the finite as the infinite, the lie as truth. The pledge of salvation lies in the rejection of any faith which claims to depict it, knowledge in the denunciation of illusion."[29] These critical theorists of the Frankfurt School were able to affirm such an excessive aniconism, for they were not concerned with justifying the perpetuation of Judaism as a living community of practice and belief. If, however, one were to evaluate the situation from that standpoint, then it would be transparent that the vibrancy of faith is not sustainable without the veracity of deception; that is to say, all propositional utterances about God, even apophatic statements of what God is not, are not only ambiguous and hyperbolic but, literally speaking, fictitious as they attempt to describe linguistically the indescribable and to delimit conceptually the illimitable. As Avishai Margalit and Moshe Halbertal observed:

> Idolatry can thus be formulated in a kind of general rule: "any nonabsolute value that is made absolute and demands to be the center of dedicated life is idolatry." . . . The internal logic of this general formulation "nothing human can be made absolute," as the core of the understanding of idolatry, threatens to include all complements of idolatry as idolatry, even the worthy God. If the knowledge of the worthy God is ultimately channeled through humans, then it cannot itself be made absolute. . . . What will stand in opposition to idolatry will not be any sense of absolute but the freedom from absolutes and the denial of ultimates; extension reaches its extreme limit.[30]

To define the opposition to idolatry as the denial of ultimates implies that one can entertain no thought about God that is not an idolatrous representation. The freedom of absolutes thus relativizes any and every theological pronouncement.

In this spirit, Simone Weil famously wrote, "Idolatry comes from the fact that, while thirsting for absolute good, we do not possess the power of supernatural attention and we have not the patience to allow it to develop. . . . Idolatry is thus a vital necessity in the cave. Even with the best of us it is inevitable that it should set narrow limits for mind and heart."[31] The rejection of idolatry is not achieved solely by affirming the belief in one God; it demands avoiding the Satanic temptation of the imagination[32] to falsify the deity by treating the relative as absolute, the earthly as heavenly, the visible as invisible, a tendency to which the ancient Israelites were especially susceptible.[33] In a blatantly hostile tone, Weil writes that idolatry is "in large measure a fiction of Jewish fanaticism," for it was the cruel followers of the "cult of Yahweh" who imputed to other peoples the crime of idolatry even though they were monotheists. Weil surmises that if the "Hebrews of the good old days" were resuscitated, they would reproach Christians for being idolaters, "taking Christ to be Baal and the Virgin to be Ashteroth." Following Colossians 3:5, Weil identifies the root of idolatry as lust, which she interprets as the "thirst for carnal goodness," and in the case of the Jews, this is expressed in their ethnocentrism: "The Hebrews had for idols, not metal or wood, but a race, a nation, something just as worldly. Their religion is in essence inseparable from such idolatry, because of their notion of the 'elect (chosen) people.'"[34]

To rectify the idolatrous nature of faith, one must reclaim kenosis on the part of the divine, the annihilation, or in Weil's terminology, the decreation that results in the spectacle of incarnation, and the corresponding self-abasement on the part of the human, the disincarnation that results from the pietistic ideal of renunciation, detachment from desire, and purging the mind of all images. To be faithful to Christ, therefore, it is necessary to experience "faithfulness *in the void*,"[35] to contemplate the inscrutable mystery that the "void is the supreme plenitude"—a mystery so sublime that even "Christ himself, for an instant, was completely without knowledge of it"— for only in this way can one discern the further paradox that the world both manifests and hides the divine, not sequentially but concurrently, that is, the divine is manifest in the world by being hidden and hidden by being manifest.[36] God is most present in the absence of God,[37] and hence, ironically, it is feasible to speak of institutionalized religion as a "hindrance to true faith" whereas atheism heralds the purification of the notion of God and the awakening of the supernatural part of the soul to the realization that the utter dissimilarity between God and all other beings imparts theological meaning to the statement that God does not exist.[38] Adopting a paradoxical logic typical of mystical intuition,[39] Weil maintains that belief in God involves the denial of God insofar as subservience to the true God is predicated on the refusal to worship images of a false God. Reminiscent of Meister Eckhart's notorious invocation, "I pray to God to make me free of God,"[40] Weil remarked that the highest form of prayer is "to pray to God . . . with the thought that God does not exist."[41]

The argument I am advancing can be profitably compared to the thesis recently proffered by Gideon Freudenthal in his *No Religion without Idolatry: Mendelssohn's Jewish Enlightenment*. Extrapolating from the specific case of Mendelssohn, Freudenthal makes a more general claim for this codependency based on his analysis of the semiotic role of the religious symbol. Summarizing his thesis, Freudenthal writes that "religion consists in the tension between Enlightenment and myth or idolatry. In a religious community, these interdependent poles may be represented by more and less enlightened and idolatrous members of a community. This structure of a community often corresponds to the ambiguity in its practitioners' minds, who either combine idolatrous and enlightened views or consciously or unconsciously waver between them."[42] Religion, in other words, cannot exist without idolatry insofar as it must comprise mythical symbols as a complement to the criterion of reason dictated by the principles of the enlightenment.[43] Freudenthal thus concludes provocatively that idolatry is a "necessary component of religion. Without idolatry religion would dissolve."[44] My own investigations of the dialogical philosophies of Judaism in the twentieth century, epitomized by Cohen, Buber, Rosenzweig, and continued in his own manner by Levinas,[45] corroborate this basic insight into the phenomenology of religious experience.

Jean-Luc Marion has similarly argued, albeit from a different theoretical framework informed by the history of Christian-Neoplatonic negative theology, that if the deity is beyond all description, then any kataphatic statement of belief would be an apophatic gesture of unbelief, indeed the undoing of monotheism, since one would have to believe in the depictions of God that one could not believe in on the notional grounds that they are illusory appearances of the inapparent, which can appear only as that which cannot appear. Insofar as incomprehensibility belongs to the "formal definition" of God, any attempt to envisage God theologically subjects God to a finite conception that is idolatry.[46] The biblical tenet regarding the invisibility of God (Exodus 33:23; John 1:18) implies not only that "nothing finite can bear his glory without perishing" but also that "a God that could be conceptually comprehended would no longer bear the title 'God.' . . . The idolatry of the concept is the same as that of the gaze: imagining oneself to have attained God and to be capable of maintaining him under our gaze, like a thing of the world."[47] Revelation of the divine thus consists of being disabused of this blasphemous illusion and fathoming that vision entails seeing that one cannot see, apprehending that one cannot apprehend. For this very reason not only is a kataphatic theology problematic but a phenomenology of religion is an impossibility—the phenomenon to be investigated under the rubric of religious experience is simply not available to human consciousness.[48] In the final chapter, I will discuss in more detail the philosophical tenability of Marion's insistence that a denominative or nonpredicative theology[49]—the *theology of absence*, "where the name is given as having no name, as not giving the essence, and having nothing but this absence to make manifest"[50]—would necessitate that we substitute praise for predication[51] and the further supposition that this praise directs the worshipper to the one whose name cannot be said, even negatively, but which calls to the worshipper, the vocative name that serves as a signpost for the indecipherable giver of "the gift of the name above all names," an obvious allusion to God's bestowing the name upon Jesus according to Philippians 2:9.[52] For the present purposes what is important to underscore is that the "apophatic anti-metaphysics"[53] implicit in Marion's thinking renders any positive description of God fallacious, and ideally, this should include the paradoxical statement—indeed the paradox of paradoxes, which he presumes "traverses the entirety of Christian theology," including such figures as Justin Martyr, Athenagoras, Clement of Alexandria, Origen, Athanasius, Gregory of Nyssa, Dionysius the Areopagite, John Chrysostom, John of Damascus, Augustine, Bernard of Clairvaux, and Thomas Aquinas[54]—that "God is known only as unknown" (*Dieu ne se connaît que comme inconnu*).[55]

Arguing a compatible position with regard to contemporary Christian praxis, Peter Rollins has written:

> This recognition of hyper-presence leads us to consider the traditional atheism/
> theism opposition, for if our beliefs necessarily fall short of that which they
> attempt to describe, then it would seem that a certain atheistic spirit is actually
> embedded within Christianity. . . . Yet the atheistic spirit within Christianity
> delves much deeper . . . for we disbelieve not only in other gods but also in the
> God that we believe in. As we have seen, we ought to affirm our view of God while
> at the same realizing that that view is inadequate. Hence we act as both theist and
> atheist. The a/theism is not some agnostic middle hovering hesitantly between
> theism and atheism but, rather, actively embraces both out of a profound faith.
> Just as Christianity does not rest between transcendence and immanence but holds
> both extremes simultaneously, so too it holds atheism and theism together in the
> cradle of faith.[56]

Rollins succinctly captures a trend that has dominated the philosophical theologies that have proliferated in recent times based in no small measure on reclaiming the long and venerated tradition of negative theology, a mode of thinking—or unthinking, as the case may be—that allows for the persistent negation of what is affirmed about God, since in saying the unsayable one continually unsays what is said. The gist of this book is to move beyond positing the agnostic middle, wherein theism and atheism continue to function as the handles of the cradle of faith,[57] or as Richard Kearney analogously expresses the matter, the middle space of anatheism, "where theism dialogues freely with atheism," a "third space" in which the "wagering between belief and nonbelief" continues without resolution.[58] The openness of the middle I seek—the middle excluded by the logic of the excluded middle—cannot be circumscribed by a "radical and recurring sense of something *more*—something ulterior, extra, and unexpected," the "infinite Other incarnate in finite others."[59] The chiasm of the space between should be characterized neither by the presence of absence nor by the absence of presence. The logic of apophasis, if permitted to run its course without the intervention of preexisting beliefs, would surpass the metaphysical dyad of presence and absence in the atheological unmasking of the mask and the consequent transcending of the need to posit some form of transcendence that is not ultimately a facet of immanence, a something more that is not in fact merely another expression of the totality of what there is, provided we understand that totality as the network of indefinite and ever-evolving patterns of interconnectivity rather than a fixed system of predictable and quantifiable data. Within that network it makes no sense to speak of an infinite other extrinsic to and incarnate in finite others; alterity is the intrinsic corollary of the diffusion of the same, the otherness at the horizon of phenomenality marked always by the sense of there being more, and therefore fewer, lived experiences that manifest the interrelatedness and interdependence of the phenomena that together constitute the multiverse.

The reliance on apophaticism has emerged in recent times as the catalyst and justification for the erection of idols of that which is beyond idolization. The naming of this namelessness is, as Thomas Altizer argued, an inherently theological naming even if it is presented under the guise of what he considers the "purest illusion" of the atheological.[60] The modern anonymous subject, who has experienced the depth of the abyss of nothingness, "can only know an anonymous God, and therefore a totally nameless God. This naming of namelessness is nevertheless a genuine naming, a naming of an ultimate and final anonymity, and thus a naming of the anonymous God."[61] Our paths diverge, however, insofar as I do not subscribe to a dialectic by which absolute negation passes into absolute affirmation, so that Nietzsche's proclamation about the death of God can be transformed into the hope for resurrection and the silence of God be broken by a new attempt to speak the name of God.[62] As Altizer put it in "America and the Future of Theology" (1963), the Christian faith that accepts the death of God is "called upon to negate all *religious* meaning, but it is the very radical nature of this negative movement which can prepare the way for the deepest epiphany of faith."[63] Reiterating the point in "Theology and the Death of God" (1964), Altizer wrote:

Dialectically, the opposites coincide, radical negation has become radical affirmation; but if the negative movement is a denial of God, then the positive movement must finally be an affirmation of God, of the God beyond the Christian God, beyond the God of the historic Church, beyond all which Christendom has known as God. A truly dialectical image of God (or of the Kingdom of God) will appear only after the most radical negation, just as a genuinely eschatological form of faith can now be reborn only upon the grave of the God who is the symbol of the transcendence of Being. . . . The transcendence of Being has been transformed into the radical immanence of Eternal Recurrence: to exist in our time is to exist in a chaos freed of every semblance of cosmological meaning or order. . . . Therefore the dissolution of the "being" of the world has made possible the renewal of the stance of eschatological faith; for an ultimate and final No-saying to the world can dialectically pass into the Yes-saying of eschatological faith.[64]

   The dialectical vocation to which Altizer is drawn—and I see no evidence that he has wavered from this position through the long durée of his career—induces the "scandal" of the *coincidentia oppositourm* such that the Yes can become a No and the No, a Yes, not by way of conflation but by juxtaposition,[65] the disappearance of the very possibility of difference in the nonidentity of the identity of opposites; that is, opposites are identical in virtue of their opposition.[66] Altizer's language pushes at the limits of reason to articulate an apocalyptic understanding of the "uniquely modern nihilism" in which the Nihil finally stands forth as the Nihil of an immanence that affords no resort to transcendence. Only through this absolute self-sacrifice and absolute self-negation "does the purely negative pole or potency of the Godhead become fully actual and real, and actual and real in ultimate disjunction from its own polar contrary. Only now do the negative and the positive poles of the Godhead become actual as true opposites, and opposites in ultimate opposition to each other. Thus, as wholly opposed to what the mystic knows as the absolute nothingness of primordial Godhead, this pure and absolute negativity is an absolutely alien negativity or an absolutely alien absolute nothingness."[67] The transfiguring power of this absolute negativity "impels a radical movement away from that very actuality which is a necessary consequence of the absolute sacrifice of the Godhead, or that actuality which in full modernity realizes itself as an absolute immanence . . . that is the necessary consequence of the pure reversal of an absolute transcendence. . . . The very advent of immanence is inseparable from the realization of the full and actual emptiness of absolute transcendence, an emptiness that is a truly alien emptiness, and one which is realized as the Nihil itself."[68] Inasmuch as the dialectical form of faith can never dissociate affirmation and negation—illustrated most dramatically in Altizer's admission that his "deepest theological goal" was to discover the coincidence of Satan and Jesus,[69] a quest, no doubt, imbued with a Blakean spirit[70]—the demise of transcendence is as much a source of suffering as it is a source of salvation; the crucifixion is itself the resurrection. Altizer thus speaks of the "ultimate breakthrough" predicated on understanding that the "absolute nothingness" of the Godhead entails an "absolute transfiguration of itself," but the latter "is only actually possible by way of a transfiguration of absolutely opposite poles or polarities, only when these opposites are fully and actually real could this transfiguration occur. These are the full opposites which pass into each other in an absolute transfiguration, and all deep and genuine dialectical thinking and vision incorporates such a transfiguration."[71]

Altizer's unwavering resolve to insist that in our nihilistic epoch the mandate of radical theology must be to name God as the unnameable is surely deserving of praise for its courage and candor. From my perspective, however, the radical theology of Altizer, much as the postmodern apophatic theologies that have dominated the marketplace of ideas within the academy, is still guilty of *theomania*, a term that I deploy, following the sense implied in the passage from Buber that serves as one of the epigraphs of this book, not to denote a delusional state wherein one believes oneself to be God but rather a relentless and maddening obsession for transcendence, even if the latter is construed as a negative presence, that is, a presence that is present only as the absence of presence. I thus concur with Mark C. Taylor's moving encomium:

> Thomas J. J. Altizer is the last theologian. As such, he is the most God-obsessed person I have ever known. To speak—truly to *speak*—with Altizer is to encounter a passion the excess of which borders on madness. . . . This is, of course, no ordinary madness; nor is it literal. The madness that pursues Altizer while he is pursuing it is a holy madness. For those blessed with holy madness, the foolishness of the world can only be overcome by reversing it in a higher madness that negates what others affirm and affirms what others negate.[72]

To the extent that the encounter with the darkness that emerges from the disbanding of transcendence—the nihilism that Altizer identifies with apocalypticism[73]—dialectically yields the resurgence of light, there is the peril of its reification as a mental idol confabulated in the imagination, even if, and perhaps especially so, what is idolized is the darkness itself, personified as Satan. The following depiction of Blake offered by Altizer could easily be applied to himself: "Blake was the first Christian atheist, and his atheism was born out of a hatred of repression and a joyous response to a new and universal epiphany of Jesus. But he was no atheist in the ordinary sense; he knew that the Christian God is every bit as real as the reality of repression, that the sovereignty and transcendence of God is created by the Fall, and that this wholly other God has died to make possible the advent of the Apocalypse."[74] Rather than fleeing from death—a characteristic that Altizer associates with Gnosticism—the task of radical theology is to confront the unspeakability of death, the abyss that does not call forth "a proclamation of the name of Christ" but "the absence of the nameability of Christ . . . indeed, the absence of all nameability whatsoever, an absence that is a necessary and inevitable absence for a full and total apocalyptic enactment."[75] Altizer's theological voyage and his unique interpretation of the incarnational trope of the kenosis of God that is the self-negation of heavenly transcendence[76]—the naming that is concomitantly an unnaming, the silence that reverberates in the totally present absence of the totally absent presence of speech[77]— has steered him to the place where he can brazenly assert that "the most actual name of God for us is truly the name of Satan. Each of us knows and speaks that name, and we speak it in truly or actually naming our darkness."[78] Needless to say, by the paradoxical logic that pertains to the absolute transfiguration of the absolute apocalypse, in naming the darkness, one names the light, since the darkness is, in the final analysis, naught but a more intense illumination of the light.

Altizer's laborious and unremitting attempt to name the unnamable and thereby reveal the divine presence in absence is, as Taylor rightly noted, a rending of the veil of God's invisibility, which is not to say making the invisible visible but rather making visible the fact that God is currently occluded and therefore not visually accessible except as nonvisible.[79] To cite Altizer's own words again: "Yes, the primary calling of the theologian is to name God, and to name that God who can actually be named by us, and if this calling has seemingly now ended, that could be because the theologian has not yet truly named our darkness, and thus not yet truly named God. While silence is now the primary path of the theologian, and above all silence about God, this is a silence which I have ever more deeply and ever more comprehensively refused, for I am simply incapable of not naming God."[80] It seems to me that in this effort to make the invisibility of transcendence visible, Altizer remains shackled by the metaphysics he thinks he has overthrown, since the invisible continues to be conceived as a presence that presents itself as nonpresent.

The relevance of my misgiving is brought into sharp relief when we consider Altizer's endeavor to commingle his radical Christian theology and Mahāyāna Buddhism around the theme of absolute nothingness or the self-emptying emptiness.[81] The earnestness of this undertaking notwithstanding, there is a critical difference in the two systems of thought that cannot be ignored. According to the former, no matter how radical or postmodern, the yearning to name the nothingness as God bespeaks the fact that the theologian remains committed to a belief in presence, even if that presence is experienced as absence, whereas according to the latter, there is no such belief, for there is neither a presence that is absent nor an absence that is present.[82] In fairness, it must be noted that Altizer frequently demonstrates that he is acutely aware of the fact that the Western concept of a theistic God cannot be readily translated into a Buddhist terminological register, and thus there is an unbridgeable difference, as we see, for example, from this observation: "Now, and for the first time in the West, an absolute Nothing is fully realized in thinking and in the imagination, and unlike every Eastern vision of an absolute nothingness, this is a Nihil which is actually and historically real, manifest and real not only in the depths of interiority but in the depths of history itself, depths calling forth a truly new Godhead, and a Godhead for the first time manifest as absolute evil."[83] Closer to the point is the following passage where the source of absolute compassion in Christianity and Buddhism are distinguished:

> But Christianity knows that reality as the depths of the Godhead, a Godhead wholly absent in Buddhism, and far more deeply absent in Buddhism than in any other religious way or tradition. Perhaps nothing is so distinctive about Buddhism than is this absence, and an absence that is not simply an absence or an eclipse of God, but far rather an absence precluding the very possibility of the presence of God, and precluding it in its own deepest power and depths. Yet Buddhism is surely not atheistic, and not atheistic because here there is no negation of God, nor even the possibility of the negation of God, for ultimately in Buddhism there is no negation whatsoever. . . . While the Christian might be baffled or offended at the absence of God in Buddhist thinking, an absence fully realized in the deepest and purest expressions of Buddhist thinking, such an absence of even a trace of pure transcendence is surely inseparable from the very purity of Buddhist thinking, which is wholly closed to the very possibility of apprehending an essential and intrinsic "other," and therefore closed to the possibility of being open to the essential and final transcendence of God.[84]

In spite of being mindful of the crucial disparity, Altizer is committed to the possibility that precisely because Buddhism lacks a theistic conception, the comparative approach can open a "universal ground" that will reinvigorate Christian theology with a deeper understanding of the kenotic dimensions of the crucifixion.[85] As he put it in his theological memoir, "a Buddhist horizon makes possible this apocalyptic understanding, and above all so a Buddhist understanding of an absolute nothingness or an absolute void, apart from which apocalypse is a meaningless surd."[86] What is critical about the amalgamation of Buddhism and Christianity, then, is that the identity of opposites, which is most purely realized inwardly in the former, can be actualized outwardly in the latter.[87]

While I accept that the dialectic affirmed by Altizer implies that the absolute negation of the absolute transcendence results in the transformation of the latter into absolute immanence—and thus the theological truth he wishes to retrieve is perforce an atheistic denial of the wholly other God[88]—I would counter that the transformation precludes the prospect of the absolute immanence dissolving the absolute transcendence absolutely, since the dictate of the *coincidentia oppositorum* is such that, in the locution cited above, opposites must be in ultimate opposition to each other and hence everything always contains its own other. In his appropriation and recasting of the Buddhist teaching, in no small measure following the lead of Japanese philosophers of the Kyoto school like Nishida Kitaro and Nishitani Keiji,[89] Altizer surmises that the transcendence of God is apprehended as the self-negation of an absolute nothingness—rendered symbolically as the death of God—that is the absolute presence and absolute absence at once; the incarnation of the kenotic Christ is a self-negation of this original self-negation.[90] The move to construct what Altizer called a "pure theology"[91] based on the hybrid of Buddhism and Christianity is doubtlessly culturally significant, but it effaces the deeper contribution of the Buddhist doctrine of nothingness as a meontology that transcends the polarities of transcendence and immanence, being and nonbeing, emptiness and fullness. That Altizer himself grasped this fundamental point is evident from his depiction of Buddhist enlightenment as the awareness of "an absence which is the is-notness of isness, or the pure nothingness of pure isness, a *coincidentia oppositorum* in which no opposites are actually present, for here there is no distance or distinction between is and is not. If that is a pure emptiness which is a pure fullness, it is full precisely by being empty, and hence there can be no actualization of emptiness, and no act which enacts anything whatsoever."[92] Or, as he put it elsewhere, "Buddhism can only know a primordial origin, an origin which is the very opposite of an actual origin, and thus an origin which voids the very possibility of an actual origin. That is a voiding which is the voiding of the very possibility of an actual nothingness."[93] If one follows the Buddhist path of annihilation, the negation is itself negated in the negation of the negation—the void voided in the voiding that is the void—and thus there is no reason to propose a negation to negate the negation.

I find myself once more in agreement with Taylor's contention that the theology of Altizer is haunted by the impossibility of theology, the realization that the move beyond darkness implies that there is no beyond to which to move.[94] The only way to be faithful to Altizer's Christian atheism and apocalyptic nihilism, therefore, is to betray it, for the death of God reaches fruition when we forget what it is that we have forgotten, a twofold oblivion that signals the end of theology and not the possibility of its rejuvenation. "As long as the specter of God haunts the world, the kenotic process that Altizer, following Hegel, charts remains unfinished. . . . For the 'No' of world negation to be negated and nihilism to be complete, we must say 'Yes' to the nothingness and emptiness hiding in the utter ordinariness and banality of contemporary culture."[95]

Along similar lines, I would contend that the apophatic theologies, as influential as they have been in forging a new synthesis of philosophy and religion, likewise should be supplanted by a more far-reaching apophasis, an apophasis of the apophasis, based on the acceptance of an absolute nothingness—to be distinguished from the nothingness of an absolute—that does not signify the unknowable One but the manifold that is the pleromatic abyss at being's core, the negation devoid of the negation of its negation, a triple negativity, the emptiness of the fullness that is the fullness of the emptiness emptied of the emptiness of its emptiness. On this score, the much-celebrated metaphor of the gift would give way to the more neutral and less theologically charged notion of an irreducible and unconditional givenness in which the distinction between giver and given collapses. To think givenness in its most elemental phenomenological sense is to allow the apparent to appear as given without presuming a causal agency that would turn that given into a gift. It is, as Derrida once wrote, to receive the improbable "grace" of clearing oneself of the double bind "of the gift, of the given gift, of giving itself."[96] I offer this book as a token of this improbable grace, an act of giving beyond the gift.

Imagination and the Prism of the Inapparent

> Look deeply into relativity and harmonize things accordingly.
> This will be a convenient way to the gate of truth.
>
> —Hung Ying-ming, *The Unencumbered Spirit*

In *Force of Imagination: The Sense of the Elemental*, John Sallis observed that "philosophy was always compelled also to exclude imagination, to set it at a distance, and even to reserve a refuge in which finally there would be protection from the threat of imagination. The dynamics of the relation of philosophy to imagination remained one of ambivalence and, though a semblance of reconciliation, even appropriation, was repeatedly made to veil the tension, it invariably broke out again in new guises."[1]

That philosophers have looked upon the imagination with suspicion is understandable. By obfuscating the boundary between reality and illusion, it is more liable to lure one into erroneous belief and impetuous behavior. The mimetic nature of imagination was understood by Plato as a sophistic attempt to imitate truth, which can be compared to the erecting of idols that are deemed false copies of reality, simulacra no more enduring than images in the mirror. From that vantage point, imagination would seem to represent philosophy's quintessential and unassimilable other, the faculty that needs to be expunged or, at the very least, marginalized. Countering that aversion, philosophers have also recognized that in the absence of imagination, there is no memory, and in the absence of memory, there is no perception or cognition. The more positive valence accorded the imagination can be traced to Aristotle, who agreed with his teacher that this faculty is for the most part fallacious but insisted nevertheless that there can be no thinking without images.

It obviously lies beyond the parameters of this introduction to offer a satisfactory review of a topic so manifold, intricate, and tangled.[2] For the purposes of the ensuing analysis, however, let me begin the tale with the major shift in orientation that occurs with Immanuel Kant. In the *Critique of Pure Reason*, Kant described human perception as a complex process that requires reason, sensation, and imagination; the latter is the hidden condition of all knowledge inasmuch as it is the mental power of figurative synthesis that fosters the interaction between the sensible and the intelligible to produce the very possibility of our experience.[3] The primary German word that Kant used to name the transcendental faculty of imagination, *Einbildungskraft*, was decoded by the likes of Hegel and Schelling as *Ineinsbildung*, that is, the power of forming a unified whole out of an indefinite multiplicity,[4] a process that Derrida accurately called the "cotranslatibility" that "marks the unity of the imagination . . . and of reason."[5] As Kant emphasized time and again, experience is the continual conjoining of perceptions. Without the synthetic function of the imagination there would be no internal coherence and hence no unity of consciousness to bridge concept and sensibility in the formation of external objects through the reproducibility of appearances. In Kant's own words: "Synthesis in general is . . . the mere effect of the imagination, of a blind though indispensable function of the soul, without which we would have no cognition at all, but of which we are seldom even conscious."[6] In the absence of imagination there would be nothing but the "blind play of representations" to which may be ascribed an eidetic magnitude that is "less than a dream."[7]

As Sallis has pointed out, "the installing of imagination at the origin of the gathering of reason" on the part of Kant entails an "encroachment of imagination upon reason" that threatened and undermined the "autonomy of reason." The imagination is accorded the "essential role in bringing forth those transcendental ideas," a "task to which reason unmixed with imagination is unequal." But once reason is mixed with imagination, reason is subverted, corrupted, and perverted. The subversive power of this encroachment is best gauged "by thematizing the relevant terms with respect to the opposition between presence and absence." Whereas reason and intuition are directed to the thing presumed to be present and thereby attempt to recover what is sensibly immediate, imagination is the faculty that represents in intuition an object that is not present. Summarizing Kant's point, Sallis notes that "the imagination irreducibly mixes presence and absence. It makes present something essentially absent, something which is not (as with intuition) recoverable by recourse to a more originary making-present." The image brought forth by the imagination makes what is presumed to be the "original" present by letting it remain absent.[8] This idea was to have major repercussions, leading eventually to the Heideggerian interpretation of the essence of truth as the unconcealment that "discloses and at the same time conceals," indeed, the mystery that is the "concealing of what is concealed."[9] In Chapter 3, I will discuss Heidegger's notion of thinking/saying in greater detail, but suffice it here to underscore that the nonrepresentational sense of truth articulated by him, a truth that comprises untruth as intrinsic to the nature of its nonshowing—the essential turn that moves us along the way to the phenomenology of the nonphenomenalizable—has its roots in the critical role that Kant assigned to the imaginative faculty.[10]

The Romantic celebration of the creative force of human imagination as the locus of the physical world is a direct outcome of the Kantian emphasis on the reproductive capacity of the imagination and the subservient position assigned to reason.[11] One of the better-known formulations of this idealization is Fichte's audacious claim that "all reality . . . is brought forth solely by imagination . . . this act of imagination forms the basis for the possibility of our consciousness, our life, our existence for ourselves, that is, our existence as selves."[12] To say that *all reality is brought forth by the imagination* is obviously attributing to that faculty a potency that would not only distinguish humans from all other sentient beings but also confer on them a demiurgic quality. Through the exercise of imagination we not only gain knowledge of the world but also impart shape to it, which bestows on us the sense of self without which we would have no fulcrum to determine the sense of the other. In his epic narrative poem *Milton*, William Blake succinctly expressed this sentiment, "The Imagination is not a State: it is the Human Existence itself."[13] The potentially infinite reach of the imaginative capacity through the act of poiesis is precisely the property that delineates the boundaries of human finitude. As Samuel Taylor Coleridge put it:

> The IMAGINATION then I consider either as primary, or secondary. The primary IMAGINATION I hold to be the living Power and prime Agent of all human Perception, and as a repetition in the finite mind of the eternal act of creation in the infinite I AM. The secondary I consider as an echo of the former, co-existing with the conscious will, yet still as identical with the primary in the *kind* of its agency, and differing only in *degree*, and in the *mode* of its operation. It dissolves, diffuses, dissipates, in order to re-create; or where this process is rendered impossible, yet still at all events it struggles to idealize and to unify. It is essentially *vital*, even as all objects (*as* objects) are essentially fixed and dead.[14]

In *The Sickness Unto Death*, Søren Kierkegaard similarly observed:

> As a rule, imagination is the medium for the process of infinitizing; it is not a capacity, as are the others—if one wishes to speak in those terms, it is the capacity *instar omnium* [for all capacities]. . . . Imagination is the infinitizing reflection, and therefore the elder Fichte quite correctly assumed that even in relation to knowledge the categories derive from the imagination. . . . The imagination is the possibility of any and all reflection, and the intensity of this medium is the possibility of the intensity of the self.[15]

The imagination is singled out as the mental faculty that is equal to all the others because it has the aptitude for infinitizing, which is to say, the capacity to explore the infinite possibilities that will unfurl in an uncertain and contingent future that is not determined by a chain of past causality, a future, moreover, that is always encountered in the moment at hand, unhinged from teleological expectation or predictability. The human self, for Kierkegaard, is the "conscious synthesis of infinitude and finitude," and its charge is "to become itself, which can be done only through the relationship to God."[16] The ultimate task of becoming oneself demands that one "become concrete," a concreteness that is achieved only through the synthesis of infinitude and finitude.[17] Through the dialectical synthesis of these opposites, the "limiting" constituent of the finite and the "extending" constituent of the infinite, the self is concretized in a two-fold movement, "an infinite moving away from itself in the infinitizing of the self, and an infinite coming back to itself in the finitizing process." In every instant, therefore, we can say of the self that it is in the "process of becoming," evolving *kata dynamin*, according to its potentiality, for it "does not actually exist," but it is "simply that which ought to come into existence."[18] At no point can we speak of stasis in the evolution of the self. The standard distinction between actuality and potentiality also breaks down insofar as the actuality of the self consists of its potentiality—it is what it is in virtue of what it shall become. The process is viewed as well under the dual aspects of necessity and possibility; if the self lacks either of these qualities, it is in a state of despair. The poetic and paradoxical formulation of Kierkegaard is worth citing verbatim:

> Just as finitude is the limiting aspect in relation to infinitude, so also necessity is the constraint in relation to possibility. Inasmuch as the self as a synthesis of finitude and infinitude is established, is κατὰ δύναμιν [potential], in order to become itself it reflects itself in the medium of imagination, and thereby the infinite possibility becomes manifest. The self is κατὰ δύναμιν [potentially] just as possible as it is necessary, for it is indeed itself, but it has the task of becoming itself. Insofar as it is itself, it is the necessary, and insofar as it has the task of becoming itself, it is a possibility.[19]

There are many more complicated layers of Kierkegaard's analysis, but what is most important for our purposes is his stance regarding the imagination as the medium through which the self becomes conscious of (or "reflects" in the twofold sense of mirroring and contemplating[20]) its infinite possibilities. Kierkegaard approvingly cites Fichte for naming the imagination as the origin of all the categories related to the acquisition of feeling, will, and knowledge on the part of the self.[21] He could have mentioned as well that Fichte portrayed the imagination as wavering between and reconciling contradictions, including that of the finite and the infinite,[22] which parallels Kierkegaard's own depiction of the imagination as the dialectical coincidence of opposites through which the finite becomes infinite, the possible necessary, the actual ideal, the concrete abstract, and the particular universal.[23]

The notion that the imagination reveals the essence of human nature through this dialectic has deep affinity with the anthropological paradigm promulgated by masters of Jewish esoteric lore. According to a recurrent exegesis in kabbalistic and Hasidic sources, *adam*, the Hebrew term for human being, is linked philologically to the expression *eddammeh le-elyon*, "I will be compared to the supernal" (Isaiah 14:14). The import of this exegesis is to provide a theosophic grounding of the priestly notion that the human bears the likeness and image of the divine (Genesis 1:26–27). In contrast to the scriptural derivation of *adam* from the word *adamah*, which signifies the earthly character of human nature (Genesis 2:7), this mystical wordplay places the superiority of the human species—instantiated prototypically in the people of Israel—in the fact that the human shape iconically mirrors the imaginal body of God.[24] According to some interpreters, the derivation of *adam* from *eddammeh* conveys as well that the distinguishing feature of the human relates to the capacity to fashion a mental image of all things in the world.[25] Kabbalists, therefore, elevated the imaginative faculty by identifying it rather than the intellect, as Maimonides notoriously argued, as the divine element within the human through which one can configure the sefirotic emanations anthropomorphically.[26] Maimonides went so far as to identify the imagination with the evil impulse, for every deficiency of reason or character is due to its action,[27] but, following Aristotelian epistemology, he could not ignore the instrumental role of the imagination in our acquisition of knowledge, and he even considered (in accord with his Muslim predecessors, especially al-Fārābī) it crucial to all prophecy with the exception of Moses.[28] However, since imagination apprehends only that which is individual or a composite based on its ability to combine sensory images, it cannot adduce a demonstration of truth, which is derived from intellectual abstraction and the differentiation of the universal from the particular. The intellect, therefore, and not the imagination is the ultimate arbiter of what is possible and impossible. The imagination considers it necessary that God is a body or a force in a body, but the intellect judges this to be impossible; the intellect considers the existence of an incorporeal God necessary, but the imagination cannot ponder such a possibility.[29]

Medieval kabbalists agreed with Maimonides that the God of Israel is not a body subject to generation and corruption; however, they proposed that the imagination is the agency by which the spiritual form is apprehended somatically, indeed in the shape of a human, the very form that makes up the gnosis of the divine name. Ironically, then, the ultimate measure of the imagination is expressed in its ability to imagine the unimaginable, to represent the unrepresentable.[30] Commensurate with the dialectic of Kierkegaard, we can say that for the kabbalists the imagination, too, is a *coincidentia oppositorum*, wherein the finite self becomes infinite as the infinite self becomes finite, the image of God that abides interiorly as the periphery that one must continuously cross in an effort to return and to take hold of one's root. Expressing the matter in the terminology utilized by Abraham Joshua Heschel, we can speak of the movement of the religious imagination as a twofold conversion, the anthropotropic turning of the divine to the human and the theotropic turning of the human to the divine.[31] However, in consonance with Henry Corbin's criticism of Heschel,[32] I would question the need to distinguish these two structures of experience by correlating anthropotropism with prophetic religion and theotropism with mystical religion. In the chiasm between these two turnings, there is the double mirroring, the mirroring of the divine in the mirror of the human and of the human in the mirror of the divine such that the imagistic antagonism to image culminates in the concealment of the imaginal at the fringe of the exposure of the imaginal.

I note, parenthetically, that it is the failure to appreciate the reciprocity of the theotropic and the anthropotropic that underlies Heschel's condemnation of the symbolic approach to religious language. According to Heschel, the elevation of the symbol to the primary mode of knowing God results in a *disavowal of transcendence*;[33] since there is ostensibly no access to the divine reality without the mediation of human metaphors, the very notion of revelation is divested of its phenomenological depth. As he puts it in *Man's Quest for God*:

> Symbolism is so alluring because it promises to rehabilitate beliefs and rituals that have become meaningless to the mind. Yet, what it accomplishes is to reduce belief to make-believe, observance to ceremony, prophecy to literature, theology to esthetics . . . The quest for symbols is a *trap* for those who seek the truth. Symbols may either distort what is literally true or profane what is ineffably real. They may, if employed in the inner chamber of the mind, distort our longing for God into mere esthetics. . . . Symbolism undermines the certainty of history, implying that even God did not succeed in conveying His will to us, and that we did not succeed in understanding His will. Man speaks in symbols; God speaks in events and commands. Realizing all this, one begins to wonder whether symbolism is an authentic category of prophetic religion. Or whether it is not a device of higher apologetics, a method of rationalization?[34]

If the truths of religions are viewed through the lens of the symbol, they become fictions, projections of the human imagination.[35] Inasmuch as symbolization is a mode of conceptualization, "an accommodation of reality to the human mind,"[36] there is no way beyond the sign/image to the transcendent reality that is incarnate in history, and one is ensnared inescapably in the solipsism of signification.[37] For Heschel, transcendence is an enigma that we sense or witness through a discernment that cannot be conceptualized or symbolized,[38] an intuition of "*the unknown within the known*, the infinite within[39] the finite, *the mystery within the order*."[40] Authentic faith is rooted in a preconceptual thinking that is "immediate, ineffable, metasymbolic."[41] Inverting the relationship of the literal and the metaphorical, Heschel notes that *what is literally true to us is a metaphor compared with what is metaphysically real to God*. Attributes applied to God are not less but more than literally real.[42] This is the import of the statement that belief in the divine is an *ontological presupposition*.[43]

In my judgment, Corbin's critical appraisal of Heschel can be extended to the matter of symbolism as well. Simply put, the understanding of the symbol and the imaginal proffered by Corbin[44] challenges Heschel's assertion that religious thought is a "sublimation of a presymbolic knowledge which the awareness of the ineffable provides."[45] On the contrary, not only is it not the case that transcendence is denied by the symbol, but the latter is the most appropriate way to retrieve that which transcends the limits of thought and expression. In contrast to Heschel's attempt to distinguish the "technique of symbolization" and the "*awareness of the ineffable*" or "*radical amazement*,"[46] I would argue that it is through the symbol that we speak the unspeakable and imagine the unimaginable. In one passage, Heschel acknowledges that the symbol does "serve as a *meeting place* of the spiritual and the material, of the invisible and the visible," but he insists nonetheless that in Judaism this role is played by ritual acts, which he describes as facilitating moments of meeting with the divine, an emphasis that reflects his view that Jewish culture is marked fundamentally by a shift from space to time,[47] a theme to which I will return in Chapter 2. A credible case can be made, however, that the symbol in traditional Jewish practice and belief, especially as deciphered through an esoteric hermeneutic, is the icon—as opposed to the idol—of the theophanic presence, which concurrently reveals what is hidden and hides what is revealed,[48] and thus it alone affords one the opportunity to encounter (in Heschel's own locution) the "aboriginal abyss of radical amazement"[49] occasioned by the mystery of the ineffable,[50] the "*allusiveness* to transcendent meaning" experienced in the "grandeur" and "spiritual radiance" of the elusive presence of the divine manifest in the world.[51] Translated into a broader ideational framework not confined by the strictures of theistic language, the imagination is the vehicle by which we exceed our social and biological environments through creative upsurges that rupture the ordinary and open the horizons of scientific, technological, and aesthetic ingenuity to the possibility of the impossible, the nonphenomenalizable that is the epistemic condition of all phenomenality, the unseeing that enframes every act of seeing, the negative ideal of the unreal that positivizes the recurrent patterns and perspectival mutations that constitute the contours of the world we deem to be real.[52]

It is through the prism of the inapparent that I will investigate the role of the imagination and the theocentric proclivity of Jewish philosophical speculation as it specifically affects the discussion on immanence and transcendence. My argument rests on the assumption that Jewish philosophical theology in the twentieth century was dominated with the dialogical concern to affirm the divine as the irreducible other vis-à-vis the world and the human in order to avert the totalizing implications of nineteenth-century idealism as exemplified by Hegel, on the one hand, and to sidestep the anthropological-psychological reductionism expressed by Feuerbach, Nietzsche, and Freud, to name three central figures, on the other hand.[53] As disparate as these two tendencies are, what they share is a move toward a radical immanentism and the eclipse of transcendence. The concern was enunciated lucidly by Heschel:

> Religion is neither the outgrowth of imagination nor the product of will. It is not an inner process, a feeling, or a thought, and should not be looked upon as a bundle of episodes in the life of man. . . . Religion is the light in which even the momentous appears as a detail. It is the ultimateness in the face of which everything seems premature, preliminary, and transitory. The pious man lives in esteem for ultimateness, in devotion to the final amid the mortal and evanescent. Religion to him is the integration of the detail into the whole, the infusion of the momentary into the lasting. . . . Religion is neither a state of mind nor an achievement of the intellect. It does not rule hearts by the grace of man; its roots lie not in his

inwardness. It is not an event in the soul but a matter of fact outside the soul. Even what starts as an experience *in* man transcends the human sphere, becoming an objective event outside him. In this power of transcending the soul, time, and space, the pious man sees the distinction of religious acts. . . . Religion, in itself, the state which exists between God and man, is neither produced by man nor dependent upon his belief; it is neither a display of human spirit nor the outgrowth of his conscience. Religion exists even if it is in this moment not realized, perceived, or acknowledged by anybody, and those who reject or betray it do not diminish its validity. Religion is more than a creed or a doctrine, more than faith or piety; it is an everlasting fact in the universe, something that exists outside knowledge and experience, an *order of being*, the *holy dimension* of existence.[54]

Heschel's insistence on the sui generis and nonreductive nature of religion as an ontic rather than a phenomenological category is in accord with a crucial element of the dialogical turn that centers around representing the divine effluence in the image of the gift. As Heschel puts it: "Thus the pious man realizes, also, that whatever he may have at his disposal has been bestowed upon him as a gift. . . . The pious man avers that he has a perpetual gift from God, for in all that comes to him he feels the love of God."[55] Religion is essentially bound up with the notion of the gift, "a divine grant to man," which must be viewed as a reality in and of itself, the holy dimension of existence, and not as a fabrication of human will or imagination.[56]

Perhaps the individual who embodied the struggle to combat the psychologization of religious belief more poignantly than anyone else was Franz Rosenzweig. In his new thinking (*neue Denken*) or experiential philosophy (*erfahrende Philosophie*), Rosenzweig sought to accomplish at least two major objectives: first, to shatter the all-encompassing One in which human and world are sublated, thereby preserving the "essential separateness" (*wesenhafte Getrenntheit*) or "transcendence" (*Transzendenz*) of each of the elements vis-à-vis the other,[57] and, second, to elude the snare of an "atheistic theology" whereby the divine is reduced to a "self-projection of the human into the heaven of myth" (*Selbstprojektion des Menschlichen an den Himmel des Mythos*).[58] Also central to Rosenzweig's endeavor, inspired especially by Kierkegaard,[59] is the conviction that God exceeds the universal; the numinous presence, which is presumed to be tangibly available to human experience (*Erlebnis*) in an ongoing way in the present and not only as a recollection of the historical event of revelation in the past, is more than a regulative principle or a rational concept. The "reality" (*Wirklichkeit*) of God, for Rosenzweig, entails an "absolute factuality" (*absoluten Tatsächlichkeit*) or "positivity" (*Positivität*).[60] I will explore this dimension of Rosenzweig's thought in greater detail in Chapter 2, but at present it is sufficient to underscore that his idea of divine facticity demands that transcendence be cast in personalist terms, which alone would justify the communal efficacy of liturgical-ritual practice as well as the sociopolitical pursuit of ethical justice.

Here it is apposite to evoke Steven Schwarzschild's statement that the "unilinear thrust of the entire course of Jewish philosophic thought" consists of the view that the "will of God and of humanity transcends the iron chains of the nature of God, humanity, and world."[61] In my judgment, the sharp contrast that Schwarzschild draws between the Jewish and Christian approaches to transcendence and immanence—the former considers the will of God as the mechanism by which what is utterly separate from the world is intimately related to it, whereas the latter posits a spatial model of incarnation, a "quasi-physical link" that, paradoxically, dichotomizes divinity and humanity[62]—is too simplistic. The crucial point nevertheless is well taken, and many Jewish thinkers have sought to protect the transcendence of God, rejecting an immanentism that would collapse the difference between the ideal and the real,[63] which can be traced historically to the atheistic stigmatization of Spinozistic rationalism that emerged from the conflict of pantheism in the exchange between Moses Mendelssohn and Friedrich Heinrich Jacobi.[64]

Influenced by the neo-Kantian idealism of Hermann Cohen and demonstrating a striking affinity with the post-Husserlian phenomenological thought of Emmanuel Levinas,[65] Schwarzschild detects an essential connection between transcendence and ethics, as God's relationship to the world is conceptualized volitionally through the law, which alone ensures divine and human freedom.[66] The immanence of sociality, accordingly, is determined from the standpoint of transcendence that surpasses the limit delineated empirically or rationally as the order of nature. God is the infinite beyond being, as Levinas tirelessly insisted, the thought that "withdraws from thought" and thus requires of thinking to think more than it can think.[67] The paradoxical language embraced by Levinas, worthy of the most arcane kabbalist,[68] is meant to forge a path that inceptually emerges from but ultimately circumvents philosophical reasoning, pushing the self-undermining of skepticism to the limits of aporia, a point that I will elaborate in the third chapter. It is, after all, with respect to the issue of unveiling the other that Levinas found Western philosophy wanting insofar as the other loses its otherness in manifesting itself as a being that is subject to comprehension. The God of the philosophers, accordingly, is a god adequate to reason, and thus transcendence is subjugated to the reign of immanence.[69] By contrast, the God of the Bible signifies transcendence that is not, properly speaking, thinkable.[70] Even so, to extend thought to the unthinkable is itself a manner of thought. The dilemma is captured pithily by Levinas, paraphrasing the statement attributed to the pseudo-Aristotelian *Protrepticus*[71] but cited by Derrida in the name of "a Greek" near the conclusion of his 1964 essay, "Violence and Metaphysics: An Essay on the Thought of Emmanuel Levinas"[72]: "Not to philosophize is still to philosophize."[73] Levinas has expressed more profoundly and persistently than any other thinker the appeal to transcendence as integral to the Jewish religious sensibility, affirming a kind of negative theology[74] (in spite of his occasional attempts to distance himself from this approach[75]) that may even come close to an ontological atheism.[76] That which he marks as otherwise than being, however, is likely to be imagined as being otherwise, that is, as a being that is other vis-à-vis being but still a being, thereby succumbing to the ontological taxonomy it is meant to undermine. In the language brought into play by Martin Kavka, the possibility of a critical meontology, positing the nonbeing of absolute otherness, is dependent on the dialectical meontology, the interpenetration of being and nonbeing.[77] On this account, nonbeing, the otherness beyond being, is not no-thing (the privation of something) but the not-yet-being (the transcendence of something and nothing).

Despite the best intentions and the astute argumentation offered by Levinas, it may just be impossible for the human mind to be delivered from this quandary: *configuring God as wholly other is itself an imaginary act by which the other is envisioned necessarily through the semblance of the same.* Levinas would surely respond that it is the inaccessibility of the other that makes the other accessible, that the presence of the other, if it is the other that is made present, must be given as the absence of the other. It is not clear, however, that this mode of givenness—which would amount in the end to an epiphany of the invisible that is discernible only through a phenomenology without a phenomenon—does not inevitably lead to the negation of alterity and the eradication of the difference between self and other.[78]

It is germane to recall in this context the observation of Ernst Bloch concerning the transcendence implied in what he refers to as "despotic theism"—in some measure he applies this as well to the rational pantheism promoted by Spinoza—the being that by nature is incomparable to anything that might appear in the immanent sphere of human experience: "And this remains decisive: *the utterly Different also holds good for the ultimate humane projections from religion.* It is only the Utterly Different which gives to everything that has been longed for in the deification of man the appropriate dimension of depth."[79] The positing of the transcendent results not in the heteronomous capitulation to an unknowable power but rather in the autonomous empowering of human agency, expressed most fantastically in the utopian hope that the mysterium of the kingdom of God can be materialized anthropologically and sociologically in a particular community of believers. "The wishful content of religion remains that of feeling at home in the *mystery* of existence, a mystery mediated with man and well-disposed to his deepest wish, even to the repose of wishes. *And the further the subject with his founders of religion penetrates into the object-mysterium of a God conceived as the supreme Outside or the supreme Above and overpowers it, the more powerfully man in his earth-heaven or heaven-earth is charged with reverence for depth and infinity.*"[80]

Bracketing the intricacies of Bloch's argument as they pertain to theopolitics, let me note that he has incisively identified the major logical flaw of apophatic theology: the positing of an absolute transcendence dissolves that very transcendence, inasmuch as the other is ascertained as other only as a projection of the self as what is other than the self. Psychically, the constitutional structure of our consciousness seemingly makes it impossible for the other to be given except as a facet of one's own egoity, since the subject can never experience the other without it being at the same time

part of his or her own experience. The peril of solipsism and the problem of account-
ing for the objectivity of the other, which ensues from the epistemological assumption that every showing of truth and being is a characteristic in the cogitatum of the
cogito, was famously addressed by Husserl in the beginning of the fifth of his *Cartesian Meditations*:

> When I, the meditating I, reduce myself to my absolute transcendental ego by
> phenomenological epoché do I not become *solus ipse*; and do I not remain that, as
> long as I carry on a consistent self-explication under the name phenomenology?
> Should not a phenomenology that proposed to solve the problems of Objective
> being, and to present itself actually as philosophy, be branded therefore as tran-
> scendental solipsism? [81]

Husserl's attempt to resolve the conundrum of the noematic-ontic mode of givenness
of the other in terms of the communalization of the constitutive intentionality of the
transcendental intersubjectivity[82]—the sphere of transcendental ownness constituted
appresentatively in each monadic consciousness that bears the other monadic con-
sciousnesses intentionally within itself and posits them as transcendental others that
coexist intrapsychically as a "community of monads" held together synthetically by
the "analogizing modification" or "associative pairing" of the psychophysical ego[83]—is
beyond our immediate concerns. What is relevant is his recognition that the transcendental idealism of phenomenology can be executed only if one unravels the riddle of
how the transcendental ego can be said to construct the other as an intentional object
that is peculiarly one's own, that is, how the other can be given as non-other. Within
the reduction to the "transcendental sphere of peculiar ownness" (*Eigenheitssphäre*),
also called the sphere of one's "transcendental concrete I-myself," all that is alien
(*Fremde*) must be bracketed, since there is no other that is not "*part of the all-embracing
constitution* in which the transcendental ego, as constituting an Objective world, lives
his life."[84] Conversely, Husserl argues, "if what belongs to the other's own essence
were directly accessible, it would be merely a moment of my own essence, and ultimately he himself and I myself would be the same."[85] Anthony Steinbock formulated
the problem at the heart of the phenomenological inquiry concisely and cogently:
"How can phenomenology account for the originality of the other subjectivity that
transcends my own experience and yet whose sense as other is constituted in and from
my intentional life? How can another ego (transcendence in the true sense) that is not
merely intended as an object in my experience be constituted precisely as other?"[86]

From Derrida's perspective, this question of the apperception of the other—a transcendent knowledge that encompasses not just other subjectivities but everything
presumed to be external to consciousness—is the *philosophical question in general*:
"*Why* is an experience which would not be lived as *my own* (for an ego in general, in
the eidetic-transcendental sense of these words) impossible and unthinkable? This
unthinkable and impossible are the limits of reason in general."[87] Derrida already

denounced Levinas on these grounds, challenging his view that Husserl allegedly missed the "infinite alterity" of the other by reducing the alter ego to the ego:

> It is the other as other which is the ego's phenomenon: the phenomenon of a certain non-phenomenality which is irreducible for the ego as ego in general (the eidos ego). For it is impossible to encounter the alter ego (in the very form of the encounter described by Levinas), impossible to respect it in experience and in language, if this other, in its alterity, does not *appear* for an ego (in general). One could neither speak, nor have any sense of the totally other, if there was not a phenomenon of the totally other, or evidence of the totally other as such.[88]

Largely due to the impact of Levinas, a plethora of scholars have written copiously and often uncritically about transcendence as the singular and inimitable alterity,[89] but few have heeded the fact that difference as such is meaningful only when discerned dialectically in light of identity. The property of any concept cannot be determined except on the basis of what is differentiated by another concept, and hence we must assume that nothing can be thought without thinking the trace of its difference vis-à-vis the other that is included in itself as what is excluded.[90]

We might well agree with Deleuze that the principle of repetition "is no longer that of the Same, but involves the Other—involves difference, from one wave and one gesture to another, and carries that difference through the repetitive space thereby constituted."[91] To be more precise, Deleuze distinguishes two forms of repetition: the repetition of the Same, which presupposes the identity of the concept or representation, and the repetition of difference, which presupposes the alterity of the idea or the heterogeneity of the a-presentation. The former involves equality, commensurability, and symmetry; the latter, inequality, incommensurability, and dissymmetry.[92] Even in the latter case, however, heterogeneity entails that we find the singularity within that which repeats, the novelty within reiteration, the return of the Same in which the Same is nothing but the recurrence of difference,[93] the ungiven that is the prerequisite of all that is given, the principle of nonphenomenality that accounts for the phenomenality of every phenomenon.[94] The concealment of the dissimilar in the pretense of the similar constitutes the elemental paradox of temporal becoming: "Repetition is truly that which disguises itself in constituting itself, that which constitutes itself only by disguising itself."[95] Hence, the "repetition of dissymmetry," writes Deleuze, "is hidden within symmetrical ensembles or effects; a repetition of distinctive points underneath that of ordinary points; and everywhere the Other in the repetition of the Same. This is the secret, the most profound repetition: it alone provides the principle of the other one, the reason for the blockage of concepts."[96]

I see nothing in Levinas or any of his myriad interpreters that would put that logical axiom into relief. Surely, when the subject matter is the divine other, the originative being that in Deleuzian terms is the "differenciator of difference,"[97] any discursive comment, even statements of negation, should be steadfastly avoided, since the unfolding of differences that is here posited as the nature of being must be without recourse to representation of any sort; the silence of not-speaking, as opposed to the silence of speaking-not, might well be the only credible response. In Levinas's own terminology, we would privilege the saying (*le Dire*) over the said (*le dit*); however, as he was well aware and often noted, there is no way to the former but through the latter, even if it is the case that the beyond being of the saying always shows itself enigmatically in the said and is thus always betrayed because the signification of the saying is not, strictly speaking, correlative with the kerygma of the said.[98] If we could envision a saying without a said, that saying would be, in Heidegger's near-mystical elocution, a "saying not-saying" (*sagenden Nichtsagen*),[99] a verbal utterance that would summon the unsaying of the said in the saying of the unsaid. Just as Levinas maintained that the "essence of language" consists in continually retracting what is said (*à dédire le dit*),[100] so Heidegger—perhaps under the influence of Meister Eckhart and Angelus Silesius[101]— insisted that the saying of thinking (*die Sage des Denkens*) must always remain unspoken (*ungesprochen*), and hence the spoken (*das Gesprochene*) is never what is said (*das Gesagte*).[102] The journey undertaken in this book is not only to unsay what has been said but also to reclaim the need to unsay the unsaying, to heed the murmuring silence, the pregnant pause wherein all being becomes the becoming of being in the moving stillness that is the space of time.

CHAPTER I

Via Negativa and the Imaginal Configuring of God

As long as there is still one beggar around, there will still be myth.

—Walter Benjamin, *The Arcades Project*

We can speak of a salient feature of modern Jewish thought as the dialogical imagination, an act of theopoiesis centered on the figural iconization of an allegedly invisible
deity in anthropomorphic and anthropopathic terms.[1] The emphasis on the dialogical,
which proceeds philosophically from the logical notion of correlation enunciated by
Cohen—what he calls in one place "a scientific elemental form of thought" (*eine wis-
senschaftliche Grundform des Denkens*)[2]— has been duly noted,[3] but what has been less
attended is that this conception bears the risk that what should not be subject to
imaginary representation invariably will be so represented, even if in the guise of the
irrepresentable. In his 1908 essay on the characteristic of Maimonidean ethics, Cohen
observed that monotheism has preserved a nexus with pantheism, a tendency that can
be overcome only when ethics dispenses with teleology.[4] To comprehend this one
must bear in mind that, for Cohen, "true teleology" gives rise to the "ethical convergence of nature and mind" (*ethische Zusammenschluß von Natur und Geist*), the proposition in light of which the history of philosophy within Judaism evolved.[5] If we affirm
reason as the origin of religious belief, as we must according to Cohen in both the
so-called earlier and later periods of his intellectual development, it is inevitable that
monotheism itself mandates that God become an object of thought that cannot be
reduced to the course of nature, which is the crux of his vehement rejection of pantheism and idealism.[6] To express the matter in a different terminological register: transcendence, which, in Cohen's elocution, is a property of the uniqueness (*Einzigkeit*) as
opposed to the unity (*Einheit*) of God,[7] signifies the utter dissimilarity and incommensurability of the divine; inescapably, however, the transcendent becomes immanent to thinking insofar as there is no way to think the unthinkable that does not
encroach on its unthinkability. How can the unthought be thought—even if merely
thought as the unthought—without the closure of the breach between being and consciousness in a fashion that approximates the idealist worldview? Prima facie, the
thought of difference should be differentiated from the difference of thought on the

grounds that the latter comprises an alterity obliterated by the former. Yet, upon closer examination, thought of difference is no different from difference of thought to the extent that one as the other entraps reason in thinking being and nonbeing from the perspective of the production of being or nonbeing in thought.[8] I surmise that Cohen has this inevitability in mind when he opines that "even Judaism could not and would not altogether resist the temptation of pantheism's sweet poison,"[9] and hence the correlation between God and human "constitutes the pantheistic element within monotheism [*der Pantheismus im Monotheismus*]."[10] The repercussions of this confession have not commanded enough scholarly attention.

VIA NEGATIVA AND THE INFINITUDE OF TRANSCENDENCE

For Cohen, the divine and the human are united—though not identified—through the very reason that preserves their difference. This is expressed most notably in the moral imperative, the pursuit of which he affirms as the "life true to monotheism" and the most "precious achievement" of reason.[11] Cohen turns to Maimonides to buttress his position,[12] since the medieval sage harbored a "basic aversion to intuitionism and mysticism," but he nonetheless affirmed the "ethical motif of pantheism" to the extent that he accepted the "unity of reason" (*Einheit der Vernunft*) as the element that joins what is ostensibly disparate, the very unity that served as the "foundation for his theory of prophecy."[13] From this it follows that "cognition is the task and telos of religion, and consequently of ethics."[14] Even if one were to accept Rosenzweig's claim that Cohen modified his earlier Kantian position by arguing for the autonomy of religion vis-à-vis ethics,[15] forging a Jewish rationalism[16] by which the ostensibly incompatible forces of Scripture and philosophy are harnessed together in such a way that the deductive reasoning of scientific discourse is significantly modified by the prophetic idiom and its decidedly nonsystematic rhetorical style,[17] one would have to admit that even in the later work it is still the cognitive value of the ethical (*Erkenntniswert der Ethik*) that alone justifies the knowledge of God (*Gotteserkenntnis*).[18] Maimonides is the paragon of one who secured the interdependence of ethics upon religion by establishing the latter on the principles that are operative in the former. Yet, as Cohen is well aware, Maimonides severely constricted our capacity to know God's substance or essence by denying the validity of positive attributes. Simply put, if an object is divested of attributes, how can it be known?[19] The apophatic dimension, accordingly, "spells something rather suspicious and oppressive" to the extent that we are "bidden to put our trust in the content of revelation, relying but upon its rational moorings, and yet we deprive rational cognition of its positive conceptuality: what foundation remains at our disposal for knowing God if we are left to operate merely with negative attributes? Would it not appear that a latent trait of aversion and of distrust against the very foundation of the God-concept, against its cognitive validity, prevailed throughout this entire Maimonidean argument?"[20] Cohen understood that if negative theology is the logical conclusion of philosophical speculation, then rationalism itself presents the greatest challenge to Judaism, which is based on a revelatory encounter and an absolute faith in the factuality of God. Cohen's solution is anchored in an innovative interpretation of the doctrine of negative theology: the attributes about God, which are specified only by revelation and thus accessible through textual exegesis rather than deductive reasoning,[21] portray the divine exclusively as a being beholden to the standard of morality.[22] The cognition of God, therefore, is the cognition of the basic premise regarding the ethical comportment of divine volition as it is expressed in the world, the ideal of providence that serves as the paradigm for human emulation.[23]

Cohen goes so far as to say that it is only in virtue of the *via negativa* that the "entire Maimonidean philosophy emerges as a unified system," for "in combating positive divine attributes," Maimonides "was motivated not merely by scholastic subtlety, nor even theological concern for maintaining the conceptual purity of divine unity, but primarily by the pure rationalism of his ethics." This insight leads Cohen to explicate Maimonidean negative theology in light of the Platonic conception of the Good as the nonfoundation (*Ungrundlegung*, τὸ ἀνυπόθετον),[24] which he claims is rendered incorrectly as "the unconditioned" (*das Unbedingte*) or "the absolute" (*das Absolute*), terms that convey the idealist sense of a rationally discernible foundation or an immutable essence. The ontological implications of these renderings contradict the intent of Plato's description of the Good as the nonhypothesis, a privative expression that denotes that which is beyond being and rational deduction.[25] In Cohen's words:

> Let us recall, however, how even Plato formulates his idea of the Good in seemingly negative terms as non-foundation. . . . I would venture to propose that in similar fashion, Maimonides by no means conceives of the negative attributes in a purely negative vein, but rather relates them to infinite judgment [*unendlichen Urteil*], which only apparently takes on the form of negation in that its formulation employs a negating principle [*Negationspartikel*]. . . . Hence, Maimonides was able to find in Plato as well as in neo-Platonism the point of departure and support for developing his own fundamental doctrine of Knowing God: it is not through negation, but rather through a negation that is only apparent [*scheinbare Negation*], that we attain a true and fast affirmation of God.[26]

For Cohen, the Platonic idea resonates as well with his understanding of the notion of origin (*Ursprung*), the transcendental ground that accords priority to what is unknown over what is known, a "new thinking" based on seeing the aught (*Ichts*) as originating in the naught (*Nichts*), which is further demarcated as the "naught of knowledge," that is, a negation that generates an affirmation in virtue of negating itself as negation and hence a negation that merely appears to be a negation, since there is no thing to negate in the unremitting becoming-other that is the true meaning of the originative principle that establishes "permanence" (*Fortbestand*) and secures "continuous preservation" (*Forterhaltung*), in contradistinction to the "first begin-ning" (*ersten Anfang*), a temporal conception that is mythological in nature.[27] This notion of the actual potential, which is the potentiality of the actual, finds its theoreti-cal grounding in the delineation of infinity as the limit-concept (*Grenzbegriff*) that fosters an ongoing critique of the penchant to subsume particularity within an all-inclusive totality.[28] The infinitude of transcendence is unknowable, not because there is some hidden essence that cannot be known, but because transcendence is expressive of the continuous manifestations of finitude by which the unlimited is delimited.[29] In Cohen's opinion, this is to be applied to Maimonides, who related the negative attri-butes to the infinite judgment that is expressed through a negating particle and thus assumes the form of negation. Following the lead of Plato and the Neoplatonic tradi-tion, Maimonides presumes that the affirmative knowledge of God is attained through the negation that is only apparently negative.[30] We can have "true knowledge of God," but this knowledge is "exclusively through negative attributes,"[31] which means the very attributes that attest to the ungrounding of the ground through which the human being can know God as the "ultrapositive infinite," the notional justification for the ethical-religious life.[32]

The intent of Cohen's interpretation of Maimonides is made clear in *Religion der Vernunft aus den Quellen des Judentums*, published posthumously in 1919. Maimonides is described as the "genuine philosopher of monotheism," insofar as he provided a "foundation for the positivity, the affirmation of being" by wedding the concepts of infinity and negation through which "privation became the infinite judgment."[33] The problem of negative attributes is elucidated "through the *connection of negation and privation*," which is to say, the attributes of privation, and not the positive attributes, are negated.[34] Affirmative propositions arise out of infinite judgments that are based on the negation of privative statements. Cohen's underlying metaphysical agnosticism—or, as some have suggested, his outright critique of ontology—is that the idea of infinity (derived from the notion of the differential and the infinitesimal calculus[35]) implies the absence of a predetermined body of knowledge rather than the lack of any partic-ular property that formed part of an integrated system and therefore could be poten-tially apprehended by reason. To negate the privation is a double negative that yields the ground of positivity, the ground that, as we have seen, is an unground, the non-foundation, an-archic. Nothing is not nothing but no thing, the indefiniteness that alone can be ascribed to the concept of God, which is the true Being (*Sein*) that can never be identical to the beings to which actual existence (*Dasein*) is attributed. In *Der Begriff der Religion im System der Philosophie* (1915), Cohen had already argued that the object of our knowledge of God is exclusively being and that existence can belong only to the negative attributes (*Nur das Sein ist Gegenstand unserer Gotteserkenntnis; das Dasein gehört unter die negativen Attribute*). Indeed, the possibility that we can think of God's essence in terms of existence is emphatically and unequivocally denied (*Gott hat nicht das Dasein*). God may be considered the "origin of existence" (*Ursprung des Daseins*), a supposition that is transmitted in the name of Maimonides, for without God there would be no existence at all (*ohne ihn gäbe es kein Dasein*).[36]

I note, in passing, that the distinction attributed by Cohen to Maimonides is reminiscent of Porphyry's differentiation between being as an entity (*on*) and the pure act of being (*einai*), between beings that exist and the ground of being. God can be described in terms of the latter but not the former, a move that allowed Neoplatonists like Proclus and subsequent Christian, Muslim, and Jewish thinkers to depart somewhat from the Plotinian conception that God is the One that is above being.[37] Cohen seems to be up to something very similar when he labels God the "originative principle of activity" (*Ursprung der Aktivität*); that is, God, the absolute originary act, is the Being whose omnipotence "negates the negativity contained in a privation" (*einer die Privation negierenden Negation erlangt*).[38] The matter can be scrutinized as well from the cosmological perspective: to speak of God as creator means that God is the "prime cause of activity" (*Urgrund der Tätigkeit*), and hence his being "can be determined in no other way than by the immanence of creation in his *uniqueness*. . . . The finite is to attain its originative principle in the infinite, in the negation of privation. . . . *Thus creation is the consequence of God's uniqueness*."[39] The monotheistic belief that the world is immanent in the divine uniqueness—or, expressed in more technical terms, that the originative principle of the finite is in the infinite—must be contrasted sharply with the pantheistic presumption that the divine uniqueness is immanent in the world—that the originative principle of the infinite is in the finite, as a Spinozistic monist would assert. The becoming of the world, consequently, is not extrinsic to the divine being even though the two cannot be identified. The import of the concept of the nothing (*das Nichts*) in the traditional belief of *creatio ex nihilo* is that the world is the "relative infinity of privation," which is a consequence not of the "nonexistent primeval substance" of matter but of the unique divine being.[40] Cohen concludes, therefore, that creation is "God's primary attribute; it is not only the consequence of the uniqueness of God's being; creation is simply identical with it. If the unique God were not creator, being and becoming would be the same; nature itself would be God." In contrast to the pantheistic collapse of the difference between being and becoming, Cohen adamantly declares that the meaning of God's uniqueness logically necessitates that "nature is the becoming that needs being as its foundation."[41]

CORRELATION AND THE A/THEOLOGY OF DIVINE UNIQUENESS

The Kantian framing of Maimonides is linked to Cohen's belief that no offense should be taken at the fact that reason is the "root of the content of revelation," since the "correlation of God and man, this correlation of the divine spirit to the human, has as an unavoidable consequence a kind of identity of logical reason in both."[42] Cohen, and following him Rosenzweig,[43] categorically rejects pantheism inasmuch as it negates the alterity of the divine by professing the identity of God and world and in so doing not only jeopardizes the possibility of cultivating the moral self[44] but also implicates the divine in a sense of beingness that is appropriate only to existents in the phenomenal realm of conditionality. Pantheism posits the being of God as identical with the universe, whereas Judaism assumes that God alone is being (*Gott allein ist das Sein*) and thus is designated distinctively as "One Who Is Being" (*der Seienden*), which involves the "*transformation of the neuter into a person*" (*Verwandlung des Neutrums in die Person*).[45] Cohen immediately admits that this transformation "makes anthropomorphism unavoidable, and the decline of Jewish thought into myth would have been unavoidable if the *fight against anthropomorphism* had not proved from the very beginning of the oral teaching to be the very soul of Jewish religious education."[46] In *Ethik des reinen Willens* (1904), Cohen proffered that the proposition that "God is spirit" (*Gott ist Geist*) has ethical value only insofar as it is preparation for the thought that "God is idea" (*Gott ist Idee*). The notion of "spirit," together with that of "person" and "life," are attributes whose roots are in myth, which is of no use to ethics. The theological meaning of spirit is to be avoided because it introduces an extraneous mythical dimension related directly to the imaginative embellishment of God as a living person.[47]

In the later composition, *Religion der Vernunft*, Cohen is more conciliatory. He still recognizes the inherent danger of anthropomorphism entailed in envisioning God as a person and not merely a neutral abstraction as one may infer from the pantheistic identification of God and nature, but he is confident that the mythic partiality will be held in check by the incessant battle against anthropomorphism that is the central concern of Judaism's oral tradition, which complements written Scripture,[48] as opposed to the incarnational dogma of Christianity, which closes the gap separating divine and human by heightening the anthropomorphic and mythological.[49] In his own words: "We do not, therefore, at this stage of our exposition need to take offense at the transformation of an abstraction into a person, especially since its connection with *being* already at least diminishes the danger that is connected with the notion of the person. God is not that which is, nor is he only the one, but the Unique One that is [*Gott ist nicht das Seiende, und auch nicht das Eine, sondern der einzig Seiende*]."[50] From the uniqueness of God one may deduce the quality of incomparability [*Unvergleichbarkeit*], and this, in turn, "entails the *distinction between being* [Sein] *and existence* [Dasein]. . . . For existence is attested by the senses, through perception. On the other hand it is reason which, against all sense-appearance, bestows actuality [*Wirklichkeit*] upon existence, discovers and elevates the nonsensible to being, and marks it out as true being."[51]

Exegetically, Cohen is drawing on the epiphany to Moses at the burning bush, in which the name of the divine is revealed as *ehyeh asher ehyeh* (Exodus 3:14),[52] which is translated *Ich bin, der ich bin*, "I am that I am." Cohen contrasts this rendering with the translation of Kautzsch, *Ich bin wer ich bin*, "I am who I am." From the ostensibly negligible grammatical difference between the two relative pronouns, Cohen elicits collaboration for his main philosophical point: we can attribute to God being but not existence or actuality.[53] Thus, in the continuation, Cohen comments that the name *ehyeh* does not denote "He is" (*er ist*) in the sense of the "perpetual and unchangeable One" (*immer Seiende und Unveränderliche*) but rather "I am the One that is" (*Ich bin der Seiende*), which is to say the one that can be named in no other way than by "I am" (*ich bin*). The name, therefore, expresses "the thought that no other being may affirm about itself this connection with *being* [*Verbindung des Seins*]. . . . In such a definite way *being* is named as that element in the name that designates the *person* of God. If this is not yet philosophy, it is certainly reason in the original sense [*Ursinn*] of the word."[54] From Cohen's perspective, the uniqueness of God is meant to neutralize the anthropomorphic repercussions of monotheism: the single God is the only Being, and hence no likeness is admissible. The point is articulated as well with reference to the most sacred of divine names in the Jewish tradition, the Tetragrammaton, which designates the Eternal One (*der Ewige*), the fundamental source of revelation (*Grundquelle der Offenbarung*), the unique being in relation to which the world is said to have no being.[55] This is not to say that Cohen adopts an acosmism that would regard the world as nothing; in his mind, the world has the ontological status of nonbeing (*Nichtssein*) insofar as the only being to which "being" can be properly assigned is God.[56] If the Unique One is so understood, then it would raise serious questions about the tenability of thinking of God in the personalist terms that Cohen assumed marked the rational nucleus of the Jewish religion and represented the critical move beyond the Kantian notion of God as a moral idea.[57] On the contrary, his conception would seem to suggest the atheological divesting of God of any kataphatic representation that could be understood except as metaphoric confabulation.

The concept of uniqueness logically compels the distinction between being (*Sein*) and existence (*Dasein*), and thus Cohen avers that the "unique being of God is such that it does not admit any mixture, any connection with sensible existence. Ontology, which is based on this connection of being and existence, contains no safeguard against pantheism; indeed, pantheism bases itself on ontology and all its main representatives."[58] The mixture of being and existence is intolerable for monotheism inasmuch as it negates the uniqueness of the divine by rendering the latter comparable to all other actual beings. This is the intent of Cohen's quip that in the eyes of monotheism "pantheism is nothing more than anthropomorphism."[59] By contrast, the notion of correlation presumes that God is other vis-à-vis the world. The idea of God itself is not meaningful without positing the existence of the world, but, at the same time, the former is meaningless if it is treated as substantially identical to the latter. The chasm is narrowed to the extent that the transcendent is immanent, which is necessitated by the fact that God serves as an ethical ideal that imposes a mutual obligation on divine and human through the mediation of the world.

Cohen attempts to avoid this problem by offering a rather unusual understanding of the rabbinic notion of the divine indwelling. The term *shekhinah*, which etymologically is from a root that means to inhabit or to dwell, imparts that all change is eliminated from God's being. Whereas the philosopher speaks of God as substance, the one who adheres to the monotheistic religion proclaims that God is *Shekhinah*, "absolute rest." Immanence, accordingly, signifies that the being of motion is made possible through the being of rest. The removal of God from all temporal becoming (*Zeitlichkeit des Werdens*), "the negative attribute of unchangeableness" (*das negative Attribut der Unveränderlichkeit*), is derived from the name *ehyeh asher ehyeh*, which he renders, as I noted above, *Ich bin, der ich bin*. Cohen emphasizes that being is determined here as the "being of an I, and not of substance that becomes the basis for the notion of matter."[60] I grant Cohen's contention that only by maintaining the distinction between the becoming of nature and the being of the divine could the metaphysics of monotheism evolve into the origin of the unique God of ethics. But the consequence of such a move is the imaginary construction of the divine being as person. I well understand that Cohen's distinction between the "being of an I" and that of "substance" indicates that God serves as the ground for the individuality of self-consciousness, which is necessary both to establish moral agency and to authenticate the religious experience of atonement (*Versöhnung*), the key notion that makes the reconciliation of the human being with God possible.[61] Still, we must ask whether this move constitutes an assault on the very idea of uniqueness, which he maintained is the staple of the uncompromising intolerance of monotheism for idolatry.[62] "God absolutely cannot be an object that can be thought of through the instruction of an image [*Bild*]. . . . He can never be known through a likeness [*Abbild*], but simply as archetype [*Urbild*], as archetypal thought [*Urgedanke*], as archetypal being [*Ursein*]."[63] Even the Jerusalem Temple is to be distinguished from the temples of polytheism inasmuch as it was not a house for God's image (*Götterbild*). The ultimate purpose for the Temple was not God but humankind, to provide the context for the infinite task of prayer, which supersedes the sacrificial cult.[64]

IMPERSONAL PERSONHOOD AND THE DISFIGURATION OF DIVINITY

Not only would Cohen undoubtedly insist that the application of personhood to the divine actuality does not result in ascribing an image to God, but, quite the contrary, it is the very gesture that precludes representation and hence safeguards the faith against the incursion of idolatry. Moreover, since the human is created in God's likeness, it could be argued that the lack of representation that issues from the attribution of personhood to the divine is the criterion that must be applied to human subjectivity; that is, the dignity of the human self would consist precisely of resistance to objectification or reification.[65] Notwithstanding the validity of these assertions, this matter needs to be interrogated on both the theological and the anthropological planes: how is a conception of personhood meaningful if it is rid of all positive description and intentionality?[66] To avoid objectifying the other is worthy of commendation, but the impersonal nature of personality that emerges from Cohen's conception seems hardly suitable psychologically or sociologically. Certainly, the theistic elements of the Jewish tradition do not support such a constraint on the imagination. Cohen himself remarked that the scriptural description of Adam's having been created in God's image "very naively intends to give to myth a monotheistic coloring." Of course, as he goes on to say, there is no image of God, and therefore the biblical account of Adam's having been created in the image and likeness of God cannot be interpreted imagistically. What is intended by this notion is that in virtue of knowledge the human is the focal point of all becoming, which is the logical consequence of God's unique being.[67] Cohen's philosophical exegesis notwithstanding, the notion of divine person problematizes the divergence between image (*Bild*) and archetype (*Urbild*) that he wished to uphold. To generate the personification of transcendence required by Cohen's own notion of divine forgiveness and goodness, which highlights a major discrepancy between religion and ethics, the archetype, the originary-image whence all images originate, would itself have to be conceived imaginally. The classifications "archetypal thought" and "archetypal being" are not sufficient to accommodate the portrayal of God as person. That Cohen wished to burn the candle at both ends, so to speak, is evident from the fact that he assents to the psalmist idea of the human being's longing to draw near to God, a longing impelled by and consummated in forgiveness, but he also proclaims that monotheism severs forgiveness from the "wholly mythological, original form of atonement."[68] I would counter that without the mythological—or perhaps mythopoeic would be the more desirable term—the discourse about divine mercy and human longing is depleted of any spiritual gravitas.

In his essay "Metaphysics and Religion" (1930), Alexander Altmann criticized Cohen on this very point. After accepting that "all religion is rooted in the experience of correlation—human-relative and divine-absolute reality," which clearly resonates with the Cohenian view, Altmann adds that religion "develops its most original formational tendencies in the reasonably volitional intention to participate."[69] The emphasis on participation demarcates the spot where Cohen's philosophy can be judged as deficient; his notion of correlation did not go far enough insofar as he did not take seriously the "absolute realization" of God as Being. As Altmann continues, "the fundamental law of religious consciousness must be that in each case the tendency toward participation is the center of religious experience, and this tendency presupposes, according to its meaning, a polarity of realities. A posture that conceives of God not as reality but as mere transcendental ideal, whether of reality or specifically of morality, hence as mere idea of reality, is philosophical but not primordially religious."[70] In the accompanying note, Altmann refers the reader to a passage in Cohen's "Religion und Sittlichkeit" and draws the following conclusion: "In all stages of the development of Cohen's philosophy of religion, the Being of God retains the sense of a mere idea that functions as a hypothesis that guarantees logically the existence and thus the reality of ethics. In spite of the sharp emphasis on the uniqueness of God in the sense of supra-phenomenal incomparability, Cohen's idea of God lacks what is religiously essential, namely, the character of transcendent reality and epistemological absoluteness."[71] In a word, according to Altmann, the transcendental philosophy of religion affirmed by Cohen, which computes transcendence as a limit concept rather than an actual reality of the primordial being, pulls God into immanence as nothing more than a construct of human reason.[72]

In the preface to the English translation of *Die Religionskritik Spinozas als Grundlage seiner Bibelwissenschaft: Untersuchungen zu Spinozas Theologisch-Politischem Traktat*, which was also originally published in 1930, Leo Strauss makes explicit what is implicit in Altmann's critique: "Above all, if the truth of Judaism is the religion of reason, then what was formerly believed to be revelation by the transcendent God must now be understood as the work of the human imagination in which human reason was effective to some extent; what has now become a clear and distinct idea was originally a confused idea. What except demonstrations of the existence of God by theoretical reason or postulations of His existence by practical reason, which were becoming ever more incredible, could prevent one from taking the last step, i.e. to assert that God Himself is a product of the human mind, at best 'an idea of reason'?"[73] In the spirit of the dialogical thinking of Rosenzweig, to whom this book is dedicated, as well as of Rudolf Otto's notion of the holy, the numinous transcendence of God "beyond experience" (*Erlebens-Jenseitigkeit*), "beyond life" (*Lebens-Jenseitigkeit*), and "beyond ideas" (*Ideen-Jenseitigkeit*)[74]—perhaps goaded by Heidegger's insistence that authentic philosophical thought must rid itself of any theological impetus[75]—Strauss notes that the experience of revelation is "not a kind of self-experience" or the "actualization of a human potentiality," but it is "something undesired, coming from the outside, going against man's grain. It is the only awareness of something absolute which cannot be relativized in any way as everything else, rational or non-rational, can; it is the experience of God as the Thou, the father and king of all men; it is the experience of an unequivocal command addressed to me here and now as distinguished from general laws or ideas which are always disputable and permitting of exceptions."[76] Even though Cohen's idea of the absolute does allow for the element of indeterminacy, it does not accommodate the diremptive aspect of the transcendent breaking into the space-time continuum and disrupting one's ordinary expectations. On the contrary, the transcendence that emerges from Cohen's religion of reason is nothing more than a cosmic principle of immanence that is mathematically calculable and scientifically predictable.

For all the disagreement between Strauss and Julius Guttmann laid out in the first chapter of his *Philosophie und Gesetz: Beiträge zum Verständnis Maimunis und seiner Vorläufer* (1935),[77] on the matter of Guttmann's condemnation of Cohen in his *Die Philosophie des Judentums* (1933) there is little dispute. Guttmann argued that in the earlier phase of his thinking, Cohen criticized Kant and transferred the idea of God from the sphere of epistemology to ethics, but the God that he affirmed is "no more than the symbol for the unity of the ethical world" and not the independent "metaphysical reality."[78] The attempt to secure the absolute transcendence of the divine against both pantheistic and moralistic immanentism—"God is the basis for the unity of nature and ethics, and thus cannot be absorbed by the world of ethics or that of nature"[79]— resulted in the "reconstruction" of God "into an idea, involving the denial of his metaphysical claims and personal character. The transcendence of God can only be the transcendence of an idea, which can of course transcend the particular separate spheres of methodical consciousness, but can never go beyond the boundaries of the latter."[80] The God-concept remains a postulate of consciousness that strips the divine of an objectivity that is critical to the volitional deity of the biblical-rabbinic faith. But even in the latter phase of his thinking, when he drew closer to Judaism and sought to promote a God concerned with human suffering, the only credible source for the purification of sin, which serves as the ultimate theological ground for the subjectivity of the individual required to justify the universality of the moral principle, Cohen could not liberate his God from the snare of an ethical idealism that precluded the possibility of positing God as the "supreme reality,"[81] the tangible object of religious experience, and thus, according to Guttmann, "there remains an unbridgeable gap between the content of religion and the philosophical creation of concepts."[82] In a similar vein, Strauss concluded that Cohen's "return to tradition" was fraught with "explicit reservations against the tradition in the name of freedom, of man's autonomy."[83] This "rehabilitation of the Enlightenment"[84] renders revelation subservient to reason, for even the identification of the latter with the law must be evaluated strictly from the vantage point of the moral edification of human beings. The revealed law thus becomes nothing more than a symbol for the "subservience of everything . . . to the ideal of holiness,"[85] which is deemed primarily as the regulative principle of morality. In spite of, or because of, Cohen's identification of reason and revelation, he could not affirm the "revealed truths or revealed laws in the precise or traditional sense of the terms."[86] For Cohen, revelatory experience unfettered by rational theology would unquestionably be subject to Kant's assumption that any "supernatural communication" (*übernatürliche Mitteilung*) or "mystical illumination" (*mystische Erleuchtung*) is a form of "exalted vision" (*schwärmerische Vision*) that signals the "death of all philosophy."[87]

The transcendence or uniqueness of God is expressive of the absolute otherness and incomparability, a privation of ontological plenitude, which leads theoretically and experientially to the nullification of theism. As Schwarzschild put it: "Cohen resumes the tradition of Maimonides, to whom he devotes much devout attention, and extends the doctrine of negative theology almost to the point where the very personalism of God vanishes."[88] Andrea Poma, a more recent expositor of Cohen's critical idealism, has come to the same conclusion, albeit in a less pejorative tone: "The idea of God or, more precisely, the idea of God's transcendence is the systematic concept of immanence, in the distinction between logic and ethics, Being and What Ought to Be, nature and morality, against any pantheistic conception of identity."[89] I have no doubt that Cohen sincerely believed that the Jewish God is the "transcendental grounding upon which all of empirical reality is predicated,"[90] but this falls short of justifying the continued depiction of this God as the personal deity of monotheistic practice and dogma, a depiction that is dependent on a far more active role of the theological imagination.

THEOMANIA AND THE ECLIPSE OF THE GIVING

A similar critique of Cohen was offered by Martin Buber in the essay "The Love of God and the Idea of the Deity" (1943). Buber chronicles Cohen's attempt to get past the Kantian sublimation of God into an idea, the principle of truth instrumental in establishing the unity of nature and morality, by giving an adequate place to the love of God in the gamut of religious faith. Nevertheless, in Buber's estimation, Cohen could not get out from under the weight of thinking that experiencing God as a living personality is to place the divine within the confines of myth. Thus even in his last work, as we have seen, to preserve the Being (*esse*; *Sein*) of God, Cohen deprives the deity of existence (*existentia*; *Dasein*). God is designated as "absolute personality," but this does not mean that God is a person, only that God loves as a personality and wishes to be loved like a personality.[91] Such a distinction, however, is not defensible; one cannot credibly speak of a reciprocal love between God and human if the former is an idea and the latter a person. Cohen's identification of the God of Abraham and the God of the philosophers was thus doomed to fail. Buber incisively notes that the purification of monotheism of all images leads to the abstraction that is the greatest imaginative representation: "For the idea of God, that masterpiece of man's construction, is only the image of images, the most lofty of all the images by which man imagines the imageless God." To love God genuinely one must sense an "actuality which rises above the idea."[92]

The danger of the role of imagination in religious faith and the psychological need to picture God anthropomorphically appears to underlie the comment in Buber's *I and Thou* that just as the infatuation of the egomaniac (*ichsüchtige Mensch*) with his self causes him to misconstrue the truth of the process of perception or affection, so the theomaniac (*gottsüchtige Mensch*) is so obsessed with the deity that he turns the Thou of the revelatory meeting into an It in the realm of experienced objects and thereby fails to grasp the nature of either the giver or the gift.[93] Like Cohen and Rosenzweig, Buber's dialogical thinking is rooted in the principle of correlation that preserves the separate identities of God, human, and world.[94] It is worthwhile recalling the nexus between the present, presence, and relation to the other established by Buber, for consideration of the temporal comportment of the moment of the encounter affords one the opportunity to understand his conception of making-present that which comes to presence without the possibility of representation that would compel theistic belief to lapse into idolatry:

The present [*Gegenwart*]—not that which is like a point and merely designates whatever our thoughts may posit as the end of "elapsed" time, the fiction of the fixed lapse, but the actual and fulfilled present—exists only insofar as presentness [*Gegenwärtigkeit*], encounter [*Begegnung*], and relation [*Beziehung*] exist. Only as the You becomes present does presence come into being. . . . Presence is not what is evanescent and passes but what confronts us, waiting and enduring. . . . What is essential is lived in the present, objects in the past.[95]

In the third part of *I and Thou*, Buber develops the notion of God as the eternal Thou, an absolute presence that can never by its own nature become an it, an object subject to spatial and temporal conditionality:

Every You in the world is compelled by its nature to become a thing for us or at least to enter again and again into thinghood. . . . Only one You never ceases, in accordance with its nature to be You for us. To be sure, whoever knows God also knows God's remoteness and the agony of drought upon a frightened heart, but not the loss of presence. . . . The eternal You is You by its very nature; only *our* nature forces us to draw it into the It-world and It-speech. The It-world coheres in space and time. The You-world does not cohere in either. It coheres in the center in which the extended lines of relationships intersect: in the eternal You.[96]

Buber recognized that if the absence beyond the world is given as presence in the world, the religious imaginaire will acquiesce inevitably to the anthropocentric personification of transcendence. In a section near the conclusion of the afterword added to *I and Thou* in 1957, Buber tackles this very issue. Acknowledging that the "actuality of faith" (*Glaubenwirklichkeit*) requires that we apply to transcendence characteristics that we take from the realm of immanence, Buber writes: "The designation of God as a person is indispensable for all who, like myself, do not mean a principle when they say 'God,' although mystics like Eckhart occasionally equate 'Being' [»*das Sein*«] with him and who, like myself, do not mean an idea when they say 'God,' although philosophers like Plato could at times take him for one—all who, like myself, mean by 'God' him that, whatever else he may be in addition, enters into a direct relationship [*unmittelbare Beziehung*] to us humans beings through creative, revelatory, and redemptive acts, and thus makes it possible for us to enter into a direct relationship to him. . . . The concept of personhood is, of course, utterly incapable of describing the nature of God; but it is permitted and necessary to say that God is *also* a person."[97]

It is noteworthy that Buber invokes Spinoza, commenting that in addition to the two modes that the philosopher identified as expressing God's infinity, nature (extension) and spirit (thought), a third should be added, which he designates by the idiosyncratic coinage "personlikeness" (*Personhaftigkeit*), a postulate that Spinoza, of course, would find philosophically offensive.[98] Buber does not shy away from the paradox: God both is and is not a person. The full scope of the discord with a linear logic of noncontradiction is appreciated when we realize that precisely because God is not a person we can speak of God as the "absolute person," that is, the "one that cannot be relativized. It is as absolute person that God enters into direct relationship to us."[99] Emulating the divine, every intersubjective relation is marked by the simultaneity of unconditional inclusivity and unconditional exclusivity.

In *Two Types of Faith*, Buber noted a basic contrast between Judaism and Christianity with respect to the anthropomorphic manifestation of the divine. In Christianity, there is one permanent image by which the invisible is seen, the person of Jesus, who represents the human countenance of the Father; in Judaism, God appears in a plethora of visions, but, since none of these persist, the divine "remained unseen in all His appearances."[100] In my judgment, Buber's assertion that the dialectic of concealment and disclosure is preserved more perspicaciously in Judaism than in Christianity is questionable, but for the purposes of this chapter this matter can be bracketed. What is more important is Buber's insight concerning the inevitable lapse of monotheism into idolatry. His words are worth citing in full:

> "Israel," from the point of view of the history of faith, implies in its very heart immediacy towards the imperceptible Being. God ever gives Himself to be seen in the phenomena of nature and history, and remains invisible. That He reveals Himself and that He "hides Himself" (Is. xlv. 15) belong indivisibly together; but for His concealment His revelation would not be real and temporal. Therefore He is imageless; an image means fixing to one manifestation, its aim is to prevent God from hiding Himself, He may not be allowed any longer to be present as the One Who is there as He is there (Exod. iii. 14), no longer appear as He will; because an image is this and intends this, "thou shalt not make to thyself any image." And to Him, the ever only personally Present One, the One who never becomes a figure, even to Him the man in Israel has an exclusively immediate relationship . . . not as an object among objects, but as the exclusive Thou of prayer and devotion.[101]

Monotheism, according to Buber, is not essentially a stance about the world, as is customarily believed, but rather the faith and piety that ensue from the "primal reality of a life-relationship." It is precisely because God remains hidden in the "exclusive immediacy" of this relationship that God is manifest in innumerable forms in space and time. To turn any of these manifestations into a fixed image is to subvert the prophetic truism that God is imageless. In Buber's language, God is the eternal Thou, the "personally present One" that can never become a figure—this is the meaning of the name of God revealed to Moses on behalf of the Israelites, *ehyeh asher ehyeh*, that is, God is the supreme subjectivity that cannot be objectified, "the One who cannot be represented," "the One who cannot be confined to any outward form."[102] This "reality of faith" is opposed by the Christian belief that "assigns to God a definite human countenance" through the historical person of Jesus. "The God of the Christian is both imageless and imaged, but imageless rather in the religious idea and imaged in actual experience. The image conceals the imageless One." From the Jewish perspective, the paradox is kept intact: the image reveals the imageless One insofar as the immediacy of the latter entails that God hides and appears concomitantly; that is, the God that is revealed is the God that is withheld.[103] As Buber put it elsewhere, "The religious reality of the meeting with the Meeter, who shines through all forms and is Himself formless, knows no image of Him, nothing comprehensible as object. It knows only the presence of the Present One."[104] It is for this reason that Buber suggests that "critical atheism" of the philosopher, the "negation of all metaphysical ideas about God," is "well suited to arouse religious men and to impel them to a new meeting. On their way they destroy the images which manifestly no longer do justice to God."[105]

Buber avows nonetheless that in order not to succumb to the voice of nihilism we need to have recourse to the "images of the Absolute, partly pallid, partly crude, altogether false and yet true, fleeting as an image in a dream yet verified in eternity."[106] Commenting on this passage, Strauss wrote the following:

> The experience of God is surely not specifically Jewish. Besides, can one say that one experiences God as the creator of heaven and earth, i.e. that one knows from the experience of God, taken by itself, that He is the creator of heaven and earth, or that men who are not prophets experience God as a thinking, willing and speaking being? Is the absolute experience necessarily the experience of a Thou? Every assertion about the absolute experience which says more than that what is experienced is the Presence or the Call, is not the experiencer, is not flesh and blood, is the wholly other, is death or nothingness, is an "image" or an interpretation; that any one interpretation is the simply true interpretation is not known but "merely believed." One cannot establish that any particular interpretation of the absolute experience is the most adequate interpretation on the ground that it alone agrees with all other experiences, for instance with the experienced mystery of the Jewish fate, for the Jewish fate is a mystery only on the basis of . . . one particular interpretation of the absolute experience. The very emphasis on the absolute experience as experience compels one to demand . . . that it be carefully distinguished from every interpretation of the experience, for the interpretations may be suspected of being attempts to render bearable and harmless the experienced which admittedly comes from without down upon man and is undesired; or of being attempts to cover over man's radical unprotectedness, loneliness and exposedness.[107]

Strauss offers a hypothetic rejoinder on the part of Buber that the atheistic suspicion about belief in the experience of the absolute is as much a belief as the theistic position.[108] What is crucial for my analysis is that Strauss offered an incisive critique of Buber's paradoxical assertion that the images of God are, at once, fictitious and true, ephemeral and enduring. In fairness to Buber, Strauss did not pay close enough attention to the point we raised above concerning what Buber imagined to be the distinctive contribution of Judaism in realizing that every image is as much a concealment as it is a disclosure. From this standpoint, Buber would have assuredly consented to Strauss's admonition that no one interpretation of the experience is sufficient to account for all the other interpretations, a view that gestures hermeneutically toward the postmodern sensibility.[109]

It is pertinent at this juncture to mention as well Buber's explication in *Good and Evil* of the biblical allegation (placed in the voice of the serpent) that by eating of the fruit of the Tree of Knowledge, the first couple became like God, knowing the opposites of good and evil (Genesis 3:5): "In the swirling space of images, through which he strays, each and every thing entices him to be made incarnate by him; he grasps at them like a wanton burglar, not with decision, but only in order to overcome the tension of omnipossibility; it all becomes reality, though no longer divine but his, his capriciously constructed, indestinate reality, his violence, which overcomes him, his handiwork and fate." Circumscribed within the precinct of the Garden of Eden, the divine reality allotted to humanity is good, but once driven out of this state, the actuality gives way to the boundless possible, which is evil to the degree that it is fictitious. Within the transcendence of the divine—and, as Buber reminds the reader, "there is no other transcendence than that of the Creator"—the opposites are transcended, but in the human domain good and evil are torn asunder, reflected psychologically in the dual aspect of the imagination, rendered in rabbinic parlance as the good inclination (*yeṣer ṭov*) and the evil inclination (*yeṣer ra*), the division that brings about the "chaotic of the possible, which is continuously, capriciously incarnating itself, over the created world."[110] Reflecting the kabbalistic and Hasidic interpretation of one of the rudimentary maxims of rabbinic anthropology, Buber accentuates that the spiritual task is to unite the two impulses by recognizing their underlying unity. What is crucial to our analysis is that this insight about the human predisposition to incarnate can be applied as well to the theopoetic propensity to imagine the transcendent in forms that are no more than a projection of our will to instantiate in form that which is formless. The presence of God is made present[111] through what we could call a process of imaging the real.[112]

IDOLATRY AND THE FIXED IMAGE OF THE DIVINE CONFIGURATION

A similar tension is discernible in Rosenzweig, whose thought I will explore in detail in the following chapter. In the Introduction, I noted briefly that the new thinking espoused by Rosenzweig—following Cohen's lead—rests on taking seriously the belief that the personal God of Judaism cannot be reduced to the natural world or to human consciousness, but he emphasizes that this personhood must be more than the regulative ideal of being, a point underscored by his repeated assertion that revelation, which is the theological category that legitimates creation and redemption—in temporal terms, the present that endows the past and the future with tensiveness—must consist of the unmediated bond between the "ever-renewed actuality" (*allzeiterneuerte*

Wirklichkeit)[113] of God and the existential facticity of the human individual that depends on the self-disclosure of the former to the latter. For Rosenzweig, belief in God's existence, as Altmann expressed his own theological outlook in the aforementioned essay from 1930, presumes the "supratranscendental real givenness of the divine appearing in a certain mode of experience . . . the specifically religious phenomenon of the divine sphere of reality that can never be reduced to transcendental-logical schema. . . . It is a specific form of experience, arising on the ground of our metaphysical stance, which lets us focus on the divine as required by its meaning in accordance with the level of its transcendence, hypostatization, and personification."[114] Altmann is not unaware of the phenomenological difficulty of maintaining that the "basic religious act discloses the sphere of an essentially transcendent absolute reality," since what is implied thereby is "a level of transcendence superior to all experienceable transcendence however interpreted metaphysically. Thus it is a transcendence that is, from the very point where it introduces itself, not experienceable."[115] Divine transcendence is removed from any attempt at relativization, and hence it cannot be enclosed within the boundaries of what may be experienced or comprehended.

Herein consists the major difference between metaphysics and religion: the domain of the former "is cognition, which is always relative," whereas the domain of the latter is the "region of the formational act that is directed toward the absolute."[116] Precisely because transcendence, when properly understood, stipulates the complete withdrawal from the phenomenalizable, we can grasp the function of religious intuition indexically as pointing the way to what is beyond the way—the sign that directs one to what is, logically speaking, insignificant. Interestingly enough, in one of his last essays that was published after his death, Altmann recounts in the name of Wittgenstein that one's faith in God "denotes the factuality of a transcendent conscious Being the surrender to whose care makes all the difference in one's life. . . . The commitment is personal and it flows from faith in a personal God."[117] In a second passage, Altmann reiterates this central tenet of the phenomenology of religious experience within a theistic framework: "Belief in God is never a merely abstract affirmation of a Supreme Being. Invariably, it entails faith in the truth of a coherent series of beliefs, strung together by a concrete image of God. Without the total *Gestalt*, that image fades away."[118] Although this image should not be understood in some "crude sense" as literal, it is still "potent and vibrant."[119] The Wittgensteinian motif of religious language-games as pictures embraced by Altmann could well serve as a summary of Rosenzweig's thinking: "To be religious is to live by pictures or, as we might say, by an inventory of images in which powerful ideas are concretized. . . . The images that form the texture of religious thought are all related to each other and form a consistent whole."[120]

Leora Batnitzky has suggested that to understand the role of image in Rosenzweig one must take into account a crucial distinction between *Vorstellung* and *Vertreter* (or the verb *vertreten*): the former denotes representation by image, and the latter a sign that is representative. The two connotations are correlated with two conceptions of idolatry: the first, which is applicable to Maimonides and Cohen, is the worship of false images of the deity, which, as a matter of course, encompasses any and every image, since God is imageless; the second, which applies to Rosenzweig, is worship of a spatially and temporally fixed image of God. In contrast to Maimonides and Cohen, Rosenzweig does not deny that images can represent God authentically; the problem is that fixating on any given image as a mode of worshipping God limits the infinite freedom of the divine to manifest itself in any form, and this, in turn, repudiates the hermeneutical value of the sign as that which marks the historically concrete relationship of God and community, the meaning of which is enacted through the liturgical actions that bind the members of that community together across the divide of time, the very actions that constitute Israel's mission as serving as witnesses of the divine revelation.[121]

Batnitzky's philological distinction has illumined a crucial but overlooked disparity between Rosenzweig and Cohen. For the former, unlike the latter, the peril of idolatry lurking at the heart of monotheism is not imagining that God assumes tangible forms in history; it is rather reifying those forms into fixed icons of worship that would obfuscate the relational and polysemic character of those forms. We should not lose sight of the fact that compared to his teacher Rosenzweig accepted a more mythopoeic approach that presumed the possibility of the invisible divinity manifesting itself in what he tellingly refers to as the figure (*Gestalt*).[122] To be sure, the image of that figure—the divine face (*göttlichen Angesicht*) in which the eternal truth of the star of redemption takes shape—is not to be conceived literally, but it is also not merely metaphorical. Insofar as it is a claim about the nature of God's reality, the figure must be experienced sensuously as a real presence. For Rosenzweig, as for the kabbalists, ascribing forms to God does not imply that the divine assumes a corruptible body. It suggests, rather, that the spiritual reality can be apprehended only through an image configured in the imagination of the visionary, an image that in its most sublime manifestation is anthropomorphic in nature. Locating these forms in the imagination is not to divest them of their objectivity or to reduce them to the subjectivity of the individual, however, since the theophanic image of that which transcends images is accorded the status of reality only inasmuch as it is imagined as real. This perspective induces the identity of symbol and symbolized, albeit an identity that preserves the difference of what is identified. The soul, accordingly, may be specularized as the garment through which the divine light is manifest by being hidden.

I will discuss this matter more elaborately in the following chapter, but suffice it here to mention Rosenzweig's observations in the brief but fecund essay on biblical anthropomorphisms written in 1928.[123] Influenced by and yet diverging from Cohen, Rosenzweig maintains that the anthropomorphic images of God in Scripture should not be construed as assertions about something (*Etwas*) that is indicative of the divine or human nature but rather as declarations about the events (*Geschehen*) of encounter between the two.[124] In a manner that is consonant with the position of Buber mentioned above, the literary anthropomorphisms, according to Rosenzweig, attest to the ontic fact that in confronting humankind the divine enters into a "momentary bodily and spiritual [*leiblich-seelische*] reality with equally concrete momentary corporeal and ensouled [*leibhaft-seelenhafte*] meeting." These manifestations do not translate into an image (*Abbild*) or a portrait (*Beschreibung*) because they display a concrete and present character (*konkret-momentanen Charakter*) that is always relative to the meeting that occurs in the present moment.[125] From Rosenzweig's standpoint, God's "self-embodying" (*Selbstverleiblichung*) and "self-spiritualization" (*Selbstvergeistigung*)—features that by his own admission bear a resemblance to the configurations (*parṣufim*) of God in kabbalistic theosophy[126]—are "the single protection against the backsliding into polytheism, which indeed is nothing but consolidation of a genuine present revelation of the real God [*wirklichen Gottes*] to a lasting image of God [*Gottesbild*]."[127] Against this background, it is of interest to ponder Rosenzweig's more extended remark on the nature of kabbalah as a reaction to the Maimonidean rejection of anthropomorphism:

> The Jewish philosophy of religion of the Middle Ages was called up to the battlefield by the grotesque confusion of the early Kabbala [*Frühkabbala*] in its wanting to count and measure out [*auszählen und ausmessen*] God's "form" [*Gottes "Gestalt"*], this inner-Jewish classic case of a genuine, that is, representative Anthropomorphism (without inverted commas). The philosophy peaks in the—so far as possible in Judaism—successful attempt of Maimonides to codify dogmatically the "incorporeality" of God. The answer is given this time by the high- and late-Kabbala [*Hoch- und Spätkabbala*]. Simply because it took over from philosophy of religion the concept of "absolutely without attributes," a Godhead to be determined only negatively [*Begriff der vollkommen eigenschaftslosen, nur negativ zu bestimmenden Gottheit*], kabbalistically expressed, the Ain Sof [the Infinite], the Absolute, it discovered under this highest rung an ever more variegated throng of heavenly rungs beneath and between.[128]

Rosenzweig goes on to say that the "last degenerations" (*letzten Ausartungen*) of the kabbalah belong to the "third epoch" of the battle against anthropomorphism within Judaism. As he further conjectures on the basis of personal experience, the answer to this perplexing problem will likely "be given by the great ones who get baptized [i.e., Jewish converts to Christianity] of the nineteenth and unfortunately also the twentieth century."[129]

Here is not the place to enter into a lengthy discourse about the affinity that Rosenzweig seems to have grasped between the anthropomorphic tendency of the kabbalistic imaginary and the incarnational appeal of Christianity for some Jews.[130] What is important to underline is that Rosenzweig clearly interpreted the Jewish esoteric tradition about the divine body, first enunciated in the *Shi'ur Qomah* tradition, to which he refers as the "grotesque confusion of the early Kabbala,"[131] and then in the latter theosophic ruminations of the "high- and late-Kabbala," in light of the distinction he makes between the theophanic forms by which God is revealed in the momentary meetings and the images by and through which these appearances are cast.[132] As exotic and extreme as the kabbalistic texts appear, they are in basic agreement with the identification of God's personality (*Persönlichkeit*) as countenance (*Antlitz*) already attested in Scripture.[133] This is the intent as well of his epigrammatic but provocative criticism of Freud's idea of the totem offered in a diary entry from 1922. Freud had it wrong to argue categorically that the totem is idolatry (*Götzendienst*) to the extent that it is always a substitute for the father (*Vaterersatz*). On the contrary, the experience of fatherhood can be considered an authentic "representation of God" (*Stellvertreter Gottes*) as long as it is understood that God cannot be contained in the image of any particular father. Regrettably, religion exhibits the inclination to reify divine appearances into images—only retrospectively from the vantage point of revelation is the idol seen as a substitution for God (*Der Götze ist nämlich nur von der Offenbarung rückwärts gesehen Gottesersatz*). Understanding idolatry as the worship of a fixed image of the divine rather than the presumed manifestation of the divine in that image leads Rosenzweig to the far-reaching conclusion that revelation is God's "own religion," which he glosses as an antireligion set "against the religion of man."[134] What Rosenzweig seems to be conveying is, in my mind, expressed more clearly in the following Heideggerian-inflected comment of Bernhard Radloff: "Only in the wake of the reduction of the image to its being-present for a subject can it be conceived an idol, for to be an idol signifies mistaking the being in its being-present for the God toward which it 'points.' But as such, in its mere being-present, the image as the *refusal* of objectivity, and as the withdrawal of being-present, is concealed."[135] But is Rosenzweig's distinction viable? Can we entertain seriously the possibility of embodiment and spiritualization on the part of God without a corresponding image-formation on the part of the human imagination? If we were to remove the latter from the equation, could we still speak meaningfully of God's appearing in the guise of discrete images?

Cohen believed that mythology is "overcome through the definition of God."[136] By contrast, for Rosenzweig, not only is this not the case, but the definition of God is impossible without mythology, and indeed, the *Star of Redemption* can be seen as an effort to reclaim the mythologic in a meaningful way philosophically, theologically, and experientially. But is Rosenzweig not subject, in the final analysis, to the same dilemma as Cohen and before him Maimonides? To speak about God would be evocative only if we subscribe to the possibility of meeting a *real God*, a God to whom phenomenological concreteness as person may be attributed. But can the human being encounter such a God without psychologically reducing that reality to a metaphorical configuration of the imagination?

CHAPTER 2

Apophatic Vision and Overcoming the Dialogical

> Truth is indivisible, hence it cannot recognize itself; anyone
> who wants to recognize it has to be a lie.
>
> —Franz Kafka, *The Blue Octavo Notebooks*

It is commonly maintained, and not without good reason, that Rosenzweig's *sprach-denken* rests upon the supposition that there are three unsublatable elements—God, human, and world—that emerge from the shattering of the all-encompassing totality presumed by German idealists to be the ultimate reality. In the 1925 essay "Das neue Denken," which was Rosenzweig's attempt to offer a guide to reading his magnum opus, *Der Stern der Erlösung*, he summarized the point concisely:

> What was put into the *Star of Redemption* was, at the beginning, the experience of factuality [*die Erfahrung der Tatsächlichkeit*] prior to all of actual experience's matters of fact. [The experience] of factuality that forces upon thinking, instead of its favorite word "really," the little word "and," the basic word of all experience . . . God and the world and man. This "and" was the first of experience; so it must also recur in the ultimate of truth. Even in truth itself, the ultimate, which can only be one, an "and" must stick; otherwise than the truth of the philosophers, which may know only itself, it must be truth for someone. If it is nevertheless to be the one, then it can be only for the One. And it thereby becomes a necessity that our truth becomes manifold and that "the" truth transforms itself into our truth. Thus truth ceases to be what "is" true and becomes that which has to be *verified* as true.[1]

The conjunctive "and" is accorded the status of being the "basic word of all experience," since the structure of experience, phenomenologically, is inexorably correlative. Not substance but relation enframes our experience—God *and* the world *and* the human, which is to say, the nature of these three elements cannot be ascertained in isolation from the other. From that point of view, the conjunction is disjunctive, for like a bridge it connects two termini by keeping them at a distance, forging nearness, as Heidegger would say, that draws nigh what remains remote.[2] Even in the oneness of the ultimate truth, the truth that is the star of redemption, the conjunction "and" must be preserved—what is most important is not to determine what the essence of truth is but to realize through the act of verification (*Bewährung*) that truth is relational; that is, it must always be truth for someone. Hence, while God's truth is one, it must be transformed into the manifold that is "our truth."[3]

In his commentary to Judah Halevi's poem on repentance for the Yom Kippur liturgy, which begins with the words *yeminkha nose awonay peshuṭah leqabbel teshuvah*, translated as *Heimkehr*, Rosenzweig emphasizes an apparently irreconcilable tension in the dialogical relationship between God and human: the former demands the first step from the latter, but the latter is constitutionally too weak to take the first step without the assistance of the former. Even on the Day of Atonement, the day of reconciliation, this tension is in place, and thus "[t]he nearness itself . . . becomes an element of the distance. The conversation between the two voices continues in that unending distance with which it began." A resolution to the dilemma is found in the termination of the final prayer of the day, the sealing of the fate (*neʻilah*), which assumes the position of the eschatological "last moment" in which "a last word" is granted to the human sinner seeking forgiveness rather than to God, to whom it is usually applied:

> The human himself, under God's eyes, gives himself the answer, which presents him with the gift of the fulfillment of his prayer of return, of homecoming for this one, anticipated last moment. At this moment he is as near to God, as close to his throne as human beings can be. In the rapture of this nearness the "You" is silent to him, not merely the You of his cry of despair, but also the You of his yearning and of his love.[4]

At the conclusion of the Day of Atonement, reflected in the last stanza of Halevi's poem, God's voice is silent, a silence that does not bespeak that the individual's desperate cry for forgiveness goes unanswered but rather that the gap between divine and human is so completely narrowed that there is only nearness without distance. In that sense, the human has the last word that is apposite for the last moment, the "word that stands behind all God's speech,—in the way in which the human can take this divine 'I' into his mouth, namely as a profession of the 'He.'" Grammatically, the first-person "I" morphs into the third-person "He" because there is no more separation, and with the collapse of all separation, the distance necessary to sustain the dialogical is overcome, and thus, in the ecstasy of the propinquity of the other to the self, the "You" of the individual's supplication and of his yearning and love falls silent.[5]

Rosenzweig's claim here would seem to contradict his own rhetorical query in the *Star*, "for what else is redemption but that the I learns to say you to the he?"[6] If dialogue is to be meaningful, it demands that there can be no proximity without remoteness, and even the redemptive moment requires that the third person be addressed in the second person, which signals familiarity and intimacy but also preserves detachment and diffidence. With typical incisiveness, Derrida captured the point when he noted in his "Interpretations at War: Kant, the Jew, the German" that "Rosenzweig's thought is characterized first and foremost by this thought of the 'and' *and* by that within it which dislocates any totalizing synthesis. It does not forbid any in-gathering [*rassemblement*] but interrupts in-gathering by the *syn* of the synthesis or of the system . . . It carries disjunction as much as it does conjunction."[7] What Derrida neglected to consider, however, is the last moment affirmed by Rosenzweig, the eschatological moment—or the liturgical sealing of Yom Kippur that anticipates that moment—wherein the conjunction is so complete that the matter of disjunction is no longer applicable. In that moment, the last word spoken by the human soul is the silence of God turning from the intimate first person to the impersonal third person. At the climactic closing of the day, when all requests for forgiveness are terminated, the prayerful pleading of the contrite sinner becomes the wordless word that stands behind all divine speech.

NEW THINKING AND KABBALISTIC MYSTICISM

In the essay "Facing the Effaced: Mystical Eschatology and the Idealistic Orientation in the Thought of Franz Rosenzweig," published in 1997, I argued that in the third part of the *Star*, especially in the sustained discussion of eternal truth in book three, Rosenzweig embraced a more mystically oriented conception that, in some measure, led to a reappropriation of the very idealism that he set out to repudiate.[8] The characterization of Rosenzweig's understanding of redemption as a kind of *theistic mysticism* was proffered by Gershom Scholem[9] and reiterated by Nahum Glatzer.[10] The more specific kabbalistic dimension of Rosenzweig's thought has been noted by a number of scholars,[11] and in the previous chapter I already had the occasion to discuss this matter when analyzing a critical remark in his brief note on anthropomorphisms. An especially interesting source that relates to this topic is the intriguing comment made by Abraham Isaac Kook preserved in a recently published letter from his son, Zvi Yehudah, written on 9 Adar 5690 (March 9, 1930).[12] As Uriel Barak suggests, Kook's comments are in all likelihood responding to the memorial address of Scholem delivered at the Hebrew University in Jerusalem on January 15, 1930, a little over a month since the passing of Rosenzweig on December 10, 1929. Scholem's eulogy, which was published in the year that it was given, would have been readily available for Kook to read. As reported by his son, Kook acknowledged the conceptual affinities between Rosenzweig and the kabbalah, and he even went so far as to say that those who are not masters of the mysteries (*ba'alei mistorin*) will not be able to comprehend his words. However, he did not consider this to be anything novel. Moreover, from his perspective, the critical issue has to be evaluated from what he deemed to be the "essence of the foundation of the kabbalah," which is the "actual drawing down of the holy spirit into reality by means of the ontological distinction of the comportment of Israel."[13] It is noteworthy that Kook discerned the speculative affinities between Rosenzweig and the kabbalah, the very affinities that figure in Kook's own mystical inclination. Even though Kook thought the experiential-theurgical dimension of the kabbalah is not accentuated by Rosenzweig, a credible case can be made that he overlooked the experiential dimension of Rosenzweig's thinking and the possibility that this was, in part, due to the influence of kabbalah.[14]

Support for my contention that the emphasis on the visual at the end of the *Star* betrays an affinity to, if not a direct influence of, kabbalah is found in a passing remark that Rosenzweig makes in his commentary to Halevi's poem *liqra't meqor ḥayyei emet aruṣah*, which he titles *Sehnsucht*:[15] "For this poet, the forerunner of the great Kabbalistic movements for whom the vision of God served as Israel's topical heritage and always to be newly actualized on the holy ground, sleep and dream are the legitimate ways to the goal."[16] This is a remarkable passage for at least two reasons. First, it demonstrates a subtle grasp of Halevi's protokabbalistic sensibilities, and second, it offers an astoundingly incisive and concise understanding of the centrality of the visionary dimension in the kabbalistic worldview.[17] What is important for our immediate concern, however, is the fact that the vision that Rosenzweig articulates in the concluding part of the *Star* is on a par with what he ascribes to Halevi and to the kabbalists. That vision, moreover, renders problematic the dialogical thinking that is dependent, as I noted in the Introduction, on the essential separateness of each of the three elements,[18] a theme that has even been used to justify labeling Rosenzweig as a precursor of postmodern discourse.[19] Rosenzweig thus made good on his promise in the conclusion of the introduction to the *Star* "to find again in this nothing, in this threefold nothing of knowledge [*diesem dreifachen Nichts des Wissens*], the All that we had to cut into pieces."[20] The All is retrieved, not as the one, all-encompassing nothing posited by idealist philosophers, but as a threefold nothing,[21] a nothing aligned individually with each of the basic terms of Rosenzweig's correlative thinking—the nothing of the knowledge of the human or the metaethical, the nothing of the knowledge of the world or the metalogical, and the nothing of the knowledge of God or the metaphysical.[22]

The mystical nature of this recovery finds support in a letter that Rosenzweig wrote to Margrit Rosenstock-Huessy on February 1, 1919, in which he described the third book of part three of the *Star* as "a 'mysticism,' but one which rests on the ground of all the unmystical which stands 500 pages before it, and then which is also neutralized again through the anti-mystical 'Gate' which yet follows after it."[23] Rosenzweig qualifies the mystical character of his account of redemption by insisting that the way he had to embark upon to get to it and the opening of the gate that follows from it are "unmystical," which is to say, they affirm the factuality (rendering the German *Tatsächlichkeit*, a critical term in Rosenzweig's thinking) of each of the three elements, that is, allowing God to be God, the human to be human, and the world to be world.[24] This qualification is necessary because Rosenzweig characterizes the mystic pejoratively as someone who harbors the self-conceit (*Mystikerdünkel*) of thinking that it is possible to cross the abyss separating the human-worldly and the divine.[25] Or, as he puts it in another passage, which betrays a glaring resemblance to Kierkegaard,[26] mysticism is "something disquietingly and even objectively dangerous," since the openness of the soul of the mystic to God renders it "invisible for the rest of the world and cut off from it. With an arrogant sense of security, the mystic turns the ring on his finger, and immediately he is with 'his' God and has nothing more to say to the world. . . . The world necessarily closes itself off to the closure of the arrogant man."[27] In a third passage, the mystic is derisively depicted as someone who is "swallowed up again in his own enclosure" rather than being open to the other and "coming alive as speaking figure."[28]

Notwithstanding these criticisms, the fact is, as Rosenzweig's own admission makes clear, the vision of the All that he offers the reader is not unrelated to the ideal of the "ecstatic mystic," who affirms that "everything is God"[29] and, as a consequence, divests the divine of its "one significant function: to be wholly other than the world."[30] Lest there be any misunderstanding, let me note that I am well aware that Rosenzweig himself marked the difference between his vision and that of the idealist and/or mystic:

> The All, which would be both everything and whole, can neither be known
> honestly nor experienced clearly; only the dishonest cognition of idealism, only the
> obscure experience of the mystic can make itself believe it has grasped it. The All
> must be grasped beyond cognition [*Erkenntnis*] and experience [*Erlebnis*], if it is to
> be immediately grasped [*unmittelbar erfaßt*]. Precisely this grasping takes place in
> the illumination of prayer [*der Erleuchtung des Gebets*].[31]

Rosenzweig finds fault with the idealist and the mystic respectively for promoting a "dishonest cognition" and an "obscure experience" of the All. By contrast, the All that he is reclaiming in his account of the eternal truth is beyond cognition and experience; it is grasped in the illumination of prayer. As Rosenzweig goes on to explain, it is through the annual liturgical cycle that the All "offers itself immediately for the beholding. In this last immediacy in which the All really comes altogether near to us, we are permitted now to restore the Name with which, in denying it, we began our work, the name of truth."[32] The truth—the All that is the Name—that had to be abandoned at the beginning is retrieved at the end. If one were to adopt a less prejudicial understanding of the mystical, it is not clear that the term should not apply to what Rosenzweig describes as the eschatological vision.

It is worth recalling that in the letter to Rudolf Ehrenberg written on November 18, 1917, the "Urzelle" (the germ cell) of the *Star*, Rosenzweig placed mysticism between "actual theology" and "actual philosophy."[33] Is this not an appropriate way to characterize his own effort in the *Star*? Consider the description of the "new philosopher" found therein: "Philosophy today requires . . . that 'theologians' do philosophy. But theologians in a different sense, of course. For . . . the theologian whom philosophy requires for the sake of its scientific character is himself a theologian who desires philosophy—out of concern for integrity. What was a demand in the interests of objectivity for philosophy will turn out to be a demand in the interests of subjectivity for theology. They complete each other, and together they bring about a new type of philosopher or theologian, situated between theology and philosophy."[34] A similar point is made in "The New Thinking": "Theology may not debase philosophy to play the part of the handmaid, yet just as degrading is the role of charwoman which . . . philosophy has become accustomed to give theology. The true relationship between these two renewed sciences . . . is one of siblings, which must in fact lead to union [of the sciences] within the persons who maintain them. Theological problems want to be translated into human [problems], while human [problems] want to be driven into the theological."[35]

INTERCONNECTIVITY AND THE SYSTEM OF PHILOSOPHY

The import of this comment sheds light on another well-known passage in the same essay wherein Rosenzweig states openly that the *Star* is primarily not a "Jewish book" or a "philosophy of religion," but it is a "system of philosophy," which sought "to bring about the total renewal of thinking."[36] Toward the end of the essay Rosenzweig recapitulates and accepts the designation of the *Star* as a "Jewish book." He explains, however, that this does not imply that it deals with "Jewish things" but that the "old Jewish words" are deployed to express what it has to say. "Like things in general, Jewish things have always passed away; yet Jewish words, even when old, share the eternal youth of the word, and if the world is opened up to them, they will renew the world."[37] The demarcation "Jewish" is indexical concomitantly of the particular and the universal; indeed, the former is meaningful only in virtue of the latter and not in the Hegelian sense of a dialectical resolution of the two such that the universal is expressed comprehensively in the particular, a *singular universality*, but rather in terms of understanding the universal as being configured continually in light of the ever-changing particular, the *universal singularity*, a universal that is, to borrow the formulation of Nancy, always calibrated from the perspective of "being-with-one-another, circulating in the *with* and as the *with* of this singularly plural coexistence,"[38] a universal that must be reckoned from the absolute incommensurability of the individual.[39] Rosenzweig himself makes a similar point:

> The world is neither a shadow, nor a dream, nor a painting; its being is being-there [*Dasein*], real being-there—created creation. The world is totally concrete [*ganz gegenständlich*], and all action in it, all "making," from the moment that it is in it, is supervening event. . . . The world is made of things; in spite of the unity of its concrete reality, it does not constitute a single object but a multiplicity of objects, precisely things. The thing does not possess stability as long as it is there quite alone. It is conscious of its singularity [*Einzelheit*], of its individuality [*Individualität*], only in the multiplicity of things. The thing can be shown only in connection

[*Zusammenhang*] with other things; it is determined by its spatial relationship with other things, within such a connection. Furthermore, as specific thing, it has no essence of its own, it does not exist in itself, it exists only in its relationships. The essence it has is not within it, but in the relationship it keeps according to its genus; it is behind its determination, and not in it that it must seek its essentiality [*Wesentlichkeit*], its universality [*Allgemeinheit*].[40]

The architectonic of Judaism is emblematic of a universality sought in the singularity and individuality of the multiplicity of things experienced somatically and concretely in the ebb and flow of temporal being. Ideally, the exemplarity that Judaism culturally imbibes in its exclusivity should be inclusively exceptional rather than exceptionally inclusive. Levinas thus well captured the essence of the *Star* in "'Between Two Worlds' (The Way of Franz Rosenzweig)," a paper read on September 27, 1959, to French intellectuals in the World Jewish Congress: "Yet this book of general philosophy is a Jewish book, which founds Judaism in a new way. Judaism is no longer just a teaching whose theses can be true or false; *Jewish existence* (and I wrote existence as one word) *itself is an essential event of being; Jewish existence is a category of being*."[41]

The *Star* comprises three of the four elements that Rosenzweig maintains are usually found in a philosophical system, logic, ethics, and aesthetics; the only element missing is philosophy of religion. However, the manner in which these topics are distributed in the book clearly indicates that it does not display the conventional understanding of a system; the presentation of the logical, ethical, and aesthetic insights are dispersed in the book rather than organized in a coherent and logical pattern.[42] We may presume, moreover, that the notion of system embraced by Rosenzweig in this description of the *Star* can be elucidated further from his comment in a letter to Rudolf Ehrenburg, dated December 12, 1917, that system does not denote an architectural structure (*System ist* nicht Architektur), which is formed by assembling individual stones whose meaning is determined only by the sense of the whole, but rather it denotes the striving (literally, the "drive and the will," *Trieb und Willen*) on the part of all individual entities (*alle andern Einzelnen*) for relationship (*Beziehung*); the viability of system is related to affirming a unity perpetually in the making, a cohesiveness that is not order but chaos, a totality that must always lie "beyond its conscious horizon." Rosenzweig notes that, in the Hegelian system, each individual position is anchored only in the whole and is thus related exclusively to two others, the one that immediately precedes it and the one that immediately succeeds it. By contrast, in the notion of the system he accepts, the genuine novelty of each temporal moment is not determined by its occupying a median position in a linear sequence between what came before and what comes after.[43] To the extent that the moment is authentically novel—an event of presence that is in excess of being present—it is experienced as the constant resumption of what is always yet to be, the return of what has never been, the vertical intervention that opens the horizontal timeline to the spherical fullness of eternity.[44]

The systematicity propounded by Rosenzweig is situated in the interstice between philosophy and theology,[45] emerging from "the intuitive knowledge of experience" of God, human, and world,[46] which serves as the epistemic basis for what is described in the final section of the *Star* as the mystic-like vision to come of the All, a seeing of the eternal star in the countenance of the configuration that is (in) truth.[47] That the vision described in the last part of the *Star* is Rosenzweig's attempt to incorporate into his system his own unique mystical experience can be confirmed by another letter to Margrit Rosenstock-Huessy from October 4, 1918, in which he described in extraordinary language having seen the star rotating around itself "with eyes and everything individual in it." By his own admission, the attempt to write down the nocturnal vision on the morning after proved to be a "wholly poor" and fragmentary recounting of the "immediate sight of the whole" (*Anblick des Ganzen*).[48] An allusion to this vision, whence the path goes forth and to which it returns, can be found in another passage in "The New Thinking." Reflecting on the nature of the philosophic book, of which the *Star* is exemplary, Rosenzweig notes that "the whole becomes surveyable at a glance." This momentary glimpse of the whole in the new thinking is to be contrasted with the conception of totality in the old thinking, insofar as the time of its occurrence "cannot be predicted" and it is not "at exactly the same point for two readers."[49] An integral part of the system that Rosenzweig constructed from his own vision revolves about "beholding the 'world-likeness in the countenance of God,'" a "seizing of all being in the immediacy of a moment and blink of an eye" in which "the limit of humanity is entered."[50] The broken All is reconfigured in this immediate sight of the whole, the whole that, like the moment in which it is seen, the blink of the eye, is the not-yet that has already been and therefore is always still to come. The assault on the necessity of a philosophical totality and the consequent turn to the concrete individual existence, the event of being, is not a rejection of system as such but a reorientation based on a system of factuality according to which universality is reshaped continuously in light of the entanglement of the web of particularity.[51]

SILENT ILLUMINATION AND THE CONCEALMENT OF REVELATION

In the remainder of this chapter, I will focus on one crucial aspect of the system, the depiction of the redemptive moment as the "silent illumination of the wholly fulfilling end" (*schweigenden Erleuchtung des voll erfüllenden Endes*).[52] The apophatic vision is an other-worldly state, the "eternal bliss" of the life-beyond-death, not a triumph of death by a return to the vicissitudes of temporal existence but rather an overcoming of time in the fullness of time that Rosenzweig describes in the ocular terms (derived from the depiction of the world to come transmitted in the name of Rav[53]) of the "pious ones" seated "with crowns upon their heads, and their eyes are turned toward the brilliance of the divinity [*Gottheit*] become manifest."[54] The end, to which is conferred the spectrality by means of which one crosses the "threshold of the supra-world [*Überwelt*], from the miracle [*Wunder*] to the illumination [*Erleuchtung*]," signifies that all three elements are transmogrified and liberated from their own ontic contingency: the human is redeemed "from all singularity and self-seeking," the world "from all thingliness," and God "from all the work of the six days of Creation and from all loving anxiety about our poor soul"; that is, God is unfettered from the imagistic garb of being portrayed "as the Lord" (*als den Herrn*),[55] the personal deity of the Jewish faith, the dialogical presence of the divine other that Rosenzweig placed at the center of his "absolute empiricism."[56] In Heideggerian terms,[57] Rosenzweig's project could be called an ontotheology, which has been succinctly characterized as "a philosophical theology in search of a philosophical foundation for the living God, a theological philosophy trying in its reflection on Being to reach a new understanding of the concrete God."[58] Naturally, I am aware of the fact that Rosenzweig was critical of the metaphysical-ontological tradition and its quest for an essence, a point to which I shall return below, but the validity of this claim should not obscure the fact that not only was his own speech-thinking meant to serve as a bridge connecting philosophy and theology, as I have already noted, but it is also an experiential mode that presumes that we can attribute a "naturalistic, existential essence" to God,[59] and consequently, he is still thinking metaphysically of being in relation to entity,[60] albeit the supreme entity that cannot be thought.[61] On both of these counts the term *ontotheology* is justified.[62]

The question I wish to put before the reader is whether Rosenzweig succeeds in promoting a way for human beings to access this essence. Does he philosophically articulate (and this is indeed the measure by which his thought needs to be judged) a foundation for belief in a living, concrete God? Expressed in his own theological vocabulary, does he account adequately for the real possibility of revelation as an experience of the immediate presence of the transcendent (or, perhaps it would be better to say, transcendence) breaking into history? Is Rosenzweig's radical empiricism sufficient to ground faith in a personal deity with a distinct existentiality, or is his own thinking susceptible to promoting an "atheistic theology," according to which the divine is reduced to a "self-projection of the human into the heaven of myth?"[63] Does he break forth from or is he inevitably trapped in the "anthropological modernity," the term he uses to name the third epoch of European philosophy—which complements "cosmological antiquity" and the "theological Middle Ages"—an epoch dominated by the "darling idea" of the "reduction" of experiences of the world and of God to the ego?[64] One might counter that Rosenzweig's embrace of apophaticism is actually an anticipation of more recent attempts to affirm "theology after ontotheology."[65] Although I am sympathetic to this point of view, in my mind it still begs the critical question, since even this form of "theological" reflection may not be exempt from the verdict that it is deeply atheological. Clarification of this matter has major implications not only for properly assessing the thought of one of the more lionized thinkers of the twentieth century but also for taking stock of the persistent theocentric bias of much of modern, and to some extent postmodern, Jewish religious philosophy, which owes its inspiration to the compelling narrative of Rosenzweig's life and his effort to revitalize the sacramental verve of Judaism in his major work.[66] Tackling this issue head on may provide an opportunity to set this course on a more even keel.

A responsible and responsive discussion of what is arguably one of the more challenging aspects of Rosenzweig's thought requires a reinvestigation of two major dimensions of his speech-thinking, the relation of hermeneutics and time, and the poetic nature of language. Without a proper grasp of these topics, readers cannot be expected to understand the turn on Rosenzweig's path that culminates in the overcoming of language, as one is rendered speechless in the face of truth, a metaphorical idiom that is hyperliteralized (perhaps due in part to the influence of kabbalistic terminology) in his attempt to render the literal metaphorically. I concur with Ricoeur's assessment that in Rosenzweig we have "a speculation that is metaphoric throughout, a metaphorics that is speculative throughout."[67] In Rosenzweig's own poetic diction, "the star that travels the path does not stand still for a moment," and thus it cannot be seen by the eye. When, however, the "moment has shut down through its becoming eternal," time permits one to see the configuration of truth in the blink of the eye. "The configuration, therefore, more than that which is elemental, more than what is real, is the directly perceptual." In this direct perception or intuition (*Anschauung*), the very factuality (*Tatsächlichkeit*) that Rosenzweig struggled to affirm,[68] that is, the ontic autonomy of the basic elementals, is "brought to its end," and "then nothing more is heard of thing [*Sache*] or of act [*Tat*]."[69] Redemption at the end restores one to creation at the beginning, and the hidden of "the everlasting primordial world [*Vorwelt*]," which became manifest in "the ever renewed world [*die allzeiterneuerte Welt*]," becomes hidden again in "the eternal supra-world [*Überwelt*]." The effort of the *Star* is to reveal this concealment as the revelation that is concealment, the "hidden aspect" that "remains all the more hidden" within God as the "revealed aspect of God dawns in us."[70] Indeed, in its deepest assonance, the theological category of revelation is overcome in the ultimate showing of the star, the luminosity of the face that reveals revelation to be the concealment of concealment, the seeing of the transcendence of seeing, the invisible manifestation of the manifest invisibility.

It has been noted that the structure of the book is not linear but circular: the author leads the reader on an excursion the end of which is a return to the beginning.[71] More profoundly, the hermeneutic at work in the *Star* reverses the temporal order, allowing for "a backward movement from the future to the past as opposed to a dialectically forward-moving argument from past to future,"[72] an idea substantiated dramatically by the opening "from death" (*Vom Tode*) and the conclusion "into life" (*Ins Leben*). In a strictly linear pattern, one would expect the progression to be from life to death; the circular course laid out by Rosenzweig starts with death and ends with life. One might say, therefore, that the *Star* puts into practice Rosenzweig's observation in "The New Thinking" that in a philosophical book "a sentence does not follow from its predecessor, but, much more likely, from its successor."[73] Even more to the point, in a second passage from that essay, Rosenzweig accepts the recommendation of one of the critics of the *Star* that the potential reader would profit by reading the book "backward and forward."[74] The author has no objection as long as one keeps in mind that it can be read from front to back as well as from back to front, thereby forming a circuitous itinerary rather than a linear trajectory. I would argue, however, that this circularity is not simply going back to where one has been, a mere repetition and recycling of patterns,[75] but it is rather a reverting to where one has never been and indeed where one can never be, which is precisely the mode of eternality that interrupts and intersects with time, thereby transforming temporality itself into a diremptive mode of luminosity, what I will call a theopoetic temporality,[76] the shining-forth of the nonrepresentable presentness that anticipates the past and recollects the future. The origin, on this account, is determined by the telos, the past shaped by the future,[77] but in such a way that both termini of the spectrum are opened—the end in the beginning and the beginning in the end. By anticipating the past and recollecting the future, we are attuned to a mode of time that deviates from the conventional sense of a chronology determined by narrative linearity.[78] It is worthwhile recalling Rosenzweig's comments in *Understanding the Sick and the Healthy: A View of World, Man, and God*, composed in 1921 as a précis of the *Star* to make it more congenial to a wider audience: an introduction to a book can never be conclusive, since its task is simply to introduce, and hence "the end to which it points serves as final verification. The end validates the beginning."[79] With these words Rosenzweig was certainly offering the potential reader a key to unlocking the intended meaning of his own work. That the end validates the beginning does not mean that the beginning is simply repeated in the end. On the contrary, the end is foretold by the beginning that cannot preview the end just as the beginning is previewed by an end that cannot foretell the beginning.

I would propose that the terms *linear circularity* or *circular linearity*, expressions that I have used to convey the dual deportment of time in kabbalistic lore as an extending line that rotates like a sphere or as a rotating sphere that extends like a line, can be applied to Rosenzweig as well. I note, in passing, that in the entry written by Rosenzweig in his diary on June 22, 1922, he remarked that his attempt to harmonize kabbalah and the "healthy human understanding" related to two key points: first, the "reality of space, that means the inadmissibility of *coincidentia oppositorum*," and second, the "reality of time, that means the inadmissibility of the category of eternity to enter somehow into the occurrence."[80] It is surely not insignificant that with respect to the central categories of space and time, Rosenzweig noted a basic similarity between kabbalah and his new thinking. For the purposes of this chapter, the matter of time is worthy of further comment.[81] Rosenzweig insists that eternity should not be affirmed at the expense of stripping time of its temporal significance, and this he understood to be an essential component of the kabbalistic orientation as well—*the inadmissibility of the category of eternity to enter somehow into the occurrence.* This statement confirms

Scholem's conjecture that the centrality of time in Rosenzweig's conception of experience resembles the emphasis placed on "time-bound thought" as a distinguishing
feature of the kabbalah offered, for instance, in a passage in one of the treatises composed in the thirteenth century by Isaac Ibn Laṭif.[82]

CONFIGURATION OF UNTRUTH IN THE MIRROR OF GOD'S TRUTH

What Scholem did not emphasize is that the premier role accorded time in the new
thinking and in the kabbalistic theosophy is connected as well to the quest for truth,
which is Rosenzweig's ultimate concern. In the final analysis, he speaks of an eternal
truth that comprehends the scope of truth as a whole, even if he continues to insist on
an "epistemological incompleteness,"[83] since the whole of truth is not accessible to us
as finite beings subject to generation and decay except as a promise and hence as a
presence that can be present only in the absence of being fully present.[84] Indeed, for
Rosenzweig, the partiality of truth is a direct outcome of the correlative logic that
demarcates the nature of being from the perspective of the relationality of events
rather than the substantiality of essences.[85]

A consequence of this critique of essentialism and the ontology of substance implied thereby[86] is that the "immediate sight" (*unmittelbare Schau*) of the "whole truth"
is available exclusively to one "who sees it in God," but this is "a seeing that is beyond
life" (*ein Schauen jenseits des Lebens*). Rosenzweig asserts nonetheless that the "living
seeing of the truth, a seeing that is life at the same time, thrives even for us only out of
the sinking into our own Jewish heart [*jüdisches Herz*] and even there only in the image [*Gleichnis*] and likeness [*Abbild*]."[87] The hermeneutic condition of human subjectivity, which is typecast by Rosenzweig in the culturally specific terms as a vision
constricted to the Jewish heart, is such that grasping the essence of truth in this
world—a seeing within of what is beyond—is always perspectival, and thus it can be
envisaged only through the veil of the image and likeness, whence we must infer that
reality is the appearance that appears to be real. Rosenzweig articulates this insight in
somewhat more technical terms, which convey a theosophic tenor, when he writes
that the eternal becomes configuration (*Gestalt*) in the truth that is the countenance
(*Antlitz*) of this configuration, the shining of the divine face (*göttlichen Angesicht*).[88]

Rendered epistemically, truth is, first and foremost, a matter of the virtuality of the
image, which both manifests and conceals, indeed manifests to the extent that it conceals and conceals to the extent that it manifests. From this it follows that untruth is
as much a part of the framing of truth as truth itself.[89] Or, in the anti-Hegelian formulation of Kierkegaard, which may have influenced Rosenzweig,[90] apropos of the
immediacy of experience, the truth arises by way of the untruth because the moment
one inquires about truth, one has already asked about the untruth.[91] Responding to
the question of whether truth is God, Rosenzweig tellingly writes:

Truth is not God [*Die Wahrheit ist nicht Gott*]. God is truth [*Gott ist die Wahrheit*]. In order to link up first of all with what was last said: Not truth itself is enthroned above reality, but God, because he is truth. Because truth is his seal, he can be One above the All and One of reality [*Wirklichkeit*]. Truth is the scepter of his reign. . . . Therefore God must be "more" than truth, as every subject is more than its predicate, each thing is more than its concept.[92]

Prima facie, the opening sentence is perplexing: how can it be that God is truth but that truth is not God? What are we to make of this distinction? Should we not presume that the symmetric property encoded in the elementary syllogism "If A is B, then B is A" would apply to the propositions "God is truth" and "Truth is God?" Consider, for example, the statement of Cohen, "Truth is God's Being [*Die Wahrheit ist das Wesen Gottes*]. . . . God is truth [*Gott ist Wahrheit*]; this means for us: only the connection of theoretical and ethical knowledge, only the connection of both sources of the scientific consciousness, is able to fulfill the idea of God."[93] One would have plausibly expected Rosenzweig to affirm in a comparable manner that if God is truth, then truth is God. What, then, is the import of the asymmetry?

Surely, Rosenzweig accepts that anything that partakes of the divine must be true. Consider his comment on Halevi's poem that begins *be-khol libbi emet u-ve-khol me'odi*, to which he gives the title *Der Wahre*: "This poem is an address to Truth, or the One who is True [*Dies Gedicht ist eine Anrede an die Wahrheit, oder an Den, der wahr ist*]—both are the same thing in the Hebrew language and for Jewish feeling. That is, neither of them make the concept of truth separate; he who says 'Truth' knows that God is it."[94] Rosenzweig insists nonetheless that God exceeds the delimitation of truth. This is the implication of his utilization of the rabbinic maxim that truth is God's seal (*ḥotamo shel ha-qadosh barukh hu emet*)[95]—the king is not identical with his seal even if the latter is invested with all the power and authority of the former. For Rosenzweig, the seal, which is the truth, denotes God's relationship to the totality and unity of the world, that by which eternity is made known in time,[96] but God is "this glory above the All and One,"[97] the eternality that supersedes life, even eternal life; indeed, God is *light* (*Licht*) and not life (*Leben*), for "he is as little alive as he is dead [*er ist so wenig lebendig wie er tot ist*] . . . and to state one or the other about him . . . betrays equal pagan partiality."[98] If we were to equate God's essence with the truth, there would still remain a "surplus" (*Überschuß*) that is "beyond his essence" (*über sein Wesen*).[99] The "factuality of truth" is such that the trust it demands leads it to confess "that it is not God [*daß sie nicht Gott ist*]. It is not it that is God [*Nicht sie ist Gott*]. But God is truth. And for its truth, truth must cite this—not that it is truth, much less that it is God, but that God is truth."[100] When properly understood, the statement that God is truth implies that truth is from God—like the illumination that originates from the light[101]—but not that truth is God, an axiom that Rosenzweig refers to as the "sentence of idealism," which is as absurd and false as the Buddhist belief that "the nothing is God" (*das Nichts ist Gott*).[102] The point is reiterated in the penultimate paragraph of the book:

> In the innermost sanctuary of divine truth where he would expect that all the world and he himself would have to be relegated to the metaphor for which he will behold there, man beholds nothing other than a countenance like his own [*ein Antlitz gleich dem eigenen*]. The Star of Redemption has become countenance that looks upon me and from out of which I look. Not God, but God's truth, became the mirror for me. God, who is the first and the last, opened the doors of the sanctuary for me that is built in the innermost center. He let himself be seen. He led me to the border of life where the sight is allowed. For no man who sees Him remains alive. So that sanctuary wherein he allowed me to see had to be a piece of the supra-world within the world itself, a life beyond life.[103]

To pass through the gate is to discern that knowing God consists of beholding the showing of the divine countenance. Attempting to comply with the scriptural response of God to Moses, "You cannot see my face, for man may not see me and live" (Exodus 33:20), Rosenzweig locates the vision at the "border of life," the point of liminality whence one can preview the supra-world in this world, a foretaste of the life beyond life. In this seeing occasioned by the reciprocal mirroring of the divine and human faces, the difference between truth and appearance is effaced to the extent that what is true is nothing more than what appears to be true. There may be a being that transcends the spatio-temporal world, but it can be specularized phenomenally only by a particular human subjectivity.

Truth, accordingly, is not a matter of correspondence between object and idea but an unveiling of the veiled that transpires within the mutual appearing and disappearing that ensues between God and the soul. That Rosenzweig was aware of the potential difficulty with this view is attested in his insistence that the truth revealed in redemption "surely does not turn into non-real truth [*uneigentliche Wahrheit*] by the fact that this countenance turned toward us, that God's share falls to our share; for even as real and most real truth it would be nothing other than—part and countenance."[104] That the divine truth is beheld only as manifest in relation to and in the very image of a human recipient does not diminish the truthfulness of what is manifest. The truth that discloses itself as the face cannot be confronted but as the face that discloses the truth. Just as in a speculum the image is real, so in the matter of divine revelation, there is no truth apart from the showing but in the showing the real is the image. This, I surmise, is the intent of Rosenzweig's statement, "In granting the fact that the existence of truth cannot be denied, there is also granted the fact that there is also untruth. The undeniability of truth and the undeniability of untruth are inseparable as facts."[105] We tend to privilege the former over the latter by imparting trust to truth and shunning untruth as error, but, in truth, the two are indissoluble.

With respect to the intermingling of truth and untruth, being and semblance, there is a conceptual kinship between Rosenzweig and Heidegger, for whom un-truth (*Un-wahrheit*) as the concealment (*Verborgenheit*) that is the un-disclosedness (*Un-entborgenheit*) belongs most properly to the essence of truth (*Wahrheitswesen*) as disclosedness (*Entborgenheit*).[106] This insight became especially pronounced in the later writings of Heidegger, but it is already in evidence in his argument in *Being and Time* that with respect to Dasein authenticity cannot be severed from inauthenticity. As Gadamer noted in "Hermeneutics and Historicism," the 1965 supplement to *Truth and Method*, the inseparability of the two is not only because fallenness is an inherent part of human existence but also because they have the "same origin" in the "first form in which . . . being itself has come into language as the antithesis of 'disclosure' and 'concealment.'"[107] Especially relevant is section 44 of *Being and Time*. Shunning the traditional correspondence theory of truth based on the agreement between the judgment of the subject and its object—epitomized in Aquinas's formulation of the essence of truth as *adaequatio intellectus et rei*—Heidegger locates the "primordial phenomenon of truth" in the disclosedness (*Erschlossenheit*) that is essential to the "basic constitution of Da-sein" as "being-in-the-world."[108] To be true thus means "to-be-discovering" (*entdeckend-sein*), which Heidegger relates to the gestures of *alētheuein* and *apophainesthai*, the laying bare that lets beings be seen in their "unconcealment" (*Unverborgenheit*) or "discoveredness" (*Entdecktheit*). Truth as *alētheia*, argues Heidegger, is the primordial appropriation (*ursprüngliche Aneignung*) of the adequative conception of truth; that is, any statement of truth is a mode of appropriation of the more primary sense of truth as discoveredness, which is Dasein's way of being-in-the-world.[109] Heidegger goes so far as to say that truth so conceived is a constitutive facet of the manner of the being of Dasein,[110] related even more specifically to the structure of care (*Sorge*), which "as *being-ahead-of-itself* [*Sichvorweg*]—already-being-in-the-world—as being together with innerworldly beings contains the disclosedness of Da-sein. *With* and *through* it is discoveredness; thus only with the disclosedness of Da-sein is the *most primordial* phenomenon of truth attained."[111]

Truth as disclosedness belongs essentially to the comportment of Dasein, and hence we can say that "Da-sein is in the truth."[112] Yet, insofar as the existential-ontological condition of "falling prey" (*Verfallen*) likewise "belongs to the constitution of being of Da-sein,"[113] we are perpetually lost in the world, lacking the perspicuity to occupy an absolute standpoint whence we could ascertain the truth without an admixture of untruth. Philosophers (and theologians) may like to pontificate about eternal verities, but the inescapable consequence of our finitude is that *all truth is relative to the being of Da-sein*.[114] The relativity of truth, however, does not signify the subjectivity of all truth, if by the latter one means the arbitrariness of the subject. Rather, what is implied is the epistemological perspectivism adopted by Nietzsche in his critique of the distinction between the true and the illusory. In Kantian terms, there is no noumenal reality beyond the phenomenal appearance—the opposite of the phenomenal world would not

be the "true world" but a "formless, unformulatable world of the chaos of sensations"[115]—
and this implies that the phenomenal itself should not be reified as something true
that exhibits unconditional value,[116] or as Nietzsche put it in one aphorism, the concept
"appearance" itself disappears when one is cognizant of the untenability of the antithesis between the thing-in-itself and appearance.[117]

The Nietzschean dimension of Heidegger's thinking is illumined by a comment
that he made in the seminar on *The Will to Power* (1936–37) concerning Nietzsche's remark that the word "semblance" (*Schein*) means "the actual and sole reality of things":

> That should be understood to mean not that reality is something apparent, but
> that being-real is in itself perspectival, a bringing forward into appearance, a
> letting radiate; that is in itself a shining. Reality is radiance. . . . Reality, Being, is
> *Schein* in the sense of perspectival letting-shine [*perspektivischen Scheinlassens*]. But
> proper to that reality at the same time is the multiplicity of perspectives, and thus
> the possibility of illusion [*Anschein*] and of its being made fast, which means the
> possibility of truth as a kind of *Schein* in the sense of "mere" appearance. If truth is
> taken to be semblance, that is, as mere appearance and error, the implication is
> that truth is the fixed semblance which is necessarily inherent in perspectival
> shining—it is illusion.[118]

It is precisely this illusionary nature of truth to which Heidegger alludes when he
writes in *Being and Time* of the invariable amalgamation of truth and untruth:

> What is discovered and disclosed stands in the mode in which it has been dis-
> guised and closed off by idle talk, curiosity, and ambiguity. . . . Beings are not
> completely concealed, but precisely discovered, and at the same time distorted.
> They show themselves, but in the mode of illusion. Similarly, what was previously
> discovered sinks back again into disguise [*Verstelltheit*] and concealment [*Verbor-
> genheit*]. *Because it essentially falls prey to the world, Da-sein is in "untruth" in
> accordance with its constitution of being.* . . . The full existential and ontological
> meaning of the statement "Da-sein is in the truth" also says equiprimordially that
> "Da-sein is in untruth." But only insofar as Da-sein is disclosed, it is also closed
> off, and insofar as innerworldly beings are always already discovered with Da-sein,
> are such beings covered over (hidden) or disguised as possible innerworldly beings
> to be encountered. . . . The fact that the goddess of truth who leads Parmenides
> places him before two paths, that of discovering and that of concealment, signifies
> nothing other than the fact that Da-sein is always already both in the truth and
> the untruth [*das Dasein ist je schon in der Wahrheit und Unwahrheit*]. . . . The
> existential and ontological condition for the fact that being-in-the-world is
> determined by "truth" and "untruth" lies in *the* constitution of being of Da-sein
> which we characterized as *thrown project* [geworfener Entwurf]. It is a constituent
> of the structure of care.[119]

The dual role of Dasein to be in truth and in untruth is linked philologically to the fact that the word for truth, *alētheia*, is a *privative* expression and, as such, connotes the sense of unconcealing, which is itself a manner of concealing.[120] The human being cannot be in truth without also being in untruth. Every apprehension, accordingly, will be a misapprehension, every uncovering a cover-up, every disclosure a closing-over. Heidegger refers to this untruth as the errancy (*Irre*) that belongs to the "inner constitution of the Da-sein into which historical human beings are admitted. . . . Errancy is the essential counteressence to the originary essence of truth. Errancy opens itself up as the open region for every counterplay to essential truth." For Heidegger, the proverb "to err is human" does not merely convey the pedestrian assurance of our making mistakes. The errancy of which he speaks alludes to the more burdensome sense of being led astray irrevocably on the path of thinking by the "forgetfulness of concealment" (*Vergessenheit des Verbergung*), the oblivion that conceals the concealment of the unconcealment concealed in the unearthing of untruth as the counteressence to the essence of truth.[121] It is important to recall Heidegger's observation that Aristotle never defended the thesis that the primary locus of truth was in the judgment, but rather he affirmed that "the *logos* is the kind of being of Da-sein which can either discover [*entdeckend*] or cover over [*verdeckend*]. This *double possibility* is what is distinctive about the truth of the logos; it is the attitude which *can also cover over*."[122]

In his later work, subsequent to the so-called *Kehre*, the turn in the 1930s,[123] Heidegger developed this conception of truth as unconcealment (*alētheia*), the letting-appear that occurs within the clearing or the lighting-up (*Lichtung*). He insists, time and again, that every disclosure is concomitantly an occlusion, since what is disclosed is also hidden, and thus the showing-forth is always an act of dissembling, the manifestation a concealment of the concealing.[124] In *The Essence of Truth* (1931–32), Heidegger writes:

> This antagonism between what is manifest [*dem Offenbaren*] and what is covered up [*dem Verdeckenden*] shows that the matter at issue is not the mere existence of unhiddenness as such. On the contrary, unhiddenness, the self showing of the shadows, will cleave more firmly to itself without knowing that the manifestness of beings occurs only through the *overcoming* of concealing [*die Offenbarkeit des Seienden* wird *eine solche nur in der* Überwindung *des Verbergens*]. Truth, therefore, is not just unhiddenness of beings such that the previous hiddenness is done away with, but the manifestness of beings is in itself necessarily an overcoming of a concealment [*sondern Offenbarkeit von Seiendem ist notwendig in sich selbst Überwindung einer Verbergung*]. Concealment belongs *essentially* to unhiddenness [*die Verbergung gehört* wesensmäßig *zur Unverborgenheit*], *like the valley belongs to the mountain*. . . . Deconcealing [*Entbergen*] is in itself a confrontation and struggle against concealing [*Verbergen*]. Hiddenness [*Verborgenheit*] is always and necessarily present at the occurrence of unhiddenness [*Geschehen der Unverborgenheit*], it

asserts itself unavoidably in the unhiddenness and helps the latter to itself. . . . But in relationship to truth this is not-unhiddenness [*Nicht-Unverborgenheit*], not-truth [*Nicht-Wahrheit*], i.e., untruth [*Un-wahrheit*] in the broad sense. The question of the essence of truth therefore changes into the question of untruth.[125]

Reiterating the theme in "The Origin of the Work of Art" (1935–36), Heidegger wrote, "Each being we encounter and which encounters us keeps to this curious opposition of presence in that it always withholds itself at the same time in a concealedness. The clearing in which beings stand is in itself at the same time concealment [*Die Lichtung, in die das Seiende hereinsteht, ist in sich zugleich Verbergung*]."[126] In the unconcealed-ness of beings, everything that appears "presents itself as other than it is [*es gibt sich anders, als es ist*]. . . . Concealment conceals and dissembles itself [*Das Verbergen ver-birgt und verstellt sich selbst*]. . . . The nature of truth, that is, of unconcealedness [*Un-verborgenheit*], is dominated throughout by denial. . . . *This denial, in the form of a double concealment* [zwiefachen Verbergens], *belongs to the nature of truth as uncon-cealedness.* Truth, in its nature, is un-truth [*Die Wahrheit ist in ihrem Wesen Un-wahrheit*]."[127] The theme is repeated epigrammatically in § 228 of the *Contributions to Philosophy (Of the Event)*, written between 1936 and 1938, "The essence of truth is un-truth" (*Das Wesen der Wahrheit ist die Un-wahrheit*), which implies that "the *negative* [Nichthafte] belongs intrinsically to truth, by no means as a sheer lack but as resis-tance [*Widerständiges*], as that self-concealing [*Sichverbergen*] which comes into the clearing as such. Thereby the originary relation of truth to beyng as event [*Ereignis*] is grasped."[128]

It lies beyond our immediate concern to delve more deeply into the intricacies of Heidegger's position. Suffice it to say that the inseparability of truth and untruth is related to his idea, in no small measure indebted to the fragment of Heraclitus *phusis kruptesthai philei*, "nature loves to hide,"[129] which Heidegger renders as "To self-revealing there belongs a self-concealing" (»*Zum Sichentbergen gehört ein Sichverber-gen*«). From the Heraclitean maxim he adduces the point that "the essence of being is such that, as a self-revealing, being reveals itself in a way such that a self-concealing—that means, a withdrawal—belongs to this revealing."[130] Nature is unconcealment, but as unconcealment it is itself a form of concealment. For Heidegger, the confluence of opposites does not signify a dialectical sublation of the dyad but rather a more ar-resting sense of sameness (*Selbigkeit*), as opposed to identicalness (*Gleichheit*), entailed in his notion of belonging-together (*Zusammengehörigkeit*).[131] Being is thus described as "the self-concealing revealing" (*das sich verbergende Entbergen*), the meaning prof-fered as the original sense of the term *phusis*;[132] nature, on this score, is not something concealed that is revealed but rather a self-revealing that is simultaneously a self-concealing. The point was well understood by Hannah Arendt: "Presence and absence, concealing and revealing, nearness and remoteness—their interlinkage and the con-nections prevailing among them—have next to nothing to do with the truism that there could not be presence unless absence were experienced, nearness without remoteness, discovery without concealment."[133] The belonging-together of concealment and unconcealment dialectically surpasses the dialectical overcoming of antimonies—the presence is an absence that is neither and therefore both present and absent—such that what is most proximate is the most remote, and what is manifest is the "constant concealment" in the double form of "refusal" (*Versagen*) and "dissembling" (*Verstellen*).[134]

Analogously, Rosenzweig was keenly aware that God's essential nature remains hidden in each of its manifestations,[135] and thus every revelation is an occlusion, every nearness a distance, every truth an untruth. The paths of the two thinkers diverge, insofar as Rosenzweig resolutely maintained that there is an ultimate—if not a substance at least an event—whose revelation cannot be reduced to a concealing of the concealment.[136] And yet, as the ensuing analysis will suggest, Rosenzweig's indebtedness to kabbalah, or at the very least the affinity of his thinking to the Jewish esoteric tradition, can be seen in his embrace of an apophatic discourse at the end of the voyage, and this in spite of his explicit rejection of negative theology at the beginning. The reclaiming of apophasis is based on the view that configuration is consequent to disfiguration, a restoring of the Yes to a No, since that which is positively affirmed in the revelatory acts of divine love—the middle when God, the first and the last, is "right nearby," and "that which is hidden becomes manifest" (*das Verborgene wird so offenbar*)—is in itself the divine essence, "whether it might be truth or nothing" (*ob es Wahrheit wäre oder Nichts*), wherein "that which is manifest becomes that which is hidden" (*das Offenbare wird zum Verborgnen*).[137] I suggest that what Rosenzweig intends by this remark is that when we glimpse the truth from the perspective of redemption, we finally discern that the disclosure of divinity is concurrently an eclipse, that every unconcealment is a concealing of the concealment that shows itself in being hidden, that every affirmation is a negation, that every gesture of kataphasis is a gesture of apophasis, that every saying is an unsaying. Contrary to a recent presentation of my opinion,[138] I never denied that there is a complex interplay between the kataphatic and the apophatic in Rosenzweig. Indeed, it is my acceptance that he attempted to take the positivity of the divine seriously that led me to the view that, in the final analysis, he succumbs to an apophasis, not because truth belongs only to God but because from the human vantage point there is no truth without untruth, no revelation without concealment, no way to configure God but through the veil of metaphoricity. In that respect, transcendence as the genuinely other cannot be experienced in its otherness. Hence, in spite of Rosenzweig's effort to utilize theological language—an obvious point that I never deny—that very language implicates him finally in what he called atheistic theology, that is, configuring God in human terms in such a way that the reality of the divine, which he presumes cannot be reduced to the human or to the world, and to which he does refer as the "wholly other," is inevitably compromised. This is what leads back at the end of the journey to the apophasis laid aside at the beginning. The essence dissipates (*zergeht*) in God's "wholly manifest act of love," the deed (*Tat*) that is "wholly in-essential [*ganz wesenlos*], wholly real [*ganz wirklich*], wholly proximate [*ganz nah*]," and thus God's presence is "freed from the rigidity of essence" and thereby fills space "to every farthest corner."[139] Precisely when the transcendent becomes immanent, the revealed is concealed, not in the banal sense that something previously unveiled is now veiled but in the more paradoxical sense that by being unveiled the veiled is itself veiled in the dissolution of what is unveiled.[140]

Rosenzweig returned to this theme in his commentary on Halevi's poem *yah anah emṣa'akha*, to which gives the title *Der Fern-und-Nahe*. The hymn—technically, an *ofan* written for *Simḥat Torah*—is animated by "one particular thought" (*einem einzigen Gedanken*), which is "the last thought that human thinking can grasp, and the first that Jewish thinking grasps: that the faraway God is none other than the near God, the unknown God none other than the revealed one, the Creator none other than the Redeemer."[141] Rosenzweig saw in Halevi's liturgical poem support for the supreme paradox of monotheism: the God that is distant is the God that is near, the transcendent God that is unknown is the immanent God that is revealed, not as two deities—a mistaken approach exemplified by the gnostic other-worldly tendency of several eminent Christian thinkers, "from Paul to Marcion to Harnack and Barth"[142]—and not even as two aspects of one deity, but as the coincidence of ostensibly contradictory opposites: it is the remote God that is near in a nearness that augments the distance, it is the concealed God that is disclosed in a disclosure that amplifies the concealment. Rosenzweig goes on to lambast the theologians—in a tone that is both humorous and acerbic he writes that the "most accurate theology is the most dangerous"—for, in the name of accuracy, they have one-sidedly emphasized transcendence by insisting that "God is Wholly Other" (*Ganz-Andre*), and thus "to talk about Him is to talk Him away . . . we can only say what He does to us." Insofar as "God can be known only in His presence [*Gegenwart*]," it must follow that "He does not permit Himself to be known in His absence [*Abwesenheit*]." For the person of faith, however, the poles of transcendence and immanence cannot be separated. To speak of the unspeakable is not to misspeak; on the contrary, it is only of the unspeakable that one can speak theologically. "When God comes near to us, of course we know only the inexpressible. . . . As long as it is inexpressible and wants to be so, it itself will take care that we cannot express it." It is only as God retreats that we can begin to express the inexpressible (*das Unaussagbare aussagen*). "In distancing Himself from us He gives Himself to us to know Him as the Faraway One [*der Ferne*]. And when He is totally distant, that is, when He has totally distanced Himself, we can even—deliver me up to the worldly arm of the law, you inquisitors of the new theology!—prove him."[143]

The reference to the possibility of the proof of God is presented tongue in cheek, a sarcastic jab at the theologians who struggle to adduce proofs of a deity thought to be wholly other, imagined in the guise of abstractions—the most perfect being, the first cause, or the ethical ideal—that are nothing more than "distressed prattle." What matters ultimately is not a theoretical debate about the nearness or farness of God but rather being able to speak "before His countenance—with the You . . . that never turns away for a moment."[144] And yet, as Rosenzweig has made clear in his interpretation of Halevi, addressing God in this intimate way is predicated on God's withdrawal, a theme that, to my ear, reflects the Lurianic doctrine of ṣimṣum, a motif with which he was certainly familiar,[145] the act of divine contraction, which is based on the paradox, whose roots go back to the early kabbalah but which is expressed explicitly by any number of sixteenth-century kabbalists, that the concealment is the cause of the disclosure and the disclosure the cause of the concealment, that every appearance of the infinite is a nonappearance, for the infinite cannot appear except as the inapparent. The naked truth is not visible unless it is enveloped in the shroud of its invisibility.[146]

This, I suggest, is the ramification of the aforementioned gloss on the reference to God's essence, "whether it might be truth or nothing." It would be reasonable to suppose that it makes a huge difference to think about that essence as truth or as nothing; indeed, they seem to be polar opposites, but from the panorama of the eternal truth, this is a distinction without a difference. The truth that becomes manifest in the redemption is the "completion of that which we experience in God's love in an enjoyable and visible presence, his Revelation, and therefore the nothing must want to be nothing other than the preliminary reference to this Revelation. . . . Exactly like truth, the nothing is of course not at all finally a self-supporting subject; it is merely a fact, the awaiting of something, it is not anything yet [Nochnichts]. . . . As the truth is only truth because it is from God, so the nothing is only nothing because it is for God."[147] To say "God is truth" is semantically equivalent to the statement that "God is the nothing." Both dicta signify that God's essence cannot be known except as the expectation of what will come to be in time. In the end, nothing is revealed to be the truth of which nothing is revealed but the possibility of something to be revealed.

HERMENEUTICS AND TIME

Let me now revisit the question of hermeneutics and time in Rosenzweig's new thinking or, as he alternatively referred to it, his "experiential philosophy" (erfahrende Philosophie).[148] The nuances of his approach can be appreciated if one compares it to the still valuable discussion in Gershom Scholem's study, "Revelation and Tradition as Religious Categories in Judaism."[149] Tradition, Scholem argued, is the "special aspect of the process that formed rabbinic Judaism," the hermeneutical method that "embodies the realization of the effectiveness of the Word in every concrete state and relationship entered into by a society."[150] The midrashic mode, which eventually assumed the taxonomic classification "Oral Torah" in the rabbinic lexicon, expands the contents of the Written Torah—and thus reinscribes the text—by applying it to new historical circumstances. Revelation, consequently, is no longer portrayed as "a unique, positively established, and clearly delineated realm of propositions;"[151] it is, rather, polysemic and multivalent, demanding "commentary in order to be rightly understood and applied—this is the far from self-evident religious doctrine out of which grew both the phenomenon of biblical exegesis and the Jewish tradition which it created. . . . A creative process begins to operate which will permeate and alter tradition—the Midrash: the more regulated *halakhic* and the somewhat freer aggadic exegesis of Scriptures, and the views of the biblical scholars in their various schools, are regarded as implicitly contained in the Written Torah."[152] The midrashic perspective makes "absolute the concept of tradition in which the meaning of revelation unfolds in the course of historical time—but only because everything that can come to be known has already been deposited in a timeless substratum. In other words, we have arrived at an assumption concerning the nature of truth which is characteristic of rabbinic Judaism (and probably of traditional religious establishment): Truth is given once and for all, and it is laid down with precision. Fundamentally, truth merely needs to be transmitted. . . . The effort of the seeker after truth consists not in having new ideas but rather in subordinating himself to the continuity of the tradition of the divine word and in laying open what he receives from it in the context of his own time. In other words: Not system but *commentary* is the legitimate form through which truth is approached."[153] Scholem goes so far as to say that this insight is the "most important principle for the kind of productivity we encounter in Jewish literature. Truth must be laid bare in a text in which it already pre-exists."[154]

The locating of rabbinic genius in the domain of commentary as opposed to system accentuates the way in which the midrashic method embraces essentially—an essentiality, I hasten to add, that is essentially inessential, as its essence is always to have been determined by what is yet to be determined—the paradox of discovering anew what was previously given. Recovering truth partakes of the epistemological paradox that what presents itself as new does so precisely because it is old, but I would modify Scholem's assessment by proffering a complementary hermeneutic based on a conception of temporality that would not necessitate a bifurcation between a "timeless substratum" of meaning and its unfolding in "historical time." Viewed from the observational post staked by Scholem, it makes perfect sense to raise a question about the possibility of immediacy in one's relationship to the divine, as the "absoluteness of the divine word" that is revealed must always be mediated—that is, translated—so that it might be received. Since every religious experience after revelation is thought to be mediated, what is experienced is the "voice of God rather than the experience of God."[155] The insight regarding the lack of immediacy in religious experience leads Scholem to conclude that tradition "creates productivity through receptivity."[156] The kabbalistic materials only bolster the idea that tradition "is founded upon the dialectic tension" of the "absoluteness" effecting the "unending reflections in the contingencies of fulfillment. Only in the mirroring in which it reflects itself does revelation become practicable and accessible to human action as something concrete." Again, the logical conclusion is drawn categorically: "*There is no immediate, undialectic application of the divine word.*"[157]

In response, I would contend that it is not necessary to bifurcate tradition and revelation in the history of Judaism in the way that Scholem suggests, nor is it obvious that the mediated and conditional status of the former inevitably entails the inability to experience the immediacy and unconditionality of the latter. I see little justification, moreover, for distinguishing the experience of the "voice of God" and the "experience of God," since the latter entails, originarily, both epistemic modalities, seeing and hearing, sometimes understood by subsequent commentators (on the basis of Exodus 20:15, "And they saw the voices") as an example of synesthesia. The dialectical resolution tendered by Scholem may be forestalled if one posits a mode of textual reasoning based on a logic that affirms the identity of opposites in the opposition of their identity—the logic of the middle path, or the "logic of not," expressed in the Mahāyāna Buddhist tradition, "A is not A, therefore it is A"[158]—rather than proposing overcoming the divergence of identity and its opposition. If we follow that route, productivity and receptivity need not be understood as antinomical; the rabbinic sensibility is another cultural formation that fosters the collusion of opposites in the sameness of their difference—*elu we-elu divrei elohim ḥayyim*, "these and those are the words of a living God."[159] If "this" and "that" are opposing positions, and both the one and the other are true, we must assume that truth contains within itself the prospect of being untrue. Such a hermeneutic, moreover, is based on a varied conception of time that likewise upholds the convergence of the ancient and novel in the variance of their semblance. As I have argued elsewhere, the rabbinic understanding of an ongoing revelation, which unfolds through an unbroken chain of interpretation, is not based on a static conception of the eternity of Torah set in opposition to time and therefore resistant to the fluctuation of historical contingency. Rather, it is predicated on a conception of temporality that calls into question the linear model of aligning events chronoscopically in a sequence stretched invariably between before and after. The rabbinic hermeneutic champions a notion of time that is circular in its linearity and linear in its circularity.[160] The study of Torah, accordingly, demands that one be able to imagine each day, indeed each moment of each day, as a potential recurrence of the Sinaitic theophany. Each interpretive venture, therefore, is a reenactment of the revelatory experience, albeit from its unique perspective.[161] Rendering in a different way the words of Goethe with which Scholem concluded his essay, "The truth that long ago was found, / Has all noble spirits bound, / The ancient truth, take hold of it" (*Das Wahre war schon längst gefunden, / Hat edle Geisterschaft verbunden, / Das alte Wahre, fass es an*),"[162] I would say that noble spirits are indeed bound by an ancient truth that was long ago found, but one can take hold of that truth only as the truth that is yet to be disclosed, a truth renewed in the moment of its genuine iteration.

It is well to recall another motto of Goethe, "understanding at the right time" (*Verstehen zur rechten Zeit*), which is invoked by Rosenzweig in "The New Thinking"[163] to corroborate his claim that understanding occurs always in the present, "time in the most temporal sense" (*Zeit im zeitlichsten Sinn*).[164] This insight runs parallel to Rosenzweig's account of revelation in the *Star*, based on the premise that "God's love is always wholly in the moment and at the point where it loves; and it is only in the infinity of time [*Unendlichkeit der Zeit*], step by step, that it reaches one point after the next and permeates the totality with soul."[165] The knot of divine love takes an infinity of time to unravel, but at the core of that love is the utterance of the divine commandment that "knows only the moment: it waits for the outcome right within the moment of its growing audible. . . . The commandment is thus—pure present [*reine Gegenwart*]. . . . Revelation is in the present [*gegenwärtig*], and indeed it is the present par excellence . . . the presently lived experience housed in the I [*des gegenwärtigen, im Ich behausten Erlebens*]."[166] In this respect, revelation may be compared profitably to music, the art form wherein "time is the dominant feature"[167] as opposed to the plastic arts that are aligned with the spatial,[168] for just as the movement of a musical composition "is the only possibility for making objective the temporal succession [*Zeitfolge*] that otherwise sinks down helplessly into the temporal point of the present [*Zeit-Punkt des Gegenwärtigen*],"[169] so the eruption of the revelatory event must "begin again already at the same moment, in the sinking away it must already begin again; its perishing must be at the same time a beginning again [*sein Vergehen muß zugleich ein Wiederangehen sein*]. . . . So this moment must have more as its content than the mere moment. The moment shows something always new to the eye every time it opens."[170] This moment, which has the potentiality to be perpetually renewed, and thus it carries within itself the "diversity of the old and new," is identified by Rosenzweig as an "hour" or the "fixed moment" in which "its end can flow again into its beginning because it has a middle, or rather many moments of the middle between its beginning and its end. With beginning, middle and end, it can become what the mere sequence of single ever new moments can never become: a circle that flows back in itself . . . . In the hour, the moment is therefore turned into that which, when it should have perished, always newly begins again and thus into the imperishable, the *nunc stans*, eternity."[171] Compressed in the "single moment" is "pure temporality" (*reinen Zeitlichkeit*)—significantly, this is demarcated as the "purely temporally lived life of Goethe"—whereby "life has become entirely temporal [*ganz zeitlich*], or, put differently, time has an entirely living, an entirely real river flowing through the vast space above the crags [*Klippe*] of the moment; no sooner can eternity fall upon time. Life, and all life, must be entirely living [*ganz lebendig*] before it can become eternal life [*ewiges Leben*]."[172] In the moment, time is fully temporal and hence eternal, a time beyond the calibration of ordinary time, but a time nonetheless, indeed the fullness of time.

Stéphane Mosès has characterized this "modality of time" in Rosenzweig as *ritual time*, which he further described as "a repetitive time, that is, a *motionless time*, a principle not of change but of permanence." The *"cycle of the liturgical year"* unveils the "transtemporal dimension" of sacred time, which is eternity, "not a time indefinitely stretched out forward but rather a total immobilization of the present instant, a state of perfect equilibrium absolutely outside the flow of time."[173] We cannot comprehend

Rosenzweig's taking of time seriously unless we factor in the possibility of experiencing what Mosès has called transtemporality, but I question the accuracy of describing the latter as immobile, repetitive, and permanent. These classifications impose on Rosenzweig a binary way of thinking that he sought to transcend. For him, there is no permanence but in change, no stasis but in process, no repetition but in innovation, no time but in eternity. In describing "the eternal moment" that bears the "destiny of an infinite now,"[174] Rosenzweig deals head on with the paradox of positing a present that is imperishable but passing, overflowing but withholding: "There is only one way out: the moment we are seeking must, since it has flown away, begin again already at the same moment, in the sinking away it must already begin again; its perishing must be at the same time a beginning again."[175] Let us recall Rosenzweig's comments inspired by Halevi's poem *yeqarah shakhnah gewyah*, which he translates as *Der Lohn*:

> Eternity can of course break into every moment, but what it then seizes is only just this moment. Life on the whole is contained in a few moments in such a way that it can grasp them in these moments. At the moment of birth as a life ahead; in one or two moments during life as a decisive one; and in death as a perfected one. Thus, only in death as a real, "present" whole. This worldly reality has life only here, and to want here to withdraw it from the clasp of eternity would mean that life never would be allowed to be an experienced whole.[176]

This text attests to the inadequacy of separating time and eternity in Rosenzweig's thinking. Eternity erupts into the moment, and, by this gesture, temporal life becomes real, a realization that comes to pass in clutching the moment of death through which life is perfected and may be experienced as whole.

The view of Rosenzweig is noticeably similar to the statement of Heschel,[177] which likely reflects the Jewish mystical tradition,[178] that "the relation of existence to time is more intimate and unique than its relation to space. . . . Time is the only property the self really *owns*. Temporality, therefore, is an essential feature of existence."[179] Having established the primacy of the temporal as the characteristic most distinctive to the human experience of the world, Heschel notes that the evanescence of time must be complemented by continuity, the "element of constancy in the inner structure of existence which accounts for permanence within temporality."[180] Insofar as the consciousness of time is contingent on a sense of duration, we must say that time "depends for its continuation on a principle that is independent of time, for time itself cannot yield permanence."[181] The secret of existence resides in this "relation of temporality to abidingness," as the human search for meaning is "a quest for the lasting."[182] The state of perdurance is realized not through the eradication of time but through its intensification:

> The way to the lasting does not lie on the other side of life; it does not begin where time breaks off. The lasting begins not beyond but *within* time; within the moment, within the concrete. Time can be seen from two aspects: from the aspect

of temporality and from the aspect of eternity. Time is the border of eternity. Time is eternity formed into tassels. . . . It is through spiritual living that we realize that the infinite can be confined in a measured line. . . . The days of our lives are representatives of eternity rather than fugitives, and we must live as if the fate of all of time would totally depend on a single moment. . . . A moment has no contemporary within temporality. But within eternity every moment can become a contemporary of God.[183]

The privileging of time over space in the spiritual physiognomy of Judaism is reiterated repeatedly in Heschel's works.[184] I will cite two other passages that shed light on Rosenzweig. The first is from *The Insecurity of Freedom*:

Things of space exhibit a deceptive independence. They show off a veneer of limited permanence. Things created conceal the Creator. It is the dimension of time wherein man meets God, wherein man becomes aware that every instant is an act of creation, a Beginning, opening new roads for ultimate realizations. *Time is the presence of God in the world of space*, and it is within time that we are able to sense the unity of all beings. Time is perpetual presence, perpetual novelty. Every moment is a new arrival, a new bestowal.[185]

The second passage is from *The Sabbath: Its Meaning for Modern Man*: "Judaism is a *religion of time* aiming at *the sanctification of time*. . . . Judaism teaches us to be attached to *holiness in time*, to be attached to sacred events, to learn how to consecrate sanctuaries that emerge from the magnificent stream of the year. . . . Jewish ritual may be characterized as the art of significant forms in time, as *architecture of time*."[186] Insofar as the Sabbath is "completely detached from the world of space,"[187] it epitomizes the mandate of ritual observance more generally to "master time in time"[188] or to consecrate "time for the sake of eternity."[189] The commandments are the "sacred deeds" through which the Jew sanctifies time and thereby enters into the eternality that is "God's time."[190]

The words of Heschel capture the gist of what Rosenzweig meant to convey regarding the relation of time and eternity exhibited in the interruptive nature of the immediacy of the revelatory moment[191] and the pietistic observance based thereon.[192] Levinas, accordingly, is closer to the mark than Mosès in describing Rosenzweig's "extasis" of temporality as the "[u]nexpected meaning of eternity within the very dimensions of time! We are very far from the atemporal signification of relations inside a system."[193] A major consequence of Rosenzweig's critique of the Hegelian totality is that "the abstract aspects of time—past, present, future—are deformalized; it is no longer a question of time, an empty form in which there are three formal dimensions."[194] The deformalization of which Levinas speaks relates to the fact that the correlation of the three modalities of time with creation, revelation, and redemption indicates that the "formal notions are not fully intelligible except in a concrete event," an insight shared by

Rosenzweig and Husserlian phenomenology[195] and, to some extent, by Heidegger's theory of temporality (*Zeitlichkeit*) as the equiprimordiality of the three modes of time: the essence of being human, the potentiality-for-Being, is determined as a future that makes present in the process of having-been.[196] For Rosenzweig, as Levinas well understood, time, and particularly the sacred time of ritual, is dialogical or, in his own terms, diachronic, since the present, time in its most temporal, is a way to face the other. Rosenzweig thus contrasts the "grammatical thinking" of the "speech-thinker" (*Sprachdenker*)[197] and the "logical thinking" of the "thinking thinker" (*denkenden Denker*) on the grounds that the former is in "need of time," which means "being able to anticipate nothing, having to wait for everything, being dependent on the other for one's own. . . . the difference between old and new, logical and grammatical thinking does not rest on loud versus quiet, but rather on needing the other and, what amounts to the same, on taking time seriously."[198] This sentiment was expressed in slightly different terminology in the following amazing passage:

> Let us be ourselves and nothing more. Such a moment of existence may be nothing but delusion; we shall, however, choose to remain within the moment, deceived by it and deceiving it, rather than live in deception above or below the moment. Let our personal experience, even though it change from instant to instant, be reality. Let man become the bearer of these shifting images. . . . Whenever I encounter man, I shall steep my countenance in his until it reflects his every feature. . . . Thus, traveling about the earth, I shall come face to face with my own Self. The innumerable masks of the innumerable instants, yours and mine, they are my countenance.[199]

Displaying his ability to collapse binaries in a manner that seems to me more effective than much of the contemporary postmodern discourse, Rosenzweig affirms that there is a self but not without the other; there is identity but not without difference; there is endurance but not without change; there is a countenance but not without masks; there is an unrelenting reality but not without shifting images. All there is to grip is the moment of existence, a moment that may be nothing but delusion, but still authenticity demands that we choose to live in that moment, to deceive and to be deceived by it. In this momentary deception, the deception of the moment, which persists as what passes, lies the possibility of fidelity to one's self and hence to the other.[200]

The indissoluble link between temporality, alterity, and transcendence in Rosenzweig was correctly discerned by Levinas: "the relation and movement where thought becomes life is not primitively intentionality but Revelation, the crossing of an absolute interval. The ultimate bound of psychism is not the one insuring the unity of the subject but, so to speak, the tying separation of society, the *dia* of the dialogue, of dia-chrony, of time that Rosenzweig aims to 'take seriously,' the tying separation we call by a well-worn name—love."[201] In the next chapter I will have more to say about

Levinas's reflections on time, but let me cite here one text that betrays his indebtedness to Rosenzweig. The passage is from the preface that Levinas wrote for the 1979 collection[202] of lectures entitled *Le temps et l'autre*:

> The main thesis caught sight of in *Time and the Other* . . . consists in thinking time not as a degradation of eternity, but as the relationship to *that* which—of itself unassimilable, absolutely other—would not allow itself to be assimilated by experience; or to that which—of itself infinite—would not allow itself to be com-prehended. . . . This impossibility of coinciding and this inadequation are not simply negative notions, but have a meaning in the *phenomenon* of noncoincidence *given* in the dia-chrony of time. Time signifies this always of noncoincidence, but also the always of relationship, an aspiration and an awaiting, a thread finer than an ideal line that diachrony does not cut.[203]

In writing of the phenomenon of noncoincidence, the given that cannot be assimilated by experience or comprehended in accord with the noetic-noematic structure of intentionality, Levinas is undeniably responding to the Husserlian internal time-consciousness.[204] Additionally, however, reverberations of Rosenzweig, albeit couched in a different terminology, can be heard in Levinas's opposing the positing of time in opposition to eternity, as well as in his emphasizing the diachronic dimension of time as an opening to the other, the transcendent that resists representation or reification.[205] Consider one more passage from Levinas in which the attuned ear will detect the trace of this influence: "My profoundest thought, which bears all thought, my thought of the infinite older than the thought of the finite, is the very diachrony of time, non-coincidence, dispossession itself: a way of 'being avowed' prior to every act of consciousness and more profoundly than consciousness, through the gratuitousness of time. . . . Inspiration is thus the prophetic event of the relation to the new."[206] In the temporal pleroma of the present envisioned by Rosenzweig, the line becomes a circle, beginning and end meet in and, as a result, eliminate the middle by inverting the projectile of time and turning one thing into its opposite.[207] The eternalization of time brought to fruition in the moment of revelation proleptically anticipates the temporalization of eternity to be realized in the hour of redemption.[208] In the interim, however, the ecstatic temporality is lived in and through the diachronic performance of ceremonial acts and especially the sacrament of prayer, by which the arrival of the end is accelerated and tomorrow is transmuted into today.[209]

Rosenzweig's thinking about time and eternity was informed, at least in part, by the rabbinic belief that one can hear again the timbre of the archaic saying in the "great historical testimony of Revelation, the necessity of which we recognized precisely from the presentness of our living experience."[210] The presentness (*Gegenwärtigkeit*) of which Rosenzweig speaks is a *tempus discretum* or, in Levinasian terms, a diachrony exemplifying dispossession, noncoincidence, deformalization, and disfiguration. As Rosenzweig put it in the "Urzelle":

So the organizing concept of this world is not the universal, neither the Arche nor the Telos, neither the natural nor the historical unity, but rather the particular, the event, *not beginning or end, but rather middle* of the world. The world is "infinite," both from beginning and from end, from the beginning infinite in space, toward the end infinite in time. Only from the middle arises a limited home in the unlimited world . . . Viewed from this perspective, beginning and end are also transformed for the first time, from limit-concepts of infinity to cornerposts of our worldly estate, the "beginning" as creation, the "end" as salvation. Thus revelation is capable of being a *middle* point [Mittel*punkt*], a fixed, middle point that cannot be displaced. . . . Revelation pushes itself into the world as a wedge; the This struggling against the This.[211]

Rejecting the old philosophical ideal, Rosenzweig replaces the universal (*Allgemeine*) with the particular (*Einzelne*), the classifiable general with the irreducibly singular, the essence (*Wesen*) with the event (*Ereignis*).[212] Reiterating the theme in *Understanding the Sick and the Healthy*, Rosenzweig wrote: "The true concern of the philosopher is with the 'essence,' the 'essential' being of his subjects. . . . The singleness and particularity [*Eigenheit*] of the subject detached from time is transformed into a statement of its particular essence [*Eigentlichkeit des Wesens*]. . . . The terms of life are not 'essential' but 'real'; they concern not 'essence' but 'fact.' In spite of this, the philosopher's word remains, 'essential.'"[213]

The actuality of each of the elemental forms is experienced in their relations to one another—only as creation, revelation, and redemption; to try to grasp any of them in its own essence would result in lack of discernment, God concealing himself, the human self closing up, and the world becoming a visible riddle.[214] The temporal location of the event is always in the middle; indeed, it is only from the delimited possibility of the midpoint (*Mittelpunkt*) of revelation that the limit-concepts of infinity at the beginning and at the end—the former correlated with space and the latter with time— are converted respectively into creation and redemption, the theological concepts that provide the cornerposts that uphold the edifice of a world of finitude.

The time of the present, therefore, is a desire for the new, which is a desire for the other,[215] a time whose continuity is marked by discontinuity with past and/or future, a time about which one can be certain only of its uncertainty,[216] since it ruptures and cuts the timeline, the moment that, in each moment, returns as something that has never been exactly on account of its always having been. "The language of love is only present [*lauter Gegenwart*]; dream and reality, sleep of the limbs and wakefulness of the heart are inextricably woven one into the other, everything is equally present [*gleich gegenwärtig*], equally fleeting [*gleich flüchtig*] and equally alive [*gleich lebendig*]. . . . A shower of imperatives descends and endows with life this eternally green meadow of the present, imperatives from different horizons, but always alluding to the same thing . . . it is always the same one imperative of love."[217] Revelation, therefore, embodies the paradox of being "always new only because it is immemorially old [*allzeit neu, nur weil sie uralt ist*]."[218] It is germane here to recall Rosenzweig's comments on Halevi's poem *ye'iruni be-shimkha ra'ayoni*,[219] which he translated as *Nachts*, since "the longed for event" occurred as "a night-vision" that "brought the poet the experience [*Erlebnis*] of the sight of God [*Gottesschau*]." The visionary phenomenon, accordingly, happens in "the state between dream and waking, a state which derives its autonomy from dream and its validity from waking."[220] The nocturnal vision—a poetological rather than a chronological demarcation—occurs in the intermediate space between appearance and reality, as Plato described the status of the *khōra*, which we perceive in a dreamlike state,[221] the space that is characterized by Derrida as the *autre temps*, the "phantastic or phantasmatic temporality," which is no longer "regulated by the time of presence-to-self as wakefulness and self-consciousness."[222] The revelatory event partakes of this oneiric temporality in which the topological metric of time is undone.[223] As the gap between past and present collapses, the poet sees God in his heart as if he were standing again at Sinai. "The experience of today confirms and repeats the historical revelation."[224]

To locate the vision of God between dream and wakefulness is analogous to the aforecited statement in the *Star*, according to which dream and reality are interwoven. These are two imagistic ways to communicate the convergence of the ideal and the real, an idea that Rosenzweig likely borrowed from Schelling[225] but which also resonates with kabbalistic symbolism. It is precisely in this convergence, moreover, that one can appreciate the reversibility of time, the construction of the future as the possibility of the past recurring in the present. For Rosenzweig, this paradox can be formulated as well in terms of language. Addressing the thorny question of the relationship of word and thing, he remarked that a thing "possesses equally the right to keep the name it has, and to receive new names. . . . And furthermore each new name must come to terms with the old ones. . . . It is man's privilege to give new names. It is his duty to use the old ones, a duty which he must perform, though unwillingly." The very continuity of humankind—materialized in the singular person and not in the abstract ideal or essence—depends on the practice of appropriating and translating old names into new terminological designations. "Mankind is always absent. Present is a man, this fellow or that one. The thing, however, is tied to all of mankind by language and by its inherent law of transmission and translation. These linguistic laws require that each new word confront the old. And where does the presence of mankind manifest itself? Not in the word of man, of course, but in that of God."[226]

From this hermeneutical standpoint, the sense of the present, enduring in its evanescence—the return of the same that is always different because always the same, the same difference—is realized in the act of interpreting the divine commands entrusted in the scriptural text, an exploit of mind that must be positioned at the interface of the verbal and the graphic, since the interpreter restores the written trace to the spoken word. Hence, for Rosenzweig, as Fishbane expressed it, "the hermeneutics of reading must therefore serve to recall man to the word of God that summons him into existence. One may therefore say that the horizon of textuality is just this divine-human speech resounding within the text."[227] The interpretive act affords one an opportunity to experience time and, more specifically, the moment, which instantiates time in its most elemental cadence, the coming again as novel repetition. The divine word reiterated with each reading of Scripture, therefore, is the word yet to be spoken, the silent sign that needs to be vocalized anew with each homiletical variation. The phenomenological cornerstone of Rosenzweig's new thinking rests on the belief in the possibility of experiencing revelation as a genuine contingency at every moment, and just as, temporally, the present is the aperture through which one accesses past and future, so, hermeneutically, revelation is the eventuality that makes creation and redemption possible.[228]

LINGUISTIC REVELATION AND METAPHORIC POIESIS

From the perspective of the history of religions, Rosenzweig grasped the dialogical potential of revelation as a linguistic occurrence[229]—he even coins the phrase the "linguistic revelation" (*sprachliche Offenbarung*)[230] as a way of marking that language is not only the primary means of the revelatory experience but its major content as well. To take in the full intimation of this claim, one must recall that Rosenzweig, following a much older perspective, views revelation as the historical spectacle of the institution of prophecy, but the latter can be understood only when considered in conjunction with the notion of miracle, which is essentially a "sign" (*Zeichen*).[231] Rosenzweig maintains that revelation "is entirely a sign, entirely a making visible and a becoming audible of the Providence originally hidden in the mute night of Creation."[232] The innately semiotic nature of revelation is expressed in the translating of the divine intent in both visual and auditory terms. The larger hermeneutical principle at work here is made explicit in the remark of Rosenzweig in his "Scripture and Luther" that all dialogic as opposed to monologic speech is an act of translation.[233] We may assume, moreover, that for Rosenzweig, in a manner conspicuously reminiscent of similar claims enunciated by Heidegger[234] and elaborated by Gadamer,[235] every act of translation is an interpretation. The emphasis on the linguistic character of revelation demonstrates the point: the saying of what was spoken is already translated, since the word of God, soundless (*laut-losen*) and dumb (*stummen*),[236] can be heard only as interpreted speech, the translation that may be viewed as more original than the original.[237] Revelation, therefore, is an inherently metaphorical process that yields, in the double sense of engendering and surrendering, an insight into the interweaving pattern of experience and interpretation.[238] It is from this spot that we can discern the mythopoetic tenor of revelation, wherein the rift between the ideal and the actual, thought and being, reality and appearance is bridged, a bridging that undergirds

Rosenzweig's celebrated use of the Song of Songs to articulate the analogical nature of the dialogical encounter between God and human. In his own words from the section dedicated to the elucidation of this biblical book:

> The allegory of love, as allegory, goes through the whole Revelation. . . . But it is supposed to be more than an allegory. . . . So it is not enough that the relationship of God to man is presented in the allegory of the lover and the beloved; God's word must immediately hold the relationship of the lover to the beloved, without the signifier making any allusion at all to the signified. And so we find it in the Song of Songs. It is no longer possible to see in that allegory "only an allegory."[239]

In characterizing the Song as an "allegory of love" and by considering it an exemplum for revelation as a whole, Rosenzweig is drawing on the traditional interpretation of this text as a transfigurative representation of God's love for Israel in the heteroerotic terms of the male lover and the female beloved.[240] Additionally, he seems to be echoing older rabbinic dicta that extol this book as the holy of holies or as being equivalent to all of Torah.[241] The Song is the "core book of Revelation" (*Kernbuch der Offenbarung*);[242] that is, it is the book that illustrates the metaphorical nature of metaphor most pristinely—its literal sense is figurative, and thus there is no way to consider truth apart from appearance, no way to expose a face without the donning of a mask. The distinction between dream and reality, what appears and what is, a distinction that, as we noted above, Rosenzweig himself affirmed in his effort to uphold the concrete singularity (*Einzelheit*) and individuality (*Individualität*) of the being-there (*Dasein*) of all that exists in the lattice of entwined relationality,[243] collapses when the divine word is thought to allude to the relationship of God and human in the erotically charged images of male lover and female beloved.[244] This, I submit, is what Rosenzweig means when he says that the allegory of love is more than an allegory: the assortment of erotic tropes discloses the face of truth in the masking of image. In Rosenzweig's own astonishingly complex and densely poetic language, "the sensuous character of the word [*die Sinnlichkeit des Worts*] is full to the brim with its divine suprasensuous meaning [*göttlichen Übersinn*], like language itself love is sensual-suprasensual [*sinnlich-übersinnlich*]. To express it another way: the allegory is not a decorative accessory for love, but essence."[245]

In picturing the divine-human correlation heteroerotically, the diction of the Song embraces the sensuous and suprasensuous in tandem, a double embrace that is the character of both the language of eros and the eros of language. Rosenzweig insists, therefore, that love is "absolutely and essentially allegory [*ganz und gar und wesentlich Gleichnis*]. It is ephemeral only in appearance, but in truth it is eternal."[246] The allegorical nature of love yields the incongruity of appearing to be transient when it is actually interminable. But this opposition is only apparent, for, in truth, the distinction between semblance and reality disappears in the simulacrum of allegorical figuration: "That appearance is as necessary as this truth; as love, love could not be eternal if it did not seem to be transitory; but in the mirror of this appearance, truth reflects it-self directly [*aber im Spiegel dieses Scheins spiegelt sich unmittelbar die Wahrheit*]."[247] The overlapping of the external and internal meaning conveys to the reader a rudi-mentary insight regarding the poiesis of Torah more generally: to speak of an unspeak-able God—the signifier that makes no allusion to a signified—is to render the imageless in poetic images that juxtapose the divergent through the prism of symbolic likeness. The word of revelation perforce must be figurative, but, in the speculum of the text, the metaphorical figuration is real, the allegory that cannot be only an allegory.[248]

This is not the appropriate place to elaborate on Rosenzweig's sense of the mythic or poetic—the two terms may be used interchangeably—but it is important to note his indebtedness to the likes of Schelling, Hamann, and Herder,[249] in privileging po-etry as the fount of philosophy[250] as well as his contention that the Jews alone possess the unity of myth that facilitates the coalescence of the universal and the particular, a hallmark of the messianic ideal.[251] As Rosenzweig writes, the "concepts of Revelation spring up for the aesthetic theory under the influence of the 'mythical' upon the 'tragic,' hence of the whole upon the spiritual content that is to be poet-ized."[252] Poetry is said to be "at home neither in time nor in space, but where time and space have their inner origin [*inneren Ursprung*], in imagistic thinking [*vorstellenden Denken*]. Poetry is not a kind of art of thought [*Gedankenkunst*], but thinking in its element as space is that of the plastic arts and time is that of music."[253] Significantly, according to Rosenzweig, poetry is not at home in either time or space but in the imagistic thinking where the temporal and spatial coordinates have their inner origin; one may conclude, therefore, that the poetic is essentially at odds with the world, that the poet is intractably in a state of uncanniness or estrangement (*Unheimlichkeit*),[254] a diasporic condition that is natural for the Jews, the "eternal people," whose promise of the holy land "never lets it feel entirely at home in any other land."[255] The metahistorical reference point in his-tory accorded the Jewish nation renders it as fundamentally alien to the vagaries of the sociopolitical world.[256]

Here it is apposite to recall Rosenzweig's remark in his "Afterword" to the transla-tion of ninety-two poems by Halevi:

> All Jewish poetry in exile scorns to ignore this being-in-exile. It would have
> ignored its exile if it ever, like other poetry, took in the world directly. For the
> world which surrounds it is exile, and is supposed to remain so to it. And the
> moment that it would surrender this attitude, when it would open itself to
> the inflow of this world, this world would be as a home for it, and it would cease
> to be exile. This exiling of the surrounding world is achieved through the constant
> presence of the scriptural word. With the scriptural word another present thrusts
> itself in front of the surrounding present and downgrades the latter to an appear-
> ance, or more precisely, as parable. Thus it is not that the scriptural word is drawn
> out as parables for illustrations of present life, but exactly reversed, that events

serve as illucidation of the scriptural word and become the parable for this scriptural word.[257]

Rosenzweig thus contrasts Jewish poetry and other forms of poetry on the grounds that the former is unavoidably exilic and therefore in a perpetual state of homelessness, whereas the latter takes on the world directly and therefore exhibits a sense of being at home. The ethnocentric difference affirmed here and the essential disjointedness experienced by the Jews—two claims that I find philosophically implausible—relates to Rosenzweig's understanding of the supremacy accorded Hebrew as the holy language. Even though Hebrew is primarily a liturgical language, it should not be considered a "dead" language, insofar as it constantly interacts with the language of daily life, and indeed it evolves over time in such a way that it never discards what has become an integral part of it. Nevertheless, its sacredness leaves the Jews with a feeling of alienation in the world, for the eternal people, in contrast to all other nations, do not identify with the language in which they converse. Just as the notion of the holy land prevents the Jews from feeling at home in any geographical space that they inhabit, so too Hebrew denies them the sense of linguistic belonging.[258] There is, therefore, "nothing more deeply Jewish than a final suspicion of the power of the word and a heart-felt confidence in the power of silence. The holiness of the holy language, in which alone he can only pray, does not allow his life to take root in the soil of a language of his own; evidence for the fact that his linguistic life [*Sprachleben*] always senses itself faraway and knows its real linguistic homeland [*Sprachheimat*] is elsewhere, in the domain of the holy language that is inaccessible to everyday speech, lies in the remarkable circumstance that the language of the everyday, at least in the mute vowel signs of Scripture [*stummen Zeichen der Schrift*], seeks to preserve contact with the old holy language long ago lost to the everyday . . . precisely in the silence [*Schweigen*] and in the silent signs of speech [*schweigenden Zeichen der Rede*] that the Jew senses that his everyday language is also still at home in the holy language of his festive hours."[259] It is against this background that we can understand the full implications of the poetic disorientation drawn by Rosenzweig: the Jewish poet is confronted by the constant presence of the scriptural word, a past that has the potential always to plunge itself into the present and thereby to downgrade the latter into an "appearance" (*Schein*) or a "parable" (*Gleichnis*). What we consider to be reality is a parabolic prism through which the word of Scripture is elucidated. The respective valence accorded reality and appearance in Western philosophical thought is inverted in Rosenzweig's thinking: what appears to be real is rendered really apparent in the speculum of the text. In this mirroring, moreover, the timeline is reversed, and the past is illumined from the present: "When a Jewish poet describes Christianity and Islam through Edom and Ishmael, he is not commenting on the present from Scripture, but rather on Scripture from the present."[260] The hermeneutical reversibility is a direct consequence of being outside of or at variance with time and space that is integral to the poetic mind-set.

The pairing of poetry (*Dichtung*) and thinking (*Denken*) in Rosenzweig's notion of imagistic thinking—a thinking-in-images—anticipates Heidegger's characterization of the thinking about being as an "original way of poeticizing" (*ursprüngliche Weise des Dichtens*), the "primordial poetry" (*Urdichtung*), which is "prior to the poetics of art."[261] We note the obvious difference between Rosenzweig and Heidegger: one looked to the Bible as the wellspring of mythopoiesis and the other to the parabolic dicta of the ancient Greeks, a language that has a particular affinity to German.[262] In spite of this divergence, the convergence is striking.[263] The resemblance is enhanced by the fact that Rosenzweig's insistence on the inseparability of the spatial and temporal coordinates in the poetic—the epic aligned with the former and the lyric with the latter—parallels Heidegger's thinking of timespace (*Zeitraum*) as the lighting/clearing (*Lichtung*) that yields the language to house, and thereby to shelter and to expose, being.[264] It lies beyond the scope of this chapter to engage this matter adequately, but suffice it to say that a key facet of the turn on Heidegger's path relates to the affirmation of poetry as the primary linguistic way of appropriating the opening of the ontological horizon, the abyss (*Abgrund*), the originary ground, which is, paradoxically, the absence of ground.[265] Both Rosenzweig and Heidegger—more pronounced in the latter's thought after the so-called turn or reversal (*Kehre*) in the mid-1930s—idealize the poet as the most suitable guide to the thinker trying to find the language that allows one to be at home in his thinking, since the poet plunges into the homelessness that will be overcome by wandering toward the state of homecoming, a portrait beholden especially to Hölderlin,[266] a common source that would easily account for the similarity of Rosenzweig and Heidegger on this crucial theme. Another congruence that is worthy of emphasis is Rosenzweig's expressing the confluence of the spatial and temporal as the convergence of the visual and verbal, an insight that resonates with Heidegger's conception of the essence of language as a saying (*Sage*) that is a showing (*Zeige*).[267] To cite the pertinent formulation of Rosenzweig: "For poetry gives figure [*Gestalt*] and discourse [*Rede*] because it gives more than either: imagistic thinking, in which both are alive together."[268]

The commingling of visible form and audible word highlights another essential similarity between revelation and poetry: the allusive idiom of the former, as the elusive intonation of the latter, is concomitantly seen and heard. The intrinsic symmetry between the two, which must be thought from this point of intersection, portends that the two modalities embrace a shared sense of temporality—just as the proper attunement to the revelatory is occasioned by an openness to the moment, so the understanding of the poetic is "strongly conditioned by a certain richness of lived experience."[269] The rapture of poetic composition, as the rupture of revelation, issues from and helps gives shape to the now of God's address where the triadic nature of time is eternalized and the unified nature of eternity temporalized.[270] We may assume that the creative spirit is personified paradigmatically in the poet, as poetry is, according to Rosenzweig, the "living art in the proper sense [*eigentlich lebendige Kunst*],"[271] and thus, like the revelation of the divine word, the poetic utterance takes place always in the moment where the verbal image resounds as the visual word, and the visual word is revisioned as the verbal image. In both cases, the spirit takes on corporeal form in the imagination of the one encountering the transcendent.

APOPHASIS AND THE ESCHATOLOGICAL
OVERCOMING OF WORD BY IMAGE

In the last part of the *Star*, Rosenzweig articulates the eschatological overcoming of word by image, the triumphant manifestation of the light that is beyond language, a visual perception or intuition at the end, the consummation of which is marked (as I have already noted) by the completion of factuality (*Tatsächlichkeit*) to the point that there is neither thing (*Sache*) nor act (*Tat*) of which to speak.[272] Rosenzweig's elocution is evidently playful: the perfection of *Tatsächlichkeit* results in the overcoming of both *Tat* and *Sache*, quite literally, a decomposition of the composite elements that make up the word's hybridity. Perhaps there is here as well an allusion to the scriptural slogan linked to the response of the ancient Israelites to the divine revelation or, more precisely, to hearing the reading of the "book of the covenant" (*sefer ha-berit*) on the part of Moses, "Let us do and let us hear," *na'aseh we-nishma* (Exodus 24:7). Before there is hearing, there is a commitment to doing, to heeding the commandment in the silent vision beyond all words. In Rosenzweig's own provocative and poetic verbalization:

> That which can be looked at is relieved of language, put into relief above it. Light does not talk; but shines [*Das licht redet nicht, es leuchtet*]. It is not at all turned in on itself; it radiates not inward but outward. Yet its radiating is also not a surrendering of itself, as language is; light does not give itself away, dispose of itself as does language when expressing itself, but it is visible while abiding entirely by itself, it does not exactly radiate outward, it only goes on radiating; it does not radiate like a fountain, but like a face, like an eye radiates, an eye that becomes eloquent without needing to open its lips. There is a silence [*Schweigen*] here that is unlike the speechlessness [*Stummheit*] of the primordial world that has no words yet, but a silence that no longer needs words. It is the silence of perfect understanding. Here, a glance means everything. Nothing teaches more clearly that the world is not yet redeemed than the multiplicity of languages.[273]

Retaining something of the aniconic rendering of revelatory experience proffered by the Deuteronomist and elaborated by a host of later Jewish exegetes, Rosenzweig depicts revelation as the emergence of language from the speechlessness of the primordial world. What is most important about the Sinaitic theophany, accordingly, is not the appearance of the glory but the communication of the divine word, although, strictly speaking, the latter is itself a form of idolatrous representation.[274] The moment of redemption, however, is marked by a transition from the verbal to the visual, as the light no longer talks but shines. Silence, in other words, is the appropriate way to describe the luminosity of the face, since it is apprehended by the aperture of the eye that gazes rather than by the opening of the lip that speaks. Although the muteness of the protocosmos and the stillness of the hypercosmos are carefully distinguished—the former is a speechlessness that has no words and the latter is a silence that no longer needs words—there is a sense in which redemption is a return to creation, for both entail the overcoming of word by light, the triumph of speech by vision.[275] As Rosenzweig puts it:

> We have already seen eternal truth sinking back into the Revelation of divine love: in all things Redemption was nothing but the eternal result of the beginning that is always set anew in the revealing love. In the love, that which was hidden had become manifest. Now this ever renewed beginning sinks back into the secret everlasting beginning of Creation. That which is manifest becomes that which is hidden. And along with Revelation, Redemption therefore also flows back into Creation.[276]

The light of the eternal truth is a reclamation of the divine fiat at creation, encapsulated in the words "Let there be light." From that perspective, one could view creation as pointing to redemption, even as redemption is anticipated in revelation. The triangulation of the three theological categories is reflected in the liturgy of the Sabbath, which celebrates creation (Friday evening), revelation (Sabbath morning), and redemption (Sabbath afternoon).[277] The Jewish Sabbath ritually incarnates the coalescence of past, present, and future, and thus it is "both sign of Creation and first Revelation, and as well and even above all anticipation of Redemption. For what else would Redemption be than this, that Revelation and Creation are reconciled!"[278] On each Sabbath the Jew proleptically initiates this reconciliation as he "follows the bidding of the prophet[279] to rest his tongue from the everyday chit-chat and learns silence and listening. And this sanctification of the day of rest through the silent hearing of God's voice must be mutual for his whole house."[280] By heeding the silent hearing, one anticipates the redemption, the future in which the past of creation and the present of revelation converge. In the life of the Jew, typified by the Sabbath, time has been proleptically redeemed. Building on the nexus between the Sabbath and the eschatological future in the rabbinic tradition, Rosenzweig concludes that the eternal people "already lives for itself as if it were the whole world and as if the world were finished; it celebrates in its Sabbaths the sabbatical completion of the world and makes it into the base and starting point of its existence."[281] The disavowal of time enacted each Sabbath does not imply an abrogation or even a dialectical surpassing of temporality but its radical deepening, an eradication of time by rooting oneself more squarely in the ground of time. Eternity is not the metaphysical overcoming of or existential escape from time; it is rather the merging of the three-dimensional structure of lived temporality through the eternalization of the present in the continuous becoming of the being that has always been what is yet to come.[282] To express the convergence of the three tenses of time in the eternity that is the truth of the divine, Rosenzweig must turn to the poetic: "The midnight that glitters in eternal starry clarity before our dazzled eyes is the same one that became night in God's bosom before all existence. He is truly the First and the Last One. Before the mountains were born and the earth writhed in labor-pains—from eternity to eternity you were God. And were from all eternity what you be in eternity: truth."[283] The end, as the beginning, is associated with midnight, an image that conveys the paradox of luminal darkness, the moment when the dark is at its brightest.

A common denominator of the three central theological categories in Rosenzweig's thought, and their corresponding temporal modes, is the interplay of concealment and disclosure. Creation is demarcated as the beginning in which God speaks and the "shell of the mystery breaks." In language that reflects the influence of Schelling but which is also strikingly close to Lurianic kabbalah, Rosenzweig speaks of creation as "God's birth from out of the foundation [*die Geburt Gottes aus dem Grunde*], his creation before the Creation [*seine Schöpfung vor der Schöpfung*]. . . . The figure [*Gestalt*] of God, until now hidden in the metaphysical beyond of myth, steps into the visible and begins to light up [*aufzuleuchten*]."[284] Creation can be regarded, therefore, as a prediction of revelation, or alternatively, revelation is the fulfillment of creation, as it is the present in which God is manifest in the "immediacy and pure presentness of the lived experience [*die Unmittelbarkeit und reine Gegenwärtigkeit des Erlebens*]. For the being that he now makes known is no longer a being beyond lived experience, this is no longer a being in secret, rather a being which has fully blossomed in this lived experience."[285] Creation and revelation are two stages in the exposure of the concealed, but redemption is characterized as the return to the origin (*Ursprung*) before the beginning (*Anfang*) of creation in which what has come to light again is concealed. The arc of time is balanced on opposite ends by two symmetrically inverse processes—the genealogical and the eschatological—the hidden becoming manifest on one side and the manifest becoming hidden on the other. Whether intentional or not, it is with respect to this construct that Rosenzweig's theopoesis divulges its deepest affinity with the kabbalistic perspective. Further support for this argument lies in the fact that the light at the end, the luminosity wherein the manifest is again hidden, is portrayed as the configuration (*Gestalt*) of the countenance (*Antlitz*) of the divine face (*göttlichen Angesicht*), a notion that corresponds to the image of the *parṣuf* that figures prominently in the theosophic symbolism of the kabbalists, especially in certain sections of zoharic literature and in the treatises that expound the kabbalah attributed to the sixteenth-century master, Isaac Luria. The proximity of Rosenzweig's characterization of truth in the image of the divine face and the kabbalistic tradition has been noted by a number of scholars.[286] Nevertheless, it is useful to cite Rosenzweig's words verbatim—already alluded to on two previous occasions in this chapter—the very words that serve as the inscription on the "gate" (*Tor*) to which one returns at the terminus of the expedition, the passageway to the "No-longer-book" (*Nichtmehrbuch*), the "everyday of life" (*All-tag des Lebens*) that is beyond the text:[287]

> That which is eternal had become configuration in the truth. And truth is
> nothing other than the countenance of this configuration. Truth alone is its
> countenance. . . . In the Star of Redemption in which we saw the divine truth
> become configuration, nothing else lights up than the countenance that God
> turned shining toward us. We shall now recognize in the divine face the Star of
> Redemption itself as it now finally became clear for us as configuration.[288]

For Rosenzweig, the world of revelation is marked by the privileging of the auditory
over the visual, illustrated by Deuteronomy 4:12, which he paraphrases as "No figure
have you seen, speech only have you heard," but the "word grows silent in the afterworld
and supra-world," such that in the redeemed world language is overcome by light, a
theme that is linked exegetically to the entreaty in the priestly blessing in Numbers 6:25,
which is rendered as "May he let his countenance shine upon you."[289] In the luminescence of the divine face is true knowledge of the truth, that is, knowing the apparent
truth as it truly appears in the constellation of truth that is the lighting-up (*Auf-
leuchten*) of God's countenance. In consonance with the prophetic, apocalyptic, and
mystical visionary traditions that stretch from Antiquity through the Middle Ages,
and in some respects consistent with the ocularcentric bias of Western philosophical
culture, Rosenzweig depicts this highest knowledge as a form of seeing wherein one
apprehends the "final clarity of transexperienced truth [*der Endklarheit der überer-
fahrene Wahrheit*],"[290] that is, a truth experienced beyond the terrain of experience.

But what does one see in this seeing? From one perspective, the response is obvious,
the luminosity of the face, but from another perspective the matter is more complex,
since this very illumination is also troped visually as the manifest becoming hidden
and verbally as the word growing into silence. How is the manifest becoming hidden
to be envisioned? Is this not a seeing of the unseen, a vision that could be accorded
only to one whose vision is blind-sighted? Is this not an affirmation that is negation? Is
Rosenzweig not culpable of embracing at the conclusion the apophasis he seemed to
reject in the opening paragraph of the first book of part one of the *Star*? "About God
we know nothing," he begins, quickly adding, "But this not-knowing is a not-knowing
about God [*Aber dieses Nichtwissen ist Nichtwissen von Gott*]. As such it is the beginning of our knowledge about him. The beginning, not the end." For Rosenzweig, it is
appropriate to place this not-knowing at the commencement of knowledge, but to do
so at the culmination, to make ignorance the end of human striving, is the "fundamental idea" (*Grundgedanke*) of negative theology, a "way that leads from a found
something [*vorgefundenen Etwas*] to the nothing [*Nichts*] and at the end of which atheism and mysticism can shake hands."[291] The concluding remark is particularly noteworthy, for, in Rosenzweig's mind, the apophasis to which the philosophical path
(exemplified by Maimonides in the Jewish tradition) leads, the proposition that God

can be defined only in his indefinable nature, is notionally on a par with both the mystical sense of the ineffable and the atheistic lack of belief, the conviction of faith and the skepticism of doubt.[292] It is instructive to recall a second passage in the *Star*, in which Rosenzweig proclaims that the basic confession of Islam, "God is God," is not a "confession of faith, but rather a confession of unbelief [*Unglaubensbekenntnis*]; in its tautology, it confesses not the revealed God, but the hidden God; Nicholas of Cusa rightly declares that both the pagan and the atheist confess this." An "authentic confession of faith" would require the "unification of two things," and hence "it always testifies that the personal experience of love must be more than a personal experience."[293] Leaving aside the patently prejudicial interpretation of Islam,[294] what is important for our purposes is to note the juxtaposition of the pagan and the atheist, which parallels the alternative pairing of the atheist and the mystic.

In this connection, it is of interest to evoke the following comment made by Derrida: "Like a certain mysticism, apophatic discourse has always been suspected of atheism."[295] Derrida bolsters his assertion by mentioning Heidegger's citation of a remark of Leibniz in a letter to Paccius on January 28, 1695, concerning Angelus Silesius, the penname of the seventeenth-century German mystic-poet Johannes Scheffler: "With every mystic there are some places that are extraordinarily bold, full of difficult metaphors and inclining almost to Godlessness [*l'athéisme*], just as I have seen in the German poems of a certain Angelus Silesius, poems beautiful besides."[296] Beyond mystical agnosticism, or the learned ignorance of Cusanus, the unsaying of apophatic discourse points to a lack of belief befitting the atheist. In a move that is typical of Derrida's penchant for paradox, he inverts the analogy. "If on the one hand apophasis inclines almost toward atheism, can't one say that, on the other hand or thereby, the extreme and most consequent forms of declared atheism will have always testified to the most intense desire of God?"[297] Parenthetically, this passage may provide some additional information to assess Derrida's depiction of kabbalah as a "kind of atheism."[298] I will discuss this text in more detail in Chapter 4, but suffice it here to note that, following the logic of this argument, the atheistic quality of Jewish esotericism relates not only to the indeterminacy of meaning but also to the subversion of the very theism that is suggested by the apophatic discourse and the affirmation of an even deeper faith in the unknowable mystery. In some measure, there is a residual here of a comment made in an unpublished essay, "L'Athéisme est aristocratique," written in what Edward Baring has labeled the Christian existentialist phase of Derrida's intellectual biography.[299] Atheism is like an aristocracy insofar as they both assert an autarchy that is modeled on the infinity of the divine. The import of the atheism affirmed by the young Derrida is attested in Simone Weil's idea of a "purifying atheism" (*athéisme purificateur*), that is, as Susan Taubes put it, a *mystical atheism* predicated on a "*religious* experience of the death of God," which yields a "theology of divine absence and nonbeing."[300] Derrida translates this finding God by losing God into the belief that divinity is the mysterious object of love beyond human reason.

Derrida's remarks are reminiscent of the observations of Nancy cited in the Preface concerning the correlative and contemporaneous invention of atheism and theism. Derrida and Nancy have well captured the paradoxical implications of apophatic discourse and the implicit reversal of absence and presence: God is most present in the place from which God is most absent. This is not to say that their own views should be equated with negative theology. The failure to distinguish their sense of the wholly other—the trace—and the positive infinity of the divine according to the Christian, Islamic, and Jewish appropriations of the Neoplatonic One is misleading.[301] My point is that they understood that an implication of the apophatic theology is that the denial of belief is the starkest avowal thereof. One might wonder whether Rosenzweig did not himself have such a reversal in mind when he states in the last paragraph of the introduction to part three of the *Star* that divine truth (*göttliche Wahrheit*) "hides from the one who reaches for it with one hand only . . . It wants to be implored with both hands. To the one who calls to it with the double prayer of the believer and of the unbeliever, it will not be denied. God gives of his wisdom to the one as to the other, to belief as to unbelief, but to both only when their prayer comes jointly before him."[302] One should also bear in mind here the well-known remark of Rosenzweig in his commentary to Halevi's poem *yonat reḥoqim naggeni ḥeṭivi*, to which he assigns the title *Die Frohe Botschaft*:

> For the expectation of the Messiah, by which and for the sake of which Judaism lives, would be an empty theologoumenon, a mere "idea," idle babble,—if it were not over and over again made real and unreal, illusion and disillusion in the form of "the false Messiah." The false Messiah is as old as the hope of the genuine one. He is the changing form of the enduring hope. Every Jewish generation is divided by him into those who have the strength of faith to be deceived, and those who have the strength of hope not to be deceived.[303] Those having faith are better, those having hope are stronger. The former bleed as sacrifices on the altar of the eternity of the people, the latter serve as priests before this altar. Until the one time when it will be the reverse, and the faith of the faithful becomes the truth, and the hope of the hoping becomes the lie.[304]

The language of faith must be coupled with the silence of doubt. To comprehend that the latter is an intrinsic dimension of the former is the key to understanding that the path of piety leads beyond the theistic representations of both Judaism and Christianity. As it happens, Derrida reached a similar conclusion in a passing reference to Rosenzweig's call to the originary *yes*, which seemingly rejects the apophatic. According to Derrida, this inceptual invocation is "an event or advent of the *yes* which might be *neither* Jewish *nor* Christian, not yet or no longer simply one or the other," and hence it brings us not to "some ontological or transcendental condition of possibility" but to what is "quasi transcendental" or "quasi ontological," which "would harmonize [*accorderait*] the originary eventness of the event with the fabulous narrative or with the fable inscribed in the *yes* as the origin of every speech (*fari*)." As the "originary word" (*Urwort*) the *yes* both "belongs to" and is "foreign to" language. What is declaimed in the beginning, therefore, is an "inaudible term," a "language without language," a word that "belongs without belonging to the whole that it simultaneously institutes and opens. It exceeds and punctures the language to which it nonetheless remains immanent: like language's first inhabitant, the first to step out of its home. . . . But one can already see its intrinsic double nature announcing itself, or more precisely, confirming itself. It is without being language; it merges without merging with its utterance in a natural language."[305]

To return to the matter of nothing, philosophy is a dead end, as it terminates in negative theology, claiming that all we can know about God is that we do not know. Rosenzweig assures the reader that the way he is taking, by contrast, will lead "from the nothing to the something [*vom Nichts zum Etwas*]." The aim of his thinking "is not a negative concept, but a most positive one. We are seeking God, as we shall later seek the world and man, precisely not within a one and universal All, as one concept among others; if we wanted this, then of course the negative theology of Nicholas of Cusa or of the man from Königsberg would be the only scientific goal; for then the negative would already be fixed as the goal at thinking's point of departure; one concept among others is always negative, at least in its opposition to the others; and if it claims to be unconditional, then science can only deal with an unconditional—nothingness."[306] Rosenzweig insightfully links the scientific goal with negative theology, whether the standard expression thereof in Nicholas of Cusa or in the less expected version of Immanuel Kant, referred to allusively as the "man from Königsberg." This identification rests on the assumption that negation is fixed as the goal in one's departure on the path. The unconditional, scientifically, could be nothing but nothingness, which rendered theologically amounts to the idealistic subsumption of God, world, and human within "the one and universal All." From Rosenzweig's standpoint, however, this presupposition must be renounced, as the three elements are correlative but ontically distinct. The God sought by the new thinking is "dependent on itself alone in its absolute factuality—if the expression is not misleading—precisely, that is, in its 'positivity.' That is why we must put the nothing of the sought-after concept at the beginning: we must get it behind us; for ahead of us lies a something as a goal: the reality of God."[307] Ostensibly, there does not seem to be any ambivalence or ambiguity on Rosenzweig's part. Apophasis must be rebuffed in favor of a kataphatic quest for what he calls the reality of God, also described as factuality and positivity. His new thinking rests on a simple proposition: "The essence of revelation is that it is a *fact*."[308]

Rosenzweig's point is consistent with the view expressed by Cohen in his 1908 essay on the ethics of Maimonides.[309] Rosenzweig does not explicitly evoke the name of Maimonides, but it is plausible to assume that he would have agreed with Cohen regarding the probable influence of the *via negativa* of the great medieval Jewish sage on the formation of the *docta ignorantia* by Cusanus,[310] although the divergence between the two is also noted.[311] Be that as it may, the crucial point that Rosenzweig shares with Cohen is the sense that if negative theology is the logical conclusion of philosophical speculation, then rationalism is itself an affront to the cognitive validity of the God-concept and a challenge to a Judaism that is ground in an absolute faith in the factuality of God based on a revelatory encounter, the creed whence all theological conceptions are to be adduced.

But Rosenzweig is more subtle than first impressions might suggest, and, as the continuation of his own text makes clear, he was indebted to Cohen's interpretation of the Maimonidean negative theology in light of the Platonic conception of the Good as the nonfoundation or, construed more literally, the nonhypothesis (*to anhypotheton*), which we discussed in the previous chapter.[312] As Rosenzweig expressed the point: "In the first place then, God is a nothing for us, his nothing [*sein Nichts*]. From the nothing to the 'something,' or, more strictly: from the nothing to what is not nothing [*vom Nichts zu dem, was nicht Nichts ist*]—for we are not seeking a 'something'— there are two ways, the way of affirmation and the way of negation. The affirmation, that is to say of what is sought after, of the not-nothing; the negation, that is to say of what is presupposed, the nothing."[313] Two ways are distinguished, the way of affirmation (*der Weg der Bejahung*) and the way of negation (*der Weg der Verneinung*), the former leads to the not-nothing (*Nichtnichts*) and the latter to the nothing (*Nichts*). What kind of affirmation is contained in this neologism, the not-nothing? The German *Nichtnichts* is even more evocative than its English rendering, since it is a compound word without any hyphenation. Rosenzweig is adamant that the two ways "are as different from each other and even as opposite to each other as—well, as precisely Yes and No."[314] This comment notwithstanding, Rosenzweig's insistence that the path progressing from nothing to something must be understood as one that traverses from nothing to not-nothing raises questions about the validity of setting the two ways in diametric opposition. If the Yes applies to not-nothing and the No to nothing, then the way of affirmation is itself a form of negation, albeit a negation of negation, a delimitation of something that exceeds language and which can thus be best demarcated in the double negative, a modality of thinking that belongs to the apophatic discourse of negative theology.[315] Rosenzweig articulates the point in the continuation of the passage:

> To affirm the not-nothing is to posit an infinite—like affirmation that takes place through negation [*wie jede Bejahung, die durch Verneinung geschieht*]: to negate the nothing is to posit—like all negation—something limited, finite, determinate. So we see the something in a twofold figure and in a twofold relationship to the nothing: on the one hand, it is its inhabitant, and on the other hand, it escapes from it. As inhabitant of the nothing, the something is the entire plenitude of all that is—not nothing . . . but as an escaped prisoner who has just broken out of the prison of the nothing, the something is nothing other than the event of this

liberation from the nothing. . . . Endlessly, then, the essence springs up from the nothing; in a sharp delimitation the action separates from it. For the essence one asks about the origin, and for action about the beginning.[316]

Affirmation takes place through negation. The "something" that is affirmed is viewed through a twofold prism in relation to the "nothing," either as inhabitant or as escapee. With respect to the former, the something is the "not nothing" (*nicht Nichts*), that is, the infinite or the "entire plenitude of all that is" (*die ganze Fülle alles dessen*), and with respect to the latter, the something is naught but the deliverance from this nothing, which yields the finite being. The something that inhabits the fullness that is within God is identified further as the "origin" (*Ursprung*), whence issues forth the "essence" (*Wesen*), whereas the something that escapes therefrom is the action (*Tat*), to which is assigned a "beginning" (*Anfang*).

The influence of Cohen's principle of origin (*Ursprungsprinzip*) on Rosenzweig's attempt to deduce a positive God-concept from an aboriginal void has been duly noted.[317] Rosenzweig was assuredly persuaded by Cohen's discussion of the concept of the originative principle, the nature of the divine being, and the problem of the nothing. Although some of the relevant material was cited in the previous chapter, it will be profitable to repeat part of the critical text here. For Cohen, in stark contrast to Heidegger,[318] the originary nothing, which he relates philologically to the Hebrew *ayin*, "in no way means merely nothing [*das Nichts*]; it means, rather, unquestionably relative infinity of privation [*das relativ Unendliche der Privation*]. The latter, however, is not found within becoming, with matter, with the nonexistent primeval substance, but rather within the unique being of God [*innerhalb des göttlichen einzigen Seins*]. . . . The finite is to attain its originative principle in the infinite, in the negation of privation."[319] The following passage attests to the fact that Rosenzweig was clearly impressed by Cohen's turn to mathematics as "an organon of thinking, precisely because mathematics does not produce its elements out of the empty nothing of the one and universal zero, but out of the nothing of the differential, a definite nothing in each case related to the element it was seeking. The differential combines in itself the properties of the nothing and of the something; it is a nothing that refers to a something, to its something, and at the same time a something that still slumbers in the womb of the nothing."[320] Insofar as the nothing and the something are conjoined within the differential, the path of affirmation of that which is not nothing and the path of negation of the nothing both emerge therefrom. Both paths "go from the nothing to the something," and thus we "recognize in the nothing the origin of the something."[321] The nothing is not an undifferentiated zero but the matrix whence the differentiation of all particular phenomena takes shape. To say that reality is grounded in the infinitesimal, therefore, means that everything emerges from a nothing, which is not really nothing at all, but the infinitely small abyss extended asymptotically between two points. This space is necessitated by the principle that one can arrive at a tangent

point P only by approaching it infinitesimally, which is to say, by making the difference between it and some other point Q infinitely small and hence infinitely distended. The gap, moreover, accounts for the curvilinear movement of each point in
relation to the tangent line, the movement that secures the principle of continuity that
shapes our experience of an inherently discontinuous world. The core of existence
is not substance but process, "the movement to and from God out of a paradoxical
nothing."[322]

Without denying the Cohenian influence, I would suggest, in addition, that there
is a conspicuous correspondence between Rosenzweig and kabbalistic theosophy.
After all, Cohen's principle is related to the appropriation of an infinitesimal calculus,
which implies, mathematically, that the origin of the objective realm is in that which
is not hypothetically.[323] For Cohen, in ascertaining the limit that is nothing we can
still be confident about our claims to know something; for Rosenzweig, the negative
points us in the direction of the ultimate knowledge, which is knowing that we
cannot know, a trail that culminates with vision overcoming language, the image
superseding the word.[324] In spite of the connection between them, Rosenzweig's
thought is to be distinguished from Cohen, insofar as the matter is not simply the
derivation of something from nothing but rather the positing of an origin that is
neither something nor nothing, an essence whose essence is not to be an essence.
This notion of an inessential essence, I surmise, corresponds to Ein Sof, the truly determinate nothing, the origin that has no limit, and the action that ensues from its nothingness to the sefirotic gradations, whose emanation from the infinite marks the
beginning of the process of delimitation. The Ein Sof of the kabbalah may be envisaged
as the self-negating negativity that yields the positivity of the entangled manifold that
constitutes the fabric of the world, the effluent emptiness that is the womb of all becoming. When seen from the perspective of the infinite, the multiplicity of finite
beings appear to be illusory, but one attuned to the nothingness that is at the core of
everything comprehends that the illusionary nature of the world is not to deny its
existence but to indicate the interconnectivity of all that exists. For the kabbalists,
the Ein Sof is the linguistic signpost that marks this interrelationality, the eternal
enfolding that is continuously unfolding in time, a process that cannot be uttered in
language because each and every thing is constantly becoming the nothing it was
not. The infinite nothingness cannot be constricted by images of affirmation or negation, since the negative images presuppose the positivity they ostensibly negate.
Hence, to say of Ein Sof that it is nothing is as erroneous as saying of it that it is
something.

My line of reasoning can be buttressed by the passage from Rosenzweig's diary that
I mentioned previously in this chapter: "The true predecessors of my problem are
nevertheless in the Kabbala. However I show that the problem of Kabbala is not specifically theological (but En Sof appears in the same way with regards to M[an] and

W[orld] and in the priority of the theological which the Kabbala presents, the real time can only be based on (that which really happens not that which unfolds itself, etc.) which contradicts the pure theory of Potency."[325] The passage, which was written in 1922, parallels the discussion in the *Star* of the infinite essence that precedes the binary division into Yes and No.[326] The beginning, Rosenzweig insists, must be the Yes, for the No would be the "No of the nothing" (*Nein des Nichts*), and "this presupposes a nothing that would be negatable, that is to say, a nothing that had already decided on a Yes." But Rosenzweig does concede that even though the beginning is the affirmative, the No is the "starting point" (*Ausgangspunkt*), the "beginning of our knowledge." It would seem that Rosenzweig wished to distinguish the ontological beginning, which is the Yes, and the epistemological beginning, which is the No. This starting point, we also learn, is "incapable of being affirmed" or "of being negated." Indeed, it is "situated before the Yes and before the No," although Rosenzweig is quick to note that the nothingness before the beginning whence there is something and nothing is not situated at all, since it is naught but the "virtual place for the beginning of our knowledge." That this "place"—or better the placeholder—has no ontic reality is underscored by Rosenzweig's assertion that it has no name and that it should not be identified as the "dark ground" (*dunkler Grund*) of Eckhart, Böhme, or Schelling. The Yes, which is the beginning, goes toward the nothing but also toward the not-nothing (*Nichtnichts*). This not-nothing is not "an autonomous given" (*selbständig gegeben*), since "absolutely nothing is given besides the nothing," and yet, it is affirmed as that which "circumscribes as its inner boundary the infinity of all that is not nothing." The infinity of all that is not nothing is identified further as the "affirmed infinity" (*Unendliches bejaht*) of God's infinite essence (*unendliches Wesen*), also demarcated as his "infinite factuality" (*unendliche Tatsächlichkeit*) and "nature" (*Physis*). In going toward the not-nothing, the Yes, "the original word of language" (*das Urwort der Sprache*), which is the beginning that contains the "unlimited possibilities" of the reality hidden within it, returns to its origin, the infinite essence of the divine nature. Although Rosenzweig describes this essence as an "infinitely affirmed Being," it is not a metaphysical substance but rather the eventfulness of the limitless possibilities that will come to exist, the not-nothing that is the "divine essence in all infinity" prior to there being a distinct something or a distinct nothing, the "infinite factuality" that is "conditioned by its nothing" and "simply at rest."[327] Rosenzweig has skillfully transposed the theosophic teaching of the kabbalists about the Ein Sof into a philosophical key.

Rivka Horwitz suggested that since Rosenzweig did not avail himself of the kabbalistic terminology in the *Star* but only in the diary entry, it is likely that he learned of the Jewish mystical teaching after composing his magnum opus.[328] In light of the recently discussed six-sonnet cycle "The Shekhinah," composed by Rosenzweig in 1911, this conjecture must be rejected. As Benjamin Pollock notes, these sonnets recast "the kabbalistic account of the primordial break within the divine that results in the exile of the Shekhinah, and of the hoped-for reunification of the Shekhinah with God in redemption."[329] Most significantly, from my viewpoint, the understanding of redemption proffered in this poetic composition entails a form of salvation from rather than within historical time. Whatever the extent of his actual literate knowledge of Jewish esotericism at this early stage in his intellectual odyssey, the young Rosenzweig displayed a keen understanding of kabbalistic eschatology based on an essentially pessimistic—one might even say gnostic—assessment of the physical world as inherently unredeemable,[330] an understanding that I have argued continued to reverberate in the last part of the *Star*, wherein Rosenzweig insists that God "is not only Redeemer, but also Redeemed," that is, redemption may be considered "self-redemption" (*Selbsterlösung*), insofar as it consists of the divine being redeemed from creation and revelation.[331] Moreover, as Idel pointed out,[332] there is a passage in the "Urzelle" that demonstrates that Rosenzweig was already familiar to some extent with the teaching of Lurianic kabbalah, specifically the "interiorization of God [*Verinnerung Gottes*], which *precedes* not merely His self-externalization [*Selbstentäußerung*], but rather even His self," an idea that he explicitly links to the "dark ground" of Schelling's thought,[333] an association, as we have seen, that he modifies in the *Star*. It is reasonable to conclude, therefore, that Rosenzweig was aware of the kabbalistic resonance of his thought from an earlier period, but for some reason he chose to conceal that in the *Star*. In a manner similar to many kabbalists, though likely indicating the influence of Cohen as well, Rosenzweig differentiates between the beginning and the origin: the former denotes a temporal moment, the point of creation of something from nothing, in contrast to the latter, which is before any temporal demarcation, the creation before creation, the essence that springs forth endlessly from the not-nothing that is the source of the nothing that is everything. With regard to this basic distinction in kabbalistic writings, there is a resemblance between Rosenzweig and Heidegger as well.[334]

In a distinctly Heideggerian turn of phrase, we should speak of Rosenzweig's *Nichtnichts* as the nothing that nothings, the nothing that reveals itself as nothing in the guise of nothing.[335] I will limit myself to several passages from *Contributions to Philosophy* to substantiate the comparison of Rosenzweig to Heidegger, which betrays the direct influence of Schelling and perhaps the indirect influence of Lurianic kabbalah.[336] The "no" of negation, writes Heidegger, is expressive of a "deeper essence" than the "yes" of affirmation,[337] "this 'negative' determination of 'nothingness'" (*diese »negative« Bestimmung des »Nichts«*), the nihilation that is prior to the distinction between the affirmable (*Bejahbaren*) and the negatable (*Verneinbaren*), indeed the conjunctive "and" that binds and separates the yes and the no in the ground of enownment—"the belonging-together of beyng and nothingness" (*die Zusammengehörigkeit von Seyn und Nichts*)—that is the "self-withdrawing" (*Sichentziehende*), "the essential occurrence of beyng" (*der Wesung des Seyns*), the "counterturning" (*Gegen-*

wendige) of "refusal" (*Verweigerung*), the "no" and the "not" (*das Nicht und Nein*) that are "more originary in beyng" (*Ur-sprünglichere im Seyn*).[338] The enowning of the event "attunes and persuasively disposes the essential occurrence of truth" by which we discern that "[t]he openness of the clearing of concealment [*die Offenheit des Lichtens der Verbergung*] is therefore originarily not the mere emptiness of vacancy [*keine bloße Leere des Unbesetztseins*]; instead, it is the disposed and disposing emptiness of the abyssal ground [*die gestimmt stimmende Leere des Ab-grundes*] which, according to the attuning intimation of the event, is a disposed abyssal ground." The emptiness, therefore, should not be conceived as lack or the "mere non-satisfaction of an expectation or wish." It is rather—from the outlook of Dasein—"the restraint" (*die Verhaltenheit*) or "the withholding in the face of the hesitant self-withholding [*das Ansichhalten vor der zögernden Versagung*] whereby time-space is grounded as the site of the moment for the decision." Attunement to this truth leads the mind to the ultimate paradox and the collapse of the distinction between nonbeing and being insofar as the emptiness of the Ab-ground "is actually the fullness of what is still undecided [*die Fülle des Noch-unentschiedenen*] and is to be decided, the abyssal ground that points to the ground, i.e., to the truth of being."[339] For Heidegger, as for Rosenzweig, the ground, which is designated the truth of being, is not a reified something but the inexhaustibility of all that is to become, the absolute necessity that is the pure potentiality, the self-negating negation that is the matrix within which all beings are disclosed in the nothingness of their being, the self-hiding that instigates the manifestation of all that is manifest, the nonshowing of every showing.[340]

The nothing that comes from the not-nothing, consequently, should not be understood in the Hegelian sense as an "unveiling of the essence of pure being" (*Wesensenthüllung des reinen Seins*)[341] but rather in the Schellingian (or kabbalistic) sense of the "self-externalization" (*Sich-äußerns*) of God from the "primordial No" (*Urnein*),[342] the "self-configuring" (*Selbts-gestaltung*) or the "self-revelation of God's freedom before Creation" (*vorschöpferische Sichselbst-offenbaren der göttlichen Freiheit*).[343] The power of God that is revealed from its hiddenness at the beginning of creation can be considered an "essential attribute," but it originates in an event that internally is an act of "pure arbitrariness" or "absolute freedom" and externally an act of "pure necessity."[344] The essential attribute is essentially inessential, since its essence consists of its being an intrinsically necessary randomness that cannot be predicted or calculated, the groundless ground of being that is not-nothing.

The two ways specified by Rosenzweig should not be set in binary opposition. As he himself writes: "That which came out as Yes appears as No, and vice versa, just as we unpack things we put into a suitcase in the order that is opposite to how we packed them. . . . the No is not the 'antithesis' of the Yes; on the contrary, facing the nothing, the No has the same immediacy as the Yes; and for its confrontation with the Yes, it does not presuppose the Yes itself, but only the emergence of the Yes from out of the nothing."[345] Rosenzweig offers a trivial example to illustrate a lofty philosophical point: the respective processes of packing and unpacking leave the impression that one order is opposite to the other, but, in fact, these orders are not oppositional at all. The sense of apparent opposition arises from the temporal sequencing, a matter that is a pure contingency and not reflective of an essential dichotomy. Analogously, as Rosenzweig emphasizes, it is possible to read a text from beginning to end or from end to beginning. As I have argued elsewhere, "the ability to read bi-directionally presumes an open circle, which of necessity entails the impossibility of determining the end from the beginning or the beginning from the end; the reversibility of the timeline does not imply closure at either terminus, but rather an ever-changing flux that desta- bilizes the model of an irreversible succession proceeding unilaterally from start to finish."[346] The same logic of reversibility is at play in Rosenzweig's description of the relationship of the Yes and the No: the latter presupposes the materialization of the former from the nothing that is something, just as the former presupposes the materialization of the latter from the something that is nothing.[347] Yes and No ap- pear to be the antithesis of one another, but they are not antithetical. Rosenzweig adamantly avers that the Yes does not come from the No as if it were "torn from God in a spasm of self-negation" (Selbstverneinung),[348] but, given his own delineation of the Yes as the not-nothing, one cannot but help comprehend this advent as an act of negation. To be sure, what is negated is not a self but an essence that can be de- marcated only as the not-nothing, that is, a nothing negated of and by its own nothingness.

Bearing this in mind, we can understand how the conclusion of the *Star* is antici- pated in its inception. In this connection, it is worth recalling the instructive remark made by Rosenzweig in "The New Thinking." Any philosophical book, he asserts, re- quires that the reader "does not understand the beginning, or, at the very least, [that one] understands it wrongly." Rosenzweig illustrates the point from the discussion regarding the concept of nothingness in the *Star*: "the 'nothingnesses,' which here seems to be only a methodological auxiliary concept, first reveals its contentful signifi- cance only in the short concluding paragraph of the volume, and its ultimate meaning only in the concluding book of the whole. What is said here is nothing other than a *reductio ad absurdum* and, at the same time, a rescue of the old philosophy."[349] The repercussion of Rosenzweig's analysis of the nothing at the beginning—the rescue of the old philosophy that his new thinking will execute—can be elicited only from the discussion at the end. The disclosure of the face of God that will shine in the eschaton is itself a form of concealment, the manifestation becoming hidden and the speech leading to silence. To be granted a vision of the face inscribed within the contours of the star is to behold the inexpressible truth. It is understandable why Rosenzweig begins with a rejection of negative theology—affirming our inability to know God is the limit to where philosophy goes—but it is not clear that he has presented the apo- phatic dimension of the philosophical tradition accurately. More importantly, his own

sense of affirmation as the negation of negation, which is reflected in his characterization of the end as a silence that no longer needs words, is itself a form of apophasis that
embraces the mystical.

As I have noted already, this end is depicted by Rosenzweig as the discernment that
God is truth. It might appear that this apprehension is kataphatic in nature: "That by
which we had to designate God's essence, the last thing that we know of him as the
Lord of what is last, of the one life perfected in supra-worldly fashion in the All: that
he is truth—this last conception of the essence slips through our fingers. For if God
is truth—what is said with this about his 'essence'? Nothing more than this, that he is
the original ground [*Urgrund*] of truth, and all truth is truth only through this, it
comes from him."[350] The essence of God is linked to his being the "ground of truth,"
and this would allegedly provide the ideational basis for a theocentric orientation,
which is articulated by Rosenzweig in his claim that the "divine essentiality [*göttliche
Wesenheit*] is really nothing more than the divine self-revealing [*göttliche Sich-
Offenbaren*]."[351] The kataphatic theology, which is similar in tone to Schelling and to
Lurianic kabbalah, can be cast propositionally in the declaration that "God is truth."
If we probe more attentively, however, we discover that Rosenzweig approaches an
articulation that is reminiscent of the *via negativa* of Maimonides: "God is truth—
this sentence with which we thought we had risen to the utmost of knowledge—if we
see more closely what truth really is, then we find that that sentence brings back to us
in different words only what is most intimately familiar of our experience; the apparent knowledge about the essence turns into the near, immediate experience of his action; that he is truth tells us finally nothing however other than that he—loves."[352]

The "apparent knowledge" (*scheinbaren Wissen*) of God's essence amounts to the
"near, immediate experience" (*nahe unmittelbare Erfahrung*) of divine action, expressed especially in the form of love, rather than any positive delineation of that
essence. "For the last truth is—it is none other than our truth. God's truth is nothing other than the love with which he loves us."[353] It should come as no surprise,
then, that Rosenzweig informs us that by gathering this "last knowledge about
God's essence . . . we could venture back . . . into that first nonknowledge [*erste
Nichterkenntnis*], into the knowledge of his nothing [*die Erkenntnis seines Nichts*],
which was our starting point."[354] In going forward, one goes back, retracing steps
to where one could have never been, and thus one discerns that the knowledge of
the divine essence apprehended at the climax is identical to the nonknowledge
available at the onset, the knowledge of his nothing, a nothing that can only be in
virtue of not being, the not-nothing.[355] Still struggling to demarcate his path as
distinct from idealistic philosophy, Rosenzweig, perhaps influenced by Kierkegaard,[356] remarks that paganism finds the "All" in that nothing, whereas revelation,
the basic postulate that accords theism meaning, taught us to recognize the "hidden God" (*verborgenen Gott*), that is, the "hidden one who is nothing other than

the not yet manifest one [*der noch nicht offenbare*]. . . . The nothing of our knowledge about him thus became for us a meaningful nothing, the mysterious prediction of what we have been experiencing in the revealing."[357] The name of truth that was discarded at the beginning of the "pilgrimage through the All" is restored in the "last immediacy in which the All really comes altogether near to us." Having rejected the idealist philosophy that rested on the "belief in the immediateness of cognition to the All and of the All to cognition," the truth can be grasped at the goal when "we have come as far as the direct view of the configuration on our road from an immediate to the nearest [*von einem Unmittelbaren zum nächsten*]." But the truth that is beheld at the goal is "nothing other than the divine Revelation that happened also for us, the ones hovering midway between ground and future. Our Truly, our Yes and Amen . . . is unveiled at the goal as the beating heart also of the eternal truth."[358]

The notion of the not-yet translates the apophatic into a kataphatic register. As Martin Kavka astutely discerned, the meontological sign of the not-yet in Rosenzweig, as in Levinas, albeit differently, entails a "temporalization of the concept of nonbeing" that "justifies a structure of messianic or eschatological anticipation."[359] By turning nothing to not-yet, the negative holds within its nonbeing the potential for all that comes to be; to decode the metaphysical idea theologically, that which is hidden reveals itself through continuous manifestations. The disclosures, however, are themselves a form of concealment, indeed the concealment of concealment, as what is revealed is always the not-nothing that is not yet something. In spite of his initial rejection of negative theology, the swerve of Rosenzweig's path winds its way to an apophasis of the apophasis: "That God is nothing becomes just as much a figurative sentence as the other one, that he is truth [*Daß Gott das Nichts sei, wird ebensosehr zu einem uneigentlichen Satz wie der andre, daß er die Wahrheit sei*]."[360] Both propositions, that "God is nothing," which is assigned to the beginning, and that "God is the truth," which is affixed to the end, must be taken figuratively. To render either literally would be to cloak the untruth exposed in the mirror of truth and lapse thereby into the mistaken dichotomization of appearance and reality.

So what, then, asks Rosenzweig, is nothing? *Was ist Nichts?* His response quintessentially performs the dialectic of concealment doubling itself to reveal what it conceals in the concealing of what it reveals: "Already in this very question the single answer that would let the nothing remain nothing is forbidden, the answer: nothing. For nothing can never designate the essence, never be predicate."[361] To inquire about the nature of nothing is to presume that nothing is something, but for nothing to be nothing, it must be no thing. Any attempt to articulate this truism, to translate nothing into propositional logic with a subject and a predicate connected by a copula will fail. Language has reached its limit, though the very failure of language holds the promise of language, the "true mystery" by which the "word speaks," an articulation that determines the boundary beyond which lies that which speech "can neither reach nor perceive," that which is "cast away from its luminous and audible sphere, into the cold dread of the nothing," the "decisive anticipation . . . where the Kingdom to come is actually coming and where eternity is actual reality."[362] Nothing is not some thing; it is the eventuality of something, indeed everything that originates in the origin that is not-nothing, the not-yet that is the "ever-repeated present, the eternal, wherein beginning and end meet, the imperishable in the today."[363] We can pronounce that "the nothing is God" (*das Nichts ist Gott*), but this sentence, Rosenzweig insists, "is as little an absurdity as the sentence of idealism that truth is God; it is simply, like the former one—false. Exactly like truth, the nothing is of course not at all finally a self-supporting subject [*selbständiges Subjekt*]; it is merely a fact [*ein bloße Tatsache*], the awaiting of a something [*die Erwartung eines Etwas*], it is not anything yet [*ein Nochnichts*]. . . . Of God alone can it be said that he is the nothing; it would be the first knowledge of his essence."[364] By now, however, we know that this claim to knowledge of the divine essence intends its very opposite, for the essence of God is such that there is no essence to be known.

As I noted above , for Rosenzweig, attested already in the "Urzelle," the organizing concept is event as opposed to essence.[365] Nevertheless, he wrote repeatedly of God's essence, though this is an essence that is not knowable, as the essence of this essence is always what shall become in having already been. Alternatively expressed, the truth of God is contained in the compresence of the three temporal modes, an idea traditionally offered by rabbinic interpreters as the meaning of the Tetragrammaton.[366] To say of God that "He is" implies that the "actual has-been," the "actual is," and the "actual becoming" are all together as one.[367] Rosenzweig cannot elude the double bind of apophasis, even as he tried to disentangle it. The signpost of redemption, "God is truth," is the only admissible answer to the theological question, "What is God?" And this answer, Rosenzweig maintains, "leads the mystical question about his supra-worldly essence, this last question, back into the living experience of his actions, so the answer 'he is nothing' leads to the abstract question about his primordial worldly essence, this first question—towards—the same experience."[368] The experience to which Rosenzweig refers is the experience of revelation, the dialogical expression of divine love, which is not a thing but an event, not spatial facticity but temporal factuality. Revelation is the immediacy that provides the cement to mend the "primeval break" of the All, for by affirming the real possibility of revelation as transcendence entering into dialogical relation with the human being in the world, the three modes of time, beginning, middle, and end, all "become equally immediate, that is to say equally incapable of being mediated, no longer to be mediated, because they are themselves already centers—and now the All, the once shattered, has grown together again."[369]

This passage must be read intertextually with the statement at the closing of the book's introduction, to which I have already referred: "The nothing of our knowledge is not a singular nothing, but a threefold one. Hence, it contains in itself the promise of definability. And that is why we may hope, as did Faust, to find again in this nothing, in this threefold nothing of knowledge, the All that we had to cut into pieces."[370] The multiplication of nothing, however, leaves one with nothing, indeed more nothing, three times more than nothing. What would be unveiled in this veiling of nothing but the unveiling of nothing? In the middle that is revelation, writes Rosenzweig, beginning (creation) and end (redemption) rise "out of their hiddenness into the manifest," but in so doing, that "which is manifest becomes that which is hidden."[371] If the hidden that is manifest becomes hidden again, if the "light breaking / darkness unutterable" at the beginning recycles to the "unutterable darkness / breaking light" at the end,[372] then Rosenzweig's new thinking is inescapably enmeshed in the duplicity of secrecy that is pivotal to apophatic theology.

The meontological temporalization of nonbeing may induce the possibility of encounter with transcendence, embodied linguistically in the erotic metaphors of the Song of Songs, but the price to be paid for grounding the openness to the other in a negative theology[373] is the potential undoing of the dialogical in the discernment that what is disclosed is the face of truth, which cannot be rendered literally but only metaphorically.[374] The eternal forms, which will be manifest in the futurity of redemption, are the figures that are "continuously brought forth by the stream of actuality fed by its three invisible-secret sources [*drei unsichtbar-geheimen Quellen*]. Indeed, in these figures those invisible secrets [*unsichtbaren Geheimnisse*] become even figural [*selbst bildhaft*], and the constant course of life rounds itself off into recurrent form."[375] The metaphysical concept of actual presence is transmuted into a semiotic trope of mythopoetic metaphoricization. But all three invisible secrets lie beyond—and indeed may be extracted ontically from—the factuality of their imaginative realization. Through the world-time of Judaism and Christianity, what is real "takes figural shape as a formed copy [*geformten Abbild*]. In their God, their world, and their man, there becomes expressible the secret of God, of man, of world, which is only experienceable, but not expressible, in the course of life. What God, what the world, what man 'is,' we do not know, only what they do, or what is done to them . . . In place of the existing substances, which are everlasting only as secret preconditions of the ever renewed actuality, enter forms [*Gestalten*] that eternally mirror this ever renewed actuality."[376] A substantialist ontology is replaced by a notion of an ever renewed actuality (*allzeiterneuerte Wirklichkeit*) that is based on the temporality lived and narrated in the "eternal clock-faces" (*ewigen Zifferblätter*) of the two liturgical communities, the eternal life of Judaism and the eternal way of Christianity. The pulse of time is measured from the perspective of this (dia)chronic mirroring, the unremitting dissimulation of forms that appear to be true in the truth of their appearance.

Derrida's observations regarding Angelus Silesius may well apply to Rosenzweig: "not only God but the deity surpasses knowledge . . . the singularity of the unknown God overflows the essence and the divinity, thwarting in this manner the oppositions of the negative and the positive, of being and nothingness, of thing and nonthing—thus transcending all the theological attributes."[377] The figurative status of the configuration of the divine face beheld in the star puts into play the possibility that the ultimate truth is that there is no truth, just as knowledge of the essence consists of becoming cognizant of the fact that there is no essence to be known. "That God is nothing becomes just as much a figurative sentence as the other one, that he is truth."[378] This dissimilitude may be the fated consequence of negative theology.[379] In spite of Rosenzweig's painstaking effort to espouse that the personal God of Judaism (and Christianity as well) cannot be "only an allegory," that revelation must consist of the unmediated bond between God and human that rests on the unique self-disclosure of the former to the latter and the consequent courage of the latter to bow down in worship before the former,[380] it is not clear that theistic language for him is anything but metaphorical, as there is no reality but the naught that is not-nothing, the nothing that is not, not even nothing. In what strikes the ear as an evidently Nietzschean tone, Rosenzweig speculated in *Understanding the Sick and the Healthy*, if *nothing* is truly the order that is the essence behind appearance, then it is possible that "appearance is everything and everything is only appearance," that "there is nothing beyond appearance, not even something 'wholly other,'" that the human being, itself reduced to mere appearance, "reflects a segment of the mirage, or, indeed (why not?) the complete mirage," that "God is merely the shadow cast by the frame of the mirror, or possibly the reflection of the mirror's glass."[381]

In the last analysis, it is legitimate to wonder whether the theism championed by Rosenzweig is not prone to being itself an *as if* construct, the "panacea for doubt" of the philosophical temperament that obscures the empirical tangibility of an event and thereby inverts "healthy common sense" into "sick reason."[382] I am well aware that the whole point of Rosenzweig's new thinking is to turn our attention away from essence to event, to ascribe to theological language the role of marking "experiences of meetings" (*Erfahrungen von Begegnungen*) rather than "experiences of an objective kind" (*Erfahrungen gegenständlicher Art*), as he put it in the note on biblical anthropomorphisms.[383] I appreciate that, from his standpoint, the anthropomorphic depictions of God guard against reverting to polytheism.[384] Rosenzweig's labors, therefore, must be judged in terms of leading the way to an experience of encountering this "real God" (*wirklichen Gottes*) rather than an experience of an essence that is naught but an "image of God" (*Gottesbild*).[385] Yet, to think in his footsteps—the thinking that is the highest mode of thanking—imposes on us the demand to inquire whether it is feasible to speak of such a meeting when our ability to assert anything positive about the "reality" of God is compromised. Is Rosenzweig not subject to the same quandary as Maimonides; that is, does the insistence on the radical incomparability of God not render all predication inappropriate, and if so, God-talk, theistically conceived, would be meaningful in some social, psychological, or political sense or perhaps as a form of apophatic discourse, the saying of the unsaid in the unsaying of the said?[386] Would apophasis not be the inevitable conclusion of such an uncompromising disbanding of the anthropomorphically inflected tropes of the tradition? But are these not the very rhetorical patterns that provide the eidetic underpinning for the ontic possibility of meeting a *real God*, a God to whom "phenomenological concreteness" (in the Levinasian sense) may be attributed?[387]

In spite of his unfaltering effort to make a credible philosophical case for the theological belief in a revelatory experience that preserves the otherness of the divine vis-à-vis the human—thereby anticipating the contemporary "rediscovery of negative theology" that has resulted in the narrowing of the gulf between theology and philosophy[388]—does Rosenzweig, ultimately, succumb to the conversion of theology into anthropology along the lines of Feuerbach, for whom the consciousness of the Infinite (which is offered as a definition of religion) amounts to the consciousness of the infinity of consciousness, and hence the God of traditional monotheism is no more than an outward projection of human nature?[389] Or, to appropriate the terminology of Habermas, is Rosenzweig not guilty of a postmetaphysical "linguistification of the sacred" that would render the ontotheological experience of the divine presence that he so passionately desired untenable?[390] Eschewing the possibility of an atheological ontology, which has been associated with Heidegger,[391] Rosenzweig seems nevertheless to be ensnared in the clench of an atheistic theology against which he fought so vociferously. Is there anything to affirm as real but the "name-less, transcendent nothing," a belief that Rosenzweig characterized as the "diseased thought" of the philistine?[392] Perhaps this is the drift of the gloss made by Rosenzweig regarding the *absolute factuality* of God, "if the expression is not misleading."[393] To the best of my knowledge, Rosenzweigian scholars have not heeded this stipulation. The expression may indeed be misleading because it is not feasible to speak of God's factuality—the "dark chaos of the particular" (*dunkles Chaos des Besonderen*)[394]—prior to or dissociated from the theopoetic confabulation of the divine in the guise of creation, redemption, and revelation.[395] Let us recall Rosenzweig's remark that the enemy "is not idealism as such," but the "assumption that it is possible for something to exist beyond reality." Realism and idealism, indeed any *ism*, are equally unacceptable, for they both promote an "essence" that abstracts from life, and hence they "fail to conciliate thought and action."[396] Is Rosenzweig subject to the very malady of spirit that he earnestly sought to alleviate? There is an aside made toward the end of "Atheistic Theology," the essay that set Rosenzweig on the course to articulate a new thinking that would uphold the possibility of revelation, which indicates that he was acutely aware of the risk of lapsing into the posture that he criticized: "That the light of God is the human soul and that only the rays of that light, which the soul needs for the illumination of its earthly way, are visible—this fundamental idea of our philosophy—was and is just as susceptible as its mystical parallels to an atheistic stamp."[397] In this utterly honest and prescient moment, Rosenzweig foresaw that the commitment to the belief that the light of God is the human soul[398] propels his own path perilously close to the "secret abysses of the nothing" (*geheimen Gründen des Nichts*),[399] the unfathomable ground where mysticism and atheism insidiously shake hands.

CHAPTER 3

Echo of the Otherwise and the Lure of Theolatry

> You constituted Time—
> I deemed Eternity
> A Revelation of Yourself—
> 'Twas therefore Deity
>
> The Absolute—removed
> The Relative away—
> That I unto Himself adjust
> My slow idolatry—
>
>   —Emily Dickinson

In the introduction to *Crossover Queries: Dwelling with Negatives, Embodying Philosophy's Others*, Edith Wyschogrod remarks that the challenge of the essays included in her collection was to promote "further inquiry into theological, ethical, and aesthetic interpretations of negatives."[1] Philosophical accounts of the negative are seen as a complex of crossings, and thus her own essays sway between efforts to overcome manifestations of the negative and claims about its irrevocability. The mandate set for postmodern thought is to persevere in tarrying with the negative à la Hegel while still seeking to erect temporary conduits in the vein of Nietzsche's vision of the "between," to set a bridge by means of which one crosses over in the negation to be affirmed in the affirmation of what is negated.[2]

In this chapter, I would like to focus on one of the principal crossings that resonate in *Crossover Queries*, the crossing that the author herself refers to as the passage from the Derridean *erotics of transcendence* to the Levinasian *ethics of transcendence*.[3] To attend properly to this crossing, I will explore the intricacies of Levinas's reflections on transcendence in the various stages of his intellectual biography. Let me commence by citing a critical extract from Wyschogrod:

> But a transcendent Absolute that is beyond consciousness necessitates an apophatic theology that may be disclosed as an unremitting yearning *for* an absent Other or as a divestiture of self *on behalf of* an Other who, as Other, never appears. Derrida's

account of naming and negative theology is essentially transgressive, an *erotics* of transcendence. When the sheer contingency of fact leads neither to an eidetic science, to the certainty of an eidos that remains invariant through all of an object's variations, nor to an erotic desire for the Other, but rather to an alterity that is beyond consciousness, the way is open for a Levinasian *ethics* of transcendence.[4]

Wyschogrod perceptively frames the innovation of Levinas, particularly the tropes of the infinite and illeity that are essential to his conception of alterity, in terms of a somewhat neglected aspect of Husserl's phenomenology that relates specifically to his discussion of God. According to Husserl, the notion of divine transcendence creates something of a phenomenological crisis because it raises the possibility of an empty intuition, that is, an intentional act of consciousness whose meaning is not determined by the plenary presence of what is intended, an intentionality that has no object of thought to which it is adequated. In Husserl's own language, the "*theological principle . . . could not be assumed as something transcendent in the sense in which the world is something transcendent*; for . . . that would involve a countersensical circularity. The ordering principle of the absolute must be found in the absolute itself, considered purely as absolute."[5] Insofar as the divine transcendence makes it impossible to speak of a "worldly God," it follows that the "immanence of God in absolute consciousness cannot be taken as immanence in the sense of being as a mental process." Consequently, there must be "within the absolute stream of consciousness and its infinities, modes in which transcendencies are made known other than the constituting of physical realities as unities of harmonious appearances."[6] The "transcendency pertaining to God" stands "in polar contrast to the transcendency pertaining to the world," since with respect to the latter we can speak of "*factual* concatenations of mental processes of consciousness . . . in which a *morphologically ordered* world in the sphere of empirical intuition becomes constituted as their intentional correlate, i.e., a world concerning which there can be classifying and describing sciences." An extraworldly divine being lacks an intentional correlate and thus cannot be subject to any scientific classification. Indeed, such a being "would obviously transcend not merely the world but 'absolute' consciousness. It would therefore be an '*absolute' in the sense totally different from that in which consciousness is* an absolute, just as it would be *something transcendent in a sense totally different* from that in which the world is something transcendent."[7] Husserl provides the foundation for Levinas's own reflections on the idea of infinity and the exclusion of transcendence, the wholly other, from the province of phenomenology and the criterion of truth as the showing of what comes to light.

INTENTIONALITY AND TRANSCENDENCE

To understand this one must ponder more carefully the transcendence of pure consciousness affirmed by Husserl. As Levinas observed in his study on Husserl published in 1930, *"Intentionality is, for Husserl, a genuine act of transcendence and the very proto-type of any transcendence."*[8] The transcendence to which Levinas alludes denotes the mind's bestowing meaning on the hyletic phenomena of the external world. We can speak, therefore, of consciousness transcending itself, since its innate structure is such that what is "perceivable immanently" is given always as "a being *for* an Ego."[9] Husserl identifies the transcendence of the pure Ego—that is, the egological transcendental consciousness that emerges after the phenomenological bracketing of the world and of the empirical subjectivity—as a *transcendency within immanency*.[10] Drawing out the implications of the Husserlian conception of intentionality, Levinas notes that the "very reality of subjects consists in their transcending themselves,"[11] for being in "con-tact with the world" is placed "at the very heart of the being of consciousness."[12] This is not to say that every act of intentionality is identical; on the contrary, intentionality is different in every case, but what is constant is that, inasmuch as it is directed toward an outside object, it entails self-transcendence. According to Levinas's interpretation of Husserl, moreover, intentionality is first and foremost a mode of affectivity and not a mode of representation, the imparting of meaning in the intuition that forges the correspondence between the noema and the noesis. As he put it in the essay "Meaning and Sense" (1964), Husserl's transcendental philosophy is a "sort of positivism which locates every meaning in the transcendental inventory . . . The hyletic and the 'mean-ing ascriptions' are minutely inventoried, as though one were dealing with an invest-ment portfolio. . . . Every absence has the given as its *terminus a quo* and *terminus ad quem*."[13] The break with Husserl is felt most acutely at precisely this pressure point. Levinas thus commented in the preface to *Totality and Infinity* (1961):

> This book will present subjectivity as welcoming the Other, as hospitality; in it the idea of infinity is consummated. Hence intentionality, where thought remains an *adequation* with the object, does not define consciousness at its fundamental level. All knowing qua intentionality already presupposes the idea of infinity, which is preeminently *non-adequation*. . . . Consciousness then does not consist in equaling being with representation, in tending to the full light in which this adequation is to be sought, but rather in overflowing this play of lights—this phenomenology.[14]

At a later juncture in the book, Levinas acknowledged that the promotion of the idea of the horizon in Husserl's phenomenology imparted to philosophical thinking the presupposition that "the truth of an existent proceeds from the openness of Being" (*la vérité de l'étant tient à l'ouverture de l'être*), whence we may infer that the "intelligibil-ity" of that existent "is due not to our coinciding, but to our non-coinciding with it. An existent is comprehended in the measure that thought transcends it, measuring it against the horizon whereupon it is profiled."[15] The real world, therefore, "is not simply a world of things correlative to perceptive acts (purely theoretical acts); the real world is a world of objects of practical use and values."[16] The determination of the transcendence of the subject from the standpoint of the practical intentionality of

affective life set Levinas on a course of thinking from which he never diverged, culminating in his more advanced articulations of ethics as first philosophy and the emphasis
he placed on the alterity of the other.[17]

A succinct formulation of the matter of intentionality and transcendence is offered
by Levinas in his 1932 essay "Martin Heidegger and Ontology," a fragment of the pro-
jected work on Heidegger that was abandoned once the latter became committed to
National Socialism:

> The problem of correspondence between thing and thought presupposes a free
> activity of thought and its isolation in relation to the object. It is precisely this
> presupposition which renders their harmony and even their contact problematic.
> "How does the subject take leave of itself to attain the object?" is what the problem
> of knowledge, in the last analysis, boils down to. Its true source is thus the concept
> of "subject" as elaborated by modern philosophy. The *cogito* presided over the sub-
> ject's birth. The *cogito* was the affirmation of the privileged nature of the subject's
> immanent sphere, of its unique place in existence; hence, the *cogito* was the
> *specificity* of the subject's connection to the rest of reality, the *sui generis* nature
> which opens up the passage from immanence to transcendence, the passage from
> ideas contained in the thinking substance to their "formal existence." . . . We
> know that in intentionality Husserl saw the very essence of consciousness. The
> originality of this view consisted in affirming not only that all consciousness is
> consciousness of something but that this striving toward something else
> constituted the entire nature of consciousness; that we must not imagine
> consciousness as something that first is and that then transcends itself, but that
> consciousness transcends itself throughout its existence.[18]

The Husserlian conception provides a model of opposing the idea of consciousness as
an ego-substance, but to the extent that intentionality necessitates a relation to objects
constituted as ontological structures within the mind—consciousness is always consciousness of something—we can speak of the intentional character of consciousness
at best as a form of "psychological transcendence."[19] By contrast, the absolute transcendence of the divine—the "transcendent Absolute that is beyond consciousness"—
would of necessity stand over and against the transcendence of the world as well as the
transcendence in immanence ascribed to the absolute consciousness of the Pure Ego,
the living presence of self present to itself in the prereflective experience of *Erlebnis*.[20]
Husserl's transcendental phenomenology lays the foundation for the notion of reflex-
ive subjectivity elaborated in post-Husserlian philosophical hermeneutics because it
recognizes that the identity of the subject cannot be deciphered apart from the dialogical relation to what is more and other than itself,[21] but it is not sufficient to account for the radical transcendence necessary to establish the ground for genuine
alterity, since what is configured as "outside" consciousness is always and already a
being that is exterior from the perspective of the interior.[22]

In an essay tellingly entitled "The Ruin of Representation" (1959), Levinas argued that the innovation of Husserl's notion of intentionality was a "double perspective" within which objects are constituted by the subject that is itself constituted by the objects it constitutes.[23] Based on this insight, he discerned the following quandary: if phenomenology ceases to be a philosophy of consciousness, then it self-destructs as phenomenology, but if it persists as phenomenology, it sublates transcendence inasmuch as there can be no given that is not an aspect of the intuitive content of the imaginative representation through which the world is constructed.[24] To the extent that the emphasis on intentionality construes the elemental event of being as disclosure on the part of the cogito—the I that thinks itself in thinking the other—phenomenology can be regarded as a method that reveals the revelation of beings, and, as such, it is fundamentally inadequate to unveil transcendence, which cannot be unveiled except through some veil.[25] In "Enigma and the Phenomenon" (1965), Levinas revisited the reluctance of the invisible, which is "beyond-being," to exhibit itself phenomenologically. The nonmanifestation of God precludes the possibility of the subject-object correlation that is inherent in the "structure of all thought." The holiness and transcendence of divinity invariably dissipate in the light of the chain of significations that make up the universe.[26]

PHENOMENOLOGY OF THE INAPPARENT: ONTOLOGICAL RESIDUALS IN LEVINAS AND HEIDEGGER

I do not think it an exaggeration to say that the phenomenological fascination with the nonphenomenalizable can be pinpointed as the essential thought that informed Levinas's critique of ontological realism—the narcissistic reduction of the other to the same[27]—throughout his life, the philosophical venture toward transcendence[28] that is referred to early on as the "matter of getting out of being by a new path."[29] Although Levinas did on occasion pay homage to Heidegger, even going so far as to call him the greatest philosopher of the twentieth century, who not only advanced phenomenology beyond Husserl but also provided a novel way of reading the history of philosophy that brought "back the unthought to thought and saying,"[30] he did not always acknowledge that his own pushing of phenomenology to the limits of the phenomenological, establishing the criteria for a postphenomenological phenomenology centered on the intentionality of the nongiven,[31] which stands upon but overturns the Husserlian conception of phenomenology as the eidetic science that interrogates the intentional structures of what is given intuitively in reflection, is indebted to, or at the very least demonstrates a strong affinity with a crucial dimension of Heidegger's attempt to think the idea of phenomenology through to its end by according equal status to the inapparent as to the apparent,[32] thereby challenging the foundational tenet that something is inasmuch as it appears.[33] In some measure, the radicalization of phenomenology to shift from the visible to the invisible is, as Dan Zahavi has argued, rooted in

Husserl's own notion of horizontality, that is, the claim that every appearance includes a plurality of other appearances, whence we may deduce that no appearance can ever be apperceived in its totality. It follows that the profile of any phenomenally constituted object is accompanied by a consciousness of profiles that are out of sight.[34] Every object of consciousness, accordingly, is a "play of presence and absence," a "synthesis of empty and filled intentions."[35] To quote Husserl's own words, "in every perception of a thing, where, by virtue of the components of indeterminateness in the apprehension, much is left open. For example, concerning the determinate color of the invisible backside, already somehow apperceived as red, is it completely, uniformly, red, or does it contain stains and streaks? Or again, concerning the form of the thing, apprehended only as something consistent, what is it really like where it passes into invisibility?"[36]

In the *Cartesian Meditations*, Husserl refers to this appearing that is concomitantly a withholding as *appresentation* or *making co-present*, that is, the "making present to consciousness a 'there too', which nevertheless is not itself there and can never become an 'itself-there.'"[37] What is appresented, therefore, "can never attain actual presence, never become an object of perception proper."[38] Every appresentation presupposes a presentation, but what is characteristic of the presentive-appresentive perception is that we must distinguish noematically between the part of the object that is genuinely perceived and the rest that is not perceived but is presumed to be appearing in its nonappearance. "Thus every perception of this type is transcending: it posits more as itself-there than it makes 'actually' present at any time."[39] The same dilemma presents itself when considering the phenomenality of experiencing another subjectivity and perhaps even more so, since the interiority of the subject preempts empirical objectification and scientific exploration[40]—an insight developed by subsequent phenomenologists, especially Michel Henry, for whom the unique manifestation of the absolute subjectivity of the ego can be designated by the oxymoron *invisible revelation*,[41] that is, the "original mode" of disclosure, "according to which phenomenality phenomenalizes itself" as the "hiding of the essence" related to the "ontological structure of reality."[42] Insofar as the transcendence of the other can never be fully concretized in the constituting consciousness of the ego, every appresented presence is in truth a blend of presence and absence, and thus, phenomenologically speaking, there is no mode of givenness that is not also a refusal to give. Paradoxically enough, the other can give itself only as not given.[43]

The concern for Heidegger similarly is to investigate not simply the plausibility of a perspectivism that prevents the full disclosure of any particular phenomenon but rather the extent to which the inapparent brings to light the appearance of all that becomes apparent. Already in a passage in *Being and Time*, Heidegger made the following observation regarding the phenomenological concept of the phenomenon: "Manifestly it is something that does not *show* itself initially and for the most part, something that is *concealed*, in contrast to what initially and for the most part shows itself, indeed in such a way that it constitutes its meaning and ground."[44] That which remains occluded in every act of self-showing (*Sichzeigen*), which Heidegger distinguishes from the act of appearing (*Erscheinen*), is not any particular being but the "being of beings" (*Sein des Seienden*). Heidegger does not disparage ontology in this context—indeed, he states explicitly that phenomenology is the "way of access to, and the demonstrative determination of, what is to become the theme of ontology"—but still he leaves no room for ambiguity with regard to the fact that the being of beings is such that it is always covered up or distorted, although it would be imprecise to mark it as a being that is hidden, a *phainomenon* that does not appear: "The being of beings can least of all be something 'behind which' something else stands, something that 'does not appear.'" Nothing, quite literally, stands behind the phenomena of phenomenology, and precisely because this is so, we can assert that "what is to become a phenomenon can be concealed." The covering-up (*Verdecktheit*), which is the "counterconcept" (*Gegenbegriff*) to the self-showing, is what makes phenomenology necessary,[45] and the paramount phenomenological datum is the invisible, which is not to be construed as a potentially visible phenomenon that is presently not manifesting itself, but rather as the nonphenomenal dimension that makes all phenomena visible by always eluding visibility.[46]

Many years later, in the conclusion of the Zähringen seminar (1973), Heidegger depicted his own phenomenology as "a path that leads away to come before . . . . and it lets that before which it is led show itself. This phenomenology is a phenomenology of the inapparent."[47] In the same seminar, Heidegger explained the "domain of the inapparent" in terms of the Parmenidean comment *esti gar einai*, "There is being," which he renders as "presencing itself presences" (*anwest nämlich Anwesen*). Acceptance of this statement results in Heidegger calling his phenomenology a "tautological thinking."[48] The matter is clarified by a comment in a letter that Heidegger wrote to Roger Munier on February 22, 1974: the one thing that is necessary is to bring thought "into the clearing of the appearing of the unapparent" (*in die Lichtung des Scheinens des Unscheinbaren*).[49] A similar theme was already implicit in Heidegger's comment in *Contributions to Philosophy* that the essential occurrence of being disclosed by the event "can be known only in that thinking which must venture the unusual—not as the peculiarity of something odd, but as the necessity of that which is most inconspicuous and in which are opened up the abyssal ground of the ground-lessness of the gods and the grounding condition of humans [*der abgründige Grund der Grund-losigkeit der Götter und der Gründerschaft des Menschen*] and in which, furthermore, something is assigned to beyng that metaphysics could never know, namely, *Da-sein*."[50]

Levinas would doubtlessly still see these passages as indicative of what he refers to in *Totality and Infinity* as the "one sole thesis" of Heidegger's *Being and Time*, "Being is inseparable from the comprehension of Being (which unfolds as time); Being is already an appeal to subjectivity. . . . To affirm the priority of *Being* over *existents* is to already decide the essence of philosophy; it is to subordinate the relation with someone, who is an existent, (the ethical relation) to a relation with the *Being of existents*, which, impersonal, permits the apprehension, the domination of existents (a relationship of knowing), subordinates justice to freedom."[51] In a second passage from this work, Levinas once more boldly declares the distinction between himself and Heidegger: "We therefore are also radically opposed to Heidegger who subordinated the relation with the Other to ontology (which, moreover, he determines as though the relation with the interlocutor and the Master could be reduced to it) rather than seeing in justice and injustice a primordial access to the Other beyond all ontology."[52] In the essay "Is Ontology Fundamental?" (1951), Levinas expressed his critique as follows:

> Comprehension for Heidegger ultimately rests on the *openness* of being. . . .
> Heidegger sees in the—in a sense formal—fact that beings (*l'étant*) are—in their
> work of being (*être*), in their very independence—their intelligibility. . . . The
> understanding of a being will thus consist in going beyond that being (*l'étant*) into
> the *openness* and in perceiving it *upon the horizon of being*. That is to say,
> comprehension, in Heidegger, rejoins the great tradition of Western philosophy: to
> comprehend the particular being is already to place oneself beyond the particular.
> To comprehend is to be related to the particular that only exists through
> knowledge, which is always knowledge of the universal.[53]

In the 1981 conversation with Philippe Nemo, Levinas characterized *Being and Time*, "one of the finest books in the history of philosophy,"[54] as a work in which Heidegger "defined philosophy in relation to other forms of knowledge as 'fundamental ontology.' . . . *Sein und Zeit* has remained the very model of ontology. . . . In what concerns Heidegger, one cannot, in fact, ignore fundamental ontology and its problematic."[55] In an interview from 1983 conducted by Raul Fornet-Betancourt and Alfredo Gomez-Muller, Levinas vehemently rejected the suggestion that Heidegger's notion of Being, which is differentiated from the multiplicity of beings, corresponds to what he demarcated as the "otherwise than being," since the latter is not a "something" but the "relation to the other, the ethical relation. In Heidegger, the ethical relation, *Miteinandersein*, being-with-another, is only one moment of presence in the world."[56] Expanding on this theme in the lecture "Transcendence and Intelligibility," originally presented at the University of Geneva on June 1, 1983, and published in 1984, Levinas asserts that the "Heideggerian critiques of metaphysics . . . proceed from the will to power." Heidegger's appeal to the end of metaphysics is predicated on his assumption that all metaphysical speculation is a "misunderstanding of the ontological difference between *being* and *being* (*étant*)" and the consequent mistake in thinking about Being from the nature of beings. In contrast, Levinas proposes that the "true signification of the end of metaphysics" would "consist in affirming that thinking beyond the given no longer amounts to bringing to light the *presence* or the *eternity* of a universe of beings or of secret or sacred principles, hidden in the prolongation of that which is given and which would be the task of metaphysical speculation to dis-cover . . . And what if its alterity or its beyond was not a simple dissimulation to be unveiled by the gaze but a non-in-difference, intelligible according to a *spiritual intrigue wholly other than* gnosis."[57]

A less prejudicial reading of the aforecited Heideggerian texts (not to mention a plethora of others that could have been marshaled as evidence) should give one pause regarding the alleged subordination of the relation with the Other to ontology.[58] What comes to presence is absence, and not an absence that is a nonpresence, that is, the negation of presence, but rather an absence rendered even more absent in the coming to presence of its absence. Heidegger's phenomenology of the inapparent demands the paradox of needing to be "attentive to what in the appearing does not appear."[59] It is worth citing Miguel de Beistegui's discussion of this important theme:

> Moving away from addressing beings in their whatness, Heidegger addresses them in terms of their being-*there*, that is, in terms of the "there is" that exceeds the merely physical contours of the individuated thing . . . . Da-sein will have designated this intangible, invisible, impalpable dimension at the heart of the tangible and the visible. It will have pointed in the direction of the "there is" that sustains and traverses every phenomenon, in the direction of the phenomenality of all phenomena, but with this remarkable characteristic that this phenomenality is itself non-phenomenal, beyond phenomenality. Heidegger's phenomenology is a phenomenology of the *inapparent*. . . . What is apparent, what appears, is only the visible side of the invisible essence of truth. Such is the reason why phenomenology, in becoming ontological, in being attentive to the truth of being and not just to beings in truth, becomes a phenomenology of the inapparent, a phenomenology of the invisible.[60]

The appearance of the inapparent is not simply the surfacing of something previously imperceptible but rather the appearance of nonappearance as such,[61] that is, the inapparent that resides in and facilitates the appearing of all things apparent,[62] the unconcealment of the concealment concealed in the concealment of the unconcealment. Levinas surely believed that his own thinking about infinity, transcendence, and alterity was a move beyond Heidegger's concern with the truth of being to the eventual affirmation of what is otherwise than being. Heidegger may have heralded the end of the metaphysical notion of presence (*Vorhanden*), but continuing to think of being as a coming-into-presence (*Anwesen*) made it impossible for him to break away from the hegemony of the very orientation he denounced.[63]

Levinas's criticism of Heidegger notwithstanding, a careful attunement to what Heidegger actually thought about the subtle relationship of presence and absence, concealment and disclosure, sufficiently narrows the gap between them.[64] In a manner that betrays a striking similarity to Heidegger, Levinas maintained, as Wyschogrod put it, that the invisible "appears as that which remains impervious to vision, not as a temporary aberration in being or something unexpressed that will later come to light."[65] The invisible is manifest as the nonmanifest that always remains hidden from sight, the trace of a presence that is never present but as the absence of presence. I am here reminded of Blanchot's comment regarding the image: the possibility of seeing coagulates into impossibility at the very center of the gaze. Vision, accordingly, is no longer viewed as "the possibility of seeing" but rather as "the impossibility of not seeing, the impossibility which becomes visible and perseveres—always and always—in a vision that never comes to an end."[66] Perhaps even more pertinent is the position adopted by Merleau-Ponty in the essay "The Intertwining—The Chiasm," included in the collection *The Visible and the Invisible*, regarding the "invisible *of* this world," which is not "a *de facto* invisible, like an object hidden behind another, and not an absolute invisible, which would have nothing to do with the visible," but rather the invisible that "inhabits this world, sustains it, and renders it visible, its own and interior possibility, the Being of this being."[67] According to a fragment penned in November 1959, "Meaning is *invisible*, but the invisible is not the contradictory of the visible: the visible itself has an invisible inner framework (*membrure*), and the in-visible is the secret counterpart of the visible, it appears only within it, it is the *Nichturpräsentierbar* which is presented to me as such within the world—one cannot see it there and every effort to *see it there* makes it disappear, but it is *in the line* of the visible, it is its virtual focus, it is inscribed within it (in filigree)."[68] For Merleau-Ponty, "the visible is pregnant with the invisible," and thus "to comprehend fully the visible relations . . . one must go unto the relation of the visible with the invisible. . . . The other's visible is my invisible; my visible is the other's invisible . . . Being is this strange encroachment by reason of which my visible, although it is not superposable on that of the other, nonetheless opens upon it, that both open upon the same sensible world."[69]

For Levinas and Heidegger we can similarly postulate invisibility as the maximum visibility, or prevision, the unseeing that is not the impossibility of seeing but the impossibility of not seeing. Moreover, in the case of both thinkers, the endeavor to break with ontology is a deeply ontological gesture, a point unfortunately missed by many interpreters.[70] The characterization of the Levinasian *il y a* by Paul Davies can be applied to Heidegger's thought as well, "a contribution to ontology that thereby ruins it, an idealist reduction rendering all idealism unfeasible."[71] Heidegger and Levinas were equally engaged in speculating about what Santiago Zabala has called the "remains of Being" or the "ontology of remnants," that is, the question of being (*Seinsfrage*)—the question of what *it* is that *is*, the "thereness" of things (*es gibt* for Heidegger and *il y a* for Levinas[72])—that persists as the most basic issue presupposed by all philosophical reflection on the nature of reality. The postmetaphysical posture deconstructs the logocentric metaphysics of presence, but it cannot completely depose metaphysics, since the problem of being keeps appearing at the very heart of philosophy.[73] Heidegger's own words leave no room for uncertainty on this matter: "For the onto-theological character of metaphysics has become questionable for thinking, not because of any kind of atheism, but from the experience of a thinking which has discerned in onto-theo-logy the still *unthought* unity [ungedachte *Einheit*] of the essential nature of metaphysics. This nature of metaphysics, however, still remains what is most worthy of thought for thinking, as long as thinking does not break off the conversation with its tradition, permeated by destiny [*geschickhaften Überlieferung*], in an arbitrary manner thus unrelated to destiny. . . . Therefore all metaphysics is at bottom, and from the ground up, what grounds [*alle Metaphysik im Grunde vom Grund aus das Gründen*], what gives account [*Rechenschaft*] of the ground, what is called to account [*Rede*] by the ground, and finally what calls the ground into account."[74]

The task is to think the Being of beings as the ground-giving unity of the manifold that exists from and in relation to the ground—the "Being which is beings" (*Sein, welches das Seiende ist*)[75]—and thus it is more accurate to speak of metaphysics as the conceptual edifice that is in need of constant rennovation rather than definitive demolition. I do not deny that Heidegger maintained that the manner of thinking guided by the key words of metaphysics should lead to the realm where these words are no longer adequate, the origin of the ontological difference between Being and beings that cannot be thought within the scope of metaphysics. However, to attain new ground one must submit continually to what has been grounded of old.[76] Drawing on a distinction that Heidegger made between overcoming (*Überwindung*) and surpassing or getting-over (*Verwindung*) by coming to terms with and being resigned to—literally, twisting towards—what is surpassed,[77] Zabala asserts, "*When we talk about Being, we will 'still' be talking about it in terms of metaphysics, because its metaphysical nature cannot be overcome, only gotten over.*"[78] Zabala does not include Levinas in his discussion of philosophers who affirmed the ontology of remnants after the destruction of metaphysics,[79] but I would argue that the contrast between overcoming and surpassing metaphysics applies to him as well.

Here it is worth recalling the observation of Derrida:

> Just as he implicitly had to appeal to phenomenological self-evidences against phenomenology, Levinas must ceaselessly suppose and practice the thought of precomprehension of Being in his discourse, even when he directs it against "ontology." . . . Ethico-metaphysical transcendence therefore presupposes ontological transcendence. The *epekeina tes ousias* (in Levinas's interpretation) would not lead beyond Being itself [*au-delà de l'Être lui-même*], but beyond the totality of the existent or the existent-hood of the existent (the Being existent of the existent) [*au-delà de la totalité de l'étant ou de l'étantité de l'étant (être étant de l'étant)*], or beyond ontic history. Heidegger also refers to *epekeina tes ousias* in order to announce ontological transcendence, but he also shows that the undetermined *agathon* toward which transcendence breaks through has been determined too quickly.[80]

Both Heidegger and Levinas, Derrida also points out, explain the manifestation of existents as "the unveiling of Being" (*au dévoilement de l'être*), which is consequent to a prior veiling.[81] The passage from Levinas cited by Derrida in support of his claim is from *Totality and Infinity*: "Preexisting the disclosure of being in general taken as basis of knowledge and as meaning of being is the relation with the existent that expresses himself; preexisting the plane of ontology is the ethical plane."[82] Derrida judiciously notes the Heideggerian underpinning of this comment. I would add that Levinas's understanding of the concealment that precedes the disclosure of being, or what he refers to in another passage from the same treatise as the production of Infinity through a "contraction" that leaves a place for the separated being (*l'être séparé*) of creation that is no longer encompassed within the totality,[83] likely reflects the kabbalistic notion of *ṣimṣum*,[84] the primordial act of constriction, interpreted especially through the prism of Ḥayyim of Volozhyn's *Nefesh ha-Ḥayyim* as the concealment of God's infinite light from human cognition rather than an actual withdrawal of that light from itself and into itself, resulting paradoxically in the formation of a vacuum within the plenum.[85] From Heidegger's perspective, the motif of the unveiling is related to the character of truth as the unconcealment (*alētheia*) in which the concealment (*lēthe*) persists as the concealing that conceals the unconcealing. Thus, being's "primordial self-illumination" fosters the "unconcealment of beings" (*Unverborgenheit des Seienden*) through darkening the light of Being (*verdunkelt das Licht des Seins*), which leads to the conclusion, "As it reveals itself in beings, Being withdraws."[86] Privileging the theme of unveiling as the way to think about being runs the risk of reducing everything that appears historically to nothing more than dissimulation. The uncovering of this truth is what Heidegger means when he writes of the "inherently eschatological" nature of Being, which is not to be understood theologically but rather phenomenologically as the "gathering (λόγος) at the outermost point (ἔσχατον)" of the essence of Being. Although clearly distinguished from messianic eschatology in either the Jewish or the Christian sense, Heidegger's notion still retains the temporal matter of anticipating the "former dawn in the dawn to come" through "what is imminent," a retrieval of the past in a future that is present, an expectation of the time "when Being gathers itself in the ultimacy of its essence, hitherto determined through metaphysics, as the absolute subjecticity [*Subjektität*] of the unconditioned will to will."[87]

Heidegger's remark calls to mind the interpretation of the Pauline discourse on the *parousia*, elicited from the fifth chapter of I Thessalonians, which he offered in the 1920–21 lecture course, "Introduction to the Phenomenology of Religion." Through an ingenious scriptural exegesis, Heidegger argues that, for Paul, the anticipation of the reappearance of the Messiah is not a matter of waiting for a future event (*zukünftiges Ereignis*). On the contrary, the "structure of Christian hope, which in truth is the relational sense of Parousia, is radically different from all expectation [*Erwartung*]."[88] The "when" of the second coming is not a moment of time in a quotidian sense but the "enactment of life" (*Vollzug des Lebens*) that occasions a "knowledge of oneself" (*Wissens um sich selbst*) lived in a "time without its own order and demarcations. One cannot encounter this temporality [*Zeitlichkeit*] in some sort of objective concept of time."[89] Heidegger's later allusion to the eschatological upholds a crucial element from his earlier theological speculation on the eschaton as the time out of time, as it were, a future that is enacted in the present as a form of gnostic self-revelation rather than a future anticipated as a historical event that is yet to come in the homogeneous sequence of quantitatively calculable and qualitatively interchangeable now-points.[90] Below I will reflect on Levinas's understanding of eschatology as instituting a relation with the infinity of being that exceeds the totality. Suffice it here to say that his view resembles Heidegger's interpretation of the eschatological as the gathering of Being in the ultimacy of its essence, the utmost point that is beyond the whole of all beings.

The issue for Levinas and Heidegger, then, was not a wholesale rejection of ontology but the need to avoid positing a totalizing ontic presence that does not allow for the possibility of ontological transcendence. As Levinas stated in the beginning of the four lectures entitled "Time and the Other," which were delivered in 1946–47 and published in 1947 in the collection edited by Jean Wahl, *Le Choix, le monde, l'existence* (Cahiers du College Philosophique), "The analyses that I am about to undertake will not be anthropological but ontological. I do believe in the existence of ontological problems and structures, but not in the sense that realists—purely and simply describing given being—ascribe to ontology."[91] In the preface to the second printing of these lectures in 1979 under the title *Le temps et l'autre*, Levinas wrote that he approved the idea of republication because he still adhered "to the main project of which it is—in the midst of diverse movements of thought—the birth and first formulation."[92] The project at which he hints is the exposition of the ontological in terms of what he calls the "dialectic of being," which involves escaping through solitude from the "general economy of being."[93] In the 1981 interview with Richard Kearney, Levinas summed up his efforts in the following way: "I am trying to show that man's ethical relation to the other is ultimately prior to his ontological relation to himself (egology) or to the totality of things that we call the world (cosmology)."[94] But, shortly after making this comment, he readily admits, "We can never completely escape from the language of ontology and politics. Even when we deconstruct ontology we are obliged to use its language."[95] Finally, in the interview with Wyschogrod, Levinas remarked, "There is, in *Otherwise than Being*, the necessary return to ontology, starting with the section on the advent of the third—the return to ontology, not ontology as such, but to the theory in general or, if you wish, justice, which must be added to charity."[96]

PHILOSOPHICAL SKEPTICISM AND THE APORIA OF REASON

For Levinas, this inexorable plight is evocative of the nature of philosophy more generally: it must question itself, deconstructing what it has constructed, unsaying what it has said. In this sense, the ancient skeptical claim that what we know is that we cannot know accentuates the essential feature of philosophy.[97] In the essay "Reflections on the Philosophy of Hitlerism," first published in French in 1934,[98] Levinas noted that skepticism is the "basic possibility for the Western spirit," insofar as the ability to doubt lies at the core of human freedom and the will to choose truth. To be free and to live truthfully "does not mean taking flight once more above contingent events that always remain foreign to the Self's freedom; on the contrary, it means becoming aware of the ineluctable original chain that is unique to our bodies, and above all accepting this chaining."[99] The "chaining" linked to this somatic awareness is the genuine freedom that is to be contrasted with the bondage (*enchaînement*) of Nazism, which promotes an ideal of certainty that promises "sincerity and authenticity" but in truth takes away the individual's confrontation with a "world of ideas" in which one can select one's "own truth" on the basis of the exercise of "free reason."[100]

Although Levinas does not mention Heidegger's name explicitly, we know from later works that he deemed Heideggerian ontology to be a "philosophy of power" that "does not call into question the same, a philosophy of injustice," which "subordinates the relationship with the Other to the relation with Being in general" and thus "remains under obedience to the anonymous, and leads inevitably to another power, to imperialist domination, to tyranny. . . . Its origin lies back in the pagan 'moods,' in the enrootedness in the earth, in the adoration that enslaved men can devote to their masters. . . . It is a movement within the same before obligation to the other."[101] The "peasant enrootedness" at the core of Heidegger's philosophy is allied both with the Nazi glorification of the "pagan" existence and its propagation of a racism that exterminates the possibility of universal ethics as well as with an "earth-maternity" that "determines the whole Western civilization of property, exploitation, political tyranny and war."[102] Indeed, in the prefatory note, written on March 28, 1990, appended to the English translation of "Quelques réflexions sur le philosophie de l'Hitlérisme," Levinas wrote that the "bloody barbarism of National Socialism . . . stems from the essential possibility of *elemental Evil* . . . inscribed within the ontology of a being concerned with being [*de l'être soucieux d'être*], a being, to use the Heideggerian expression, 'dem es in seinem Sein um dieses Sein selbst geht.' "[103]

The concluding reference is to the depiction of Dasein in § 22 of *Being and Time* as the being "which in its very being is concerned about that being" of the world.[104] Subsequently, I will evaluate the evenhandedness of Levinas's assessment of the ontological in Heidegger, but what I wish to emphasize here is that one can detect in Heidegger an approach to thinking that highlights in the same way as Levinas the nexus between freedom and skepticism. For instance, in one context, explicating Hegel's description of the presentation of phenomenal knowledge as a "thorough skepticism," Heidegger notes that the original meaning of *skepsis* is an act of seeing by which we pursue the "Being of beings" through scrutinizing the representation (*Darstellung*) of beings as they come to light in the realm of appearance.[105] In uncovering the appearance of appearance, the truth of the untruth of phenomenal knowledge is manifest as an essential facet of the mind's questioning advance toward absolute knowledge: "Skepsis takes hold of consciousness itself, which develops into skepticism, and skepticism, in the appearance of phenomena, brings the shapes of consciousness forth and transforms one into another. Consciousness is consciousness in the mode of self-producing skepticism."[106] The very history of consciousness is marked by the dual movement of skepticism as the negation that routinely casts doubt on what is posited by reason on the basis of appearance and then itself becomes undone by the affirmation that renders the doubt dubious. Skepticism is not to be regarded simply as "an attitude of the isolated human subject" resolved to examine everything autonomously and to never rely on another's authority, but it is rather the more elemental and universal task of thought to look over "the whole expanse of phenomenal knowledge" in the form of the "enlargement" (*Erweiterung*) of the *ego cogito* to "the reality of absolute knowledge," an augmentation of consciousness that "requires and is preceded by skepsis into the vastness that opens up when unconditioned subjectivity appears to itself."[107] That Heidegger remained faithful to this view—even though he rejected the larger Hegelian framework—is attested in his remark, "For us, then, the essence of the undoubtable can very well be doubtful [*Das Wesen des Unbezweifelbaren* kann somit *für uns sehr wohl zweifelhaft sein*]." From the premise that the essence of the undoubtable can be doubted we can adduce that the only thing that cannot be doubted is that everything can be doubted, a condition that Heidegger cleverly tropes as the sense we feel when "we are not at home in our habitat [*wir in unserer Behausung nicht zuhause sind*]."[108] In the 1955 essay "On the Question of Being," Heidegger commented that Nietzsche depicted nihilism as "this most uncanny of all guests [*dieses unheimlichsten aller Gäste*]" because "as the unconditional will to will, it wills homelessness [*Heimatlosigkeit*] as such. This is why it is of no avail to show it to the door, because it has long since been roaming around invisibly inside the house."[109] This account of nihilism can be extended to philosophy, which displays the inherent quality of lacking an inherent quality, the feeling of homelessness that can be experienced only when one is at home,[110] or in the articulation of Novalis, the sense of "homesickness" that results in "the *urge to be everywhere at home*,"[111] belonging by not-belonging, as Derrida articulated the point: "Philosophy has a way of being at home with itself [*chez elle*] that consists in not being at home with itself, whence this double bind with respect to the philosophical."[112]

In the dialogue with Françoise Armengaud centered around the particular question of Jewish philosophy, Levinas seemed to verbalize a similar theme: "Philosophical discourse will appear as a way of speaking addressed to completely open minds who require totally explicit ideas, a discourse in which all that is normally taken for granted is said. . . . But one day it is discovered that philosophy is also multiple, and that its truth is hidden, has levels and goes progressively deeper, that its texts contradict one another and that the systems are fraught with internal contradictions."[113] Prima facie, one is inclined to view the task of the philosopher as someone who must render the truth about the human condition coherently and explicitly, a mode that would seemingly clash with a religious sensibility based on scriptural truth, which tends to be expressed in an implicit manner that demands ongoing interpretation and lacks a sense of harmony and uniformity. A more circumspect approach, however, recognizes that the truth of philosophy is hidden and multivocal in nature and that it, too, requires an incessant examination of itself through which the inconsistencies disclose that any system is beleaguered by incongruities. "To philosophize," writes Levinas, "is to trace freedom back to what lies before it, to disclose the investiture that liberates freedom from the arbitrary. Knowledge as a critique, as a tracing back to what precedes freedom, can arise only in a being that has an origin prior to its origin [*une origine en deçà de son origine*]—that is created."[114] The movement proper to the "essence of knowing" is not grasping an object but being able to question it, to penetrate beneath its own condition. From the ethical standpoint, this "knowing whose essence is critique cannot be reduced to objective cognition; it leads to the Other. To welcome the Other is to put in question my freedom."[115] What philosophy represents, therefore, is the relentless attempt to subvert itself, to interrogate its own presuppositions, to think what cannot be thought, the unthought, which is not a thought that presently has not been entertained but in the future will be, but rather that which endures in the face of the Other as what can never be adequately thought except as what remains to be thought, the untruth that pervades all truth,[116] which translates hermeneutically into the potential to yield new meaning unremittingly in the curvature of time.[117] The intrinsically aporetic nature of philosophical knowledge is the anarchic foundation for Levinasian ethics. As he put it in *Totality and Infinity*: "The essence of reason consists not in securing for man a foundation and powers, but in calling him in question and in inviting him to do justice."[118] Returning to this theme in *Otherwise than Being or Beyond Essence* (1974), Levinas writes: "It is by the approach, the one-for-the-other of saying [*l'un-pour-l'autre du Dire*], related by the said [*le Dit*], that the said remains an insurmountable equivocation, where meaning refuses simultaneity, does not enter being, does not compose a whole. The approach, or saying, is a relationship with what is not understood in the together . . . . A subversion of essence, it overflows the theme it states, the 'all together,' the 'everything included' of the said. Language is already skepticism."[119] To mark language as the bearer of skepticism is to call into doubt the juxtaposition of being and language that has informed Western philosophy from its pre-Socratic beginnings. Neither Heidegger nor Levinas could completely break out from the anthropocentric understanding of the nature of beings and the privileging of language,[120] but both problematize the matter by viewing the purpose of language as bringing to the fore the unsaid of the saying at the core of every said.[121]

Levinas continued to think about the aporia of reasoning from multiple perspectives, since no one perspective is adequate to articulate the full reverberation of a thinking whose task it is to surpass thinking. Indeed, as Levinas makes clear in *Totality and Infinity*, the pattern of thought he adopts undermines both the Aristotelian logic of noncontradiction and the Hegelian logic of dialectic: "The whole of this work aims to show a relation with the other not only cutting across the logic of contradiction, where the other of A is the non-A, the negation of A, but also across dialectical logic, where the same dialectically participates in and is reconciled with the other in the Unity of the system."[122] The "relation with the Other," therefore, is predicated on an "overturning of formal logic."[123] I propose that this overturning served as the an-archic foundation for a phenomenology of transcendence, the metaphysical desire for the invisible, through the different stages of Levinas's thinking. This is not to deny that there were conceptual and terminological shifts in Levinas over the course of time, especially from the first major treatise, *Totality and Infinity*, to the second, *Otherwise than Being*, but this should not be overstated to the point of positing a turn that would preclude the threads of continuity that tie together the different segments of his intellectual evolution.[124] Consider Levinas's remark in the preface to the German translation of *Totality and Infinity*, written on January 18, 1987:

> *Totality and Infinity, an Essay on Exteriority*, which appeared in 1961, opens a philosophical discourse which was continued in *Otherwise than Being or Beyond Essence* in 1974, and *De Dieu qui vient à l'idée* [On God Who Comes to the Mind] in 1982. Certain themes of the first work are repeated or renewed, or return in other forms, in the last two; certain intentions are specified in them. For the substance of this discourse, which began twenty-five years ago and which forms a whole, these are non-contingent and no doubt instructive variations, but it is not possible to give an account of them in the brevity of a preface.[125]

Levinas goes on to note two crucial differences between the discourse in the early and later works, and especially pertinent to our discussion is the first of these, which consists of the fact that *Otherwise than Being* "avoids the ontological—or more exactly, *eidetic*—language which *Totality and Infinity* incessantly resorts to in order to keep its analyses . . . from being considered as dependent on the empiricism of a psychology."[126] In spite of this shift, Levinas insists on the integrity of vision that runs throughout his works. Along similar lines, it is worth recalling Levinas's words in *Of God Who Comes to Mind*: "The ontological language employed in *Totality and Infinity* . . . is ontological because it wants above all not to be psychological. But in reality, it is already a search for what I call 'the beyond being,' the tearing of this equality to self which is always being—the *Sein*—whatever the attempts to separate it from the present."[127]

FROM EXCENDENCE TO TRANSCENDENCE

The effort to move beyond the Heideggerian sense of transcendence—in Levinas's mind a continuation of Husserl's phenomenological investigations[128]—as the subjective self-relation linked to Dasein's understanding of its own being as primarily a verbal possibility, a conception of the human condition that dictates enclosure in a world without any possibility of transcendence that is not a transcendent immanence,[129] the subordination of the infinite to the finite that Levinas eventually framed as the "outcome of a long tradition of pride, heroism, domination, and cruelty," which found its sociopolitical expression in National Socialism,[130] is already evident in "Martin Heidegger and Ontology." Criticizing the idealist position in both its Kantian and Hegelian dimensions, Levinas insists that the relation of subject to object cannot be reduced such that the "object is encompassed in consciousness, to one of these supertemporal relations we know in an ideal world." This "decisive step" facilitates the "true passage into subjectivity—in all its opposition to being, that is to say, in its opposition to temporal substance. . . . This step is taken by means of an evasion of time."[131] Challenging the philosophical systems that conceal the subject from its "true subjectivity," Levinas notes that for Heidegger time "is not a characteristic of the *essence* of reality, a *something*, or a property; it is the expression of the *fact of being* [*fait d'être*] or, rather, it is that *fact of being* itself. In a way it is the very dimension in which the existence of being comes about. *To exist is to be 'temporalized' [se temporalizer].*"[132] The French *se temporalizer* renders the German *sich zeitigen*, which "*serves to highlight better the specific sense of time, which is not a 'something' that exists or unfolds, but which is the very 'effectuating' of existence.*"[133]

At this incipient phase, Levinas anticipated his later thinking by maintaining, in the wake of Heidegger, that traditional philosophy excluded the matter of time from the purview of the transcendent being.[134] Even Husserl's transcendental phenomenology falls short, for while he may have well established the dynamics of internal time-consciousness, not enough attention is paid to the alterity of the other person, which, in the mind of Levinas from early on, is far more important in the shaping of one's experience of time than the self-temporalization of intentional consciousness. "The relationship with the Other is the absence of the other; not absence pure and simple, not the absence of pure nothingness, but absence in a horizon of the future, an absence that is time."[135] The term *ontology* can be used to depict the theory of time, but Levinas makes clear that this is not to be identified either with realism or with the study of the essence of being. Indeed, the Heideggerian connotation of ontology "is opposed to that-which-is in the very sense of *the fact that it is* and its specific mode of being," and hence it results in discerning the difference between the subject and object as it pertains to existence, that is, "the very manner of *being-there* [*être-là*]," which is not to be conflated with the sense of that which is, literally, the existing object (*l'objet étant*). To progress beyond the epistemological to the ontological outlook, from the indifference to time in the subject-object relation to an appreciation of the temporal comportment of human consciousness as the being who understands the "being of a be-ing" (*das Sein des Seienden*), it is necessary that the "ontological determination of the subject . . . must seek a temporal sense in the transcendence of the subject in relation to itself."[136] The "ontological foundation of the contemporary notion of subjectivity," therefore, contests the claim, which can be traced to Plato, that the subject/object structure is the "originary form of the transcendence of soul through self-relation." By taking time more seriously in assessing the nature of being, one will "better understand this proximity of the existential determination of man—through the fall, through finitude—to his determination as an immanence having to transcend itself."[137] Levinas displayed an incisive understanding of Heidegger's anthropology: the essence of being human is simultaneously his existence, his way of being, but his way of being is essentially his being-there, a mode of self-temporalizing, which is designated by the term *Dasein* (being right-there, *l'être ici-bas*) rather than *Daseiendes* (a be-ing right-there, *l'étant ici-bas*).[138] The term *transcendence*, for Heidegger, is reserved for this "act of taking leave of oneself to reach objects," the "leap accomplished beyond 'be-ings' [*étants*] understood in an *ontic* sense toward ontological being." The very structure of being in the world, consequently, is to transcend oneself (*Être dans le monde c'est se transcender*).[139]

In the essay "On Escape" (1935), Levinas coined the neologism *excendence* to denote the rudimentary event of being human as the need to break free from the imprisonment of being, to get away from the absoluteness of existence without the telos of a final destination[140]—even the possibility of taking refuge in either the traditional sense of the transcendent God or in nothingness is not adequate, since the former is the infinite and self-sufficient being, but a being nonetheless, and the latter, too, is the "work of a thinking essentially turned toward being."[141] The paradox for Levinas is that we are compelled to get out of the confines of the self, but there is nowhere to go, a condition that demarcates the existential status of the human being typified especially in the case of the Jew—Levinas repeatedly emphasizes in his so-called confessional writings that the Jewish predicament is the human predicament, and thus his concern with the specificity of the Jew is meant to illumine the universal status of humanity—who is a stranger in this world.[142] Even more poignantly, the paradox entails the awareness that escape is possible because of its very impossibility, not in the Heideggerian sense of death as the ultimate end that is the *possibility of impossibility* but in the Blanchotian sense of dying as the "never-ending ending" that is the *impossibility of possibility*, that is, the constitution of self that is possible only to the extent that it is impossible—to be oneself is to discern that one is never free to be oneself apart from a complex network of intersubjective relationships in light of which the "I" is constantly losing its ipseity, constantly dying the death of itself to be born as the other of its own self.[143] In that sense, as Blanchot put it,

> death is man's possibility, his chance, it is through death that the future of a finished world is still there for us; death is man's greatest hope, his only hope of being man. This is why existence is his only real dread, as Emmanuel Lévinas has clearly shown, existence frightens him, not because of death which could put an end to it, but because it excludes death, because it is still underneath death, a presence in the depth of absence . . . Death works with us in the world; it is a power that humanizes nature, that raises existence to being, and it is within each one of us as our most human quality; it is death only in the world—man only

knows death because he is man, and he is only man because he is death in the process of becoming. . . . As long as I live, I am a mortal man, but when I die, by ceasing to be a man I also cease to be mortal, I am no longer capable of dying, and my impending death horrifies me because I see it as it is: no longer death, but the impossibility of dying.[144]

One year prior to "On Escape," Levinas had already observed in "Reflections on the Philosophy of Hitlerism" that in the current political atmosphere the essence of being human "no longer lies in freedom, but in a kind of bondage [*enchaînement*]." As I noted above, in this early essay, Levinas described this freedom to be one's true self not as a flight from the contingencies of life but as becoming aware of and accepting the yoke of being chained to our embodiment.[145] The escape is understood, moreover, in terms of the conception of destiny that sets one free from the limitation of history by embracing the "true present," in and through which the past can be modified or effaced. Levinas looks to Judaism as the cultural formation that bears this message through the notion of "repentance that generates the pardon that redeems." In light of this possibility, time "loses its very irreversibility."[146] The prospect of repentance champions the reversibility of time insofar as it is predicated on the viability of wiping the past clean to generate a genuinely novel beginning. The novelty of the present is not at variance with the past; newness is feasible only to the extent that the past is retrieved so that it may be altered—inverting the causal timeline, we can speak of the effect of what comes after as conditioning the cause of what comes before. Recall Levinas's own observation in *Totality and Infinity* that separation "is not reflected in thought, but produced by it. For in it the *After* or the *Effect* conditions the *Before* or the *Cause*; the Before *appears* and is only welcomed."[147] This reversal underlies the Jewish ideal of repentance, which is the basis for the "mystical drama" put forth by Christianity: "The Cross sets one free; and through the Eucharist, which triumphs over time, this emancipation takes place every day. The salvation that Christianity wishes to bring us lies in the way it promises to reopen the finality brought about by the flow of moments of a past that is forever challenged, forever called into question, to go beyond the absolute contradiction of a past that is subordinate to the present."[148] The religious basis for liberalism, the political antidote to fascism, is the Jewish notion of repentance and its mystical embellishment in the Christian doctrine of the suffering of the savior on the cross. Human freedom, "which is infinite with regard to any attachment and through which no attachment is ultimately definitive,"[149] must be based on a genuinely open future, but the latter depends on the possibility of escaping from the encumbrance of the past by altering it in the present.

In the preface to *Existence and Existents* (1947), Levinas deployed the term *excendence* again but in a manner that resounds to some extent with the apophaticism of the Neoplatonic tradition:[150] "The Platonic formula that situates the Good beyond being . . . signifies that the movement which leads an existent toward the Good is not a transcendence by which that existent raises itself to a higher existence, but a departure from Being and from the categories which describe it: an *ex-cendence*. But excendence and the Good necessarily have a foothold in being, and that is why Being is better than non-being."[151] Being is still privileged to nonbeing, but the aim is to be transported away from being, not to the transcendence of a higher existence, whether understood in the traditional theological sense or in the Heideggerian positing of a Being beyond beings. Levinas is notably critical of Heidegger's notion of transcendence as ecstasy, the "being outside of oneself," since this requires the "leaving of an inwardness for an exteriority," the "movement of the inside toward the outside" that may not be the "original mode of existence."[152] The latter, which is signified by Levinas's signature expression, *il y a*, "there is," is the "apparition of an existent," an impersonal existence to which no name can be affixed because it is a "pure verb," the function of which "does not consist in naming, but in producing language, that is, in bringing forth the seeds of poetry which overwhelm 'existents' in their position and their very positivity."[153] The time of the verb is the "absolute character of the present," the presence that is constituted by its evanescence rather than its duration.[154] Poetry, above all forms of art, divulges this tensiveness of articulation, for, as Levinas later expressed the matter in "Edmond Jabès Today" (1972–73), rather than occupying place, the poet is burdened with evading place, or what he calls embracing the "opening of space," and hence the inspiration of the poetic saying is the "de-claustration of all things, the de-nucleation of being,"[155] an idea that anticipates his depiction of poetry (in contradistinction to Heidegger[156]) as the Saying that is a solicitation of and speaking to the other, or as he put it in "Paul Celan: From Being to the Other" (1972), a movement "from place to the non-place," the "attempt to think transcendence," which unfolds in the antimony of "a leap over the chasm opened in being, to whom the very identity of the leaper inflicts a refutation."[157]

The language of the poem, applying Levinas's description of Blanchot to his own conception of *il y a*,[158] "is what appears—but in a singular fashion—when all the real has been denied: realization of that unreality. Its way of being, its nature, consists in being present without being given, in not delivering itself up to the powers, since negation has been the ultimate human power, in being the domain of the impossible, on which power can get no purchase, in being a perpetual dismissal of the one who discloses it. . . . The poetic language that moved the world aside lets the incessant murmur of that distancing reappear, like a night manifesting itself in the night."[159] The poem facilitates the "unique adventure of a transcendence beyond all the horizons of the world" and thus "leads without leading" to the shore of the unthinkable, a destination that cannot be reached except as that which cannot be reached.[160] Nomadism and exile are thus essential to the poetic excursion to the "place of going astray, to the uninhabitable,"[161] the quest for the unreal that is the deepest recess of the real.[162] Elsewhere Levinas refers to the itinerant and diasporic nature of poiesis as the "infinite adventure" of transcendence as self-transcendence,[163] insofar as the poet grasps himself or herself as a stranger, the "singular de-substantiation of the I" that allows for the recognition of the other, which, in turn, engenders the saying without a said.[164] Reiterating the point in *Otherwise than Being*, Levinas writes: "Language would exceed the limits of what is thought, by suggesting, letting be understood without ever making understandable [*en laissant sous-entendre, sans jamais faire entendre*], an implication of a meaning distinct from that which comes to signs from the simultaneity of systems or the logical definition of concepts. This possibility is laid bare in the poetic said [*le dit poétique*], and the interpretation it calls for ad infinitum [*à l'infini*]."[165] We are caught here in an unassailable paradox: language always exceeds the limits of what can be thought, inasmuch as it is a bridge to the other, the "hither side of identity" (en deçà *de l'identité*) that "is not reducible to the for-itself [*pour soi*],"[166] and hence it can let things be understood only without making them understandable. Meaning consists of implication or allusion rather than the conventional forms of signification determined by the criteria of systematic simultaneity and logical conceptualization. The model is the poetic word—also referred to as "the prophetic said" (*le dit prophétique*)—which, like the Tetragrammaton, is endlessly spoken because inherently unspeakable, infinitely interpreted because innately inscrutable.[167]

The work of art typifies Levinas's notion of *il y a* as an encounter with the "bare fact of presence" that "arises behind nothingness . . . neither *a being*, nor consciousness functioning in a void, but the universal fact of the *there is*, which encompasses things and consciousness."[168] In this ecstatic encounter with the there is, which is reminiscent of William James's notorious description of the infant's experience as "one great blooming, buzzing confusion,"[169] the ego "is swept away by the fatality of being," and there "is no longer any outside or any inside."[170] The complete exposure to being in the vigilance of the night—Levinas relates this phenomenologically to the state of insomnia—results in the depersonalization of the self, the state of consciousness without a subject.[171] But this is not to be identified completely with the obfuscation of boundaries associated with the oneiric: "The *there is*, the play of being, is not played out across oblivion, does not encase itself in sleep like a dream. . . . This reverting of presence into absence does not occur in distinct instants, like an ebb and flow."[172] In "Reality and Its Shadow" (1948), Levinas seems to have modified his view somewhat, for he utilizes the dream metaphor to depict the nature of the experience of *il y a* both as an aesthetic object and as an ontic paradigm to circumscribe the materialization of what is real:

> To be "among things" is different from Heidegger's "being-in-the-world"; it constitutes the pathos of the imaginary world of dreams—the subject is among things not only by virtue of its density of being, requiring a "here," a "somewhere," and retaining its freedom; it is among things as a thing, as part of the spectacle. It is exterior to itself, but with an exteriority which is not that of a body, since the pain of the I-actor is felt by the I-spectator, and not through compassion. Here we have really an exteriority of the inward.[173]

The "pathos of the imaginary world of dreams" is an especially suitable way to express the characteristic of "there is"—the quality of being "among things"—for within the dreamscape exteriority cannot be imagined except from the standpoint of interiority, since the phantasmagoria of the dream are indistinguishable from the identity of the dreamer. Conversely, insofar as the dreamer cannot be distinguished from the phantasmagoria of the dream, we should speak of the disappearance of the dreamer's subjectivity in the folds of the dream.[174] Levinas, in part inspired by the "depths of Shakespearean tragedy," notes the essential connection between the night and the spectral allure of phantoms that appear only in the dark, signifying the "return of presence in negation" that moves one constantly toward the "limit between being and nothingness where being insinuates itself even in nothingness."[175] Appropriating the language of Luce Irigaray, we can say that nocturnality, the spatio-temporal condition of the dream, exemplifies an "ecstatic *jouissance*," the "beyond" that surpasses "all unveiled-unveiling clarity," a "night which is thicker than any forces yet revealed." The "nocturnal beyond" is not a darkness to be characterized as an absence, for that "would still subject it to the opposition of light and shade, to the ambivalences of noon and midnight, the rhythms of the rising and the setting of suns." Within the darkness of night the "illumination and protection of the secret are retained-contained together, inseparable." The nocturnal luster, which is the "source of lightning," glistens in the "excess of what is withheld from vision."[176] In this invisible surfeit, the brute factuality of "there is," we cannot differentiate the interiority of the subject from the exteriority of the object. The inside is outside precisely because there is no outside that is not inside.

The intent of Levinas's comments seem to me to correspond to the eloquently expressed observation of Nancy:

> The sleeping *self* does not appear: it is not phenomenalized, and if it dreams of itself, that is . . . according to an appearing that leaves no room for a distinction between being and appearing. Sleep does authorize the analysis of any form of appearance whatsoever, since it shows itself to itself as this appearance that appears only as non-appearing . . . In this non-appearing, one single thing shows itself. But it does not show itself to others, and in this precise sense it does not appear. . . . The sleeping self is the self of the thing in itself: a self that cannot even distinguish *itself* from what is not "self," a self without self, in a way, but that finds or touches in this being-without-self its most genuine autonomous existence.[177]

The model of the *self without self* can be applied to the *il y a*, which is, to borrow the evocative expression of Bettina Bergo, the *zero-point of ontology*,[178] the ground whence existents arise, the event through which the act expressed by the verb "to be" becomes a being designated by a substantive.[179] For Levinas, the nocturnal darkness represents the "presence of absence," the "impersonal, nonsubstantive event of the night," the (non)sense of there-being without there being anything discrete, "like a density of the void, like a murmur of silence. There is nothing, but there is being, like a field of forces. Darkness is the very play of existence which would play itself out even if there were nothing."[180] Levinas depicts the *il y a* by this "paradoxical existence" that is neither something that is nothing nor nothing that is something, "the existential density of the void itself, devoid of all being, empty even of void, whatever be the power of negation applied to itself. . . . A presence of absence, the *there is* is beyond contradiction; it embraces and dominates its contradictory."[181] In the first lecture included in *Time and the Other*, Levinas similarly characterizes the "fact that there is [*il y a*]" as the "absence of everything" that "returns as a presence, as the place where the bottom has dropped out of everything, an atmospheric density, a plenitude of the void, or the murmur of silence."[182] The *il y a* denotes the "indeterminate ground," the "ambience of being," the anonymous "field of every affirmation and negation," which "cannot be expressed by a substantive but is verbal," the "existing without existents" that is the "absence of all self, a without-self [*sans-soi*]."[183]

Positivity, therefore, lies in its negativity—a quality that Levinas assigns to love, an "essential and insatiable hunger," illustrated by the scriptural image of the burning bush that feeds the flames but is not consumed (Exodus 3:2).[184] The event of *there is* takes place always in the present, the time that is the "negation or ignorance of time, a pure self-reference, a hypostasis." In this hypostatic present, wherein the subject is free with regard to the past and the future, freedom consists of responsibility, a "positive enchainment to one's self . . . . the impossibility of getting rid of oneself."[185] Hence, in contrast to Heidegger, Levinas maintains that freedom is not "an event of *nihilation*; it is produced in the very 'plenum' of being through the ontological situation of the subject."[186] The flight from being is the freedom that comes about through being enchained to the self whence one aspires to flee, the dialectic of the presence of absence implied in the conception of excendence: exiting from being while retaining a foothold in being, striving for what is both totally other than and the same as the self.

AWAITING WITHOUT AN AWAITED: MESSIANIC PATIENCE AND THE FUTURAL UNDERGOING

In the aforementioned lectures on time and the other delivered in 1946–47, Levinas set out to demonstrate that time is not, as Heidegger taught,[187] "the achievement of an isolated and lone subject, but that it is the very relationship of the subject with the Other."[188] The intrinsic nexus between time and the other is summarized by Levinas in the 1979 preface to *Time and the Other*:

> *Time and the Other* presents time not as the ontological horizon of the *being of a being* [*l'être de l'étant*] but as a mode of the *beyond being* [*l'au delà de l'être*], as the relationship of "thought" to the other [*Autre*], and—through the diverse figures of the sociality facing the face of the other person: eroticism, paternity, responsibility for the neighbor—as the relationship to the Wholly other [*Tout Autre*], the

Transcendent, the Infinite. It is a relation or religion that is not structured like knowing—that is, an intentionality. Knowing conceals re-presentation and reduces the *other* to presence and co-presence. Time, on the contrary, in its dia-chrony, would signify a relationship that does not compromise the other's alterity, while still assuring its non-indifference to "thought."[189]

In contrast to the traditional conception of the abstract eternity of God, an intemporal mode of being that confers upon the lived duration (*la durée vécue*) of the present its full sense by "dissimulating the fulguration of the instant,"[190] Levinas insists on "thinking time not as a degradation of eternity, but as the relationship to *that* which—of itself unassimilable, absolutely other—would not allow itself to be assimilated by experience; or to *that* which—of itself infinite—would not allow itself to be com-prehended. . . . It is a relationship with the In-visible, where invisibility results not from some incapacity of human knowledge, but from the inaptitude of knowledge as such—from its in-adequation—to the Infinity of the absolutely other, and from the absurdity that an event such as coincidence would have here. The impossibility of co-inciding and this inadequation are not simply negative notions, but have a meaning in the *phenomenon* of noncoincidence *given* in the dia-chrony of time."[191]

Time is beset by the paradox of "a distance that is also a proximity."[192] The closer one gets to the time to which one has been advancing, the further one is from the onset of that time, as the basic component of time is such that it is always still to come, the now that is not yet because the not yet is now. Translated into ethical terms, the temporal is determined principally by the relationship to the other,[193] but that relationship can never be an event wherein the self and the other coincide, since the other to which the self is related always exceeds the capacity of that self to know or to experience. The perpetual motion of the temporal torrent is an expression of the desire that is engendered by the transcendence of the other transcending itself, the "true adventure of paternity," which Levinas calls "trans-substantiation," the process that "permits going beyond the simple renewal of the possible in the inevitable senescence of the subject. Transcendence, the for the Other, the goodness correlative of the face, founds a more profound relation: the goodness of goodness."[194] In an obviously polemical tactic, Levinas chooses the term "trans-substantiation" to criticize the Christian idea of the host bread and sacramental wine changing into the body and blood of Jesus. The expression denotes the relation to the other, which is not "an idyllic and harmonious relationship of communion, or a sympathy through which we put ourselves in the other's place." The other resembles us, but the alterity of the other is always constituted by its exteriority, and hence "the relationship with the other is a relationship with a Mystery,"[195] which Levinas further relates to the nature of eros[196] and to the quality of modesty that is associated with the feminine.[197] Correspondingly, the responsibility implied by the diachronic demands "allegiance to the unequalled." It is in this sense of noncoincidence that time is understood as the relationship with the invisible, the infinity of the absolutely other, which gives rise to "an awaiting without an awaited, an insatiable aspiration."[198]

One can decode this description as a phenomenological recasting of the traditional requirement imposed on the Jew to wait temporally for the redemption as the event that apparently cannot transpire in time but which is nonetheless constitutive of the nature of time. The messianic hopefulness, on this score, exemplifies the deportment of time as the constant return of the present that instantiates the expectation of what can never be actualized, inducing the longing for the advent of the (non)event,[199] the present that Levinas depicts as the "mastery of the existent over existing," an occurrence that "can no longer be qualified as experience," a phenomenon that is, technically speaking, "beyond phenomenology."[200] It is for this reason that in the preface to *Totality and Infinity* Levinas writes that the "real import" of prophetic eschatology

> does not introduce a teleological system into the totality; it does not consist in teaching the orientation of history. Eschatology institutes a relation with being *beyond the totality* or beyond history [*l'être* par delà la totalité *ou l'histoire*], and not with being beyond the past and the present. . . . It is a relationship with *a surplus always exterior to the totality*, as though the objective totality did not fill out the true measure of being, as though another concept, the concept of *infinity*, were needed to express this transcendence with regard to totality, non-encompassable within a totality and as primordial as totality.[201]

The eschatological vision does not foretell the end of history, as it is conventionally understood, but rather the "relation with the infinity of being," "the breach of the totality, the possibility of a *signification without a context*."[202] This is not to say that Levinas entirely abandoned the teleological aspect of Jewish messianism.[203] On the contrary, he alludes to it when he writes in another passage in *Totality and Infinity* of "the infinite time of triumph without which goodness would be subjectivity and folly."[204] That the "infinite time of triumph" is indeed a messianic reference is confirmed by another, less cryptic statement from the same treatise: "Messianic triumph is the pure triumph; it is secured against the revenge of evil whose return the infinite time does not prohibit."[205] On the one hand, the messianic triumph, which demands an infinity of time to be instantiated, consists in the victory of good over evil, but, on the other hand, not even infinite time can categorically prevent the reemergence of evil. Without the infinite time of triumph there would be no objective standard of the good; however, even if one posits such a triumph there is no guarantee that evil will be utterly conquered.

Fundamental to the rabbinic sensibility—even if not universally or monolithically affirmed—is the belief in the Messiah's impending coming at any moment; this moment, however, is a "now" that does not belong to the ordinary calibration of time— the now that is awaited is awaited because it can never take place, and hence deferment is endemic to messianic consciousness.[206] One is here reminded of Benjamin's notion

of the now-time (*Jetztzeit*) articulated in the sixteenth of the aphorisms gathered together under the title "On the Concept of History," a present that is not a transition
from one point on the timeline to the next but the rupture "in which time takes a
stand [*einsteht*] and has come to a standstill."[207] The historian, in particular, is entrusted with the task of establishing "a conception of the present as now-time shot
through with splinters of messianic time."[208] Benjamin explicitly connects this idea of
the now-time and the disenchantment with the future to Jewish messianism in the
last section of this work: "We know that the Jews were prohibited from inquiring into
the future: the Torah and the prayers instructed them in remembrance. . . . This does
not imply, however, that for the Jews the future became homogeneous, empty time.
For every second was the small gateway through which the Messiah might enter."[209]
In the beginning of his "Theological-Political Fragment," Benjamin made clear that
this messianic present, which both guarantees and denies the possibility of the future
being realized in time, is outside of history:

> Only the Messiah himself completes all history, in the sense that he alone redeems,
> completes, creates its relation to the messianic. For this reason, nothing that is
> historical can relate itself, from its own ground, to anything messianic. Therefore,
> the Kingdom of God is not the telos of the historical dynamic; it cannot be
> established as a goal. From the standpoint of history, it is not the goal, but the
> terminus [*Ende*]. Therefore the secular order cannot be built on the idea of the
> Divine Kingdom, and theocracy has no political but only a religious meaning. To
> have repudiated with utmost vehemence the political significance of theocracy is
> the cardinal merit of Bloch's *Spirit of Utopia*.[210]

Many other thinkers have expressed this peculiar and paradoxical dimension of
Jewish soteriology, but for our purposes I will cite Schwarzschild, whose views reflect
the influence of Cohen's asymptotic and noneschatological or anti-apocalyptic notion
of the messianic future,[211] which involves the perpetual delay of the occurrence even as it
secures its constant possibility. Commenting on the twelfth of the thirteen Maimonidean principles, "I believe with full faith in the coming of the Messiah, and, though he
tarry, I anticipate him, nonetheless, on every day, when he may come," Schwarzschild
noted that "the logic of this formulation entails that . . . the Messiah will always not
yet have come, into all historical eternity. It is his coming, or rather the expectation of
his coming, not his arrival, his 'advent,' that is obligatory Jewish faith. . . . Jewishly,
the Messiah not only has not come but also will never have come—that he will always
be coming."[212] In my estimation, this corresponds to Levinas's notion of diachrony as
the "matter of waiting without an awaited," the aspiration that grows stronger in its
insatiability the more it is fulfilled.[213]

It lies beyond the scope of this chapter to delve into the minutiae of Levinas's understanding of the messianic,[214] but let me state briefly that his rejection of the portrayal of the savior "as a person who comes to put a miraculous end to the violence in

the world, the injustice and contradictions which destroy humanity"[215] lends support
to my conjecture that his conception of diachrony is a philosophical appropriation of
the traditional Jewish dogma. From a close reading of several talmudic texts speculating on the nature of the Messiah in the chapter "Messianic Texts" in *Difficult Freedom*, Levinas infers the following: "Judaism does not therefore carry with it a doctrine
of an end to History which dominates individual destiny. Salvation does not stand as
an end to History, or act as its conclusion. It remains *at every moment* possible."[216] That
the messianic deliverance does not summon the cessation of historical time is precisely
what makes its eventuality viable at every moment, but this necessitates a radical
transformation of the eschatological reduction of time to eternity:[217] "Judaism, reaching out for the coming of the Messiah, has already gone beyond the notion of a mythical Messiah appearing at the end of History, and conceives of messianism as a personal
vocation among men."[218] The shift from Messiah as a distinct person to messianism as
a personal vocation for all of humanity—the traditional image of the suffering of the
redeemer is expanded to each individual's duty to bear sacrificially the responsibility
for the suffering of others[219] and in this sense, as Levinas interprets a dictum attributed to R. Naḥman,[220] "if he is among the living, he could be someone like me"
(אי מן חייא הוא כגון אנא): "to be Myself is to be the Messiah," for only one who can say
"Me" is capable of taking on the suffering of the world,[221] and thus "each person acts
as though he were the Messiah"[222]—is an outcome of the diachronic conception of temporal transcendence as a movement toward the infinity of the wholly other, the "ethical
adventure of the relationship to the other person,"[223] a course set forth by a "pluralism
that does not merge into unity."[224]

Salvation, Levinas wryly remarked, "does not require the satisfaction of need, like
a higher principle that would require the solidity of its bases to be secured."[225] Signifi-
cantly, the need to be saved and the need to be satisfied are correlated respectively with
Jacob and Esau. One wonders whether Levinas tacitly has in mind the traditional ty-
pological understanding of these figures as Judaism or the Synagogue (Israel) and
Christianity or the Church (Edom). Be that as it may, the main point is that, for
Levinas, there is no presumption of a termination of suffering in history. In the lecture
"The State of Cesar and the State of David" (1971), Levinas aligns himself with the
"non-apocalyptic Messianism" of Maimonides.[226] The rabbinic-philosophical viewpoint sheds light on the implausibility of dreaming that the ideal can be fulfilled in
events promised by a state. In consonance with Rosenzweig, Levinas maintains that
the perspective of Judaism shatters the "Platonic confidence in the possibility that the
rational political order would have in ensuring the end of all exile and all violence and,
in peacetime, bringing about the happiness of contemplation."[227] That there can be no
climax to the historical process implies that the possibility for salvation is always real.
The term *always* (*toujours*), as Levinas remarked in "Revelation in the Jewish Tradition" (1977), signifies natively "the sense of great patience, of its dia-chrony and temporal transcendence. A sobering up that is 'always' deeper and, in this sense, the

spirituality of the spirit in obedience."[228] The hope of the "temporal transcendence of
the present toward the mystery of the future"[229] depends on letting go of the belief
that an eschaton may be reached and a new era without affliction and misfortune
ushered in. Messianic awakening consists of being liberated from this eschatological
expectation and realizing that the consummation of the goal is in the waiting for the
goal to be consummated, a truism that conveys the secret of the nature of time:[230]

> Waiting for the Messiah is the actual duration of time. Or waiting for God. But
> now waiting no longer testifies to an absence of Godot who will never come. It
> testifies, rather, to the relation with something that cannot enter into the present,
> because the present is too small for the Infinite.[231]

To wait for the Messiah is not to wait for something or someone; it is to wait for the
sake of waiting, and hence it requires the patience that is the *length of time*, "an awaiting without anything being awaited, without the intention of awaiting." In swallow-
ing its own intention, patience attests to the inevitable deferral of the temporal: "Time
is deferred, is transcended to the Infinite. And the awaiting without something
awaited (time itself) is turned into responsibility for another."[232] A comparison to
Blanchot is here once again warranted:

> Waiting is always a wait for waiting, wherein the beginning is withheld, the end
> suspended, and the interval of another wait thus opened. The night in which
> nothing is awaited represents this moment of waiting. The impossibility of waiting
> belongs essentially to waiting. . . . Waiting begins when there is nothing more to
> wait for, not even the end of waiting. Waiting is unaware of and destroys that
> which it awaits. Waiting awaits nothing.[233]

Parenthetically, we would do well to contemplate the intricate connection between
prayer and temporality understood as this awaiting without an awaited. A full exposition of this matter lies beyond the scope of this chapter, but suffice it to say that the
gesture of worship itself can be understood from this vantage point: the less of a response, the more impassioned the invocation. To gauge the efficacy of prayer from the
criterion of receiving a reply—the analogue to waiting for someone or something—is
not to understand prayer at all. When conjured theistically, prayer ensnares one inescapably in a trap of metaphoricity, and hence the face of the other, presumed to be
incapable of representation, is shrouded anthropomorphically and anthropopathi-
cally. But the true purpose of prayer is not to request of a supposedly willful God to
fulfill one's needs or to lavish praise and adoration on that God; it is, on the contrary,
to overcome the theopoetic need to project the human ego into a conception of a personal deity that exercises providential care and governance over history and the natural world. In Levinas's words, "Transcendence *finds* by ever remaining a search (this is
its life) and even patience, passive to the point of forgetting its own demand—or
prayer—in the pure length and the pure languor and the silence of time."[234]

Commenting on the rabbinic tradition that it is forbidden to utter the Tetragrammaton as it is written, Levinas asks rhetorically, "But is not this withdrawal, contemporaneous with presence, maintained in the proximity of prayer?"[235] The liturgical practice preserves the absence in the presence by requiring that the name be pronounced through its epithet. Interestingly, at this precise juncture, Levinas appeals to the kabbalah.[236] Repeating this theme elsewhere, Levinas cogitates "whether prayer, before being the saying of a said, is not a way of invoking or searching or desiring, irreducible to all apophatic or doxic intentionality and to all derivations or types of intentionality."[237] Prayer thus conceived is a "way of searching for something that cannot enter into any relation as an ending," a "near-reference to an unnameable God," which "would be distinguished not only from thematizing and objectivizing intentionality, but even from dialogue's questioning, for it would in no way be equivalent to the position of an ending." The intentionality derived from prayer "would be the originary thinking-of-the-Absent-One."[238] Insofar as prayer performatively reenacts the "first fact of existence," which is neither being-in-itself (*en soi*) nor being-for-itself (*pour soi*), but being-for-the-other (*pour l'autre*), it is the model for the offering of any word without expectation of response or fulfillment of desire.[239] Somewhat counterintuitively, Levinas elicits from the *Nefesh ha-Ḥayyim* of Ḥayyim of Volozhyn that Jewish worship, the "service of the heart," is "prayer without demand," for the worshipper "never asks for anything for oneself"; true prayer is not about gratification of need but rather the "elevation of the soul," by which one "dis-inter-ests oneself" (*se dés-inter-esser*) and "loosens the ties of that unconditional attachment to being. . . . For the self (*moi*), prayer means that, instead of seeking one's own salvation, one secures that of others."[240] The liturgical and eschatological converge inasmuch as both underscore that the redemption of the world is sanctioned through the subjugation of the egoistic self in bearing the suffering of the other and the suffering of God, who suffers through that suffering.

The messianic promise shares with death the qualities of being an "*affectivity without intentionality*,"[241] an "awaiting or anticipation, without any anticipating aiming; it must thus be considered as having engulfed its intentionality of awaiting, in an awaiting that is patience or pure passivity . . . a non-taking upon oneself or a non-assumption of what is equivalent to no content,"[242] the "affection of the present by the nonpresent."[243] Levinas's portrayal of eros in its "feminine epiphany" can be applied to his idea of messianic time: "The violence of this revelation marks precisely the *force* of this absence, this *not yet*, this less than nothing, audaciously torn up from its modesty, from its essence of being hidden. A *not yet* more remote than a future, a temporal *not yet*, evincing degrees in nothingness."[244] Can we imagine a not yet that is not temporal? What, then, does Levinas wish to impart by referring to a temporal not yet that is more remote than a future? Death is not the goal toward which the human being is oriented, the finitude that is the abrogation of time, but it is the perpetual deferment that is the very nature of time, the "postponement" (*ajournement*) that is a "mode of existence and reality of a separated being that has entered into relation with the Other. This space of time [*espace du temps*] has to be taken as the point of departure."[245] For Levinas, death is not a confrontation with the anxiety of the "nihilation of nothingness" but rather facing "what is *against me*," "one of the modalities of the relation with the Other,"[246] a "menace that approaches me as a mystery; its secrecy determines it—it approaches without being able to be assumed, such that the time that separates me from my death dwindles and dwindles without end, involves a sort of last interval which my consciousness cannot traverse, and where a leap will somehow be produced from death to me. The last part of the route will be crossed without me; the time of death flows upstream; the I in its projection toward the future is overturned by a movement of imminence, pure menace, which comes to me from an absolute alterity."[247] These words portend that the transcendence of death—the moment that I can never cross and thus is always other in relation to the consciousness of self—constitutes the essence of temporality. As he writes in the essay "Intentionality and Sensation" (1965), "Should we not understand transcendence in the etymological sense of the term, as a passing over, an overstepping, a gait, rather than as a representation, without thereby destroying the essential of the metaphorical sense of this term? Transcendence is produced by kinaesthesis: thought goes beyond itself not by encountering an objective reality, but by entering into this allegedly distant world. . . . A diachrony stronger than structural synchronism."[248]

TEMPORAL TRANSCENDENCE, DEATH, AND THE DIACHRONY OF NONCOINCIDENCE

The connection between transcendence and time, essential to Levinas's critique of both Husserl and Heidegger,[249] rests on the following paradox: death is the presence of the future in the present because the future is always to come and therefore can never be now.[250] Rather than viewing the essence of being human à la Heidegger as the being-toward-death, the possibility of impossibility, death cannot be but as the "phenomenon of the end" that is the "end of the phenomenon"[251]—this is its interminable way of being—and thus "it is always possible, possible at each moment. . . . Such will be the complete concept of death: the most proper possibility, an unsurpassable possibility, isolating, certain, indeterminate. . . . It is a matter of maintaining this possibility *as* a possibility; one must maintain it without transforming it into a reality."[252] Death points to the "pure future,"[253] the "unlimited infinity of the future,"[254] the "impossible thought,"[255] that is, the thought of the impossible possibility, the pure possibility, the possibility of possibility that actualizes the transcendence of the fecundity of there being (*il y a*) in relation to a future that is "irreducible to the power over possibles."[256] It follows that the essence of time is not, as Heidegger thought, the "finitude of being" but rather "its infinity."[257] To express the matter in a different terminological register, the possibility of death is the possibility of the possible that materializes in the plurality of existents expressing an existing that is not in conformity with the logic of a monadic unity.[258] Transcendence is the very *consciousness of the possible*, the "original iteration" insinuated in the observation of Husserl that what temporalizes is already temporalized.[259] A more robust and seemingly less critical formulation of this facet of Husserl's internal time consciousness is given by Levinas in *Otherwise than Being*:

> This specific intentionality is time itself. There is consciousness insofar as the sensible impression differs from itself without differing; it differs without differing, is other within identity. . . . Differing within identity, modifying itself without changing, consciousness glows in an impression inasmuch as it diverges from itself, to *still* be expecting itself, or *already* recuperating itself. Still, already—are time, time in which nothing is lost. The past itself is modified without changing its identity, diverges from itself without letting go of itself . . . To speak of consciousness is to speak of time.[260]

In *Totality and Infinity*, Levinas similarly expounded the nature of time as the *other within identity* in conversation with Bergson's notion of the *élan vital* as the continuous duration: "The work of time goes beyond the suspension of the definitive which the continuity of duration makes possible. There must be a rupture of continuity, and continuation across this rupture. . . . Reality is what it is, but will be once again, another time freely resumed and pardoned."[261] There is continuity, but there is also rupture; indeed, embracing a logic of the *coincidentia oppositorum*, Levinas states that *there must be a rupture of continuity, and continuation across this rupture*. The "ultimate and living metaphor" (*la métaphore ultime ou vive*) that may be elicited from the Bergsonian idea of *durée* is that the flow of time cannot be captured (as Husserl maintained) in the reminiscence of the past or expectation of the future in the imagination; the temporality of time is the always-present future that can never be exhausted by the anticipation of its coming (*à-venir*), the going toward the God of time that is prophecy (*prophétie qu'il faut entendre comme l'à-Dieu du temps*).[262]

It is curious that Levinas expresses the nature of the flux in the religious or legal terms of being pardoned. The use of theological language is even more blatant in the continuation of the passage from *Totality and Infinity*: "Resurrection constitutes the principal event of time. There is therefore no continuity in being. Time is discontinuous; one instant does not come out of another without interruption, by an ecstasy."[263] The theme of resurrection, one might say, is here resurrected to enunciate that the principal event of time is a matter of discontinuity and the ecstasy of interruption.[264] The balance achieved previously is here abandoned for a more one-sided characterization: time is inherently discontinuous. The diremptive nature of time is reinforced by the observation that "death and resurrection constitute time," a "formal structure" that "presupposes the relation of the I with the Other and, at its basis, fecundity across the discontinuous which constitutes time." Levinas redresses the imbalance to some degree by portraying the fecundity of the "infinition of time" as the "recommencement in discontinuous time" that "brings youth." For Levinas, the temporal cannot be separated from the anthropological insofar as the metrics of time is measured in the ethical relation to the other. Hence it is not surprising that he immediately reverts to religious and legal language: "Time's infinite existing ensures the situation of judgment, condition of truth, behind the failure of the goodness of today."[265] If it will take an infinite time for the truth to be told, then we can presume there can be no getting to the terminus of having told the truth. To this dilemma, Levinas responds: "Truth requires both an infinite time and a time it will be able to seal, a completed time. The completion of time is not death, but messianic time, where the perpetual is converted into eternal. . . . Is this eternity a new structure of time, or an extreme vigilance of the messianic consciousness?"[266] Levinas does not answer the question. But, as we have seen, the messianic truth he is prepared to embrace is dependent on accepting that there is no end to history. Eternity, therefore, would have to be a structure of time rather than its deconstruction.[267]

It is apposite to mention a passage in *Otherwise than Being* in which Levinas avails himself of messianic language to characterize the temporal sway of being:

> This diachrony of time is not due to the length of the interval, which representation would not be able to take in. It is a disjunction of identity where the same does not rejoin the same: there is non-synthesis, lassitude. The for-oneself of identity is now no longer for itself. . . . The subject is for another; its own being turns into for another, its being dies away turning into signification. . . . In such a resolution not a world but a kingdom is signified. But a kingdom of an invisible king, the kingdom of the Good whose idea is already an eon. The Good that reigns in its goodness cannot enter into the present of consciousness, even if it would be remembered. In consciousness it is an anarchy. The Biblical notion of the Kingdom of God—kingdom of a non-thematizable God, a non-contemporaneous, that is, non-present, God—must not be conceived as an ontic image of a certain "époque" of the "history of Being," as a modality of essence. Rather, essence is already an Eon of the Kingdom. . . . It signifies in the form of the proximity of a neighbor and the duty of an unpayable debt, the form of a finite condition. Temporality as ageing and death of the unique one signifies an obedience where there is no desertion.[268]

The gauge of the diachronic is not the duration of the interval but the disjunction of identity that transforms the for-oneself of subjectivity into the for-another of intersubjectivity, a resolution that signifies the kingdom of the Good, which is identified as the biblical Kingdom of God, that is, the kingdom of an invisible king, a nonthematizable God that cannot be present or contemporaneous. The transcendence of this God is signified in the responsibilities one harbors in relation to the imminence of the neighbor. The finitude of temporality is measured by the yardstick of the duties that the subject infinitely suffers for the proximate other, an obedience from which there can be no absconding.

EPIPHANY OF THE FACE: SAYING THE UNSAID IN UNSAYING THE SAID

Many of the themes outlined above regarding the nature of transcendence are developed in greater detail in the two major works of Levinas, *Totality and Infinity* and *Otherwise than Being*. As he expressed the matter in the former composition, the face of the other, which is manifest in the voice that comes from "another shore" (*autre rive*), teaches about transcendence, the "presence of infinity breaking the closed circle of totality."[269] Transcendence is the "total alterity" that "does not shine forth in the *form* by which things are given to us," and as such it is "the vision of the very openness of being" (*la vision de l'ouverture elle-même de l'être*) that "cuts across the vision of forms and can be stated neither in terms of contemplation nor in terms of practice. It is the face [*visage*]; its revelation is speech [*parole*]."[270] Whereas vision is "essentially an adequation of exteriority with interiority," the "exteriority of discourse cannot be converted into interiority. The interlocutor can have no place in an inwardness; he is forever outside."[271]

The shift from image to discourse in Levinas's postphenomenological phenomenology—a phenomenology that moves beyond the understanding of truth as disclosure, a bringing to light of presence, the end of metaphysics, and in its place upholds the alterity of transcendence, the welcoming of the face and the doing of justice as the ultimate events that reveal the nonadequation of the idea of infinity vis-à-vis consciousness[272]—is rooted in an adaptation of the biblical and rabbinic suspicion of images as a means of promoting idolatry.[273] Eschewing the traditional apophaticism, Levinas notes that the "incomprehensible nature of the presence of the Other . . . is not to be described negatively. Better than comprehension, *discourse* relates with what remains essentially transcendent."[274] Through discourse we find a bridge to the other. In what appears to be a veiled criticism of Heidegger, Levinas writes, "Speaking, rather than 'letting be,' solicits the Other. Speech cuts across vision."[275] The face of the other that is absolutely other—the presence that always overflows the sphere of the same, "the infinitely more contained in the less" (*l'infiniment plus contenu dans le moins*)[276]—is not visible to my gaze, but it can be addressed by me in the verbal recitation of the saying (*le Dire*), which, as Levinas reminds the reader in *Otherwise than Being*, is never identical to what is said (*le Dit*).[277] The philosophical exaltation of language compresses all experiences to the "horizon of their thematization" to achieve some "equilibrium of meaning" necessitated by religions, sciences, and technologies, but in truth this process is "an incessant unsaying of the said [*un incessant dédit du Dit*], a reduction to the saying always betrayed by the said, whose words are defined by non-defined words [*les mots se définissent par des mots non-définis*]; it is a movement going from said to unsaid [*mouvement allant de dit en dédit*] in which the meaning shows itself, eclipses and shows itself."[278] Repeating an image that he deployed in *Totality and Infinity*, Levinas writes that the voice that comes from "the other shore" (*l'autre rive*) must always interrupt "the saying of the already said [*le dire du déjà dit*]. . . . The said in which everything is thematized, in which everything shows itself in a theme, has to be reduced to its signification as saying, beyond the simple correlation which is set up between the saying and the said."[279] Language, therefore, demonstrates a twofold comportment: as *saying* it is "an ethical openness to the other," and as that which is *said*, it is "reduced to a fixed identity or synchronized presence—it is an ontological closure to the other."[280] Despite the change in nomenclature, the appeal to the saying over the said corresponds to Levinas's earlier description of the epiphany of the face as an act of linguistication that turns the "sensible, still graspable . . . into total resistance to the grasp. . . . The face, still a thing among things, breaks through the form that nevertheless delimits it."[281]

In passing, I note that even with regard to the Levinasian distinction between the saying and the said there are interesting parallels to Heidegger in spite of Levinas's denial.[282] Of the many relevant references, I will cite a passage in which Heidegger addresses the nature of "the Saying" (*die Sage*) as the unfolding of "the being of language" (*das Wesen der Sprache*): "To say means to show, to make appear, the lighting-concealing-releasing offer of world [*Zeigen, Erscheinen lassen, lichtend-verbergend-freigebend Darreichen von Welt*]."[283] The Saying of which Heidegger speaks is a matter of phenomenological showing, insofar as to say is to show, but this speaking/showing and the thinking by which it is engendered are not to be regarded as objectifying representation characteristic of the natural sciences: "Thinking rather is that comportment [*Verhalten*] that lets itself be given [*dasjenige geben läßt*], by whatever shows itself in whatever way it shows itself, what it has to say of that which appears. Thinking is not necessarily a representing of something as an object."[284] The showing/saying is not the ordinary "linguistic expression added to the phenomena after they have appeared" but rather the "way to language" that "sets all present beings free into their given presence [*befreit Anwesendes in sein jeweiliges Anwesen*], and brings what is absent into their absence [*entfreit Abwesendes in sein jeweiliges Abwesen*]."[285]

Heidegger applies the term *Ereignis*, usually translated as "appropriation" or "enowning," to name the "moving force" in the "*Showing of Saying*" (*Zeigen der Sage*) that "yields the opening of the clearing [*das Freie der Lichtung*] in which present beings can persist and from which absent beings can depart while keeping their persistence in the withdrawal." We are not to think of this "yielding owning" (*erbringende Eignen*) in standard causal terms, for what shows itself in the Saying "is neither the effect of a cause, nor the consequence of an antecedent." It follows that the appropriation "cannot be represented as an occurrence or a happening—it can only be experienced as the imparting in the Showing of Saying [*nur im Zeigen der Sage als das Gewährende erfahren*][286]. . . . The appropriating event [*Ereignen*] is not the outcome (result) [*Ergebnis (Resultat)*] of something else, but the giving yield [*Er-gebnis*] whose extending giving [*reichendes Geben*][287] alone is what gives us such things as a 'there is' [*Es gibt*], a 'there is' of which even Being itself stands in need to come into its own as presence."[288] What is made to appear in this saying/showing—mystifyingly referred to as the releasing-proffering of the world—comes to presence in the lighting/clearing (*Lichtung*) that shelters the concealing in the disclosing. Thus, in the *Contributions to Philosophy*, Heidegger informs the reader that he considered "most essential" to his notion of "the grounding" (*die Gründung*) or "the inceptual thinking" (*das anfängliche Denken*) the fact that "the opening qua clearing [*die Eröffnung als Lichtung*] brings into play the self-concealing [*das Sichverbergen*], whereby the sheltering of truth [*die Bergung der Wahrheit*] receives its ground and impetus."[289]

Levinas's insistence that Heidegger's existential analysis is still subordinate to the ontological fails to take into account the complexities of his critique of the metaphysics of presence[290] in the ascendancy of the notion of *Ereignis* in his thinking, the expression that Heidegger himself referred to in a note to the 1949 edition of the "Letter on Humanism" (1947) as the "guiding word" (*Leitwort*) of his thinking since 1936,[291] the very term that Levinas enlists and translates as *événement* to express his sense of the present as the act of "eventing."[292] In another note to the same text, Heidegger articulates his perspective gnomically: "Being as event of appropriation [*Ereignis*], event of appropriation: the saying [*Sage*]; thinking: renunciative saying in response [*Entsagen*] to the saying of the event of appropriation."[293] That this is the term that signals the move beyond the ontological is shown clearly in Heidegger's remark in the summary of the 1962 lecture "Time and Being" that *Ereignis* "is not a new formation of Being in the history of Being," but it indicates that "Being belongs to and is reabsorbed within Appropriation [*das Sein in das Ereignis gehört und dahin zurückgenommen wird*]," whence it follows that "the history of Being is at an end for thinking *in* Appropriation, that is, for the thinking which enters into Appropriation . . . is no longer what is to be thought explicitly."[294] From the standpoint of *Ereignis*, metaphysics as "the history of the imprints[295] of Being [*die Geschichte des Seinsprägungen*]" is seen as "the history of the self-withdrawal of what is sending in favor of the destinies . . . an actual letting-presence of what is present [*jeweiligen Anwesenlassens des Anwesenden*]." Metaphysics as the history of Being is the "history of the concealment and withdrawal of that which gives Being." To enter into the thinking of *Ereignis* is to end this withdrawal, and the "oblivion of Being" (*Seinsvergessenheit*) is superseded by the "awakening into Appropriation" (*Entwachen in das Ereignis*).[296] As Thomas Sheehan has argued, Heidegger's thought in toto can be viewed as a "phenomenological reduction of being to meaning," and the two critical terms, *facticity* in the earlier period and *Ereignis* in the later period, both denote "the a priori appropriation of man to the meaning process."[297]

Many more passages from Heidegger could have been cited, but the material I have adduced is sufficient to make the point that Levinas's critique of Heidegger's alleged ontology ignores the more mature phases of his thinking and, indeed, smacks of a hermeneutical partiality that borders on deliberate obscuration. Thus, in the Nemo interview of 1981, after praising *Being and Time*, Levinas proclaimed that "the later work of Heidegger, which does not produce in me a comparable impression, remains valuable through *Sein und Zeit*. Not, you well know, that it is insignificant; but it is much less convincing." Levinas quickly added that this less enthusiastic reaction is not due to Heidegger's "political engagements" and his "participation in National-Socialism," decisions neither forgotten nor forgiven.[298] Along similar lines, in the 1983 interview with Fornet-Betancourt and Gomez-Muller, Levinas again acknowledged his inability to forget the pain caused by Heidegger's joining the National Socialist party in 1933, but he still labeled him "the greatest philosopher of the century, perhaps one of the greatest philosophers of the millennium," noting in particular his admiration for *Being and Time*, which he calls the "summit of phenomenology." Levinas admits that he was "less familiar" with the "later Heidegger," but he nevertheless raises concern that it displays "a discourse in which the human becomes an articulation of an anonymous or neutral intelligibility, to which the revelation of God is subordinated."[299] Even in his last reflections on Heidegger, the lecture "Dying For . . . ," delivered in March 1987 at the Collège International de Philosophie in Paris, Levinas concentrated solely on Heidegger's early treatise.[300] Levinas does occasionally mention "the late philosophy" (*la dernière philosophie*) of Heidegger, and from the recently published notebooks there is ample evidence that he was reading works composed after Heidegger's so-called turn,[301] but he dismisses the more mature thinking summarily as more evidence of the ontological suppression of the ethical and the specification of human existence in terms of the mystery that is defined solely by power.[302]

In a passage from his notebooks, Levinas remarks that consequent to "the glorious departure of *Sein und Zeit* to the discovery of being," in the *Holzwege* Heidegger "wanders after the protracted investigations of being."[303] In a second passage, Levinas affirms that, for Heidegger, speech (*parole*) already presupposes a "copresence" and "preliminary relationship with others" in the "same world" as that of the speaker, but the "essence of language" was still located in the act of "signification," which is further described as the ontological demarcation of the "something as something" (*etwas als etwas*), a point that is supported by reference to Heidegger's *Holzwege* and to his interpretation of Hölderlin,[304] a likely reference to *Erläuterungen zu Hölderlins Dichtung*.[305] What is noteworthy for our purposes is that the Heideggerian expression cited by Levinas, *etwas als etwas*, is actually from *Being and Time*, including the section of the text[306] that Levinas engages in the very next paragraph in the notebooks.[307] It seems reasonable to me to offer this as evidence that Levinas read later works of Heidegger through the lens of his first philosophical monograph.

Very telling in this regard is Levinas's response to Florian Rötzer's question about which "central thought" of Heidegger he felt he had developed. Levinas begins by admitting his admiration for the way that Heidegger employed the Husserlian method in *Being and Time*, and he then comments on the importance—he even calls it an

"eternal truth"—of the ontological difference between being and beings; he concludes, however, on a negative note by referring to those "who don't believe in the
Ereignis, or who don't accept the fourfold as the center of every thinking,"[308] two
concepts that are prominent in the later Heidegger. A comparable assessment was offered by Levinas in the interview with François Poirié. As he readily admits regarding
Heidegger's *Being and Time*, "Still today all this is more precious to me than the last
speculative consequences of his project, the end of metaphysics, the themes of *Ereignis*, the *es gibt* in its mysterious generosity. What remains is Heidegger's ingenious
application of phenomenological analysis discovered by Husserl and, alas, the horror
of 1933."[309] Relevant as well is the critique of Heidegger in the following passage in
Otherwise than Being. Even though it seems that Levinas is alluding to the literary
flourishes of the later Heidegger, his condemnation still focuses on the privileging of
the ontological, the reduction of the other to the same, and the paganistic feigning of
a transcendence in the guise of ecstatic moments that are no more than mirages,
echoes, and reflections of self:

> In all the compunction of Heidegger's magical language and the impressionism of
> his play of lights and shadows, and the mystery of light that comes from behind
> the curtains, in all this tip-toe or wolf stepping movement of discourse, where the
> extreme prudence to not frighten the game perhaps dissimulates the impossibility
> of flushing it out, where each contact is only tangency, does poetry succeed in
> reducing the rhetoric? Is not essence the very impossibility of anything else, of any
> revolution that would not be a revolving upon oneself? Everything that claims to
> come from elsewhere, even the marvels of which essence itself is capable, even the
> surprising possibilities of renewal by technology and magic, even the perfections of
> gods peopling the heights of this world, and their immortality and the immortal-
> ity they promise mortals—all this does not deaden the heartrending bustling of
> the *there is* [*l'écoeurant remue-ménage de l'*il y a] recommencing behind every
> negation.[310]

Levinas disparagingly applies the language of Ecclesiastes to Heidegger, characterizing his thought as "Vanity of vanities, all is vanity, nothing is new under the sun."[311]
But the fact is that Levinas does not delve into the intricacies and complexities of the
later work of Heidegger, which offers a perspective that is much closer to his own criticisms of ontology and the attempt to ground the meaning of human existence in a
saying—"the primordial belonging of the word to being" (*die anfängliche Zugehörig-
keit des Wortes zum Sein*)[312]—that gestures toward the Being that is otherwise than
being.[313] Let us recall Heidegger's statement in *Identity and Difference*: "Being shows
itself as the unconcealing overwhelming [*entbergende Überkommnis*]. Beings as such
appear in the manner of the arrival that keeps itself concealed in unconcealedness [*in
der Weise der in die Unverborgenheit sich bergenden Ankunft*]. . . . The difference of Being
and beings, as the differentiation of overwhelming and arrival, is the perdurance of

the two in *unconcealing keeping in concealment* [entbergende-bergende Austrag beider]."[314]

Typical of this turn is Heidegger's claim that the nature of substance, which may be elicited from the Greek *ousia*, is most properly rendered as "presencing" (*Anwesung*) as opposed to "presentness" (*Anwesenheit*): "What is meant here is not mere presence [*Vorhandenheit*], and certainly not something that is exhausted merely in stability; rather: *presencing*, in the sense of coming forth into the unhidden [*im Sinne des Hervorkommens in das Unverborgene*], placing itself into the open [*das Sichstellen in das Offene*]."[315] Presencing does not entail a presence subject to representation based on the subject-object relation. On the contrary, the coming to presence (*An-wesen*) is a turning toward the human essence (*Menschenwesen*) that finds its consummation in the thinking of Being that calls forth the crossing out of Being (*der kreuzweisen Durchstreichung des Seins*), and hence, as Heidegger graphically illustrated in the essay "On the Question of Being," the "thoughtful look" into the realm wherein being "dissolves into the turning" that is "worthy of question" requires that the word "being" be written in such a way that it is crossed out.[316] It is in this sense of surpassing—to which the label "meta-physics" can be applied—that the Being of beings is given, and thus we can say that "nothing belongs, in its being absent, to presencing."[317] Derrida rightly observed that, for Heidegger, the crossing out of "being"—the placing under erasure, *sous rature*, as he reformulated this Heideggerian practice[318]—is a "mark of deletion" that summons the "questioning of what constitutes our history and what produced transcendentality itself," but it is not a "merely negative symbol." It is rather the "final writing of an epoch. Under its strokes the presence of a transcendental signified is effaced while still remaining legible. . . . In as much as it de-limits onto-theology, the metaphysics of presence and logocentrism, this last writing is also the first writing."[319]

The play of presence and absence is the key to grasping Heidegger's understanding of the comportment of truth as disclosedness, the double negative that yields a positive, the withdrawal of the withdrawing, the unconcealment (*alētheia*) that is the concealment of the concealing (*lēthe*), which conceals itself so that it may be revealed. Explicating the *first beginning* as the "disentanglement [*Entwindung*] out of the still unexperienceable turning [*unerfahrbaren Kehre*]," Heidegger writes,

ἀλήθεια "is" φύσις, in which the concealment is itself concealed [*die Verbergung selbst verbirgt*], such that pure emergence [*reine Aufgehen*] appears and such that the emergence seems to be pure presence [*reine Anwesung*]. . . . In the first beginning, which must once emerge, the inceptuality [*die Anfängnis*] remains concealed, and thus the truth (of being) is here related (in a concealed way) to the concealed and is the unconcealedness of emergence [*die Unverborgenheit des Aufgangs*], i.e., unconcealedness as emergence [*als Aufgang*]. Therein essentially occurs already the letting go of semblance, appearance, and seeming [*die Loslassung des Scheinens und Erscheinens und des Anscheins*], especially since emergence, if apprehended for itself, is encountered in such a way that the apprehending must be pure letting-appear [*reine Scheinenlassen*].[320]

Truth is juxtaposed with nature insofar as the manifestation of the latter arises from the concealing of the concealment, the unconcealedness that is the emergence of the semblance of presence apprehended in the letting-appear of the letting-go of appearance. Heidegger thus insists, as I noted in the previous chapter, that "un-truth" is "most proper to the essence of truth." The un-truth, the "concealment of beings as a whole," precedes—in Heidegger's precise language, "is older" (*ist älter*) than—"every opened-ness [*Offenbarkeit*] of this or that being," indeed, even older than "letting-be itself [*das Seinlassen selbst*]." This letting-be, the "it gives" (*es gibt*), is the mystery (*Geheimnis*) of the "concealing of what is concealed as a whole, of beings as such . . . not a particular mystery regarding this or that, but rather the one mystery—that, in general, mystery (the concealing of what is concealed) [*die Verbergung des Verborgenen*] as such holds sway throughout the Da-sein of human beings. In letting beings as a whole be, which discloses and at the same time conceals, it happens that concealing appears as what is first of all concealed [*die Verbergung als das erstlich Verborgene erscheint*]."[321] This leads Heidegger to presume that even though the "primordial" knowledge revolves about the possibility of discerning the "being of language" from the "language of being" (*Das Wesen der Sprache: Die Sprache des Wesens*),[322] it is nevertheless the case that "the being of language nowhere brings itself to word as the language of being." Heidegger concludes, therefore, that "the essential nature of language flatly refuses to express itself in words [*das Wesen der Sprache es gerade verweigert, zur Sprache zu kommen*]—in the language, that is, in which we make statements about language. If language everywhere withholds its nature in this sense, then such withholding is in the very nature of language [*dann gehört diese Verweigerung zum Wesen derSprache*]."[323] As Heidegger put it elsewhere:

> Everything spoken [*Gesprochene*] stems in a variety of ways from the unspoken [*Ungesprochenen*], whether it be something not yet spoken [*noch-nicht-Gesprochenes*], or whether it be what must remain unspoken [*ungesprochen*] in the sense that it is beyond the reach of speaking. . . . What is unspoken is not merely something that lacks voice, it is what remains unsaid [*Ungesagte*], what is not yet shown [*Gezeigte*], what has not yet reached its appearance [*ins Erscheinen Gelangte*]. That which must remain wholly unspoken is held back in the unsaid, abides in concealment as unshowable [*verweilt als Unzeigbares im Verborgenen*], is mystery [*Geheimnis*].[324]

Language is the mystery of what is spoken of the unspoken, the unsaid in every saying, the unshowable in every showing.

The degree to which Levinas flattened the complexity of Heidegger and as a consequence obscured the propinquity of their thinking can be seen from the following attempt to distinguish the perspectives of Heidegger and Blanchot along the lines that for the former writing is to lead to the "truth of being," whereas for the latter it is to lead to the "errancy of being." Levinas accepts that "an alternance of nothingness and being" occurs in the Heideggerian truth of being, but he insists nonetheless that there is a critical difference: Blanchot, contrary to Heidegger, calls it non-truth rather than truth.[325] Elaborating the point, Levinas draws the convergence and divergence between Heidegger and Blanchot more sharply:

> Heidegger's late philosophy consists predominantly in the interpretation of the essential forms of human activity—art, technology, science, economy—as modes of truth (or the forgetting of it). The fact that, for Heidegger, the approach to that truth, the response to that call, is made by wandering byways, and that error is contemporaneous with truth—the fact that the revelation of being is also its dissimulation: all this shows a very high degree of proximity between Heidegger's notion of being and that realization of unreality, that presence of absence, that existence of nothingness that, according to Blanchot, the work of art, the poem, allows us to express. But in Heidegger's view truth—a primordial disclosure— conditions all wanderings, and that is why all that is human can be said, in the final analysis, in terms of truth—[to] be described as "disclosure of being." In Blanchot, *the work uncovers, in an uncovering that is not truth*, a darkness. In an uncovering that is not truth! . . . Truth conditioned by errancy, errancy conditioned by truth: a distinction without a difference? I think not.[326]

For the purposes of our discussion let me note that Levinas's account of the later Heidegger is colored by what he perceived to be the "fundamental dogma of Heideggerian orthodoxy," the "priority of being [*être*] in relation to beings [*l'étant*]," which disregards the ethical in favor of the ontological.[327] Heidegger's world, therefore, is one in which "justice does not condition truth," and thus, using a well-known stereotype among Jewish survivors of the Holocaust to depict Hitler and the Nazis,[328] Heidegger is compared to Amalek, the nemesis of Israel, whose "existence prevents the integrity of the Divine Name—that is, precisely, the *truth of being*."[329] Levinas appropriates an older aggadic motif, rooted in Scripture, which views Amalek as the force of absolute evil[330] that diminishes the Tetragrammaton.[331] Through his philosophical exegesis, Levinas applies the malevolence of Amalek, which he anachronistically identifies as an expression of anti-Semitic persecution,[332] to Heidegger's thought: his tireless reduction of truth to being culminates in the inability to establish the truth of being.

This bias informs Levinas's distinction between Heidegger and Blanchot on the matter of truth. Even if one were to concede that Heidegger did not accord the proper place to ethics, Levinas's presentation of Heidegger's view of truth is a gross simplification. To circumscribe Heidegger's thought the way Levinas does fails to appreciate that for Heidegger himself, as I discussed at length in the previous chapter, truth cannot be extricated from untruth. Lest there by any misunderstanding, let me be clear that I do not deny that Blanchot's conception of truth in art can be read as a critique of Heidegger's assertion that truth is in essence untruth, which, as Levinas pointed out, amounts to an act of violence against the truth that belongs to the world.[333] I do, however, question whether the idea of truth as untruth is so distant from the assertion that the truth of being always entails the nontruth of the otherwise than being.[334] According to the aporetical logic that Heidegger applies to the origin that precedes both the absence of presence and the presence of absence—the nihilation that nihilates the something of nothing in the nothing of something, the opening enclosure that enables the succession of light and dark but is itself neither luminous nor dim, much like *il y a* in Levinas and Blanchot[335]—in the clearing that is truth, what is uncovered is the paradox that both undermines the epistemological distinction between truth and nontruth and undercuts the ontological distinction between being and nonbeing.[336] Thus, for instance, in the diary that Heidegger wrote chronicling his first trip to Greece in 1962, he commented on the Heraclitean description of Apollo, *He neither reveals, nor hides but rather he shows*: "To show means to let something be seen, which as such [that is, as visible] is kept at the same time covered and protected. Such a showing is the proper happening in the field of ἀλήθεια, which founds the sojourn in the antechamber of the holy."[337] Heidegger has offered in these words an abridged account of his doctrine of truth as the manifestation of that which remains concealed in its coming to be manifest.

Much more could be said about this complex of ideas, but for the purposes of this analysis two points need to be emphasized. First, Heidegger articulated a notion of truth that cannot be disentangled from an equally originary untruth, whence it follows that the primary saying is concurrently an unsaying, the showing an unshowing, the disclosure a concealment, the presence an absence. Second, the ocular and auditory dimensions of the enowning cannot be separated, insofar as the "Saying is showing." Showing would suggest the need to gaze upon what comes forth, but Heidegger insists that to "belong to Saying," a belonging that contains the "actual presence of the way to language," one must learn how "to listen."[338] For something to come to light, it must get a hearing.[339]

In all of these matters, Heidegger anticipated many of the notes sounded by Levinas. I willingly acknowledge that the ethical import of Levinas's concern is not pronounced in Heidegger, and thus it is important not to conflate their views, even though Levinas himself once acknowledged in a moment of unusual candor in the interview with Rötzer that his notion of the face, the cornerstone of his ethics, is a continuation of Heidegger's analysis of the hand in his concept of the ready-to-hand (*Zuhandenheit*) that marks Dasein's relation to the things we encounter or make use of in the world[340] or, as he insightfully put it elsewhere, the "incarnation of thought" (*incarnation de la pensée*).[341] Also germane is Levinas's observation in "Diachrony and Representation" (1982) that Heidegger's interpretation of the Anaximander fragment in *Holzwege* "puts into question the 'positivity' of the *esse* in its *presence*, signifying, bluntly, encroachment and usurpation! Did not Heidegger—despite all he intends to teach about the priority of the 'thought of being'—here run up against the original significance of ethics?"[342]

The most critical similarity—indeed the similarity that helps draw attention to the disparity—is that both affirm a primary sense of language[343] linked to the event of saying through which being is simultaneously affirmed and negated. As Derrida already noted: "For Levinas, as for Heidegger, language would be at once a coming forth [*éclosion*] and a holding back [*réserve*], enlightenment [*éclairement*] and obscurity [*occultation*]; and for both, dissimulation would be a conceptual gesture."[344] The saying is a sign that points to what is beyond signification and must properly be identified as the being that is otherwise than being. For Levinas, this alterity is to be sought in the gradual advance toward the face-to-face encounter with the other, but already in Heidegger, if one is sufficiently heedful, the dialogical character of language is evident. Indeed, in *Being and Time*, Heidegger emphasized the primacy of hearing to the existential possibility of human speech:

> Hearing is constitutive for discourse. And just as linguistic utterance [*sprachliche Verlautbarung*] is based on discourse [*Rede*], acoustic perception [*akustische Vernehmen*] is based on hearing [*Hören*]. Listening to . . . is the existential being-open [*existenziale Offensein*] of Da-sein as being-with for the other [*als Mitsein für den Anderen*]. Hearing even constitutes the primary and authentic openness [*Offenheit*] of Da-sein for its ownmost possibility of being, as in hearing the voice of a friend whom every Da-sein carries with it. Da-sein hears because it understands [*Das Dasein hört, weil es versteht*].[345]

The claim that hearing marks the primary understanding—the authentic mode of language[346]—through which Dasein remains open to the voice of another exhibits a basic kinship with Levinas's insistence regarding the saying as the way to behold the face of the other, which "gives itself phenomenally yet remains exterior to experience."[347] Interpreting the words of Levinas that speech cuts across vision, Wyschogrod writes: "It can be argued that for Levinas the face as precept or image must be 'disconnected' from the face as signification, not in the interest of extracting a pure or absolute consciousness, but rather as showing that spatial configurations fail to disclose the meaning of the face, its discursiveness and ethical authority."[348] Wyschogrod is to be given credit for contextualizing the shift in Levinas in terms of the aniconism that has shaped Jewish faith through the generations. And especially important is Maimonides. Levinas is likely to have been influenced by the Maimonidean translation of visuality into discourse.[349] As Maimonides well understood, sacralization of the image has the potential for idolatry, which consists of ascribing corporeality to God or, in the more technical philosophical terminology of Avicenna adopted by him, the necessary existent, whose oneness entails a simple, incomposite nature. The masses require the figural imagination to convey this truth—they cannot entertain the existence of something that is not a body—but this very figuration disfigures the truth insofar as the truth is beyond configuration.[350] For the philosophically enlightened, figurative images are to be read figuratively, unmasked for what they are, feeble attempts of the human imagination to bequeath images to that which has no image.

A striking example of this strategy is found in Maimonides's explanation of the scriptural claim that God spoke to Moses face-to-face, *we-dibber yhwh el mosheh panim el panim* (Exodus 33:11) as "the hearing of a speech without the intermediary of an angel," that is, without the intervention of the imaginative faculty.[351] Maimonides adduces this by citing two other verses, one that describes God's speaking to the people of Israel face-to-face (Deuteronomy 5:4) and another that describes the Israelites hearing the voice of words but seeing no figure (ibid., 4:12). In a second passage, Maimonides explains the depiction of Moses knowing God face-to-face, *we-lo qam navi od be-yisra'el ke-mosheh asher yeda'o yhwh panim el panim* (Deuteronomy 34:10), as denoting an unmediated encounter, which is not the case with all other prophets.[352] Wyschogrod insightfully observed that Levinas's use of the image of the face to mark the relation with the other beyond imagistic representation is based on Maimonides's "metonymic expansion" of the term *panim*.[353] She notes, however, that even though Levinas is indebted to the aniconicity endorsed by Maimonides, he does not presume that we can ascertain knowledge of the other through rational intuition and inference.

I would add, parenthetically, that there seems to be operative in both Maimonides and Levinas a presumed correlation between space and vision, on one hand, and time and hearing, on the other. In what sense can the privileging of the temporal-aural over the spatial-ocular secure the possibility of accessing the infinite other as the trace of transcendence that is disruptive of the sphere of being? From the Maimonidean perspective, there is a transmutation of the visual into the verbal, but even the latter should be insufficient to speak of the transcendent. Attributing speech to God is no less problematic for Maimonides (or, for that matter, Levinas) than imagining the possibility of seeing an image of God; both equally take on a form of anthropomorphization that is idolatrous when literalized or ontologized as real. Nevertheless, reflecting the long-standing bias in Jewish sources, both Maimonides and Levinas view the visual as more dangerous than the auditory, and hence they interpret the scriptural account of Moses speaking to God face-to-face as a metaphoric denotation of the dialogic relationality that in truth defies any figurative representation. Just as Maimonides explained that God's declaration that his face will not be seen signifies that the true reality of the necessary of existence cannot be grasped, so Levinas uses the image of the face to denote the unknowability of what is, strictly speaking, no thing but "the *event of being*" (*l'*événement d'être) that "passes over to what is other than being" (*l'autre de l'être*), "being's other," the "otherwise than being" (*autrement qu'être*), which is the "very difference of the *beyond*, the difference of transcendence."[354] Levinas opts to reform phenomenology by utilizing language that is replete with aniconic resonances and critical of the ocularcentric tendency to favor vision. The infinite is envisaged in a/theophanic terms as "the echo of the *otherwise*" (*l'echo de l'*autrement) issuing from "the *hither side of ontology*" (en deçà de l'ontologie),[355] which does not denote an indefinite extension of the finite (following Kant) but an actuality (in line with Descartes), albeit an actuality that can never be actually delimited, as it is always other, always beyond what we can know or think, the "exorbitant ultramateriality" that is inexhaustible.[356] Even to call it an "it" is misguided and underlines the inadequacy of language to convey the nature of the face that repudiates any attempt to contain it imagistically.

The more mature undertaking of Levinas to privilege the metaphysical transcendence beyond ontology flows naturally out of his earlier inquisitiveness concerning the apparent entrapment of human subjectivity in a world without any transcendence other than transcendence within immanence. In *Time and the Other*, he explicitly describes the transcendence of light, which stands metaphorically for reason or consciousness, as being "wrapped in immanence. The exteriority of light does not suffice for the liberation of the ego that is the self's captive."[357] Philosophical idealism has run its course. To approach the infinite, the thought that "withdraws from thought," one must "understand more than one understands" and "think more than one thinks."[358] A particularly bold account of this agnosticism—perhaps skepticism would be the better term[359]—is found in the essay "From Consciousness to Wakefulness" (1974), where Levinas questions whether lucidity, generally thought to be the measure of perfect knowledge, is the "most awakened wakefulness," which he further describes as the "inassimilable disturbance of the Same by the Other—an awakening that shakes the waking state—a disturbance of the Same by the Other in difference." This, he adds, is the appropriate description of transcendence, a "relation between the Same and the Other that cannot be interpreted as a state, not even as the state of lucidity, a relation that must be granted to vigilance, which, as anxiety, does not rest in its theme, in representation, in presence, in Being." Transcendence is this "order, or disorder, in which reason is no longer knowledge or action but in which, unseated by the Other from its state—unseated from the Same and from being—it is ethical relation with the other person, proximity of the neighbor."[360] An alternate enunciation of the matter is found in *Otherwise than Being*: "Transcendence, the beyond essence which is also being-in-the-world [*à l'au-delà de l'essence qui est aussi* être-*au-monde*], requires ambiguity, a blinking of meaning [*clignotement de sens*] which is not only a chance certainty [*une certitude aléatoire*], but a frontier both ineffaceable and finer than the tracing of an ideal line."[361] The emphasis on the ethical, therefore, is consequent to the apophatic: the uncertainty or the random certainty, the sporadic meaning, associated with the divine Other, the ineffaceable and subtle frontier that is concomitantly invisble and visible, beyond essence and being-in-the-world, results in the turn toward the human other. In Levinas's interview with Wyschogrod conducted on December 31, 1982, he remarked that it is in virtue of nonappearing, the staging (*mise en scène*) of the infinite in the construction of social relations, that he was willing to call his thinking a form of phenomenology, which he related more specifically to "Husserl's recovery of the concrete horizon."[362]

IMAGINING TRANSCENDENCE AND THE THREAT OF THEOLATRY

The critical question I will raise in this section is whether the preference accorded the acoustic over the visual helps one avoid lapsing into the very objectification of the other, against which Levinas cautioned frequently in his writings and lectures. Put differently, can we preserve an outside that cannot be rendered phenomenologically accessible from the inside if we presume the ability to "hear" transcendence or the infinity that is otherwise than being? Does such hearing maintain the excess that superintends the totality, the more that is less, the face that is both the exposure of the other and its refusal to be exposed? To paraphrase Levinas, the presence of the other would perforce consist in the other divesting itself kenotically of the form in which it is manifest,[363] the showing that is variously expressed as the face that speaks, the opening within the opening, the "suffering of the eye overtaxed by light," the wakefulness to life, the "transcendence that cannot be reduced to an experience of transcendence, for it is a seizure prior to every *position* of subject and to every perceived or assimilated content."[364] Philosophy itself is transformed by this understanding insofar as it becomes the "language of transcendence and not the tale of experience: a language in which the teller is part of the tale, thus a necessarily personal language, to be understood beyond what it says, that is, to be interpreted."[365] Phenomenological acuity gives way to a midrashic sensibility: language is determined by the notion of a saying that is always more than what is said and hence elicits endless interpretation,[366] a cornerstone of Levinas's diachronic conception of time, the simultaneity of past and future in the present, which he paradoxically describes as "the relation with God who is in excess of the relation with the Other but is, however, in the relation with the Other."[367] Rabbinic hermeneutic practice, as Levinas describes it, is a mode of interpretation that "necessarily includes that seeking without which the non-said, inherent in the texture of what is declared, would be extinguished by the weight of the texts and sink into their letters."[368]

In line with the venerable aniconism of the Jewish tradition, Levinas extols sound over light,[369] privileging the auditory to the ocular, and hence, in language that overtly vilifies the incarnational foundation of Christian logocentrism,[370] he notes that "the real presence of the other . . . is fulfilled in the act of hearing, and derives its meaning from the role of transcendent origin played by the word that is offered. It is to the extent that the word refuses to become flesh that it assumes a presence amongst us."[371] In *Totality and Infinity*, Levinas had already expressed the matter by noting that the "Transcendent, infinitely Other, solicits us and appeals to us . . . The Other is not the incarnation of God, but precisely by his face, in which he is disincarnate [*désincarné*], is the manifestation of the height in which God is revealed."[372] The Christological doctrine is similarly appropriated and undermined in *Otherwise than Being*: "In the approach of a face the flesh becomes word [*la chair se fait verbe*], the caress a saying. The thematization of a face undoes the face and undoes the approach. The mode in which a face indicates its own absence in my responsibility requires a description that can be formed only in ethical language."[373] Finally, and perhaps most boldly, in "The Thinking of Being and the Question of the Other," Levinas expresses his misgivings regarding the Christian dogma: "A being-affected by the invisible—by what is invisible to the point of not letting itself be represented, or thematized, or named, or pointed out as a 'something' in general like a this or a that and, consequently, 'the absolutely non-incarnatable,' that which does not come to 'take form' [*prendre corps*], and which is unsuited to hypostasis—a being-affected beyond being and beings, and beyond their distinction or amphibology; the infinite eclipsing ess*a*nce."[374]

Faithful to this dogma of disincarnation, Levinas would later contrast—in my judgment, somewhat disingenuously[375]—his notion of *il y a*, "there is," with Heidegger's *es gibt*, in the following way in an interview with Philippe Nemo:

> For me . . . "there is" is the phenomenon of impersonal being: "it." . . . It is something resembling what one hears when one puts an empty shell close to the ear, as if the emptiness were full, as if the silence were a noise. It is something one can also feel when one thinks that even if there were nothing, the fact that "there is" is undeniable. Not that there is this or that; but the very scene of being is open: there is. In the absolute emptiness that one can imagine before creation—there is.[376]

Levinas embraces a paradoxical language that has interesting parallels with both kabbalistic and Buddhist cosmologies: the ultimate source of being, what he calls "there is," is the impersonal surge of indiscriminate being that precedes all discriminate being, the emptiness that is full, the rumbling silence of the absent presence that disappears in the appearance of its present absence. Interestingly, Levinas elucidates this phenomenon from a childhood memory of experiencing the silence of his bedroom as the adults continue in their wakeful life. When pressed by his interlocutor on the comparison to Heidegger's *es gibt* and the sense of munificence implied thereby, Levinas emphatically denies the suitability of such anthropomorphizing:

> I insist in fact on the impersonality of the "there is"; "there is," as "it rains," or "it's night."[377] And there is neither joy nor abundance: it is a noise returning after every negation of this noise. Neither nothingness nor being. I sometimes use the expression: the excluded middle. One cannot say of this "there is" which persists that it is an event of being. One can neither say that it is nothingness, even though there is nothing.[378]

The comportment of *il y a* is such that it violates the Aristotelian logic of the excluded middle: it is neither nothing nor something. One cannot even say of "there is" that it is an event of being. Indeed, it is too much to say that it is nothingness, even though there is, in truth, nothing, for nothingness (*néant*) is "merely the negation of the negation, which 'preserves' (*aufhebt*) the being that it denies."[379] As Levinas put it in an essay published in *Deucalion* 1 (1946) and then incorporated into the collection *De l'existence à l'existant*, published the following year, the expression il y a names the "impersonal, anonymous, yet inextinguishable 'consummation' of being, which murmurs in the depths of nothingness itself . . . We have not derived this notion from exterior things or the inner world—from any 'being' whatever. For *there is* transcends inwardness as well as exteriority; it does not even make it possible to distinguish these."[380] It is the experience of the night that presents us with a phenomenological opening to this sense of the dissolution of all forms, the "total exclusion of light," an absence that "invades like a presence." And yet, Levinas insists, the nothing confronted in the night "is not that of pure nothingness. There is no longer *this* or *that*; there is not 'something.' But this universal absence is in its turn a presence, an absolutely unavoidable presence."[381] One should not view these words in a Hegelian fashion as if the presence were the "dialectical counterpart" of absence that could be grasped through thought. What Levinas is conveying is the sense of nocturnality in which there is neither being nor nonbeing, the absence that is present by being absent as the presence that is absent by being present, the nothing to which we can respond only in silence.

The "rustling" of *il y a* provokes a sense of horror as it "bears down on us in insomnia" with the "*impersonal vigilance*" of the "anonymity of the night." But this horror should not be confused with "an anxiety about death."[382] And here Levinas marks the crucial difference between himself and Heidegger:

> The horror of the night, as an experience of the *there is*, does not then reveal to us a danger of death, nor even a danger of pain. That is what is essential in this analysis. The pure nothingness revealed by anxiety in Heidegger's analysis does not constitute the *there is*. There is horror of being and not anxiety over nothingness, fear of being and not fear for being; there is being prey to, delivered over to something that is not a "something." When night is dissipated with the first rays of the sun, the horror of the night is no longer definable. The "something" appears to be "nothing."[383]

Echoing this theme in the Nemo interview, Levinas maintained that the nothing of *il y a* is the opposite of the "absolute negation" that is death. The experience of "there is" is a "maddening" horror from which it is totally impossible to escape just as it is impossible for the insomniac to escape from the state of wakefulness in which he or she can both say and not say that it is the "I" that cannot fall asleep. In the state of insomnia, consciousness is depersonalized in a manner that sheds light on the impersonalization of the "it" that is the character of "there is."[384]

In "Violence and Metaphysics," Derrida observed the complex way in which Levinas's thinking about ethics is conditioned by the apophatic tradition of Western philosophy and thus incriminates him in the ontotheology he sought to undermine—the being delineated as beyond being (*epekeina tes ousias*) is a being nonetheless.[385] Negative theology remains a negative ontology, insofar as it persists, as the case of Meister Eckhart demonstrates, in "acknowledging the ineffable transcendence of an infinite existent." The thought of Being implied in affirming the hyperessentiality of transcendence fails to surpass all "ontic determinations."[386] Is Derrida correct that the Levinasian "ethical-metaphysical transcendence" presupposes an "ontological transcendence"?[387] In the dialogue with Armengaud, Levinas insisted that the "original ethical signifying of the face," which is embodied in the twin commandments of the love of God and the love of one's neighbor, is "without any metaphor or figure of speech, in its rigorously proper meaning—the transcendence of a God not objectified in the face in which he speaks; a God who does not 'take on body,' but who approaches precisely through this relay to the neighbor—binding men among one another with obligation, each one answering for the lives of all the others."[388] In conjunction with this view, he notes that the *via negativa* in Maimonides opened the door to casting the positive knowledge of God as the attributes of actions, which are encapsulated in the characteristics of *ḥesed*, *mishpaṭ*, and *ṣedaqah*, rendered respectively by Levinas as the "ethical behavior" of "good will," "judgment," and "fairness" in relation to the other. This is the highest possible theological knowledge one can have and the means to realize the commandment of *imitatio dei*.[389] The point is reinforced in Levinas's interview with Wyschogrod, wherein he recalled that at the end of the *Guide* (III.54) Maimonides affirmed the supremacy of the ethical ideal anchored in the attributes of divine action in the world, an ideal that Levinas calls the "law of nonreciprocity" or "asymmetry" demanded by the relation with the other.[390]

Appealing to the *via negativa* and emphasizing that God is unknowable and therefore beyond our linguistic and conceptual limits would seemingly provide a buffer against the defective representations. In contrast to Cohen's interpretation of the Maimonidean negative theology, for Levinas, the medieval sage limited our capacity to know God, for ascribing positive attributes to the divine is tantamount to abolishing belief in the existence of the deity.[391] Ironically, however, the incorporation of apophaticism on his part only enhanced the degree to which the insistence of an encounter with transcendence incriminates one in the mistaken kataphatic depiction of the meontological.[392] Despite the lofty ambition underlying Levinas's plea to inaugurate ethics rather than ontology as the discursive underpinning for the possibility of the human experience of the divine as well as the imperative that issues from the infinite responsibility each of us must have for another human being in his or her specificity,[393] the correlation of alterity and transcendence in the manner he conceives it may already be too much of an effacement of the nonphenomenalizable, too much figuring of the unfigurable, too much of a hazard of making the anti-idolatry of formlessness into a form of idolatry by incarnating the disincarnate and ascribing interest to the disinterestedness of what is ostensibly beyond being.

That Levinas was aware of this possible pitfall is most strikingly attested in the section called "The Metaphysical and the Human" in *Totality and Infinity*.[394] In a manner similar to the assertion of Nancy cited in the Preface that "monotheism is in truth atheism,"[395] Levinas asserts that "the monotheist faith" (*la foi monothéiste*), if truly faithful, must eradicate all vestiges of myth, and, hence, incongruously, it implies a metaphysical atheism (*l'athéisme métaphysique*).[396] On this accord, the anti-idolatrous and aniconic truth of Judaism is best served by affirming an orthopraxis that requires heeding the demand of holiness without assenting to theological dogma. Several years prior to the publication of *Totality and Infinity*, Levinas expressed the matter in the lecture "A Religion for Adults," given in 1957 at the Abbey of Tioumliline in Morocco:

> Jewish monotheism does not exalt a sacred power, a *numen* triumphing over other numinous powers but still participating in their clandestine and mysterious life. The God of the Jews is not the survivor of mythical gods. . . . Monotheism marks a break with a certain conception of the Sacred. It neither unifies nor hierarchizes the numerous and numinous gods; instead it denies them. As regards the Divine which they incarnate, it is merely atheism.[397]

A very bold statement indeed: vis-à-vis the idolatrous celebration of the sacramental power of the gods, which is viewed as a form of violence, the monotheism established by Abraham is atheism. In what strikes the ear as utopian enthusiasm, Levinas characterizes the idea of infinity, which is set against the God of positive religions, as the "*dawn of a humanity without myths*." Transcendence, therefore, is distinguished from a "union with the transcendent by participation," the mythopoeic idea that still informs "believers of positive religions."[398] Even though Levinas insists that *correlation does not suffice as a category for transcendence*, inasmuch as the "idea of Infinity implies the separation of the same with regard to the other,"[399] he seems to follow the correlative dialogic of Cohen, Buber, and Rosenzweig when he writes that revelation is "discourse," which requires "a separated being" (*un être séparé*) as the interlocutor. "To hear the divine word," accordingly, "does not amount to knowing an object; it is to be in relation with a substance overflowing its own idea in me . . . Discourse, which is at the same time foreign and present, suspends participation and, beyond object-cognition, institutes the pure experience of the social relation, where a being does not draw its existence from its contact with the other." The emphasis on the social relation is meant to call attention to the fact that the "dimension of the divine opens forth from the human face," and thus it is a "relation with the Transcendent free from all captivation by the Transcendent" (*Une relation avec le Transcendant—cependant libre de toute emprise du Transcendant*).[400] The idea of infinity requires this sense of separation so profoundly that the very atheism it entails may lead to the forgetfulness of the idea of infinity. Indeed, the possibility of the "forgetting of transcendence" is necessary for separation.[401] The epiphany of transcendence borders on atheism to the extent that the being of that transcendence is cancelled out, an idea that Levinas anchors in the Jewish tradition concerning the writing of the ineffable name:

> Approaching [God] through a proper name is to assert an irreducible relation to knowledge which thematizes, defines or synthesizes and which, through these very acts, understands what this knowledge correlates as being, as finite and as immanent. It is to understand revelation both as a modality which paradoxically preserves transcendence from what is revealed, and consequently as something that goes beyond the capacity of an intuition, and even of a concept. . . . The square letters are a precarious dwelling from which the revealed Name is already withdrawn; erasable letters at the mercy of the man who traces or copies out. A writing . . . in which transcendence is cancelled out, an epiphany bordering on atheism.[402]

As Levinas put it in a relatively early characterization of the *il y a*, responding to Durkheim's notion of the "impersonality of the sacred in primitive religions": "Rather than to a God, the notion of the *there is* leads us to the absence of God, the absence of any being."[403]

On the anthropological level as well, Levinas criticizes the egoistic sense of subjectivity by appealing to "the atheism of the I" (*l'athéisme du moi*), which "marks the break with participation and consequently the possibility of seeking a justification for oneself, that is, a dependence upon an exteriority without this dependence absorbing the dependent being. . . . In the quest for truth, a work eminently individual, which always, as Descartes saw, comes back to the freedom of the individual, atheism affirms itself as atheism [*l'athéisme s'affirmait comme athéisme*]."[404] What is the import of this tautology? How could atheism affirm itself except as atheism? What Levinas wishes to emphasize is that the "ultimate knowing" of the self is not determined by the egoism of the *for itself* but rather by the questioning of the self that arises in the turning of the self to what is prior to the self, the presence of the Other. That "privileged heteronomy" of the Other invests the self with the spontaneity of freedom that is essential to the creatureliness of what it is to be human. The "marvel of creation," which Levinas depicts in the traditional idiom of *creatio ex nihilo*, "results in a being capable of receiving a revelation, learning that it is created, and putting itself in question." The formation of "moral being," therefore, implies the atheism of which we spoke, but at the same time extending beyond atheism, which consists of the sense of "shame for the arbitrariness of the freedom that constitutes it."[405]

With this turn to the ethical, we can appreciate better the link between monotheism and atheism: "The atheism of the metaphysician means, positively, that our relationship with the Metaphysical is an ethical behavior and not theology, not a thematization, be it a knowledge by analogy, of the attributes of God." Levinas is willing, therefore, to depict the "total Transcendence of the other" as "the invisible but personal God" (*le Dieu invisible, mais personnel*).[406] The possibility of an invisible being is plausible, but it is not easy to conjure the notion of a personal being that is invisible unless one resorts to the positing of spiritual entities that would embroil Levinas in an ontotheological conception of the infinite he sought to avoid in affirming an inapparent illeity that resists representation. To be sure, as Wyschogrod noted, in speaking about the resolute transcendence of the other, Levinas deployed the third-person pronoun *il* rather than the second-person *tu* in order to eschew "the language of intimate relation, thereby distinguishing himself from the interpretation of the divine/human encounter as depicted by Martin Buber."[407] Notwithstanding the legitimacy of this distinction, even according to Levinas, the *invisible but personal God* cannot be approached outside of "human presence"—indeed, divine invisibility implies not only that God is "unimaginable" but that God is accessible only in the pursuit of justice, "the uprightness of the face to face" (*la droiture du face-à-face*), and hence ethics is identified as "the spiritual optics" (*l'optique spirituelle*)[408]—and yet it cannot be reduced to a fabrication of human consciousness without compromising its alterity.

The avowal that God is inextricably bound to the interhuman makes it difficult, if not well-nigh impossible, to separate the theocentric and anthropocentric dimensions of the Levinasian project and renders, in my mind, the contention that Levinas assented to a purely secular philosophy of intersubjective transcendence dubious.[409] As Levinas himself observed, "the distinction between transcendence toward the other man and transcendence toward God should not be made too quickly,"[410] even though in the same context he qualifies this claim by asserting that the term *transcendence* is employed without any "theological presupposition."[411] Elsewhere, however, Levinas observes that "theology or the intelligibility of the transcendent . . . announces itself in the very wakefulness of insomnia, in the vigil and troubled vigilance of the psyche before the moment when the finitude of being, wounded by the infinite, is prompted to gather itself into the hegemonic and atheist Ego of knowledge."[412] In the interview with Wyschogrod, Levinas approves of the latter's suggestion that "the staging of religion is the same as the staging of ethics" and maintains that his "central thesis" turns on appreciating that the "structure that is divinity" is the constitution of society, for divinity is naught but going toward another human being.[413] Is the price enacted here not the attenuation of transcendence and the adaptation of what should be unknown to the demands of societal norms? The tension of which I speak comes to a head in Levinas's contention that the infinite "speaks" (*il parle*) followed by the disclaimer that "he does not have the mythical format that is impossible to confront."[414] In my judgment, to allege that the infinite speaks, let alone solicits and appeals to human beings, is to implicate the infinite in the very myth making that Levinas tries to avoid and thus threatens to entangle ethics in the ontotheological framework.

METAPHORIC INCARNATION AND POETIC ABSTRACTION

Let me reiterate that I am fully aware that the discourse with God, according to Levinas, is a language that "leads above being" (*elle-mène au-dessus de l'être*),[415] begetting, in Wyschogrod's locution, a "supra-ontological metaphysics."[416] I am also cognizant that the image of the face utilized by Levinas is meant to intimate an alterity that cannot be known or named, the "wholly open" that "is in the trace of illeity," that which "is beyond the visible that offers itself to our gaze, or to the power of representation."[417] The metaphors of discourse and the face nevertheless are modes of personifying infinity that may assault the neutrality and incommensurability of otherness. As Levinas expresses it in another comment: "The face speaks [*Le visage parle*]. The manifestation of the face is already discourse. . . . The eyes break through the mask—the language of the eyes, impossible to dissemble. The eye does not shine; it speaks."[418] Even if we were to accept the notion that the *speaking* ascribed to the face or to the eye is not a conventional language made of words but rather the linguistic marking of the relationship of proximity that always contains a surplus of signification—and consequently, as Levinas stated in his interview with Wyschogrod, there is no ascription of a special power to language vis-à-vis being as we find in Jewish mysticism or the idea central to Heideggerian poetics that the "whole of language bears the ultimate secret of the absolute"[419]—it is still a mode of figuratively representing the "uncontainable"[420] that theoretically exceeds any figuration. Simply put, the disclosure of transcendence in any form of revelatory giving suggests that the mind submits in the end to imaging the unimaginable rather than remaining speechless in apophatic unknowing and aporetic suspension. It is of interest in this regard to mention the following entry in Levinas's recently published notebooks: "*Accomplissement. Symbole. Notions essentielles pour l'évasion de l'existence. Sacrement. Figuration.*"[421] The way to transcendence—the escape from existence—is accomplished through the symbol, which, for Levinas, is not an "image of a veiled reality" (*image de l'être voilé*) but the "prefiguration of the implementation" (*préfiguration de l'accomplissement*).[422] The performative nature of the symbolic, which is expressive of the "wondrous fecundity" (*fécondité miraculeuse*) of time,[423] necessitates the figurative confabulation of the impersonal—or perhaps the transpersonal[424]—transcendence beyond configuration.

That Levinas was conscious of this dilemma is evident as well from an additional remark he made to Wyschogrod: "it is absolutely necessary to compare the incomparable, and, in consequence, to think in language. In speech, alongside of Saying there absolutely must be a said."[425] The pre-original saying, which is beyond being, always shows itself enigmatically in the said, and it is thus always betrayed by any statement of signification that intends a meaning of being.[426] The true peril, however, is that the said continuously engulfs the Saying, for without the said—a specific cultural demonstration such as the Bible, which Levinas presumed to be an illustration of a "said that is inspired," the "sacred language"[427]—there is no access to the Saying. In kabbalistic terms, there is no seeing without a garment, and even the nameless is accessible only through the investiture of the name. For Levinas, the disclosing of the face of the neighbor always "escapes representation," inasmuch as "it is the very collapse of phenomenality" (*il est la défection même de la phénoménalité*), and hence the disclosing thereof is an abandoning of self that is "more naked than nudity" (*plus nu que la nudité*).[428] But the face is also "weighted down with a skin" (*visage s'alourdissant de peau*) through which it breathes, and this skin, to some extent, enclothes the nakedness of the face. The skin is "the divergency between the visible and the invisible [*l'écart entre le visible et l'invisible*], quasi-transparent, thinner than that which would still justify an expression of the invisible by the visible." The face, therefore, is simultaneously "an enormous presence and the withdrawal of this presence" (*une présence énorme et le retrait de cette présence*). This retreat is "not a negation of presence" or even "its pure latency"; that is, it is not something that is not, a presence that is presently absent, but rather the "alterity" that is "without common measure with a presence or a past assembling into a synthesis in the synchrony of the correlative."[429] Wyschogrod astutely noted that the Levinasian notion of infinity ensures the axiom that the "otherness of the other person cannot be sublated and is construed as a species of an-iconic transcendence . . . The submissiveness of the subject becomes, for Levinas, the condition of an ethics that has been theologized and a theology that has been ethicized."[430] The determinant of a moral life rests on this disincarnate notion of alterity and the insuperable difference between self and other, and yet, the business of ethics entails comprehending the self as an incarnate being not only gripped by its own suffering and death but marked by the "most passive, unassumable, passivity" (*la passivité la plus passive, l'inassumable*), the "subjectivity or the very subjection of the subject," the "exposedness of the subject to another," the "disinterestedness" (*désintér-essement*) and "proximity" vis-à-vis the neighbor, to the point of "being obsessed with the oppressed who is other than myself."[431]

Here we come upon the positive connotation of the incarnation of consciousness that Levinas affirms in *Otherwise than Being* in his analysis of the phenomenon of recurrence, which is to be sought "beyond or on the hither side of consciousness and its play, beyond or on the hither side of being which it thematizes, outside of being, and thus in itself as in exile."[432] The provocative claim that for the self to be in itself it is as if it were in exile—*en soi comme en exil*—challenges the Hegelian notion of self-consciousness, based on the "reduction of subjectivity to consciousness," as well as the Husserlian conception of the immanent time of consciousness, whereby the self is the "ideal pole of an identification across the multiplicity of psychic silhouettes kerygmatically proclaimed to be the same by virtue of a mysterious schematism of discourse."[433] The self "does not enter into that play of exposing and dissimulations which we call a phenomenon (or phenomenology, for the appearing of a phenomenon is already a discourse). The oneself takes refuge or is exiled in its own fullness, to the point of explosion or fission, in view of its own reconstitution in the form of an identity in the said. . . . . . The oneself cannot form itself; it is already formed with absolute passivity."[434] The incarnation of subjectivity is measured by the weight and burden of this "passivity more passive still than any passivity" (*passivité plus passive que toute passivité*), the being-for-the-other that necessitates "the de-posing or de-situating of the ego" (*la dé-position ou la de-stitution du Moi*), the corporealization of a self despite it-self predicated on the attachment and the vulnerability one undergoes in being ex-posed to the other,[435] "something irreversibly past, prior to all memory and all recall,"[436] the "unexceptionable homeland of dialectical negativity," the "negativity characteristic of the *in itself* [*l'*en soi] without the openness of nothingness," the "recurrence by con-traction,"[437] that is, the "recurrence to oneself out of an irrecusable exigency of the other, a duty overflowing my being, a duty becoming a debt and an extreme passivity prior to the tranquility, still quite relative, in the inertia and materiality of things at rest. It is a restlessness and patience that support prior to action and passion."[438] Incar-nation, in a word, is Levinas's way of naming the exteriority of self and consequent exposure to alterity, the "trace of the diachrony of the one-for-the-other," the "trace of *separation* in the form of inwardness, and of the for-the-other in the form of responsi-bility." Identity of self is not achieved through "self-confirmation" but "as a signification of the one-for-the-other," a "deposing of oneself" (*déposition de soi*), which is "the incarna-tion of the subject [*l'incarnation du sujet*], or the very possibility of giving [*la possibilité même de donner*], of dealing signifyingness [*de* bailler *signifiance*]."[439]

The implications of the Levinasian idea of incarnation are drawn concisely by Wyschogrod: "If Levinas is to retain the transcendence of alterity while avoiding the pitfalls of noumenality, he must have recourse to phenomena that, as it were, erase their own phenomenality, images given empirically yet apprehended discursively in nonpredicative fashion."[440] The ethics of transcendence may involve an irreconcilable tension between the metaphorical tropes of the face and the trace, the former demar-cating the embodied corporeity demanded by the specificity of the other and the latter the disincarnation that is necessary to safeguard the glory of the infinite as the other that is forever beyond our grasp. If spiritual optics is an imageless vision that is "bereft of the synoptic and totalizing objectifying virtues of vision,"[441] should this not culmi-nate in an atheological showing, an apophatic venturing beyond the theomorphic need to configure the transcendent to the disfiguration of facing the face that neces-sarily is no face because it cannot be faced, the contemplation of the meta/figure, the inessential essence that is (non)human? I am mindful of the fact that in describing the beyond being, Levinas insists that systems are interrupted by the "superlative" that exceeds them rather than by the "negation of concepts."[442] Levinas's ambivalence to-ward apophasis is evident as well in his statement that the trace left by the infinite is not "the residue of a presence," for if that were so, then "its positivity would not pre-serve the infinity of the infinite any more than negativity would."[443] Even so, it does appear that just as the idolatrous moment in art occurs when the good is absorbed by the form,[444] so for Levinas the rejection of representation with regard to the face leads him to a figuration of the disfigured through the utilization of copious images to un-derscore the insufficiency of imagery.[445] Can there be a way to accommodate in resem-blance the positive theistic depictions of the divine without acquiescing to idolatry? Is the human imagination capable of escaping the web of metaphoricity, or will it continue to be coerced into constructing images of the unimaginable in the sublime hope of representing the unrepresentable and thinking the unthinkable?

A meticulous scrutiny of Levinas's comments on the nature of metaphor scattered in his writings indicates that he would respond negatively to my rhetorical query. He was adroitly aware that metaphor, which is labeled the form of "poetic abstraction" through which the "innumerable significations" of an object of representation are incarnated,[446] is the only vehicle of language available to us that leads beyond experience to the relationship with the Other (*relation avec l'Autre*), theologically rendered as "being with God" (*être avec Dieu*)[447] or as an "orientation toward God" (*orientation vers Dieu*).[448] Levinas began his lecture on metaphor in the Collège philosophique on February 26, 1962, by noting that the word—derived from the Greek *metapherein*, to put one thing in place of another—etymologically indicates the "transfer of meaning" (*un transfert du sens*), which he explicates as the "semantic elevation" (*une élévation sémantique*) that entails "the passage from a basic and down to earth sense to a more nuanced and more noble sense, a miraculous surplus" (*le passage d'un sens élémentaire et terre à terre à un sens plus nuancé et plus noble, un miraculeux surplus*),[449] the excess (*dépassement*) of the trace that is "the essential event of language in-the-face-of-the-Other" (*l'événement essentiel du langage est en-face-de-l'Autre*).[450]

Years before Levinas remarked that metaphor is the "essence of language" that resides in the "impulsion to the extreme in the superlative that is always more superlative than transcendence."[451] All linguistic signification is metaphorical insofar as it "leads upward" (*elle mène vers là-haut*), the "irreducible movement" that transports one beyond to "the infinity of the Other" (*l'infini de l'Autre*), which is the "foundation of human spirituality."[452] Just as one could not hear the voice of God without metaphor, so there would be no metaphor without God (*Sans métaphore on ne peut pas entendre la voix de Dieu. . . . Il faut retourner la réflexion: sans Dieu il n'y aurait pas de métaphore*). God, on this account, can be designated the "very metaphor of language," the "thought that rises above itself" (*Dieu est la métaphore même du langage—le fait d'une pensée qui se hausse au-dessus d'elle-même*). This is not to say that God is merely a metaphor but rather that there is no movement toward him except through metaphor (*Ce qui ne veut pas dire que Dieu n'est qu'une métaphore. Car il n'y a d'autre métaphore que le mouvement qui porte vers Lui*),[453] and thus God can be depicted as the metaphor par excellence[454] or as the metaphor of metaphors.[455] Translated into a different jargon, God is the trace of the trace, the trace of what is nothing apart from being a trace.[456] By speaking of the Absolute that is beyond being in this manner, Levinas is affirming both the intractable metaphoricity of theological discourse and its ineludible demetaphorization, the double sense captured in the word *à-Dieu*, going toward God that is at the same time bidding farewell to the world,[457] being transported elsewhere that is nowhere at all. Metaphor can be defined as "the reference to absence" if it is understood that this absence is not "another given" that is either "still to come" or "already past" but an absence that can never be present, the imperceptible meaning that "would not be the consolation for a delusive perception but would only *make perception possible*,"[458] the illeity that is "situated beyond the calculations and reciprocities of economy and of the world," an illeity whose presence is determined by an absence on account of which we can assert that "being has a sense," albeit a sense "which is not a finality."[459] Based on this manner of reckoning, the quintessential metaphor is the idea of infinity, for to think this term is to refuse its very thinkability.[460] In the end, metaphor is the supreme measure of human thought—indeed, the superhuman element in language (*le surhumain dans le langage*)[461]—and the only way to overcome metaphor is through metaphor, as Levinas remarked, "*La métaphore—le dépassement métaphorique—reste cependant à la mesure de la pensée.*"[462] Metaphor signifies the movement in language toward infinity about which there is no language, the response to the other that always exceeds what is said.[463] Levinas alludes to the same paradox years later when he noted that metaphor is the "amplification of thought" (*une amplification de la pensée*), the movement "that persists as movement while no longer being movement" («*Mouvement de la pensée» reste du mouvement tout en n'étant plus mouvement*).[464]

EMBODIED NAKED AND THE DEMETAPHORIZATION OF THE FACE

By identifying metaphor as the impulse in language that guides one to the transcendent other beyond language, one might be tempted to assume that Levinas is guilty of the position epitomized in the well-known statement of Heidegger, "The metaphorical exists only within metaphysics [*Das Metaphorische gibt es nur innerhalb der Metaphysik*],"[465] and implied as well in the last section of Derrida's "White Mythology," which is entitled *La métaphysique—relève de la métaphore*.[466] A thorough exposition of the role of metaphor in Heidegger and Derrida is a topic that is obviously too vast and complex to treat adequately here.[467] What I would emphasize, however, is that even though Levinas characterized metaphor as a form of transposing or carrying-over, the link he forges between the metaphorical and what might be called the metasemantic is not indicative of the representationalism that has informed the metaphysical bias of Western philosophy based on a binary distinction between the literal and the figurative meanings, which corresponds to the distinction between the sensible and the nonsensible realms.[468] For Levinas, the movement of metaphor is the act of signification by which one has recourse to the Infinite, an infinity that "does not present itself to a transcendental thought, nor even to meaningful activity, but presents itself in the Other; the Other faces me and puts me in question and *obliges* me by his essence qua infinity. That 'something' we call signification arises in being with language because the essence of language is the relation with the Other."[469] Through metaphor one is transported to the "hither side," the beyond essence or otherwise than being, the movement of language that starts "from the trace retained by the said, in which everything shows itself" and through which the "indescribable is described."[470] This trace, which is the face of the Other, is a "trace of itself" (*trace de lui-même*), a "trace expelled in a trace" (*trace expulsée dans la trace*),[471] the doubling of the trace, which is "the very signifyingness of signification" (*la signifiance même de la signification*)[472] that "does not signify an indeterminate phenomenon" but rather the "non-indifference to another" (*non-indifférence pour l'autre*), "the one-for-the other" (*l'un-pour-l'autre*),[473] an invitation to be exposed to the other, an "exposure of this exposedness," which is exposed in the "expression of exposure," identified as the "saying."[474] Metaphor is the mode of ambiguity by which the presence of the face signifies its absence and the absence of the face its presence, the gesture of saying that marks the breaking point (*rupture*) where the "essence is exceeded by the infinite" but also the place of binding (*nouement*).[475] The "glow of the trace" is thus distinguished from the "appearing of phenomena," for the "trace is sketched out [*se dessine*] and effaced [*s'efface*] in a face in the equivocation of a saying. In this way it modulates the modality of the transcendent."[476] The transport of the metaphoric facilitates this modulation on the basis of an essential complicity between the visible and the invisible, the known and the unknown: the Infinite "is revealed without appearing, without *showing* itself as Infinite,"[477] the imagelessness that haunts every image, the face that is concomitantly the trace of the nonmanifest in the manifest and of the manifest in the nonmanifest.

Hent De Vries has argued that the perspective on transcendence to be elicited from the writings of Adorno and Levinas "is more paradoxical—indeed, is surreptitious—and permanently runs the risk of idolatry and blasphemy. This is not due to a lack of consistency or rigor in their philosophical projects: rather, of the *tertium datur* there can be neither truth or falsity, since this dimension is at once indestructible or irrepressible and undecidable or aporetic. It can only be 'said' through 'unsaying' and cannot be 'unsaid' without entangling it—once again—in the 'said' that the 'unsaying' interrupts, only immediately to betray itself in turn, ad infinitum."[478] Although de Vries acknowledges the "echo" or "resonance" of monotheistic religion in Levinas's characterization of the infinitely Other and thus accepts that this "central motif" in Judaism "in part determines the tone and texture of his philosophical thinking," he nonetheless insists that Levinas did not construct, reconstruct, or deconstruct "a religious philosophy in the systematic, let alone dogmatic, theological sense. Therefore, religious tradition cannot weigh decisively in an evaluation of the contribution of his figures of thought to a minimal theology whose modus operandi lies in the diminishing yet still remaining dimension of the almost invisible, the nearly untouchable, the scarcely audible, *in pianissimo*."[479] While I agree that one cannot elicit a systematic or dogmatic theology from Levinas, I do not concur that the impact of his Jewish faith was as limited as de Vries argues. On the contrary, it seems to me that it is precisely this commitment that renders his metaphysics of transcendence problematic and suspect of succumbing to theolatry. I thus respectfully take issue with the conclusion reached by de Vries:

Levinas's late work consistently explores a modality of transcendence which can dispense with the complementary false affirmatives of a complete negativity of the same (and hence absence of the other) or an unambiguous positivity (and hence presence) of the other. The trace makes plausible the diminishing but still remaining intelligibility of the discourse concerning transcendence in general and God in particular without once again burdening philosophy with a questionable ontotheology, the metaphysics of presence or absence to which theism and its analogues, yet likewise atheism with its naturalisms and humanisms, fall prey. A far more complicated relationship between infinity and fulfillment holds among all these historical, traditional and modern, dogmatic and enlightened, doctrines.[480]

I do not accept the surmise of de Vries that Levinas's thought "touches profoundly on that of an open, that is to say, negative dialectical speculation: micrologically encircling a transcendence in immanence or immanence in transcendence that is, at the same time, a transcendence of transcendence and, hence, an immanence thought and experienced *otherwise*."[481] I do not see evidence for the transcendence of transcendence that would lead to the immanent positivity without recourse to the positing of the negative qua negative, that is, the negative that in no way is reduced to the positive, the transcendence that is transcendentally immanent only by being immanently transcendent. Only in relation to this surplus can we speak of the creation as a "transcendental condition."[482] Alternatively, transcendence is marked linguistically by the word "face" (*visage*) because it conveys the "negation of the world by speaking of the world" (*négation du monde en parlant du monde*).[483] It seems to me this move is absolutely necessary to preserve Levinas's insistence that the "encounter in dialogue" is a "thought thinking beyond the world."[484]

I understand full well that the trope of invisibility is used by Levinas, as he writes in *Otherwise than Being*, to depict the nonpresence of the Good,[485] the event of being that is beyond the binary of ipseity and alterity, and to enunciate the fact that subjectivity—the inimitable unicity of self that withdraws from essence and thus is without the identity of an ego coinciding with itself[486]—is irreducible to consciousness and thematization. Proximity, therefore, is "the relationship with the other, who cannot be resolved into 'images' or be exposed in a theme. . . . Not able to stay in a theme, not able to appear, this invisibility which becomes contact and obsession is due not to the nonsignifyingness of what is approached, but to a way of signifying quite different from that which connects exposition to sight." Signification relates to the characteristic of transcendence beyond visibility, which is expressed in the "surplus of responsibility" that one must bear for the other, the "very signifyingness of signification, which signifies in saying before showing itself in the said."[487] Although I appreciate that the other cannot be "tamed" or "domesticated" thematically, I am not convinced that this notion of invisible subjectivity is sustainable as a foundation for the ethical relationship as described by Levinas. The admonition of Wyschogrod is well placed: "Kant's formless and figureless imperatives are supplanted by the figure of the unfigurable, the face of the other, which despite Levinas's caveats about its aniconicity, attains ethical significance because the other is a vulnerable being of flesh and blood."[488] The "glory of the Infinite" to be staged in the social arena implies that transcendence, the beyond essence, is concurrently a being-in-the-world (*A la transcendance—à l'au-delà de l'essence qui est aussi être-au-monde*).[489] Levinas insists nevertheless that the "diachrony of transcendence," the "saying beyond being and its time" (*en Dire d'au-delà de l'être et son temps*), cannot "enter into the unity of transcendental apperception," and therefore the "transcendence is not convertible into immanence."[490] Here it is relevant to mention Janicaud's contrast between the "overcoming of intentionality" and the "opening of phenomenology to the invisible" that one finds respectively in Merleau-Ponty and Levinas. The sole methodological guide directing Merleau-Ponty is the "patient interrogation of the visible," a way that "presupposes nothing other than an untiring desire for elucidation of that which most hides itself away in experience." Merleau-Ponty was "passionately" committed to the phenomenological inasmuch as he assiduously sought "to think phenomenality intimately, the better to inhabit it," in order to open "our regard to the depth of the world." By stark contrast, in the case of Levinas, "the directly dispossessing aplomb of alterity supposes a nonphenomenological, metaphysical desire. . . . It supposes a metaphysico-theological montage, prior to philosophical writing. The dice are loaded and choices made; faith rises majestically in the background."[491] One may object to the overly dramatic tone used by Janicaud, but the substance of his comment is accurate. The invisible affirmed by Levinas is not the invisible of the visible, a doubling back and deepening of the sensible, but the invisible alterity of the God of the biblical tradition, and, consequently, "theology is restored with its parade of capital letters," a theology that "dispenses with giving itself the least title" but which "installs itself at the most intimate dwelling of consciousness."[492]

I accept the need to contrast the metaphysical transcendence affirmed by Levinas in *Totality and Infinity* and the transcendence without metaphysics in *Otherwise than Being*,[493] but the notion of illeity of the latter is analogous to the *invisible but personal God* of the former. Indeed, already in *Totality and Infinity*, Levinas wrote that the "relationship with exteriority," the "beyond being" (*au-delà de l'être*), "consists not in being presented as a theme but in being open to desire [*à se laisser désirer*]; the existence of the separated being which desires exteriority no longer consists in caring for Being. To exist has a meaning in another dimension than that of the perduration of the totality; it can go beyond being."[494] The relation with this exteriority is not realized in the Spinozistic monism, the "universality of thought," but in the pluralism that ensues from the "goodness of being for the Other, in justice."[495] Even so, the desire for the dimension of what is beyond being—the desire that consists of being open to desire, "the metaphysical desire" (*le désir métaphysique*) to which Levinas refers in the very beginning of the first section of *Totality and Infinity*, a "desire for the invisible" (*le désir de l'invisible*), a tending "toward *something else entirely* [*tout autre chose*], toward the *absolutely other* [*l'absolument autre*]"⁴⁹⁶—necessitates the "surpassing of being starting from being" (*le dépassement de l'être à partir de l'être*).⁴⁹⁷ The other must persist in its otherness, and therefore alterity defies an immanentization that would do away with transcendence. It is from this standpoint, as I noted above, that Levinas deploys language that is tacitly critical of the incarnational foundation of Christian logocentrism and affirmative of the traditional Jewish aniconism.⁴⁹⁸

The transcendental apperception in Husserlian phenomenology is not sufficient to account for the radical transcendence necessary to establish the ground for genuine alterity—the "blinking and dia-chrony of enigma"—since what is configured as "outside" consciousness is exterior only from the perspective of the interior, and hence immanence will always triumph over transcendence.⁴⁹⁹ As an enterprise that probes the conditions that make it possible for a phenomenon to be a phenomenon, phenomenology is deficient in its ability to reveal transcendence beyond phenomenality. The inapparent can appear only to the extent that it is subsumed under the taxon of the apparent—what appears as inapparent appears nonetheless.⁵⁰⁰ In *Otherwise than Being*, Levinas offers a tantalizing undoing of theism along this line of inquiry: "Is not the inescapable fate in which being immediately includes the statement of being's *other* not due to the hold the *said* has over the *saying*, to the *oracle* in which the said is immobilized? Then would not the bankruptcy of transcendence be but that of a theology that thematizes the *transcending* in the logos [*la faillite d'une théologie thématisant, dans le logos, le* transcender], assigns a term to the passing of transcendence, congeals it into a 'world behind the scenes' [*'arrière monde'*], and installs what it says in war and in matter, which are the inevitable modalities of the fate woven by being in its interest?"⁵⁰¹ And in an even bolder statement in the 1976 lecture "In Praise of Insomnia": "We then interpreted this breaking open of experience in witnessing, this agitation of the Same by the Other, as the *diachrony* of time. This is a time that would lend itself [*se donnerait*] to our understanding as a reference to God—as the *to-God* itself [*l'à-Dieu meme*]—before being interpreted as a pure deficiency or as a synonym of the perishable or the noneternal. That is, what gives itself to be understood as that which is diametrically opposed to the traditional idea of God."⁵⁰²

These statements, and others that could have been cited, imply that Levinas sought to surmount the ontotheological understanding of God as person while holding on to that very understanding in order to ground his ethics. There is no denying that the process is an attenuation of the imagination. Thus, in one of the few places where he mentions the imaginary prowess explicitly, he writes: "It is from moral relationships that every metaphysical affirmation takes on a 'spiritual' meaning, is purified of everything with which an imagination captive of things and victim of participation charges our concepts. The ethical relation is defined, in contrast with every relation with the sacred, by excluding every signification it would take on *unbeknown* to him who maintains that relation. . . . Everything that cannot be reduced to an interhuman relation represents not the superior form but the forever primitive form of religion."[503] The need to strip religious language of every investiture of imagination extends for Levinas to an apophasis of the apophasis, that is, to severing transcendence from the "word-less, negative theology."[504] Thus, he adamantly declares that the "non-presence of the infinite is not only a figure of negative theology. All the negative attributes which state what is beyond the essence become positive in responsibility, a response answering to a non-thematizable provocation and thus a non-vocation, a trauma."[505] Negative attributes are not simply limiting; there is metaphorical force to negation.[506] With respect to this interpretation of the Neoplatonic apophatic tradition, Levinas is closer to Cohen than he is to Rosenzweig, even if he thought of his own thinking as continuing the path of the latter's critique of totality.[507]

It is on this very point, moreover, that Levinas breaks with the correlation between thought and the world posited by Husserl and the phenomenological assumption that "appearing" is a "giving itself" to intentional consciousness.[508] The "thought awakened to God" is described as a thought that "aspires to a *beyond*, to a *deeper than oneself*—aspiring to a transcendence different from the *out-of-oneself* that the intentional consciousness opens and traverses."[509] The thinking he is seeking "is neither assimilation of the Other to the Same nor integration of the Other into the Same, a thinking which does not bring all transcendence back to immanence . . . What is needed is a thought which is no longer constructed as a relation of thinking to what is thought about, in the domination of thinking over what is thought about; what is needed is a thought which is not restricted to the rigorous correspondence between noesis and noema and not restricted to the adequation where the visible must be equal to the intentional aim (*la visée*), to which the visible would have to respond in the intuition of truth; what is needed is a thought for which the very metaphor of vision and aim (*visée*) is no longer legitimate."[510]

In disputing the implicit solipsism of Husserlian intentionality, Levinas was undoubtedly influenced by the ruminations on transcendence proffered by his close friend and colleague Jean Wahl.[511] According to Wahl, there is a form of transcendence (or, to be more precise, *transdescendence* as opposed to *transascendence*) that is a movement "directed toward immanence, whereby the transcendence transcends itself" (*lorsque la transcendance se transcende elle-même*). Perhaps the greatest transcendence is that which consists of transcending the transcendence, that is to say, of falling back into immanence (*Peut-être la plus grande transcendance est-elle celle qui consiste à transcender la transcendance, c'est-à-dire à retomber dans l'immanence*). The attainment of the "second immanence" appears "after the destroyed transcendence" (*après la transcendance détruite*), but that transcendence "is never completely destroyed, never completely transcended," resting in the "background of spirit like the idea of a lost paradise," the bereavement for which generates the hope and longing for a presence that constitutes the "value of our attachment to the here-below."[512] Immanence is valorized as something positive only insofar as it points to the absolute, nameless one,

the mystery that transcends all existing realities in the world. Utilizing another terminological distinction made by Wahl, we can differentiate between the "transcendent
immanence of perception" and the "immanent transcendence of ecstasy." The former
is correlated with the silence of positive ontology "in which the mind is nourished by
things," and the latter with the silence of negative ontology, the "mystical event,"
wherein the "mind achieves union with its own highest point, which is at the same
time the highest point of the world."[513] In this highest point, objectivity and subjectivity converge in their mutual dissolution, and one is led dialectically to the self-
transcending transcendence, the transcendence that transcends and thereby preserves
itself in the immanence that is the web of interrelational entities.[514]

One can easily detect the importance of these reflections on Levinas's ongoing endeavor to communicate as effectively as possible his theory of transcendence. As I have
emphasized, it cannot be denied that he sought to affirm a transcendence that is not
to be relocated absolutely in the terrain of immanence—neither transcendent immanence nor immanent transcendence captures the drift of Levinas's insight. As he put it
pithily in a conversation with Nemo, "The term 'transcendence' signifies precisely the
fact that one cannot think God and being together."[515] Whatever his ultimate intent,
the rhetoric of his texts indicates, however, that he could not avoid characterizing
transcendence in personal terms that efface the clear distinction between human and
divine and thus jeopardize the concept of alterity as the transcendent that is truly
other.

Quite nobly and admirably, Levinas described monotheism as a "supernatural gift"
of seeing that beneath the variety of the different historical traditions (Judaism, Christianity, and Islam), one person is absolutely like another person, and thus the word of
one God is what "obliges us to enter into discourse" in the hopes of forming a "homogeneous humanity." From Levinas's perspective, tolerance issues from the power of
monotheism, and this is what has made the "economy of solidarity" possible.[516] Lamentably, it is not clear that the current sociopolitical state of the world leaves much
hope that this kind of cohesion can be realized on the basis of monotheism and this in
spite of what we today call the global economy. The exigency of the moment may call
for the need to subjugate the monotheistic personification of God and the corresponding egoistic depiction of self, and this would demand a sweeping and uncompromising purification of the idea of the infinite from all predication. Would this not fulfill
Levinas's own aspiration for a heterological thought of pure difference, the "thinking
of the absolute without this absolute being reached as an end?"[517] Might this not
finally prompt the dawning of a humanity without myths, an era in which the three
Abrahamic religions could all accept that the monotheistic faith in its deepest assonance implies a metaphysical atheism? Only then would our notion of God be liberated from the last remnants of a phenomenological theology such that we may discard
all metaphorical language, even the nonmetaphorical metaphoricization of the face as
the nonappearing of the infinite other. Perhaps in this undoing we can genuinely

welcome the enigma of illeity, the "way of the Ab-solute" that is "foreign to cognition,"[518] that "which is 'too great' for the measure or finitude of presence, revelation,
order and being, and which consequently, as neither being nor non-being, is the 'excluded third party' of the beyond of being and non-being . . . perhaps also expressed
by the word God"[519]—the dissolution of the belief in a face that is not itself a mask
that justifies the continued use of theistic images to depict transcendence[520]—and
thereby open the possibility to the "blessing of multiplicity" referred to by Levinas in
the Wyschogrod interview, the conviction that "there are many more relations of love
in the world when there is plurality."[521]

Within the confines of this difference—to discern that Jew, Christian, and Muslim
are the same in virtue of being different—we can find the stirrings of the difficult
freedom that is the burden and honor of the "universalist particularism" at the heart
of Israel's messianic mission, which may in fact be the persistent resistance to any messianic fulfillment. It is worth recalling the cautionary words of Peter Gordon regarding Rosenzweig's view of redemption and the eternal future that is "permanently
proleptic" inasmuch as it is always not-yet: "To call this doctrine universalist seems
misleading, since it downplays the paradox that universalist hope can only function
on the basis of present exclusion."[522] This, it seems to me, is the tragic dimension of
Jewish messianism, epitomized in the aphorism of Kafka, cited already in a Levinasian sense by Blanchot,[523] that the Messiah will come on the day after he has arrived,
not the last day but on the very last day.[524] The *very last day*—the day that can never
come to pass in the wavering of time, the day that succeeds the last day, the day that
requires the pure patience of awaiting without something awaited.

CHAPTER 4

Secrecy of the Gift and the Gift of Secrecy

A truth at which one should arrive
Forbids immediate utterance,
And tongues to speak it must contrive
To tell two different lies at once.

—W. H. Auden,
"Reflections in a Forest"

In this chapter I will discuss the nexus of secrecy, the gift, and the apophatic in the thought of Derrida. Many scholars have weighed in on these themes, but I will reexamine them from the particular vantage point of the relation to Jewish mysticism that one may cull from the Derridean corpus. While my focal point is Derrida's understanding of kabbalah as an expression of polysemy and atheism, the ramifications of the ensuing analysis should put into sharp relief the theological appropriation of deconstruction attested in any number of *theo-philosophies of transcendence*[1] that have proliferated in the course of the last few decades, many of them centered especially on the metaphor of the gift.

UNHEIMLICHKEIT AND THE SPECTER OF JEWISH EXISTENCE

Our analysis must begin with the observation that notwithstanding the occasional references to the kabbalah in Derrida's writings, which assuredly are not marginal or inconsequential, Derrida never offered a sustained analysis of Jewish mysticism, nor has he intimated that a grasp of this material is critical for understanding his philosophic orientation. On the contrary, one of the most explicit statements of Derrida on the topic is an outright denial of such influence:

> I don't have anything against mysticism, it even interests me a lot, but in any case happily or unhappily, as you wish, I'm not mystical and there's nothing mystical in my work. My work is precisely the deconstruction of values that ground mysticism, i.e., presence, the look, absence of the sign, ineffability. When I say I am no mystic, above all no Jewish mystic, as Habermas maintains somewhere . . . I'm not only

personally not mystical, but I question whether anything I write has the least trace of mysticism. In that case there are many misunderstandings, not only between me and Habermas, but also between me and many German readers, so far as I can see. In part that's because German philosophers don't read my texts directly, but refer to secondary, American interpretations. When Habermas, for example, talks about my Jewish mysticism, he refers to an American book by Susan Handelman, which in my view is undoubtedly interesting, but very problematical in respect to the claim that I'm a lost son of Judaism. . . . Therefore, I don't demand that people read me as if they could transport themselves before my texts into an intuitive ecstasy, but I demand that people be more careful with the mediations, more critical in translation and with detours through contexts that are often very far from mine.[2]

The first thing to note is the essentializing tenor underlining Derrida's remarks concerning mysticism, a somewhat surprising move given his repeated emphasis on the need not to essentialize phenomena. The second thing to note is Derrida's unequivocal rejection of being referred to specifically as a Jewish mystic. One has to be struck by the self-assurance expressed by a thinker known for his unambiguous celebration of ambiguity! One can only conjecture that the label "mystic" in general, and the more specific pigeonholing "Jewish mystic," assigned to him by Habermas,[3] an opinion that Derrida claims inaccurately to be based on a book by Handelman,[4] hit a deep nerve. What was it that Habermas actually said that warranted such a categorical denial on the part of a man who wrote categorically against the possibility of rendering judgments categorically?

The context within which Habermas broaches the topic of Derrida's closeness to Jewish mysticism is the comparison and distinction he draws between deconstruction and the "movement of Heidegger's thought." Derrida's grammatology, according to Habermas, is still beholden to laying bare the "inverted foundationalism" of Heidegger "by once again going beyond the ontological difference and Being to the differance proper to writing, which puts an origin already set in motion yet one level deeper. . . . As a participant in the philosophical discourse of modernity, Derrida inherits the weaknesses of a critique of metaphysics that does not shake loose of the intentions of first philosophy." For Derrida, in contrast to Heidegger, it is "not the authority of a Being that has been distorted by beings, but the authority of a no longer holy scripture, of a scripture that is in exile, wandering about, estranged from its own meaning, a scripture that testamentarily documents the absence of the holy."[5] Habermas recognizes that the position embraced by Derrida is more subversive, and thus he "stands closer to the anarchist wish to explode the continuum of history than to the authoritarian admonition to bend before destiny."[6] It is with regard to this point that Habermas interjects that Derrida continues the tradition of Jewish mysticism by developing a "heretical exegesis of scripture" rather than following in the footsteps of Heidegger by retrieving a neo-paganism that would lead to a moment "beyond the beginnings of monotheism."[7] Utilizing Scholem's explanation of the kabbalistic approach to revelation, Habermas concludes that "Derrida's grammatologically circumscribed concept of an archewriting whose traces call forth all the more interpretations the more unfamiliar they become, renews the mystical concept of tradition as an ever *delayed* event of revelation. . . . Earnestly pursued deconstruction is the paradoxical labor of continuing a tradition in which the saving energy is only renewed by expenditure."[8] Building on Handelman's claim that Derrida's critique of Western logocentrism is a "reemergence of Rabbinic hermeneutics in a displaced way,"[9] Habermas notes,

> It is of great importance . . . that Derrida, unlike Heidegger, does not get the motif of a God that works through absence and withdrawal from the Romantic Dionysius reception (via Hölderlin), so as to be able to turn it—as an *archaic* motif—against monotheism. Rather, the active absence of God is a motif that he gets (via Levinas) from the Jewish tradition itself. . . . The work of deconstruction fosters an unacknowledged renewal of a discourse with God that has been broken off under *modern* conditions of an ontotheology that is no longer binding. The intention is, then, not to overcome modernity by having recourse to archaic sources, but to take specific account of the conditions of modern postmetaphysical thought, under which an ontotheologically insulated discourse with God cannot be continued.[10]

Derrida was not pleased with either the attempt to situate deconstruction as an endless play of textual interpretation within the scope of rabbinic hermeneutics—to deem it a kind of "Jewish science"[11]—or with the claim that it is a postmetaphysical renewal of discourse with God. The strong opposition to the marker "Jewish mystic," moreover, is based on his general rejection of mysticism, which he understands as a "state of intuitive ecstasy" by and through which one encounters an unspeakable presence, a presence that is absent, but a presence nonetheless. I will return to this critical point when I discuss the distinction that Derrida makes between negative theology and dénégation. What I would emphasize here is that Derrida's disapproval of being called a mystic is related to his contention that mysticism is a phenomenon that inevitably reinforces an ontotheological perspective.

Running the risk of stating the obvious, Derrida's strong reaction to Habermas and Handelman is a reflection of his very complicated relationship to Judaism. The degree of Derrida's alienation from Jewish tradition is discernible in many places in his writings, including, for instance, in his reflection on the childhood trauma he suffered in Algiers when he was thrown out of school together with other Jewish children:

> From that moment—how can I say it—I felt as displaced in a Jewish community, closed unto itself, as I would in the other (which they used to call "the Catholics"). . . . Symmetrically, oftentimes, I felt an impatient distance with regard to various Jewish communities, when I have the impression that they close in upon themselves, when they pose themselves as such. From all of which comes a feeling of non-belonging that I have doubtless transposed.[12]

Derrida's rupture from the textual and linguistic culture of Judaism is attested as well in an interesting way in the aside he made in an oral conversation about prayer: "And I was, of course, rebelling when I was a young Jewish boy in Algeria, and they forced me to pray in a language which was totally unintelligible to me. But, I think that at that moment, I understood something essential of the prayer. One can pray without understanding the words. . . . For me Hebrew is this. And it has to do with the book too. Because, of course, for the same reason pure prayer should be improvised."[13]

In spite of—indeed, precisely on account of—this estrangement from his Jewish identity, the latter imparted to Derrida the idiosyncratic way of belonging by not-belonging. In the previous chapter, I cited a passage from Derrida in which he characterized philosophy in these exact terms.[14] In other texts, the nature of secrecy is linked to this paradox.[15] Thus, for instance, Derrida comments on "the *Unheimlichkeit* of the *Geheimnis*" in *The Gift of Death*: "It is perhaps there that we find the secret of secrecy, namely, that it is not a matter of knowing and that it is for no-one. A secret doesn't belong, it can never be said to be at home or in its place [*chez soi*]."[16] Juxtaposing these different passages, we can surmise that, for Derrida, Judaism is not primarily a demarcation of ethno-religious identity but rather a literary trope that signifies what cannot be signified, the secret that characterizes the way of being human in the world. I revisit the matter of secrecy below, but suffice it here to underscore that the secret is not a mystery that is inherently unknowable but rather the unknowability that issues from there being nothing ontologically or metaphysically that is to be known, the open secret that there is no secret. Judaism thus provided Derrida with an existential template by which he could articulate the pretense of the secret, the sense of being in place by having no place. As Derrida expressed the matter in *Of Hospitality*:

> What is called the "mother" tongue is already "the other's language." If we are saying here that language is the native land, namely, what exiles, foreigners, all the wandering Jews in the world, carry away on the soles of their shoes, it is not to evoke a monstrous body, an impossible body, a body whose mouth and tongue would drag the feet along, and even drag about under the feet. It is because this is about the *step*, once again, of progression, aggression, transgression, digression.[17]

The epithet "wandering Jews" does not apply exclusively to those born into or converted to Judaism; it denotes rather the inherent homelessness of the human condition, the exilic nature of having no nature, an essential indeterminacy that is without any determinate essence.[18] Hélène Cixous, fellow French Jew growing up in Algeria and Derrida's lifelong friend, offered a poignant portrait of his struggle:

> Between the Jew and him the Jew they tell him he is, between what, without qualms and without consideration, one is accustomed to term Jewish he has always insisted on introducing the tip [*la pointe*] of a precaution in order to fend off the verdict's fatality the truth-saying of the verdict, this sense of being condemned and executed that is ineluctably engendered by the incredible circumcision scene.

Circumcised without his consent, before any word, before passivity even. The
point, the identifiable, the undeniable, the whole of his philosophy contests it. The
minute he risks capture, he begins to struggle. He will never agree to be taken
either for a Jewish Jew, or as a photo, at least not without putting up a fight.[19]

Circumcised without consent—an arresting image, to be sure, but one that is rather
negligible, since no infant Jewish boy can be thought of as offering consent to be circumcised. Not only is such a proposition ludicrous, but the nature of circumcision
entails that the baby being circumcised is offered like an animal sacrificed on the altar.
For Derrida, as Cixous suggests, circumcision is not a one-time occurrence. Each moment that he is alive, Derrida is compelled to relive the initial incision that he dog-
gedly resists, bearing the mark of that which refuses demarcation, struggling against
being classified as the one that defies classification.

LAST OF THE JEWS, COVENANTAL CUT, AND
WRITING THE IMPOSSIBLE

It goes without saying that Derrida did not position himself as a "Jewish" writer or
even as someone who writes primarily about themes of Jewish concern. On the contrary, he expressed the view that he is inside the tradition only by being outside it, that
for him the covenant (*alliance*) is a cut that has torn him apart from the very thing to
which he is bound.[20] As he instructs himself in the entry of December 30, 1976, in
Circonfession, "*leave nothing, if possible, in the dark of what related me to Judaism, alliance broken* (Karet) *in every aspect, with perhaps a gluttonous interiorization, and in
heterogeneous modes: last of the Jews, what am I* [le dernier des Juifs, que suis-je] [. . .]
the circumcised is the proper [le circoncis est *le propre*]."[21]

It is significant that Derrida glossed the comment about the broken covenant with
the Hebrew *karet*, for in ancient Israel this term referred to the gravest of punish-
ments, being permanently cut off from the community of Israelites, a reversal, one
might say, of the rite of circumcision, by which males were attached to the community. Inverting and subverting the meaning of the traditional idiom, Derrida understands circumcision as the incision that loosens him from rather than binds him to the
Abrahamic community into which he was born. Of course, in being severed he somehow remains bound; indeed being bound for him consists in being severed.[22] "Circumcision is a determining cut. It permits cutting but, at the same time and in the
same stroke [*du même coup*], remaining attached to the cut."[23] In virtue of this cut that
binds, Derrida identifies himself as the "last of the Jews" (*le dernier des Juifs*), which
does not signify someone who is no longer a Jew, whether through assimilation or
conversion, and not even a modern-day Marrano. In passing, I note that in another
passage from *Circonfession*, Derrida does embrace this image to describe his peculiar
relationship to Judaism: "I confided it to myself in Toledo . . . that if I am sort of a

marrane of French Catholic culture . . . I also have my Christian body . . . I am one of those *marranes* who no longer say they are Jews even in the secret of their own hearts, not so as to be authenticated *marranes* on both sides of the public frontier, but because they doubt everything."[24] Historically, the Marrano was outwardly Christian and inwardly Jewish, but for Derrida, the Marrano is one who denies his Judaism even on the inside, indeed even in the innermost interiority of the heart. The Marrano is so oblivious of and skeptical with regard to his Jewishness that he is unaware of denying that he is a Jew whether in public or in private.

Cixous suggested that when Derrida declared himself the last of the Jews "it was the Marrano he was calling, the Marrano that he already was although he didn't know it. One of those Jews without knowing it and without knowledge, Jew without having it, without being it, a Jew whose ancestors are gone, cut off, as little Jewish as possible, the disinheritor, guardian of the book he doesn't know how to read."[25] The classification "last of the Jews," therefore, like the Marrano status, implies that Derrida is still cognizant of being a Jew, albeit a *truly false Jew*,[26] that is, a Jew whose Jewish identity is problematic, since he does not harbor the possibility of meaningfully perpetuating the tradition. As Derrida himself writes, "I am perhaps not what remains of Judaism [*qui reste du judaïsme*], and I would have no trouble agreeing with that, if at least people really wanted to prove it . . . but after all what else am I in truth, who am I if I am not what I inhabit and where I take place [*qui suis-je si je ne suis pas ce que j'habite et où j'ai lieu*] . . . today in what remains of Judaism to this world . . . and in this remainder I am only someone to whom there remains so little that at bottom, already dead as son with the widow [*déjà mort comme fils auprès de la veuve*], I expect the resurrection of Elijah, and to sort out the interminably preliminary question of knowing how they, the Jews and the others, can interpret circumfession, i.e. that I here am inhabiting what remains of Judaism, there are so few of us and we are so divided."[27] The messianic resonance here cannot be missed unless one is utterly tone-deaf. What is particularly noteworthy is that death surrounds the messianic hope, as Derrida describes himself "already dead as son with the widow," expecting the resurrection of Elijah, a name that traditionally denotes the prophet who heralds the coming of the Messiah and the imaginal form present at each circumcision, but it is also the author's Hebrew name.[28]

The intent of Derrida's eschatological leanings and the portrait of the apocalyptic ideal—"an apocalypse without apocalypse, an apocalypse without vision, without truth, without revelation"[29]—are formulated lucidly in *Specters of Marx*: "Well, what remains irreducible to any deconstruction, what remains as undeconstructible as the possibility itself of deconstruction is, perhaps, a certain experience of the emancipatory promise; it is perhaps even the formality of a structural messianism, a messianism without religion, even a messianic without messianism, an idea of justice—which we distinguish from law or right and even from human rights—and an idea of democracy—which we distinguish from its current concept and from its determined predicates today."[30] In the essay "Faith and Knowledge: The Two Sources of 'Religion' at the Limits of Reason Alone," Derrida elaborated this notion of "messianicity without messianism" as an aspiration that entails the "opening to the future or to the coming of the other as the advent of justice, but without horizon of expectation and without prophetic prefiguration. . . . Possibilities that both open and can always interrupt history, or at least the ordinary course of history. . . . This messianic dimension does not depend upon any messianism, it follows no determinate revelation, it belongs properly to no Abrahamic religion (even if I am obliged here, 'among ourselves,' for essential reasons of language and of place, of culture, of a provisional rhetoric and a historical strategy of which I will speak later, to continue giving it names marked by the Abrahamic religions)."[31]

Messianicity, which implies the hope of the "coming of the other . . . as a singular event when no anticipation sees it coming,"[32] is "older than all religion, more originary than all messianism."[33] The very prospect of religion endures in the "space and time of a spectralizing messianicity beyond all messianism."[34] In a lecture honoring Levinas delivered in Paris on December 7, 1996, Derrida refers to his view as a "structural or *a priori* messianicity," which is not an "ahistorical messianicity, but one that belongs to a historicity without a particular and empirically determinable incarnation. Without revelation or without the dating of a given revelation."[35] From these passages, and undoubtedly others that could have been cited, we see how far removed Derrida's eschatological stance is from traditional forms of Jewish messianism. Nevertheless, not only has he been impelled to employ some of the standard idioms, but he has also grasped the paradoxical corollary of the temporal comportment of the achronic future implied in the Jewish belief: the possibility of the Messiah's coming is predicated on the impossibility of the Messiah's arrival, inasmuch as the "*eskhaton* whose ultimate event (immediate rupture, unheard-of-interruption, untimeliness of the infinite surprise, heterogeneity without accomplishment) can exceed, *at each moment*, the final term of a *phusis*, such as work, the production, and the *telos* of any history."[36] In spite of Derrida's effort to disentangle eschatology from teleology, he insists, "There has to be the possibility of someone's still arriving, there has to be an *arrivant* . . . someone absolutely indeterminate . . . who may be called the Messiah."[37] For Derrida, messianicity involves the constant advent of what is to come (*a-venir*), a present perpetually postponed to the future (*l'avenir*), a giveness always yet to be given, the wholly other (*tout autre*) that refuses incorporation into any totalitarianization of the same, "the to-come of the event that cannot be thought under the given category of event."[38] As he puts it elsewhere: "The affirmation of the future to come: this is not a positive thesis. It is nothing other than the affirmation itself, the 'yes,' insofar as it is the condition of all promises or of all hope, of all awaiting, of all performativity, of all opening toward the future, whatever it may be, for science or for religion."[39]

Insofar as Derrida's messianicity is predicated on the continual deferral of a future that can never appear—and hence it entails the "irreducible paradox" of "waiting without horizon of expectation,"[40] akin to the Levinasian depiction of messianic hope as an awaiting without an awaited, discussed in the previous chapter—he refers to it as a doctrine of "hauntology," the haunting "apparition of the inapparent," which disrupts ontology.[41] The messianic figure, therefore, is ghostlike, the inapparent that appears in the (dis)appearance of its having once appeared. "But one has to realize the ghost is there, be it in the opening of the promise or the expectation, *before its first apparition*: the latter had announced itself, from the first it will have come second. *Two times at the same time*, originary iterability, irreducible virtuality of this space and this time. That is why one must think otherwise the 'time' or the date of an event."[42] To be a Jew means to live as this phantom, the simulacrum of the simulacrum that appears from the first as second, the trace of the trace, the retrace at the beginning that is the repetition of the same that is always different.

That Judaism came to play a vital role in Derrida's description of the method of deconstruction can be asserted with confidence. Perhaps this is enunciated most explicitly in his lengthy study "Violence and Metaphysics: An Essay on the Thought of Emmanuel Levinas." The ruminations of Levinas, Derrida tells the reader, "make us tremble," for by attempting to think Judaism and Greek philosophy together a subversive role is assigned to the former, particularly in terms of a challenge to the dominant ontology or metaphysics of presence that underlies the logocentric perspective.[43] "At the heart of the desert, in the growing wasteland, this thought, which fundamentally no longer seeks to be a thought of Being and phenomenality, makes us dream of an inconceivable process of dismantling and dispossession."[44] The ethical relationship to the other as infinitely other is the one experience that is "capable of opening the space of transcendence and of liberating metaphysics. . . . It is opening itself, the opening of opening, that which can be enclosed within no category or totality."[45]

In the end of the essay, Derrida raises several questions aimed at destabilizing the dichotomy between Hebraism and Hellenism implied in the citation by Matthew Arnold placed at the beginning of the essay, ending with the words of James Joyce[46] that affirm the coincidence of the presumed opposites:

> Are we Jews? Are we Greeks? We live in the difference between the Jew and the Greek, which is perhaps the unity of what is called history. We live in and of difference, that is, in *hypocrisy* [*Nous vivons dans la différence entre le Juif et le Grec, qui est peut-être l'unité de ce qu'on appelle histoire. Nous vivons dans et de la différence, c'est-à-dire dans l'*hypocrisie] . . . Are we Greeks? Are we Jews? But who, we? Are we (not a chronological, but a pre-logical question) first Jews or first Greeks? . . . And what is the legitimacy, what is the meaning of the copula in this proposition from perhaps the most Hegelian of modern novelists: "Jewgreek is greekjew. Extremes meet"?[47]

Prima facie, one might think that the hybridity suggests that to be a Jewgreek or a Greekjew, one must be both, but when these expressions are appropriately deconstructed, they signify that if one is to be either a Jew or a Greek, one must occupy what Derrida elsewhere refers to as the space of the "*between*," wherein the "architecture" is "neither Greek nor Judaic,"[48] a space that must be prior to the division of Jew and Greek, identified by Geoffrey Bennington as Egypt, since both the Israelites and the Spartans allegedly were displaced from that place.[49] In an attempt to go beyond the jewgreek identity, with its cultural roots respectively in Jerusalem and Athens, Bennington suggests that Egypt is symbolically the "place" of deconstruction, a surmise that is based primarily on Derrida's own admitted fascination with Egyptian hieroglyphics. Bennington also proposed that the demarcation "Egyptian" may relate to the fact that Derrida is North African. Viewing things from this perspective leads Bennington to gloss the Joycean locution appropriated by Derrida as follows: "Jewgreek is greekjew: but greekjew is Egyptian. . . . Jewgreek is neither Greek nor Jew as mix or *Aufhebung*. I call the non-teleological becoming Greek of the Jew, or the non-originary having been-Jew of the Greek, 'Egypt.' "[50] This alternative cultural marking is adopted as well by Peter Sloterdijk in his *Derrida, an Egyptian*, but for him, the term is not related to Derrida's biography; it serves rather—in great measure due to both Freud's thesis in *Moses and Monotheism* about the cultural and national identity of Moses as an Egyptian and Thomas Mann's portrayal in *Joseph and His Brothers* of Joseph as the hetero-Egyptian interpreter of dreams through the science of signs—as "the term for all constructs that can be subjected to deconstruction—except for the pyramid, the most Egyptian of edifices. It stands in its place, unshakeable for all time, because its form is nothing other than the undeconstructible remainder of a construction that, following the plan of its architect, is built to look as it would after its own collapse."[51]

Leaving aside the matter of Egypt, if we can assume that "Jew" and "Greek" denote respectively the particular and the universal, then we are right in characterizing that space as the chasm in which the singularity of the individual is both particular and universal and therefore neither particular nor universal in any absolute sense. To imagine an alterity of an absolute nature—as if Judaism were the "infinitely other" vis-à-vis Hellenism, the nonphilosophical complement to the philosophical logos—is not tenable. The separation of Athens and Jerusalem can never be total, nor can their differences be completely reconciled; the relationship is better conceived in terms of "a same which is not identical, and which does not enclose the other" (*d'un même qui n'est pas l'identique et qui ne renferme pas l'autre*),[52] words that imply a logic that is very close to Heidegger's notion of belonging-together, which we discussed in the previous chapter. Derrida's exact words are crucial and worth citing again: "*We live in and of the difference between Jew and Greek*, which is perhaps the unity of what is called history. We live in and of difference, that is, in *hypocrisy*."[53] There is no authenticity that is not two-faced, no sincerity that is not pretense, no identity without ambivalence. It is for this reason that the claim to dwell in the space of the difference between Jew and Greek, the very unity of our historical reckoning, is in fact a form of hypocrisy.

Derrida reiterated his perspective when addressing the question of his Jewish identity in an interview with Elisabeth Weber. Not willing to tackle the issue of Judaism in all of its intricacies and complexities, he concentrates instead on circumcision:

> A wound has already taken place that marks an incision in the body; it forbids you this distance or this play which consists in turning around.[54] The game is no longer possible. And yet this hopeless challenge . . . perhaps engages precisely what is going on, at any rate describes the figure, very difficult to represent, for me as much as anyone, of *my* experience or the experience of my relationship to . . . I don't venture to say Judaism—let's say, to circumcision . . . for me "circumcision" could mean on the one hand the singular alliance of the Jewish people with their God, but just as well, on the other hand, it could figure a sort of universal mark that we find not only in men but also in women and in all the peoples of the world, whether or not they have thought of themselves as chosen or singular. . . . And basically, however I interpret or one interprets the fact that, I'm told, I was born Jewish or am circumcised, I always find once again, I always find *myself* once again confronted with a problem of figure, a *cas de figure*, as we say in French. It's not only a problem of rhetoric, a case of figure, if at the same time Judaism is an absolutely singular trait not shared by all men and all women, but represents itself, as Judaism, as the figure of the human universal.[55]

Universalizing the most particularizing ceremonial practice of the Jewish tradition, Derrida acknowledges that circumcision could signify the "singular alliance of the Jewish people with their God,"[56] but it is clear that the meaningfulness of the rite for him consists of the fact that it can "figure" rhetorically as a "universal mark."[57] To his credit, he does emphasize that the notion of an inward circumcision of the heart is expressed by the prophet Jeremiah and thus has textual roots in Judaism independent of Christianity.[58] Both emulating and rejecting the Pauline viewpoint,[59] Derrida does not go so far as to substitute circumcision of the spirit for circumcision of the flesh,[60] but he interprets the latter in such a way that it accomplishes the overcoming of gender and ethnic difference usually associated with the former. Paraphrasing the baptismal formula in Galatians 3:28, we can say that for Derrida, all distinctions are erased in the circumcised body—understood figurally and not literally[61]—and hence there is neither Jew nor Greek, neither male nor female.[62] The idea of chosenness, accordingly, is not indicative of a singularity that separates Jews and non-Jews, but rather it is a sign of the "human universal" that binds Jews and non-Jews together, the "figure of exemplarity" that makes it possible for Derrida to say "I am Jewish," by which he means "I am testifying to the humanity of human beings, to universality, to responsibility for universality."[63] As Derrida put it in the lecture he delivered as part of the colloquium "Judéités: Questions pour Jacques Derrida," held at the Jewish Community Center in Paris on December 3–5, 2000, exemplarism "would consist in acknowledging, or claiming to identify, in what one calls the Jew the exemplary figure of a universal structure of the living human, to wit, this being originally indebted, responsible, guilty. As if election or counter-election consisted in having been chosen as guardian of a truth, a law, an essence, in truth here, of a universal responsibility. The more jewish the Jew [*plus le Juif est juif*], the more he would represent the universality of human responsibility for man, and the more he would have to respond to it, to answer for it."[64]

The rationale of extreme exclusivity is transformed into a principle of maximal inclusivity, and thus the notion of the "chosen people" denotes being "in an exemplary way, witnesses to what a people can be." Derrida promptly notes the paradoxical logic that proceeds from arguing that the particularity of Jewish election entails the universal: self-identity "consists in not being identical to myself, in being foreign," and hence "the less you are Jewish, the more you are Jewish." The Jew, in a word, personifies the "identity as non-self-identity." This leads Derrida to draw the following startling, and counterintuitive, conclusion: "*Jews who base their Jewishness on an actual circumcision, a Jewish name, a Jewish birth, a land, a Jewish soil, etc.—they would by definition be no better placed than others for speaking in the name of Judaism.*"[65] Jews are coerced to affirm simultaneously that they are Jewish and not Jewish, for the otherness of the Jew perforce must comprise its own other, the universal that exceeds the particular in which it is contained. It is in this spirit that Derrida recalls the aforecited statement from *Circonfession* that he is the "last of the Jews";[66] that is, he represents the "death of Judaism, but also its one chance of survival,"[67] inasmuch as he discerns that his identity as a Jew entails not knowing exactly what it is to be authentically Jewish, that he belongs to Jewish culture by essentially "not belonging."[68] It is this aporia that forges an inherent link between the method of deconstruction and identifying Jewish singularity as the locus of exemplarity:

> Being-jew would then be something more, something other than the simple lever . . . of a general deconstruction; it would be its very experience . . . . It would be its hyper-exemplary experience, ultimately, eschatologically, or perversely exemplary, since it would implicate the credit or, if you prefer, the faith that we would place in exemplarity itself. . . . I insist on saying "I am jew" or "I am a Jew," without ever feeling authorized to clarify whether an "inauthentic" Jew, or, above all, an "authentic" Jew . . . . Willing or pretending to be neither an inauthentic Jew, nor an authentic Jew, nor a quasi-authentic Jew, nor an imaginary Jew . . . . Well, I know that I do not know that, and I suspect all those who believe they know of not knowing, even if, in truth, they do know more—I know—much more than I. . . . I insist on presenting myself as a Jew, on saying and declaring myself [*à dire et à me dire*] "I am jew," neither authentic nor inauthentic nor quasi-authentic, given that I do not know what I mean, that I could criticize, disavow, "deconstruct" everything that I might mean.[69]

Derrida admits that many of the topics that engaged his critical sensibilities can be traced to his Jewish heritage. Moreover, as he rightly notes, the effort to emancipate himself from the dogma of revelation and of election can be interpreted as the very content of these dogma.[70]

In the dialogical exchange with Maurizio Ferraris, Derrida expands on the theme of belonging by not-belonging: "I am a Jew from Algeria, from a certain type of community, in which belonging to Judaism was problematic, belonging to Algeria was problematic, belonging to France was problematic, etc. So all this predisposed me to not-belonging."[71] The same motif is articulated by Derrida in his explication of Celan's view that the Jew does not possess any innate properties: "The Jew is also the other, myself and the other; I am Jewish in saying: the Jew is the other who has no essence, who has nothing of his own or whose own essence is not to have one."[72] From this perspective, Derrida's patently absurd and presumptuous declaration "I am the last of the Jews"[73] carries the mockery and irony of assuming that he is the most Jewish because he is the least Jewish,[74] which may imply that he is "more than jewish" (*plus que juive*) or "other than jewish" (*autre que juive*);[75] that is, he can remain within Judaism only by abandoning it. In this sense, Christ could be considered prototypically the last of the Jews.[76] Concerning the secret of his Jewishness, Derrida wrote:

> As if—a paradox that I will not stop unfolding and that summarizes all the torment of my life—I had to keep myself from judaism [*me garder du judaïsme*] in order to retain within myself something that I provisionally call jewishness. The phrase, the contradictory injunction, that would thus have ordered my life seemed to say to me, in French: "garde-toi du judaïsme—ou même de la judéité." Keep yourself from it in order to keep some of it, keep yourself from it, guard yourself from being jewish in order to keep yourself jewish or to keep and guard the Jew in you. Guard yourself from and take care of the Jew in you [*prends garde au Juif en toi*]. Watch and watch out [*re-garde*], be vigilant, be watchful, and do not be Jewish at any price. Even if you are alone and the last to be jewish at this price, look twice before claiming a communal, even national or especially state-national, solidarity and before speaking, before taking sides and taking a stand *as a Jew*.[77]

With a flare for the sensational, Derrida refers to the need to preserve his Jewishness by distancing himself from Judaism as *the torment of his life*. The larger political implications of this predicament are made explicit: to take one's stand as a Jew, indeed as the last of the Jews, one has to be reluctant to claim communal or national, let alone state-national, solidarity with other Jews. Paradoxically enough, to keep oneself Jewish—to shield the Jew within—means to guard oneself from being Jewish at any price. Inexorably, in the case of the Jew, as Derrida remarked in his study on Edmond Jabès, there is a "noncoincidence of the self and the self" (*non-coïncidence de soi avec soi*), for the "Jew's identification within himself does not exist. The Jew is split, and split first of all between the two dimensions of the letter: allegory and literality."[78]

We cannot say with certitude whether or not Derrida thought of himself as the unique hybrid, the mongrel Egyptian, who is jewgreek by being greekjew. A position akin to this has been proffered by John Caputo in *The Prayers and Tears of Jacques Derrida: Religion without Religion*. To be more precise, Caputo, echoing the views of Habermas and Handelman mentioned above, is of the opinion that although Derrida does not write in the name of a Jew, his work is nonetheless "driven by a Jewish passion." His compositions constitute his own diaspora, in which the "dispersion and dissemination of his psyche are the very substance of his Jewishness."[79] I do not agree with Caputo's argument that the "genuinely religious import of deconstruction" is related to a prophetic or messianic concern with justice,[80] but he has offered us a helpful opening on our path. In contrast to his emphasis, I will concern myself with the specific question of Derrida's relation to Jewish mysticism. To comprehend this aspect of his thought, however, we must begin by considering how Judaism functions as a disruption that causes a breach in the edifice of Western philosophy, the *différance*, the incessant not-saying of what it is that one is saying. And here again we return to the cut of circumcision, the alliance predicated on fissure. "His entire philosophy," wrote Cixous, "will perhaps have been a rehashing of the innumerable figures of the Circumcision figure, or perhaps it speaks only of that in an incessant kaleidoscope of changes or maybe it is itself but one link in the chain of substitutions, one can always dash around the ring or the circle to try and find the inexistent door."[81]

Although the status of Jewish existence becomes in the hands of Derrida primarily a philosophical rather than an ethnic nomenclature, it is clear that the more universalistic categorization is enrooted in the particularity of his own existential facticity. The extent to which Derrida felt detached and estranged from the patrimony of his youth may be gauged from another brutally honest, and somewhat bleak, comment in his notebooks, "and the last of the Jews that I still am is doing nothing here other than destroying the world on the pretext of making truth" (*et le dernier des Juifs que je suis encore ne fait rien d'autre ici que détruire le monde sous pretext de faire la vérité*).[82] Derrida returned to the question of his Jewish upbringing in *Le monolinguisme de l'autre: ou la prothèse d'origine*, a study originally published in 1996 based on an oral presentation from April 1992. At one point he candidly observes, "Such, in any event, would have been the radical lack of culture from which I undoubtedly never completely emerged. From which I emerge without emerging from it, by emerging from it completely without my having ever emerged from it."[83] In the continuation of this passage, Derrida admits that he was not capable of breathing new life into an ossified and necrotized Judaism, since he carried the "negative heritage" of an "amnesia," which he never had the courage, strength, or means to resist, and because he did not feel he was qualified to do the original work of the historian. Significantly, Derrida tacitly owns up to the fact that historical scholarship in the study of Judaism, which is based on the philological competence that has eluded his grasp, could have redemptive or restorative value. In an astonishing moment of self-disclosure, Derrida concedes that he has been influenced by "an insidious Christian contamination: the respectful belief in inwardness, the preference for intention, the heart, the mind, mistrust with respect to literalness or to an objective action given to the mechanicity of the body, in short, a denunciation, so conventional, of Pharisaism."[84] By his own admission, Derrida's attitude toward Judaism reflects a bias against Pharisaic literalism, a well-attested motif in the history of Jewish-Christian polemic.

This stark self-portrait of one who depicts the specific behavioral patterns of Judaism as parochial would seem to leave little room to consider Derrida in any meaningful way a living link in the chain of Jewish mysticism, which has unwaveringly affirmed the central significance of ritual behavior, even if the ultimate emphasis is placed on its inner and symbolic meaning. And yet, the matter is more complex, inasmuch as many kabbalists have affirmed that the abrogation of law is its most perfect fulfillment, that beyond nomian observance is a law that exceeds the strict adherence to the lawfulness of the law. It is feasible to view Derrida's position as consistent with kabbalistic hyper-nomianism.[85] Just as the kabbalists locate the lawless law in the supreme aspect of the divine pleroma, the place of pure mercy and forgiveness wherein it is no longer viable to distinguish guilt and innocence, so Derrida wrote about the nonjuridical dimension of the gift (*don*) of forgiveness (*pardon*) as the law beyond the law.[86] We must think of this possibility as inherently embracing the impossible—the moment the matter is uttered its truth rests on being false. It is precisely this impossibility of appropriation that yields the possibility of writing. As Derrida confides to us about his own autobiographical praxis, "*only write here what is impossible, that* ought *to be the impossible-rule*" (n'écrire ici que l'impossible, ce *devrait* être la régle-impossible).[87]

To grasp the intent of this comment, one must bear in mind that, for Derrida, inscription more generally, and not simply autobiographical writing, constitutes the signature of being that "remains an other whose law demands the impossible. It does not demand this thing or that, something which could turn out to be impossible. No, it demands the impossible, and demands it because it is impossible, and because this very impossibility is the condition of the possibility of demand." To write I must confront the "thing that would be other, the other thing" (*la chose serait donc l'autre, l'autre chose*), which "gives me an order or addresses an impossible, intransigent, insatiable demand to me, without an exchange and without a transaction, without a possible contract. Without a word, without speaking to me, it addresses itself to me, to me alone in my irreplaceable singularity, in my solitude as well. I owe to the thing an absolute respect which no general law would mediate [*un respect absolu que ne médiatise aucune loi générale*]: the law of the thing is singularity and difference as well. An infinite debt ties me to it, a duty without funds or foundation. I shall never acquit myself of it. Thus the thing is not an object; it cannot become one."[88]

The "rule of the impossible" (*la régle-impossible*) hinges on the fact that the writer is indebted to bear through verbal discourse the other that addresses one without speaking, the thing that can never become object, the presence that cannot be represented except as the absence of the presence that it could not presently be. In a profoundly tragic turn, Derrida observes that inscription requires the "muteness of the thing" (*le mutisme de la chose*), for the thing that must be written is an "insatiable *thou must*" (tu dois *insatiable*) that "remains beyond exchange and priceless."[89] The thing imposes itself as that which must be written, and yet it offers no specific direction or content; it demands to be heard from the depth of its muteness. Had the other spoken, there would be an exchange and an ensuing contract binding writer and what is written, but in its muteness, there is an asymmetry that defies the circuitry of exchange, the indebtedness of the gift that cannot be negotiated contractually. I will have more to say about the gift and the impossibility of representation at a later stage of this analysis. For the time being, it is sufficient to note that the rule of the impossible cannot be followed unless it be broken, for writing the impossible, the only writing that is possible, indeed the impossibility that facilitates the possibility of writing, is a rule about breaking rules, a law that can be implemented only in its eradication. We have arrived at the spot where Derrida is most proximate to and yet most distant from the kabbalistic worldview.

POLYSEMY, ATHEISM, AND THE APOPHATIC OVERCOMING OF ONTOTHEOLOGY

Ironically, perhaps the most expedient way to approach the topic of Derrida and the kabbalah is by remaining silent. This reticence is due neither to the traditional paradox of negative theology—how to speak of the unspeakable transcendence of the One beyond sensible image and intelligible concept—nor to the contemporary challenge of deconstruction—how to speak at all when the meaning of words is never incontestably clear.[90] The difficulty I face is far more prosaic: with all his considerable literary accomplishments, Derrida did not overtly profess expertise in any area of Judaic studies, let alone an area that is limited to a handful of specialists spread about several continents.[91] Nevertheless, in various places in his copious writings, Derrida utilizes kabbalistic themes. Here I will note three such occurrences in the section called "The Column" in the collection of essays published as *Dissemination*: (1) the zoharic motif of the ungraspable column of air, which is related to the demarcation of the ten sefirotic emanations as a column of numerations; (2) the Lurianic symbol of the "pneumatic layer" (*ṭehiru*) in which the contraction (*ṣimṣum*)—the dramatic crisis of self-determination within God—occurs; and (3) the messianic Torah of invisible letters written in white fire in the blank spaces encompassing the visible letters written in black fire, which is associated especially with the Hasidic master, Levi Isaac of Berditchev.[92] Derrida even offers a taxonomy of the Jewish occult tradition: "The Kabbalah is not only summoned up here under the rubric of arithmosophy or the science of literal permutations . . . it also cooperates with an Orphic explanation of the earth."[93]

The reference to arithmosophy calls attention to the fact that the kabbalistic term *sefirot* is derived etymologically from *safar*, "to count." That Derrida understood that the *sefirot* are not ordinary numeric ciphers is evident from the fact that he also claims that they correspond "to the ten archetypal names or categories." Even so, their primary intent is mathematical, a point accentuated by Derrida's further observation, "The tree of the *sephiroth*, an engraving of the whole, reaches down into the En Sof, 'the root of all roots'; and this structure is entirely recognizable in *Numbers*. That would be only one of the numerous textual grafts through which the Kabbalah is reproduced there; numerous: plural, disseminated."[94] The arithmetic connotation of the *sefirot* denotes the multivocality of meaning that is disseminated midrashically in an ongoing dispersal through the apparently endless succession of time.[95] As Derrida playfully puts it, "*Numbers* are thus a kind of cabal or cabala in which the blanks will be anything but provisionally filled in, one surface or square always remaining empty, open to the play of permutations, blanks barely glimpsed as blanks, (almost) pure spacing, going on forever and not in the expectation of any Messianic fulfillment."[96] Anticipating his latter affirmation of messianicity without messianism, Derrida claims that the Torah to be revealed by the Messiah, the "new Torah," is the text that can never be delimited, since it is writ in the white spaces of infinity in which the black letters become indiscernible. Portraying the sefirotic gradations as numerations is meant, therefore, to underline the polysemic nature of the text, the ambiguity that precludes the possibility of establishing a single true or original meaning that can be brought into presence.

The quality of polysemy is linked as well to the characterization of kabbalah as the "science of literal permutation." It is reasonable to infer that this expression is a translation of the Hebrew *ḥokhmat ṣeruf ha-otiyyot*, the "wisdom of letter combination," a cornerstone of the ecstatic-prophetic kabbalah of Abraham Abulafia.[97] However, it is necessary to emphasize that in the context in which Derrida utilizes this definition he also engages the technical theosophic symbolism elicited, at least in part, from zoharic literature. More importantly, the literal permutation is another name for the Derridean principle of dissemination. Support for this interpretation may be gathered from the passage in the letter of Mallarmé to Verlaine, dated November 16, 1885, cited by Derrida in the same collection, where the "Orphic explanation of the Earth" is glossed as "the poet's sole duty and the literary game par excellence."[98] Both aspects of the kabbalah, the numeric and the linguistic, allude to the sense of "textuality," which implies the quality of "numerous plurivocality," the "absolutely disseminated" that "evinces a kind of atheism."[99]

Derrida's interpretation of the kabbalah as arithmosophy and as the science of letter combination is related to the conception of the infinite finitude of *différance*,[100] and thus he asserts that number, a cipher for the sefirotic enumerations, is the "only thing" that the "so-called atheists have believed in."[101] If atheism is correlated with the polysemic, we can educe that theism represents an essentializing or monosemic reading.[102] In Chapter 2, we had the occasion to discuss another passage wherein Derrida juxtaposes atheism, mysticism, and apophatic discourse. The common thread that ties the two texts is the understanding of atheism as a disruptive and dissociative power that destabilizes the totalizing system of meaning and thereby renders every linguistic assertion ambivalent and every affirmation of certitude ambiguous. To characterize mysticism in general, or Jewish mysticism in particular, as atheistic thus does not imply the commonplace connotation of the denial of God's existence but rather the idiosyncratic sense of a synonym for textual multivalency. Derrida's position is in accord with Umberto Eco's labeling the kabbalistic understanding of the Torah—based exclusively on the citation and analysis of sources in Scholem's "The Meaning of Torah in Jewish Mysticism"—as a "radically secularized hermeneutics where the text is no longer transparent and symptomatic, since it only speaks of its possibility of eliciting a semiosic 'drift' . . . the text must be (with a more radically Kabbalistic option) *deconstructed*, until fracturing its own expressive texture. Thus the text does not speak any longer of its own 'outside'; it does not even speak of itself; it speaks of our own experience in reading (deconstructively) it. . . . In this ultimate epiphany of the symbolic mode, the text as symbol is no longer read in order to find in it a truth that lies *outside*: the only truth (that is, the old Kabalistic God) is the very play of deconstruction. The ultimate truth is that the text is a mere play of differences and displacements."[103] Interpreting the aforementioned statement of Levi Isaac of Berditchev about the white letters of the messianic Torah, which is characterized as well by the Lacanian notion of the symbolic as the chain of signifiers, Eco observes that the "new deconstructionist practices" will allow for "the new and atheistic mystics of the godless drift, to rewrite indefinitely, at every new reading, the new Torah."[104]

Elsewhere I have argued that the kabbalistic and Derridean notions of polysemy have to be distinguished on the grounds that the unfolding of the text's potentially infinite meaning would not be imaginable to a kabbalist if he did not presume that all of the interpretations were enfolded in the originary text to which a discrete, albeit aporetic, signifier is assigned, that is, the ineffable name, YHWH, the name that declaims in its (non)utterance the nameless that is spoken when unspoken and unspoken when spoken.[105] Even though the ineffability of this name secures the paradox that it is the name that cannot name except by not-naming, the paradox of denomination,[106] it would still be considered by Derrida as an illustration of the transcendental signifier, the originary text, a palimpsest from its inceptual inscripting/erasure—the multiple readings etched on its surface constitute the writing-over, the spectrality of the invisible emerging from beneath the layers of the visible, the disclosure of truth in the concealment of image through the concealment of truth in the disclosure of image.

I accept that for the kabbalist exegete, the infinite, which is circumscribed in the text, is the theme that cannot be thematized but as that which ceaselessly thematizes itself through concealing its concealment, disappearing in the advent of its coming-to-view, the nonshowing that is the spectacle of mystical vision. Although a credible case can be made that the kabbalistic and deconstructionist hermeneutics share the view that there is no core intentionality to the text, the two tactics of reading nevertheless differ on the question of the possibility of demarcating a domain beyond the text. The eclecticism of the kabbalah is a facet of heterosemiotic uniformity, its singularity a consequence of a monological pluralism. The diversity of opinions is not indicative of "various ontological schemes" informing "different hermeneutical modes of interpretation"[107] but rather a shared ontology that informs a common hermeneutic, which rests, at least in its traditional formulations, on an ontological assumption that postmodern readers would likely find objectionable: there is a presence that exceeds the text, a presence that is always a nonpresence, insofar as it can be present only by being absent, and hence it can never be represented, but it is a presence nonetheless, the secret manifest in the nonmanifestation of the secret, the nothing about which one cannot speak in contrast to there being nothing about which to speak, the unsaying of apophasis as opposed to the dissimulation of dénégation. To interpret the kabbalists as if they were advocating a total collapse of divinity into the fold of the text, thereby effacing the transcendence of the beyond-being, the form of the formless, as suggested by Eva Tavor Bannet's comparison of the deconstructed God of Derrida's *différance* and the kabbalists' Ein Sof,[108] is an evocative reading, but it does not mean that it is the most responsible either historically or philologically.

From the Derridean perspective the kabbalistic Ein Sof is a "negative mode of presence"[109] and thus remains, as he argued with respect to Meister Eckhart's affirmation of the nothingness that is the Godhead beyond God, "enclosed in ontic transcendence. . . . This negative theology is still a theology and, *in its literality at least*, it is concerned with liberating and acknowledging the ineffable transcendence of an infinite existent."[110] Or, as Derrida put it in the lengthy essay "How to Avoid Speaking: Denials," which was first delivered in June 1986 as the opening lecture of the colloquium on "Absence and Negativity," organized by the Hebrew University and the Institute for Advanced Studies in Jerusalem,[111] when discussing the *via negativa* promulgated by the Neoplatonist who wrote under the pseudonym Dionysius the Areopagite, "As for the *hyper* of the superessential (*hyperousios*), it has the double and ambiguous value of what is above in a hierarchy, thus both beyond and more. God (is) beyond Being but as such is more (being) than being: *no more being and being more than being: being more*."[112] Deconstruction and negative theology are contrasted, since the latter "seems to reserve, beyond all positive predication, beyond all negation, even beyond being, some superessentiality, a being beyond being."[113] Elaborating the point, Derrida writes:

> What "differance," "trace," and so on, "mean-to-say"—which consequently *does not mean to say anything*—would be "something" "before" the concept, the name, the word, that would be nothing, that would no longer pertain to being, to presence or to the presence of the present, or even to absence, and even less to some hyperessentiality. Yet the ontotheological reappropriation always remains possible . . . One

can always say: hyperessentiality is exactly that, a supreme being that remains incommensurable with the being of all that is, that *is* nothing, neither present nor absent, and so on. If in fact the movement of this reappropriation appears irrepressible, its ultimate failure is no less necessary.[114]

Ostensibly, medieval kabbalah is open to the same critique: Ein Sof is the *being beyond being*, the being that surpasses the plethora of discriminate beings that make up the multiverse, but it is still the "being of the One as non-being," in the language of Badiou,[115] and thus there appears to be no way to elude an "ontotheological reappropriation." In light of this interpretation of the kabbalistic symbol, we can better understand Derrida's gloss of a passage from Heidegger's "Letter on Humanism," written to Jean Beaufret in 1946, "But if the human being is to find his way once again into the nearness of being [*Nähe des Seins*], he must first learn to exist in the nameless [*Namelosen*],"[116] with the following aside: "Did not the Kabbala also speak of the unnameable possibility of the Name?"[117] Remarkably, Derrida discerned a connection between the residual ontotheology of the Jewish esoteric tradition and Heidegger centered about the thought of being and the articulation of the name that is no name.

However, one might challenge the distinction Derrida draws between the apophaticism of the kabbalah and the dénégation of deconstruction by questioning the interpretation of *hyperessentiality* in his earlier work. The semantics of Neoplatonic and kabbalistic texts is ambiguous enough—a criterion that a deconstructionist hermeneutic should be compelled by the impulse of its own intellectual agenda to support—to allow for a different explication of the meaning of the word "beyond" in the description of the One as the metabeing. The words *hyperousia* or *superessentia* do not denote a being or an entity subject to a substantialist metaphysic or to an ontological monism but rather the "non-being" that is "more-than-being," the "non-substance" that is "more-than-substance."[118] The expression *being beyond being* is an apophatic pronouncement, a speaking-away, which is to say it connotes not simply the affirmation of what is negated but also the negation of what is affirmed: the being that is beyond being is a being only insofar as it is not a being—its being, in other words, is not to be. As Michael Sells has argued, "Apophasis is a discourse in which any single proposition is acknowledged as falsifying, as reifying. It is a discourse of double propositions, in which meaning is generated through the tension between the saying and the unsaying."[119]

It should be recalled that Derrida himself in his later reflections on the subject noted that negative theology is "a language that does not cease testing the very limits of language, and exemplarily those of propositional, theoretical, or constative language."[120] The inadequacy of language forces us to continue to speak of the One as if it were a being, but the apophatic utterance is a form of "disontology," the term employed by Sells to name "the ongoing discursive attempt to gain a momentary liberation from the delimitations of predication and reference as represented by thus and not thus."[121] The possibility of such utterances ensues from the mystical union wherein "the transcendent is undone," and neither the soul nor the deity can be calibrated from the routine angle of the boundaries of self-identity.[122] Words invariably prove to be deficient—there is no way to unsay what needs to be said except by saying the unsaid. It is not only that every act of unsaying presupposes a previous saying or that every saying demands a corrective unsaying,[123] but, more paradoxically, *every saying is an unsaying*, for what is said can never be what is spoken insofar as what is spoken can never be what is said. "To speak in order to say *nothing*," quipped Derrida, "is not not to speak. Above all, it is not to speak to no one."[124] As I have remarked in a previous publication, the mystical element as it evolved in medieval Judaism, Christianity, and Islam ensued "from the juxtaposition of the kataphatic and apophatic, that is, a mysticism that steadfastly denies the possibility of ascribing any form to the being beyond all configuration, indeed the being to whom we cannot even ascribe the attribute of being without denying the nature of the (non)being. . . . The juxtaposition of the kataphatic and apophatic has fostered the awareness on the part of the ones initiated in the secret gnosis that mystical utterance is an unsaying, which is not the same as the silence of not-speaking, but rather that which remains ineffable in being spoken."[125] In making claims about the ineffability of the infinite through the act of speaking-not, mystics of the three monotheistic faiths availed themselves of images of negation—that is, "images that are negative but no less imagistic than the affirmative images they negate"—to illustrate the negation of images.[126]

Based on this criterion we can conjecture that the nothing of infinitude affirmed by the kabbalists is conceived meontologically as being-other-than-what-is-conceived, but in being so conceived, this being-not, which is to be distinguished from not-being, is the object of contemplation. What is contemplated is not a what at all, not this and not that, and not even the negation of this and that, but the absolutely other vis-à-vis all existents, the nihility that is prior to the distinction of being and nonbeing—in the formulation of the kabbalists, *lo yesh we-lo ayin*[127]—and therefore beyond both affirmative and negative propositions. To cite one of many examples: in his commentary on the *sefirot*, Shem Tob Ibn Shem Tob (1380–1440) wrote, "I have also found in the book of R. Simeon ben Yoḥai that he called the Root of all Roots *ein sof*, and this is an honorable name by which to discern its existence, and to know that it has no boundary and that it is not grasped by any thought or idea, and we are not to say that it is either something or nothing, and not anything, and this name negates from it everything that speculation necessitates to negate."[128] This text, and others that could have been cited, attest that infinitude in kabbalistic lore cannot be objectified or thematized ontotheologically—indeed, as some kabbalists emphasized, even the name *ein sof* is too constricting,[129] or as others put it, there is no linguistic signifier whatsoever, no letter or even the ornamental tittle atop the *yod*, that can signify the Ein Sof[130]—and thus it is difficult to think of the Ein Sof in Neoplatonic terms as the *hyperousios*, at least if the latter is understood à la Derrida's explanation as the presence that presents itself as nonpresent. If the infinite is truly neither something nor nothing, then it is not merely a presence that presents itself as nonpresent, but it is a nonpresence that is outside the either/or structure that informs the economy of the binary of presence and absence; it is, in short, the chiasm that resists both the reification of nothing as something and of something as nothing. To speak of this nothingness as the absence of presence is as inadequate as it is to speak of it as the presence of absence; it is technically beyond both affirmation and negation, neither something that is nothing nor nothing that is something. Infinity both is what it is not and is not what it is because it neither is what it is not nor is not what it is.

SECRECY, THE NAME, AND THE CRYPTOGRAPHIC
NATURE OF LANGUAGE

In "The Eyes of Language: The Abyss and the Volcano," a sustained reading of a letter from Scholem to Rosenzweig, Derrida summons the lore of kabbalah—interpreted through the Scholemian lens—to articulate the view that the "power of language" is

> an enveloped virtuality, a potentiality that can be brought or not to actuality; it is hidden, buried, dormant. . . . This is indeed an explicit motif in certain trends of the Kabbalah. The magical power of the name produces effects said to be real and over which we are not in command. The name hidden in its potency possesses a power of manifestation and of occultation, of revelation and encrypting [*crypte*]. What does it hide? Precisely the abyss that is enclosed within it. To open a name is to find in it not something but rather something like an abyss, the abyss as the thing itself.[131]

The name simultaneously reveals and conceals, for what is revealed by the name is the concealment, the something that is *like* an abyss, the abyss *as* the thing itself. Derrida deploys these prepositions to highlight the inescapable metaphoricity of language; the name cannot unearth the thing itself but only the likeness of the thing; indeed, the name that cannot be named indicates that there is nothing to unearth but the boundless chain of likenesses of nothing. In this matter we can detect the influence of the kabbalistic speculation on the name.

Here it is relevant to recall Derrida's ruminations on the *tallit*, the traditional Jewish prayer shawl, in *Veils*, a work coauthored with Cixous. Although Derrida does not refer explicitly to kabbalistic literature in that discussion, he embraces the fundamental paradox of concealing and revealing in his account of the fringe garment that hides nothing but which nevertheless calls forth to memory the obligation to heed the command, the unshowing that fosters envisioning the sign of the covenantal law that must be appropriated by the individual through the gaze because it can never be owned by another, the paradox that marks the way of dissimulation, the doubling of the secret in the withholding of the bestowal of the withholding:

It veils or hides nothing, it shows or announces no Thing, it promises the intuition of nothing. Before seeing or knowing [*le voir ou le savoir*], before fore-seeing or fore-knowing, it is worn in memory of the Law. You still have to see it in another way for that, have it to yourself, have oneself [*s'avoir*] that skin, and see it indeed . . . So there would be, on sight, *your* sight ("see," "look"), an appropriation ("to you," "you will have," "for you"), a taking possession. But this is the property (the for-self) that at bottom does not belong and is there only to recall the Commandments. . . . As if everyone discovered his own shawl to his own sight, and right on his own body, but only with a view to hearing and recalling the law, of *recalling* oneself to it or of *recalling* it to oneself. And so to do more or something different, through memory, than "seeing." Each time is signed the absolute secret of a shawl—which can of course, at time for prayer, say the precepts, be lent, but not exchanged, and especially not become the property of someone else. The secret of the shawl envelops one single body. One might think that it is woven *for* this one body proper, or even *by* it, from which it seems to emanate, like an intimate secretion, but this is less through having engendered it thus right up close to oneself than through having already opened it or given it birth into the divine word that will have preceded it. For a secretion, as is well known, is also what separates, discerns, dissociates, dissolves the bond, holds to the secret.[132]

In the autobiographical *Circonfession*, Derrida refers enigmatically to the acronym of Pardes, first used by medieval kabbalists to name the four levels of meaning in Scripture,[133] which he decodes in the following manner: *peshaṭ* is the "*literality denuded like a glans*" (la littéralité dénudée comme un gland); *remez*, the "*crypt, allegory, secret, diverted word*" (crypte, allégorie, secret, parole détournée); *derash*, the "*morality, homily, persuasive and pulpit eloquence*" (la moralité, l'homélie, l'éloquence persuasive et de chaire); and *sod*, the "*profound, cabbalistic*" (profound, cabbalistique) meaning. After delineating these four levels, which he tellingly labels "*the quaternary model of a paradisiac discourse of Jewish 'rationality'*" (le modèle quaternaire d'un discours paradisiaque de la "rationalité" juive), Derrida remarks: "*although I've got the* PaRDeS *of this partition 'in my blood,' it does not correspond exactly to the one imposing itself on me, some laborious translation of it is not forbidden.* [. . .] *it was the last time, the mirror on my right, her left, sudden terror faced with the secret to be kept, of no longer being able to form the letters and words, fear of absolute inhibition through fear of betraying oneself.* [. . .] *it was like a beehive sponge of secrets, the buzzing rumor, the mixed-up noises of each bee, and yet the cells near to bursting, infinite number of walls, internal telephone.*"[134] In both *Dissemination* and *Circonfession*, Derrida turns to the kabbalistic tradition to elicit support for the notion of an amorphous text, that is, a text whose language is no longer broken conventionally into discrete words, a pretext, we might say, that serves as the hermeneutical basis for polysemy, the "white fire" of the primordial Torah, which is infinite and thus not fixed in any form,[135] the "text written in letters that are still invisible."[136] This idea is linked, moreover, to the notion of secrecy, a theme that Derrida consciously relates to the kabbalah.[137]

The key here lies in understanding Jewish mysticism primarily in semiological terms, with particular emphasis on the mystical experience of contemplative envisioning, which rests on the ontic presumption regarding the textualization of reality, that is, the idea that the most basic stuff of existence consists of the twenty-two letters of the Hebrew alphabet, and these twenty-two letters are comprised within the four letters of the name YHWH, the mystical core of the text of Torah. The divine being, and by insinuation all beings of the worlds that are the manifest occlusion of that being, is circumscribed in the book that is signified by the proper name *par excellence*. The proper name, which may also be apperceived as the prism through which the *sefirot* are variously configured, signifies what lies beyond signification, even beyond signification by any of the letters. The name, itself a curious phenomenon insofar as its ineffability necessitates that it can be articulated only through the cloak of its epithet, leads one to the nameless, the in/significant other that demarcates all that is signified, the inaudible voice that differentiates all that is articulated. This portrait of YHWH, which may be elicited from medieval kabbalistic literature, bears comparison with views expressed by Derrida regarding the nature of language as the mode by which we name the unnameable. However, in the case of the former this is identified as an essence that cannot be named, whereas in the case of the latter it is a linguistic marking of the fact that there is no essence but merely a polyphony of names, an illimitable string of signifiers.

To clarify my position, I note that in an essay published in 1982, "Derrida, Jabès, Levinas: Sign-Theory as Ethical Discourse," Shira Wolosky argued that in the studies on Jabès and Levinas included in *L'écriture et la différance*, which appeared in 1967, Derrida owned up to the relationship between his grammatological scheme and the theory of language found in kabbalistic writings. I will not investigate each of the passages to which she refers as support for her argument, but the gist of my concern is that it is not obvious that Derrida's exegetical remarks on either Jabès or Levinas are meant to be taken as clear-cut statements of his own views. Let me offer one example of the methodological problem. After citing Derrida's remark "Jabès is conscious of the Cabalistic resonances of his book,"[138] Wolosky comments on "a consciousness which Derrida shares, and which can be applied to his own work as well. Jabès' path, which Derrida also follows, leads into the kabbalistic world of linguistic mysticism, where claims for grammatological primacy open into an extensive and radical system."[139] There is nothing in Derrida's remarks that would substantiate this claim definitively. It is conjectural, at best, to assert that the kabbalistic resonances of the poetic fragments of Jabès apply equally well to Derrida; the latter's observations are a commentary on the former, a commentary that is written on the basis of attentive reading, but as commentary there is distance between text and interpreter, a distance that can never be entirely overcome in the hermeneutical act, no matter how astute one's interpretive prowess. As Derrida himself puts it in this very essay on Jabès, writing is a "tearing of the self toward the other within a confession of infinite separation."[140] To assume unreservedly, as Wolosky does, that Derrida's reflections about Jabès can be transferred to him without disruption, one would have to efface all difference between reader and text, an effacement that would fly in the face of the deconstructionist hermeneutic.

In a study published in the same year, "History as Apocalypse," Thomas Altizer adopted a similar view, going so far as to propose that in the essays on Jabès and Levinas, Derrida "unveiled his own ground in Lurianic Kabbalism, perhaps the most deeply modern or postmodern of all forms of mystical thinking." Altizer names *ṣimṣum* and *shevirat ha-kelim* as the two Lurianic doctrines that are "related to Derrida's thinking."[141] Perceptively, he notes that Derrida conjoined these two themes in his explication of Jabès's use of the scriptural motif of the shattering of the stone tablets by Moses when he beheld the Israelites worshipping the Golden Calf: "The breaking of the Tables articulates, first of all, a rupture within God as the origin of history. . . . God separated himself from himself in order to let us speak, in order to astonish and to interrogate us. He did so not by speaking but by keeping still, by letting silence interrupt his voice and his signs, by letting the Tables be broken."[142] Drawing an inference from this incisive exegesis of Jabès, Altizer concludes that this "Kabbalistic vision of God's contraction or self-withdrawal (*zimzum*) is surely one decisive source of Derrida's ground in a groundless beginning, a preprimordial 'hole' rather than a primordial plenum, which Derrida can speak of as the 'original exile' from the kingdom of being."[143] I am prepared to grant that Derrida is correct in ascribing kabbalistic import to the views of Jabès expressed in *Le livre des questions*.[144] What is at stake, however, is how to interpret this affinity as it relates to Derrida's own views. As I noted above, it is not at all certain that the explication of Jabès is meant to be read demonstrably as an account of his opinions, and I am not confident that ascribing to him the positing of a groundless beginning, an absence that precedes presence, is the most felicitous way to translate the deconstructionist critique of metaphysics.

Support for the influence of kabbalah on Derrida, however, may be culled from other passages in his writings where there appears to be a convergence of kabbalistic symbolism and his own thought, particularly some of the aforementioned technical motifs in sixteenth-century Lurianic kabbalah, the notion of the trace (*reshimu*) in the primordial space (*ṭehiru*) that results from the contraction (*ṣimṣum*) of the infinite from itself unto itself.[145] The point has not gone unnoticed in scholarly literature. Harold Bloom, for instance, proposed an influence of kabbalistic hermeneutics on Derrida's critical notion of *différance*: "Though he nowhere says so, it may be that Derrida is substituting *davhar* for *logos*, thus correcting Plato by a Hebraic equating of the writing-act and the mark of articulation with the word itself. Much of Derrida is in the spirit of the great Kabbalist interpreters of Torah, interpreters who create baroque mythologies out of those elements in Scripture that appear least homogeneous in the sacred text."[146] In another context, Bloom compared the kabbalistic notion of "writing before writing," articulated especially in Lurianic theosophy, and the Derridean notion of the trace. Bloom casts kabbalah as a "theory of *writing*" akin to this brand of French criticism, emphasizing, in particular, the denial of an absolute distinction between writing and speech shared by both. Yet, he is mindful to draw the following contrast: "Kabbalah too thinks in ways not permitted by Western metaphysics, since its God is at once *Ein-Sof* and *ayin*, total presence and total absence, and all its interiors contain exteriors, while all of its effects determine its causes. But Kabbalah stops the movement of Derrida's 'trace,' since it has a *point* of the primordial, where presence and absence co-exist by continuous interplay."[147] In a third study, Bloom reiterates the affinity between the "over-determined" conception of language as a "magical absolute" in kabbalistic tradition and the "*absolute* randomness" of language in the "linguistic nihilism" advocated in deconstruction.[148]

On balance, it strikes me that the scales of judgment regarding the relationship of Derrida to Jewish esotericism should be tipped in the direction of confluence rather than influence, but even presuming the former is not without problems. To illustrate this point let me note that in "How to Avoid Speaking: Denials," Derrida discusses negative theology as it has been formulated in the history of Christian mysticism, focusing most notably on Pseudo-Dionysus and Meister Eckhart, but he does not mention a word about kabbalah or Jewish mysticism. Lest one protest that this observation is trivial, let us recall that Derrida himself makes a point of noting that in the address he cannot treat negative theology "in a tradition of thought that is neither Greek or Christian," that is, in "Jewish and Arab thought."[149] With respect to these traditions, Derrida must perform the gesture of disavowal or dénégation,[150] speaking by unspeaking, which is appropriate to the subject at hand. Thus, in a second passage from this composition, Derrida interrupts his discussion of the relationship of avoidance that pertains to Heidegger and the apophasis of Dionysius the Areopagite and Meister Eckhart with the comment "*To say nothing*, once again, of the mystics or theologies in the Jewish, Arab, or other traditions."[151] To say nothing—not for the first time but *once again*—the saying of nonsaying must always be a matter of reiteration, since what is spoken in this speaking is what has been previously unspoken.[152]

To appreciate the importance of this parenthetical musing, we must recall that in this lecture Derrida displayed that he was sensitive to the geographical locale in which he gave his talk; indeed, he grappled with the philosophical intent of what it meant to be in Jerusalem. There is, Derrida reminds us, a certain impossibility of being in this place, an impossibility that he associates with the traditional formula uttered at the end of the Passover seder, "Next year in Jerusalem"; that is, Jerusalem, symbolically, is the place to which one must always be going, and thus it embodies deferring the pledge and postponing the promise indefinitely, an experiential feature of the structure of the messianic architectonic.[153] Precisely in the place where one cannot be except by anticipating being there is it most suitable to speak of what cannot be spoken. Interestingly, Derrida referred to this lecture "as the most 'autobiographical' discourse I have ever risked . . . It is necessary to surround with precautions the hypothesis of a self-presentation that passes by way of a lecture on the negative theology of others. But if one day I had to tell my story, nothing in this narrative would begin to speak of the thing itself if I did not come up against this fact; I have never yet been able—lacking the ability, the competence, or the self-authorization—to speak of what my birth . . . should have brought closest to me: the Jew, the Arab."[154] Bracketing the important issues of cultural and linguistic identity that emerge from this revealing note, and especially the somewhat perplexing tag of ethnicity "the Jew, the Arab,"[155] let me reiterate the main point for the purposes of this chapter: Derrida shies away from comporting himself as someone who can discourse about Jewish mysticism even in the lecture on apophasis delivered in Jerusalem, a site that would have naturally facilitated a discussion of this matter in Jewish and/or Islamic mysticism.[156] This statement must give pause to all those involved in the effort to discern Derrida's relationship to the mystical dimensions of Judaism. One cannot simply ignore the fact that Derrida has not taken upon himself the responsibility of discussing this matter because he does not feel at ease and in control of the relevant material that would have to be deconstructed.[157] The more engaging question, then, is how the study of Derrida and the study of kabbalah can mutually illumine one another.

(UN)VEILING THE VEIL: KABBALISTIC ESOTERICISM AND DERRIDEAN DECONSTRUCTION

To assess this question properly, we must again raise the issue of the compatibility of Derrida's enterprise and theories of interpretation that have been operative in various forms of Jewish textual practice, as I think this is the appropriate context within which to place kabbalah. To approach the relationship of Derrida to Jewish mysticism without getting a handle on Derrida and Judaism would amount to what Alfred North Whitehead called the fallacy of misplaced concreteness, that is, mistaking the part for the whole. If there is an efficacious way to think about Derrida in terms of Jewish mysticism, then it will have to be approached from within the broader context of his relationship to the religious and intellectual culture of the Jews.

In her book published in 1982, *The Slayers of Moses: The Emergence of Rabbinic Interpretation in Modern Literary Theory*, Handelman argued that Derrida's deconstructive method could be viewed as a form of "Jewish heretic hermeneutics."[158] It is, more accurately, in Derrida's notion of writing as *différance*, the dissemination of the word through the infinite play of signification occasioned by the rejection of a transcendental signifier, that Handelman finds a coalescence of the main themes of this hermeneutic, to wit, castration or mutilation of the phallus, which is linked to circumcision, rebellion, irrevocable loss, displacement, and breaking the covenant.[159] On the basis of

a passage in *Glas*, Handelman suggested that Derrida's choice of writing, and by intimation the notion of text, to oppose the logocentrism of Western thought is related to
the veiled Torah scroll that is unveiled from behind the curtain at a climactic moment
in the Jewish liturgical service.[160] I note, incidentally, that Wolosky independently
cited the same text as proof that Derrida's life experience as a Jew provided the "stance
for a radical re-vision of Hellenic assumptions."[161] Subsequently, I shall return to the
image of unveiling the veiled in kabbalistic hermeneutics, paying special attention to
the concurrence of the themes of writing, circumcision, and exposition of secrets. For
the moment what is worthy of note is that there is something compelling to the argument that the primacy accorded the written text over the spoken word, the affirmation
of the grammatological as opposed to the logocentric, may have, at least in part, been
informed by Derrida's visceral familiarity with Jewish ritual experience.

The crucial question, however, is, should the deconstructionist hermeneutic be
compared theoretically to rabbinic claims regarding the polysemous nature of Torah
as the originary script decoded in the displacements and contraversions of midrashic
reading, a textual strategy greatly expanded and embellished in medieval kabbalah?
Can we accept the further suggestion of Handelman, following Bloom, that Derrida's
notion of the trace, the "elusive originating-nonoriginating mark of meaning," is similar to the kabbalistic conception of the divine name (described by Scholem) as the
meaningless, primordial language, encoded in the text of Torah, which assumes
meaning only through the mediation of multivalent interpretations?[162] There are, as
we have seen, passages in Derrida that would corroborate this claim. We should also
bear in mind that Derrida himself makes explicit the connection between the Greek
privileging of logos as spoken word and the Johannine notion of the word become
flesh.[163] Of the many examples that illustrate the point, consider the following remark
in *Of Grammatology*: "The difference between signified and signifier belongs in a profound and implicit way to the totality of the great epoch covered by the history of
metaphysics, and in a more explicit and more systematically articulated way to the
narrower epoch of Christian creationism and infinitism when these appropriate the
resources of Greek conceptuality."[164] In semiotic terms, the son is the phonic sign of
the father, who would be identified as the transcendental signified. Conventional sign-
theory, with its privileging of the spoken word over the written text, derives from the
ontological scheme of Greek metaphysics reinforced by the Christological doctrine of
incarnation. Are we justified in assuming that the emphasis placed on writing as the
primary act of God's creativity and the consequent notion that being may be compared to a book, which derives from ancient Hebraic wisdom, provides an alternative
to the ontotheology that has prevailed in Hellenistic culture?

Here it is instructive to consider Derrida's criticism of Heidegger toward the conclusion of "Faith and Knowledge": "Ontotheology encrypts faith and destines it to the
condition of a sort of Spanish Marrano who would have lost—in truth, dispersed,
multiplied—everything up to and including the memory of his unique secret. Em-

blem of a still life: an opened pomegranate, one Passover evening, on a tray." The pomegranate, we are told in the same context, denotes the "granulated, grainy, disseminated, aphoristic, discontinuous, juxtapositional, dogmatic, indicative or virtual, economic; in a word, more than ever telegraphic" articulation of meaning.[165] Surely it is not insignificant that the symbol that Derrida chooses for the method of deconstruction, which provides a way beyond the ontotheological obstruction of faith, is a Jewish ritual object linked to Passover, the festival that commemorates the past liberation and anticipates the future redemption. This passage lends support to Caputo's suggestion that the nomadic play that is basic to deconstruction reflects the ontic condition of the Jew as other, the uprooted, displaced wanderer who lives in the hope of a promise that, paradoxically, is fulfilled only to the extent that it is recurrently impeded. Derrida notes that the itinerant quality of the Jew is portrayed by the symbol of the tabernacle, the necessarily impermanent place wherein the divine glory is disclosed as the presence that cannot be iconically represented, the arcanum in and through which the infinite is envisioned as the invisible nothing—not the invisible visible, the secret that is presently hidden and therefore kept out of sight, but the absolute invisibility that "takes secrecy beyond the secret," the encrypted nonvisible that falls outside the register of visuality (the sonorous, the musical, the phonic, the tactile, the odoriferous) and yet enframes and inhabits all things visible[166]—that defies imaginary depiction.

> The tabernacle gives its name and its place to the Jewish family dwelling. That establishes the Jewish nation. The Jewish nation settles in the tabernacle, adores therein the sign of God and his covenant. . . . Now the tabernacle . . . remains a signifier without signified. The Jewish hearth forms an empty house. Certainly, sensible to the absence of all sensible form, the Jews have tried to produce an object that gave in some way rise, place, and figure to the infinite. But this place and this figure have a singular structure: the structure encloses its void within itself, shelters only its own proper interiorized desert, opens onto nothing, confines nothing, contains as its treasure only nothingness: a hole, an empty spacing, a death. . . . No center, no heart, an empty space, nothing. One undoes the bands, displaces the tissues, pulls off the veils, parts [écarte] the curtains: nothing but a black hole or a deep regard, without color, form, and life. . . . The Jewish Geheimnis, the hearth in which one looks for the center under a sensible cover [enveloppe]—the tent of the tabernacle, the stone of the temple, a robe that clothes the text of the covenant—is finally discovered as an empty room, is not uncovered, never ends being uncovered, as it has nothing to show.[167]

In this passage, there is much that is said about what cannot be said, the text of the covenant that is continuously uncovered, since there is nothing visible that demands to be recovered. The process of unveiling has no terminus—what is unveiled is the veil that there is nothing that is veiled but another veil. How do we apply this image of nothing at the center but empty space to a text or, more specifically, to the stone tablets upon which were inscribed the Ten Commandments? Is the "text of the covenant" not a concrete form that renders the image of "nothing to show" inappropriate? For Derrida, it appears, even these stones may be construed as "nothing but a black hole." Extending this insight, the medium upon which any text is written is the white space that is as critical to the determination of significance as the black letters of text.[168] Alternatively expressed, meaning is never fixed by authorial intent; on the contrary, the deconstructionist method is predicated on a presumably unbridgeable gap—the hole in the middle—between the intention of the writer and the interpretation posited by the reader. With regard to the hermeneutical question, the author cannot claim privileged status, for sense can be articulated only through multiple voices engaged in the persistent play of interpretation:

> Dissemination endlessly opens up a *snag* in writing that can no longer be mended, a spot where neither meaning, however plural, nor *any form of presence* can pin/pen down [*agrapher*] the trace. Dissemination treats—doctors—that *point* where the movement of signification would regularly come to *tie down* the play of the trace, thus producing (a) history. The security of each point arrested in the name of the law is hence blown up. It is—at least—at the risk of such a blowup that dissemination has been broached/breached. With a detour through/of writing one cannot get over.[169]

The notion of secrecy is employed by Derrida to characterize the polysemy of signification enacted in the *différance* wrought by dissemination. That is, by "secret" Derrida does not refer to either the unknowable transcendence (the *hyperousios* of negative theology) or to an irretrievable hidden truth (the *mysterium* of esoteric gnosis); the secret, in his mind, relates to the fact that meaning can never be determined with incontrovertible certainty, and thus we cannot speak of immutable content in isolation from the event of reading, which always deals with the "absolute singularity, the infinite separation of what binds me or exposes me to the unique, to one as to the other, to *the One as to the Othe*r."[170] The secret implicates one in the "vicious circle" that the unavowable is the only speech that may be avowed, and "thus one never avows . . . especially when one avows."[171] If we are to speak of an inherent secretive nature of language, it signifies the surplus of signification to be determined through a multivocality of voices. Consider the following account of apophasis:

> The apophatic is not here necessarily dependent on negative theology, even if it makes it possible, too. And what we are attempting to put to the test is the possibility, in truth the impossibility, for any testimony to guarantee itself by expressing itself [*s'énonçant*] in the following form and grammar: "Let us testify that . . ." We testify [*témoignons*] to a secret that is without content, without a content separable from its performative experience, from its performative tracing.[172]

The Jewish stricture against representing the deity visually within the inner sanctum of the tabernacle and temple is interpreted by Derrida as an allusion to the hermeneutical dynamic that partakes of the structure of secrecy: the text cloaked behind the curtain can never cease being uncovered inasmuch as the meaning discovered in the text is what comes to light by being unremittingly recovered.

Above all else, the Jew as other functions symbolically as bearing the character of writer, for writing, *écriture*, is not a return to origin but a recurrent retracing of one's steps to the text, the homeland where one has never been, a marking of absence, a delimiting of the limitless, the saying of something without saying anything, erasing the inscription under the inscripting of erasure. It is for this reason, as I have already noted, that on a number of occasions in his compositions Derrida turns his gaze on circumcision, the primordial cut that traditionally binds the Jewish male to the covenantal community, the differentiating mark, the mark of difference, the inscription of singularity, the proper name that can be pronounced only once, in a moment that is unique, the present that is always to come for it has always already been, a presence that cannot be represented even as absence. For Derrida, the cut of circumcision signifies autobiographical self-representation,[173] the ring of double affirmation, the circle of return wherein the same recurs because it is different. And it is exactly here that one finds, in my judgment, the element of Derrida's thinking that can be applied most fruitfully to kabbalistic symbolism, the link between circumcision, inscription, and obliteration, the re/marking of the mark occluded in its demarcation.

As I have suggested in a number of studies, the primary site of contemplative visualization in kabbalistic praxis is the circumcised phallus, which must be concealed in its exposure.[174] The link between circumcision and secrecy in the esoteric teaching can be viewed as an elaboration of the rabbinic emphasis on the need to conceal the *membrum virile*, an aspect of the etiquette of modesty (*ṣeniʿut*) required of the Jewish male.[175] In kabbalistic lore, the concealment of the phallus on pietistic grounds served as the ritual foundation for the symbolic interpretation of circumcision as embodying the hermeneutical play of secrecy; that which is hidden (*ṣeniʿuta*) is divulged exclusively to those who are humble (*ṣenuʿin*), for they know the art of concealing the concealment in disclosing the disclosure.[176] Circumcision, therefore, may be viewed as the sacrament through which the Jew enacts the role of dissimulation by cutting away the foreskin to inscribe the covenantal sign, *ot berit*, the "letter of the covenant," which Derrida names the "sign (or simulacrum) of castration,"[177] a sacrificial marking imprinted by taking away, the presence represented through its own absence. The paradox is fully expressed in the repeated insistence on the part of kabbalists that it is forbidden to gaze on the phallus, which is laid bare in the second part of the circumcision ritual, the act of *periʿah*, the tearing and stripping back of the inner mucosal lining of the foreskin to expose the corona.[178] Inscripting the sign occasions erasure of the name that cannot be written. This claim rests on the assumption that what is revealed of the secret is manifest in its concealment and what is concealed thereof is hidden in its manifestation.

In a manner consonant with kabbalists, Derrida proposes that the symbolic underpinning of the literal cut of circumcision is the figurative incision of the letter in the flesh, an act of engraving that stands tropologically for writing. I note, parenthetically, that the thematic connection between circumcision and writing in Derrida's thought incriminates him in a phallocentrism that is also characteristic of kabbalistic sources. This is somewhat ironic as Derrida challenged the phallocentric nature of the logocentrism of Western metaphysics, insisting on the need to attend seriously to the problematic of sexual difference by assigning to the woman a bona fide role as other rather than subsume her under the masculine dominance of the same. The matter is cast as the dissimilarity between the phallogocentrism of hermeneutical anxiety and the feminine displacement of reading.[179] Relevant to this discussion is Derrida's assertion that no text "completely escapes" the rubric of phallocentricism.[180] Although no mention is made in that context to circumcision, it seems reasonable to make this connection in light of Derrida's utilization of circumcision as a rhetorical trope to characterize writing and reading. Be that as it may, when circumcision is viewed through the Derridean lens, it assumes a metaphorical meaning without diminishing its concrete sense; indeed, the very sense of somatic concreteness is transfigured in a manner akin to what one finds in Jewish mystical tradition: the nature of corporeality is conceived semiotically. In contrast to the Christological doctrine of incarnation, which is predicated on the identification of a particular historical figure as the embodiment of God's word, the Jewish esoteric tradition proffers an incarnational doctrine predicated on the notion of divine body as scriptural text, which is the Tetragrammaton.

Needless to say, Derrida does not embrace the kabbalistic idea in all of its symbolic density, eschewing, as he does, any metaphysical, let alone theosophic, conception of transcendence. Nevertheless, he does affirm two of the main elements of the worldview of kabbalists. First, it is axiomatic for Derrida's deconstruction that the materiality of being is textual. Consider this formulation: "The nonquestion of which we are speaking is the unpenetrated certainty that Being is a Grammar; and that the world is in all its parts a cryptogram to be constituted or reconstituted through poetic inscription or deciphering; that the book is original, that everything *belongs to the book* before being and in order to come into the world; that any thing can be born only by *approaching* the book, can die only by failing *in sight of* the book; and that always the impassible shore of the book is *first*."[181] To place the book at the beginning is not to lapse back into a logocentric positing of an origin or a transcendental signified, for there is no book that is not composed by traces of another book, and so on in an endless chain of significations. The book is first, at the beginning, but the beginning, paradoxically, cannot begin and remain the beginning, since to be the beginning it must have already begun.[182] The beginning, then, must be conceived as a breaking point, an interference, the instigation of the "discontinuous series of instants and *at-*

tractions."[183] If, however, the book at the beginning, which is the beginning of the book, has no beginning, then writing the book has no end, and, consequently, meaning cannot be fixed in any resolute fashion. "To risk meaning nothing is to start to play, and first to enter into the play of différance which prevents any word, any concept, any major enunciation from coming to summarize and to govern from the theological presence of a center the movement and textual spacing of differences."[184] To commence with a book, therefore, is to mandate interpretation as the incipient evocation: "The necessity of commentary, like poetic necessity, is the very form of exiled speech. In the beginning is hermeneutics."[185]

The second similarity to traditional kabbalah relates to the special role that Derrida ascribes to the Tetragrammaton in illumining the language of secrecy and the secrecy of language. From the biblical narrative of the Tower of Babel, Derrida adduces that this name simultaneously "imposes and forbids translation. . . . Translation then becomes necessary and impossible, like the effect of a struggle for the appropriation of the name, necessary and forbidden in the interval between two absolutely proper names."[186] The Tetragrammaton, therefore, is designated the "translatable-untranslatable name,"[187] that is, translatable inasmuch as it is ineffable and hence cannot be voiced except through cognomens, yet, untranslatable insofar as it names the wholly other and absolute singularity[188] that cannot be named.[189] From the specific case of the Tetragrammaton, "the proper name which is never proper,"[190] we can extrapolate about the concomitant necessity and impossibility of translating every proper name, a double bind that is indicative of language per se.[191] The ineffable name paradigmatically exemplifies the role of *dénomination*—"at the same time to name and to unname"[192]—implicit in every linguistic utterance, the unsaying that makes each saying (im)possible:

> God's name would then be the hyperbolic effect of that negativity or any negativity that is consistent in its discourse. God's name would fit everything that cannot be broached, approached, or designated, except in an indirect and negative way. Every negative sentence would already be haunted by God or by the name of God, the distinction between God and God's name opening up the very space of this enigma.[193]

Perhaps the greatest affinity between Derrida's grammatology and kabbalistic hermeneutics is captured in the tradition reported by the Hasidic master, R. Ṣadoq ha-Kohen of Lublin: "Thus I have received that the world in its entirety is a book that God, blessed be he, made, and the Torah is the commentary that he composed on that book."[194] This dictum is embedded deeply in the Jewish idea that God's creative act is essentially linguistic, in fact that divine creativity is an act of written composition. The first book that God writes is the world, and the second the Torah. This statement implies, in a quintessentially Jewish manner, that the first book, the text of the cosmos, requires a commentary, Scripture, and that commentary, we can well imagine, begets other commentaries that not God but human beings create in a seemingly endless effort to reveal the hidden depths concealed in the original traces of God's writing that make up the universe. R. Ṣadoq's comment, while perhaps not consciously intended in this manner, subverts any hermeneutical theory that posits a final truth, a foundation that ends all play of meaning. In perfectly good Derridean fashion, we may say that the way back leads not to an original truth but rather to an origin that is a text that needs to be interpreted by another text. In the beginning there is interpretation. The necessity of commentary thus constitutes the very texture of existence from the Jewish standpoint. There is nothing that is not inscribed within the book and therefore open to interpretation, not even God's being. One is here reminded of the provocative observation of Derrida, "there is nothing outside of the text" (*il n'y a pas de hors-texte*).[195] All transcendence is reduced to textuality.

The textualization of body is related by Derrida, as it is by numerous kabbalists over the centuries, to circumcision, for the latter is the act by means of which the flesh is engraved and the individual receives a proper name. Derrida provides a way to get beyond the "great war between Judaism and Christianity," as he put it in *Archive Fever*, that is, the debate regarding the literal versus the figurative interpretation of the ritual of circumcision, excision of flesh, on the one hand, and immersion in baptismal water, on the other. The sign of circumcision, like the phylacteries, which Derrida describes as "archives of skin or parchment covered with writing," is "right on the body . . . but with a being-right-on that this time does not exclude the detachment and the untying of the ligament, of the substance, and of the text simultaneously."[196] The text of the inscripted body for Derrida yields the body of the scripted text, and just as the former arises as a consequence of a violent infringement upon the flesh, so the latter is written in the disrupting rupture of eruption. The Jewish rite is hyperliterally preserved by Derrida, for the mark of circumcision is the primal cut of discernment that differentiates one from the other and leaves the other inaccessible in its otherness, a mark that is "at once both endowed with and deprived of singularity."[197] Circumcision thus functions as a figure of speech for the method of deconstruction, since the latter is analogously understood as a cut, a tearing off and taking apart, a setting of boundaries traversed by turning the inside outside and the outside inside.[198] In an entry in *Circumfession*, Derrida relates the main themes of his writings, some of whose titles are specified by name, to the ancient Jewish rite of passage: "*Circumcision, that's all I have ever talked about, consider the discourse on the limit, margins, marks, marches, etc., the closure, the ring (alliance and gift), the sacrifice, the writing of the body, the* pharmakos *excluded or cut off, the cutting/sewing of* Glas, *the blow and the sewing back up . . . yes but I have been, I am and I always will be me and not another, circumcised* [oui mais j'ai été, je suis et je serai toujours, moi et non un autre, circoncis]."[199]

The link between circumcision and writing is treated more fully by Derrida in his study "Shibboleth for Paul Celan," published in 1986. The main thesis is summed up in this statement: "There must be circumcision, circumcision of the word, writing, and it must take place once, precisely, each time one time, the one time only."[200] The choice of the Hebrew term *shibbolet* is based on the use of this sign in the testing of the Ephraimites by the men of Gilead in Judges 12:6. The indication that one was from Ephraim was the pronunciation of the word as *sibbolet*. The *shibbolet*, as Derrida expresses the matter in another essay, is a "solid barrier of a social division,"[201] for the way of speaking serves as an idiomatic mark to distinguish between those who belong and those who do not belong to a particular speech community. The *shibbolet* has a double edge, for it cuts two ways; that is, the tear it makes in the fabric of being facilitates entry to the indigenous by turning away the alien. Predictably, the double edge is related to circumcision, which is concomitantly a "mark of belonging and of exclusion."[202] By virtue of circumcision the Jew becomes *"at one and the same time,* both the alleged universality of Jewish witnessing . . . and the incommunicable secret of the Judaic idiom, the singularity of 'his name, his unpronounceable name.' "[203] Derrida's reflections are anchored in the fact that it is customary to proclaim the name of the Jewish infant boy publicly at the time of circumcision, but unlike the normal function of the name, in the case of the Jew the name names what cannot be pronounced, the distinctiveness of alterity, the embodiment of difference, otherness, estrangement, homelessness, and inscrutability. The Jew gives witness—stubbornly it seems—to the universal through an absolute singularity.[204] "But does one ever circumcise without circumcising a word? a name? And how can one ever circumcise a name without doing something to the body? First of all to the body of the name which finds itself recalled by the wound to its condition as word, then as carnal mark, written, spaced, and inscribed in a network of other marks, at once both endowed with and deprived of singularity."[205]

The homology of circumcision of the foreskin and circumcision of the tongue in Jewish mystical sources—attested already in *Sefer Yeṣirah*—underlies Derrida's identification of the Jew as poet. In support of this claim, however, he refers not to these texts but to the assertion of Marina Tsvétayeva, "All poets are Jews," cited by Paul Celan as an epigraph to "Und mit dem Buch aus Tarussa," the final poem in the 1963 collection *Die Niemandrose*,[206] which brings to mind the statement of Blake in "The Marriage of Heaven and Hell" that the people of Israel "taught that the Poetic Genius . . . was the first principle and all the others merely derivative."[207] It is in this sense that, according to Derrida, the poet/writer participates in the "enigma of circumcision,"[208] the circumcised word that is "incised and excised, which may be the body of a language and which in any case always binds the body to language: the word which is entered into, wounded in order to be what it is, the word cut into, written because cut into, caesuraed in its origins, with the poem."[209] The literal circumcision as the determinate mark of Jewish ethnicity is rescinded and replaced by the hyperliteral understanding of circumcision as a trope for writing, "an incision in the body of language," the opening of the word to the other, the door that "opens history and the poem and philosophy and hermeneutics and religion. Of all that calls itself—of the name and the blessing of the name, of yes and of no, it sets turning the ring, to affirm or to annul."[210]

Here a note of caution is in order: the view that all poets are Jews does not imply its inverse, for it is certainly not the case that all Jews are poets. All poetic language may be deemed Jewish in essence, but this "promises itself only through dis-identification, that expropriation in the nothing of that non-essence," which is the essence of the Jew. Every language to be poetic, accordingly, must be circumcised by the rabbi, who thereby becomes a poet.[211] In his essay on Jabès, Derrida differentiates between rabbi and poet. While both agree about the necessity of exegesis, they reflect two distinct interpretive stances, the former representing heteronomous allegiance to the law and the latter autonomous independence from the law. "Between the fragments of the broken Tables," Derrida writes, "the poem grows and the right to speech takes root."[212] Although both types are legitimate responses to the "original opening of interpretation,"[213] it is the poetic that justifies the characterization of the writer as Jew. Poetic autonomy presupposes the shattering of the tablets of law, but this freedom is not absolute, for even the outlaw remains bound to the law—if there were no law, how could one be outside the law and hence an outlaw? For the poet, the lawful breaching of the law is intricately connected to language. "The poet, in the very experience of his freedom, finds himself both bound to language and delivered from it by a speech whose master, nonetheless, he himself is."[214]

In my judgment, this insight corresponds to what I have called the hypernomian tendency in kabbalistic literature, which can be expressed concisely as the insight that the law is fulfilled most perfectly in its abrogation.[215] Expressing matters in a manner that is even closer to Derrida, kabbalists have discerned that the lawful repudiation of law is intertwined with the presumption that in its utter otherness the Godhead is unrepresentable but still the measure of all that is representable, a measure that is meted most pristinely in the ordinance prohibiting representation. From this peculiar Jewish-inspired exegesis, law generically is delineated as the measure that puts things in place by circumscribing them in the limit that must be trespassed. In the face of what cannot be represented, all representation of the other is transgressive, but without representation of the other there would be no law to abrogate.[216] Transgression thus lies in the hub of the law, for trespassing the law determines the boundaries of the law.[217] Moreover, for kabbalists, as for Derrida, the issue of law and its overcoming is related to the problem of language and its transcendence: "Inclining, but not going beyond incline or inclination, not even or almost (*beinahe zur Gottlosigkeit hinneigend*), and the oblique slope [*penchant*] of this *clinamen* does not seem separable from a certain boldness of language [*langue*], from a poetic or metaphoric tongue."[218] Just as the path to overcome the law is by way of undergoing the law, the unsayable can be heeded merely by way of what is said, albeit spoken as the unspoken, a paradox that is ritually instantiated in the Jewish custom of vocalizing the ineffable name by its circumlocution. The unpronounceability "keeps and destroys the name; it keeps it, like the name of God, or dooms it to annihilation among the ashes."[219]

SECRECY AND THE APORIA OF THE GIFT

The transgressive element, and particularly the connection between it and linguistic representation, is also helpful in ascertaining the association of secrecy and illicit sexual relations that figures prominently in the kabbalistic tradition and whose reverberation is discernible in Derrida's thinking. Uncovering the secret is linked thematically to the laying bare of the apocalyptic unveiling, the disclosure of what has been enveloped and withdrawn, held in reserve. The "gesture of denuding" and "affording sight" (*donner à voir*) to what was hidden is akin to the uncovering of the genitals in the incestuous liaisons prohibited by the priestly law.[220] More specifically, Derrida asserts that transgression discloses an essential link between the gift and secrecy, a theme found in an archaic mythical fragment preserved in *Sefer ha-Bahir*, considered by scholars to be one of the oldest works of kabbalah to circulate on the European continent. I have had the opportunity to examine this passage elsewhere, utilizing Derrida's reflections, so in this context I will only briefly recapitulate the main points of the argument.[221]

In an effort to explain the first word of the Torah, *bere'shit*, "in the beginning," the bahiric pericope[222] offers a parable about a king who gives his daughter as a gift in marriage to his son. What in the nature of this bestowal necessitates its being characterized as a giving of a gift? Indeed, according to rabbinic law, which one can presume would have been upheld by the author(s) of this passage in the *Bahir*, marriage is a contractual arrangement, and thus it would be superfluous to speak of a woman being offered as a gift when she is betrothed to a man. The clue is provided in the concluding remark of the king to the prince, "Do with her as you wish." To appreciate the intent of this comment, it would be useful to recall Derrida's remark on the nature of the gift as that which opens the circle of economy, the *aneconomic* that disrupts the exchange of goods, so as to defy reciprocity or symmetry,[223] for "the *given* of the gift (*that which* one gives, *that which* is given, the gift as given thing or as act of donation) must not come back to the giving (let us not already say to the subject, to the donor). It must not circulate, it must not be exchanged, it must not in any case be exhausted, as a gift, by the process of exchange, by the movement of circulation of the circle in the form of return to the point of departure. . . . It is perhaps in this sense that the gift is the impossible."[224]

The paradox of the gift—to be distinguished from the Husserlian sense of *Gegebenheit*, the givenness of things[225]—is such that as soon as it is "identified as a gift, with the meaning of a gift, then it is cancelled as a gift. It is reintroduced into the circle of exchange, and destroyed as a gift."[226] For the gift to be a gift, it must be free of this economic calculability, but to be so free, neither the one who gives nor the one who receives can be conscious of the giving. The phenomenon of the gift may appear only within the horizon of its absence. The nexus of secrecy and the gift ensues from the fact that the bestowing of the gift occurs precisely as the impossibility of the gift presenting itself as a gift, an event that is "totally heterogeneous" to either theoretical or phenomenological identification.[227] The paradoxical phenomenality proper to the gift is marked by Derrida as the impossibility of the double bind: "For there to be gift, it is necessary that the gift not even appear, that it not be perceived or received as gift [*pour qu'il y ait don, il faut que le don n'apparaisse même pas, qu'il ne soit pas perçu comme don*]."[228] The givenness of the gift, therefore, consists of its being not-given; that is, the gift is revealed as gift to the extent that it is concealed as gift in being revealed.[229] Derrida elucidates the aporia of the gift by drawing a more specific connection between language, textuality, and the dynamic of giving and taking:

> The definition of language, of a language, as well as of the text in general, cannot be formed without a certain relation to the gift, to giving-taking [*donner-prendre*]. . . . Reduced to its barest formality, the structural principle . . . is that all semantic ambivalence and the syntactico-semantic problem of giving-taking are not situated only within language, the words of language or the elements of a textual system. Language is also an example of it as is any textual determination. In short, one must not only ask oneself . . . how it is possible that to give and/or to take are said this way or that way *in* a language, but one must also remember first of all that language is as well a phenomenon of gift-countergift [*don-contre-don*], of giving-taking—and of exchange. . . . Everything said in language and everything written about giving-taking in general *a priori would fold back* on language and writing as giving-taking. Giving *would come back, come down* to taking and taking to giving, but this would come back to fold itself over not only on language or writing but toward the text in general, beyond its linguistic or logocentric closure, beyond its narrow or common meaning.[230]

The bahiric parable can be profitably read through the lens of Derrida's account of the gift and particularly its link to the temporalization of language in the dynamic of bestowing and receiving, opening and closing.[231] That the prince is given the princess as a gift by the king signifies that the act of giving is not a symmetrical relation. Nothing the son does can reciprocate the action of the father, for there is no exchange of commodities, no mutual giving and taking. Moreover, the son who receives the daughter as gift cannot donate this gift to another; the daughter belongs exclusively to the son, and there is no way to assuage this sense of custodianship. Finally, in the absence of reciprocity, the recipient of the gift assumes complete control and mastery over that which is given; insofar as the donor renounces all claims of ownership and possession with respect to the gift, the act of giving exceeds the circle of economy. In the bahiric passage, the excessive power of gifting is expressed as an entitlement with a distinctly sexual nuance—the prince is instructed by his father to do as he pleases with the princess. Indeed, the symbolic import of the parable blatantly contradicts the normative strictures of biblical law, for the taboo of siblings mating (Leviticus 18:9) is undermined by the relationship that is described between the son and the daughter of the king. The secret alluded to here, which later kabbalists relate to the talmudic mystery of illicit sexual relations (*sitrei arayot*),[232] is that the sexual prohibitions necessary to preserve the fabric of human society can be, indeed must be, transgressed in a symbolic manner in the divine realm.[233] In that sense, the gift of wisdom is truly the impossible, that which defies the limits of temporal possibility inscribed within the parameters of law. The only time of the gift is the present, the paradoxical instant that is an effraction in the linear circularity of time.[234]

But there is an additional element in Derrida's analysis of the gift and secrecy that can be applied to kabbalistic hermeneutics. The gift is marked by

> structural paradoxes, the stigmata of the impossibility . . . So as not to take over the other, the overtaking by surprise of the pure gift should have the generosity to give nothing that surprises and appears *as* gift, *nothing that presents itself as present, nothing that is* [rien qui se présente comme présent, rien qui soit]; it should therefore be surprising enough and so thoroughly made up of a surprise that it is not even a question of getting over it, thus of a surprise surprising enough to let itself be forgotten without delay. . . . The secret of that about which one cannot speak, but which one can no longer silence [*Le secret de ce don't on ne peut pas parler, mais qu'on ne peut plus taire*].[235]

The paradox of the gift is that it is always "the gift of something that remains inaccessible, unpresentable, and as a consequence secret. . . . The gift is the secret itself, if the secret *itself* can be told. Secrecy is the last word of the gift which is the last word of the secret."[236] Just as the disclosure of the secret undermines its claim to being a secret, so the gifting of the gift is revoked in the giving of the gift. The "unconditional respect" of the secret, Derrida tells us, in an obvious challenge to Kantian epistemology, is that the "secret is not phenomenalizable. Neither phenomenal nor noumenal."[237] The secret is not something that can be unveiled, since it "remains inviolable even when one thinks one has revealed it." The secret is "nonprovisional, heterogeneous to all manifestation. This secret is not a reserve of potential knowing, a potential manifestation. And the language of ab-negation . . . *necessitates* doing the impossible, necessitates going there where one cannot go."[238] To be a secret the secret must persist as secret, mute and impassive, and thus one can speak of the secret *ad infinitum* without disrupting its secrecy. Indeed, it is the ineffability of the secret that generates a potentially unlimited sequence of attempts to articulate the secret.[239] "No more secrecy means more secrecy [*plus de secret, plus de secret*]: that is another secret of secrecy."[240]

The duplicity of the secret as the saying of what cannot be said, the hermeneutical condition of *différance*, is illustrated by the biblical narrative of the *aqedah*, Abraham's attempted sacrifice of Isaac (Genesis 22:1–19). Commenting on Kierkegaard's observation that Abraham responds briefly to Isaac but really does not speak because, as the

single individual standing in absolute relation to the absolute, he cannot say anything
of a universal nature that could make the particularity of the event understandable,[241]
Derrida writes that he "speaks in order not to say anything about the essential thing
that he must keep secret. Speaking in order not to say anything is always the best technique for keeping a secret [*Parler pour ne rien, dire, c'est toujours la meilleure technique
pour garder un secret*]."[242] Extrapolating a general principle from the specific example
adduced by Kierkegaard, Derrida concludes that by speaking what cannot be spoken,
the secret is preserved in the sacrifice of the sacrifice.

The secret for the kabbalists, too, necessarily exemplifies this double bind: the
secret can be a secret only if it is hidden, but the secret can be hidden only if it is revealed.[243] Again, to quote Derrida, the secret is "the thing to be dissimulated, a thing
that is neither shown nor said, signified perhaps but that cannot or *must* not first be
delivered up to self-evidence."[244] The secret is thus linked to dénégation; that is, the
secret of necessity is the negation that negates itself. In this doubling of the negative,
the secret both is what it is not and is not what it is, a dissimulation that dissimulates
in the concealment of concealment that is the disclosure of disclosure—what is disclosed is nothing but the concealment.

> There is a secret of denial and a denial of the secret. The secret as such, *as secret*,
> separates and already institutes a negativity; it is a negation that denies itself. It
> de-negates itself. This de-negation does not happen to it by accident; it is essential
> and originary.[245]

The secret's text is woven in and from the interweave of veiling and unveiling, dissimulation and exposure. Precisely with respect to overcoming this dichotomy by occupying a space between does bestowing the gift illumine the secret. The secret can be
safeguarded only if it has been divulged and thus is no longer a secret, and, similarly,
the gift can be given only if it is received and thus is no longer a gift. It follows that the
secret remains untold in the telling, the gift withheld in the giving.[246]

The way of withholding-bestowal elicited from examining the secret and the gift
illumines Derrida's understanding of language as an encircling cut, a circum/cision,
that tears the fabric to which one is bound, the opening of space that fosters the possibility of piecing together the peace of the whole that has been ruptured. In one passage, Derrida relates this process to the act of translation: "translation-proof, grace
would perhaps come when the writing of the other absolves you, from time to time,
from the infinite *double bind* and first of all—such is the gift's condition—absolves
itself, unbinds itself from this double bind."[247] To be unbound of the double bind,
opening up to receive the gift that, strictly speaking, cannot be given, is elsewhere referred to by Derrida in the technical Eckhartian term *Gelassenheit*,[248] the "serenity of
abandonment," which is the "rarest secret" beyond all knowledge, even knowledge of
the name, since nothing is given to God (*à Dieu*), not even the saying of Adieu.[249]

"One can have doubts about it from the moment when the name not only is nothing, in any case is not the 'thing' that it names, not the 'nameable' or the renowned, but also risks to bind, to enslave or to engage the other, to link the called, to call him/her to respond even before any decision or any deliberation, even before any freedom. . . . According to a formula that haunts our tradition from Plotinus to Heidegger . . . and to Lacan . . . the gift of the name gives that which it does not have [*le don du nom donne ce qu'il n'a pas*], that in which, prior to everything, may consist the essence, that is to say—beyond being—the nonessence, of the gift [*l'inessence du don*]."[250] Through the gifting of what cannot be given, the performative act of calling God by the name that cannot be uttered, the spontaneous irruption of prayer, indeed the entreaty to pray, is made possible: "So, when this break, this interruption happens in the everyday life, on the exceptional moment of prayer, we are going back to the name, to the name of name, to the Jewish God who has . . . a number of names, a nameless name, or a placeless place, and so on and so forth. We don't simply address someone, we pray to someone— God if you want, some unique one, to allow us to pray . . . It's praying after the prayer— *prier après la prière*—which is the prayer before the prayer, the prayer for the prayer."[251]

If we are to speak of the influence of Jewish mysticism on Derrida, it would be in the concomitant bestowing and withholding, which resonates with the dialectic of disclosure and concealment that marks the way of kabbalistic hermeneutics.[252] Particularly germane is Derrida's comment that the play of words in the ostensibly tautological expression *tout autre est tout autre*—the rule of the universal exception predicated on the link between alterity and singularity—"seems to contain the very possibility of a secret that hides and reveals itself at the same time within a single sentence and, more than that, within a single language."[253] The dialectic underlies the decidedly apophatic sense of unbinding the double bind that facilitates the liturgical utterance of the unutterable name, the name that "names nothing that is, neither this nor that,"[254] the name that consists of the essence that is beyond being (*au-delà de l'être*), the nonessence, of the gift.[255] Yet, it is particularly with regard to this kenosis of language that the critical difference between traditional kabbalah and Derridean deconstruction becomes apparent. For the kabbalist, divine alterity does not entail the displacing of the onto-topological figuration of the superessentiality of God's being. In kabbalistic writings, the invisible absence of God, the withdrawal from the spectrum of the visible, signifies the divine presence most fully, whereas, for Derrida, absence is not merely an absence of what is present even if what is present is truly absent; it is rather the absence of both absence and presence. Simply put, kabbalists are occupied with naming the absence, whereas Derrida insists on the absence of naming.[256] If there can be any faith at all, it must be predicated on the likelihood that there is nothing in which to believe, the metaphysical skepticism that serves as the a/theistic premise for a "nondogmatic doublet of dogma, a philosophical and metaphysical doublet, in any case a *thinking* [pensant] that 'repeats' the possibility of religion without religion [*sans religion la* possibilité *de la religion*]."[257] Prayer itself is possible only to the extent that it embraces this impossibility: "If we were sure that at the other end of the prayer God would show up, and that we produce the addressee, that wouldn't be a prayer. The possibility that God remains eternally absent, that there might be no addressee at the other end of my prayer is the condition of the prayer. . . . So, that's why I would go so far as to say there should be a moment of atheism in the prayer."[258]

In traditional kabbalistic lore, the esoteric implication of prayer likewise involves an atheistic moment, insofar as liturgical worship, mystically conceived, entails the contemplative ascent that culminates with the subjugation of the finite will of the worshipper to the infinite will. In this state of absorption into the divine nothingness, liturgical words lose their referential meaning, for there is no other to be addressed dialogically, and, consequently, theism gives way to a monism in which the very purpose of prayer is disrupted. Prayer is thus marked by the invocation of the nameless that cannot be invoked, but such an invocation is based ultimately on the paradox of an absence that is present only in its absence, a true nothing, one might say; in deconstruction, this dialectic is no mystery, for the mysterious necessitates the lack of any lack, an absence that cannot be represented even as absence. When there is naught but lack, there is no ground even to speak of lack, let alone the lack of lack, and consequently, all that remains of the theological mystery is the rhetoric of secrecy, since as a matter of substance, there is no secret but the secret that there is no secret.

Here it is apposite to recall the following remarkable self-appraisal in *Circonfession*, "the constancy of God in my life is called by other names, so that I quite rightly pass for an atheist [*si bien que je passe à juste titre pour athée*], the omnipresence to me of what I call God in my absolved, absolutely private language being neither that of an eyewitness nor that of a voice doing anything other than talking to me without saying anything, nor a transcendent law or an immanent *schechina*, that feminine figure of a Yahweh who remains so strange and so familiar to me, but the secret I am excluded from, when the secret consists in the fact that you are held to secrecy by those who know your secret [*quand le secret consiste en ceci que vous êtes tenu au secret par ceux qui savent votre secret*] . . . and do not dare admit to you that this is no longer a secret for them, that they share with you the open secret [*le secret de polichinelle*]."[259] Derrida's precise words "I quite rightly pass for an atheist" do not imply a reappropriation of religious discourse and the affirmation of the nameless divinity that one may address through prayers and tears.[260] Without any ambiguity Derrida asserts that he is not privy to revelation of either a visual or an auditory nature; he cannot affirm the transcendent law or the immanent presence. That which goes by the name "God" is the secret that he is both bound to and excluded from, in fact, excluded by being bound thereto, the open secret that the belief consists of doubt. To pass as an atheist means to accept the radical finitude of the constitution of time as the ever-passing moment that cannot be past, present, or future, the notion of time as the trace of what comes to be as what is no more.[261]

RETRACING THE TRACE OF THE TRACE

To express the matter in another terminological register: the notion of the trace is endorsed by both kabbalists and Derrida, but with the critical difference that, for the former, the originary trace can be traced back ontologically to the infinite, the luminous darkness, exposed through its occlusion in the multiplicity of differentiated beings, a superabundance whose absence signifies the presence of a being so full that it must be empty. On occasion Derrida's formulations seem more congenial to the kabbalistic apophasis. Thus, in the essay "Form and Meaning: A Note on the Phenomenology of Language," first published in 1967, he gives an account of the trace related in part to the "closure of metaphysics" implied in some of the dicta of Plotinus:

> Form (presence, evidence) would not be the final recourse, the last instance, to which every possible sign would refer—the *archē* or the *telos*; but rather . . . the *morphē, archē,* and *telos* would still turn out to be signs. In a sense—or a non-sense—that metaphysics would have excluded from its field, while nonetheless being secretly and incessantly related to it, the form would already and in itself be the *trace (ichnos)* of a certain non-presence, the vestige of the formless, announcing and recalling its other to the whole of metaphysics—as Plotinus perhaps said. The trace would not be the mixture or passage between form and the amorphous, between presence and absence . . . but that which, in escaping this opposition, renders it possible because of its irreducible excess.[262]

It is noteworthy that, in this context, Derrida was still willing to speak of the trace of a "non-presence" or the "vestige of the formless," an "irreducible excess" that escapes the opposition of presence and absence. To speak of the trace in this manner strikes me as a perfectly appropriate locution to apply to the kabbalistic materials. In a similar vein, Derrida commented in the 1968 essay "Différance" on Heidegger's notion of the "early trace" (*die frühe Spur*) of difference that "effaces itself from the moment that presence appears as a being-present" (*das Anwesen wie ein Anwesendes erscheint*)[263] in a manner that could be applied to the kabbalistic idea of the trace especially as it was articulated in the Lurianic sources:

> The trace is not a presence but is rather the simulacrum of a presence that dislocates, displaces, and refers beyond itself. The trace has, properly speaking, no place, for effacement belongs to the very structure of the trace. . . . In addition, and from the start, effacement constitutes it as a trace—effacement establishes the trace in a change of place and makes it disappear in its appearing . . . In the

language of metaphysics the paradox of such a structure is the inversion of the metaphysical concept which produces the following effect: the present becomes the sign of signs, the trace of traces. . . . It is a trace, and a trace of the effacement of a trace.[264]

Whereas the trace for Heidegger and the kabbalists may still be called a simulacrum of a presence, the trace of the effacement of a trace, for Derrida, as he states explicitly in *Of Grammatology*, there is no origin of which the trace is a trace except for the origin that is constituted reciprocally by a nonorigin, which is not to say the obfuscation of origin but rather the abjuration of there being any origin. To refer to the trace as the "disappearance of origin" would be too much of a metaphysical imposition. Hence, "to wrench the concept of the trace from the classical scheme, which would derive it from a presence or from an originary nontrace and which would make of it an empirical mark, one must indeed speak of an originary trace or arche-trace. Yet we know that that concept destroys its name and that, if all begins with the trace, there is above all no originary trace."[265] What Derrida denies is precisely what the kabbalists affirm: the originary trace marks the beginning that both reveals and conceals the nontrace of the origin, the imprint of infinity that is prior even to the withdrawal of the light.

In Derrida's mind, the trace affirmed by kabbalists and Heidegger is a "negative mode of presence," whereas his trace "gives us to think beyond the closure" and therefore "cannot be simply absent."[266] But is this a fair assessment? Is it not possible to characterize the originary trace in the kabbalistic and Heideggerian pathways along the lines of the heterological sign of excess that "must elude mastery,"[267] the wholly other that can in no way appear or be named, the supplementary stroke (*trait*) that retreats (*re-trait*) in the withdrawal (*retrait*) of its tracing?[268] It seems to me plausible to apply to both the kabbalists and Heidegger the delineation of the trace as that which is "produced as its own erasure" and is thus "neither perceptible nor imperceptible,"[269] the vestigial sign that is subject to an "indefinite process of supplementarity,"[270] since it cannot be retraced to any origin that is not itself also a "trace of the trace," the *différance* etched in a "mode of writing" that is from its inception "without presence and without absence,"[271] an "inscription prior to writing, a protowriting without a present origin, without an *arche*."[272] On this score, all representation must be considered a "de-presentation,"[273] a conclusion that resounds with the kabbalistic tenet regarding the imaginal deformation of the formless in the form of the sefirotic emanations, the representation of the unrepresentable in the vocalization of the ineffable—insofar as kabbalists maintain that the *sefirot* are contained in the Tetragrammaton, the latter serves as the model to convey the confluence of the visual and the auditory, for just as the ineffable name is uttered in the epithet that preserves its ineffability, so the invisible image is portrayed in the form that shelters its invisibility.[274]

Traditional kabbalists—in line with the apophaticism of Neoplatonic negative theology—do assume there is a reality beyond language, the superessential infinity that transcends reason and speech. I do not think, however, that the kabbalists would assent to the asymmetrical proposition that without the One there is no multiplicity but without multiplicity there can still be the One.[275] This is not to deny that Ein Sof can be thought of as the One that contains all things, but it is not correct to speak of it as the One that can be abstracted from the many. The (non)essence of the One must be reckoned from the absolute incommensurability of individual entities. The goal of the mystical quest is to be conjoined to the infinite, to reverse the order of creation by transforming something into nothing, the same other returning always as what has never been but as already other to the same. The hiddenness of the infinite, therefore, does not signify the transcendence that protects the theistic dogma of divine separateness; on the contrary, the concealment relates to the mystery of the disclosure of the nothing in the limitless cycle of generation and decay that has neither beginning nor end. From this perspective, nothingness can be regarded as the temporal sway of eternal becoming, the fullness of time that is continuously emptying itself in the coming to be of what passes away persistently. In the nothingness of Ein Sof, time is eternalized in the nonpresent present, the present that can never be present and thus can never be absent.

The nothing is the unnameable and unknowable essence that permeates and yet escapes all beings, or, translated in Heideggerian terms, the groundlessness above time and space that is the elemental ground of the temporal-spatial world, the pleromatic vacuum that is neither something nor nothing but the not-being that continually comes to be in the ephemeral shadow play of being,[276] the void wherein everything possible is actual because what is actual is nothing but the possible,[277] the sheltering-concealing[278] wherein the real is what appears to be real,[279] the clearing in relation to which being is no longer distinguishable from nothing, the matrix within which all beings are revealed and concealed in the nihilation of their being. The Ein Sof may be called, borrowing the language of Nishitani, *transmetaphysical*, the One that must be thought beyond thinking, the One that exists beyond being, the One that is the negation of the One. When representation ceases to be representation, we discern—albeit through the lack of discernment—that the One is an emptiness that "refuses all objectification" and thus cannot even be named "the One." The "true nothingness" is "beyond the representation of both 'being' and 'nothingness.' . . . The unobjectifiable nothingness and the phenomena of various things are trans-metaphysically one. Nothingness is identical with the world of difference."[280] Nothingness is the substratum out of which all differentiated beings arise and in which their mutual relationality is grounded, and hence the most suitable logic—designated as *sokuhi*—is based on the absolute identification of the is and the is not. Diagramed symbolically, we would say A is A; A is not-A; therefore A is A.[281] The inherent insubstantiality of all things implies, in turn, the principle of codependent origination (*pratītyasamutpāda*): no thing has an intrinsic or independent reality apart from the causes and conditions through and from which it arose. In line with the logic of the middle way (Madhyamaka), Nishitani presumes that because everything is inherently empty, all things are mutually interdependent, and thus he posits a mode of reality—what he calls the "circuminsessional relationship"—that is beyond the binary of being and nothing.[282]

In a manner analogous to the Mahāyāna notion of the indiscriminate emptiness (śūnyatā) as the discriminate thusness (tathātā) of all that exists, the Ein Sof of the kabbalah can be envisaged as an emptiness that overcomes all differentiating thought and thus must be emptied of the distinction between empty and full—the self-emptying emptiness that is not empty in virtue of being empty[283]—the abyss of infinity that is accessible only meontologically as the nihilating nonground that is neither being nor nonbeing, neither existence nor nonexistence, the nothingness to which neither identity nor nonidentity can be attributed.[284] The trace of this nonground arises as an effacing of the trace that is the groundlessness of the ground, an effacing in which the faceless appears as the erasure of erasure and the consequent writing of the nameless name, the name that cannot be declaimed except through its epithet, which is not the refusal of the name but rather the crossing out that facilitates the endless marking of the name. Kabbalistically, the writing of the name is the erasure of the nameless, just as the erasure of the name is the writing of the nameless. The differing and deferring subordinates metaphysics to metaphor, privileging thereby absence over presence, but the supplemental differend—the pharmakon, the trace, or the spectral—instable and meandering as it might be, is still established by syntactic rules. The logical conundrum that Derrida cannot elude is the fact that for something to be discerned as indeterminate, indeterminacy itself must be determined. Expressed somewhat crudely, his crusade against essentialism is nothing short of essentialist; his sponsorship of heterogeneity is strikingly homogenous.[285] Derrida's description of metaphor as "indefinitely constructing its destruction" points to the fundamental paradox of deconstruction as a theory of literature: what is scripted is simultaneously, and always, constructed and destructed, destructed in its ongoing construction and constructed in its abiding destruction, producing "its essence as its own disappearance, showing and hiding itself at the same time."[286] The kabbalistic sources, in like manner, proffer a notion of the inessential textual essence, the ineffable name, a text whose essence it is to lack an essence, a text that embodies the light of infinity and therefore endlessly discloses itself through the concealment of its disclosure.

In the last interview Derrida granted, which took place several months prior to his death, he conjured a familiar topos to reflect on the nature of his own career as a writer: "If I had invented my writing, I would have done so as a perpetual revolution. For it is necessary in each situation to create an appropriate mode of exposition, to invent the law of the singular event, to take into account the presumed or desired addressee; and, at the same time, to make as if this writing will determine the reader, who will learn to read (to 'live') something he or she was not accustomed to receiving from anywhere else."[287] The goal specified by Derrida, to ruminate over the uniqueness of each reader, is surely laudable, but it is still reasonable to ask philosophically about the feasibility of this aspiration. What kind of law might the *law of the singular event* be? Can law ever be so radically individuated? In an essay dedicated to elucidating Kafka's celebrated parable "Before the Law," Derrida addressed the issue directly: "There is a singularity about relationship to the law, a law of singularity which must come into contact with the general or universal essence of the law without ever being able to do so. Now this text, this singular text . . . names or relates in its way this conflict without encounter between law and singularity, this *paradox* or *enigma* of being-before-the-law."[288] Given the fact that law by definition must exact some form of general applicability, for if a law were applied to only one individual, it would not fulfill the prerequisite of legality and would simply be a matter of habit—as Derrida himself observed in one essay, "law is always a law of repetition, and repetition is always submission to law"[289]—the insistence on a law of singularity without any relation whatsoever to generality is absurd and incoherent. He speaks of this encounter between law and singularity as the enigma or paradox of being-before-the-law, but, by his own understanding (influenced by Heidegger's description of the human experience of death) of the possibility of the impossible,[290] this is an impossibility that is not even possible as impossible, an impossible possibility, the experience of which Derrida offers as a definition of deconstruction,[291] but it is rather an impossible impossibility that is neither possible nor impossible and therefore completely irrelevant. A writing that truly erases itself in its inscription would have to be an invisible writing, a writing that left no traces because it was never written, what Derrida himself—explicating Celan's words from the poem "À la pointe acérée," *Ungeschriebenes, zu/Sprache verhärtet*[292]— refers to as the "without writing, non-written, the unwritten" (*sans écrit, anécrit, non-écrit*).[293]

To contemplate the gesture of not-writing (*pas d'écriture*)—the graphic equivalent to the phonic description of apophasis as the voiceless voice (*la voix blanche*)[294]—is quite different from the mandate to think about writing as an ambiguous marking of the trace. The latter may be viewed as a prescript or as a postscript—the coming before is already a coming after having come before—an inscription of the invisible, which is not an entity that cannot be seen because it is hidden, but seeing that there is nothing to be seen but the unseeing, the white space, the blind spot, the condition for there to be any visibility at all, whereas the former is not an inscription, not a marking, nothing that leaves any trace. As Derrida reminds us, "Trace as memory is not a pure breaching that might be reappropriated at any time as simple presence; it is rather the ungraspable and invisible difference between breaches."[295] It is one thing to argue that the imperative of writing is to give space for singular events, to invent something new in every original iteration, but it is quite another thing to say that the singularity of what is to be written can have no relationship to the universal. In what language would such a text be inscripted? Derrida does entertain the possibility of an "inscription prior to writing, a protowriting without a present origin,"[296] a motif that he connects, as we have seen, to the midrashic idea of a primordial Torah inscribed as white fire upon back fire, a "text written in letters that are still invisible."[297] Even if we grant that the not-writing is identical to this arche-writing, a writing-before-writing, it still would be necessary to account for the translation of invisible letters of the trace into a text that can communicate to others. Does not the demand for absolute concreteness in writing elide into (or revert to) an absolute abstraction?[298]

In his earlier work, Derrida had it right: *otherness introduces determination and puts a system into circulation.* Indeterminacy itself is determined as indeterminate by the canons of some form of determination that has been determined to be valid relative to a particular economy of sociopolitical meaning. In an interview with Christian Descamps published in *Le Monde*, January 31, 1982, Derrida reaffirmed this insight by utilizing his signature notions of *différance* and the trace: "Differance or the trace does not present itself, this almost nothing of the unpresentable is what philosophers always try to erase. It is this trace, however, that marks and relaunches all systems."[299] The reader can always discover fissures in a text that cannot be dominated by systematic discourse, but it is through the latter that the former come into view, the very process that initiates the deconstruction of the system.[300] As one interpreter of Derrida astutely noted, "pure heterogeneity, pure difference, pure becoming . . . cannot be apprehended as such: a degree of admixture with their theoretical counterparts (homogeneity, identity, simultaneity) is required for apprehension to become possible."[301] With this formulation, we are closer to the kabbalistic conception of textual embodiment, the view that the substance of everything consists of the permutation of the letters, which articulate and thereby incarnate the word or wisdom of the infinite light that is beyond visual and verbal representation, the text that is infinite precisely because it can undergo endless embellishments. All of reality is this text, which is the effaceable but inerasable name, the transcendent signifier that is without sign, other than perhaps as the sign that continually eludes signification. In marking this divergence between traditional kabbalah and Derridean deconstruction, we establish the terms necessary for a dialogical encounter between two disparate modes of discourse equally devoted to entrusting the gift of secrecy in the secret giving of the gift.

CHAPTER 5

Immanent Atheology and the Trace of Transcendence

The idea, the dream of God,
The dream of the chasm of night
They name God,
Would be simply—
So they tell me—to become
This life. He is summoned
By what he imagines: there, up ahead,
In a gaze. The dream, the desire,
Born from these ravines, from these formless blocks,
From this deep-down trickling of a spring
—God—
Is that something might well up
Through the blood, the cry, the whole body
Toward what as yet he does not have:
A face, eyes.

—Yves Bonnefoy, *Still Blind*

In this chapter, I will continue the investigation of the apophatic by turning to the role of immanence and transcendence in the thought of Edith Wyschogrod. It will take some time before the full measure of Wyschogrod's contributions to the disciplines of philosophy and religious studies is appreciated. Needless to say, there have already been some major works of scholarship that have critically engaged various aspects of her multifaceted and interdisciplinary thought. In particular, her status as one of the premier interpreters of Levinas—she was the first to publish a full-length monograph on him in English—has been duly noted. Additionally, there have been essays that have called attention to her interventions in the fields of phenomenology, postmodernism, aesthetics, ethics, politics, and historiography. What has been less scrutinized is her status as a creative Jewish thinker. The ensuing analysis attempts to fill that lacuna by charting some of the ways in which she offers a deconstructive Jewish philosophy that I will call, borrowing her own taxonomy, an "immanent a/theology."[1]

FISSURE AND THE APORIA OF INCOMMENSURABLE FAITHS

I commence my reflections by evoking Wyschogrod's comment on the fact that in the essay "How to Avoid Speaking: Denials," Derrida by his own admission intentionally avoided discussing the apophatic element in the Jewish and Islamic traditions and was thereby compelled "to speak of it without speaking of it."[2] As I noted in the previous chapter, Derrida glossed this part of the lecture by noting that it may have been the most autobiographical presentation he had ever delivered, adding, regrettably, that he lacked the ability, competence, and authority to speak of the legacy of his birth encapsulated in the hybrid identity Jew-Arab.[3] Obviously, this is a deeply ironic passage: by not openly discussing the tradition of apophasis in Judaism or Islam, Derrida performatively enacted the very topic of his lecture, for with respect to what cannot be spoken, not to speak is the pertinent gesture of speaking. Wyschogrod is thus completely justified in her own exegetical surmise: "Derrida pointedly avoids discussing the apophasis found in the Jewish and Islamic traditions relevant to his own life, arguing that not to speak of them is itself a form of attestation. Yet it is precisely with regard to the missing traditions that one might apply Derrida's term 'the logic of the supplement,' the hidden presuppositions that drive his analyses, to his account of apophasis and denegation."[4] I submit that the sentiment expressed by these words can be applied to the role of Judaism in Wyschogrod, even though the situation is not totally analogous, inasmuch as she does often attend to Jewish figures and themes more overtly. My point is, rather, that what drives her postphenomenological and poststructural analyses is her philosophical grappling with her Jewishness. This is not to parochialize her thought; on the contrary, it seems to me that she saw the particular as the only feasible way to implement the universal without reducing the other to the identity of the same.

To some degree, Wyschogrod's perspective is congruous with Levinas's notion of a "universalist singularity," that is, the "primordial event in Hebraic spirituality" that sponsors a universalism predicated on the principle that "to be with the nations is also to be for the nations,"[5] or, expressed somewhat more abstractly, a universalism grounded in the preservation of the singular, the "oneself" that is "prior to the distinction between the particular and the universal."[6] The "paradox of Israel" is the promotion of an "exceptional message" that is nevertheless "addressed to all," the "peculiarity beyond universality . . . made manifest well before the distinction between the particular and the universal makes its appearance in the speculation of logicians."[7] For Levinas, this is not simply a theme he advocated in his "confessional" or "Jewish" writings and lectures;[8] the claim that the individual destiny of the Israelite nation is its universalism is the conceptual underpinning of the reciprocity between philosophy and Judaism.[9] As he put it in the interview with Armengaud:

> Does the distinction between Judaism and philosophical reflection immediately emerge as a major conflict? We may start out . . . in a world in which Judaism was lived, and in a very natural way: not at all, or not only, in what is called piety or rigorous ritualism, but above all with the sense that belonging to humanity means belonging to an order of supreme responsibility. An order in which non-Jewish books also are perceived as being concerned with the meaning of life—which is contiguous with the meaning of human existence and already, perhaps, with the meaning of being. . . . Philosophy speaks of it also, but in another language, that always strives to be explicit, adjusting its terms to one another and formulating problems where there are breaks in the coherence. But has the handing down of the Scriptures ever taken place without transmission through that language of interpretation, which is already disengaged from the verses that sustain it, always to be found in the gaps between utterances?[10]

According to Levinas, we should not correlate philosophy and Judaism respectively with the symbolic and the literal, the universal and the singular. Jewish texts are always aligned with midrash, and philosophical texts retain something of the literal particularity. The hermeneutical principles underlying Jewish texts and philosophy are not so disparate even though they are not identical.

Leaving no room for uncertainty on this strategic point, Levinas commented: "I do not commit the error of denying the radical difference in spirit between the Scriptures and philosophy. But, having emphasized their agreement in fact at a certain moment in time . . . I am now ready to speak . . . of their *essential* connection in human civilization altogether, which is measured or hoped for as peace among men."[11] This dimension of Levinas's thought is captured poignantly by Jill Robbins:

> For Levinas, the Talmud dissimulates not just an ethical discourse but, more specifically, a "philosophical" discourse, an alternative intelligibility that is antitotalizing and that goes against the grain of the dominant philosophical conceptuality in the West. This is to say that within Levinas's confessional writings, the Talmud, written in Hebrew, as it were, dissimulates a "Greek" dimension. Conversely, insofar as Levinas's philosophical writings make reference to "Hebrew" ethics, they do so necessarily in "Greek" . . . In short, what Levinas had described in Rosenzweig as a double movement, first toward Christianity, then toward Judaism, that is, as a necessary confrontation with Christian conversion, could be formulated with regard to Levinas's hermeneutic of Judaism as a necessary intrication of "Hebrew" ethical thought in the "Greek." It is as if the very distinction between Hebrew and Greek can only be thought from within the "Greek."[12]

Wyschogrod succinctly summarized the Levinasian position in similar terms: "If Judaism is to do its job, it must be understood; it must somehow enter into this universal language that it cannot do without; philosophy, in turn, must become Judaized."[13]

These words can be applied to Wyschogrod's own thinking, even though, contra Levinas, she did not seek a synthesis of Jewish revelation and Greek thought.[14] On balance, I would proffer that her approach is characterized better by Derrida's appropriation of Joyce's hybrid expressions "Jewgreek" or "Greekjew," which we discussed in the previous chapter. The words of Derrida fittingly characterize not only the path of Wyschogrod's philosophical thought but her existential demeanor in the world as well. Let us remember the "autobiographical ruminations" that Wyschogrod offered in the lecture "Religion as Life and Text: Postmodern Re-figurations." Beginning from the provocative stance that her childhood can be thought of as the "overcoming of an oscillation between transgression and transcendence," the former injecting negation related to the "not" of sheer facticity or brute materiality and the latter the "not" of moral interdiction that comes in the form of the constraint of the other, Wyschogrod reflects on how the overcoming of this double negative of ignorance and injury can be used to explain her entry into the study of religion.[15]

Three points in Wyschogrod's narrative recitation are most germane. First, from her parents she inculcated the emphasis on mastering scientific knowledge (*Wissenschaft*) "in the sense of cultural erudition and knowledge of the human subject made transparent through the insights of literature and psychology." Second, from her maternal grandparents she experienced the piety of "synagogue worship and home rituals," whence she discerned "a celebratory affirmation of God's covenant with Abraham surrounded by that penumbra of sadness built into Judaism because Israelite history's dark moments are included in its observances." The significance of this influence is apparent from Wyschogrod's confession that this "incorporation of the past into the present" would rule her own accounts of "a scission or split in time, of a present that can never be wholly present, and of a future that holds in front of itself an archaic past." I will return to Wyschogrod's view on temporality, but what is worthy of emphasis here is that by her own admission a decisive facet of her thinking about time is informed by a pronounced sensibility in Jewish ceremonial practice. Third, from several Protestant aunts, described as being of Huguenot descent, Wyschogrod had some taste of a "Christian presence" in her life, centered especially on the "redemptive events of the Gospel," which presented "opportunities for joyous celebration." Receiving annual Christmas gifts opened for Wyschogrod the "aporia of incommensurable faiths," the "manifestation of difference," a "fissuring" that she tried to articulate in her work.[16] Derrida wrote of living in the difference between Jew and Greek, and Wyschogrod of living in the difference between Jew and Christian, but, for all intents and purposes, it is the same difference. Attunement to Wyschogrod's thinking requires one to inhabit the cleft of this fissure, to dwell in the indelible disparity between the two Abrahamic traditions.

POSTMODERNISM, DÉNÉGATION, AND THE UNDOING OF UNDOING

I will begin my analysis of Wyschogrod's contribution to a postmodern Jewish immanent atheology by saying a word about her use of the term *postmodern*. In the essay "Hasidism, Hellenism, Holocaust: A Postmodern View,"[17] Wyschogrod states that "postmodern" has both a methodological and an ontological connotation. The former refers to "strategies for decoding the canons of reason in order to expose reason's duplicity expressed in its tactics of self-concealment," whereas the latter "signifies the dismantling of the understanding of being and time that has dominated Western thought from its Greek beginnings to the present. A focus upon negation is the opening move in the overturning of traditional ontology." Wyschogrod is quick to point out that if negation is simply the obverse of being, then it becomes itself a property of being that may be subsumed under "a system of meaning whose ontological foundations remain intact." The negation that she wishes to affirm is an "unmediated heterology, an otherness, of deep negation," that is, a truly radical alterity wherein and whereby the negative is itself so utterly negated that, in the words of Derrida cited by Wyschogrod,[18] it "can no longer be called negative," which presumes the renunciation of some positive, a negation that is beyond both the negation of the affirmative and the affirmation of the negative.

By her own admission, Wyschogrod notes that her thinking sways between efforts to overcome manifestations of the negative and claims about its irrevocability and that an especially important influence haunting her project is Hegel's struggle with the negative as "the possibility of the nonexistence of the totality of all that is currently seen as world or as the maximal intensity of disvalue that can be attributed to the world."[19] In the Hegelian dialectic, history culminates with the "emergence of an all-encompassing Absolute . . . an ontological and logical vacuum that has sucked into itself all that is and sees itself as having brought to completion the work of historical and philosophical negation, thereby obviating the need for further inquiry into the labor of the negative."[20] Sublation of the negative in its ultimate overcoming is thus intrinsic to each moment of the World-Spirit's history. The latter, in Hegel's own words, wins its truth "by looking the negative in the face and tarrying with it,"[21] which is to say, Spirit's unfolding is "contingent upon a continual undoing."[22] But if the labor of the negative is this continual undoing, can the undoing ever be undone in an unsurpassable negation? An attempt to respond to this query is offered in the following passage from *Spirit in Ashes: Hegel, Heidegger, and Man-Made Mass Death*:

> The negation of the Absolute, therefore, must itself be absolute, and the difference generated by this negation must itself be an absolute difference. Hegel all too quickly

passes over the uniqueness of the negation when what is negated is the Absolute itself. Negation of this sort is without voice; it can only be interpreted as silence and therefore mystery. . . . For Hegel such a negation is unthinkable. But if it could be imagined, it could only become actual in the annihilation of man as it has begun to occur in the death event. The extermination and extinction of man is the negation of the Absolute, not the Biblical Absolute, but Hegel's fully immanent Absolute. No further revelation, no Divine Word is now possible, since there is no beyond. This negation is manifest as unique and ultimate silence—not the awesome quiet of cosmic space to which Pascal alludes but a historical absence of speech, the silence that supervenes upon speech. The traces of this silence are to be found in language, in the speech of the death-world and its survivors where death attaches to every signifier. Were we to imagine this negation in the language of traditional religion, we could only use the language of religious mystery. From this point of view the death event, with its nadir at the death-world, would necessarily become the ultimate mystery and resist inclusion into an Absolute which could no longer be a positive Absolute.[23]

Hegel's dialectic is such that every presence becomes what it is by negating what it is not, and hence every negation brings some presence in its wake. The idea of negativity in Hegel, therefore, "is harnessed to the logic of presence so that the idea of the negative as reserve, pure loss, silence—that which is irrecoverable—is foreign to Hegel. Instead, the negative is brought into plenary presence carried forward by the dialectical activity of Spirit."[24] What is unthinkable for Hegel is the dialectical overcoming of the dialectic that results in the negation of the Absolute, a negation so profound that it generates an absolute difference—the Derridean *différance*[25]—in which all difference is annihilated, the pure void, neither something nor nothing, in which all presence is eradicated. The negation of negation theologically entails the obliteration of transcendence that results from the Nietzschean slaying of God and, anthropologically, the extermination of human beings attested most brazenly by the Nazi death camps.

Wyschogrod identifies the double negative—the negation of the negation that is the Absolute—with the "non-negotiable negative" implied by the event of Auschwitz, in Adorno's thinking, or, according to Lyotard, the "negation of the negative."[26] Wyschogrod would concur with Adorno's critique of Hegel's "positive negation," that is, that the "nonidentical" cannot be obtained as "something positive" or by "a negation of the negative," for equating the "negation of negation with positivity" is the "quintessence of identification."[27] The conclusion reached by Adorno could well serve as a summary of Wyschogrod's own view: "To negate a negation does not bring about its reversal; it proves, rather, that the negation was not negative enough. . . . The thesis that the negation of a negation is something positive can only be upheld by one who presupposes positivity—as all-conceptuality—from the beginning."[28] The Hegelian system depends on the dialectical principle that "to negate negation is positive," but the "empirical substance of dialectics," endorsed by Adorno, "is not the principle but the resistance which otherness offers to identity."[29] If one speaks of the nothing as nothing, one negates the negation and thereby renders the negative into a positive. What is necessary, therefore, is to negate the negation of the negative, to reclaim a negativity that no longer contains its own other within the identity of the same. Analogously, from Wyschogrod's perspective, the unprecedented possibility of the total abolition of human subjectivity necessitates that the ultimate negation can no longer be sublated by the movement of Spirit in history.[30] The undoing of the undoing occasions a negative that is no longer subject to negation, since its own negativity would have been positively negated, whence it follows that the binary opposition of being and nonbeing is dismantled and primacy no longer given to the positive or to the negative. The nihilatory inferences of the Holocaust are not meant to reinstate a "discursive negation" to express the unsayable along the lines of traditional negative theology but rather "to bring to the fore the problem of unsayability" by raising questions concerning the plausibility of the descriptive and analytic functions of language routinely presumed by historical consciousness.[31]

In compliance with Derrida, Wyschogrod accepts that the "idea of difference yields deeper insight into negation itself," that "difference acquires meaning only because we become aware of negation through the *play* of differences which leaves tracks or traces in that which is present . . . But a negation so profound that all presence would be snuffed out would annihilate difference as well. Difference and presence alike depend on continuity of the world. Without it, alterity would be reduced to the same."[32] It is precisely this task of "thinking a negation that cannot be thought" that forges an intrinsic connection between the Holocaust and the postmodern sensibility. The unmasking of rationality, which is indispensable to the postmodern ethos, is instantiated by the event of the Holocaust, which prototypically signifies what Wyschogrod calls the "death-world," based on an inversion of the Husserlian conception of the life-world (*Lebenswelt*).[33] Ironically, the questioning of reason that emerges from one of the darkest chapters of the history of the Jews casts light on a deeper structure that Wyschogrod identifies as the Jewish proclivity for multivocality and the constant interrogation of texts to derive new meaning. In her reading of the Jewish tradition, there is a conspicuous tolerance for polysemy; Jewish sources, like theological texts more generally, when read through the Lacanian psychoanalytic lens, can be viewed as "manifesting multiple strands of meaning which become intelligible through an analytic process."[34] Using this criterion, the manifold meanings are entertained as credible so long as it is recognized that all of them are true. "As a religion of the text," she writes, "Judaism is compatible with the intertexuality of hermeneutical and poststructuralist interpretation."[35] Jewish exegesis, accordingly, would allow in Derridean terms for a "textual dissemination" that, in contrast to "discursive polysemy," implies an "implacable difference," a "textual stream whose interpretations cannot be brought to closure."[36] On another occasion Wyschogrod astutely notes a critical distinction between deconstruction and the hermeneutical assumptions undergirding a Jewish postmodernism:

> This privileging of the text is not an affirmation that there is nothing outside the text, a point stressed by Derrida, but rather a focus upon text as the site (or non-site) of meaning and as opening out into infinite interpretive possibilities. This notion is foreign to the traditions of Western philosophy but not to rabbinic thought with its underlying assumption that God consults the Torah to create the world (thus affirming that before the beginning there was the text). What is more, the written Torah is looked upon as an extreme condensation whose explication is unfolded in the Talmud and later rabbinic writings in an ongoing hermeneutical process, although not a process without rules. The blurring of the boundary between *what* is to be interpreted and its interpretation results in a vastly expanded textual field.[37]

Notwithstanding this difference, Wyschogrod concedes that recent French aesthetics and traditional Jewish modes of interpretation are indebted to deconstruction insofar as both "lie outside literary critical orthodoxies and proceed otherwise than by way of the canons of standard philosophical discourse, appealing to association and a variety of rhetorical tropes as critical tools."[38]

There is another dimension of Wyschogrod's discussion of the negative that strikes me as essentially Derridean. I refer to her acceptance of Derrida's insisting that the deconstructive logic of dénégation be distinguished from traditional negative theology.[39] On the one hand, the *via negativa* presumes a "theological center about which nothing can be said because language is inadequate to this fullness of being," and, on the other hand, the negativity of a deconstructed atheology entails an apophasis that turns the fullness upside down by emptying it of its own fullness; the emptiness at the core, in other words, is not simply the privation of an ontological plenitude, the negative relative to something positive, but rather the center, which is "construed as an absence," not an absence of some potentially present presence that is presently absent, the absence that presents itself as nonpresent, but rather an absence that can never be present except as the absence of any possible presence, the chiasm of being that resists the reification of nothing as something or of something as nothing.[40] Hermeneutically, the "logic of the text" is altered by this absence and thus "opens previously unthinkable configurations, an errancy, wandering or leaching of meaning that is irrecoverable as that which is fully present."[41] As she puts it elsewhere, the mark of postmodernism "is not sheer ineffability, but a negation that deconstructs language so that, to borrow a metaphor from the Hasidic master Nahman of Bratslav, language itself stutters."[42] To stutter, we know, is not to remain silent; it is to speak, albeit in such a way that what is spoken is never what is said, an "apophatics of denial," in Derrida's locution, a "self-deconstructing speech."[43] Wyschogrod highlights the ethical repercussion of the halting nature of speech: "Language is not only communication but always already inter-diction, the no-saying of a speech that prohibits, even if such prohibition is on behalf of the other."[44] The language of negation—the no-saying of the stutterer as opposed to the mute speechlessness of one who cannot speak—can be cast in ocular terms as the negative epiphany, a seeing of nothing to be seen, the invisible that is beyond the opposition visible/nonvisible,[45] the nonphenomenalizability that shapes the sensible world of human experience. Beholding the unseen and heeding the unsaying are the means necessary to scale the heights of the sacred and to plumb the depths of the cataclysm. In the heterological nonspace of *différance*, there is no discrepancy between the sacred and the cataclysmic: one, as the other, directs the mind to the void that is not amenable to linguistification, conceptualization, or confabulation.[46]

Speaking-not, that is, speaking not to speak rather than not speaking to speak, is akin, as Wyschogrod acknowledges in "Intending Transcendence: Desiring God," to Derrida's dénégation, "a negation that denies itself," the negativity instituted by the "secret of denial" that is concurrently the "denial of the secret," a dissimulation that shows itself in "dissimulating its dissimulation," the saying of the divine name that "can only be said in the modality of this secret denial."[47] The choice of illustrating the apophatic utterance by the example of unsaying the name, that is, saying the name by not saying it, plainly reflects the specific liturgical practice of Jews to vocalize YHWH through its epithet Adonai. Wyschogrod exposes this indebtedness in her observation that Derrida's explication of Angelus Silesius in *Sauf le nom* "both conceals and reveals a crucial theological tenet of rabbinic discourse: the terms used to refer to God, his biblical names, are charged with the utmost sanctity. For the negative theologian, Derrida contends, the name erases itself before what it names, thereby safeguarding the named. . . . The name may be written but not read aloud, so that it is as utterance that the name remains secret."[48] To substantiate her conjecture, Wyschogrod cites a few rabbinic sources that accentuate the mystery and unpronounceability of the name; many more could have been listed, including especially a plethora of kabbalistic texts. As we noted in the previous chapter, Derrida himself invokes the kabbalah to corroborate the notion that language, like the ineffable name in the Jewish tradition, consists of the concomitant power of manifestation and occultation; that is, the name reveals by concealing and conceals by revealing.[49] For our purposes what is most noteworthy is the fact that Wyschogrod links three seemingly discrete subjects by noting a "crisis of language" that is bound up with the ineffability of God's name in rabbinic thought, the impossibility of naming "God's hyperessentiality" in the apophatics of negative theology, and the "empty intuition" in Husserlian phenomenology, the object of intention "whose meaning is not borne out by the plenary presence of what is intended."[50]

The thread that ties all three together is a destabilization of language that ensues from the "yearning for the unnameable, a desire for a kenosis that remains impossible, for a transcendence that can only be experienced as a failed immanence."[51] The final words echo the following statement in Levinas's essay "The Idea of the Infinite in Us," which Wyschogrod cites in full at the end of her study: "Transcendence is no longer a failed immanence. It has the sort of excellence proper to Spirit: perfection, or the Good."[52] But what does Levinas mean when he writes that *transcendence* is not a *failed immanence*? He seems to be reacting to the Husserlian idea that what is configured as transcendent to consciousness is always and already a being that is outside from the perspective of what is inside, the periphery in virtue of which the exteriority of the immanent is configured noematically as the interiority of the transcendent. In Levinas's mind, as we explored in Chapter 3, the idea of transcendence in immanence that emerges from the correlation of thought and world prevalent in Husserlian phenomenology, and the consequent assumption that the "linguisticality of phenomena" is constituted by the intentionality of consciousness,[53] fall short of the belief, well rooted in religious traditions, that the infinite is the absolutely other that cannot shine forth in the forms of the phenomenal world.[54] Levinas well expressed the dilemma that tenaciously traps human consciousness in its attempt to think transcendence: "How can the Other . . . appear, that is, be for someone, without already losing its alterity and exteriority by that way of offering itself to view?"[55] As he elaborates in another passage:

> How and where is there produced, within the psyche of experience, the major break capable of accrediting an *other* as irreducibly other [*autre*] and, in this sense, as *beyond*, even though in the tissue of the thematized thinkable every rending preserves or renews the texture of the Same? How can a thought go *beyond* the world that is precisely the way by which the being that it thinks is assembled, whatever the heterogeneity of its elements and the variety of their modes of being? How can the transcendent signify "the wholly other," easy to say, certainly, but which the common fund of the thinkable and of discourse restores to the world and as a world?[56]

Levinas consents to the possibility that immanence is the "supreme grace of spiritual energy,"[57] but he insists nonetheless that the mystery of transcendence is undermined if it is thought to be wholly subsumed in the immanence of being. As Wyschogrod rightly observed, "The transcendence of the trace is not present in the world. It is, according to Levinas, the presence of what in effect has never been there, for in order to have been there, the transcendent would have had to belong to the order of being."[58] If all transcendence is brought back to immanence, this would imply the undesirable assimilation or integration of the Other into the Same.[59] To be sure, the glory of the infinite is embodied corporeally in the world.[60] This proximity, however, is not manifest primarily as the corporealization of the incorporeal in nature but as the body of sociality constructed from ethical relationships. To think of immanence in this way is to uphold the integrity of the disincarnation of the transcendent[61] and to secure thereby the alterity beyond consciousness that alone justifies the shift to the Levinasian *ethics of transcendence* from the Derridean *erotics of transcendence* in which the absent Other runs the risk of being subject to immanentization as the object of desire.[62]

EROTICS OF TRANSCENDENCE, SAINTLY TRANSGRESSION, AND THE IMPOSSIBLE HOPE

In spite of the pervasive influence of Levinas on Wyschogrod, it seems to me that her own contribution to the philosophy of religion in general, and to Judaism in particular, is in some vital aspects closer in spirit to the erotics of transcendence than to the ethics of transcendence. It is worthwhile recalling the judicious assessment of Altizer:

> Even though Wyschogrod is a genuine theological thinker, nothing is more absent from her discourse than the word *God*, except insofar as she speaks forcefully of the death of God, a death which she understands theologically . . . Nor does she divorce the death of God from her own quest for a new ethics, and it is here that she differs most deeply from Levinas. While she absorbed Levinas's discovery of the *il y a*, an *il y a* that Levinas defines as Being in the absence of beings, Wyschogrod can apprehend an ethical role of the *il y a*, which is to denucleate the self as a complex of mental acts and render the self receptive to alterity. Alterity seemingly vanishes in postmodernity, and this is a fundamental ground of our ethical crisis, but this is an emptying which is the very opposite of self-emptying, and one inseparable from the modern realization of the death of God. Now if this is a realization which Levinas totally refuses, Wyschogrod herself refuses such a refusal.[63]

From a Levinasian perspective, the atheological postmodernity[64] that one may educe from Wyschogrod's work succumbs to the demarcation of transcendence as a failed immanence. Insofar as the "identifying mark of Nietzschean postmodernism is its sheer refusal to traffic in transcendence," Wyschogrod agrees with Deleuze that the "illusoriness of transcendence consists either in rendering immanence immanent to something other than itself or in locating transcendence within immanence."[65] Neither of these attempts to transcend transcendence would have been satisfactory to Levinas. In this regard it is instructive to consider carefully Wyschogrod's gloss on Levinas's conception of the face as the trace of transcendence: "It exhibits the track or spoor of an archaic transcendence or, alternatively, *from my point of view and not that of Levinas*, the track of the totality of humankind or of all sentient beings, past, present, and future, none of which can be brought into plenary presence."[66] In no uncertain terms, Wyschogrod distinguishes her understanding of transcendence from that of Levinas: the otherwise than being becomes the totality of beings that can never be conceptualized as a knowable plenum. At best, then, Wyschogrod, like Deleuze,[67] can affirm an immanent theory of ethics and desire.[68]

The specific affinity to Derrida can be detected in Wyschogrod's insistence that an "unalloyed transcendence can only be expressed in contemporary discourse as an erotics, a hope *per impossibile* to trump these cataclysms."[69] In light of the calamitous events in the twentieth century, coupled with the post-Nietzschean tendency to "an erotics of immanence," which is predicated on the absolute "absence of transcendence,"[70] the only tenable way to speak meaningfully about transcendence is through the erotic, for the latter represents the possibility of the impossible par excellence, and thus it bears within its bosom the "hope against hope," which Wyschogrod interprets as the "interface of possibility and improbability"; that is, the first hope indicates what is possible, the second that it is improbable.[71] Hope is not the promise of the constantly deferred happiness but rather the hope for a present, albeit a present that cannot come to pass because it is "always already marked by difference."[72] Hope, phenomenologically, is "bound up with that which is not yet," and therefore it is always the gift of the future.[73] Wyschogrod thus called for a "fundamental rethinking of hope" that will preclude the expectation of happiness stipulated by either eudaemonistic ethics or political utopianism. "If hope is a gift, the gift too must be reenvisaged in terms of a relation between its gratuitousness, on the one hand, and its inevitable involvement in the sphere of economy, on the other. What is more, a gift does not depend upon its precondition but is purely contingent."[74]

In her discussions of hope, the gift, and the future, Wyschogrod frequently cites Derrida.[75] The influence is perhaps most palpable in her wrestling with his notorious claim (discussed in the previous chapter) that "the very conditions that produce the gift render it impossible." Wyschogrod counters that if we trust our "preconceived comprehension" of the term, then the gift entails the threefold participation of donor, object, and recipient, and consequently, "the gift is self-nullifying in that the recipient is always already enmeshed in a system of exchange. Should the recipient return the gift, she has converted the gift into a loan; if the recipient fails to return the gift, she is placed under obligation: 'I owe X a counter-gift or at least thanks,' or its opposite, 'X was in my debt; he has now repaid it so I owe him nothing.' . . . Once it is recognized that a gift has been given, there is no emerging from the *cul de sac* I have described. Only by forgetting, not recognizing the gift as gift, can there be gift."[76] Wyschogrod elucidates the point by inducing the homonymy of the English "gift" and the German *Gift*,[77] "poison"; that is, the burden of the conversion of the gift into a loan turns receiving a gift into something poisonous for the recipient and the donor. Most significantly, the Derridean notion seems to doom the role of the heterological historian as the "giver of the gift" of recounting events of the past—thereby giving voice to the voiceless victims of tyranny and violence—with the "poisoned gift of historical deception" that raises doubt about the facticity of the historian's narrative. The resolution of the dilemma is found in Derrida's own charge that we must acquiesce to the "transcendental illusion of the gift" and accede thereby to the "aleatory character of existence." Paraphrasing the imperative of Derrida, which is cited verbatim by Wyschogrod,[78] one must commit oneself to the gift, even if such a commitment is the destruction of the gift as that which lies outside the circular contract of the economy of exchange.[79]

In the final analysis, Wyschogrod's conception of hope and the redemptive potential of remembering and retrieving the past in the ever-deferred not yet of the "messianic now"[80] through the writing of history—an excess by which the invisible dead others "undo or unwrite the predicative and iterative historical narrative" and thus open "the dimensions of the more, of an unincorporable infinite"[81]—is fashioned on Derrida's depiction[82] of the inexhaustible craving for a presence that can never be made present:

> Hope then is the hope for presence. Although the historian may already be persuaded of the impossibility of getting hold of the present, this impossibility continually vitiates itself. . . . It is this inextinguishable longing for the present and the impossibility of laying hold of it that constitutes hope. Hope relates to a future that is always yet to come but may never arrive. To remain hope, hope must desire the possible, yet it wants what escapes the domain of possibility, the plenitude of a presence that cannot be appropriated.[83]

Wyschogrod's language is overwhelmed by Derrida's notion of the messianic promise of the impossible, the possibility that is in no other way possible but as impossible, an unconditional opening to a future that is inherently indeterminate and endlessly deferrable, a future that issues from the negative infinity of time. Contrary to the attempts to discern a religious turn in Derrida's thinking, to utilize his thought to buttress a religion beyond religion, the messianicity that he affirms is by his own admission a decidedly "atheological heritage,"[84] the impossible possibility that stems from the likelihood that the future that is coming threatens not to be that for which one has hoped.[85] Wyschogrod summons this Derridean trope to explain the words of Moses to Aron in Schoenberg's opera, "You know why you will not see the Promised Land / Because you did not really need to see it— / You beheld it as you took on God's voice through me and grasped God's way / . . . So you lost God's land but had been already in it."

> The promised land is not any land, not an original space or time but a there that is not there, a past that has already passed by and cannot be made present, cannot be awaited as such, and yet, impossibly, must be awaited. This is Moses' promise of what cannot arrive, in Derrida's terms,[86] "the impossible itself . . . this *condition of possibility* of the event is also its *condition of impossibility* . . . the messianic without messianism, that guides us here like the blind."[87]

This, in a nutshell, is what is at stake in Wyschogrod's depiction of the erotic as hope *per impossible*: just as the very possibility of hope consists of its being impossible, so too the exorbitance of eros—what Wyschogrod calls the "voluptuary structure of desire"[88]—comports as the excessiveness that is constituted by a lack that can be satiated only as that which can never be satiated. Whereas Levinas maintained with an air of certainty that the "excess can express itself in the disinterested desire for the Other who is in the trace of transcendence,"[89] Wyschogrod seems less sanguine. The negation implied in the desire for an unreachable God cannot be easily "cordoned off from the cataclysms of history,"[90] and hence, as we have already noted, it is not self-evident that transcendence can be experienced except as a failed immanence. Wyschogrod does incorporate something of the Levinasian perspective (coupled with the view of desire enunciated by Deleuze and Guattari) in her insistence that desire is necessary to the radical altruism of the saintly life,[91] manifest in the outpouring of compassion fueled by ascetic renunciation, which may be expressive of the adulation of the erotic rather than the contempt of the body,[92] but even here she is wary, counseling that an unlimited desire is "incompatible with altruism because the Other . . . constitutes a limiting condition of desire. The Other can never coincide with the desire that intends her/him."[93]

The point is made in a different conceptual register by Altizer:

> Now it is not insignificant that Levinas . . . should have called forth a primordial or pre-primordial ethics that ends every possible ethics, nor insignificant that the thinking of Levinas is so deeply Neoplatonic . . . While Wyschogrod is drawn to Plotinus, she nevertheless resists Neoplatonism, and therein inevitably resists Levinas as well, perhaps most clearly in opening herself to a genuinely apocalyptic horizon. . . . Nothing is clearer in Wyschogrod's work than that she calls out not simply the groundlessness of all established ethics, but the very vacuity of our given ethical categories, thus placing in question all of our ethical language, and inevitably raising the question of whether any ethical language at all is possible for us.[94]

One may quibble with the categorical classification of Levinas as a Neoplatonist,[95] but the main point of Altizer's comment is correct: Wyschogrod could not accept the Levinasian notion of an unknowable illeity, the otherwise than being, as the ground of ethics. Altizer himself seems to backtrack from this important difference between the two thinkers when he remarks, "It cannot be denied that Levinas is a theological thinker, and while he has a Jewish reluctance to write the word *God*, that Infinite which is his deepest ground is clearly God, a ground which Wyschogrod, too, accepts."[96] It is not obvious to me that Wyschogrod would have, in fact, assented to this formulation. I do not see evidence that she affirmed the infinite with Levinas's conviction, nor do I think it is appropriate to brand her as a theological thinker unless the theology is understood atheologically. Closer to the mark, although still somewhat imprecise, is a third comment of Altizer:

> For Wyschogrod the ultimate ground of alterity is the Infinite, but can we say "God" in response to that ground, and can this be only a silent saying anterior to speech? This kind of saying could account for Wyschogrod's apparent silence about God, but if this is a silence evoked for us by the death-world, must we only speak

silently about God because for us to speak openly or decisively about God would necessarily be a speaking of an absolute No? And not only an absolute No, but an absolute No wholly removed from an absolute Yes, or before which an absolute Yes could only be wholly silent and unsaid.[97]

Those familiar with Altizer's death of God theology will hear resonances of his own thinking in his summation of Wyschogrod. As I have already noted, I would question the legitimacy of attributing to her the belief that the infinite is the ultimate ground of alterity, especially if that infinite is identified with God. Moreover, I would propose that the blatant silence about God on her part is not a speaking silently about the absolute No in the vein of negative theology but rather the atheological silence of there being no absolute No of which to speak or not to speak and certainly no absolute Yes that could be spoken only through the deep silence of unsaying. To give witness to the fact that there is something rather than nothing is to avow that there is neither something to negate nor nothing to affirm. I would go so far as to say that Wyschogrod's interpretation of the apophatic dimension of Levinas at times displays the distinctive stamp of Derrida. Consider the account of transcendence that she offers in the email exchange with Caputo on postmodernism and the desire for God:

> For Levinas, the Other is the other person, whose very existence places a demand of noninjury upon me, an ethical demand that I read in the face-to-face relation with the Other. But it has not gone unnoticed that the Other is in the track or trace of transcendence, which, for Levinas, is construed in terms of a God who has always already passed by, who cannot be made present. This allows for a transcendence that . . . is seen in conformity with rabbinic tradition. Ethics is first philosophy, and the Old One, the Ancient of Days, is . . . cordoned off. But the *imago dei* (to be construed an-iconically, in conformity with Jewish tradition) is not a representation of God but an invisible writing that more than hints at an immanentist theology.[98]

The focal point of ethics is the Other in the intersubjective sphere, but the otherness of the other person—indeed, the very personhood of the Other—is secured only insofar as it is the trace of transcendence, which, as Wyschogrod correctly notes, is identified by Levinas as the theistic God, the "Ancient of Days" (Daniel 7:13, 22), the deity that cannot be reified or made present, expressed temporally as one that is permanently in a state of having "always already passed by," an exegetical gloss on Exodus 33:22–23. Most importantly, the concluding aside about the aniconic rendering of the *imago dei* as an invisible writing that points to an immanentist theology strikes me as a curious grafting of Derrida onto Levinas.

Along similar lines, the Derridean dimension of Wyschogrod's immanent atheology is attested in her affirming a transgressive erotics of transcendence shaped by the indelible desire for what can be present only by its absence, an idea that is consistent with what she identifies as the dominant Jewish "fear of idolatry,"[99] the "anathema pronounced upon the sacralization of the image," the "dread of the simulacrum," typified by Maimonides in "his fear that there may be no way to distinguish true from imaginary things."[100] While the aniconism is surely a key aspect of Levinas's thought, I do not recall that he ever depicts transcendence as a transgressive erotics, a move that transforms the aniconism into a more spirited iconoclasm. The iconoclastic undertone of Wyschogrod's atheological postmodernism can be seen in her shrewd explication of Schoenberg's take on the sin of the golden calf: the danger of this image did not consist of its "ontological status" or its being an artifact expressing an "excess of imagination" but rather in the effort to establish it as the fixed icon that would "restrict the dissemination of images and the conjurations that give rise to them. At the same time, it is an attempt to substitute itself for the infinite semantic potential of writing, of a particular system of signs that is the law as incised upon tablets that are broken but rearise spectrally."[101]

At a later juncture in the conversation with Caputo, Wyschogrod comes to the point of the erotics of transcendence explicitly. Providing a brief account of Levinas's background in the nineteenth-century quarrel between eastern European Hasidim, with their emphasis on ecstatic prayer, and the reaction thereto in the priority given to talmudic study on the part of the Lithuanian Mitnagdim, she notes that Levinas shared the latter's distrust of Hasidic fervor, the "white heat of religious emotion." In a moment of candor, Wyschogrod admits that she shares "Levinas's suspicion of the frenzy, religious and secular," but she "cannot identify entirely with an immanentism of the trace or with Buber's Romantic version of Hasidism."[102] It lies beyond my immediate concern to unpack all the ramifications of this statement. The most important point to emerge therefrom is that the Levinasian position—the "immanentism of the trace," which implies that transcendence cannot be encountered directly in the phenomenal world except as that which disturbs its surface like the ruffling of a stone thrown into a pool[103]—is as unacceptable to Wyschogrod as is Buber's romanticization of Hasidism either (as may be culled from his earliest writings) as an expression of pietistic rapture and enthusiasm, the aboriginal spirit of Hebraic prophecy that accords with the world-affirmation of the Dionysian ecstaticism proposed by the youthful Nietzsche, or (as may be elicited from his later writings) as the quintessential realization of the dialogical encounter with the eternal Thou.[104] In contradistinction to both of these options, Wyschogrod beckons

> an ineradicable desire, which is indeed a desire for the Other, but also a desire for desire, a desire that intensifies as it falls back on itself. Described by Diotima in Plato's *Symposium* and reinscribed in recent French thought (e.g., in Derrida's essay "Plato's Pharmakon"), this desire is an ineluctable yearning that knows nevertheless that it yearns for that which may burn and destroy, a risk caught in the story of Moses that remains determinative for the rabbis and so captivated Augustine, who

yearned to speak with God face to face. *I call what is lacking in Levinas the erotics of transcendence.* Both adopting and distancing myself from Levinas, I suggest that the desire for transcendence reflects the hubris of asking and the humility of knowing that what is asked for cannot be granted.[105]

The erotics of transcendence is illumined both by Diotima's depiction of Eros spoken through the voice of Socrates in Plato's *Symposium* and the wish of Moses reported in Exodus 33 to see God's face. From these two ostensibly disparate sources, Wyschogrod skillfully articulates the quality of risk that is inherent in the desire for transcendence, that is, the risk that inexorably one will be burned and destroyed by the object of desire. Moreover, hubris and humility are associated with this desire, hubris for making such a request in the first place and humility for knowing that it cannot be fulfilled. Even as Levinas fears the transference of eros to transcendence because this might end up in the mystical enrapture of the self in God, resulting in annihilation, like the moth that is consumed by the fire that encircles it,[106] Wyschogrod is prepared to embrace such a transference as vital to an erotics of transcendence, the desire that "is inherently unfulfillable (akin to but not identical with Derrida's passion for the impossible). It is a desire that is always already (messianically) ahead of itself but also remains a desire for the archaic . . . It is a desire for the eternal return of the same (the past by way of the future, the future always already the past), but is not a desire for a static eternity. The messianic is in the trace of a past that cannot be made present."[107]

We are accustomed to thinking of the messianic in eschatological terms, as a turning toward and striving for the future. Wyschogrod, however, maintains that the messianic is "ahead of itself" but also a "desire for the archaic," a paradox that prompts her to enunciate what strikes me as an essentially Deleuzian version of Nietzsche's doctrine of the eternal return of the same[108]—an interpretive move that she makes explicit in *An Ethics of Remembering*[109]—that is, the recycling of time, the recurring difference that makes the past available through the future and the future through the past, but without positing an originary presence at the beginning or a final resolution at the end. The future thus is always coming as what can never arrive, and the past always retrieving what could never have been present.[110] The same that returns is the very difference that repudiates the possibility of there being any self-same identity to return. What is experienced phenomenologically as temporal continuity in reaching backward through memory and extending forward through anticipation is constructed hermeneutically in the moment that cuts the timeline by looping pastness, presentness, and futurity in a threefold bond of eternal discontinuity. Time's passing, consequently, is not overcome by the dissolution of temporal transience in an ocean of eternity but by abiding in the persistent demise of what has never been but what is ever to come, the eternal cycle of recurring difference, wherein being becomes interminably in the terminable becoming of being.

Here it is advantageous to mention Wyschogrod's depiction of the "saintly struggle on behalf of the other" as a "wrestling with time," a mode of temporalization that she labels "the time that is left."[111] The meaning of this expression is made clear from a passage in *Saints and Postmodernism*. According to Heidegger, death signifies each individual's ownmost possibility because no one can die for another. What he neglects, however, is that "the force of the relation to my own death derives from an awareness of *the time that is left*, the gap between my life now and the event that is my dying and is yet to come. . . . When my death is thought of in this way as the always dwindling time that is left to me rather than as the coming to an end of my life, then the death of the Other and my death become *commensurable*. . . . The other's death and mine are now integrated into a common framework in that each of us has a certain portion of time still outstanding."[112] In the most elemental sense, to exist for a human being is to have time left over, a residual that is always calibrated from the standpoint of the event of dying, "the time that lies ahead before each life comes to an end."[113] With respect to this futurity, there is no appreciable phenomenological difference between one's own death and the death of another, since in each case the event of dying signals that there is time left to one's life, even if it is no greater than a nanosecond. Rather than creating a fissured sense of self vis-à-vis the other, as the marker of the time that is left, death opens up the possibility of a *commensurable temporality*, the meantime—the time between what is occurring now and what is to come—that can serve as the space of alterity that overcomes the exclusive concentration on the egoistic instinct for self-preservation and self-interest.

For saintly altruism to be effective, the suffering of the other must cease before the demise of the saint or of the other. Wyschogrod evinces proof from the language of Jewish and Christian hagiography, wherein the fluctuating time of earthly life is emphasized as the arena for redemptive change rather than the fixed time of eternal life. This "ever-diminishing time span," she concludes, "bears directly on saintly singularity in that this singularity can in part be defined as the complex of occurrences that come to pass between the beginning and the end of the saint's activity. The time of a saintly life as expressed in hagiographic narrative is the time-before-it-is-too-late that is, as Kierkegaard claims, lived forward but remembered backward."[114] As a genre of narrativity, hagiography is a textual phenomenon—whether performed orally or in writing—that bridges the chasm of temporal distances by retelling the story of the saint's life. In this reinscription of the tale, both the teller and the addressee have the opportunity to experience the sense of temporality marked as the *time that is left* and as the *time-before-it-is-too-late*, that is, the temporal deportment of lived timed as "pure flux or passage."[115] The saint lives thoroughly in a present that is, simultaneously, an anticipation of the future and a recollection of the past. The contemporaneity to which Wyschogrod alludes is clarified by the following comment in *Saints and Postmodernism*: "Hagiographic narrative exhibits a tripartite chronological ordering: the time of the matter narrated, the life of the saint from birth to death with both its quotidian and exceptional episodes; 'authorial' time, or the time of recounting; and the order of time into which the story falls, that of the listener or reader. . . . It is only through narrative articulation that events are disclosed as such and take on the character of an ontological matrix."[116]

Not surprisingly, the ontological and discursive surfeit of hagiographic textuality can also be expressed spatially. Invoking the figure of Teresa of Avila,[117] Wyschogrod depicts the excess of desire as a relentless moving from despair to jouissance, a nomadic wandering in the interior castle in which God is inside by being forever outside, the "proximate One" that can never be linguistically demarcated or conceptually thematized.[118] The reference to Teresa's itinerant state calls to mind Wyschogrod's assertion in *Saints and Postmodernism* that the "absence of dwelling" is a "central feature of many hagiographic accounts." Saintly existence is a way of being in the world marked by drifting, dispersion, and diaspora—in some measure an *imitatio Christi* according to the description of the Son of Man as having nowhere to lay his head (Matthew 8:20, Luke 9:58)—characteristics that afford the saint the possibility of transcending the "essence of man" by taking on the "sheer animal sentience,"[119] and by so doing, the saint emulates God, becoming "an outside that is inside" and thus occupying the "empty nonplace 'inhabited' by the Other."[120]

In Levinas's thought, as we discussed in Chapter 3, nomadism is intrinsic to the poetic way of being in the world: it is not the inflexible physical structures that constitute the essence of human habitation—a patent criticism of Heidegger's promulgation of a pagan enrootedness in the earth[121]—but rather the makeshift desert shelters, the impermanent lodging that signifies that it is the moral concern for the face of the Other and not the sedentary ownership of property that is the ultimate source of meaning.[122] For Wyschogrod, the saint's migrant condition is linked to the animality that supersedes humanity and imitates divinity, an obvious reversal of the longstanding bias whereby the divine image is interpreted as the marker that differentiates the human from all other sentient beings. Beyond this important about-face, it should also be noted that the peripatetic nature of the human is tied innately to the image, the simulacrum, which should not be conceived Platonically as a false copy but rather in Deleuzian fashion as the virtual reality that eludes classification.[123]

Furthermore, Wyschogrod's mentioning Teresa of Avila intimates that, unlike Levinas, she is willing to affirm the potentially fanatic passion of the mystical—the "desire that has no specifiable object, a desire that desires the desire of the Other, whose desire is infinite"[124]—as a plausible sort of postmodern spirituality. In response to Caputo's prodding, she employs the expression *le désir de Dieu* to express the erotics of transcendence, since it is sufficiently ambiguous to convey both God's desire for the human and the human desire for God. Wyschogrod is prepared to utilize this theological language, but she cautions that as postmoderns we are not free to return to the essentialism of a "premodern religiosity."[125] Mindful of Levinas's concern, Wyschogrod insists that the exaltation and zeal exemplified by Hasidic masters and Christian saints, especially in light of the horrors of the twentieth century, must be tempered by ethical responsibility. "We cannot evade the ecstatic, but we can in flesh and blood feel the constraint of alterity."[126] Wyschogrod is thus apprehensive about "saintly abjection," such as anorexia, for this is a form of narcissism that turns the saint into a self-loathing being, who seeks to be "taken up into the compensatory love of God," resulting in the reduction of the concern for the other's destitution to an endless quest to overcome one's own dejection.[127] The "discourse of postmodern ecstatics," therefore, will be pervaded by ambiguity if alterity is absent from that discourse.[128]

I would contend, however, that Wyschogrod's own postmodern discourse directed to the desired Other is riddled with ambiguity. Thus, expressing more doubt than Levinas with respect to the question of transcendence and confidence in the decree of the divine voice, Wyschogrod concedes that we cannot know for certain that "we have been commanded," but even so "we are constrained."[129] Constrained, no doubt, by the other. And yet, as Wyschogrod admits, the differential cogency of postmodernism—in contrast to the pleromatic postmodernisms that are guilty of totalizing monisms concealed within pluralisms—requires that alterity be thought "in terms of lack, absence, and negation. But, it could be asked, is alterity nothing but negation and lack, a nonplace from which a certain speech, the speech of the other, issues?"[130] Responding to her own hypothetical question, Wyschogrod turns to the altruism of saints because the object of saintly life can be envisioned precisely in terms of this lack, that is, a "positivity bound up with living for the other."[131] However, as Wyschogrod hastily adds, to allow the "nonconceptualizable Other to be the object of saintly work," there must be a "subject" of saintly life, some sense of a singular being identified as the agency that can relieve the suffering of others through acts of compassion. In a postmodern moment, when the metaphysical conception of consciousness has been fractured, even this solution is not without complication: "The conditions for saintly life as something singular must be stipulated and the kind of ideality deconstructive analysis undermines must be detached from the term *singularity* by bringing to light the difficulties connected with individuation."[132]

Wyschogrod proceeds to offer a semantic distinction between saintly singularity, on the one hand, and the concept of individuality that remains ontically logocentric, on the other, but she admits that the former itself cannot be construed without resorting "to the notion of a larger whole characterized by suffering and privation."[133] Both self and other are constituted as deprivation, a bind of double negation: the other manifesting through negation the negativity of the destitution that the self seeks to negate. The lives of saints, therefore, "exhibit two types of negation: the negation of self and the lack of what is needful but absent in the life of the Other."[134] In this regard, the saint is exemplary of the kenotic comportment of the human condition: the constitution of self is dependent on emptying oneself to satisfy the need that is expressive of the other's very existence. "The negativity of destitution is not a secondary 'phenomenon' of lack but something primordial, the always already riven character of suffering, and displays itself as such to the saint. This mode of negation is to be distinguished from the negation that belongs within the totality of a system . . . Nothing whatsoever precedes the destitution of the other."[135] In that destitution the other's singularity is displayed as the positivity deployed as negativity, the *supra-ontological* or *me-ontic* being, the inherent deficiency—the absent absence that is present in its absence—in virtue of which "the other is always already the object of a desire that exceeds any expectation of fulfillment."[136] Once again, we see that the depiction of saintly desire as excessive is a marker of the voluptuary structure of human desire[137] more generally: just as the satiation of desire perforce only generates more desire, so the will to will is manifest most potently in the will not to will. The apophatic and the ascetic here converge: to speak-away, the unsaying at the core of every act of saying, is a verbal exploit on a par with the satisfaction of desire through the unremitting purging of desire. The very alterity that segregates the self and the other is what bridges them: the self is the same as the other in virtue of their being different. Sameness thus consists of difference, a nondialectical identity of opposition. Consequently, the suffering of the other will always be greater than the intention to relieve it. For Wyschogrod, this is the *infrastructure of saintly experience*:

> The singularity of the other speaks from the nonplace of the difference between the saint's desire and the other's own suffering, so that the other's singularity is always an excess, more than can be encompassed by saintly intention. What is absolutely other gives itself to the saint as this excess. The other, then, as seen by the saint, is the one whose suffering exceeds any saintly effort at amelioration. . . . From this perspective, saintly singularity is desire released from the bonds of a unifying consciousness, a desire that is unconstrained and excessive yet guided by the suffering of the other . . . In actuality, no saint can always carry such generosity through to the end.[138]

Wyschogrod adamantly insists that the postmodern saintliness must be distinguished from premodern saintliness. It is not viable "to return nostalgically and uncritically to an older ethos," for nostalgia is nothing but a form of historical amnesia. "The postmodern saintly life as a new path is not a proposal to revert to an older hagiographic discourse, least of all to hide behind its metaphysical presuppositions. It is instead a plea for boldness and risk, for an effort to develop a new altruism in an age grown cynical and hardened to catastrophe: war, genocide, the threat of worldwide ecological collapse, sporadic and unpredictable eruptions of urban violence, the use of torture, the emergence of new diseases."[139] The quest for the postmodern saintliness in Wyschogrod does not depart from its anarchic moorings; there is no metaphysical monism concealed beneath her pluralistic conception of the real, as she alleges in the case of the antinomianism of Deleuze and Guattari.[140] And even though she undoubtedly avoids the "private economy of interiorized ecstasy" attributed to Kristeva,[141] in the end, her thought requires the supplanting of nomological discourse by the discourse

of the Other, since there is no transcendence in which the ethics of alterity and acqui-
escence to the law might coincide.

CRUCIFORM ATHEOLOGY

A theme that runs throughout much of Wyschogrod's work is the problem of thinking transcendence in the absence of a transcendent ground, a thinking that she characterizes, in the wake of Nietzsche, as joyful insofar as it is a thinking unburdened by
the gravitas of the logic of presence. Prima facie, to think transcendence in the absence of a transcendent is, in Levinasian terms, to think otherwise than being. Upon
closer examination, however, this discernment translates atheologically into a "world
that is scriptic but without Scripture, a field of laterally interpenetrating texts."[142] It is
hardly an arbitrary coincidence that the move away from the ontology of presence is
described in metaphors that are predominantly textual and graphic. Ostensibly,
Wyschogrod sought to establish the historical accuracy of hagiographic narratives in
order to confirm the veracity of the moral practices of the saintly life, which could
serve as the touchstone for a postmodern ethics.[143] But it is not clear to me that she
succeeds any more than Derrida—whatever their true ambitions[144]—in being able to
get out from under the burden of the hermeneutical supposition that strongly questions the feasibility of reconstructing historical context in such a way that allows the
historian to access extratextual ontic referents. Hence, commenting on Mark Taylor's
Erring in language that is a fusion of Heidegger, Derrida, and Levinas, Wyschogrod
writes of a "postmodern historicality" that "takes cognizance of the traces inscribed in
texts, the tracks or spoors that must be hunted down in order to think what is as yet
unthought of in them."[145] The emphasis on thinking the unthought as the principal
deed of the historian shifts the balance to a textualized event.

The implication of this shift for future speculation on the relationship between
Christianity and Judaism is drawn boldly and profoundly: Christian thinkers can no
longer confine themselves to interpreting the Hebrew Bible typologically as a prefig-
urement of what is revealed in the New Testament, but rather the "whole field of
Jewish textuality" should become the "discursive space in which Christianity must
ceaselessly confront and re-articulate itself." This propensity engenders a "wandering
across the limen that separates Judaism and Christianity, a boundary that is always
already breached through the crossover of texts."[146] It seems reasonable to relate the
use of the metaphor of wandering to the roving nature of the saint, which we previously discussed, and the breaching of boundary between Judaism and Christianity to
Wyschogrod's autobiographical musing. It is apposite to note her observation that
"theistic belief may but need not be a component of the saint's belief system."[147] I do
not think it is far-fetched to conclude that Wyschogrod saw her own philosophic meandering as an expression of a postmodern saintliness. Taking the directive to heart,
Wyschogrod ventures on her own speculative wandering to produce an "erring theol-

ogy" centered about a deconstructive reading of the concept of liminality as it pertains to space as the limen of exile, time as the limen of the Sabbath, and people as the limen of ingathering. These three liminalities are correlated with the theological categories of creation, revelation, and redemption. Consciously emulating Rosenzweig, Wyschogrod imposes one triad atop the other to form the cruciform of the six-pointed star, the constellation of an immanent atheology.[148]

In discussing the first of these liminalities, Wyschogrod demonstrates an insightful grasp of a central motif in Jewish thought, the portrayal of creation as an act of writing, a theme that resonates with the primacy that a "deconstructionist postmodernism" bestows on the grammatological as a "nihilatory and primordial power of language."[149] Particularly striking is Wyschogrod's comprehension of the kabbalistic recasting of the rabbinic idea that the world was created by means of the Torah. She juxtaposes the Lurianic myth of creation through the self-contraction (ṣimṣum) of the infinite, which is accurately depicted as "a wandering forth of God across the limen, an exile of the divine self from itself," and the notion that the divine emanations are linguistic and numerical ciphers "reaching down into the En-Sof." Divine writing is thus a form of exile, an othering that results in the delimiting of the limitless within the concatenation of the worlds.[150] The theosophic model is applied existentially to the status of the Jewish people: "Just as God others himself, so exile is always already the condition also of Israel's existence." Beyond chronicling the historical banishments that Jews have endured through the course of history, Wyschogrod interprets the "serpentine traces" of the diasporic predicament in ontic terms: "Only in and through this wandering is Israelite identity formed, an identity-in-difference shaped by the nomadic existence of the desert. . . . But this errancy is the mark of pain and death, that which is insurmountable in existence and must be acknowledged in a fully immanent atheology."[151] The fate of the vagrant identity might well express the lack of closure frequently celebrated as one of the prime characteristics of the postmodern state of affairs, but we should not lose sight of the fact that it also betokens an interminable suffering to the extent that exile has no foreseeable end. The life of incessant migration signifies openness in an almost archetypal manner, but it also indicates rootlessness and the want of protective shelter. Taken literally, homelessness is indicative of socioeconomic inequity of grave import; taken figuratively, it bespeaks being banished without God and without world, roaming about without the benefit of a circumference in which one is enclosed and nourished. Cognizant of this very problem, Wyschogrod underscores that in the "fully deconstructed atheology exile is not only endless wandering but also the circulation of productive forces. . . . Exile is vigilance for and towards social justice."[152] The potentially detrimental effect of the inherent exilic status of the Jew is turned into a constructive mandate to pursue the moral ideal.

The second of the liminalities concerns temporality. In the immanent atheology, the difference between present time and end time will "express itself within time as redeemed time." As is often the case, the rhetorical style of Wyschogrod is grossly understated. The conception she extracts from Jewish sources is a subtle appropriation and subversion of traditional eschatological speculation. There is no escape from time, and if we are to speak of a redemption of time, then time will have to be redeemed through time. Wyschogrod illustrates the point by drawing on the symbolic association of Sabbath and the redemption: "The Sabbath, conceived as outside time within time is a redeemed temporality. Marked by the fissures of exile, it nevertheless opens out the possibility of an eternally recurring time of mercy and grace."[153] In consonance with the views of Rosenzweig and Heschel discussed in Chapter 2, Wyschogrod refers paradoxically to the Sabbath as "outside time within time," a temporal cognate to her spatial understanding of the saint emulating God's radical exteriority by residing in the world as the outside that is inside, which, of course, logically entails the inverse; that is, to be the outside that is inside, one must be the inside that is outside. Insofar as the Sabbath epitomizes this paradox, it provides the paradigm of a redeemed temporality, which is further specified as "an eternally recurring time of mercy and grace." This corresponds to what we noted above as Wyschogrod's acceptance of the Deleuzian interpretation of Nietzsche's doctrine of eternal recurrence, albeit with the added proviso that the cycle of motion and rest is determined by the qualities of mercy and grace.

To draw out the deeper philosophical significance of the Sabbath as a prolepsis of redeemed time, Wyschogrod alludes to the kabbalah again: "The Kabbalistic account of divine emanation and self-exile must be read in conjunction with the biblical account of creation as the alternation of crafting and respite. But Kabbalistic theology is fully speculative interpreting the creation as spatial continuity and divine self-contraction within the pleroma." It is obvious that Wyschogrod has in mind the Lurianic cosmology, which I briefly discussed above. What is of special interest is that she argues that the kabbalistic teaching "presages" and "becomes fully clarified in Hegel's interpretation of the relation of time to space." Hegel argued that space has two aspects, the "existence of uninterrupted continuity" and the "existence of things in their separateness." The discreteness of objects, their differentiation into separate entities, is related, more specifically, to the property of punctiformity, the "dot-quality" that "gives rise to lines and planes." This attribute, however, cannot be expressed spatially; it can exist only as time.[154] Wyschogrod's point can be clarified by a passage in *Spirit in Ashes*, where she analyzes the "punctiformity of space as the truth of space" in Hegel: "From the standpoint of space, punctiformity is the negation of continuity, and time the negation of the negation. . . . Time is what it is not, space, in the form of its ideality."[155] The existence of discrete objects requires that space be both an "uninterrupted continuity" and the "negation of this continuity," a negation that is effectuated by means of the temporal. To identify time as the truth of space means that the extended beings that become in space are made of time, the template through which the exteriority is internalized and the interiority externalized. Wyschogrod is to be given credit for connecting the kabbalistic account of God contracting the infinite essence into a dot with the Hegelian idea of the extension of space into the punctiformity of time. The Sabbath, in her reading, "expresses the turning of space into time, the respite from creation as the temporal self-articulation of identity-in-difference."[156]

The third liminality is the ethnic-nationalistic boundary that separates peoples. Wyschogrod takes on one of the most vexing problems that have challenged Judaism through the ages, the emphasis on singularity and difference, which is expressed most audaciously by the images of chosenness and election. The deconstruction of this limen involves affirming "an ingathering of peoples, an ingathering in which all nations have become nomadic."[157] In an ingenuous reversal, Wyschogrod universalizes the idiomatic marker of Jewish specificity—the dissemination of the Jews among the nations endows them with the status of the saint, for they are "neither inside nor outside," and, as a consequence, the nations are endowed with this status as well. The ultimate expression of the penchant to stray is the "overcoming of death," which is the "boundary that separates interior from exterior, absence from presence." In terms of the immanent atheology, this conquest of mortality is expressed in the vision of Isaianic peace, the eventual end to violence, and the "identity-in-difference" realized through the "nomadic crossing over of nations."[158]

In conclusion, we can say that the Jewish atheology put forward by Wyschogrod—in no small measure due to the impact of the Deleuzian analysis of Nietzsche's "nomad thought"[159]—is illustrative of what is known as *psychical nomadism*, the practice of taking what one needs from a system and leaving behind what one finds unappealing. But even what she adopts—the three basic elements that have molded the composition of that faith for millennia, the boundaries of spatiality, temporality, and ethnicity—is subject to a radical deconstruction and transvaluation. The crossing of the spatial is reinscribed as the ideal of the nomadic, a state of perpetual dispossession that signals the quest for social justice; the crossing of the temporal as the ideal of redeemed time, to be outside of time and yet inside time, indeed to be inside by being outside; and the crossing of the ethnic as the breakdown of distinctions and the overcoming of death through the cessation of violence. The common denominator to all three acts of reinscription is the resisting of the binary logic and the establishment of an identity-in-difference. The atheology is qualified as "immanent" because there is no recourse to a transcendence that is external to nature, no metaphysical presence that is not a part of the physical universe. Transcendence signals exteriority but not as a substance that lies outside the totality. It is relevant to recollect here that, for Wyschogrod, the importance of finding evidence for *unio mystica* in kabbalistic sources lies in reinterpreting the phenomenon negatively such that "it renders possible the plunging of the individual soul into the abyssal, apocalyptic nonground of the divine, nonground because the abyss cannot become an ontological foundation or anchorage."[160] We can aver transcendence in relation to this abyss, the nonground, the inside that is outside by being the outside that is inside.

Can a Jewish immanent atheology as delineated by Wyschogrod, the "philosophy of deep negation,"[161] show its face in time and space? Can we imagine an actual liturgical community embodying these deconstructions as a living cultural matrix? Thinking in the footsteps of Levinas, Wyschogrod notes the centrality of the rabbinic interpretation[162] of the Israelite's response to Moses, "All that the Lord has spoken we will do and we will hear" (Exodus 24:7): "Doing does not merely express a priority of *praxis* over *theoria* but of a peculiar and unique praxis which itself bypasses analyses of activity beginning with Aristotle who understands activity as the domination of the present, as beginning, as teleologically organized. . . . The law is accepted before being subjected to scrutiny; at the same time to do is, paradoxically, already to hearken."[163] Can there be a viable postmodern Jewish ritual—a doing before hearing that is "entirely freed from *telos*," a "rupture with the means-end scheme of ordinary activity"[164]—if there is no commanding voice, no transcendence but transcendence within immanence? Is the identity-in-difference espoused by Wyschogrod sustainable, or does it alter the nature of Judaism so fundamentally that it could not satisfy the command to instruct your children, that is, the stipulation to transmit the tradition across the generations? I have my misgivings, and even Wyschogrod expressed doubt about this possibility in her questioning whether the call to "return to text" by postmodern Jewish philosophers, thinking in the shadows of the carnage of the Shoah, can "be productive of joy (even if not unalloyed) any more than the vanished world of Hasidism that Buber tried to recreate?"[165] Elsewhere she cautioned, "To gain the pleromatic fullness of ecstasy requires a present that forgets history, because who in the century of man-made mass death could attain ecstasy without amnesia?"[166] Her own attempt to insist on a heterological history, a history that does not efface the other, is an effort not to capitulate to this amnesia, but is it possible to respond in the affirmative to her question, to experience ecstasy without some measure of forgetfulness? More broadly, is a Jewish renewal of covenant possible without a massive loss of memory even in the context of the ritualized commemoration of the past? What cannot be doubted is that Wyschogrod demonstrated great courage in raising these issues in her own restless contemplative adventures, daringly seeking to formulate a suitable, and I think it warranted to add neo-kabbalistic,[167] atheology for the post-Holocaust landscape. Only time, I suppose, will tell whether the philosophical tale she has told has the power to lure us onto a path where time may be redeemed through our own excursions in time.

CHAPTER 6

Undoing (K)not of Apophaticism:
A Heideggerian Afterthought

TO STAND, in the shadow
Of a scar in the air.

Stand-for-no-one-and-nothing.
Unrecognized,
for you
alone.

With all that has room within it,
even without
language.

—Paul Celan, *Breathturn*

The inquiry of apophasis, transcendence, and immanence in the Jewish thinkers discussed in the previous chapters is idiomatic of a much larger question that has hovered over the whole of this monograph. In my judgment, recent attempts to harness the apophatic tradition of Western Neoplatonism together with Derridean deconstruction in order to construct a viable postmodern negative theology,[1] a religion without religion,[2] are not radical enough. Not only are many of these philosophies of transcendence guilty of a turn to theology that defies the phenomenological presupposition of an immanent phenomenality, as Janicaud argued,[3] but they fall short on their own terms inasmuch as they persist in employing metaphorical language that personalizes transcendence and thereby runs the risk of undermining the irreducible alterity and invisibility attributed to the transcendent other. It is reasonable to argue that we must marshal the best metaphors in an effort to imagine what technically cannot be imagined, but such efforts ensnare the human mind in representing the unrepresentable and imaging the imageless by the production of images that, literally speaking, are false, and in so doing, the very allure of the alleged transcendence is severely compromised.

Rather than expanding the analogical imagination in envisioning transcendence—a spatial image of a horizon rooted in an outdated cosmology—the spiritual ultimatum of the hour, the epochal duty, as I have argued elsewhere,[4] is the need to overcome it, to rid monotheism not only of the psychological tug to personify the impersonal but also of what Corbin called the "pious illusion of negative theology" and the pitfall of "metaphysical idolatry."[5] In Freudian terms, we must cease idealizing the father in the image of ourselves, to which we might add that the problem has only been augmented by idealizing the mother in an incontestably noble effort to redress gender imbalance by positing images of the feminine to signify the heterogeneity intended to liberate transcendence from a dominative and homogenous masculinity. The counsel of Ricouer still seems relevant and may well serve as guidance for the future: "In our time we have not finished doing away with *idols* and we have barely begun to listen to *symbols*. It may be that this situation, in its apparent distress, is instructive: it may be that extreme iconoclasm belongs to the restoration of meaning."[6]

APOPHASIS OF APOPHASIS: SILENCING GOD-TALK

If we were to apply this unrestrained smashing of all idols without political prejudice or psychological need, then the more fruitful use of the apophatic rhetoric in our moment would be to get beyond the anthropocentric bias to undo both the masculine and the feminine imaginaries that have informed our depictions of the deity. As Catherine Keller remarks, "For apophasis in its own terms would be more aptly called the exposure of theological *idols*—the unsaying of divine attributes inasmuch as they mistake finite constructions such as gender for the infinite."[7] If the turn to apophasis results in a "*theological* critique of theological idolatry,"[8] then this should also include avoiding gendering the negative or the ineffable as feminine.[9] To do so is to reify the feminine as yet one more theological idol, albeit the idol that is the negation of all idols. I agree that sensitivity to the matter of gender "exposes our carnal finitude to the cosmic excess that bears us,"[10] but why should that excess be troped as female? The obvious answer is that it has been intellectually and morally mandatory to redress centuries of cultural imbalance reflected in linguistic habits, patterns of thinking, and modes of behavior. The feminine, quite justly, has assumed the role of the counter-symbol that represents resistance to the totalizing symbolic order of the phallic signifier.[11] Translated theologically, woman is the not-All, the "infinite disquiet" of the divine essence, as Derrida expressed it, which renders problematic the dominant masculine language of speculative dialectic and common liturgical practice.[12] But is not the price exacted for this strategy an assault on the very apophasis that is summoned to generate a new feminist discourse? At an earlier juncture the "cure for idolatry" may have been served by this attempt to gender the God beyond being and naming as female, but by now we must be intrepid enough to admit that the *intimate radicalism of the apophatic infinity*[13] should lead us theoretically to the end of such speculation, whether protofeminist or postfeminist. Keller is not unaware of this critique. Thus she speaks evocatively of the "unsaying of gender"[14] and utilizes the work of Judith Butler to articulate the point: "The sturdy notion of gender that supported not only the exposure of the idol but the introduction of female icons in theology has come unsaid, *undone*, within feminist theory. . . . If I can argue for an apophasis of gender, an unsaying of the concept of 'gender' that shatters its confident access to a bounded pair of positive semantic fields, Man and Woman, it would be in part because Butler declared 'the trouble with gender.' "[15] A bolder apophatic theology—or perhaps atheology would be the better term—should call for a more wholesale iconoclasm, an undoing of the undoing, as it were, a radical shattering of all idolatry, including icons of the aniconic. From the perspective of the absolute nothingness beyond existence and nonexistence, it is all the same difference, and hence the infinite nihility should not be imaginatively confabulated as either male or female.[16] Redressing the imbalance by erecting idols of the infinite—even if conceived in a nonsubstantialist way as the watery and fluctuating potentiality of the abyss—that are gendered as both male and female only compounds the problem by contributing to the creation of a cloud of darkness that shrouds the luminosity of the darkness in which all binaries, including the dyad of sexuated difference, are completely transcended, not in the coincidence of opposites but in their unmitigated erasure.

Reflecting on the role of feminist theologians, Keller writes, "We may be performing an honorable role, not unlike that of death of God theologians qua *theology*; we are exposing the idol of monotheism within His own household. We do not then return the gift out of ingratitude but out of exhaustion—as though our alchemy had failed to transmute the poison."[17] As I have already acknowledged, I concur that the feminist critique has exposed the idolatry of the dominant masculine representations of the deity, but I do not see how emphasizing the feminine can serve as a transmutation of the poison. Is it not the case that the portrayals of God as female are just as idolatrous as the portrayals of God as male, even if we grant the anti-essentialism that is essential to the project and agenda of feminist theology? Keller once more advocates a "feminist apophasis," an unsaying of God, which will be crucial to a new God-talk, although she is mindful of the pitfalls of simply returning to the negative theology embedded in the Christian Neoplatonic hierarchies, and thus she appeals to the deconstructive engagement with apophatic theology as a useful protection against lapsing into a deepening of monotheistic patriarchy. In her felicitous words: "If there is a specifically feminist apophasis, it will hover with both positive and negative wings over the face of the abyss. For the abyss, upon closer meditation, is not an empty void awaiting a word of difference—but our always already differential, always already engendering fluidity—what I have called the *tehom*."[18]

Keller insists that the feminist unsaying of the divine patriarch must avoid terminating in a silence that would not only be akin to the death of God theology but would also disempower women and repeat a patriarchical tendency to reduce women to muteness. What is called for is a "carnal apophasis," which may then serve as the "intercarnal gift" that feminist theology can offer to the enterprise of returning to God, the insight that nothing determinate can be said of God but that we can still avail ourselves of God as the "gifted metaphor for the space itself, in which truth might be told."[19] The gift, on this account, "is neither the undecidability itself nor the impossible as such. The gift would be the particular possibility that offers itself, that lures us to receive it, to *realize* it. To embody it."[20] I can surely appreciate the desire and/or need to cast the gift as the lure of possibility as a corrective to the focus on the gift and the impossible, but I would counter that the apophatic gesture should culminate in the unsaying of the unsaying and that the true possibility of the gift consists in recognizing that there is no possibility of a gift, just the possibility of the unconditional giving of the abyss in which both giving and receiving are no longer discernible. The language of the gift invariably embroils one in the theopoetic fabrication of false idols. Admirably, for Keller, the feminist contribution of the "currently unavoidable gift discourse" is to accentuate the "asymmetrical reciprocity" expressed most poignantly in the ability to not accept the gift.[21] I would humbly submit nonetheless that the gift of refusal is better served by refusing the very discourse of the refusal of the gift.

Recent appeals to polydoxy and the embrace of diverse truths are unquestionably more agreeable than either an orthodox insistence on a single truth or the categorical heterodox rejection of all truth, which, ironically, is as wedded to the belief in certitude as the orthodoxy it rejects.[22] And yet, the avowal of the so-called *manifold of the polydox theology* may threaten the immanent relationality that it wishes to affirm by demarcating the "incarnational depth of the world" as the "mystery of the divine manifold."[23] Unless the word "divine" is just a figurative or mythopoeic way to speak of nature—and hence the theism would be a terminological ruse camouflaging pantheism or panentheism—then the manifold, in Nancy's terms the *singularly plural coexistence*,[24] should resist any recourse to transcendence even if the latter is understood, in Henry's language, as an "*immanent* revelation" of a presence that must remain invisible.[25] In his defense for an anatheism that "signals the possibility of God after God," Kearney notes that "it allows for the alternative option of its impossibility," by which he means that the transcendence of the divine involves a "*surplus* of meaning" that educes "a process of an interpretation" that can never entirely remove the "strangeness" of God. Human beings are prone to imagine the unknowability of God in multiple ways. "The absolute requires pluralism to avoid absolutism."[26] On hermeneutical grounds I would argue that a genuine unknowing, unencumbered by a theopolitical agenda—whether to the right, to the left, or to the center—should yield a twofold (a)gnosis that would make it difficult, if well-nigh impossible, to speak of any doxa about matters divine. While the celebration of pluralism is indisputably laudable, it should not be assumed that it is universally applicable; polydoxy is not superior to orthodoxy if the beliefs promulgated under the pretext of plurality regurgitate erroneous claims, as in the case of envisioning immanence from the standpoint of transcendence. A moral critique of monotheism is not accomplished merely by advocating for a theology of multiplicity;[27] what is desirable is a purging of all theological constructs that are idols of misrepresentation.

It is time to uphold an even deeper apophasis, an apophasis of the apophasis, a bearing of silence that is not only the negation of affirmation, or even the negation that is negated, but the negation that is neither a *non privativum* nor a *non negativum*, as Heidegger put it, interpreting the expression *ouk edexanto*, "they received not," in 2 Thessalonians 2:10, as an "enactmental not" (*vollzugsmäßige Nicht*):

> The "enactmental not" is not a refusal of enactment [*Vollzugsabweisung*], not a setting-oneself-outside of the enactment. The "not" concerns the position of the complex of enactment [*die Stellung des Zusammenhangs des Vollzugs*] to the relation which is motivated from out of it. The meaning of the "not" can be clarified only out of the historical context. . . . The thoughts of negative theology grew from similar motifs of the "beyond yes and no" [*Jenseits von Ja und Nein*].[28]

To appreciate Heidegger's point, one must mull over the scriptural context. The author of this text predicts that prior to the coming of Christ on the day of the Lord, there will be an apostasy heralded by the revelation of the "man of lawlessness," the "son of perdition," who proclaims himself to be God (2 Thessalonians 2:3–4). The lawless one eventually will be slain by Christ, but before evil is defeated, the Satanic power works through signs that are meant to deceive the wicked, who have refused to love the truth (ibid., 7–10). The act of refusal is what Heidegger calls the "enactmental not." The deception, as he sees it, is related to the fact that "the Antichrist appears as God," and hence to escape the Antichrist one must enter "into the complex of enactment of the religious situation."[29] This enactment, however, includes in its purview its own negation—the repudiation of truth in succumbing to the duplicity of the lie that dissimulates as truth.

If I understand Heidegger correctly, he seems to be embracing in this early text— the passage is from the "Phenomenological Explication of Concrete Religious Phenomena in Connection with the Letters of Paul," the second part of the "Introduction to the Phenomenology of Religion," the course that he taught in the winter semester 1920–21—a view that has affinity with Rosenzweig's assertion that the true religious event, the act of "prayer," necessitates the two hands of belief and unbelief.[30] A genuine Christian life, Heidegger taught in a second passage from these lectures, is plagued by "constant insecurity" that is not coincidental but necessary. This is the gnostic import of Paul's dictum that "the day of the Lord will come like a thief in the night" (1 Thessalonians 5:2): those who seek security and peace (ibid., 5:3) are caught up with the menial "tasks of life," leaving them "in the dark with respect to knowledge of themselves," whereas the "sons of the light and of the day" (ibid., 5:5) cannot experience the diurnal but through immersion in the nocturnal, even though they are not of the night or of the darkness.[31] Insofar as the "complex of the enactment with God" (*Vollzugszusammenhang mit Gott*)—faith in the resurrected Christ—is fulfilled by the individual believer, who "authentically stands" in the "now" (*to nun*), and not in "the anticipation of a special event that is futurally situated in temporality,"[32] the potential for despair is part and parcel of the eschatological hope.[33] What Heidegger is alluding to is the *parousia*, which for him is not a matter of waiting for the second coming, understood as the literal return of Christ, but the "obstinate waiting," which, together with the "transformation before God," is inherent in the "enactment of the factical life" that is integral to faith. Rather than seeing these two elements as oppositional, the waiting itself is a consequence of the transformation, the sense of futurity that one experiences in the present when one is in the presence of the being-present of God (*Gegenwärtigsein Gottes*).[34] The waiting, therefore, is not a waiting for some event in the offing that will repeat what happened in the past but rather an expectation of the future erupting in the moment as an inimitable replication, the "having-become" (*das Gewordensein*) that is at the same time a "new becoming" (*neues Werden*).[35] Heidegger alludes to this eschatological realization of duplication qua difference in the statement "Christian experience lives time itself" (*Die christliche Erfahrung lebt die Zeit selbst*)[36] and in the parallel formulation, "Christian religiosity lives temporality" (*die Christliche Religiosität lebt die Zeitlichkeit*).[37] According to the theological pondering of the youthful Heidegger, as I noted in Chapter 3, the *parousia* is not a temporal event in the ordinary sense but the enactment of life that endows time with an "entirely special character," that is, a mode of temporality that has no temporal order and thus is not "objectively graspable."[38]

Underlying the concurrence of the *already* of the historical resurrection and the *not-yet* of the *parousia*, which is not a future event that can be computed or calculated chronoscopically, is a conception of temporality as a linear circle that is reminiscent of the Rosenzweigian interpretation of redemption discussed in Chapter 2. Not surprisingly, Heidegger distinguishes Christian and Jewish eschatological perspectives on this basis. In one passage, he admits that the "basic direction" of this eschatology is "already late Judaic" (*schon spätjüdisch*), but he immediately adds that the "Christian consciousness" is a "peculiar transformation thereof."[39] The degree to which Heidegger viewed this transformation as a radical break is underscored in a second passage: "In late-Judaism [*Spätjudentum*], the anticipation of the Messiah refers primarily to such a futural event [*zukünftiges Ereignis*], to the appearance of the Messiah at which other people will be present." The Jewish hope is tied to the "event complex that is to be expected" (*erwarteten Ereigniszusammenhang*), and the Christian to the "complex of enactment" (*Vollzugszusammenhang*) that is fully realized in the present in light of the fact that the Messiah has already come historically.[40] Although acknowledging that the author of 4 Ezra showed some acquaintance with the Christian prevalence, the clear-cut distinction that Heidegger makes is rooted in the age-old prejudicial contrast between Jewish literalism and Christian spiritualism. Borrowing terms coined by

Asher Biemann,[41] we can say that for Heidegger, Jewish eschatology is expressive of chronological time and Christian eschatology of kairetic time; that is, the fullness of time is realized not in the dénouement of a linear process but in the incursion of each moment that disrupts the temporal sequence. From this perspective the Jew lacks the midpoint that conjoins and disjoins the beginning and the end to which the Christian can lay claim. As I have argued in a number of my studies, a more nuanced understanding of Jewish messianism narrows the gap that Heidegger presumed separated Judaism and Christianity.[42] Thus I agree in the main with the contention of Simon Critchley that Heidegger's locating the origins of Pauline eschatology in the soil of Judaism allows "for a bringing together of Messianic temporality, rooted in the *ho nun kairos*, the time of the now, which Agamben links to Benjamin's idea of *Jetztzeit*, now-time, and Heidegger's conception of the *Augenblick*, the moment of vision—which, of course, was Luther's translation of *kairos* in Paul."[43] I would add, however, that Heidegger himself did not envisage this possibility; on the contrary, his remarks indicate unambiguously that he presumed that the Christian transformation of the Jewish sensibility brought about varying conceptions of temporality that fundamentally divided Jews and Christians.

To engage this matter responsibly will take us too far afield. What is important to emphasize again is that Heidegger's understanding of the comportment of time basic to the *parousia* assumes that to live time in this way is to live, as Paul, a life of distress, to be beset constantly by suffering.[44] The believer is "stuck in the worldly,"[45] but he realizes that it is a place of alienation and fallenness.[46] Moreover, as we have seen, Heidegger was keenly aware of the fact that believers awaiting the *parousia* are susceptible to the deception of the Antichrist appearing in the form of Christ, and hence they run the risk of being "absolutely annihilated" and losing their authentic life, which figuratively may be called the afterlife (*Postexistenz*). "The appearance of the Antichrist in godly robes facilitates the falling-tendency of life [*die abfallende Lebenstendenz*]; in order not to fall prey to it, one must stand ready for it. The appearance of the Antichrist is no mere passing occurrence, but rather something upon which each one's fate is decided—even that of the already-believing."[47] For the one of faith this appearance can be considered a revelation in which Christ and Antichrist are distinguished. "The great presentation [*Aufmachung*] in which the Antichrist appears facilitates faith for the believers, if they already are decided. . . . The expectation must already be such that through faith, the deception of the Antichrist will be recognized as deception."[48] The anguish consists, however, in the fact that in the interim state of waiting—the "before" that is indispensable to the waiting for the future that is already present—there is always the danger that even the sons of light, who have enacted the life of faith, may be duped and capitulate to the darkness that is the world.

In the *Introduction to Metaphysics*, Heidegger proclaimed a similar idea by noting that if faith in God "does not continually expose itself to the possibility of unfaith, it is not faith but a convenience."[49] The true believer must be constantly open to the possibility of doubt, and hence, as he put it in *The Metaphysical Foundations of Logic*, not only may "ontic faith in God" be "at bottom godlessness [*Gottlosigkeit*]," but the "genuine metaphysician," who incessantly questions why there is something rather than nothing, may "be more religious than the usual faithful, than the members of a 'church' or even than the 'theologians' of every confession."[50] In this matter we can learn from the poet whose nearness to god is qualified as "reserving" insofar as it is determined by the presence of absence. Thus the poet is "without fear of appearing godless" but must nonetheless "remain near to the god's absence, and wait long enough in this prepared nearness to the absence till out of the nearness to the absent god there is granted an originative word to name the high one."[51] Perhaps the boldest formulation of Heidegger's position is found in the following passage in *Mindfulness*:

> Godlessness [*Gott-losigkeit*] does not consist in the denial and loss of a god, but in the groundlessness of the godhood of gods [*der Grund-losigkeit für die Gottschaft der Götter*]. Therefore, the pursuit of customary worship and its consolations and uplifting can all the time be godlessness; equally godless is the replacement of such worship by enticing "lived-experiences" [*Erlebnissen*] or paroxysms of emotion [*Gefühlswallungen*]. . . . Only when man learns to have an inkling that it is not for him to decide on godlessness but that godlessness is the highest loss for gods themselves, only then does he enter the path of mindfulness [*Besinnung*] which shows him how godding as retro-attainment [*Rückfindung*] of godhood enowns itself solely out of be-ing. Only where explaining and obfuscating dominate; only where beings press forth unto the beingness of the represented, can the opinion arise that gods are the result of *divinization*, be it divinization of "nature," or of human drives and powers (*animal rationale*). Where at the mercy of such divinization gods are merely the object of opining and procuring, one day it must come to de-godding . . . the inexorable counterpart of *explaining* the godhood of gods, that is, derivation of gods from a divinization.[52]

Most importantly for our purposes is the distinction Heidegger makes between the process of divinization (*Vergötterung*) or godding (*Götterung*), whence the godhood of the gods is reified as an object through the envisaging of beings (*Vor-stellen des Seienden*) out of the oblivion of being (*Vergessenheit des Seyns*), and the process of de-godding (*Entgötterung*), whence the godhood of the gods is divested of these objectifications and restored to the grounding of its truth as the sheltered-concealed opening, the enownment of being. Godlessness is not, as one might expect, identical with the denial or loss of god, what we conventionally call atheism, but it is the obliteration of the ground of the godhood, the abground, which exceeds the presentation of the godly as the "higher being," the "being that is beyond beings" (*Über-seienden*), or the being that "lies over and beyond man" (*Über-menschliche*).[53] What we have here is a more sophisticated articulation of the thematic connection forged by Heidegger in the early work between the act of renunciation and negative theology. Indeed, from his perspective, the root of apophasis, which he intriguingly notes evolved in a "pale form" in medieval mysticism, is to be located textually in the *enactmental not*, an enactment of the refusal to enact, an expression of inexpressibility that is beyond the expressible and the inexpressible.

This more radical negation presumes neither a presence that is absent nor an absence that is present; there is simply nothing of which not to speak, and hence it should occasion the end of God-talk, even of an apophatic nature, a mode of speech predicated on the seemingly absurd proposition that what is said is never what one is saying. The exigency of the moment—to subjugate the theistic anthropomorphization of God and the corresponding egoistic theomorphization of self—demands a sweeping and uncompromising purification of the idea of infinity from all predication, including the ecological tendency to deify the cosmos in incarnational language as the embodiment of a "relational" or an "intracosmic" transcendence.[54] Poeticizing about the divine in such a fashion may well be an "act of constantly opening horizons of possibility," as Kearney optimistically put it, but there is no imperative to transpose those "gifts of possibility" into the "divine gift as creation"[55] unless one is theologically predisposed to reclaim this traditional construal of infinity. The Christological underpinning of the gift image is made explicit in another study by Kearney:

> [T]he sacramental move . . . marks an opening towards a God whose descent into flesh depends on our response to the sacred solicitation of the moment. This calls for a special attentiveness to infinity embodying itself in daily acts of eucharistic love and sharing. An endless crossing over and back between the infinite and infinitesimal. Here the highest deity becomes, kenotically, the "very least of these." The Word becomes everyday flesh. On-going and interminable gift. Transubstantiation.[56]

Structurally, givenness requires giving and the given, but not everything given is a gift. To portray the latter in postmodern terms as a bestowal on the part of divinity liberated from the straightjacket of ontotheology does not mitigate the problem of presuming that what is given is a gift, which in turn rests on the even more laden assumption that the giving is expressive of some form of generosity or grace on the part of the giver. To speak, for instance, as Caputo does, of a "*postmodern turn* in theology when the meditation upon *theos* or *theios*, God or the divine, is shifted to events"[57] may be satisfying emotionally as a way to retrieve an aspect of the theological creed cast in a contemporary jargon, but it is not satisfying phenomenologically, which as a rigorous science calls for the relentless interrogation of any and every belief that is part of the constitution of our lifeworld.[58]

From the particular vantage point of this study, a second remark of Caputo is especially pertinent: "Events are little gifts, and postmodern thinking seeks to keep them free of big deals, which would sell them out. . . . Theology keeps its ear close to the heart of the pulse of pulsations of the divine in things."[59] Big or little, the notion of the gift as it is here deployed is philosophically problematic. This is not an impartial term, and it cannot be entertained seriously unless one personifies the agency of giving. Caputo insists that the event (characterized by an interesting blend of Deleuze, Derrida, and quantum physics) is "a kind of anonymous impulse, a prepersonal transcendental field," and hence "what is distinctive about postmodern theology is that this prepersonal, prehuman field is taken to be a domain of the divine, a sacred surface that is lined with divine strings of force or sparked by divine impulses charged with divine intensities."[60] Utilizing the word "gift" to characterize the nature of the event has the liability of entangling one in a web of metaphoricity that renders questionable the ability to access a "prepersonal" and "prehuman" field that is purportedly the domain of the divine. The event is described as "an irruption, an excess, an overflow, a gift beyond economy, which tears open the closed circles of economics,"[61] but these characteristics are dependent, as Caputo himself acknowledges, on experiencing the event as a desire for God, for something astir in the name of God, for something he knows not what, something for which he prays day and night.[62] The apophatic theopoiesis here affirmed derives from the assertion of nothing-to-assert that is an assertion nonetheless, albeit one that performs an allegorical dissimilarity. The ultimate datum of this utterance may be the "God beyond God," as Meister Eckhart proposed centuries ago,[63] or the "God without God," in the more audacious language of Husserl,[64] but even these articulations of the unutterable leave us beholden to the very theism they seek to subvert. In a strict Deleuzian sense, the singular immanence of the event prohibits the ascription thereto of the language of gift or overflow that point to some transcendent causal force.[65] Of the event what can be said is nothing that could be spoken. To call it a desire for God, even if the latter term is offered only as the semiotic signpost to mark the nonphenomenalizable that evades speech and knowledge, goes way beyond what is justified by the phenomenological parameters of the event.

HEIDEGGER'S VENTURE: GIVING THE GIFT UNGIVEN

What is necessary, although by no means easy to achieve, is the termination of all representation, even the representation of nonrepresentability, a heeding of silence that outstrips the atheological as much as the theological, the unsaying of the unsaying that thinks transcendence as the immanent other beyond theism and atheism. By tendering the disclosure of transcendence in the form of the revelatory giving of the gift, the mind reverts to imaging the unimaginable rather than remaining quiescent in aporetic suspension. There is no need—philosophically or scientifically—to posit a gift issuing from an invisible source that hypothetically crosses the domain of the visible, as Marion has argued in numerous studies explicating the theme of the saturated phenomenon,[66] an ontic incursion of the atemporal and aspatial that is denominated theologically as an epiphany. I concede that the force of life (for want of a more suitable term) can be assigned the quality of givenness, and this minimally involves the reciprocity of the given and the giving. Nonetheless, there is no compelling reason to deduce further that the givenness, which is an indispensable component of our spatiotemporal conceptualization of materiality, dictates that there is a gift, and in the absence of a gift, there is certainly no need to posit one who gives. If one protests that it is possible to conceive of the giver freed from the constraints of the mediation of giving, I would retort that the intercession of a giver in any shape is a metaphysical deduction imposed on the originary giving. Logically, we are not obliged to speak of the givenness—in Heideggerian terms, the *es gibt*, "it gives," the ontological determinant that must remain ontically indeterminable in order to safeguard the pure givenness from which all transcendence that is not enfolded in the immanence of the phenomena has been bracketed[67]—as the gift of divine creation, and plainly no justification exists to postulate an experience of revelation by means of which one could chance upon a transcendent being diremptively breaking into the phenomenal sphere of becoming. It is beneficial to recall Derrida's gloss on the title of one of the epigrams in the fourth book of *Der cherubinische Wandersmann* by Angelus Silesius,[68] "God is above all gifts" (*Gott über alle Gaben*): "It is even said of him that he is not what is *given there* in the sense of *es gibt*: He is not what gives, he is beyond all gifts [*il n'est pas ce qui donne, il est au-delà de tous les dons*]."[69]

To be sure, on occasion Heidegger did avail himself of the image of the gift in conjunction with the notion of givenness, and, as Derrida rightly pointed out, this locution "still announces or recalls too much the dispensation of God, of man, or even that of Being."[70] But a judicious reading of the relevant sources in both the early and later periods of Heidegger's thinking raises serious questions about the appropriation of the Heideggerian notion of the gift for theological objectives. Let me illustrate the point by referring to a passage from the lecture "Das Ding," delivered on June 6, 1950, at the Bayerischen Akademie der Schönen Kunste. In seeking to determine the nature of thingness, Heidegger turned his focus on the object of the jug. What constitutes the thinghood of the jug is its twofold comportment as the void that holds and the vessel that pours out. The nature of giving ensues from the belonging–together— the juxtaposition of what remains apart—of the holding and the outpouring:

> The twofold holding [*zwiefache Fassen*] of the void rests on the outpouring [*Ausgießen*]. In the outpouring, the holding is authentically how it is. . . . The holding of the vessel occurs in the giving of the outpouring [*Schenken des Gusses*]. . . . The nature of the holding void is gathered in the giving. . . . The giving, whereby the jug is a jug, gathers in the twofold holding—in the outpouring. We call the gathering of the twofold holding into the outpouring, which, as a being together [*Zusammen*], first constitutes the full presence of giving [*das volle Wesen des Schenkens*]: the poured gift [*das Geschenk*].[71]

There is much to comment on here, including the striking resonance of the dual character of the thing as holding and outpouring, on the one hand, and the attributes of grace and judgment according to kabbalistic lore, on the other hand, the masculine potency to overflow and the feminine capacity to receive. What I will concentrate on, however, is the depiction of the outpouring in the image of the *poured gift*. Heidegger's use of the metaphor is somewhat misleading: if there is no giver apart from the giving, it makes little sense to speak of a gift unless it is understood that the term connotes nothing but the *full presence of giving* in which there is neither giver nor given.[72] In Heideggerian terms, presence is concomitantly an absence; the being of the phenomenon shows itself in the nonshowing of the phenomenon of the being—the apparition appears in the unconcealedness of the concealment of its appearance. Hence, what Heidegger calls "the destiny of being" (*das Seinsgeschick*) is the "proffering" of being that endures by "simultaneously withdrawing into its essence."[73]

The nature of this self-concealing revealing is illumined by the fragment of Heraclitus, cited by Hippolytus, "Time is a child playing a game of draughts; the kingship is in the hands of the child" (*aion pais esti paizon, pesseuon; paidos he basileie*).[74] The *Seinsgeschick*—the release (*Loslassen*)[75] or the flinging loose (*Loswurf*) of beings that is the venture (*das Wagnis*) of Being[76]—is the time that is like the child that plays, the playing that constitutes the nobility of the child, the dare to surrender to the risk and chance that is the game.[77] There is no rhyme or reason to the world-play (*Weltspiele*):

> It plays, because it plays [*Es spielet, weil es spielet*]. The "because" withers away in the play. The play is without "why." It plays since it plays. It simply remains a play: the most elevated and the most profound. But this "simply" is everything, the one [*das Eine*], the only [*Einzige*]. Nothing *is* without *ground/reason* [Grund]. Being and ground/reason: the same [*das Selbe*]. Being, as what grounds, has no ground [*Sein als gründendes hat keinen Grund*]; as the abyss [*Ab-Grund*] it plays the play that, as *Geschick*, passes being and ground/reason to us.[78]

With these words, which conclude the last of the thirteen lectures based on the course "Der Satz vom Grund," offered at the University of Freiburg in 1955–56, Heidegger responds to the question raised in the fifth lecture when he juxtaposed the Leibnizian principle *Nihil sine ratione*, "Nothing is without reason," and the poetic aphorism of Angelus Silesius "Ohne warum" ("Without Why") from the first book of *Der cherubinische Wandersmann*, "*Die Ros ist ohn warum; sie blühet, weil sie blühet,/ Sie acht nicht ihrer selbst, fragt nicht, ob man sie siehet*," "The rose is without why: it blooms because it blooms, / It pays no attention to itself, asks not whether it is seen."[79] On the face of it, the poet's mystical adage diametrically opposes the philosopher's principle of sufficient reason (*principium reddendae rationis*). However, as Heidegger plumbs the depth of thought preserved in this fragment, he extracts a more profound way to understand the principle of logic. In stating that "the rose is without why" and that "it blooms because it blooms," Angelus Silesius "does not want to deny that the blooming of the rose has a ground" but only that it is "without a *reddere rationem*, a rendering of reasons."[80] The rose, in other words, "can simultaneously have a ground and be without grounds."[81] Through this manner of speaking by "not-speaking" (*Nichtsagens*),[82] the poet instructs us about what remains concealed and unsaid in the principle, that it is "an uttering of being" (*ein Sagen vom Sein*), which speaks of the Being of beings, shedding light thereby on the truth that "Being is ground-like" (*Sein ist grundhaft*). The principle avers, therefore, not that "being has a ground" (*Sein hat einen Grund*) but rather that "*being in itself essentially comes to be as grounding*" (Sein west in sich als gründendes).[83]

We may infer that it is grossly inaccurate to construe the Heideggerian gift in the standard sense; on the contrary, the phenomenological status of givenness allows us, at best, to posit the giving, not a something that is given and definitely not a gift. The primacy of givenness in Heidegger is evident from his signature depiction of being as *es gibt*, but he is to be distinguished from Husserl insofar as he accentuates the extent to which the appearing of every phenomenon is concurrently a disappearing, the self-showing of being that is a concealment of nonbeing; what is given in the giving is gathered within the withdrawal of its givenness.[84] As Heidegger put it in the lecture "Zeit und Sein," given on January 31, 1962, at the Studium Generale, University of Freiburg:

> To think Being explicitly requires us to relinquish Being as the ground of beings in favor of the giving which prevails concealed in unconcealment [*im Entbergen verborgen*], that is, in favor of the It gives [*Es gibt*]. As the gift [*Gabe*] of this It gives, Being belongs to giving. As a gift, Being is not expelled from giving. Being, presencing [*Anwesen*] is transmuted. As allowing-to-presence [*Anwesenlassen*], it belongs to unconcealing; as the gift of unconcealing it is retained in the giving. . . . Being *is* not [*Sein* ist *nicht*]. There is, It gives Being as the unconcealing of presencing [*Sein gibt Es als das Entbergen von Anwesen*].[85]

The gift is the giving of Being that allows beings to appear, but it is at the same time a withdrawal of giving. The withdrawal is what facilitates the transmission or destiny (*Schickung*) by which Being holds back in its sending forth and thus remains concealed in the unconcealment. On this crucial point, I might add, there is continuity between the earlier and later phases of Heidegger's thinking. Consider the following passage in *Die Grundprobleme der Phänomenologie*, the text of the lecture course that Heidegger delivered at the University of Marburg in 1927, several months after the publication of *Sein und Zeit*:

> What can there be apart from nature, history, God, space, number? We say of each of these, even though in a different sense, that it *is*. We call it a being. . . . Beyond all these beings *there is nothing* [*Außer diesem Seienden* ist nichts]. Perhaps there *is* no other being beyond what has been enumerated, but perhaps there is still something else that *is given* [aber vielleicht gibt es *doch noch etwas*], something else which indeed is not [*was zwar nicht* ist] but which nevertheless, in a sense yet to be

determined, *is given* [*was es aber gleichwohl in einem noch zu bestimmenden Sinne gibt*]. . . . In the end something is given [*gibt es etwas*] which *must* be given if we are to be able to make beings [*Seiendes*] accessible to us as beings and comport ourselves toward them, something which, to be sure, is not but which must be given [*etwas, da zwar nicht ist, das es aber geben muß*] if we are to experience and understand any beings at all. We are able to grasp beings as such, as beings, only if we understand something like *being* [Sein].[86]

This passage is an elaboration of the critical expression *es gibt* introduced by Heidegger in his magnum opus as well as the related distinction between being (*Sein*) and beings (*Seiendes*), which I discussed briefly in Chapter 3. Being is the ontological criterion that makes possible the ontic experience of beings that encompass the totality of all that exists. At a loss for adequate language, Heidegger speaks of this Being beyond all beings as a "something" (*etwas*) that "is given" (*gibt es*) but that "is not" (*nicht ist*); that is, Being gives in such a way that the given is always yet to be determined and hence is not an identifiable object subject to *Gegenwärtigen*, the "comportment toward something present," the "having-there of something present," which "expresses itself in the now."[87] Heidegger distinguishes two forms of givenness: a being that is given as that which lies present before us (*vorgegeben*) or being itself as it is given in the "pre-ontological understanding of being" (*vorontologischen Seinverständnis*). Notwithstanding the fact that both the way in which Being is given (*der Vorgabe von Sein*) and the way in which beings are given (*der Vorgabe von Seiendem*) can become objects (*Gegenstand*),[88] there is an essential difference; the former can never be objectified in the manner that applies to the latter. This is the import of Heidegger's comment that beyond all beings *there is nothing*; indeed there is no thing. Hence, building on an observation of Plato,[89] Heidegger insists that the positive sciences can approach Being only in a dreamlike way (*traumhaft*) and not in a "waking vision" (*wachen Gesichtetes*), for they are "unable to give an account of what a being is as a being. The concept of being and of the constitution of the being of beings is a mystery to them."[90]

Reflecting in his "Letter on Humanism" on the meaning of the expression *es gibt* as it was used in *Being in Time*, Heidegger wrote:

> For the "it" that here "gives" is being itself [*das Sein selbst*]. The "gives" names the essence of being that is giving [*das gebende*], granting its truth. The self-giving into the open, along with the open region itself, is being itself. At the same time "it gives" [»*es gibt*«] is used preliminarily to avoid the locution "being is" [»*das Sein ist*«]; for "is" is commonly said of something that is [*was ist*]. We call such a thing a being. But being "is" precisely not "a being." . . . And yet Parmenides, in the early age of thinking, says ἔστι γὰρ εἶναι, "for there is being." The primal mystery [*das anfängliche Geheimnis*] for all thinking is concealed in this phrase. . . . Because being is still unthought, *Being and Time* too says of it, "there is / it gives."[91]

Es gibt denotes that the giving of being is the being of giving, the self-giving (*Sichge-ben*), the giving of the giving that is the being of being. Within this circularity the "it" and the "gives" are transposable: what "it," the being, gives is the essence of being that is giving. Inasmuch as being (*das Sein*) is not "a being" (*das Seiende*), not a something that is, Heidegger opts for the expression *es gibt*, "it gives," in place of the more expectable *das Sein ist*, "being is." For Heidegger, the German *es gibt*, as the Greek of the Parmenidean dictum *esti gar einai*, alludes to the primal mystery of being that is "still unthought" (*noch ungedacht*), that is, the thought that can never be thought definitively but must be thought anew by every thinker in each moment of thinking, the thought that is always on the way to being thought.[92]

In his philosophical ruminations after the turn, Heidegger searched for more appropriate words to name this event of giving—the most significant term to emerge was *Ereignis*, the enowning or appropriating that is the giving-yield of the there is[93]—that is not a thing, the event of beingness that engenders speech but is itself prior to the alliance between being and language that has dominated Western metaphysics. It is true that Heidegger could not liberate himself from the reigning bias of philosophy to privilege language and, as a consequence, the human being. He did, however, alter that bias by shifting the emphasis such that language is prior to the human being—language is, in his celebrated image, the house of being in which the human dwells as the one that guards or shepherds the truth of being.[94] From Heidegger's perspective, the special status of human language is related to the fact that things come to be through their being named,[95] but he insists that the advent of being precedes both language and human existence. In the aphorism "Beyng and Language" (*Das Seyn und die Sprache*) in *Contributions to Philosophy*, he surmises that the human being and language "both *belong* equiprimordially [*gleichursprünglich*] to beyng," and in virtue of that belonging-together the human is "the steward of the truth of *beyng*" (*Wächter der Wahrheit des Seyns*).[96]

The nature of language to which Heidegger alludes is disclosed in his comment that it is "the echo which belongs to the event."[97] In contrast to the representational function assigned to language in classical metaphysical ontology, here speech is not envisioned primarily as a demarcation of the event in substantialist terms but rather as its echo, a reverberation that follows the event that issues from—indeed is thrown by—the abyssal ground (*Ab-grund*). Attunement to this echo imparts to the human being "the stewardship of the truth of beyng," which is tantamount to the essence of what it is to be a human. "The human being belongs to beyng as the one appropriated by beyng itself for the sake of the grounding of its truth." Language is the vehicle through which one is authentically grounded in the grounding that originates in "the essential occurrence of beyng."[98] Insofar as that occurrence cannot be predetermined or predicted, the essential nature of language, too, is characterized by indeterminacy and openness. Prior to serving as a symbolic marking of things, language originarily—from the perspective of its origination in the sheltering-concealing of the open—is a saying that echoes what has been previously unsaid in the giving-forth of the event of being, whence it follows that the essence of language can "never be determined otherwise than by naming the origin of language. Accordingly, it is impossible to proffer essential definitions of language while at the same time maintaining that the question of its origin is unanswerable."[99] The origin of language can be named only as that which cannot be named. The ground of language, therefore, is silence, "the most concealed holding to the measure [*das verborgenste Maß-halten*] . . . in that which is most internal and most extensive, the positing of measures [*Maß-setzung*] as the originating essential occurrence of what is fitting and of its joining (the event)."[100]

In another section from *Contributions to Philosophy*, "Language and the inventive thinking of beyng" (*Das Erdenken des Seyns und die Sprache*), Heidegger states that "the truth of beyng" cannot be spoken by "ordinary language," but he also raises doubt that a "new language" could be devised for such a purpose. What is requisite "to say the language of beings as the language of beyng" is to cultivate the capacity to hear, that is, to speak by listening rather than by speaking,[101] a gesticulation that Heidegger calls "bearing silence" (*Erschweigung*) or "sigetics" (*die Sigetik*), the "prudent lawfulness of the silence-bearing activity," a logic that is commensurate to "the truth of the essential occurrence of beyng," a truth that is "the intimating-resonating concealment (the mystery) of the event (the hesitant withholding). . . . For every saying arises from beyng and speaks out of the truth of beyng." The essence of what may be called the language of being is grasped in the sigetic art of keeping still in the face of the mystery, although Heidegger expresses disdain even for this "label," which he has offered for "those who still think by 'pigeonholing' and who believe they posses knowledge only if what is said has been categorized."[102] The bearing silence, therefore, is a mode of saying that is a not-saying; indeed, all that is sayable about beings is transcended by the open-ended unfolding of the event of being, the hesitant withholding that can never be exhausted by an economy of presence.[103] If we go on speaking of something "that is" with regard to the event of being, then that something is always yet-to-be, the being that is otherwise-than-being, neither a present absence presently absent nor an absent presence absently present.

If we are attentive to the fact that being itself is the "self-withdrawing" (*Sichentziehende*) that essentially occurs as the refusal (*Verweigerung*) of being, then we can appreciate that the "highest gift" (*höchste Schenkung*) is identical to this "nullity" (*Nichtiges*), that it is "on account of *this negativity* of beyng itself [dieser Nicht*haftigkeit des Seyns selbst*] that 'nothingness' [*das "Nichts"*] is full of that *assigning* 'power' the enduring of which is the origin of all 'creating' (beings coming to be more fully)."[104] We may elicit from this passage that the gifting of being is the nothingness that is the refusal of being,[105] the "abyssal ground" that is the "hesitant self-withholding of the ground" (*die zögernde Versagung des Grundes*) wherein "the originary emptiness [*ursprüngliche Leere*] opens up and the originary *clearing* [*ursprüngliche* Lichtung] occurs,"[106] the excess (*Über-maß*) in the essence of being that springs from the self-concealment (*Sichverber-*

gen) "of all quantification and measurement," the "self-withdrawing [*Sichentziehen*] of *measuring out*,"[107] which marks the temporal comportment of the gateway of each moment as "the collision of future and past,"[108] the constant return of what has always been what is yet to come. In language that echoes Nietzsche's doctrine of the eternal recurrence of the same, Heidegger writes: "The eternal is not the incessant [*das Fort-währende*]; it is instead that which can withdraw in a moment so as to recur later. What can recur: not as the *identical* [*das* Gleiche] but as the newly transforming [*neue Verwandelnde*], the one and the unique, i.e., beyng, such that it is not immediately recognized, in this manifestness, as the same [*das Selbe*]!"[109] Hans Blumenberg's suggestion[110] that Nietzsche's idea of recurrence is a mythic response to the culminating question of the metaphysical tradition as expressed by Leibniz, "Why something rather than nothing?" (*Cur aliquid potius quam nihil?*), can be applied as well to Heidegger's notion of repetition. Heidegger's own reflections on time indicate that, like Nietzsche, he embraced an idea of repetition based on difference, and this in spite of his critique of the Nietzschean eternal return as being bound up with the "fundamental metaphysical position" of Western thinking,[111] a point famously argued by Deleuze.[112] The following Deleuzian depiction of Nietzsche could well serve as a succinct summary of Heidegger's view:

> Eternal return cannot mean the return of the Identical because it presupposes a world (that of the will to power) in which all previous identities have been abolished and dissolved. Returning is being, but only the being of becoming. The eternal return does not bring back "the same," but returning constitutes the only Same of that which becomes. Returning is the becoming identical of becoming itself. Returning is thus the only identity, but identity as a secondary power; the identity of difference, the identical which belongs to the different, or turns around the different. . . . Repetition in the eternal return, therefore, consists in conceiving the same on the basis of the different.[113]

In this vein, Heidegger writes explicitly that to repeat means "to *let* the *same*, the uniqueness of beyng, become a plight *again* and *thereby out of a more original truth*. 'Again' means here precisely 'altogether otherwise' [*ganz anders*]."[114] With regard to being, "the same," which is contrasted with "the identical,"[115] is precisely the retrieval of the inception that is perpetually different.[116] The secret of time is expressive of the truth—apperceived at all times through the semblance of untruth—that the impermanence of becoming alone is the permanence of being; what is given is steadfastly the same because interminably different.[117] From this perspective the "*one who seeks has already found*"; that is, "the *original seeking* [das ursprüngliche Suchen]"—the seeking for origin—is a "*grasping of what has already been found, namely, the grasping of what is self-concealing* [Sichverbergenden] *as such*."[118] The temporalization apposite to the appropriative event, marked by the anomaly of the "again" that is "altogether otherwise," is a "remembering expectation" (*erinnernde Erharren*), the abandonment (*Verlassenheit*) to the moment wherein "remembering a hidden belonging to beyng" is "expecting a call of beyng," the "dispensation of the (hesitant) self-withholding," which "a-byssally grounds the domain of decision" and "also makes possible a bestowal as an essential possibility, grants bestowal a space."[119] The concealing-projecting of the abyss gives in such a way that the intensiveness of time is exteriorized as the extensionality of space.

In "Zeit und Sein," Heidegger writes that "the giving that determines all" is the fourth dimension of time, the interplay (*Zuspiel*) of past, present, and future, which "brings about to each its own presencing [*Anwesen*], holds them apart thus opened and so holds them toward one another in the nearness [*der Nähe*] by which the three dimensions remain near one another."[120] The true nature of time is related to this fourfold, and in that sense we can translate the "there is" as "it gives time" (*es gibt die Zeit*), the giving (*das Geben*) that is "an extending which opens and conceals. As extending is itself a giving, the giving of a giving is concealed in true time."[121] There is thus a homology between the giving in the statement "It gives being" (»*Es gibt Sein*«) and the giving in the statement "It gives time" (»*Es gibt Zeit*«). The giving in both dicta is "a sending [*Schicken*] and a destiny [*Geschick*] of presence in its epochal transmutations. . . . Thus true time appears as the 'It' of which we speak when we say: It gives Being. The destiny in which It gives Being lies in the extending of time."[122]

But what is the nature of the "it?" Reluctant to go into detail, Heidegger pushes language to its limit: "The It, at least in the interpretation available to us for the moment, names a presence of absence [*ein Anwesen von Abwesen*]."[123] The *presence of absence* does not signify something absent that will be made present but rather the presence that is present as the *absence of presence*, the appearance of Being withheld in the givenness of its being. Hence we can think the "it" only "in the light of the kind of giving that belongs to it: giving as destiny [*das Geben als Geschick*], giving as an opening up which reaches out [*das Geben als lichtenden Reichen*]." What determines the belonging–together (*Zusammengehören*) of time and being is the event of appropriation.[124] This event is not an occurrence as such but the condition that makes any occurrence possible.

> Accordingly, the It that gives in "It gives Being," "It gives time," proves to be Appropriation. . . . Giving [*Geben*] and its gift [*Gabe*] receive their determination from Appropriating. . . . For as we think Being itself and follow what is its own, Being proves to be destiny's gift of presence [*Gabe des Geschickes von Anwesenheit*], the gift granted by the giving of time [*das Reichen von Zeit*]. The gift of presence is the property of Appropriating [*Die Gabe von Anwesen ist Eigentum des Ereignens*].[125]

Heidegger states with no ambiguity that "logical classifications" (*logische Ordnungsbeziehungen*) are irrelevant—or, in his exact words, "mean nothing"—in the attempt to enter the space of this discourse.[126] One must embark on a different path of thought in order to think the belonging–together of time and being such that one will be attuned to the fact that the destiny of the latter is the extending of the former. The term *gift* is used by Heidegger to name this advent of the event, the given-being of the being-given, which takes shape within the timespace contingency. But to presume that this gift is an entity would induce viewing the act of giving as an ontic process that reduces Being to one of the beings spawned by the abyssal ground, which, as Heidegger tells us, is neither emptiness nor fullness.[127] Needless to say, the further assumption that creation writ large can be viewed as a gift is a lapse into the ontotheological positing of a transcendental causality, the ground of being, which is topologically exterior to the world.[128] Nothing could be more remote from Heidegger's meditation on the Being that is the total dismissal of being, the Being that is the clearing in which being and nonbeing are yet to be differentiated, the Being that is nothing. The "sending" of *Ereignis* is thus always also a "keeping back" (*Ansichhalten*), an "extending" that is always also a withholding (*Vorenthalt*). Insofar as the "modes of giving" most peculiar to *Ereignis* are "determined by withdrawal," every giving will be indicative of a refusal to give, every conferral expressive of a denial to confer.[129]

In light of Heidegger's clarity on this point, I cannot accept Marion's assertion that "by baptizing" (*en baptisant*)—a curious and hardly innocent choice of language—the "it" as *Ereignis*, Heidegger violates his own interdiction and obfuscates the enigma by affixing a name to it.[130] According to Marion, by assigning beingness to *Ereignis*, Heidegger discards the pure reduction of the phenomenological givenness taken on its own terms.[131] Elsewhere Marion adroitly summarizes Heidegger's position by noting that "the giving (*Geben*) gives to presence the gift (*Gabe*), so completely and radically that this gift alone occupies presence and, in appearing, necessarily masks its own donation . . . because giving can never appear as something given since it exhausts and accomplishes itself in allowing to appear—it does not occupy the opening, because it opens it."[132] But here again, Marion insists that Heidegger moves away from the full implications of the phenomenality of the "it gives" by falling back on *Ereignis*, a transposition that leads to the setting aside of the "register of donation."[133] By "thrusting donation back onto *Ereignis*," Heidegger stopped his own advance toward overcoming metaphysics and failed to follow the path of the "contrasting game of giving and the gift" to "an entirely other dimension than being" and the "surpassing of representational thinking."[134]

I would contend, contra Marion, that the Heideggerian *Ereignis* preserves and amplifies the enigma of givenness by insisting that Being conceals itself in the unconcealment of its concealment, and hence the gift that is given can be given only as what cannot be given. Every bestowal is a withholding, every disclosure an occlusion. I would go so far as to say that the absolute event of *Ereignis* can be thought of apocalyptically[135] as the advent of the event that can take place only as a nonevent;[136] that is, the eventfulness conveyed by the nonmanifest manifestation of the manifest nonmanifestation of Being can transpire only in the recoil of its transpiring. Appropriation, on this score, is the dissolution of an ineliminable nothingness—the depresencing of a presence that can never be represented—embedded in the divestiture of the nothing that is indifferently identical in virtue of being identically different.

The disagreement with Marion registered here is not merely a pedantic squabble. His contention that the gift "precedes" and "abandons" the ontological difference between Being and beings—or in the poetic images he enlists, the "gift crosses Being/being" and thereby opens up to the event of charity, which "remains unspeakable according to the language of Being," by "liberating being from Being"[137]—can be discovered in Heidegger. Marion does, of course, credit Heidegger for thinking the correlation of the gift and giving with Being/being, attested in the expression *es gibt*, but he criticizes him for understanding the "enigmatic It" of the gift as arising "from the appropriation of Time to Being, hence also of being to Being."[138] The model of the gift that he proffers has the advantage of distorting the ontological difference "by disappropriating in it what the *Ereignis* appropriates; being remains in its appropriation to Being . . . . Beings, hence Being/being, hence also *ousia*, over and above what is given to them by the pure and simple giving of the *Ereignis*, discover themselves taken up again, as unbeknown to them and from the point of view of another aim."[139] Marion supplants Heidegger's appropriation with his conception of disappropriation, which preserves the distance that he will name not Being but "God," *Dieu*, written with the third letter crossed out with an X, the sign of the cross or the Greek letter *chi*, which is the first letter of the word Χριστός. Presumably, a response to the Heideggerian practice of the crossing out of being,[140] the orthographic anomaly of Marion reveals that God, the "term of distance," appears "only in the disappearance of his death and resurrection." This alone is the giving that "offers the only accessible trace of He who gives."[141] I will return in the next section to the barefaced Christocentrism of Marion's treatment of the gift, but here I wish to emphasize that his misreading of the notion of *Ereignis* as a regression to an ontological mode of thinking not only obscures his indebtedness to Heidegger's breakthrough but also leads to an unfortunate exaggeration regarding the novelty of his affirmation of the invisibility of the gift as its supreme visibility.[142]

GIVENNESS AND THE DISAPPEARANCE OF THE GIFT

Marion is unquestionably one of the most influential thinkers promulgating the metaphor of the gift (*le don*) in philosophical and theological discourse. In the following comment, he relates this image to the Jewish tradition, perhaps due the influence of Derrida:[143]

> The Name has no name in any language. No language says it or understands it. This is why the Jew never pronounces the tetragrammaton, which he nevertheless reads. By orally substituting other titles for it, one indicates that the Name does not belong to our language but comes to it from elsewhere. The Name appears as a

gift, where, in the same gesture, the unthinkable gives us a name as that in which it gives itself, but also as a gift that gives the unthinkable, which only withdraws in the distance of the gift. The name therefore delivers the unthinkable, as the unthinkable that *gives* itself; the same unthinkable also gives *itself*, and hence withdraws within the anterior distance that governs the gift of the Name. The Name delivers and steals away in one and the same movement.[144]

The ineffable name serves as a model to illumine the paradoxical nature of the gift as that which can be manifest only to the extent that it is withheld. Thus, in language that is in basic accord with the Derridean perspective, which we discussed in the previous chapters, Marion argues that for the gift to become actual it would be "inescapably transformed into its contrary, according to a threefold assimilation to exchange and commerce," that is, the triadic structure of donor, object, and recipient essential to the bestowal of the gift. What comes to light is a "radical phenomenal instability that gives the gift the appearance of a phenomenon but leaves it incapable of being constituted as an objective phenomenon." The conception of giving underlying the gift is such that for it to appear, it must disappear, since once given, the giver is rewarded, the recipient indebted, and the gift occludes its character as gift by becoming an object in the economy of exchange:

> Either the gift appears as actual but disappears as a gift, or it remains a pure gift but becomes unapparent, nonactual, excluded from the instance of things, a pure idea of reason, a simple noumenon incompatible with the conditions of experience. . . . Either the gift remains true to givenness but never appears or it does appear, but in the economy of an exchange, where it is transformed into its contrary—to be precise, an exchange, a given that is returned (*do ut des* [I give so that you will give]), something given for a return and returned for a given, part of the trade and management of goods. Exchange is imposed as the truth of the gift, and cancels it. By submitting itself to an economy, the gift exchanges its essence as gift for an actuality that denies it—precisely in exchange. For an economy economizes the gift.[145]

The gift loses its sense of being a gift when it is subject to the economy of exchange determined by the threefold structure of giver, recipient, and given. For the gift to be gift, it must free itself from the reciprocity between donor and beneficiary. "As reduced to the givenness in it, the gift is accomplished in an unconditioned immanence, which not only owes nothing to exchange, but dissolves its conditions of possibility."[146]

Givenness (French: *donation*; German: *Gegebenheit*), as Marion summarized the basic principle of Husserlian phenomenology, "breaks out because the appearing of appearance becomes the apparition *of* what appears—in short, launches what appears onto its own appearing. . . . Appearances no longer mask what appears; they give it its own aspect so that it may appear."[147] Phenomenologically, the mandate is not only to let the intentional objects appear—to get back to the things themselves—but also to let the appearing of the appearance appear, for only in such a way can it be fathomed that givenness is the criterion that determines the essence of the phenomenon—what it is for X to be is for X to appear, but for X to appear, X must be given.[148] The gift of which Marion speaks stems from the phenomenality of givenness construed in this manner of showing the unshowing, the deformalization of the phenomenological sense of the phenomenon:

> The fold of givenness [le pli de la donation], in unfolding itself [en se dépliant],
> shows the given that givenness dispenses [montre le donné que dispense la donation].
> For the phenomenon, showing itself is equal to unfolding the fold of givenness in
> which it arises as a gift. Showing itself and giving itself play in the same field—the
> fold of givenness, which is unfolded in the given.[149]

The given has no justification apart from the givenness whence it is given, and consequently, the given is without any principle that justifies its being given. Pure givenness gives of itself,[150] not as an ontic given and without a metaphysical or an ontotheological foundation.[151] To the extent that a gift is really given, it becomes a phenomenon independent of the giver: "This disappearance of the giver does not result from any recalcitrance on the part of the recipient, but from the very definition of the gift given; it is not ingratitude that causes the exclusion of the giver, yet this exclusion ultimately results by virtue of the very phenomenality of the gift given, in itself exclusive and appropriating."[152]

For the gift to appear as that which cannot appear, it must withdraw from the giver understood à la the Cartesian inconcussum quid as the unchanging ground of a transcendental and constitutive ego: "As long as the ego remains, givenness remains inaccessible; it appears only once the ego giver is bracketed."[153] Going one step further, Marion conjectures that to appear as given, not only the giver but the gift itself must disappear. "Givenness would therefore remain intact—would appear as givenness—only at the price of the disappearance [la disparition] or nonappearance [l'inapparence] of the gift given. Such a nonappearing [non-apparition] of the gift in no way implies renouncing its phenomenality."[154] The gift, accordingly, can never be seen; indeed, the paradoxical logic of the "eidetic law" decrees that the "gift becomes more invisible as it gives itself more effectively. It disappears precisely in direct proportion to its appearing."[155] In a manner that resonates with the view of Heidegger discussed above,[156] Marion asserts that the true gift nullifies itself inasmuch as it recedes from the givenness of the gift:

> In effect, just as the gift appears only if the giver disappears, the gift thus aban-
> doned ends by masking in itself not only the giver but the very process of the
> gift. . . . Paradoxically, a gift truly given disappears as given, too. . . . What is

specific to the gift—once we grant that it implies relinquishment in order to appear—thus consists in disappearing as given, and in allowing nothing more to appear than the neutral and anonymous presence, left without any origin, of a thing, of a being, or of an object, coming only from itself, never from elsewhere— nor originating from a giver or from a process of giving. The major aporia of the gift derives from this paradox: the gift given can appear only by erasing in its phenomenon its giver, the process of its gift, and, ultimately, its entire gift-character.[157]

The gift, then, reveals givenness quintessentially as the apparent nonappearance of the saturated phenomenon, the hyperplenitude, whose "ownmost property is to render thinkable the measure of manifestation in terms of givenness," the criterion that Marion identifies as "the one and only paradigm of phenomenality."[158] The saturated phenomenon receives this accolade because it instantiates the paradox of "the counter-appearance" (la contre-parence) and "the visibility that is against what is [visually] intended" (la visibilité à l'encontre de la visée);[159] that is, "its essentially unforeseeable character" (son caractère essentiellement imprévisible) entails that it "cannot be aimed at" (ne peut se viser).[160] On account of these qualities the saturated phenomenon effectuates the reversal of the relationship between givenness and showing: "In this case, phenomenality is calibrated first in terms of givenness, such that the phenomenon no longer gives itself in the measure to which it shows itself, but shows itself in the measure (or, eventually, lack of measure) to which it gives itself."[161] The visibility of the given increases in inverse proportion to its invisibility, and thus envisioning the phenomenon of revelation can be viewed—in the spirit of the apophatic mystical tradition—as an act of blindness, the seeing of what cannot be seen, an event that "gives itself without manifesting itself for the curious spectator."[162] The gift qua saturated phenomenon "gives itself as absolute, that is, as free from any analogy with common law phenomena and from any predetermination by a network of relations, with neither precedent nor antecedent within the already seen (the foreseen) . . . But this opening denial, and thus this disfiguration, still remains a manifestation. Thus, in giving itself absolutely, the saturated phenomenon gives itself also as absolute: free from any analogy with the experience that is already seen, objectivized, and comprehended."[163] The saturated phenomenon represents the "ultimate possibility" of phenomenology, for it is "not only the possibility that surpasses actuality, but the possibility that surpasses the very conditions of possibility, the possibility of unconditioned possibility—in other words, the possibility of the impossible."[164]

With respect to this issue, Marion, unlike Derrida and Heidegger, introduces God into his phenomenology of the gift: the depiction of the saturated phenomenon coming into phenomenality without the world recognizing or accepting it[165] is an obvious allusion to the incarnation of the Logos in Christ.[166] Elsewhere, Marion is more explicit about his theological intentions: "The phenomenological figure of 'God' as the being-given par excellence, hence as the abandoned, can be outlined by following the guiding thread of givenness itself. As the given par excellence, 'God' is given without restriction, without reserve, without restraint."[167] The unreserved giving—the being-given that is the being-abandoned—supplies the rationale for identifying the gift as God. Insofar as this giving is without limit, the "absolute presence that follows from it saturates any horizon, all horizons, with a dazzling evidence. Now, such a presence without limit (without horizon), which alone suits givenness without reserve, cannot present itself as a necessarily limited object." The saturated phenomenon is displayed in the "atonal tonality of bedazzlement," wherein the presence of God "shines by absence." Rather than contradicting the phenomenality of the givenness, the unknowability attests to its supremacy. " 'God' becomes invisible not in spite of givenness but by virtue of that givenness. . . . The phenomenon par excellence on account of that very excellence lays itself open to not appearing—to remaining in a state of abandon."[168] Givenness finds its culmination in what is not-given, just as the appearing of the inapparent is the most conspicuous form of appearance.

The question that we must pose is one that Marion himself raises: does the phenomenology of givenness so conceived implicate one in "the revival of transcendence in its most resolutely metaphysical, if not to say theological sense?"[169] This fear would seem to be alleviated by Marion's insistence that the fact that a gift can also be called a "present" does not imply that the gift is a presence.

> The *parousia* certainly governs *presence* [*la* présence], but it does not always control the *present* [*le* présent]. The present does not owe everything to presence, and could quite possibly owe it nothing at all. The question of givenness is not closed when presence contradicts the gift: it is, in contrast, opened to the possibility of the present without presence—outside Being [*hors d'être*].[170]

By his own admission, Marion is here offering an interpretation inspired by but in opposition to Derrida's aporia of the gift. A knot of negation becomes apparent from the fact that the truth of the gift is equivalent to the nongift; that is, the being of the gift, when brought to light, abolishes the gift. The choice of the term *parousia* to illustrate "the possibility of a present without presence" (*la possibilité du présent sans présence*) is surely not coincidental or inconsequential. This is clearly a deliberate attempt on Marion's part to introduce a theological dimension into his phenomenological analysis of pure giving.[171] As Caputo expressed the matter, "For the gift has a kind of *ex opere operato* quality for Marion—it works by itself—prior to the agency of the donor or recipient, rather like a Catholic sacrament."[172]

The dogma of the second coming of Christ sheds light on the convergence and divergence with the paradox of the gift. The *parousia* exemplifies the temporality of what is present as what is to come, the expectation of the already but not yet presence that is present by being absent, which opens up the phenomenon of givenness to the possibility of a present without presence that is outside Being. In contradistinction to the visible immanence associated with the presentness of the presence that is endemic to the routine gift,[173] the *parousia* is an invisible transcendence that gives itself by not giving itself,[174] a sacrificial gesture of kenosis,[175] mirrored in the ascetic dispossessing of self-negation.[176] The phenomenon of revelation, the "saturation of saturation," is thus named "the *abandoned*" (*l'abandonné*), insofar as "the excess of the gift [*l'excès du don*] assumes the character of shortage [*l'aspect de la pénurie*]."[177] Sacramentally, the eschatological gift of presence is enacted proleptically in the Eucharist,[178] the rite that brings to the disposability of the present moment the irreducible presence of Christ— the revelatory present that bears in its bosom past and future, the Alpha of creation and the Omega of redemption—in the community of believers that partake of the mystery of communion with God.[179] In this manner, the theology of transubstantiation—the word become flesh so that the flesh may become word[180]—escapes the criticism of the reification of the eucharistic presence and avoids "the supreme as well as subtly dissimulated idolatry, the spiritual idolatry where consciousness becomes to itself the idol of Christ."[181]

Marion is well aware that the task of thinking the "eucharistic presence without yielding to idolatry" is made difficult by the fact that the "very enterprise that claimed to criticize an apparently metaphysical eucharistic theology" results in the "metaphysical completion" of idolatry.[182] Nevertheless, according to Marion, it is possible to impede the idolization of the eucharistic presence to the degree that we are mindful of the fact that this is a presence that can be fully present only by not being fully present; the nonpresence of the presence presupposes a dispossession of the here and now that informs the ordinary conception of time.[183] Marion thus stresses the notion of distance by which the exteriority of Christ can be made present in the substance of the host without collapsing the difference so that it is reified as a presence and turns into an idol.[184] The eucharistic presence, accordingly, betrays the "privileged temporalization of time," the time of the present that is the fullness of the gift given by Christ under the species of the consecrated bread and wine. In the eucharistic gift there is a coalescence of the three modalities of time: the presentness of the present is adduced from memorializing the pledge of the past as awaiting the promise of the future.

The theological treatment of the Eucharist, as opposed to an anthropological or a metaphysical orientation, underscores that the gift constitutes the presence that is experienced not as an "available permanence" but "as a new sort of advent."[185] Doctrinally, the *parousia* provides the believer with the opportunity to implement the Pauline practice of forgetting what is behind and straining toward what is ahead, pressing on toward the goal of resurrection (Philippians 3:13–14). The stretching forward (*epektasis*) encapsulates the temporalization of the future, which "determines the reality of the present in the very mode of the advent. The eucharistic gift relies, so to speak, on the tension that raises it since and for the future."[186] Marion finds in the Christian symbolism the consummating expression of the gift of presence as the charitable bequeathing of the present of time that is the true essence of the time of the present:

The initial demand—to think presence as a present, and the present as a gift—now finds an infinitely more concrete content. Presence must be received as the present, namely, as the gift that is governed by memorial and *epektasis*. Each instant of the present must befall us as a gift: the day, the hour, the instant, are imparted by charity. . . . Of time in the present, it can well be said that one must receive it as a present, in the sense of a gift. But this implies also that we should receive this present of the consecrated Bread as the gift, at each instant, of union with Christ.[187]

Nonpresence is thus brought to presence "at each instant, as the gift of that very instant, and, in it, of the body of the Christ in whom one must be incorporated. . . . The eucharistic present thus organizes in it, as the condition of its reception, the properly Christian temporality, and this because the eucharistic gift constitutes the ultimate paradigm of every present."[188] The temporality of the gift is one in which "the present, always already anterior to and in anticipation of itself, is received to the extent that the past and the future, in the name of the Alpha and the Omega, give it. Which means: what is named (and wrongly criticized) under the name of 'real presence' founders in the metaphysical idolatry of the *here and now* or else must be received according to the properly Christian temporality."[189]

Marion has translated into overt theological language what he deems to be the true philosophic explanation of the gift of the present as the time wherein the identifiable absence of the expectation of the future presence is received:

The present at last is accomplished, not as an enduring permanence, but as a present that is given, in short as a present that is received, not as a presence subsisting in itself. . . . The present that is given accomplishes the present instant, precisely because it overflows presence. What is more: the arrival from elsewhere is not only accomplished in the present, it gives me my first present. With its passage, at last something—once again—happens. This gift of the precise present results from the arrival of an elsewhere within the indefinite future of my expectation. . . . The expectation of *this* elsewhere thus does not only temporalize me; it identifies me by assigning me to my own—that which must happen for me (or us) tells me who I am (or who we are). The temporality of the expectation of an elsewhere defines originary individuality and, eventually, originary community.[190]

The Christocentrism of Marion's position is so blatant that it does not merit belaboring the point; the words speak for themselves. It is nevertheless incumbent on me to make the following methodological observation: it is one thing to use phenomenology to buttress one's theological commitments but quite another thing to argue that a particular theological tenet accommodates the phenomenological truth more than any other tradition, which is precisely what Marion has done in his assertion that one finds the epitome of the phenomenological nature of the gift as that which appears in the mode of what gives itself only in the Eucharist and *parousia*.[191] At the very least, it is not at all self-evident that the "eucharistic gift constitutes the ultimate paradigm of every present." I concur with Janicaud's assessment that Marion's "recourse to phenomenology is constantly biased by both a 'call' that is purportedly original and a reference, imposed on the reader, to religious experience. It is a question here . . . of a Christian phenomenology [*phénoménologie chrétienne*], but whose properly phenomenological sense must fall away, for a nonbeliever, midway through the journey."[192]

In different terminology James K. A. Smith offered a similar critique:

> Marion's "religious phenomenon" is collapsed into a *theological* phenomenon; correlatively, his (albeit impossible) phenomenology of religion slides towards a very possible, and very particular, theology. The result is both a *reduction* of religion to theology, and also *particularization* of religion as Catholic or at least Christian—which, of course, is also a kind of reduction, a reduction which reduces the size of the kingdom and bars the entrance to any who are different. Part of my project will be to locate the *ethical* issues behind these apparently benign discussions of method, suggesting that behind Marion's understanding of the phenomenology of religion lies a certain kind of *in*justice.[193]

Smith is correct that Marion has narrowly defined religion by reducing it to its "theological sedimentation" and that, as a consequence, he particularizes or colonizes the religious phenomenon "as quite Christian—at best, monotheistic, and at worst, down right Catholic. . . . This *particularization* is yet another kind of *reduction*: a reduction which reduces the size of the kingdom, which keeps the walls close to Rome and makes it impossible for any who are different to enter."[194] Marion's restricting the phenomenology of religion to the saturated phenomenon, which is identified most paradigmatically as the theophany of Christ, results in religion being "reduced and particularized—or, more aptly, colonized in the name of a Christian imperialism . . . Marion's *piety* leaves no room for difference and will not permit any other gods to appear, indeed, one may be concerned that this pious phenomenology of religion is not beyond crusading to eliminate such paganism."[195]

Lest there be any misunderstanding, let me state unequivocally that the issue for me is not the appropriateness of phenomenology to investigate the invisible as a decisive dimension of the visible; on the contrary, the inclination to move from the apparent to the inapparent is an intrinsic aspect of the phenomenological inspection of the nature of givenness. Hence, I acquiesce to Marion's assertion that phenomenology can be called upon to make decisions about the type of phenomenality that would render the theological phenomenon such as the unnameable and unknowable God thinkable, but it cannot make decisions about the actuality of that phenomenon.[196] The difficulty, however, is delimiting the invisible by which the visible is manifest theologically, arguing that the religious phenomenon is the "privileged index of the possibility of phenomenality"[197] and, even more perniciously, identifying Christian symbolism as the only acceptable language to deal with that which is given invisibly.[198]

It is worth recalling here the response of Marion to the question of Richard Kearney in a conference at Villanova University in September 1997 regarding the religious and theological nature of the gift that informed his speculation on giving and givenness: "Well, I shall disappoint you by saying that right now, at this stage of my work, I have to emphasize that I am not interested in the gift and I am not interested in the religious meaning of the gift. . . . In fact, I was interested in the gift when writing theology, some ten years ago or more. But, with *Reduction and Givenness*, the question of the gift turned out to be profoundly modified for me by the discovery of the issue of givenness, *Gegebenheit*, in phenomenology, and by phenomenology I mean Husserl, and by Husserl I mean the early Husserl, the Husserl of the *Logical Investigations*."[199] As Marion characterizes his own project, he has shifted from the focus on the gift and its theological repercussions to an attempt "to re-read phenomenology as such as the science of the given" as an alternative to investigating the phenomenon as an object or as a being.[200] In this dialogue Marion admits that "theological items," such as the Eucharist, "could appear as phenomena, too, because they have at least something in common with all the other phenomena, at different degrees, viz., to appear as given." Even so, he insists that the primary focus is on "the phenomenological dimension of givenness."[201] Notwithstanding this explicit disclaimer,[202] Marion's publications since the time this remark was uttered demonstrate that he neither disposed of his interest in the gift nor ever shook loose of the preference ascribed to revelation, and particularly the revelation of Christ, as the premier example of the saturated phenomenon. Prompted by Kearney's question regarding this privileging of revelation,[203] Marion candidly responded, "Indeed, I think it is possible to describe, in the horizon of the phenomenology of givenness, what I would call the empty and just possible figure of revelation, which makes sense as a possibility within phenomenology. I suggest that revelation—of course, for me, the revelation of Christ, but also any kind of revelation, if there are other claims to revelation—can acquire phenomenological status and match other kinds of phenomena. In that precise sense, the distinction between the field of philosophy and the field of theology . . . could be bridged to some extent. . . . The gift, that is, the phenomenon as given, is also, I would say, a dimension of the experience of the world including the possibility of revelation too."[204]

Tellingly, in another passage, Marion owns up that to make the invisible gift visible, a phenomenology of the invisible—in line with what was enunciated by Heidegger in *Being and Time* but developed in greater depth in his later thought—is necessary but not sufficient, since "the unseen can only be grasped by theology." Even this stipulation is brazenly qualified: "At least if by theology we mean Christian theology in its profound privilege of having its origin in a Revelation," a point supported exegetically by the verse "one can receive only what is given him from heaven" (John

3:27).[205] The theological principle that "every gift comes from God" illumines the phenomenology of the gift more generally, and the former is epitomized in the Christian conviction that God "gives nothing less than himself in the form of Christ."[206] The Eucharist, therefore, is "the paradigm of every gift of charity," for "the reduction of the gift to contingent and common reality, which are consigned to disappear, and become transparent, allows the donor (Christ) to appear, who in turn, by his own kenosis, makes possible the appearance of the Father. The real presence *de-realises* in fact the matter of the gift, which, in return and paradoxically, renders its donor phenomenal and makes the entire process of donation appear."[207]

For Marion, the Christian narrative is not one of any number of legitimate theologies; it is the only veritable theology, the prototype of theology, inasmuch as it imbibes the truth that to speak of God means that God is both the origin and objective of the theological discourse, that God "simultaneously speaking and spoken, gives himself as the Word, as the Word given even in the silent immediacy of the abandoned flesh."[208] The preeminence of Christianity "does not stem from singularity of meaning . . . but from what, precisely, authorizes this eminent singularity, namely, the very position given to meaning, to its statement, and to its referent. . . . Christ does not say the word, he says *himself* the Word. . . . He says himself, and nothing else, for nothing else remains to be said outside of this saying of the said, saying of the said said par excellence, since it is proffered by the said-saying."[209] Unlike Levinas, according to whom there can never be a convergence of the saying and the said, since the saying is never what is said, Marion presents Christ as the embodiment of this very coincidence that fills "the gap between the sign and the referent."[210] As the Son that speaks the unspeakable Said of the Father, the *Verbum Dei*,[211] Christ fulfills the essential mission of theology to be "a *logos* of the *Logos*, a word of the Word, a said of the Said."[212]

In spite of Marion's deflection of those who have criticized him, as well as a handful of scholars who have come to his defense, I am not persuaded that the criticism has been effectively invalidated. His effort to shift the "danger" from a "theologization of phenomenality" to a "transcendental phenomenalization of the question of God" is not convincing. The latter, after all, rests on his assumption—the phrasing of which in the interrogative is itself questionable since it seems to be the foregone conclusion upon which the investigation is based—that "the fact of Revelation provokes and evokes figures and strategies of manifestations and revelation that are much more powerful and more subtle than what phenomenology, even pushed as far as the phenomenon of revelation (paradox of paradoxes), could ever let us divine."[213] For Marion, "there is nothing astonishing in the fact that one inquires after God's right to inscribe himself within phenomenality. What is astonishing is that one should be stubborn—and without conceptual reason—about denying him this right, or rather that one is no longer even surprised by this pigheaded refusal."[214] Try as he may, there is no phenomenological basis to inquire *after God's right to inscribe himself within phenomenality*—if there is such a God (and I will here not enter into the problematic nature of

Marion's uncritical acceptance of the traditional gender taxonomy), the discipline of phenomenology cannot provide the means to speak of that God's right to self-inscribing. Marion wants it both ways: on the one hand, the topography of revelatory experience is to be determined by a dispassionate exploration of the phenomenological nature of givenness; on the other hand, revelation presumes the possibility of an experience that supersedes the bounds of phenomenality, the appearance of which can appear only unapparently, the given that is given as what cannot be given.[215]

The prospect of revelation as the paradox of the saturated phenomenon, particularly as it is embodied in the figure of Christ, has driven Marion's phenomenological studies of givenness, even if the rhetorical presentation leaves the impression that the order is reversed, so that the phenomenological inquiry of the saturated phenomenon culminates in the paradox of revelation, "one that concentrates in itself—as the figure of Christ establishes its possibility—an event, an idol, a flesh, and an icon, all at the same time. Saturation passes beyond itself, exceeds the very concept of maximum, and finally gives its phenomenon without remainder or reserve."[216] The assertion that the figure of Christ alone establishes the possibility of revelation cannot be vindicated phenomenologically; it is a theological creed that precedes the phenomenological investigation. The path of phenomenology may wind its way to the appearance of the inapparent, but to identify the phenomenon that refuses to be confined within the phenomenological reduction exclusively as Christ falls outside the jurisdiction of a phenomenologist. To claim to see by not seeing the invisibility of the visible is germane to the phenomenological vocation; the same cannot be said for the claim to see by not seeing the visibility of the invisible. Moreover, for all of Marion's effort to distinguish between the icon of invisibility,[217] which is proper to Christianity, and metaphysical idolatry, it seems to me that his own portrayal of the eucharistic gift comes close to slipping into an idolatry that renders very dubious the apophatic attempt to salvage a God without being, a God not subject to ontotheology.[218]

THE GIFT UNGIFTED: GIVING BEYOND THE GIVER AND THE GIVEN

The mythopoeic power of imagining the force of life as a gift and the lingering psychological need to render transcendence metaphorically are not difficult to comprehend. But, from a strictly philosophical perspective, the eventfulness of giving is far more neutral than what the image of the gift would suggest. I agree with Derrida that there is no necessary "semantic continuity" between the use of *Gegebenheit* in phenomenology and the problem of the gift.[219] Marion's presumption that there is such a continuity leads to the obfuscation of the line separating phenomenology and theology. To cite Derrida's pointed criticism of Marion's undertaking: "My hypothesis concerns the fact that you use or credit the word *Gegebenheit* with gift, with the meaning of gift, and this has to do with—I will not call this theological or religious—the deepest ambition of your thought. For you, everything that is given in the phenomenological sense, *gegeben, donné, Gegebenheit,* everything that is given to us in perception, in memory, in a phenomenological perception, is finally a gift to a finite creature, and it is finally a gift of God."[220] The phenomenological identification of givenness with the gift is driven by this anthropo-theologization.[221] I am not swayed by Marion's rejoinder to Derrida: "I am not trying to reduce every phenomenon to a gift and then to say that, after that, since this is a gift, and given to a finite mind, then there is perhaps a giver behind it all. . . . My project attempts, on the contrary, to reduce the gift to givenness, and to establish the phenomenon as given."[222] Givenness may be the "immanent structure of any kind of phenomenality," inasmuch as everything that appears must appear as given, but the enframing of that givenness as a gift requires an agency that is still circumscribed as transcendent to or immanent within the horizon of Being in spite of Marion's protestation that his "proposal remains merely philosophical and without any theological presupposition."[223] What gives just gives, not as a gift but as the inevitable consequence of there being something rather than nothing, the fundamental datum of existence that remains inexplicable in spite of the most imaginative efforts on the part of philosophers and physicists to explain it. Moving beyond the binary logic implied in what Heidegger considered to be the ultimate question of Western metaphysics, we would say that the something that is given is the very nothing that gives, and hence that something is nothing to the extent that nothing is something. In the giving, there is giving—nothing more, nothing less. Just as the rose blooms because it blooms, so the giving gives, not as gift but as giving, without will, intention, or design. Both object and subject, the given and the giver, are subsumed in the giving, which is indistinguishable from the givenness.[224]

In the ungifting of the gift, we detect that the exterior can be experienced as interior only relative to an interior experienced as exterior. My thinking is in accord with William E. Connolly—influenced as he is by many of the same thinkers, including Merleau-Ponty, Whitehead, and Deleuze—who writes that "every specific temporal field periodically comes into contact with other force-fields that have hithertofore been outside it. Or, put another way, there is always an outside to a particular field of immanence, even if the outside is not invested with divinity."[225] One need not petition some form of transcendence to preserve a sense of mystery or to maintain the openness of human experience. We can account for both mystery and openness by ascertaining the "deep metaphysics" from within physics,[226] a transcending of transcendence that affirms transcendence only as it is circumscribed within an "immanent realism in a world of becoming."[227] Again utilizing Connolly's language, we can speak of a *mundane* transcendence to name "any activity outside a nonhuman force-field or human awareness that may then cross into it, making a difference to what the latter becomes or interacting with it in fecund or destructive ways, often without being susceptible to full representation before the crossing or explanation by means of efficient causation after it."[228] The mundane transcendence, as opposed to a *radical* transcendence, still entertains the possibility of something or a process "outside of immanence, but it does not translate into divinity."[229]

I conclude by making explicit the question that has infused the animating spirit of the philosophical excursion undertaken in this book. Is it possible to posit a divine partner to human dialogue that is not, in the final analysis, reduced to a confabulation of the imagination that would, in Levinasian terms, result in the *transcendence of idolatry* or the *idolatrous transcendence*?[230] Thinking in the footsteps of Derrida, Mark C. Taylor astutely observed that as long as the otherness of God is conceived oppositionally or dialectically, then altarity (in the spelling that he prefers to the more typical "alterity") would prompt a "difference that makes no difference. Since difference identifies itself as an oppositional identity, its ostensible otherness is really a covert sameness." The altarity that we need to imagine is the "unthought otherness" that is beyond the dichotomy of identity and difference, a mode of unthinking that "is not anti-theological or atheistic but is a/theological." Atheology is distinguished from negative theology on the grounds that the *via negativa* is the inverse of the *via positiva* and therefore substantively changes nothing. "Negation is covert affirmation, emptiness implicit fullness, and absence covert presence. A/theology, by contrast, seeks to think the unthinkable margin of difference that is the condition of the possibility and impossibility of all affirmation and negation, emptiness and fullness, presence and absence."[231]

But is an atheological position in the manner described by Taylor possible? As the musings of this book have shown, the perseverance of the dialogical depiction of transcendence, even as it is acknowledged that the latter cannot be thematized except as the nonthematizable, intimates that a vestige of theism remains and that it is not possible to think the unthought otherness without being caught in the paradoxical labyrinth of contemplating the other as precisely what is not the same and therefore the same other. To think "the *thought* of the other as other," as Derrida well understood, entails thinking the "unthinkable unity of light and night," a collapse of opposites such that the "other" signifies "phenomenality as disappearance" (*la phénoménalité comme disparition*),[232] the "nonphenomenal phenomenon" (*du phénomène de sa non-phénoménalité*) that comes to light in the darkness of the "appearing which dissimulates its essential dissimulation [*apparaître qui dissimule sa dissimulation essentielle*] . . . hiding that which is hidden in the other [*cache ce qui en l'autre est le caché*],"[233] the double concealment, the concealing of the concealing, by which nothing is revealed but that there is nothing to reveal.

In an effort to contemplate the concept of God after postmodernity, a path beyond theism and atheism, Calvin O. Schrag noted, "If the conversation about God as truly otherwise than a grammar of beings and Being, outside the economy not only of metaphorical and ontological reflection but also that of the poetic imagination, is to continue, we will need to maneuver a semantic shift on our discourse about the Deity." Levinas, in particular, is singled out insofar as his "transposition of transcendence from an ontological into an ethical key opens new possibilities for thinking about God as the other than the other."[234] Although I agree that the Levinasian transcendence stipulates this substitution of ethics for ontology, I do not agree, as I argued at length in Chapter 3, that Levinas succeeds in truly thinking of God as other than the other, since God remains within the economy of the metaphorical and thus is not completely dissociated from ontological imagery, even if conceptualized as that which is incomparable to all other beings. One can apply the critical appraisal of Schrag to Levinas: "God as a person, even if in the superlative sense of personhood, remains a being among other beings, subject to the ontological and ontic determinations drawn from an analysis of finite beings in general. God conceived in this manner quickly becomes a subject for the assignation of anthropomorphic properties."[235] Schrag excluded Levinas from this judgment, but I think there is just cause to include him. Be that as it may, Schrag cast a spotlight on the philosophical dilemma that proponents of postmodern theologies need to confront: is it possible to think of God as other than other? Is the human mind not caught in an insurmountable trap in the effort to imagine the otherwise than being without capitulating to representing the other in the image of the same? Can we cogitate alterity even as the alterity that cannot be cogitated? For Schrag, it is feasible to put forward "a thought experiment that involves a shift away from God-talk, an overture to a new grammar and new semantics, accompanied by a new hermeneutics of praxis, all of which will revolve around an acknowledgement of and response to 'the Gift.'"[236]

The tenability of the shift to a "new semantics" turns on assuming "the notion of the gift as transcendent, otherwise than being, beyond the infinite and the finite as metaphysical schema. This transcendence of the gift, in its concrete expression of a love devoid of any expectation of repayment, is an aneconomic transcendence."[237] The transcendent nature of the gift does not prevent Schrag from identifying love as the "quintessential exemplification of the gift, in the form of a caritas, a charity that is unconditional, expecting nothing in return, not even the repayment of loving the one who loves." While seemingly impossible to actualize in the world, this aneconomic and anomian love is the transcendent gift that must become "efficacious within the immanental economies that are based on moral reciprocity, distributive justice, and political equality."[238] Weaving his own version of a postmodern incarnational ethic from the thread of the "accentuation of love as a gift without exchange,"[239] Schrag concludes, "And it is this unconditional alterity issuing a call to the inhabitants of a conditioned economy that comes to mind in the wake of our inquiries into a discourse of the God above God, God without Being, the religious without religion, and the call of conscience in the face of the neighbor."[240] Beautiful as this sentiment might be, its philosophical veracity is the question that must be assessed and interrogated. Ostensibly, the metaphysical grammar centered around God has been replaced by the semantics of the gift, the otherwise than being without conditionality, beyond the economy of exchange and the expectation of return. But is it plausible to conceive of such a gift without ascribing it to an agency that would mitigate against its impenetrable transcendence?

On what basis can we assume a force of charitable love at work in the universe without anthropomorphizing its source? Does the idea of the gift skirt the metaphysical and ontological problems associated with the traditional theistic deity?

Influenced by postmodern delineations of intersubjective relations, Kearney has similarly addressed this topic by distinguishing between person and persona; the former refers to the aspects that an individual shares empirically, biologically, and psychologically with others, and the latter is the otherness of the other, the utterly singular facet—typified in Levinas's *la trace d'autrui*—that is beyond the intentional horizons of the retention and protention of signifying consciousness. This beyondness, however, "spurs language to speak figuratively about it, deploying imagination and interpretation to overreach their normal limits in efforts to grasp it—especially in the guise of metaphor and narrative."[241] Borrowing this terminology, we can say that the predominant sway of contemporary philosophical religious thought continues to configure the divine other as persona. The centrality of the exploitation of metaphor and narrative in this configuration highlights the tenacity of the imagination and the theolatrous impulse that lies coiled in the crux of theism. Worshipping the one God without images was predicated on smashing the idols of the other gods, but if this one God were to be truly deprived of all imagery, including the apophatic image of no image, then there would be nothing not to see and, consequently, nothing to venerate as what cannot be seen. Invisibility itself would finally be reckoned iconologically as visible in virtue of its invisibility, a disrobing of the naked truth fully attired in the cloak of untruth.[242] As Derrida put it:

> Our *apocalypse now*: there would be no more chance, save chance itself, for a thought of good and evil whose announcement would come to *gather* itself in order to be with itself in a revelatory speaking; (no) more chance, unless a chance, the unique, chance itself, for a collection of truth, a *legein* of *alētheia* that would no longer be a legendary unveiling; and (no) more chance even for such a gathering of gift, *envoi*, destiny (*Schicken*, *Geschick*), for the destination of a "come" whose promise at least would be assured of its own proper event.[243]

Apocalyptic hope is cast in post-Heideggerian terms as the *legein* of *alētheia*, the gathering of truth, the disconcealment concealed in the nothing of the future revealed as the event that is always to come, the promise of the not yet inundating the present with anticipation of what cannot be anticipated except as unanticipated, the calculation of the incalculable that releases one from the sense of futurity dictated by the temporal density of the tensive destiny of the past. To attend the invocation of this promise—the promise fulfilled in the abeyance of its fulfillment—one must be awakened to the fact that there is no gift to receive but the gift of discerning that there is no gift other than the giving that gives with no will to give and no desire to be given.

NOTES

Preface

1. Alain Badiou and Slavoj Žižek, *Philosophy in the Present*, edited by Peter Engelman, translated by Peter Thomas and Alberto Toscano (Cambridge: Polity Press, 2010), pp. 26–48.

2. In this regard, my thinking is in step with the Derridean sense of *différance*, which is an undermining of rather than an opposition to the Hegelian dialectic. See Christina Howells, *Derrida: Deconstruction from Phenomenology to Ethics* (Cambridge: Polity Press, 1999), p. 134.

3. Mark Johnston, *Saving God: Religion after Idolatry* (Princeton: Princeton University Press, 2009), p. 18. It is beyond the parameters of this book to delve in more detail into the idolatrous practices of the ancient Near East. For a philosophical analysis of sundry aspects of the phenomenon in biblical and postbiblical literature, see Moshe Halbertal and Avishai Margalit, *Idolatry*, translated by Naomi Goldblum (Cambridge, MA: Harvard University Press, 1992). See also Zainab Bahrani, *The Graven Image: Representation in Babylonia and Assyria* (Philadelphia: University of Pennsylvania Press, 2003), which examines idolatry in the larger context of visual arts in Mesopotamian culture.

4. Johnston, *Saving God*, p. 63.

5. Ibid., p. 19.

6. Ibid., p. 51.

7. Ibid., p. 23.

8. Ibid., p. 39.

9. To some extent, Johnston is aware of the dilemma, and thus he writes that "this demand, for religion without idolatry, or more realistically, for a less idolatrous religion, is internal to monotheism itself" (ibid., p. 40). At most, what we can hope for is less idolatry, not its complete eradication. In recent years, more biblical scholars have openly embraced the notion that the ancient Israelites believed in a corporeal God and that the prohibition against making images of the divine for cultic purposes was not due to God's invisibility but rather to the fact that human beings had the ability to see God. See James Kugel, *The God of Old: Inside the Lost World of the Bible* (New York: Free Press, 2003), pp. 106–107. Of the many other relevant studies, I mention two works that strike me as

261

emblematic of the interpretive shift: Michael Fishbane, *Biblical Myth and Rabbinic Mythmaking* (Oxford: Oxford University Press, 2003), and Benjamin D. Sommer, *The Bodies of God and the World of Ancient Israel* (Cambridge: Cambridge University Press, 2009). Fishbane's reconsideration of myth and monotheism (expressed in the biblical, rabbinic, and zoharic corpora) rests on a nuanced understanding of the anthropomorphisms and anthropopathisms underlying the morphological appearances of God that should be viewed as modalities of the divine personality. For his part, Sommer summarizes his thesis as follows: "Divine embodiment, paradoxically, emerges from this study as far more important to Judaism than to Christianity. For the Tanakh, for rabbinic literature, and for important strands in Jewish mysticism, God has always been a corporeal being. For Christianity, in contrast, God deigned to take on a body at a particular moment in time; existence in a body was part of the eternal essence of divinity. In short: Christians believe in incarnation, whereas the Tanakh simply believes in embodiment" (*The Bodies of God*, p. 136). In light of the distinction that Sommer draws between embodiment and incarnation, he argues that my description of Jewish notions of incarnation (citing Elliot R. Wolfson, *Through a Speculum That Shines: Vision and Imagination in Medieval Jewish Mysticism* [Princeton: Princeton University Press, 1994], p. 395) should be emended (*The Bodies of God*, p. 127 n. 64). A thorough response is beyond the parameters of this note, but let me state briefly that in my judgment the semantic distinction between embodiment and incarnation as presented by Sommer is a distinction without a difference. Regrettably, the author has not demonstrated that he has grasped the true intent of my use of the term *incarnation* or the notion of the imaginal body upon which it is based, that is, a body whose corporality cannot be defined as either literal or metaphorical. For a sophisticated discussion of idolatry and aniconism in the different layers of the scriptural canon, see David H. Aaron, *Biblical Ambiguities: Metaphor, Semantics, and Divine Imagery* (Leiden: Brill, 2001), pp. 125–192.

10. Johnston, *Saving God*, p. 1.

11. Ibid., p. 44 n. 9.

12. A whole other dimension, which I will not explore here, is the intolerance and violence that are correlative to the evolving monotheism and the rejection of other gods and the nations that worship them. Concerning this topic, see Regina M. Schwartz, *The Curse of Cain: The Violent Legacy of Monotheism* (Chicago: University of Chicago Press, 1997); Jan Assmann, *Of God and Gods: Egypt, Israel, and the Rise of Monotheism* (Madison: University of Wisconsin Press, 2008), pp. 28–52, 106–126; idem, *The Price of Monotheism*, translated by Robert Savage (Stanford: Stanford University Press, 2010), pp. 8–30.

13. Johnston, *Saving God*, p. 66.

14. Ibid., p. 25 (emphasis in original).

15. Ibid., p. 187.

16. Yochanan Muffs, *The Personhood of God: Biblical Theology, Human Faith and the Divine Image* (Woodstock: Jewish Lights, 2005), p. 3 (emphasis in original).

17. Ibid., p. 4.

18. Ibid., p. 12.

19. Jean-Luc Nancy, "A Deconstruction of Monotheism," in *Religion: Beyond a Concept*, edited by Hent de Vries (New York: Fordham University Press, 2008), p. 383.

20. Ibid., p. 386. For a critique of the theistic conception, see H. J. Adriannse, "After Theism," in *Religion: Beyond a Concept*, pp. 392–412.

21. Jean-Luc Nancy, *Dis-Enclosure: The Deconstruction of Christianity*, translated by Bettina Bergo, Gabriel Malenfant, and Michael B. Smith (New York: Fordham University Press, 2008), p. 15. See Jean-Luc Nancy, "Preamble: In the Midst of the World; or, Why Deconstruct Christianity?" in *Re-treating Religion: Deconstructing Christianity with Jean-Luc Nancy*, edited by Alena Alexandrova, Ignaas Devisch, Laurens Ten Kate, and Aukje Van Rooden (New York: Fordham University Press, 2012), pp. 7–10, esp. 8: "A vector of atheism does indeed cut across the great religions, not insofar as they are religious but insofar as they are all contemporary . . . with the exit from human sacrifice and with the Western turn in world history, and thus also in philosophy, which is atheism articulated for itself—these religions have witnessed a complete recasting of the 'divine,' a recasting whose deep driving force pushes toward the removal, if not of the 'divine,' then at least of 'God.'" See as well Nancy's revealing remark in "On Dis-enclosure and Its Gesture, Adoration: A Concluding Dialogue with Jean-Luc Nancy," in *Re-treating Religion*, pp. 331-332: "In this book [*Adieu* by Jean-Christophe Bailly], there is an expression that I think is charming, and that I have remembered ever since I read it: 'Atheism has not managed to irrigate its own desert.' So, ultimately, I am responding to the call of this phrase: I am trying to irrigate and to bring water into the desert of atheism." On the depiction of the Catholic God as the "god of the death of God, the god who withdraws from all religion (from every bond with a divine presence) and who departs into his own absence," see Jean-Luc Nancy, *The Ground of the Image*, translated by Jeff Fort (New York: Fordham University Press, 2005) p. 11. Compare the statement of Deleuze cited in Philip Goodchild, "Why Is Philosophy So Compromised with God?" in *Deleuze and Religion*, edited by Mary Bryden (New York: Routledge, 2001), p. 156: "in a sense, atheism has never been external to religion: atheism is the artistic power at work on religion."

22. Jean-Luc Nancy, *The Inoperative Community*, edited by Peter Connor, foreword by Christopher Fynsk (Minneapolis: University of Minnesota Press, 1990), p. 113.

23. Jean-Luc Nancy, *The Creation of the World or Globalization*, translated and with an introduction by François Raffoul and David Pettigrew (Albany: State University of New York Press, 2007), p. 69.

24. Ibid., p. 71.

25. It is noteworthy that Nancy, ibid., p. 70, refers briefly to the Lurianic doctrine of ṣimṣum to illustrate the point that "the 'nothing' of creation is the one that opens in God when God withdraws in it . . . in the act of creating. God annihilates itself [*s'anéantit*] as a 'self' or as a distinct being in order to 'withdraw' in its act—which makes the opening of the world."

26. Ibid., p. 70.

27. Henri Atlan, *The Sparks of Randomness*, vol. 2: *The Atheism of Scripture*, translated by Lenn J. Schramm (Stanford: Stanford University Press, 2013), pp. 346–347. I am in agreement with the following remark of Lorenz B. Puntel, *Being and God: A Systematic Approach in Confrontation with Martin Heidegger, Emmanuel Levinas, and Jean-Luc Marion*, translated by and in collaboration with Alan White (Evanston: Northwestern University Press, 2011), p. 252: "To be sure, the word 'God' has been and continues to be connected with a great many different conceptual contents. At least for the most part, however, it has been and continues to be used to designate a person, no matter how that person is more precisely understood or articulated."

28. Carl Raschke, *Postmodernism and the Revolution in Religious Theory: Toward a Semiotics of the Event* (Charlottesville: University of Virginia Press, 2012), pp. 6–8 (emphasis in original). A similar approach is taken by Santiago Zabala, "Introduction: A Religion Without Theists or Atheists," in Richard Rorty and Gianni Vattimo, *The Future of Religion*, edited by Santiago Zabala (New York: Columbia University Press, 2005), pp. 8–9: "To surpass metaphysics means, according to Rorty and Vattimo, to stop inquiring into what is real and what is not; it means recognizing that something is better understood the more one is able to say about it. Problems are resolved with irony, privately exercised vis-à-vis one's own predecessors rather than vis-à-vis their relation to truth. . . . Postmetaphysical thought fundamentally aims at an ontology of weakening that reduces the weight of the objective structures and the violence of dogmatism."

29. Max Horkheimer and Theodor W. Adorno, *Dialectic of Enlightenment: Philosophical Fragments*, edited by Gunzelin Schmid Noerr, translated by Edmund Jephcott (Stanford: Stanford University Press, 2002), p. 17. Compare Theodor W. Adorno, *Negative Dialectics*, translated by E. P. Ashton (New York: Seabury Press, 1973), pp. 401–402: "The idea of truth is supreme among the metaphysical ideas, and this is where it takes us. It is why one who believes in God cannot believe in God, why the possibility represented by the divine name is maintained, rather, by him who does not believe." On the presentation of Adorno's thought as the critique of idolatry and the upholding of an extreme iconoclastic rejection of images, see Hent de Vries, *Minimal Theologies: Critiques of Secular Reason in Adorno and Levinas*, translated by Geoffrey Hale (Baltimore: Johns Hopkins University Press, 2005), pp. 601–606, 629–630. See also Russell Jacoby, *Picture Imperfect: Utopian Thought for an Anti-Utopian Age* (New York: Columbia University Press, 2005), pp. 127–128. On viewing the critical theory of the Frankfurt school as a reformulated Jewish negative theology, see Ilan Gur-Ze'ev, "Adorno and Horkheimer: Diasporic Philosophy, Negative Theology, and Counter-Education," *Educational Theory* 55 (2005): 343–365, and the more recent assessment by James Gordon Finlayson, "On Not Being Silent in the Darkness: Adorno's Singular Apophaticism," *Harvard Theological Review* 105 (2012): 1–32.

30. Halbertal and Margalit, *Idolatry*, p. 246.

31. Simone Weil, *Gravity and Grace*, introduction and postscript by Gustave Thibon, translated by Emma Crawford and Mario von der Ruhr (London: Routledge, 2002), p. 60. The text is repeated verbatim in Simone Weil, *The Notebooks*, translated by Arthur Wills

(London: Routledge, 2004), p. 130. In other passages in her writings, Weil utilized the well-known Platonic metaphor of the cave to depict the sensible world of illusion and false appearance, which is adverse to reality and truth. See, for instance, Weil, *The Notebooks*, pp. 356–357.

32. Weil, *Gravity and Grace*, p. 54: "We must get rid of the illusion of possessing time. We must become incarnate. Man has to perform an act of incarnation, for he is disembodied (*désincarné*) by his imagination. What comes to us from Satan is our imagination."

33. Simone Weil, *Lettre à un religieux* (Paris: Éditions Gallimard, 1951), p. 72; English version in Simone Weil, *Awaiting God: A New Translation of* Attente de Dieu *and* Lettre à un religieux, translated by Bradley Jersak, introduction by Sylvie Weil (Abbotsford, BC: Fresh Wind Press, 2012), p. 198. On idolatry as mistakenly ascribing absolute value to a reality confined to this world, see Simone Weil, *The Need for Roots: Prelude to a Declaration of Duties Towards Mankind*, translated by Arthur Wills, with a preface by T. S. Eliot (London: Routledge, 2002), pp. 115 and 127. See also Simone Weil, *First and Last Notebooks*, translated by Richard Rees (London: Oxford University Press, 1970), p. 308: "No human being escapes the necessity of conceiving some good outside himself towards which his thought turns in a movement of desire, supplication, and hope. Consequently, the only choice is between worshipping the true God or an idol. Every atheist is an idolater—unless he is worshipping the true God in his impersonal aspect. The majority of the pious are idolaters." On atheism, see further the sources cited below in n. 38.

34. Weil, *Lettre à un religieux*, pp. 17–19; English translation in Weil, *Awaiting God*, pp. 172–173. Weil's antagonistic and prejudicial dicta about Judaism have been the focus of various studies of which I will here offer a representative list: Emmanuel Levinas, *Difficult Freedom: Essays on Judaism*, translated by Seán Hand (Baltimore: Johns Hopkins University Press, 1990), pp. 133–141, 144, 161; David McLellan, *Utopian Pessimist: The Life and Thought of Simone Weil* (New York: Poseidon Press, 1990), pp. 149–154; Thomas R. Nevin, *Simone Weil: Portrait of a Self-Exiled Jew* (Chapel Hill: University of North Carolina Press, 1991); Gillian Rose, *Judaism and Modernity: Philosophical Essays* (Oxford: Blackwell, 1993), pp. 211–223.

35. Weil, *The Notebooks*, p. 148 (emphasis in original). See Lissa McCullough, "The Void: Simone Weil's Naming of Evil," in *Wrestling with God and with Evil: Philosophical Reflections*, edited by Hendrik M. Vroom (Amsterdam: Rodopi, 2007), pp. 25–41.

36. Weil, *The Notebooks*, p. 149. Compare the depiction of the "presence of decreation" in idem, *Gravity and Grace*, pp. 38–39: "God could create only by hiding himself. Otherwise there would be nothing but himself. . . . It is necessary to uproot oneself. To cut down the tree and make of it a cross, and then to carry it every day." See the discussion on self-effacement, op. cit., p. 41: "God can love in us only this consent to withdraw in order to make way for him, just as he himself, our creator, withdrew in order that we might come into being." The theme is reiterated in Simone Weil, *Intimations of Christianity Among the Ancient Greeks* (London: Routledge, 1998), p. 183: "For in creating God renounces being all, He abandons a bit of being to what is other than Himself. Creation

is renunciation by love. The true response to the excess of divine love does not consist in voluntarily inflicting suffering upon oneself . . . . The true reply consists only in consenting to the possibility of being destroyed, that is to say, in the possibility of total disaster, whether that disaster actually happens or not." Weil's depiction of the creation as the withdrawal of God bears an interesting affinity with the kabbalistic idea of *ṣimṣum*, developed most prominently by Isaac Luria and his disciples in the sixteenth century. See Wladimir Rabi, "La conception weilienne de la création: Rencontre avec la kabbale juive," in *Simone Weil: Philosophe, historienne et mystique*, edited by Gilbert Kahn (Paris: Éditions Aubier Montaigne, 1978), pp. 141–160; Richard A. Freund, "La tradition mystique juive et Simone Weil," *Cahiers Simone Weil* 10 (1987): 289–295, esp. 292–293; Maurice Blanchot, *The Infinite Conversation*, translation and foreword by Susan Hanson (Minneapolis: University of Minnesota Press, 1993), pp. 116–118; Nevin, *Simone Weil*, pp. 249–250; Lissa McCullough, "Simone Weil's God: A Radical Christianity for the Secular World," Ph.D. dissertation, University of Chicago, 1999, pp. 122–137; Henry Leroy Finch, *Simone Weil and the Intellect of Grace*, edited by Martin Andic, foreword by Annie Finch (New York: Continuum, 1999), pp. 108–109.

37. Weil, *Gravity and Grace*, p. 106. Compare Weil, *The Notebooks*, p. 151: "Of two men who have no experience of God, he who denies him is perhaps nearer to him than the other. The false God who is like the true one in everything, except that we do not touch him, prevents us from ever coming to the true one. . . . We have to believe in a God who is like the true God in everything, except that he does not exist, for we have not reached the point where God exists." See the discussion of the paradox of the presence and the absence of God in Weil's thought in Blanchot, *The Infinite Conversation*, pp. 114–116.

38. Weil, *Gravity and Grace*, pp. 114–115: "There are two atheisms of which one is a purification of the notion of God. . . . Of two men who have no experience of God, he who denies him is perhaps nearer to him than the other. . . . We have to believe in a God who is like the true God in everything, except that he does not exist, since we have not reached the point where God exists. . . . Religion in so far as it is source of consolation is a hindrance to true faith: in this sense atheism is a purification. I have to be atheistic with that part of myself which is not made for God. Among those men in whom the supernatural part has not been awakened, the atheists are right and the believers wrong." The final part of this passage appears with slight variation in Weil, *The Notebooks*, p. 238. Compare Weil, *Awaiting God*, p. 154: "The degree of intellectual honesty that I am obligated to because of my particular vocation requires that my thoughts are indifferent to all ideas without exception, including for example materialism and atheism; equally welcoming and equally reserved with regard to all of them—as water is indifferent to objects that fall into it." Also pertinent is the comment in Weil, *Intimations of Christianity*, p. 184: "Whatever a person's professed belief in regard to religious matters, including atheism, wherever there is complete, authentic and unconditional consent to necessity, there is fullness of love for God; and nowhere else." And see Weil, *First and Last Notebooks*, p. 84: "One of the most exquisite pleasures of human love—to serve the loved one without his knowing it—is only possible, as regards the love of God, through atheism."

Compare the passage cited above at the end of n. 33. See Susan A. Taubes, "The Absent God," *Journal of Religion* 35 (1955): 6–16; McLellan, *Utopian Pessimist*, pp. 198–199, 209.

39. Weil provides the key to her hermeneutic in *Gravity and Grace*, p. 102: "Method of investigation: as soon as we have thought something, try to see in what way the contrary is true." The theological foundation for this hermeneutic is in Weil's belief that "in the domain of the transcendent contradictions are possible" (*First and Last Notebooks*, p. 269).

40. *The Complete Mystical Works of Meister Eckhart*, translated and edited by Maurice O'Connell Walshe, revised with a foreword by Bernard McGinn (New York: Crossroad Publishing, 2009), p. 424. It is worth recalling Weil's commendation of Eckhart in *Awaiting God*, p. 149: "When authentic friends of God, such as Meister Eckhart in my opinion, repeat words they heard in secret amidst the silence during union with God, and are in disagreement with the teachings of the Church, it is simply that the language of the marketplace is not that of the nuptial chamber." For a recent analysis of Weil's apophatic subjectivity in light of the Dionysian and Eckhartian traditions of negative theology, see William Robert, "A Mystical Impulse: From Apophatics to Decreation in Pseudo-Dionysius, Meister Eckhart and Simone Weil," *Medieval Mystical Theology* 21 (2012): 113–132. I note, finally, that a similar ideal of venturing beyond God as an expression of one's mystical devotion was expressed by Angelus Silesius, *The Cherubinic Wanderer*, translation and foreword by Maria Shrady, introduction and notes by Josef Schmidt, preface by E. J. Furcha (New York: Paulist Press, 1986), p. 39: "Where is my dwelling place? Where I can never stand./ Where is my final goal, toward which I should ascend?/ It is beyond all place. What should my quest then be?/ I must, transcending God, into the desert flee." The title of the aphorism is "One must go beyond God," or in the original German, *Man muss noch über Gott*. See *Angelus Silesius*, text selection and commentary by Gerhard Wehr (Wiesbaden: Marixverlag, 2011), p. 32. As a second example, consider the aphorism "Beyond Divinity" (*Die Über-Gottheit*), in *The Cherubinic Wanderer*, p. 39: "What men have said of God, not yet suffices me,/ My life and light is One beyond divinity."

41. Weil, *Gravity and Grace*, p. 20.

42. Gideon Freudenthal, *No Religion without Idolatry: Mendelssohn's Jewish Enlightenment* (Notre Dame: University of Notre Dame Press, 2012), p. 15.

43. Ibid., p. 19.

44. Ibid., p. 197.

45. On the influence of the German-Jewish dialogical philosophy on Levinas, coupled with existentialism and French Hegelianism, see the pertinent remarks of Bettina Bergo, *Levinas Between Ethics and Politics: For the Beauty that Adorns the Earth* (Pittsburgh: Duquesne University Press, 2003), pp. 18–21. See Ch. 3 n. 407.

46. Jean-Luc Marion, *In Excess: Studies of Saturated Phenomena*, translated by Robyn Horner and Vincent Berraud (New York: Fordham University Press, 2002), pp. 154–155. See also Jean-Luc Marion, *God Without Being: Hors-Texte*, translated by Thomas A. Carlson, with a foreword by David Tracy (Chicago: University of Chicago Press, 1991), pp. 25–52.

47. Jean-Luc Marion, "In the Name: How to Avoid Speaking of 'Negative Theology,'" in *God, the Gift, and Postmodernism*, edited by John D. Caputo and Michael J. Scanlon (Bloomington: Indiana University Press, 1999), p. 34.

48. Jean-Luc Marion, "The Saturated Phenomenon," in *Phenomenology and the "Theological Turn": The French Debate* (New York: Fordham University Press, 2000), pp. 176–177. For a critique of Marion's view, see James K. A. Smith, "Liberating Religion from Theology: Marion and Heidegger on the Possibility of a Phenomenology of Religion," *International Journal for Philosophy of Religion* 46 (1999): 17–33; idem, *Speech and Theology: Language and the Logic of Incarnation* (New York: Routledge, 2002), pp. 7–10, 41, 54–55, 94–98. Finally, let me note that I am not persuaded by the attempt of John Panteleimon Manoussakis, *God after Metaphysics: A Theological Aesthetic* (Bloomington: Indiana University Press, 2007), p. 160 n. 2, to defend Marion on the basis that phenomenology has become the "inherited property of a school with its by-laws and self-proclaimed police" rather than a "method of thinking." Unfortunately, Manoussakis misses the point of the criticism, and thus his defense falls short of the mark. The issue is not that religious beliefs can be the legitimate subject of phenomenological inquiry but that delimiting those beliefs to a specific tradition to which the particular thinker adheres does threaten the degree to which phenomenology retains its status as a rigorous science dedicated to the ongoing and unimpeded elucidation of rudimentary principles. More generally, Manoussakis's own project to construct a new paradigm based on the aesthetic counterexperience that one may encounter in the antimony of incarnation, purportedly a reversal of Platonism, insofar as it overturns the metaphysical hierarchy of the supersensuous and the sensuous and inverts the ancillary relationship of the image (the Son) to the invisible original (the Father), is guilty of the same subjugation of phenomenology to theology. The author claims that his "analysis is faithfully phenomenological, even when it ventures to trespass phenomenology's limitations" (p. 5), but he fails to see that his phenomenological investigations of seeing, hearing, and touching God—the "impossible possibility of thought" (p. 13)—are all colored by a preexisting Christian faith, which is shaped in particular by the scriptural texts he considers to be sacred. I find quite astonishing and somewhat disingenuous Manoussakis's statement that his recourse to scriptural verses is not due to the fact that he views them as the "embodiment of any doctrinal truth, but rather because they are texts that, in our tradition, have informed our concepts and ideas about God" (p. 5). Can one seriously entertain that, for Manoussakis, these two possibilities are distinguishable? Is a theological belief elicited from Scripture not viewed by him as a doctrinal truth? In the final analysis, the phenomenology put forward by Manoussakis is an exercise in biblical hermeneutics. See Ch. 6 n. 223.

49. On denomination—denaming or unnaming—as the third way between apophatic negation and kataphatic affirmation, see Marion, "In the Name," pp. 24–28, and Derrida's comments in response to Marion, op. cit., pp. 45–46. For further discussion, see John D. Caputo, "Apostles of the Impossible: On God and the Gift in Derrida and Marion," in Caputo and Scanlon, *God, the Gift, and Postmodernism*, pp. 189–191; Anselm

K. Min, "Naming the Unnameable God: Levinas, Derrida, and Marion," *International Journal for Philosophy of Religion* 60 (2006): 107–113; Smith, *Speech and Theology*, pp. 129–133.

50. Marion, "In the Name," p. 37.

51. Ibid., pp. 28–30.

52. Ibid., p. 42. The expression "the gift of the name above all names" is part of Marion's citation from St. Basil of Caesarea, *Against Eunomius*, 2.8 (*Patrologia Graeca* 29, 585b), which is an exegetical gloss on the verse from the hymn in the second chapter of Philippians. The passage from St. Basil serves as well as the epigraph for Marion's essay. Notably, Marion departs from his source, which, citing the scriptural text verbatim, speaks of God having "bestowed" (Greek: *echarisato*; Latin: *largitus*) the name on Jesus. Through Marion's prism this bestowing assumes the nature of a gift, a misreading that obviously reflects his theological predilection. For a more precise rendering, see St. Basil of Caesarea, *Against Eunomius*, translated by Mark Delcogliano and Andrew Radde-Gallwitz (Washington, DC: Catholic University Press of America, 2011), p. 140. On the Jewish-Christian theologoumenon regarding Jesus bearing the hypostasized name of the nameless God, see Guy G. Stroumsa, "A Nameless God: Judaeo-Christian and Gnostic 'Theologies of the Name'," in *The Image of the Judaeo-Christian in Ancient Jewish and Christian Literature*, edited by Peter J. Tomson and Doris Lambers-Petry (Tübingen: Mohr Siebeck, 2003), pp. 230–243, esp. 236–239.

53. The term is employed by Kevin W. Hector, *Theology without Metaphysics: God, Language, and the Spirit of Recognition* (Cambridge: Cambridge University Press, 2011), pp. 15–24. Hector presents Marion and Caputo as two distinct expressions of apophatic antimetaphysics.

54. Marion, "In the Name," pp. 34–35. The names I have listed are the ones mentioned by Marion, but the "anthology of citations" could have been greatly augmented; indeed, in his words, it could have been extended "ad infinitum" (p. 35).

55. Jean-Luc Marion, *Being Given: Toward a Phenomenology of Givenness*, translated by Jeffrey L. Kosky (Stanford: Stanford University Press, 2002), p. 243; *Étant donné: Essai d'une phénoménologie de la donation* (Paris: Presses Universitaires de France, 1997), p. 338. See as well Marion, "In the Name," p. 36: "God therefore can be known only as not being known." With respect to this point, Marion posits an agreement between deconstruction and Christian theology.

56. Peter Rollins, *How (Not) to Speak of God* (London: Paraclete Press, 2006), p. 26. See idem, *The Fidelity of Betrayal: Towards a Church Beyond Belief* (London: Society for Promoting Christian Knowledge, 2008), pp. 105–126.

57. In a more recent work, Rollins, speculating on the baptismal language invoked by Paul in Galatians 3:28, attempts to move beyond the binary of Christian and non-Christian. See Peter Rollins, *Insurrection* (New York: Howard Books, 2011), pp. 163–180. This move would be closer to my own philosophical and existential sensibilities.

58. Richard Kearney, *Anatheism: Returning to God After God* (New York: Columbia University Press, 2010), p. 184.

59. Ibid., p. 183 (emphasis in original).

60. Thomas J. J. Altizer, *The New Gospel of Christian Atheism* (Aurora: Davies Group Publishers, 2002), p. 7.

61. Thomas J. J. Altizer, *Godhead and the Nothing* (Albany: State University of New York Press, 2003), p. 3.

62. In many of his writings, Altizer has reflected on the status of the nothingness of God in his radical theology and the theological need to name that namelessness. For the most sustained analysis, see Altizer, *Godhead and the Nothing*. For a critical summary and assessment of Altizer's death of God theology, see Mark C. Taylor, "Betraying Altizer," in *Thinking Through the Death of God: A Critical Companion to Thomas J. J. Altizer*, edited by Lissa McCullough and Brian Schroeder (Albany: State University of New York Press, 2004), pp. 11–28; idem, *After God* (Chicago: University of Chicago Press, 2007), pp. 199–205; idem, "Foreword: The Last Theologian," in Thomas J. J. Altizer, *Living the Death of God: A Theological Memoir* (Albany: State University of New York Press, 2006), pp. xi–xviii. See also Cyril O'Regan, *Gnostic Return in Modernity* (Albany: State University of New York Press, 2001), pp. 65–76; idem, *Theology and the Spaces of Apocalyptic* (Milwaukee: Marquette University Press, 2009), pp. 75–77.

63. Thomas J. J. Altizer and William Hamilton, *Radical Theology and the Death of God* (Indianapolis: Bobbs-Merrill Company, Inc., 1966), p. 13 (emphasis in original).

64. Ibid., pp. 100–103.

65. Ibid., p. 109. With respect to the topic of the coincidence of opposites and the dialectic of the sacred and profane, Altizer's thinking betrays the influence of Eliade. See Thomas J. J. Altizer, *Mircea Eliade and the Dialectic of the Sacred* (Philadelphia: Westminster Press, 1963), pp. 81–104.

66. Thomas J. J. Altizer, *Genesis and Apocalypse: A Theological Voyage Toward Authentic Christianity* (Louisville: Westminster/John Knox Press, 1990), p. 93.

67. Altizer, *Godhead and the Nothing*, p. 153.

68. Ibid., p. 154. On Altizer's death of God and the sacrificial exchange, see Raschke, *Postmodernism*, pp. 96–103.

69. Altizer, *Living the Death of God*, pp. 4–5. See ibid., pp. 8–9, 35–40, 180. For a fuller discussion of Christ and Satan, see Altizer, *Genesis and Apocalypse*, pp. 161–173.

70. Altizer, *Living the Death of God*, pp. 59–60, 67–68; idem, *Genesis and Apocalypse*, pp. 169–170; idem, *The Contemporary Jesus* (Albany: State University of New York Press, 1997), pp. 128–137; idem, *The New Apocalypse: The Radical Christian Vision of William Blake* (Aurora: Davies Group Publishers, 2000), pp. 5–6, 72–74, 122–124; idem, *Godhead and the Nothing*, pp. 71–72.

71. Altizer, *Living the Death of God*, p. 167.

72. Taylor, "Foreword," pp. xi–xii (emphasis in original).

73. The point is affirmed in many passages. See, for instance, Altizer, *Living the Death of God*, p. 173.

74. Altizer, *The New Apocalypse*, p. 122.

75. Altizer, *Genesis and Apocalypse*, p. 182.

76. Altizer, *The New Gospel*, p. 45, and the extended discussion of the self-annihilation of God, op. cit., pp. 97–122.

77. The identity of silence and speech is explored at length in Thomas J. J. Altizer, *The Self-Embodiment of God* (New York: Harper & Row, 1977). The author's thesis is summarized on p. 83: "Silence comes to a final end when its otherness as silence is fully and finally spoken. Then the otherness of silence, that otherness which is the otherness of speech, becomes unspeakable. Yet it becomes unspeakable only by being spoken. . . . Silence ends when it is spoken, and it actually ends only inasmuch as it is spoken, only insofar as it embodies and enacts itself. . . . This occurs when silence itself becomes its own other, when it fully enacts itself as speech." Compare Thomas J. J. Altizer, *Total Presence: The Language of Jesus and the Language of Today* (New York: Seabury Press, 1980), p. 97, and David Jasper, "In the Wasteland: Apocalypse, Theology, and the Poets," in *Thinking Through the Death of God*, pp. 185–195, esp. 191–192.

78. Altizer, *Living the Death of God*, p. 180.

79. Taylor, "Foreword," p. xvii.

80. Altizer, *Living the Death of God*, pp. 177–178.

81. Thomas J. J. Altizer, *Oriental Mysticism and Biblical Eschatology* (Philadelphia: Westminster Press, 1961), pp. 113–151, esp. 137–145; idem, "Emptiness and God," in *The Religious Philosophy of Nishitani Keiji*, edited by Taitetsu Unno (Berkeley: Asian Humanities Press, 1989), pp. 70–81; idem, *Genesis and Apocalypse*, pp. 93–106. For a critical discussion of the role of Buddhism in Altizer's radical theology, see Janet Gyatso, "Compassion at the Millennium: A Buddhist Salvo for the Ethics of the Apocalypse," in *Thinking Through the Death of God*, pp. 147–167.

82. The distinction I have made here corresponds to the critical analysis in Mark C. Taylor, "Altizer's Originality: A Review Essay," *Journal of the American Academy of Religion* 52 (1984): 569–584.

83. Altizer, *Godhead and the Nothing*, p. 70. See also idem, *The New Apocalypse*, pp. 122–123; idem, *Genesis and Apocalypse*, p. 97. And compare idem, *The Genesis of God: A Theological Genealogy* (Louisville: Westminster/John Knox Press, 1993), p. 149: "While an apocalyptic nothingness may well be the opposite of a Buddhist nothingness, and is so if only because of the actuality of its occurrence, that occurrence does release a pure and total nothingness, and a nothingness which apocalypticism knows as the end of the world."

84. Altizer, *The Contemporary Jesus*, pp. 164–165.

85. Altizer, "Emptiness and God," pp. 70–71.

86. Altizer, *Living the Death of God*, p. 57.

87. Altizer, *Godhead and the Nothing*, p. 93.

88. Taylor, *After God*, pp. 200–201: "In Altizer's dialectical vision, 'true' theology is inescapably atheistic. God, however, does not simply disappear; rather, a particular notion of God—more specifically, neoorthodoxy's wholly other God—dies in an act of self-emptying that issues in a realized eschatology that totally transforms the present."

89. Consider the following declaration in Altizer, *Living the Death of God*, p. 58: "Certainly I was profoundly affected by these Buddhist thinkers. Here is pure theology,

and a pure theology that is a universal theology, even employing the death of God in the Crucifixion as a way to a uniquely Buddhist Emptiness, and this was the very point at which the deepest dialogue occurred between my Buddhist friends and myself. Yes, I have attempted to evolve a Buddhist Christian theology, but this was previously accomplished by Nishida and the Kyoto School, and there are ways in which my theology is a reflection of theirs, just as it is also a reflection, even if a pale one, of our deepest Western visions of an absolute nothingness. Nihilism itself realizes a truly new meaning here, and even a truly holy meaning, and just as an apophatic mysticism can know Godhead itself as an absolute nothingness, and therefore know an absolute nothingness as an absolutely holy nothingness, our deepest modern visionaries have called forth an absolute nothingness which is a holy nothingness, and holy precisely as that nothingness itself."

90. Altizer, *The Contemporary Jesus*, p. 166.

91. See passage cited in n. 89.

92. Altizer, *Genesis and Apocalypse*, p. 97.

93. Altizer, *The Genesis of God*, p. 152.

94. Taylor, "Betraying Altizer," p. 11.

95. Ibid., p. 27.

96. Jacques Derrida, "On a Newly Arisen Apocalyptic Tone in Philosophy," in *Raising the Tone of Philosophy: Late Essays by Immanuel Kant, Transformative Critique by Jacques Derrida*, edited by Peter Fenves (Baltimore: Johns Hopkins University Press, 1993), p. 118.

Introduction: Imagination and the Prism of the Inapparent

1. John Sallis, *Force of Imagination: The Sense of the Elemental* (Bloomington: Indiana University Press, 2000), p. 43.

2. The scholarly literature on the role of the imagination more generally in the history of Western philosophy is vast, and here I mention only one particularly impressive study: Eva T. H. Brann, *The World of the Imagination: Sum and Substance* (Boston: Rowman & Littlefield Publishers, Inc., 1991).

3. Immanuel Kant, *Critique of Pure Reason*, translated and edited by Paul Guyer and Allen Wood (Cambridge: Cambridge University Press, 1999), A102, p. 230. Compare Immanuel Kant, *Prolegomena to Any Future Metaphysics That Will Be Able to Present Itself as Science*, edited by Günter Zöller, translated by Peter G. Lucas and Günter Zöller (Oxford: Oxford University Press, 2004), p. 197. For a representative list of studies dealing with the imagination in Kant's critical idealism, see Wilfrid Sellars, "The Role of Imagination in Kant's Theory of Experience," in *Categories: A Colloquium*, edited by Henry W. Johnstone (University Park: Pennsylvania State University Press, 1978), pp. 231–245; Richard Kearney, *The Wake of Imagination: Toward a Postmodern Culture* (Minneapolis: University of Minnesota Press, 1988), pp. 167–177; Rudolf A. Makkreel, *Imagination and Interpretation in Kant: The Hermeneutical Import of the Critique of Judgment* (Chicago: University of Chicago Press, 1990); Sarah L. Gibbons, *Kant's Theory of Imagination: Bridging Gaps in Judgment and Experience* (Oxford: Oxford University

Press, 1994); Sallis, *Force of Imagination*, pp. 66–67; Jane Kneller, *Kant and the Power of Imagination* (Cambridge: Cambridge University Press, 2007).

4. Jan Johann Albinn Mooij, *Fictional Realities: The Uses of Literary Imagination* (Amsterdam: John Benjamins Publishing Co., 1993), p. 29 n. 34; Michael G. Vater, "Schelling's Neoplatonic System-Notion: 'Ineinsbildung' and Temporal Unfolding," in *The Significance of Neoplatonism*, edited by R. Baine Harris (Albany: State University of New York Press, 1976), pp. 275–299; idem, "F. W. J. Schelling: Further Presentations from the System of Philosophy (1802)," *Philosophical Forum* 32 (2001): 375–376. On the expression *In-Eins-Bildung*, see John Llewelyn, *The Hypocritical Imagination: Between Kant and Levinas* (London: Routledge, 2000), pp. 3–4; Jacques Derrida, *Eyes of the University: Right to Philosophy 2*, translated by Jan Plug and others (Stanford: Stanford University Press, 2004), pp. 68–69.

5. Derrida, *Eyes of the University*, p. 68.

6. Kant, *Critique of Pure Reason*, A78, p. 211.

7. Ibid., A112, p. 235.

8. John Sallis, *Delimitations: Phenomenology and the End of Metaphysics* (Bloomington: Indiana University Press, 1986), pp. 32–33.

9. Martin Heidegger, *Pathmarks*, edited by William McNeill (Cambridge: Cambridge University Press, 1998), p. 148; *Wegmarken* [GA 9] (Frankfurt am Main: Vittorio Klostermann, 1996), p. 193.

10. Compare Immanuel Kant, *Lectures on Metaphysics*, translated and edited by Karl Ameriks and Steve Naragon (Cambridge: Cambridge University Press, 1997), 28:236–237, pp. 54–55. In that context, Kant distinguishes *imagination* and *Einbildungsvermögen*; the former, which is rendered as "reproductive imagination," consists of the ability to combine past representations or images based on experience, and the latter is the ability to produce new images independent of the actuality of objects.

11. Sallis, *Force of Imagination*, pp. 68–69.

12. Johann Gottlieb Fichte, *Science of Knowledge with the First and Second Introductions*, edited and translated by Peter Heath and John Lachs (Cambridge: Cambridge University Press, 1982), I, 227, p. 202.

13. William Blake, *The Complete Poetry and Prose of William Blake,* newly revised edition, edited by David V. Erdman, commentary by Harold Bloom (Berkeley: University of California Press, 1982), p. 132.

14. Samuel Taylor Coleridge, *Biographia Literaria or Biographical Sketches of My Literary Life and Opinions*, vol. 7 of *The Collected Works of Samuel Taylor Coleridge*, edited by James Engell and W. Jackson Bate (Princeton: Princeton University Press, 1983), 1:304 (emphasis in original).

15. Søren Kierkegaard, *The Sickness Unto Death: A Christian Psychological Exposition for Upbuilding and Awakening*, edited and translated, with introduction and notes, by Howard V. Hong and Edna H. Hong (Princeton: Princeton University Press, 1980), pp. 30–31. My own analysis has benefited from the discussion in Arnold B. Come, *Kierkegaard as Humanist: Discovering My Self* (Montreal: McGill-Queen's University

Press, 1995), pp. 152–177. On the dangers of the imagination in Kierkegaard's writings, including anxiety and the extreme infinitization that borders on madness, see Simon D. Podmore, *Kierkegaard and the Self Before God: Anatomy of the Abyss* (Bloomington: Indiana University Press, 2011), pp. 108–111, 130–131, 156–159. See also the analysis of the borderline of madness in John Llewelyn, *Margins of Religion: Between Kierkegaard and Derrida* (Bloomington: Indiana University Press, 2009), pp. 7–30.

16. Kierkegaard, *The Sickness Unto Death*, pp. 29–30.

17. Ibid., p. 30.

18. Ibid.

19. Ibid., p. 35.

20. Ibid., p. 37.

21. Compare Johann Gottlieb Fichte, *Foundations of Transcendental Philosophy (Wissenschaftslehre) nova methodo (1796/99)*, translated and edited by Daniel Breazeale (Ithaca: Cornell University Press, 1992), pp. 74–75: "Every act of reflection is an act of self-determining, and the reflecting subject immediately intuits this act of self-determining. But it intuits this act through the medium of the imagination, and, accordingly, it intuits it as a sheer power of self-determination. By means of this abstract act of thinking (as a power) the I arises for itself as 'something'—something purely spiritual, something exclusively ideal—and becomes conscious of its own activity of pure thinking and willing, and becomes conscious of it as such . . . This act of reflection, however, is an act of self-determining; but the previously described act of imagination is an act of the I, and it is therefore determinate. Consequently, in one and the same undivided act, pure thinking is made sensible by the imagination, and what is made sensible by the imagination is determined by pure thinking (reciprocal interaction of intuiting and thinking)."

22. Fichte, *Science of Knowledge*, I, 217–218, pp. 194–195: "Imagination is a faculty that wavers in the middle between determination and nondetermination, between finite and infinite. . . . The task was that of uniting the opposites, self and not-self. By the power of imagination, which reconciles contradictions, they can be perfectly united."

23. On the unity of the universal and the particular in the self, compare Søren Kierkegaard, *Either/Or*, edited and translated, with introduction and notes, by Howard V. Hong and Edna H. Hong, 2 vols. (Princeton: Princeton University Press, 1987), 2: 263–264.

24. A *locus classicus*, which had a major impact on later sources, is Isaiah Horowitz, *Shenei Luḥot ha-Berit ha-Shalem*, edited by Meyer Katz (Haifa: Yad Ramah Institute, 2006), 3:18 and 135. See also Judah Loewe of Prague, *Derekh Ḥayyim*, edited by Joshua David Hartman, vol. 3 (Jerusalem: Makhon Yerushalayim, 2007), pp. 330–331. Needless to say, many more sources could have been cited.

25. See the text from Simḥah Bunem of Przysucha's *Qol Simḥah* cited in Wolfson, *Through a Speculum*, p. 78.

26. The identification of the divine image as the intellect appears in several places in the Maimonidean oeuvre, of which I will here mention only one source: Moses Maimonides, *The Guide of the Perplexed*, translated with an introduction and notes by Shlomo Pines, with an Introductory Essay by Leo Strauss (Chicago: University of

Chicago Press, 1963), I.1, pp. 21–23. According to Maimonides, both biblical words *ṣelem* and *demut*, rendered respectively as "image" and "likeness," refer to the rational faculty; the former term denotes the "natural form" and the latter "likeness in respect of a notion." By contrast, Abraham Abulafia deviates from his philosophical mentor by arguing that "image" signifies the intellect and "likeness" the imagination, playing, no doubt, on the philological connection between *demut* and *dimyon*. See Elliot R. Wolfson, "Kenotic Overflow and Temporal Transcendence: Angelic Embodiment and the Alterity of Time in Abraham Abulafia," in *Saintly Influence: Edith Wyschogrod and the Possibilities of Philosophy of Religion*, edited by Eric Boynton and Martin Kavka (New York: Fordham University Press, 2009), pp. 121 and 279 n. 50.

27. Maimonides, *The Guide*, II.12, p. 280.

28. Ibid., II.36, p. 369. There are numerous studies of Maimonidean prophetology and specifically the role of imagination. For a comprehensive discussion that takes other scholarly analyses into account, see Howard Kreisel, *Prophecy: The History of an Idea in Medieval Jewish Philosophy* (Dordrecht: Kluwer Academic Publishers, 2001), pp. 148–315, esp. 239–257.

29. Maimonides, *The Guide*, I.73, pp. 209–211.

30. Wolfson, *Through a Speculum*, pp. 270–325.

31. Abraham Joshua Heschel, *The Prophets* (New York: Harper & Row, 1962), pp. 440–442. Compare Abraham Joshua Heschel, *God in Search of Man: A Philosophy of Judaism* (New York: Farrar, Straus & Cudahy, 1955), p. 416: "Spirit is a *direction*, the turning of all beings to God: *theotropism*. It is always more than—and superior to— what we are and know" (emphasis in original). On the decentering of human subjectivity and the privileging of the theocentric orientation, see Robert Erlewine, "Rediscovering Heschel: Theocentrism, Secularism, and Porous Thinking," *Modern Judaism* 32 (2012): 176–178.

32. Henry Corbin, *Creative Imagination in the Ṣūfism of Ibn ʿArabī*, translated by Ralph Manheim (Princeton: Princeton University Press, 1969), pp. 108–109. It is worth recalling Corbin's French translation of a section of *The Prophets* that appeared in *Hermès* 3 (1939): 78–110. On the personal and intellectual relationship between Heschel and Corbin, see Edward K. Kaplan and Samuel H. Dresner, *Abraham Joshua Heschel: Prophetic Witness* (New Haven: Yale University Press, 1998), pp. 234–236, 257–259, 300; Paul B. Fenton, "Henry Corbin et la mystique juive," in *Henry Corbin: Philosophies et sagesses des religions du livre: Actes du Colloque "Henry Corbin," Sorbonne, les 6–8 Novembre 2003*, edited by Mohammad Ali Amir-Moezzi, Christian Jambet, and Pierre Lory (Turnhout: Brepols Publishers, 2005), pp. 157–161.

33. The expression is used by Heschel in *Who Is Man?* (Stanford: Stanford University Press, 1965), p. 83.

34. Abraham Joshua Heschel, *Man's Quest for God: Studies in Prayer and Symbolism* (New York: Scribner, 1954), pp. 142–143. The passage is cited and analyzed by Lawrence Perlman, *Abraham Heschel's Idea of Revelation* (Atlanta: Scholars Press, 1989), pp. 107–108.

35. Heschel, *God in Search of Man*, p. 127.

36. Ibid., p. 115.

37. Heschel, *Man's Quest for God*, p. 129. See Edward K. Kaplan, "Sacred versus Symbolic Religion: Abraham Joshua Heschel and Martin Buber," *Modern Judaism* 14 (1994): 213–231, esp. 216–217, where the author connects Heschel's negative assessment of Buber with Rosenzweig's implicit criticism in "Atheistic Theology" (see Ch. 1 n. 93). See also Edward K. Kaplan, *Holiness in Words: Abraham Joshua Heschel's Poetics of Piety* (Albany: State University of New York Press, 1996), pp. 82–84; and Shai Held, "Reciprocity and Responsiveness: Self-Transcendence and the Dynamics of Covenant in the Theology and Spirituality of Abraham Joshua Heschel," Ph.D. dissertation, Harvard University, 2010, pp. 148–149 n. 79.

38. Heschel, *God in Search of Man*, p. 108.

39. The text reads "the infinite with the finite," but from the context we can assume this is a typographical error, and thus I have taken the liberty of correcting it to "the infinite within the finite."

40. Heschel, *God in Search of Man*, p. 114.

41. Ibid., p. 103. Compare ibid., p. 115: "Any genuine encounter with reality is an encounter with the unknown, is an intuition in which an awareness of the object is won, a rudimentary, *preconceptual* knowledge. Indeed, no object is truly known, unless it was first experienced in its unknown-ness. . . . The living encounter with reality takes place on a level that precedes conceptualization, on a level that is responsive, *immediate*, *preconceptual*, and *presymbolic*" (emphasis in original).

42. Heschel, *God in Search of Man*, p. 180.

43. Ibid., p. 121.

44. For discussion of Corbin's notion of the *mundus imaginalis* and the role of the symbol, see Elliot R. Wolfson, "*Imago Templi* and the Meeting of the Two Seas: Liturgical Time-Space and the Feminine Imaginary in Zoharic Kabbalah," *RES: Anthropology and Aesthetics* 51 (2007): 121–125. On the interpretation of symbols in Corbin's presentation of the Shi'ite Imam, see Christian Jambet, *Le caché et l'apparent* (Paris: Éditions de l'Herne, 2003), pp. 123–143. See also Tom Cheetham, *The World Turned Inside Out: Henry Corbin and Islamic Mysticism* (Woodstock: Spring Journal Books, 2003), pp. 55–83; idem, *Green Man, Earth Angel: The Prophetic Tradition and the Battle for the Soul of the World*, foreword by Robert Sardello (Albany: State University of New York Press, 2005), pp. 63–117.

45. Heschel, *God in Search of Man*, p. 116.

46. Heschel, *Man's Quest for God*, p. 139.

47. Ibid.

48. Jambet, *Le caché et l'apparent*, pp. 43–67; Cheetham, *The World Turned Inside Out*, pp. 113–139.

49. Abraham Joshua Heschel, *Man Is Not Alone: A Philosophy of Religion* (New York: Farrar, Straus & Young, 1951), p. 13.

50. Ibid., pp. 4–6, 11–16, 58–59. Compare Heschel, *God in Search of Man*, pp. 64–65.

51. Heschel, *Man Is Not Alone*, p. 22. It behooves me to mention one passage—ignored, to the best of my knowledge, by others who have written about the status of the symbol in Heschel—where a somewhat different perspective on symbolism seems to be at play. In the preface to *Man's Quest for God*, pp. xii–xiii, Heschel makes the following comment: "In worship we discover that the ultimate way is not to have a symbol but *to be a symbol*, to stand for the divine. The ultimate way is to sanctify thoughts, to sanctify time, to consecrate words, to hallow deeds." To be sure, this comment is sandwiched between passages wherein Heschel articulates his criticism of the symbol as being a product of human fancy that obfuscates our ability to experience the divine reality, but it is telling that he does ascribe a positive role in describing the ritual task of becoming a symbol as opposed to having a symbol. If I understand Heschel correctly, in this passage he does appear to be adopting a view more congenial to the Corbinian perspective.

52. Elliot R. Wolfson, *A Dream Interpreted within a Dream: Oneiropoiesis and the Prism of Imagination* (New York: Zone Books, 2011), p. 41. My discussion there is indebted to Merleau-Ponty; see references, p. 312 n. 112, to which I would add Diana Coole, *Negativity and Politics: Dionysus and Dialectics from Kant to Poststructuralism* (London: Routledge, 2000), pp. 122–155. See also Elliot R. Wolfson, *Language, Eros, Being: Kabbalistic Hermeneutics and Poetic Imagination* (New York: Fordham University Press, 2005), pp. 195–196 and the notes cited therein.

53. On the turn to the dialogical in Rosenzweig, Buber, Levinas, and Heschel, see the pertinent comments of Martin Kavka, "The Meaning of That Hour: Prophecy, Phenomenology, and the Public Sphere in the Early Writings of Abraham Joshua Heschel," in *Religion and Violence in a Secular World*, edited by Clayton Crockett (Charlottesville: University of Virginia Press, 2006), pp. 124–125.

54. Abraham Joshua Heschel, "The Holy Dimension," *Journal of Religion* 23 (1943): 119–120 (emphasis in original).

55. Heschel, *Man Is Not Alone*, p. 291.

56. Heschel, "The Holy Dimension," p. 119.

57. Franz Rosenzweig, "The New Thinking," in *Philosophical and Theological Writings*, translated and edited, with notes and commentary, by Paul W. Franks and Michael L. Morgan (Indianapolis: Hackett Publishing Company, Inc., 2000), p. 119; Franz Rosenzweig, *Der Mensch und sein Werk: Gesammelte Schriften III. Zweistromland: Kleinere Schriften zu Glauben und Denken*, edited by Reinhold Mayer and Annemarie Mayer (Dordrecht: Martinus Nijhoff, 1984), p. 146.

58. Franz Rosenzweig, "Atheistic Theology," in *Philosophical and Theological Writings*, p. 17; *Zweistromland*, p. 692.

59. Franz Rosenzweig, *The Star of Redemption*, translated by Barbara Galli (Madison: University of Wisconsin Press, 2005), p. 13. References to the original German are from Franz Rosenzweig, *Der Mensch und sein Werk: Gesammelte Schriften II. Der Stern der Erlösung*, with an introduction by Reinhold Mayer (The Hague: Martinus Nijhoff, 1976).

60. Rosenzweig, *Star of Redemption*, p. 31; *Stern der Erlösung*, p. 25.

278 NOTES TO PAGE 9

61. Steven Schwarzschild, *The Pursuit of the Ideal: Jewish Writings of Steven Schwarzschild*, edited by Menachem Kellner (Albany: State University of New York Press, 1990), p. 71.

62. Ibid., p. 72.

63. A typical expression of this sentiment is found in the essay "Symbolism and Jewish Faith" in Abraham J. Heschel, *Moral Grandeur and Spiritual Audacity*, edited by Susannah Heschel (New York: Farrar, Strauss, Giroux, 1996), pp. 82–83: "Nothing is more alien to the spirit of Judaism than the veneration of images. . . . To Jewish faith there are no physical embodiments of the supreme mysteries. . . . The world is not of the essence of God, and its expression is not His. The world speaks to God, but that speech is not God talking to Himself. . . . The realization that the world and God are not of the same essence is responsible for one of the great revolutions in the spiritual history of man." For Heschel, the principle of immanence or God's presence in history is linked to the human being, who is created in God's image and thus has the capacity to become a symbol of the divine in the world. See ibid., pp. 84–86.

64. Moshe Schwarcz, "Atheism and Modern Jewish Thought," *Proceedings of the American Academy for Jewish Research* 44 (1971): 127–150, esp. 131–143. The exchange between Jacobi and Mendelssohn is presented in detail by Michah Gottlieb, *Faith and Freedom: Moses Mendelssohn's Political Thought* (Oxford: Oxford University Press, 2011), pp. 59–111.

65. Schwarzschild, *The Pursuit of the Ideal*, pp. 312–313 n. 76, marks the similarity of Cohen and Levinas. See ibid., p. 233. Another parallel between Schwarzschild and Levinas is that both viewed the Jewish people as the ideal of perfect humanity in an effort to neutralize the ethnocentrism by locating the universal in the singular and the singular in the universal. See ibid., p. 246, and the criticism of Levinas's position on the state of Israel on p. 343 n. 76. For comparative analyses of Cohen and Levinas, see Ze'ev Levy, "Hermann Cohen and Emmanuel Lévinas," in *Hermann Cohen's Philosophy of Religion: International Conference in Jerusalem 1996*, edited by Stéphane Moses and Hartwig Wiedebach (Hildesheim: Georg Olms, 1997), pp. 133–143; Christoph von Wolzogen, *Emmanuel Levinas: Denken bis zum Äußersten* (Freiburg: Verlag Karl Alber, 2005), pp. 179–189; Edith Wyschogrod, *Crossover Queries: Dwelling with Negatives, Embodying Philosophy's Others* (New York: Fordham University Press, 2006), pp. 405–422; Leora Batnitzky, *Leo Strauss and Emmanuel Levinas: Philosophy and the Politics of Revelation* (Cambridge: Cambridge University Press, 2006), pp. 75–93; Dana Hollander, "Is the Other My Neighbor? Reading Levinas Alongside Hermann Cohen," in *The Exorbitant: Emmanuel Levinas Between Jews and Christians*, edited by Kevin Hart and Michael A. Signer (New York: Fordham University Press, 2010), pp. 90–107. See also the affinities between Cohen and Levinas noted in Hermann Cohen, *Ethics of Maimonides*, translated with commentary by Almut Sh. Bruckstein, foreword by Robert Gibbs (Madison: University of Wisconsin Press, 2004), pp. xxviii, xxix, xxxiv, 51, 82, 142, 175; and consider the comments of Pierre Bouretz, *Witnesses for the Future: Philosophy and Messianism*, translated by Michael Smith (Baltimore: Johns Hopkins University Press, 2010), p. 79.

66. Schwarzschild, *The Pursuit of the Ideal*, pp. 63, 69–71, 75–76. Compare the analysis of ethics and monotheism in Lenn E. Goodman, *God of Abraham* (New York: Oxford University Press, 1996), pp. 79–114, and Myriam Bienenstock, "Hermann Cohen über Freiheit und Selbstbestimmung," in *Religious Apologetics—Philosophical Argumentation*, edited by Yossef Schwartz and Volkhard Krech (Tübingen: Mohr Siebeck, 2004), pp. 509–529.

67. Emmanuel Levinas, *Basic Philosophical Writings*, edited by Adriann T. Peperzak, Simon Critchley, and Robert Bernasconi, translated by Alphonso Lingis and Richard A. Cohen (Bloomington: Indiana University Press, 1996), p. 76.

68. A number of scholars have written about the possible influence of kabbalistic lore on Levinas, focusing especially on the *Nefesh ha-Ḥayyim* of Ḥayyim of Volozhyn, the disciple of Elijah ben Solomon, the Gaon of Vilna. See Elliot R. Wolfson, "Secrecy, Modesty, and the Feminine: Kabbalistic Traces in the Thought of Levinas," in *The Exorbitant*, pp. 52–73, and reference to other scholars cited on p. 250 n. 1. Since my essay originally appeared in the *Journal of Jewish Thought and Philosophy* 14 (2006): 193–224, I did not have the opportunity to see the study of Jacob Meskin, "The Role of Lurianic Kabbalah in the Early Philosophy of Emmanuel Levinas," in *Levinas Studies: An Annual Review*, vol. 2, edited by Jeffrey Bloechl (Pittsburgh: Duquesne University Press, 2007), pp. 49–77. And see now Matthew Del Nevo, "The Kabbalistic Heart of Levinas," *Culture, Theory and Critique* 52 (2011): 183–198, esp. 191–198.

69. Emmanuel Levinas, "The Trace of the Other," translated by Alphonso Lingis, in *Deconstruction in Context*, edited by Mark C. Taylor (Chicago: University of Chicago Press, 1986), pp. 345–359.

70. Emmanuel Levinas, "God and Philosophy," in *The Levinas Reader*, edited by Seán Hand (Oxford: Blackwell, 1989), p. 168.

71. The dictum, which is related by Derrida to several passages from Levinas's *Difficile liberté*, is a modification of Fragment B6, preserved in the pseudo-Aristotelian *Protrepticus*, as noted by Robert Bernasconi in the translation of "God and Philosophy" in Levinas, *Basic Philosophical Writings*, p. 188 n. 2, citing Anton-Hermann Chroust, *Aristotle: Protrepticus—A Reconstruction* (Notre Dame: University of Notre Dame Press, 1964), pp. 48–49. Chroust provides the history of the statement in Alexander of Aphrodisias and subsequent Neoplatonic commentators. For additional sources, see Ingemar Düring, *Aristotle's Protrepticus: An Attempt at Reconstruction* (Gothenburg: Acta Universitatis Gothoburgensis, 1961), pp. 113–114, and the brief comment on p. 178.

72. Jacques Derrida, *Writing and Difference*, translated, with an introduction and additional notes, by Alan Bass (Chicago: University of Chicago Press, 1978), p. 152 [*L'écriture et la différence* (Paris: Éditions du Seuil, 1967) p. 226]: "If one has to philosophize, one has philosophize; if one does not have to philosophize, one still has to philosophize (to say it and think it). One always has to philosophize [*S'il faut philosopher, il faut philosopher; s'il ne faut pas philosopher, il faut encore philosopher (pour le dire et le penser). Il faut toujours philosopher*]."

73. Levinas, "God and Philosophy," p. 167.

74. See Derrida, *Writing and Difference*, pp. 141–142; Jeffrey L. Kosky, "Contemporary Encounters with Apophatic Theology: The Case of Emmanuel Levinas," *Journal for Cultural and Religious Theory* 1 (2000), available at www.jcrt.org; idem, *Levinas and the Philosophy of Religion* (Bloomington: Indiana University Press, 2001), pp. 40–42; Theodore de Boer, "Levinas and Negative Theology," in *Théologie négative*, edited by Marco M. Olivetti (Milan: CEDAM, 2002), pp. 849–859; Min, "Naming the Unnameable God," pp. 100–103; Michael Fagenblat, *A Covenant of Creatures: Levinas's Philosophy of Judaism* (Stanford: Stanford University Press, 2010), pp. 111–139.

75. See Kosky, *Levinas and the Philosophy of Religion*, pp. 204–205 n. 15.

76. John Llewelyn, "Am I Obsessed by Bobby? (Humanism of the Other Animal)," in *Re-Reading Levinas*, edited by Robert Bernasconi and Simon Critchley (Bloomington: Indiana University Press, 1991), p. 239. See also Donald L. Turner and Ford Turrell, "The Non-Existent God: Transcendence, Humanity, and Ethics in the Philosophy of Emmanuel Levinas," *Philosophia* 35 (2007): 375–382, esp. 376–377. For Levinas's critique of theology, see also Richard A. Cohen, "Against Theology, or 'The Devotion of a Theology Without Theodicy': Levinas on Religion," in *The Exorbitant*, pp. 74–89, esp. 78–83.

77. Martin Kavka, *Jewish Messianism and the History of Philosophy* (Cambridge: Cambridge University Press, 2004), pp. 53–65, esp. 64.

78. See the insightful analysis of this point in Dan Zahavi, *Self-Awareness and Alterity: A Phenomenological Investigation* (Evanston: Northwestern University Press, 1999), pp. 189–194, esp. 191–192.

79. Ernst Bloch, *The Principle of Hope*, translated by Neville Plaice, Stephen Plaice, and Paul Knight, 3 vols. (Cambridge, MA: MIT Press, 1986), p. 1195 (emphasis in original).

80. Ibid., p. 1196 (emphasis in original).

81. Edmund Husserl, *Cartesian Meditations: An Introduction to Phenomenology*, translated by Dorion Cairns (The Hague: Martinus Nijhoff, 1977), § 42, p. 89.

82. Ibid., § 49, p. 107. See ibid., § 56, p. 130: "To this community there naturally corresponds, in transcendental concreteness, a similarly open *community of monads*, which we designate as *transcendental intersubjectivity*. We need hardly say that, as existing for me, it is constituted purely within me, the mediating ego, purely by virtue of sources belonging to my intentionality; nevertheless it is constituted thus *as* a community constituted also in every other monad (who, in turn, is constituted with the modification: 'other') as the same community—only with a different subjective mode of appearance—and as necessarily bearing within itself the same Objective world. Manifestly it is essentially necessary to the world constituted transcendentally in me (and similarly necessary to the world constituted in any community of monads that is imaginable by me) that it be a *world of men* and that, *in each particular man*, it be more or less perfectly constituted *intrapsychically*—in intentional processes and potential systems of intentionality, which, as 'psychic life,' are themselves already constituted as existing in the world" (emphasis in original). Compare Edmund Husserl, *Ideas Pertain-*

ing to a Pure Phenomenology and to a Phenomenological Philosophy. Second Book: Studies in the Phenomenology of Constitution, translated by Richard Rojcewicz and André Schuwer (Dordrecht: Kluwer Academic Publishers, 1989), § 18, pp. 82–89, and the analysis of transcendental solipsism and its overcoming in Elisabeth Ströker, *Husserl's Transcendental Phenomenology*, translated by Lee Hardy (Stanford: Stanford University Press, 1993), pp. 117–145. See also James Richard Mensch, *Intersubjectivity and Transcendental Idealism* (Albany: State University of New York Press, 1988), pp. 15–18, 23–55; Dan Zahavi, *Husserl's Phenomenology* (Stanford: Stanford University Press, 2003), pp. 109–125.

83. Husserl, *Cartesian Meditations*, § 51, p. 115, § 54, p. 118, § 55, pp. 120–121, § 56, p. 130. See ibid., § 55, pp. 125–126: "The Objective world has existence by virtue of a harmonious confirmation of the apperceptive constitution . . . a confirmation thereof by the continuance of experiencing life with a consistent harmoniousness, which always becomes re-established as extending through any 'corrections' that may be required to that end." On the notion of the intersubjective subjectivity and the intramonadic community, see Dan Zahavi, *Husserl and Transcendental Intersubjectivity: A Response to the Linguistic-Pragmatic Critique*, translated by Elizabeth A. Behnke (Athens: Ohio State University Press, 2001), pp. 62–84. See especially the passage from Husserl cited by Zahavi, op. cit., p. 78: "For what 'it is an other' says for me throughout, however, is only: it exists by virtue of my constitution. Thus it is evident that transcendentally speaking, the being of others depends on my being. However, it simultaneously belongs to the sense of others who exist for me that the same thing holds for them. Thus the world is constituted for me and for others—and by means of them, an intersubjective world—in such a way that everything that is, depends on my being, yet also on the being of others—who exist for me." Proverbially speaking, Husserl wanted to burn the candle at both ends: all that exists depends on the individual consciousness, but the latter itself is dependent on the being of others. In this manner, the threat of solipsism is corrected by an assumed intersubjectivity that is inherent to the very structure of subjectivity. See Husserl, *Cartesian Meditations*, § 60, p. 139: "A priori, my ego, given to me apodictically—the only thing I can posit in absolute apodicticity as existing—can be a world-experiencing ego only by being in communion with others like himself: a member of a community of monads, which is given orientedly, starting from himself. In that the Objective world of experience shows itself consistently, other monads show themselves consistently to be existent." Elsewhere Husserl depicted the ground of intersubjectivity in what he called the "primal ego," the preegological ego in which all egos coincide on the level of the "continual, original, streaming constitution" of the constant now prior to their "constituted objectification as enduring temporal entities." In this respect, it is the temporality of an original, nonobjective, and nondifferentiated present that provides the foundation for the intersubjective coincidence of the self and the others. See James Richard Mensch, *After Modernity: Husserlian Reflections on a Philosophical Tradition* (Albany: State University of New York Press, 1996), pp. 57–66, esp. 64–65, and the more extensive analysis in idem, *Intersubjectivity*, pp. 204–306.

84. Husserl, *Cartesian Meditations*, § 44, p. 93.

85. Ibid., § 50, p. 109.

86. Anthony J. Steinbock, *Home and Beyond: Generative Phenomenology after Husserl* (Evanston: Northwestern University Press, 1995), p. 65.

87. Derrida, *Writing and Difference*, p. 131 (emphasis in original).

88. Ibid., p. 123 (emphasis in original).

89. Here I offer a modest list of the enormous number of relevant studies: Bernard Forthomme, *Une philosophie de la transcendance: La métaphysique d'Emmanuel Lévinas* (Paris: J. Vrin, 1979); Edith Wyschogrod, *Emmanuel Levinas: The Problem of Ethical Metaphysics*, second edition (New York: Fordham University Press, 2000), pp. 90–102; Etienne Feron, *De l'idée de transcendance à la question du langage: l'itinéraire philosophique de Levinas* (Grenoble: J. Millon, 1982); Adriaan T. Peperzak, *Beyond: The Philosophy of Emmanuel Levinas* (Evanston: Northwestern University Press, 1997), pp. 72–120, 162–170; Theodore de Boer, *The Rationality of Transcendence: Studies in the Philosophy of Emmanuel Levinas* (Amsterdam: J. C. Gieben, 1997); Rudi Visker, *Truth and Singularity: Taking Foucault into Phenomenology* (Dordrecht: Kluwer Academic Publishers, 1999), pp. 235–273; Francis Guibal, "La transcendance," in *Emmanuel Lévinas: Positivité et transcendance*, edited by Jean-Luc Marion (Paris: Presses Universitaires de France, 2000), pp. 209–238; John E. Drabinski, *Sensibility and Singularity: The Problem of Phenomenology in Levinas* (Albany: State University of New York Press, 2001), pp. 43–81; Catherine Chalier, *La trace de l'infini: Emmanuel Levinas et la source hébraïque* (Paris: Cerf, 2002), pp. 77–106, 253–267; Robert Bernasconi, "No Exit: Levinas' Aporetic Account of Transcendence," *Research in Phenomenology* 35 (2005): 101–117; Bettina Bergo, "Ontology, Transcendence, and Immanence in Emmanuel Levinas' Philosophy," *Research in Phenomenology* 35 (2005): 141–177; Samuel Moyn, *Origins of the Other: Emmanuel Levinas Between Revelation and Ethics* (Ithaca: Cornell University Press, 2005), pp. 182–186; Claire Katz, " 'Before the Face of God One Must Not Go With Empty Hands': Transcendence and Levinas' Prophetic Consciousness," *Philosophy Today* 50 (2006): 58–68; Catherine Keller, "Rumors of Transcendence: The Movement, State, and Sex of 'Beyond,' " in *Transcendence and Beyond: A Postmodern Inquiry*, edited by John D. Caputo and Michael J. Scanlon (Bloomington: Indiana University Press, 2007), pp. 129–150, esp. 133–134, 137–139; Sarah Allen, *The Philosophical Sense of Transcendence: Levinas and Plato on Loving Beyond Being* (Pittsburgh: Duquesne University Press, 2009). For a critique of Levinas's conception of transcendence and the beyond being, see Puntel, *Being and God*, pp. 284–302.

90. Rodolphe Gasché, *The Tain of the Mirror: Derrida and the Philosophy of Reflection* (Cambridge, MA: Harvard University Press, 1986), p. 129.

91. Gilles Deleuze, *Difference and Repetition*, translated by Paul Patton (New York: Columbia University Press, 1994), p. 23.

92. Ibid., pp. 23–24.

93. Ibid., pp. 90–91, 242–243.

94. Miguel de Beistegui, *Immanence: Deleuze and Philosophy* (Edinburgh: Edinburgh University Press, 2010), pp. 52–53.

95. Deleuze, *Difference and Repetition*, p. 17.

96. Ibid., p. 24.

97. Ibid., p. 32.

98. Emmanuel Levinas, *Otherwise Than Being or Beyond Essence*, translated by Alphonso Lingis (Dordrecht: Kluwer Academic Publishers, 1991), pp. 19 and 95. I have also consulted the original *Autrement qu'être ou au-delà de l'essence* (Dordrecht: Kluwer Academic Publishers, 1974), pp. 23 and 48. Consider the comment of Levinas in Wyschogrod, *Crossover Queries*, p. 284, cited in Ch. 3 at n. 425.

99. Martin Heidegger, *Identity and Difference*, translated and with an introduction by Joan Stambaugh (New York: Harper & Row, 1969), p. 142. Stambaugh renders the German *sagenden Nichtsagen* on p. 73 as "a telling silence." The translation I have followed is found in Robert Bernasconi, *The Question of Language in Heidegger's History of Being* (Atlantic Highlands: Humanities Press, 1985), p. 77. See Wolfson, *Language, Eros, Being*, p. 22. Unfortunately, I mistyped the German expression as *sagendes Nichtsagen*, but it is given correctly on p. 418 n. 208. The same mistake appears in the aforecited work of Bernasconi, and it is likely that this is what led to my careless error.

100. Emmanuel Levinas, *Totality and Infinity: An Essay on Exteriority*, translated by Alphonso Lingis (Dordrecht: Kluwer Academic Publishers, 1969), p. 30; *Totalité et infini: Essai sur l'extériorité* (The Hague: Martinus Nijhoff, 1961), p. xviii.

101. Concerning Heidegger's relation to these thinkers, see John D. Caputo, *The Mystical Element in Heidegger's Thought* (Athens: Ohio State University Press, 1978), pp. 97–103, 140–217. For some other attempts to analyze Heidegger's indebtedness to the mystical theology of Eckhart, see Reiner Schürmann, "Trois penseurs du délaissement: Maître Eckhart, Heidegger, Suzuki: Part One," *Journal of the History of Philosophy* 12 (1974): 455–477; idem, "Trois penseurs du délaissement: Maître Eckhart, Heidegger, Suzuki: Part Two," *Journal of the History of Philosophy* 13 (1975): 56–60; idem, *Meister Eckhart: Mystic and Philosopher* (Bloomington: Indiana University Press, 1978), pp. 192–213; John van Buren, *The Young Heidegger: Rumor of the Hidden King* (Bloomington: Indiana University Press, 1994), pp. 53, 55, 63, 99–102, 113–122, 297–313; Sonya Sikka, *Forms of Transcendence: Heidegger and Medieval Mystical Theology* (Albany: State University of New York Press, 1997), pp. 143–186, 248–249, 266–267, 272, 276–277; Sean J. McGrath, *The Early Heidegger and Medieval Philosophy: Phenomenology for the Godforsaken* (Washington, DC: Catholic University of America Press, 2006), pp. 120–121, 128–129, 131–142, 144–148, 230–231; Barbara Dalle Pezze, *Martin Heidegger and Meister Eckhart: A Path Towards Gelassenheit*, with a foreword by Timothy O'Leary (Lewiston: Edwin Mellen Press, 2008).

102. Martin Heidegger, *Poetry, Language, Thought*, translation and introduction by Albert Hofstadter (New York: Harper & Row, 1971), p. 11; *Aus der Erfahrung des Denkens* [GA 13] (Frankfurt am Main: Vittorio Klostermann, 2002), p. 83.

Chapter 1: Via Negativa *and the Imaginal Configuring of God*

1. On the terms "theopoetic" and "theopoiesis," see Amos N. Wilder, *Theopoetic: Theology and the Religious Imagination* (Philadelphia: Fortress Press, 1976), p. iv; David L. Miller, "Theopoiesis," in Stanley R. Hopper, *Why Permissions and Other Poems: Transformations of Theology in Poetry* (Atlanta: Scholars Press, 1987), pp. 1–12; idem, *Hells and Holy Ghosts: A Theopoetics of Christian Belief* (Nashville: Abingdon Press, 1989); idem, *Christs: Meditations on Archetypal Images in Christian Theology* (New Orleans: Spring Journal Books, 2005), p. xviii; Stanley R. Hopper, "Introduction," in *Interpretation: The Poetry of Meaning*, edited by Stanley R. Hopper and David L. Miller (New York: Harcourt, Brace and World, 1967), pp. ix–xxii, esp. xix; Catherine Keller, *God and Power: Counter-Apocalyptic Journeys* (Minneapolis: Fortress Press, 2005), pp. 140, 145–146, 149–152.

2. Hermann Cohen, *Der Begriff der Religion im System der Philosophie*, introduction by Andrea Poma, second, revised edition [*Werke* 10] (Hildesheim: Georg Olms Verlag, 2002), p. 47.

3. The motif of the uniqueness of God and the idea of correlation in Cohen has been discussed by numerous scholars. As a representative list, see Alexander Altmann, "Hermann Cohens Begriff der Korrelation," in *In zwei Welten: Siegfried Moses zum fünfundsiebzigsten Geburtstag*, edited by Hans Tramer (Tel-Aviv: Verlag Bitaon, 1962), pp. 377–399, reprinted in Alexander Altmann, *Von der mittelalterlichen zu modernen Aufklärung: Studien zu jüdischen Geistesgeschichte* (Tübingen: J. C. B. Mohr, 1987), pp. 300–317; Andrea Poma, *The Critical Philosophy of Hermann Cohen*, translated by John Denton (Albany: State University of New York Press, 1997), pp. 171–198; idem, *Yearning for Form and Other Essays on Hermann Cohen's Thought* (Dordrecht: Springer, 2006), pp. 61–85. See also Wolzogen, *Emmanuel Levinas*, pp. 151–160; Dieter Adelmann, *Einheit des Bewusstseins als Grundproblem der Philosophie Hermann Cohens: Vorbereitende Untersuchung für eine historisch-verifizierende Konfrontation der Fundamentalontologie Martin Heideggers mit Hermann Cohens „System der Philosophie"* (Potsdam: Universitätsverlag Potsdam, 2012), pp. 137–142.

4. Cohen, *Ethics of Maimonides*, p. 19; "Charakteristik der Ethik Maimunis" in Hermann Cohen, *Kleinere Schriften IV, 1907–1912*, edited and introduced by Hartwig Wiedebach [*Werke* 15] (Hildesheim: Georg Olms Verlag, 2009), p. 177. I am aware that Cohen's attitude to Spinoza and pantheism evolved over the years, but for the purposes of this analysis it is only the harshly critical stance espoused in the later writings that is of interest, and thus I will not discuss his earlier flirtation with pantheism as a preliminary stage to monotheism. See Hermann Cohen, "Einheit oder Einzigkeit Gottes," in *Kleinere Schriften VI, 1916–1918*, edited and introduced by Hartwig Wiedebach [*Werke* 17] (Hildesheim: Georg Olms Verlag, 2002), p. 525, and "Spinoza über Staat und Religion, Judentum und Christentum," in *Kleinere Schriften V, 1913–1915*, edited and introduced by Hartwig Wiederbach [*Werke* 16] (Hildesheim: Georg Olms Verlag, 1997), pp. 290–372, and the brief comments of Franz Rosenzweig, "Über den Vortrag Hermann Cohens 'Das Verhältnis Spinozas zum Judentum,'" in *Zweistromland*, pp. 165–167. See

Benjamin Elliot Sax, "Language and Jewish Renewal: Franz Rosenzweig's Hermeneutic of Citation," Ph.D. dissertation, University of Chicago, 2008, pp. 164–168. For the wider intellectual context, see Franz Nauen, "Hermann Cohen's Perceptions of Spinoza: A Reappraisal," *AJS Review* 4 (1979): 111–124; David Janssens, *Between Athens and Jerusalem: Philosophy, Prophecy, and Politics in Leo Strauss's Early Thought* (Albany: State University of New York Press, 2008), pp. 31–36; Benjamin Lazier, *God Interrupted: Heresy and the European Imagination Between the World Wars* (Princeton: Princeton University Press, 2008), pp. 73–110; Bouretz, *Witnesses for the Future*, pp. 23–30; and the comprehensive analysis in Mark Kaplowitz, "'The Gravest Obstacle and Thus a Great Misfortune': Hermann Cohen's Interpretation of Spinoza," Ph.D. dissertation, New York University, 2010. In considering Cohen's neo-Kantian perspective on Spinoza, it is worth recalling the remark of Heidegger, *Identity and Difference*, p. 47–48 (German text, pp. 113–114): "Spinoza appeals always afresh to the whole thinking of German Idealism, and at the same time provokes its contradiction, because he lets thinking begin with the absolute. Kant's path, in contrast, is different, and is even more decisive than Spinoza's system for thinking of absolute idealism and for philosophy generally." Heidegger's approach to Spinoza is a matter I hope to take up in a future study. On Heidegger's attitude toward Spinoza and the rejection of typecasting his philosophy as "Jewish," see the brief but illuminating comments in Rüdiger Safranski, *Martin Heidegger: Between Good and Evil*, translated by Ewald Osers (Cambridge, MA: Harvard University Press, 1998), p. 256. On the Nazi condemnation of the works of Spinoza, see Yvonne Sherratt, *Hitler's Philosophers* (New Haven: Yale University Press, 2013), pp. 76, 80, 106. I will not enter here into the larger question of Heidegger's relationship to National Socialism, a topic that has produced a considerable bibliography.

5. Cohen, *Ethics of Maimonides*, p. 21; "Charakteristik," p. 178.

6. Cohen, *Ethics of Maimonides*, p. 27; "Charakteristik," pp. 181–182. It is of interest to recall here the comment of Gershom Scholem, *Major Trends in Jewish Mysticism* (New York: Schocken, 1954), p. 38: "Authoritative Jewish theology, both mediaeval and modern, in representatives like Saadia, Maimonides and Hermann Cohen, has taken upon itself the task of formulating an antithesis to pantheism and mystical theology. . . . In this endeavor it has shown itself tireless."

7. Cohen, *Der Begriff der Religion*, pp. 26–27; idem, "Einheit oder Einzigkeit Gottes," in *Kleinere Schriften VI, 1916–1918*, pp. 523–529, 605–611, 639–644; English translation in *Reason and Hope: Selections from the Jewish Writings of Hermann Cohen*, translated by Eva Jospe (New York: W. W. Norton, 1971), pp. 90–101; idem, *Religion of Reason Out of the Sources of Judaism*, translated, with an introduction by Simon Kaplan, introductory essay by Leo Strauss, introductory essays for the second edition by Steven S. Schwarzschild and Kenneth Seeskin (Atlanta: Scholars Press, 1995), pp. 35–49; *Religion der Vernunft aus den Quellen des Judentums*, second edition (Frankfurt am Main: J. Kaufmann Verlag, 1929), pp. 41–57.

8. It is for this reason that I am not entirely convinced of the attempt of Poma, *Yearning for Form*, pp. 313–379, to interpret Cohen in a postmodern fashion, specifically

in light of Deleuze's idea of difference and repetition. I do not see how Cohen ultimately gets out of the circle of being and thought. Even the meontological, the emphasis on nonbeing, does not effectuate a genuine difference separating what is and what is thought. However, I do accept the part of Poma's argument that emphasizes that pure thought, and by extension pure being, is not subject to the mediation of representation and the reduction of all difference to the concept of identity. For a different but related attempt to underscore multivocality as a distinctive feature of Cohen's reasoning, see Almut Sh. Bruckstein, "Joining the Narrators: A Philosophy of Talmudic Hermeneutics," in Steven Kepnes, Peter Ochs, and Robert Gibbs, *Reasoning After Revelation: Dialogues in Postmodern Jewish Philosophy* (Boulder: Westview Press, 1998), pp. 105–121, esp. 118, and the expansion of this methodology in Daniel H. Weiss, *Paradox and the Prophets: Hermann Cohen and the Indirect Communication of Religion* (Oxford: Oxford University Press, 2012), pp. 64–90.

9. Cohen, *Ethics of Maimonides*, p. 19; "Charakteristik," p. 177.

10. Cohen, *Ethics of Maimonides*, p. 32; "Charakteristik," p. 184. Here it is also worth recalling the following passage in Cohen's "Spinoza über Staat und Religion, Judentum und Christentum," in *Kleinere Schriften V 1913–1915*, p. 425, where a distinction is upheld between mysticism and pantheism on the grounds that the former occasions a dissatisfaction with the transcendence of the unique God, but the latter as such does not necessarily contradict monotheism. In light of so many harsh comments about pantheism, especially in the acosmic version of Spinoza, it is surely significant that according to this text pantheism, in contrast to mysticism, is not inherently opposed to monotheism. Concerning this passage, see Leo Strauss, "Cohen's Analysis of Spinoza's Biblical Science (1924)," in *Leo Strauss: The Early Writings (1921–1932)*, translated and edited by Michael Zank (Albany: State University of New York Press, 2002), pp. 151 and 169 n. 73.

11. Cohen, *Ethics of Maimonides*, pp. 21, 29; "Charakteristik," pp. 178, 182.

12. See Arthur Hyman, "Maimonidean Elements in Hermann Cohen's Philosophy of Religion," in *Hermann Cohen's Critical Idealism*, edited by Reinier Munk (Dordrecht: Springer, 2005), pp. 357–370, esp. 368–370. See the rather acerbic attack on Cohen's "unhistorical interpretation" of Maimonides in Leo Strauss, "How to Begin to Study Medieval Philosophy," in *The Rebirth of Classical Political Rationalism: An Introduction to the Thought of Leo Strauss—Essays and Lectures by Leo Strauss*, selected and introduced by Thomas L. Pangle (Chicago: University of Chicago Press, 1989), pp. 207–208. For other assessments of Cohen and Maimonides, see Roland Goetschel, "Le paradigme Maimonidien chez Hermann Cohen," in *The Thought of Maimonides: Philosophical and Legal Studies*, edited by Ira Robinson, Lawrence Kaplan, and Julien Bauer (Lewiston, NY: Edwin Mellen Press, 1990), pp. 384–403; Almut Sh. Bruckstein, "On Jewish Hermeneutics: Maimonides and Bachya as Vectors in Cohen's Philosophy of Origin," in *Hermann Cohen's Philosophy of Religion: International Conference in Jerusalem 1996*, edited by Stéphane Moses and Hartwig Wiedebach (Hildesheim: Georg Olms Verlag, 1997), pp. 35–50, esp. 40–46; Kavka, *Jewish Messianism*, pp. 67–114; Alfred L. Ivry, "Hermann Cohen, Leo Strauss, Alexander Altmann: Maimonides in Germany," in *The Trias of*

Maimonides: Jewish, Arabic, and Ancient Culture of Knowledge, edited by Georges Tamer (Berlin: Walter de Gruyter, 2005), pp. 175–183; Aaron W. Hughes, "Maimonides and the Pre-Maimonidean Jewish Philosophical Tradition According to Hermann Cohen," *Journal of Jewish Thought and Philosophy* 18 (2010): 1–26; James Diamond, "Exegetical Idealization: Hermann Cohen's Religion of Reason Out of the Sources of Maimonides," *Journal of Jewish Thought and Philosophy* 18 (2010): 49–73.

13. Cohen, *Ethics of Maimonides*, pp. 32–33; "Charakteristik," p. 184.

14. Cohen, *Ethics of Maimonides*, p. 66; "Charakteristik," p. 201.

15. Franz Rosenzweig, "Einleitung," in Hermann Cohen, *Jüdische Schriften*, vol. 1 (Berlin: C. A. Schwetschke & Sohn, 1924), pp. xlv–xlvi, reprinted in Rosenzweig, *Zweistromland*, pp. 206–207. See the critical evaluation of Rosenzweig's thesis in Adelmann, *Einheit des Bewusstseins*, pp. 73–83.

16. See the telling remark in Barbara E. Galli, *Franz Rosenzweig and Jehuda Halevi: Translating, Translations, and Translators*, foreword by Paul Mendes-Flohr (Montreal: McGill-Queen's University Press, 1995), p. 199; German original: Franz Rosenzweig, *Der Mensch und sein Werk: Gesammelte Schriften IV. Sprachdenken im Übersetzen, 1 Band: Jehuda Halevi. Fünfundneunzig Hymnen und Gedichte*, edited by Reinhold Mayer and Annemarie Mayer (Dordrecht: Martinus Nijhoff, 1984), p. 54. Commenting on Halevi's poem that begins *be-khol libbi emet u-ve-khol me'odi*, which he titles *Der Wahre*, Rosenzweig notes that the first words are based on the command to love God in Deuteronomy 6:5, "which here now becomes the love of truth and yet retains all the sensual and suprasensual [*sinnlich-übersinnliche*] ardour of love for God. And he who has understood this 'and yet' will know what 'Jewish rationalism' is about, and that this rationalism may be very rational, and yet can never be as rational as it—is Jewish. Whoever has known Hermann Cohen—he also will know this." For alternative renderings, see Franz Rosenzweig, *Ninety-Two Poems and Hymns of Yehuda Halevi*, translated by Thomas Kovach, Eva Jospe, and Gilya Gerda Schmidt, edited and with an introduction by Richard A. Cohen (Albany: State University of New York Press, 2000), p. 37; *The Commentaries of Franz Rosenzweig to Ninety-Five Poems of Judah Halevi*, translated and annotated by Michael Swartz (Jerusalem: Magnes Press, 2011), p. 79 (Hebrew). On the expression "sensual and suprasensual," *sinnlich-übersinnliche*, see the passage from the *Star* cited in Ch. 2 at n. 245.

17. For a provocative attempt to reconsider the "incompatible voices" of Scripture and philosophy in Cohen's *Religion of Reason*, see Weiss, *Paradox and the Prophets*. The larger question of the viability of qualifying philosophy by any particular cultural identity, whether Jewish, Christian, Muslim, Hindu, Buddhist, and so on, has been discussed by many scholars. The topic as it pertains to Jewish thinkers has also been analyzed by a variety of thinkers. For example, see Ze'ev Levy, *Between Yafeth and Shem: On the Relationship between Jewish and General Philosophy* (New York: Peter Lang, 1987), pp. 95–131; and the recent examination in Willi Goetschel, *The Discipline of Philosophy and the Invention of Modern Jewish Thought* (New York: Fordham University Press, 2013), pp. 1–57. My own view accords with the position taken by Rose, *Judaism and Modernity*,

pp. 11–24, summarized on p. 18: "I discern and propose a different *tertium quid*: that the relation between philosophy and Judaism be explored neither in terms which presuppose self-identity nor in terms of mutual opposition but in terms of their evident loss of self-identity—when they are cast into crisis, chronic and acute; when they are exposed at their deepest difficulty."

18. Cohen, *Ethics of Maimonides*, p. 74; "Charakteristik," p. 205. See the exposition in William Kluback, *Hermann Cohen: The Challenge of a Religion of Reason* (Chico: Scholar's Press, 1984), pp. 41–76; idem, *The Idea of Humanity: Hermann Cohen's Legacy to Philosophy and Theology* (Lanham: University Press of America, 1987), pp. 20–26. For a different perspective on the relationship of religious belief and ethics in the respective teachings of Kant and Cohen, see Rose, *Judaism and Modernity*, pp. 121–123.

19. Cohen, *Ethics of Maimonides*, pp. 67–68, 70–71; "Charakteristik," pp. 202–203.

20. Cohen, *Ethics of Maimonides*, p. 83; "Charakteristik," p. 207.

21. Cohen's exact words are worth citing here (*Ethics of Maimonides*, p. 68; "Charakteristik," p. 202): "there are no other divine attributes than those posited by revelation. It is philosophy's impotence that is exposed here" (*Es giebt keine anderen Attribute, als welche die Offenbarung aufstellt; die philosophie ist es, die hier als ohnmächtig erklärt wird*). See the explication of this passage in Bruckstein, "On Jewish Hermeneutics," p. 43.

22. Cohen, *Ethics of Maimonides*, p. 69; "Charakteristik," p. 203. Cohen's innovative reinterpretation of Maimonides's *via negativa* is obscured somewhat in the summary presentation in Leora Batnitzky, *Idolatry and Representation: The Philosophy of Franz Rosenzweig Reconsidered* (Princeton: Princeton University Press, 2000), pp. 18–21. See, however, Schwarzschild, *The Pursuit of the Ideal*, pp. 144–145; Kenneth Seeskin, *Searching for a Distant God: The Legacy of Maimonides* (Oxford: Oxford University Press, 2000), pp. 102–105; Kavka, *Jewish Messianism*, pp. 106–114; Randi Rashkover, *Revelation and Theopolitics: Barth, Rosenzweig, and the Politics of Praise* (London: T & T Clark International, 2005), pp. 16–17.

23. Cohen, *Ethics of Maimonides*, pp. 71, 74; "Charakteristik," pp. 203–204.

24. Cohen, *Ethics of Maimonides*, pp. 86–87; "Charakteristik," p. 209. Compare Hermann Cohen, *Logik der reinen Erkenntnis*, introduction by Helmut Holzhey [*Werke* 6] (Hildesheim: Georg Olms Verlag, 2005), pp. 87–89. On Cohen's Platonic, as opposed to Aristotelian, interpretation of Maimonides, see Leo Strauss, *Philosophy and Law: Contributions to the Understanding of Maimonides and His Predecessors*, translated with an introduction by Eve Adler (Albany: State University of New York Press, 1995), pp. 129–131, and idem, *Leo Strauss on Maimonides: The Complete Writings*, edited with an introduction by Kenneth Hart Green (Chicago: University of Chicago Press, 2013), pp. 179–180, 191–205. Strauss's reading of Cohen on Maimonides is assessed in Almut Sh. Bruckstein, "Hermann Cohen. *Ethics of Maimonides*: Residues of Jewish Philosophy—Traumatized," in *Hermann Cohen's Ethics*, edited by Robert Gibbs (Leiden: Brill, 2006), pp. 119–121, and Leora Batnitzky, "Hermann Cohen and Leo Strauss," in *Hermann Cohen's Ethics*, pp. 200–210; idem, *Leo Strauss and Emmanuel Levinas*, pp. 104–112; Benjamin Aldes Wurgaft, "How to Read Maimonides after Heidegger: The Cases of

Strauss and Levinas," in *The Cultures of Maimonideanism: New Approaches to the History of Jewish Thought*, edited by James T. Robinson (Leiden: Brill, 2009), pp. 353–383; Kenneth Hart Green, *Leo Strauss and the Recovery of Maimonides* (Chicago: University of Chicago Press, 2013), pp. 28–29, 132–133.

25. Cohen, *Ethics of Maimonides*, pp. xxxiv, 10–11 ("Charakteristik," p. 170), and the critical notes accompanying the text.

26. Cohen, *Ethics of Maimonides*, pp. 86–88; "Charakteristik," pp. 209–210. See *Leo Strauss on Maimonides*, pp. 205–210; Bruckstein, "On Jewish Hermeneutics," pp. 42–46. See also Poma, *The Critical Philosophy*, pp. 176–184.

27. Cohen, *Religion of Reason*, p. 69; *Religion der Vernunft*, p. 79. On Cohen's concept of origin, see Walter Kinkel, "Das Urteil des Ursprungs: Ein Kapitel aus einem Kommentar zu Hermann Cohens Logik der reinen Erkenntnis," *Kantstudien* 17 (1912): 274–382; Pierfrancesco Fiorato, *Geschichtliche Ewigkeit: Ursprung und Zeitlichkeit in der Philosophie Hermann Cohens* (Würzburg: Königshausen & Neumann, 1993), pp. 5–52, esp. 32–39; Rose, *Judaism and Modernity*, pp. 117–118; Reiner Wiehl, "Das Prinzip des Ursprungs in Hermann Cohens 'Religion der Vernunft aus den Quellen des Judentums,'" in *„Religion der Vernunft aus den Quellen des Judentums": Tradition und Ursprungsdenken in Hermann Cohens Spätwerk: Internationale Konferenz in Zürich 1998*, edited by Helmut Holzhey, Gabriel Motzkin, and Hartwig Wiedebach (Hildesheim: Georg Olms Verlag, 2000), pp. 63–75; Poma, *The Critical Philosophy*, pp. 90–97; Hartwig Wiedebach, "Wissenschaftslogik versus Schöpfungstheorie: Die Rolle der Vernichtung in Cohens Ursprungslogik," in *Verneinung, Andersheit und Unendlichkeit im Neukantianismus*, edited by Pierfrancesco Fiorato (Würzburg: Königshausen & Neumann, 2009), pp. 47–67; Asher D. Biemann, *Inventing New Beginnings: On the Idea of Renaissance in Modern Judaism* (Stanford: Stanford University Press, 2009), pp. 41–43, 68–69.

28. Compare the analyses of Bruckstein in Cohen, *Ethics of Maimonides*, p. 59; Hartwig Wiedebach, *The National Element in Hermann Cohen's Philosophy and Religion*, translated by William Templer (Leiden: Brill, 2012), pp. 53–63; Adelmann, *Einheit des Bewusstseins*, pp. 129–133. On the concept of specificity in Cohen's religion of reason as a mediation of the tension between the universal and the particular, see the monograph by Sophie Nordmann, *Du singulier à l'universel: Essai sur la philosophie religieuse de Hermann Cohen* (Paris: J. Vrin, 2007). See also Yehoyada Amir, "Particularism and Universalism in the Religious Philosophy of Hermann Cohen," *Jerusalem Studies in Jewish Thought* 19 (2005): 643–675 (Hebrew). Finally, it is worth recalling the astute observation of Arthur A. Cohen, *The Natural and the Supernatural Jew* (New York: Pantheon Books, 1962), pp. 101–102: "The passion to be individual and authentic emerged in Cohen's proud recovery of Judaism, but the passion to be universal was—in that particularly German syndrome—fated to be finally the desire to be the best German. As a result Cohen never succeeded in overcoming that particularist universalism which passes as German culture in favor of that universal particularism which is Judaism."

29. Bruckstein, "On Jewish Hermeneutics," p. 38.

30. Cohen, *Ethics of Maimonides*, pp. 87–88; "Charakteristik," pp. 209–210.

31. Cohen, *Ethics of Maimonides*, p. 91; "Charakteristik," p. 212.

32. Kavka, *Jewish Messianism*, pp. 109–110; Hughes, "Maimonides," pp. 8–9.

33. Cohen, *Religion of Reason*, p. 62; *Religion der Vernunft*, p. 72.

34. Cohen, *Religion of Reason*, p. 63; *Religion der Vernunft*, p. 73.

35. The topic is worked out most fully in Hermann Cohen, *Das Prinzip der Infinitesimal-Methode und seine Geschichte*, introduction by Peter Schulthess [*Werke* 5] (Hildesheim: Georg Olms Verlag, 2005). See Ch. 2 n. 323.

36. Cohen, *Der Begriff der Religion*, p. 47.

37. Alexander Altmann, "The God of Religion, the God of Metaphysics and Wittgenstein's 'Language-Games,'" *Zeitschrift für Religions- und Geistesgeschichte* 39 (1987): 301. It is of interest to note that Altmann, op. cit., pp. 304–305, elicits a similar approach from Heidegger's plea for a new metaphysics that turns away from the concern for beings toward an openness to Being. In one of his first essays, "Metaphysik und Religion," published in 1930, Altmann raised the question of the relevance of Heidegger. See the English version of this study in Alexander Altmann, *The Meaning of Jewish Existence: Theological Essays 1930–1939*, edited by Alfred L. Ivry, introduction by Paul Mendes-Flohr, translated by Edith Ehrlich and Leonard H. Ehrlich (Hanover: University Press of New England, 1991), pp. 7–10, and discussion of the intellectual milieu in which this essay was written, including the pronounced impact of Heidegger, in Thomas Meyer, *Zwischen Philosophie und Gesetz: Jüdische Philosophie und Theologie von 1933 bis 1938* (Leiden: Brill, 2009), pp. 108–119. The impact of Heidegger's notions of destiny (*Schicksal*) and heritage (*Erbe*) on Altmann's idea of the understanding of Jewish existence (*Daseinsverständnis*) in his essay "What Is Jewish Theology?" (1933) is discussed by Martina Urban, "Persecution and the Art of Representation: Schocken's Maimonides Anthologies of the 1930s," in *Maimonides and His Heritage*, edited by Idit Dobbs-Weinstein, Lenn E. Goodman, and James A. Grady (Albany: State University of New York Press, 2009), pp. 167–170. In "The God of Religion," p. 306 n. 87, Altmann refers to his earlier study. My own engagement with Heidegger in the study of the phenomenology and hermeneutics of Jewish esotericism and the use made of him by Altmann in articulating his own theology is a matter that cannot be pursued here. I hope to elaborate on this topic in a monograph I am currently writing, tentatively entitled *Heidegger and the Kabbalah: Hidden Gnosis and the Path of Poiesis*. My indebtedness to Altmann has been graciously noted by Steven Wasserstrom, "Melancholy Jouissance and the Study of Kabbalah: A Review Essay of Elliot R. Wolfson, *Alef, Mem, Tau*," *AJS Review* 32 (2008): 392–393.

38. Cohen, *Religion of Reason*, p. 64; *Religion der Vernunft*, p. 73.

39. Cohen, *Religion of Reason*, pp. 64 and 66; *Religion der Vernunft*, pp. 73 and 76.

40. Cohen, *Religion of Reason*, p. 66; *Religion der Vernunft*, p. 76.

41. Cohen, *Religion of Reason*, p. 67; *Religion der Vernunft*, p. 77. On this dimension of Cohen's thought, see Kluback, *The Idea of Humanity*, pp. 222–223.

42. Cohen, *Religion of Reason*, pp. 82–83; *Religion der Vernunft*, p. 96.

43. Rosenzweig, *Star of Redemption*, p. 24.

44. Hermann Cohen, *Ethik des reinen Willens*, with introduction by Peter A. Schmid [*Werke* 7] (Hildesheim: Georg Olms Verlag, 2008), pp. 339–340.

45. Cohen, *Religion of Reason*, p. 41; *Religion der Vernunft*, p. 48.

46. Cohen, *Religion of Reason*, pp. 41–42 (emphasis in original); *Religion der Vernunft*, p. 48.

47. Cohen, *Ethik des reinen Willens*, p. 453. Cohen's position on the relationship of the Bible and myth can be profitably compared to the comments in *Leo Strauss on Maimonides*, pp. 182–183.

48. Cohen's representation of rabbinic Judaism reflects the opinion held by many prominent German Jewish thinkers of the nineteenth and early twentieth centuries. Needless to say, more recent studies have challenged this portrayal on grounds that some of the rabbinic sages clearly adopted a more mythical dimension of the divine, even attributing a bodily form to God in a manner that Cohen would have reckoned idolatrous and heretical.

49. Kluback, *Hermann Cohen*, pp. 45–46. In the 1917 essay "Der Jude in der christlichen Kultur," Cohen discusses at length incarnation and pantheism. He depicts the Christological doctrine to be a form of "mediational pantheism" (*vermittelter Pantheismus*), which he distinguishes from both pagan pantheism and the monotheism of Judaism. The dogma of incarnation thus marks the unequivocal break with Judaism, which affirms the absolute otherworldliness (*Jenseitigkeit*) and incomparability (*Unvergleichbarkeit*) of God. Cohen argues, moreover, that Luther transformed the Christian tradition by treating Christ as an "ideal figure of faith" (*Idealfigur des Glaubens*), a belief grounded neither in historical nor literary fact but in an ideal form, which is a construction of reason. The emphasis on the principle of *sola scriptura* frees the Protestant from a literalistic faith in scriptural texts. See Cohen, *Kleinere Schriften VI, 1916–1918*, pp. 430–431, 438–439; Alan Mittelman, " 'The Jew in Christian Culture' by Hermann Cohen: An Introduction and Translation," *Modern Judaism* 23 (2003): 65–66, 69.

50. Cohen, *Religion of Reason*, p. 42 (emphasis in original); *Religion der Vernunft*, pp. 48–49.

51. Cohen, *Religion of Reason*, p. 44 (emphasis in original); *Religion der Vernunft*, p. 51.

52. Concerning the philosophical exegesis of this verse, see references cited in Altmann, "The God of Religion," p. 297 n. 40. On Cohen's interpretation as exemplary of the larger question concerning the relationship of being (*hawayah*) and time (*zeman*), see Francesca Albertini, *Das Verständnis des Seins bei Hermann Cohen: Von Neukantianismus zu einer jüdischen Religionsphilosophie* (Würzburg: Königshausen & Neumann, 2003), pp. 117–122.

53. The point is summarized succinctly by Wyschogrod, *Crossover Queries*, pp. 408–409: "For Cohen, ideality derives its source from logical necessity: the highest expression of this necessity is the God of monotheism. At no point, however, does the concept of God acquire actuality, for were God to become actual he would take on the ontological structure appropriate only to phenomenal existents. The concept of actuality for Cohen means relating thought to sensation and must be excluded from the concept of God. God can, in that sense, have no actuality."

54. Cohen, *Religion of Reason*, pp. 42–43; *Religion der Vernunft*, pp. 49–50.

55. Cohen, *Religion of Reason*, p. 43; *Religion der Vernunft*, p. 50.

56. Cohen, *Religion of Reason*, p. 44; *Religion der Vernunft*, p. 50. See Julius Guttmann, *Philosophies of Judaism: The History of Jewish Philosophy from Biblical Times to Franz Rosenzweig*, introduction by R. J. Zwi Werblowsky, translated by David W. Silverman (New York: Holt, Rinehart, and Winston, 1964), pp. 364–365.

57. Jehuda Melber, *Hermann Cohen's Philosophy of Judaism* (New York: Jonathan David, 1968), pp. 65–66.

58. Cohen, *Religion of Reason*, pp. 44–45; *Religion der Vernunft*, p. 52.

59. Cohen, *Religion of Reason*, p. 45; *Religion der Vernunft*, p. 52.

60. Cohen, *Religion of Reason*, p. 46; *Religion der Vernunft*, p. 53. Compare Hermann Cohen, "Das heilige Geist," in *Kleinere Schriften V, 1913–1915*, p. 463; English translation in *Reason and Hope*, p. 152.

61. Cohen, *Religion of Reason*, pp. 165–215; *Religion der Vernunft*, pp. 192–251. See the extensive analysis of Michael Zank, *The Idea of Atonement in the Philosophy of Hermann Cohen* (Providence: Brown Judaic Studies, 2000); Rivka Horwitz, "Two Models of Atonement in Cohen's 'Religion of Reason': One According to Ezekiel, the Other 'Joyful in Sufferings' According to Job," in „*Religion der Vernunft aus den Quellen des Judentums*," pp. 175–190; Norman Solomon, "Cohen on Atonement, Purification and Repentance," in *Hermann Cohen's Critical Idealism*, pp. 395–411.

62. Cohen, *Religion of Reason*, p. 52; *Religion der Vernunft*, p. 60. See Goetschel, "Le paradigme Maimonidien," pp. 384–393; Kenneth Seeskin, "Hermann Cohen on Idol Worship," in „*Religion der Vernunft aus den Quellen des Judentums*," pp. 107–116; Robert Erlewine, "Hermann Cohen and the Humane Intolerance of Ethical Monotheism," *Jewish Studies Quarterly* 15 (2008): 148–173, esp. 161–163; idem, *Monotheism and Tolerance: Recovering a Religion of Reason* (Bloomington: Indiana University Press, 2010), pp. 154–155.

63. Cohen, *Religion of Reason*, p. 57; *Religion der Vernunft*, p. 66.

64. Cohen, *Religion of Reason*, p. 384; *Religion der Vernunft*, p. 447.

65. Seeskin, "Hermann Cohen on Idol Worship," pp. 110–111. For a fuller treatment of the philosophical problem with the popular religious conception of a personal God, see Seeskin, *Searching for a Distant God*, pp. 142–176, and esp. 154–157, where the views of Cohen, Buber, and Rosenzweig are discussed.

66. In some measure, this corresponds to one of the criticisms of Cohen's *Logik der reinen Erkenntnis* made by Joseph B. Soloveitchik in his dissertation. See Josef Solowiejczyk, "Das reine Denken und die Seinskonstituierung bei Hermann Cohen," Ph.D. dissertation, Friedrich-Wilhelms-Universität zu Berlin, 1932, pp. 85–91, and the analysis in Reiner Munk, *The Rationale of Halakhic Man: Joseph B. Soloveitchik's Conception of Jewish Thought* (Amsterdam: J. C. Gieben Publisher, 1996), pp. 48–51.

67. Cohen, *Religion of Reason*, p. 86; *Religion der Vernunft*, p. 100.

68. Cohen, *Religion of Reason*, pp. 212–214; *Religion der Vernunft*, pp. 248–250. The concept of nearness is connected to the ideal of correlation insofar as one must infinitely

draw near to the infinite in such a way that the difference is never finally overcome. See also Cohen's essay "Die Lyrik des Psalmen," in *Kleinere Schriften V, 1913–1915*, pp. 165–198, esp. 183–184. The description of proximity resonates with Cohen's asymptomatic understanding of the messianic future, a topic well discussed in scholarly literature. See Bouretz, *Witnesses for the Future*, pp. 58–65, and other references cited in Ch. 3 n. 211.

69. Altmann, *The Meaning of Jewish Existence*, p. 14.

70. Ibid., p. 15.

71. Ibid., p. 159 n. 40.

72. Ibid., p. 13.

73. Leo Strauss, *Spinoza's Critique of Religion* (New York: Schocken Books, 1965), p. 8. For discussion of Strauss's criticism of Cohen's perspective on revelation, see Batnitzky, *Leo Strauss and Emmanuel Levinas*, pp. 95–99. A similar appraisal is offered by Cohen, *The Natural and the Supernatural Jew*, pp. 85–89. For a reading of Cohen that challenges Strauss's contention that the return to Judaism requires the overcoming of philosophy, see Rose, *Judaism and Modernity*, pp. 111–125, esp. 113.

74. Strauss, "On the Argument with European Sciences (1924)," in *Leo Strauss: The Early Writings*, p. 111. For the influence of Otto's notion of the holy on the young Strauss, see discussion of Zank in *Leo Strauss: The Early Writings*, pp. 75–79; Janssens, *Between Athens and Jerusalem*, pp. 20–23.

75. See Rodrigo Chacón, "German Sokrates: Heidegger, Arendt, Strauss," Ph.D. dissertation, New School for Social Research, 2009, pp. 239–241. Strauss's complex relation to Heidegger has been the focus of many studies, of which I here list a modest sampling: James F. Ward, "Political Philosophy and History: The Links between Strauss and Heidegger," *Polity* 20 (1987): 273–295; Steven B. Smith, "'Destruktion' or Recovery? Leo Strauss's Critique of Heidegger," *Review of Metaphysics* 51 (1997): 345–377; Heinrich Meier, *Leo Strauss and the Theologico-Political Problem*, translated by Marcus Brainard (New York: Cambridge University Press, 2006), pp. 49–51; Catherine Zuckert, "Leo Strauss: Jewish, Yes, but Heideggerian?" in *Heidegger's Jewish Followers: Essays on Hannah Arendt, Leo Strauss, Hans Jonas, and Emmanuel Levinas*, edited by Samuel Fleischacker (Pittsburgh: Duquesne University Press, 2008), pp. 83–105; Daniel Doneson, "Beginning at the Beginning: On the Starting Point of Reflection," in *Heidegger's Jewish Followers*, pp. 106–130; Lawrence Vogel, "Overcoming Heidegger's Nihilism: Leo Strauss and Hans Jonas," in *Heidegger's Jewish Followers*, pp. 131–150, esp. 141–148; Wurgaft, "How to Read Maimonides," pp. 362–364, 375–380; Richard Velkley, "On the Roots of Rationalism: Strauss's Natural Right and History as Response to Heidegger," *Review of Politics* 70 (2008): 247–259; idem, *Heidegger, Strauss, and the Premises of Philosophy: On Original Forgetting* (Chicago: University of Chicago Press, 2011); Martin Woessner, *Heidegger in America* (Cambridge: Cambridge University Press, 2011), pp. 54–66. For Strauss's own account of the impact of Heidegger and his estimation of him as the greatest philosopher of the twentieth century, in spite of the thematic link he draws between Nazism and *Sein und Zeit*, see the lecture notes published as Leo Strauss, "An Introduction to Heideggerian Existentialism" in *The Rebirth of Classical Political Rationalism*, pp. 27–31.

76. Strauss, *Spinoza's Critique of Religion*, p. 8. The argument presented here parallels the contention of Strauss that for medieval philosophers the attempt to show the harmony between reason and revelation always presumed the primacy of the latter. See Strauss, *Philosophy and Law*, pp. 58–59. For discussion of Strauss's complex stance on the relationship of reason and revelation, see Kenneth Hart Green, *Jew and Philosopher: The Return to Maimonides in the Jewish Thought of Leo Strauss* (Albany: State of New York University Press, 1993), pp. 94–95, 122–123; idem, *Leo Strauss and the Rediscovery of Maimonides*, pp. 72–73; Eugene R. Sheppard, *Leo Strauss and the Politics of Exile: The Making of a Political Philosopher* (Waltham: Brandeis University Press, 2006), pp. 70–71; Janssens, *Between Athens and Jerusalem*, pp. 54–61; Randi L. Rashkover, "Justifying Philosophy and Restoring Revelation: Assessing Strauss's Medieval Return," in *Encountering the Medieval in Modern Jewish Thought*, edited by James A. Diamond and Aaron W. Hughes (Leiden: Brill, 2012), pp. 229–257, esp. 230–233. On the affinity between Rosenzweig and Strauss on revelation and divine transcendence, see Batnitzky, *Leo Strauss and Emmanuel Levinas*, pp. 62–67. See also Kenneth Hart Green, "Editor's Introduction: Leo Strauss as a Modern Jewish Thinker," in *Jewish Philosophy and the Crisis of Modernity: Essays and Lectures in Modern Jewish Thought*, edited with an introduction by Kenneth Hart Green (Albany: State University of New York Press, 1997), pp. 25–28.

77. On the controversy between Strauss and Guttmann, see Meyer, *Zwischen Philosophie und Gesetz*, pp. 19–106, esp. 57–104; Batnitzky, *Leo Strauss and Emmanuel Levinas*, pp. 109, 120, 182–186; Green, *Leo Strauss and the Rediscovery of Maimonides*, pp. 105–107.

78. Guttmann, *Philosophies of Judaism*, p. 354.

79. Ibid., p. 356.

80. Ibid., p. 357.

81. Ibid., p. 358.

82. Ibid., p. 367. See the succinct but incisive discussion of Guttmann's criticism of Cohen in Strauss, *Philosophy and Law*, pp. 46–47. And see the discussion of the idea of idealism in Adelmann, *Einheit des Bewusstseins*, pp. 227–243.

83. Strauss, *Philosophy and Law*, p. 27.

84. Ibid., p. 28.

85. Strauss, "Introductory Essay," in Cohen, *Religion of Reason*, pp. xxxv–xxxvi.

86. Ibid., p. xxiii.

87. Immanuel Kant, "On a Newly Arisen Superior Tone in Philosophy," in *Raising the Tone of Philosophy*, pp. 62 and 71, and see the comments of Derrida, "On a Newly Arisen," pp. 123–124, 143–144.

88. Schwarzschild, *The Pursuit of the Ideal*, p. 71.

89. Poma, *Yearning for Form*, p. 300. In that context, Poma is interpreting a passage from *Ethik des reinen Willens*, but I think his words can be applied as well to Cohen's presentation of God in *Religion der Vernunft aus den Quellen des Judentums*.

90. Bruckstein, "On Jewish Hermeneutics," p. 38.

91. Martin Buber, *Eclipse of God: Studies in the Relation Between Religion and Philosophy* (New York: Harper & Row, 1952), pp. 53–61.

92. Ibid., p. 62. See discussion of this dimension of Buber's dialogic principle in Israel Koren, *The Mystery of the Earth: Mysticism and Hasidism in the Thought of Martin Buber* (Leiden: Brill, 2010), pp. 320–322.

93. Martin Buber, *I and Thou*, a new translation, with a prologue and notes by Walter Kaufmann (New York: Charles Scribner's Sons, 1970), p. 164; *Ich und Du* (Heidelberg: Verlag Lambert Schneider, 1974), pp. 136–137. The passage is cited as the opening epigraph of this book. The dialogical orientation is at variance with Buber's earlier embrace of the notion of God's realization that ostensibly opposes the understanding of revelation based on a deity that is independent of human projection and, in some measure, is guilty of atheism, as Rosenzweig tacitly assumed in the 1914 essay "Atheistic Theology." See Paul Mendes-Flohr, *From Mysticism to Dialogue: Martin Buber's Transformation of German Social Thought* (Detroit: Wayne State University Press, 1989), p. 180 n. 247.

94. Buber, *I and Thou*, p. 143 (*Ich und Du*, p. 113): "God embraces but is not the universe; just so, God embraces but is not my self [*Gott umfaßt das All, und ist es nicht; so aber auch umfaßt Gott mein Selbst, und ist es nicht*]. On account of this which cannot be spoken about, I can say in my language, as all can say in theirs: You. For the sake of this there are I and You, there is dialogue, there is language, and spirit whose primal deed language is, and there, in eternity, the word."

95. Buber, *I and Thou*, pp. 63–64; *Ich und Du*, pp. 19–20.

96. Buber, *I and Thou*, pp. 147–148 (emphasis in original); *Ich und Du*, pp. 117–119. Buber's depiction of God as the absolute presence encountered in the moment was developed, in part due to the influence of Rosenzweig, in the fifth of the eight lectures he delivered at the *Freies Jüdisches Lehrhaus* in Frankfurt between January 15 and March 12, 1922. See Rivka Horwitz, *Buber's Way to "I and Thou": An Historical Analysis and the First Publication of Martin Buber's Lectures "Religion als Gegenwart"* (Heidelberg: Verlag Lambert Schneider, 1978), pp. 36, 107–110. On the presence of God and the relation of time and eternity, see also Buber's remarks in the seventh lecture, op. cit., p. 131, and the relevant comments on Buber's idea of the realization of God in the ever-present moment of revelation, which is compared to Nietzsche's doctrine of "the eternal return of the same," in Mendes-Flohr, *From Mysticism to Dialogue*, pp. 118–119.

97. Buber, *I and Thou*, pp. 180–181 (emphasis in original); *Ich und Du*, p. 158.

98. Buber offered a sustained critique of Spinoza in the essay "Spinoza, Sabbatai Zevi and the Baal-Shem" (1927) included in *The Origin and Meaning of Hasidism* (New York: Horizon Press, 1960), pp. 90–112, and see the analysis in Koren, *The Mystery of the Earth*, pp. 287–293.

99. Buber, *I and Thou*, pp. 181–182; *Ich und Du*, p. 159. Compare Buber, *Eclipse of God*, p. 28: "Thus the personal manifestation of the divine is not decisive for the genuineness of religion. What is decisive is that I relate myself to the divine as to Being which is over against me, though *not* over against me *alone*. . . . He who refuses to limit God to the transcendent has a fuller conception of Him than he who does so limit Him. But he who confines God within the immanent means something other than Him." The reality of

faith, according to Buber, means "living in relationship" to the "absolute Being" that one believes in unconditionally (p. 31).

100. Martin Buber, *Two Types of Faith: A Study of the Interpretation of Judaism and Christianity*, translated by Norman P. Goldhawk (New York: Macmillan Company, 1951), p. 129.

101. Ibid., p. 130.

102. Ibid., pp. 130–131. Compare Martin Buber, *Moses: The Revelation and the Covenant*, with introduction by Michael Fishbane (Amherst, NY: Humanity Books, 1998), pp. 51–53: "As reply to his question about the name Moses is told: *Ehyeh asher ehyeh*. This is usually understood to mean 'I am that I am' in the sense that YHVH describes himself as the Being One or even the Everlasting One, the one unalterably persisting in his being. . . . It means: happening, coming into being, being there, being present, being thus and thus; but not being in an abstract sense. . . . YHVH indeed states that he will always be present, but at any given moment as the one as whom he then, in that given moment, will be present. He who promises his steady presence, his steady assistance, refuses to restrict himself to definite forms of manifestation; how could the people even venture to conjure and limit him! . . . That Ehyeh is not a name; the God can never be named so; only on this one occasion, in this sole moment of transmitting his work, is Moses allowed and ordered to take the God's self-comprehension in his mouth as a name." See ibid., pp. 117–118: "The saga of the Fathers . . . has something to tell of human figures, in which YHVH lets himself be seen. But there is nothing super-natural about them, and they are not present otherwise than any other section of Nature in which the God manifests himself. What is actually meant by this letting-Himself-be-seen on the part of YHVH has been shown in the story of the Burning Bush; in the fiery flame, not as a form to be separated from it, but in it and through it . . . . And it is in precisely such a fashion . . . that the representatives of Israel come to see Him on the heights of Sinai. . . . He allows them to see Him in the glory of His light, becoming manifest yet remaining invisible." See also Martin Buber, *Kingship of God*, third edition, translated by Richard Scheimann (Amherst, NY: Humanity Books, 1990), pp. 105–106.

103. Buber, *Two Types of Faith*, pp. 131–132.

104. Buber, *Eclipse of God*, p. 45.

105. Ibid., p. 46.

106. Ibid., p. 119.

107. Strauss, *Spinoza's Critique of Religion*, pp. 11–12. On Strauss's criticism of Buber's privileging the "immediate experience of God," see Janssens, *Between Athens and Jerusalem*, pp. 23–24.

108. Strauss, *Spinoza's Critique of Religion*, p. 12.

109. On the attempt to read Strauss as a postmodern political thinker, see Catherine H. Zuckert, *The Truth about Leo Strauss: Political Philosophy and American Democracy* (Chicago: University of Chicago Press, 2006), pp. 80–114.

110. Martin Buber, *Good and Evil: Two Interpretations* (New York: Charles Scribner's Sons, 1952), p. 92. For an analysis that builds on the Buberian typology, see Kearney, *The Wake of Imagination*, pp. 37–61.

111. Understanding the traditional idea of the divine presence in the world as a human activity of making God present has resonance with Buber's conception of the realization (*Verwiklichung*) of God either through the experience (*Erlebnis*) of the individual (in the mystical phase of Buber's thinking) or through the community (*Gemeinschaft*) between human beings (in the dialogical phase). See Mendes-Flohr, *From Mysticism to Dialogue*, pp. 72–73, 95–96, 106–107, 113–119.

112. In the essay "Distance and Relation" (1950), Buber speaks of the capacity of *imagining the real*, by which he means "the capacity to hold before one's soul a reality arising at this moment but not able to be directly experienced. Applied to intercourse between men, 'imagining' the real means that I imagine to myself what another man is at this very moment wishing, feeling, perceiving, thinking, and not as a detached content but in his very reality, that is, as a living process in this man." See Martin Buber, *The Knowledge of Man: A Philosophy of the Interhuman*, edited with an introductory essay by Maurice Friedman, translated by Maurice Friedman and Ronald Gregor Smith (New York: Harper & Row, 1965), p. 70. On the human aptitude for figuration through artistic images, see ibid., pp. 149–165, and Zachary Braiterman, *The Shape of Revelation: Aesthetics and Modern Jewish Thought* (Stanford: Stanford University Press, 2007), pp. 42–44. See also Martina Urban, *Aesthetics of Renewal: Martin Buber's Early Representation of Hasidism as Kulturkritik* (Chicago: University of Chicago Press, 2008), pp. 102–103.

113. Rosenzweig, "The New Thinking," p. 132; *Zweistromland*, p. 156. The fuller text is cited in Ch. 2 at n. 376.

114. Altmann, *The Meaning of Jewish Existence*, pp. 10–11.

115. Ibid., pp. 12–13.

116. Ibid., p. 15.

117. Altmann, "The God of Religion," p. 291.

118. Ibid., p. 292.

119. Ibid., p. 294.

120. Ibid. For a more recent attempt to juxtapose Rosenzweig and Wittgenstein on the matter of religious language-games as pictures and the larger theoretical problem of anthropomorphism, see Cora Diamond, "Wittgenstein on Religious Belief: The Gulf Between Us," in *Religion and Wittgenstein's Legacy*, edited by Dewi Z. Phillips and Mario von der Ruhr (Burlington: Ashgate, 2004), pp. 99–138, esp. 123–128, and Paul Franks, "Talking of Eyebrows: Religion and the Space of Reasons after Wittgenstein, Rosenzweig, and Diamond," in *Religion and Wittgenstein's Legacy*, pp. 139–160, esp. 144–155. For other relevant comparative studies of Rosenzweig and Wittgenstein, see Hilary Putnam, "Introduction," in Franz Rosenzweig, *Understanding the Sick and the Healthy: A View of World, Man, and God*, translated and with an introduction by Nahum Glatzer (Cambridge, MA: Harvard University Press, 1999), pp. 3–9; idem, *Jewish Philosophy as a Guide*

to Life: Rosenzweig, Buber, Levinas, Wittgenstein (Bloomington: Indiana University Press, 2008), pp. 9–36; Paul Franks, "Everyday Speech and Revelatory Speech in Rosenzweig and Wittgenstein," *Philosophy Today* 50 (2006): 24–39.

121. Batnitzky, *Idolatry*, pp. 20–24, 32, 53. As Batnitzky acknowledges, her discussion—indeed, the title of her book—is informed by the analysis in Halbertal and Margalit, *Idolatry*, pp. 37–66. For a different approach to the role of form in Rosenzweig's thinking, see Braiterman, *The Shape of Revelation*, pp. 44–59.

122. Rosenzweig, *Star of Redemption*, pp. 124, 441; *Stern der Erlösung*, pp. 125, 465.

123. The text was published initially in *Der Morgen* 4, Heft 5 (1928) and a second time in Franz Rosenzweig, *Kleinere Schriften* (Berlin: Schocken Verlag, 1937), pp. 525–533. I have consulted the German text in Rosenzweig, *Zweistromland*, pp. 735–741.

124. Franz Rosenzweig, "A Note on Anthropomorphisms in Response to the *Encyclopedia Judaica*'s Article," in *God, Man, and the World: Lectures and Essays*, edited and translated by Barbara E. Galli, with a foreword by Michael Oppenheim (Syracuse: Syracuse University Press, 1998), p. 138; *Zweistromland*, p. 737.

125. Rosenzweig, "A Note on Anthropomorphisms," p. 144; *Zweistromland*, p. 741. See Barbara Galli, "Rosenzweig Speaking of Meanings and Monotheism in Biblical Anthropomorphisms," *Journal of Jewish Thought and Philosophy* 2 (1993): 157–184; Michael Oppenheim, *Mutual Upholding: Fashioning Jewish Philosophy Through Letters* (New York: Peter Lang, 1992), pp. 83–116; idem, *Speaking/Writing of God: Jewish Reflections on the Life with Others* (Albany: State University of New York Press, 1997), pp. 28–41; idem, "Foreword," in Rosenzweig, *God, Man, and the World*, pp. xxiii–xxxii. For an analysis of anthropomorphism and imagery, see Michal Schwartz, *Metapher und Offenbarung: Zur Sprache von Franz Rosenzweigs Stern der Erlösung* (Berlin: Philo, 2003), pp. 53–56.

126. Moshe Idel, "Franz Rosenzweig and the Kabbalah," in *The Philosophy of Franz Rosenzweig*, edited by Paul Mendes-Flohr (Hanover: University Press of New England, 1988), pp. 169–171. A slightly revised version has been published in Moshe Idel, *Old Worlds, New Mirrors: On Jewish Mysticism and Twentieth-Century Thought* (Philadelphia: University of Pennsylvania Press, 2010), pp. 165–167. Henceforth, I will refer to the revised text.

127. Rosenzweig, "A Note on Anthropomorphisms," pp. 144–145; *Zweistromland*, p. 741.

128. Rosenzweig, "A Note on Anthropomorphisms," p. 143; *Zweistromland*, p. 740.

129. Rosenzweig, "A Note on Anthropomorphisms," pp. 143–144; *Zweistromland*, pp. 740–741.

130. See Idel, *Old Worlds*, pp. 166–167; Sandu Frunză, "Aspects of the Connection Between Judaism and Christianity in Franz Rosenzweig's Philosophy," in *Essays in Honor of Moshe Idel*, edited by Sandu Frunză and Mihaela Frunză (Cluj-Napoca: Provo Press, 2008), pp. 200–227, esp. 221–222.

131. See Franks, "Everyday Speech," p. 35. A more extensive discussion of Rosenzweig's attitude to the *Shi'ur Qomah* speculation, examined from the perspective of his overall understanding of biblical anthropomorphisms, is offered by Franks, "Talking of

Eyebrows," pp. 150–154. Franks notes, *inter alia*, that even though Rosenzweig's "approach to biblical talk about God" is "quite opposed" to Maimonides and "much closer" to Wittgenstein, he nonetheless "endorses Maimonides' judgement of the *Shiʿur Qomah* traditions" (p. 150). In my view, the matter is more complex. Rosenzweig is obviously critical of the extravagant nature of the anthropomorphic measurements of God's body in the *Shiʿur Qomah* texts, but he also is able to relate it to what he would surmise to be a "genuine" or "representative" mode of anthropomorphizing. Moreover, in spite of the seemingly vast difference between the Maimonidean and Rosenzweigian interpretations of scriptural discourse about the divine, both thinkers end up affirming a contemplative seeing beyond language as the culminating mode of liturgical worship, as I argue in the next chapter. I have previously noted the conceptual affinities between Rosenzweig and the kabbalists with respect to the mythopoetic construction of the symbolic form of the divine anthropos ("Facing the Effaced: Mystical Eschatology and the Idealistic Orientation in the Thought of Franz Rosenzweig," *Zeitschrift für Neuere Theologiegeschichte* 4 [1997]: 79–80), a discussion that, lamentably, although not surprisingly, is completely ignored by Franks in his analysis of the development of the *Shiʿur Qomah* anthropomorphisms in the Idrot sections of the zoharic compilation, but this should not blind one from perceiving the notional proximity of the *via negativa* of Maimonides, which itself exerted a great impact on the kabbalistic sensibility, and the apophaticism affirmed by Rosenzweig. On the repercussions of the Maimonidean apophatic theology on the kabbalists, see Elliot R. Wolfson, "*Via Negativa* in Maimonides and Its Impact on Thirteenth-Century Kabbalah," *Maimonidean Studies* 5 (2008): 393–442.

132. It is of interest to compare Rosenzweig's position to that of Mendelssohn, who judged kabbalah to be guilty of idolatry, insofar as its emphasis on symbols is predicated on the semiotic error of attributing the properties of the signified to the sign. See Freudenthal, *No Religion without Idolatry*, pp. 168–172.

133. Rosenzweig, "A Note on Anthropomorphisms," p. 141; *Zweistromland*, p. 739.

134. Franz Rosenzweig, *Der Mensch und sein Werk: Gesammelte Schriften I. Briefe und Tagebücher*, edited by Rachel Rosenzweig and Edith Rosenzweig-Scheinmann, with the participation of Bernhard Casper, vol. 2: *1918–1929* (The Hague: Martinus Nijhoff, 1979), pp. 770–771. Regarding this passage, see Batnitzky, *Idolatry*, pp. 22–23; Eric L. Santner, *On the Psychotheology of Everyday Life: Reflections on Freud and Rosenzweig* (Chicago: University of Chicago Press, 2001), p. 123 n. 53, and the brief allusion in Stéphane Mosès, "Franz Rosenzweig in Perspective: Reflections on His Last Diaries," in *The Philosophy of Franz Rosenzweig*, p. 187. See also Braiterman, *The Shape of Revelation*, pp. 228–229.

135. Bernhard Radloff, "Preliminary Notes on Divine Images in the Light of Being-Historical Thinking," in *Heidegger, Translation, and the Task of Thinking: Essays in Honor of Parvis Emad*, edited by Frank Schalow (Dordrecht: Springer, 2011), p. 168 (emphasis in original). See Ch. 6 n. 35.

136. Cohen, *Religion of Reason*, p. 65; *Religion der Vernunft*, p. 75.

Chapter 2: Apophatic Vision and Overcoming the Dialogical

1. Rosenzweig, "The New Thinking," p. 135 (emphasis in original); *Zweistromland*, p. 158. On the notion of verification, see Martin Kavka, "Verification (*Bewährung*) in Franz Rosenzweig," in *German-Jewish Thought Between Religion and Politics: Festschrift in Honor of Paul Mendes-Flohr on the Occasion of His Seventieth Birthday*, edited by Christian Wiese and Martina Urban (Berlin: Walter de Gruyter, 2012), pp. 167–183.

2. See Martin Heidegger, *The Metaphysical Foundations of Logic*, translated by Michael Heim (Bloomington: Indiana University Press, 1984), p. 221 (*Metaphysische Anfangsgründe der Logik im Ausgang von Leibniz* [GA 26] [Frankfurt am Main: Vittorio Klostermann, 1978], p. 285): "The human being is a creature of distance! And only by way of the real primordial distance that the human in his transcendence establishes toward all beings does the true nearness to things begin to grow in him. And only the capacity to hear into the distance summons forth the awakening of the answer of those humans who should be near." See also Heidegger, *Poetry, Language, Thought*, pp. 177–178 (*Vorträge und Aufsätze* [GA 7] [Frankfurt am Main: Vittorio Klostermann, 2000], p. 179): "Nearing is the presencing of nearness [*Nähern ist das Wesen der Nähe*]. Nearness brings near—draws nigh to one another—the far and, indeed, *as* the far [*Nähern nähert das Ferne und zwar als das Ferne*]. Nearness preserves farness. Preserving farness, nearness presences nearness in nearing that farness" (emphasis in original). And see Martin Heidegger, *Elucidations of Hölderlin's Poetry*, translated by Keith Hoeller (Amherst: Humanity Books, 2000), p. 42 (*Erläuterungen zu Hölderlins Dichtung* [GA 4] [Frankfurt am Main: Vittorio Klostermann, 1996], p. 24): "The nearness that now prevails lets what is near be near, and yet at the same time lets it remain what is sought, and thus not near. We usually understand nearness as the smallest possible measurement of the distance between two places. Now, on the contrary, the essence of nearness appears to be that it brings near that which is near, yet keeping it at a distance [*erscheint das Wesen der Nähe darin, daß sie das Nahe nahebringt, indem sie es fern-hält*]. This nearness to the origin is a mystery." On Heidegger's conception of nearness, see Krzysztof Ziarek, *Inflected Language: Toward a Hermeneutics of Nearness: Heidegger, Levinas, Stevens, Celan* (Albany: State University of New York Press, 1994), pp. 9–12, 46–55. A similar sentiment was expressed by Paul Celan, *The Meridian: Final Version—Drafts—Materials*, edited by Bernhard Böschenstein and Heino Schmull with assistance from Michael Schwarzkopf and Christiane Wittkop, translated and with a preface by Pierre Joris (Stanford: Stanford University Press, 2011), p. 96: "The near is at the same time the infinitely distant; if it has the opacity of what stands opposite it, it also has the brightness of the faraway." For the German text, see Paul Celan, *Der Meridian: Endfassung—Entwürfe—Materialien*, edited by Bernhard Böschenstein and Heino Schmull with assistance from Michael Schwarzkopf and Christiane Wittkop (Frankfurt am Main: Suhrkamp Verlag, 1999), p. 96.

3. See Galli, *Franz Rosenzweig and Jehuda Halevi*, p. 378. As Galli points out, op. cit, pp. 382–385, the relationship of the one truth—and the corresponding one language—to the present human experience of multiple languages is the basis for Rosenzweig's dialogical grammar and his theory of translation based thereon.

4. Galli, *Franz Rosenzweig and Jehuda Halevi*, pp. 196–197; Rosenzweig, *Jehuda Halevi. Fünfundneunzig Hymnen und Gedichte*, pp. 49–51. Compare Rosenzweig, *Ninety-Two Poems*, pp. 29–33; Rosenzweig, *The Commentaries of Franz Rosenzweig*, pp. 72–74.

5. Galli, *Franz Rosenzweig and Jehuda Halevi*, pp. 196–197; Rosenzweig, *Jehuda Halevi. Fünfundneunzig Hymnen und Gedichte*, p. 51; Rosenzweig, *Ninety-Two Poems*, p. 33; Rosenzweig, *The Commentaries of Franz Rosenzweig*, pp. 73–74.

6. Rosenzweig, *Star of Redemption*, p. 292; *Stern der Erlösung*, p. 305.

7. Jacques Derrida, *Acts of Religion*, edited, with an introduction, by Gil Anidjar (New York: Routledge, 2002), p. 143.

8. Wolfson, "Facing the Effaced," pp. 39–81. For a more typical presentation of Rosenzweig, and one that unfortunately did not take my study into account, see Michael Mack, "Franz Rosenzweig's and Emmanuel Levinas's Critique of German Idealism's Pseudotheology," *Journal of Religion* 83 (2003): 56–78. See also Peter E. Gordon, "Rosenzweig Redux: The Reception of German-Jewish Thought," *Jewish Social Studies* 8 (2001): 8–9, 32–33; Reyes Mate, *Memory of the West: The Contemporaneity of Forgotten Jewish Thinkers*, translated by Anne Day Dewey, edited by John R. Welch (Amsterdam: Rodopi, 2004), pp. 76–92.

9. Gershom Scholem, *The Messianic Idea in Judaism and Other Essays in Jewish Spirituality* (New York: Schocken Books, 1971), p. 322.

10. Nahum N. Glatzer, "Was Franz Rosenzweig a Mystic?" in *Studies in Jewish Religious and Intellectual History Presented to Alexander Altmann on the Occasion of His Seventieth Birthday*, edited by Siegfried Stein and Raphael Loewe (University, Alabama: University of Alabama Press, 1979), p. 131. Although Glatzer applies the Scholemian characterization "theisitic mysticism" to Rosenzweig, he categorically denies that he was a mystic. See, additionally, the comments of Nahum N. Glatzer in the "Introduction" to his *Franz Rosenzweig: His Life and Thought* (Philadelphia: Jewish Publication Society of America, 1953), p. xxvii. In contrast to Leo Baeck, Hermann Cohen, and Martin Buber, "Rosenzweig is distinguished . . . by his more radical break with the past and his renascence of theological concepts that were last alive in the long-forgotten sphere of independent, dialectical Kabbalah. (This parallel, first recognized by Gershom G. Scholem, is doubly significant, since Rosenzweig never was a mystic)." On the depiction of the *Star* as promoting a philosophically mystical doctrine, see also Kenneth Hart Green, "The Notion of Truth in Franz Rosenzweig's *The Star of Redemption*: A Philosophical Enquiry," *Modern Judaism* 7 (1987): 317–318.

11. Wolfson, "Facing the Effaced," pp. 74–81. The question of the influence of kabbalah on Rosenzweig has been discussed by several other scholars. See Gershom Scholem, "Franz Rosenzweig and His Book *The Star of Redemption*," in *The Philosophy of Franz Rosenzweig*, pp. 20–41, esp. 35–39; Warren Zev Harvey, "How Much Kabbalah in *The Star of Redemption*?" *Immanuel* 1 (1987): 128–134; idem, "Why Philosophers Quote Kabbalah: The Cases of Mendelssohn and Rosenzweig," *Studia Judaica* 16 (2008): 118–125, esp. 122–124; Idel, *Old Worlds*, pp. 159–167; Eveline Goodman-Thau, *Aufstand*

der Wassen: Jüdische Hermeneutik zwischen Tradition und Moderne (Berlin: Philo Verlagsgesellschaft, 2002), pp. 118–157; Rivka Horwitz, "From Hegelianism to a Revolutionary Understanding of Judaism: Franz Rosenzweig's Attitude Toward Kabbala and Myth," *Modern Judaism* 26 (2006): 31–54, and the slightly different version "A Revolutionary Understanding of Judaism: Franz Rosenzweig's Attitude to Kabbalah and Myth," in *Franz Rosenzweigs »neues Denken«: Internationaler Kongreß-Kassel 2004*, edited by Wolfdietrich Schmied-Kowarzik, 2 vols. (Freiburg: Verlag Karl Alber, 2006), pp. 689–712 (Hebrew version in *Judaism, Topics, Fragments, Faces, Identities: Jubilee Volume in Honor of of Professor Rivka Horwitz*, edited by Haviva Pedaya and Ephraim Meir [Beer-Sheva: Ben-Gurion University of the Negev Press, 2007], pp. 43–71); Stéphane Mosès, *System and Revelation: The Philosophy of Franz Rosenzweig*, foreword by Emmanuel Lévinas, translated by Catherine Tihanyi (Detroit: Wayne State University Press, 1992), pp. 279–285; Bouretz, *Witnesses for the Future*, pp. 157–158. The similarity of Rosenzweig's view of language to the kabbalah, which is compared as well to the position of Heidegger, was noted by Jürgen Habermas, *Philosophical-Political Profiles*, translated by Frederick G. Lawrence (London: Heinemann, 1983), p. 24. See also the tantalizing remark of Paul Ricoeur, *Figuring the Sacred: Religion, Narrative, and Imagination*, translated by David Pellauer, edited by Mark I. Wallace (Minneapolis: Fortress Press, 1995), p. 93, that the "closing pages of *The Star* . . . call upon the esoterism of the cabala and the *Zohar* in exact symmetry to the discussion of Hegel and Schelling in Part One." For Ricoeur, the configuration (*Gestalt*) of the star as the "eternal truth" in the third part of Rosenzweig's book is best explained as a "speculation borrowed from Jewish esoterism" (p. 96), a speculation that is essentially metaphorical (p. 97). Ricoeur's view, as he acknowledges, is based on the assessment of Mosès, *System and Revelation*, p. 285, that Rosenzweig's depiction of the divine truth in the shape of a human face is an "evocation so specifically connected to the spiritual world of the Kabbala" that it "shows the deep kinship of Rosenzweig with the mystical tradition of Judaism." Concerning Rosenzweig's image of the divine face and a possible influence of kabbalah, see below, n. 286. See Barbara E. Galli, "Franz Rosenzweig's Theory of Translation Through Kabbalistic Motifs," in *The Legacy of Franz Rosenzweig: Collected Essays*, edited by Luc Anckaert, Martin Brasser, and Norbert Samuelson (Leuven: Leuven University Press, 2004), pp. 189–197; idem, "Rosenzweig's All, Kabbalistically Reflected," in *Franz Rosenzweigs »neues Denken«*, pp. 713–724. In both of these studies, Galli is heavily dependent on my work in assessing the kabbalistic dimensions of Rosenzweig's thinking. The same can be said of Barbara E. Galli, "Poetics of Time in Rosenzweig and Kafka," in *Faith, Truth, and Reason: New Perspectives on Franz Rosenzweig's »Star of Redemption«*, edited by Yehoyada Amir, Yossi Turner, and Martin Brasser (Munich: Verlag Karl Alber, 2012), pp. 259–275, but in this case she does not mention my work at all. Galli has dedicated a whole monograph, *On Wings of Moonlight: Elliot R. Wolfson's Poetry in the Path of Rosenzweig and Celan* (Montreal: McGill Queens University Press, 2007), to an exploration of some aspects of my thinking expressed in select poems and scholarly writings. See also Renate Schindler, *Zeit, Geschichte, Ewigkeit in Franz Rosenzweig's Stern der Erlösung* (Berlin:

Parerga Verlag GmbH, 2007), pp. 232–235, and the additional references cited below in n. 264.

12. Uriel Barak, "Rabbi A. I. Kook on the Nature of Franz Rosenzweig's Connection to Kabbalah," *Da'at* 67 (2009): 97–116 (Hebrew).

13. Ibid., p. 99.

14. Horwitz, "From Hegelianism," p. 32.

15. Galli, *Franz Rosenzweig and Jehuda Halevi*, pp. 20–21; Rosenzweig, *Jehuda Halevi. Fünfundneunzig Hymnen und Gedichte*, p. 27; Rosenzweig, *Ninety-Two Poems*, p. 10; Rosenzweig, *The Commentaries of Franz Rosenzweig*, p. 39.

16. Galli, *Franz Rosenzweig and Jehuda Halevi*, p. 187; Rosenzweig, *Jehuda Halevi. Fünfundneunzig Hymnen und Gedichte*, p. 227; Rosenzweig, *Ninety-Two Poems*, p. 11; Rosenzweig, *The Commentaries of Franz Rosenzweig*, p. 40.

17. I have dedicated many of my studies to elucidate the point, but none as expansively as Wolfson, *Through a Speculum That Shines*. Halevi is discussed on pp. 173–187.

18. For a critique of my reading, see Benjamin Pollock, *Franz Rosenzweig and the Systematic Task of Philosophy* (Cambridge: Cambridge University Press, 2009), pp. 258–311.

19. Galli, *Franz Rosenzweig and Jehuda Halevi*, pp. 317–318. A reading of Rosenzweig as a postmodern philosopher was proffered by Robert Gibbs, *Correlations in Rosenzweig and Levinas* (Princeton: Princeton University Press, 1992), pp. 10, 20–22, 55, 120, but see the challenge offered by Gordon, "Rosenzweig Redux," p. 33. Another attempt to interpret Rosenzweig as a postmodern Jewish thinker is offered by Yudit Kornberg Greenberg, *Better Than Wine: Love, Poetry, and Prayer in the Thought of Franz Rosenzweig* (Atlanta: Scholars Press, 1996), pp. 139–150.

20. Rosenzweig, *Star of Redemption*, p. 29; *Stern der Erlösung*, p. 24. It is of interest to recall the remark of Karl Löwith, "F. Rosenzweig and M. Heidegger on Temporality and Eternity," *Philosophy and Phenomenological Research* 3 (1942): 55–56, that Rosenzweig and Heidegger shared the aim of replacing the "all-too-many things" with "the one that is necessary at a time which is driving toward decisions because the traditional contents of modern civilization no longer prove indisputable." For the revised version, see idem, *Nature, History, and Existentialism*, edited by Arnold Levison (Evanston: Northwestern University Press, 1966), pp. 54–55. A German version of the essay with significant variations was published as Karl Löwith, "M. Heidegger und F. Rosenzweig. Ein Nachtrag zu 'Sein und Zeit,'" *Zeitschrift für philosophische Forschung* 12 (1958): 161–187. In addition to Löwith, the intellectual convergences and divergences between Heidegger and Rosenzweig have been made by a number of scholars: Guttmann, *Philosophies of Judaism*, pp. 368 and 448 n. 42; Else-Rahel Freund, *Franz Rosenzweig's Philosophy of Existence: An Analysis of* The Star of Redemption (The Hague: Martinus Nijhoff, 1979), pp. 7–8, 89, 132, 146; Steven S. Schwarzschild, "Franz Rosenzweig and Martin Heidegger: The German and the Jewish Turn to Ethnicism," in *Der Philosoph Franz Rosenzweig (1886–1929): Internationaler Kongreß-Kassel 1986*, 2 vols., edited by Wolfdietrich Schmied-Kowarzik (Freiburg: Verlag Karl Alber, 1988), pp. 887–889; Alan Udoff, "Rosenzweig's Heidegger Reception and the

re-Origination of Jewish Thinking," in *Der Philosoph Franz Rosenzweig*, pp. 923–950; Mosès, *System and Revelation*, pp. 291–293; Richard A. Cohen, "Authentic Selfhood in Heidegger and Rosenzweig," *Human Studies* 16 (1993): 111–128; Galli, *Franz Rosenzweig and Jehuda Halevi*, pp. 304–305; Peter E. Gordon, "Rosenzweig and Heidegger: Translation, Ontology, and the Anxiety of Affiliation," *New German Critique* 77 (1999): 113–148; idem, *Rosenzweig and Heidegger: Between Judaism and German Philosophy* (Berkeley: University of California Press, 2003); idem, "Redemption in the World: Authenticity and Existence in Rosenzweig and Heidegger," in *Franz Rosenzweigs »neues Denken«*," pp. 203–215; idem, "Franz Rosenzweig and the Philosophy of Jewish Existence," in *The Cambridge Companion to Modern Jewish Philosophy*, edited by Michael L. Morgan and Peter E. Gordon (Cambridge: Cambridge University Press, 2007), pp. 130–131; Wolzogen, *Emmanuel Levinas*, pp. 147–150; Alexander García Düttmann, *The Gift of Language: Memory and Promise in Adorno, Benjamin, Heidegger, and Rosenzweig*, translated by Arline Lyons (Syracuse: Syracuse University Press, 2000), pp. 5–34; Wolfdietrich Schmied-Kowarzik, "Dasein als 'je meines' oder Existenz als Aufgerufensein. Zur Differenz existenzphilosophischer Grundlegungen bei Martin Heidegger und Franz Rosenzweig," in *Die Jemeinigkeit des Miteins. Die Daseinsanalytik Martin Heideggers und die Kritik der soziologischen Vernunft*, edited by Johannes Weiss (Konstanz: UVK, 2001), pp. 197–217, reprinted in Wolfdietrich Schmied-Kowarzik, *Rosenzweig im Gespräch mit Ehrenberg, Cohen und Buber* (Freiburg: Verlag Karl Alber, 2006), pp. 197–216; idem, "Rosenzweig als Vorläufer von Heidegger und ihrer beider Nachfolge Schellings," *Philosophische Rundschau* 52 (2005): 222–233; Bernhard Casper, *Das dialogische Denken. Eine Untersuchung der religionsphilosophischen Bedeutung Franz Rosenzweigs, Ferdinand Ebners und Martin Bubers* (Freiburg: Verlag Karl Alber, 2002), pp. 74, 81, 83–84 n. 32, 100 n. 48, 120, 130, 139 n. 79, 143 n. 87, 174–175, 333–335; Hassan Givsan, "Rosenzweig und Heidegger," in *Franz Rosenzweigs »neues Denken«*, pp. 179–202; Martin Brasser, "Die verändernde Kraft des Wörtchens 'ist': Heideggers Kasseler Vorträge und Rosenzweigs neues Denken," in *Franz Rosenzweigs »neues Denken«*, pp. 216–227; Wayne J. Froman, "Rosenzweig and Heidegger on 'the Moment' ('der Augenblick')," in *Franz Rosenzweigs »neues Denken«*, pp. 228–246; Jules Simon, *Art and Responsibility: A Phenomenology of the Diverging Paths of Rosenzweig and Heidegger* (New York: Continuum, 2011). See the reference to the study by Casper cited below, n. 212, and other sources mentioned in nn. 263 and 334–335. Consider the reservations (aimed primarily at Casper) expressed by Harold M. Stahmer, "'Speech-Letters' and 'Speech-Thinking': Franz Rosenzweig and Eugen Rosenstock-Huessy," *Modern Judaism* 4 (1984): 61.

21. My view should be contrasted with the more standard position expressed concisely and clearly by Gibbs, *Correlations*, pp. 38–39: "Negative theology for Rosenzweig is the demonstration that each thing we know does not fit God. . . . This move produces the relative nothing, the starting point of Rosenzweig's reflection. Rosenzweig displays that philosophy has now made this negative move in each of the three spheres. But *The Star of Redemption* as a whole becomes a motion away from this threefold ignorance." For an articulation closer to my own, see Pollock, *Franz Rosenzweig*, pp. 144–149, 157–169.

22. Norbert Samuelson, "The Concept of 'Nichts' in Rosenzweig's *Star of Redemption*," in *Der Philosoph Franz Rosenzweig*, pp. 643–656. See also the brief introduction to the selection from Rosenzweig's *Star* included in William Franke, *On What Cannot Be Said: Apophatic Discourses in Philosophy, Religion, Literature, and the Arts*, vol. 2: *Modern and Contemporary Transformations*, edited with theoretical and critical essays by William Franke (Notre Dame: University of Notre Dame Press, 2007), pp. 139–144. For points of difference between my approach and that of Franke, see below, nn. 315 and 374. On the influence of Kant with regard to the threefold formulation of the nought in Rosenzweig, see Freund, *Franz Rosenzweig's Philosophy of Existence*, pp. 87–88.

23. Franz Rosenzweig, *Die "Gritli"-Briefe. Briefe an Margrit Rosenstock-Huessy*, edited by Inken Rühle and Reinhold Mayer, with a preface by Rafael Rosenzweig (Tübingen: Bilam Verlag, 2002), p. 227, cited in Pollock, *Franz Rosenzweig*, p. 260 n. 3, and then again, with analysis, on p. 306.

24. Rosenzweig, "The New Thinking," p. 115; *Zweistromland*, p. 143. See ibid., pp. 116–117 (*Zweistromland*, p. 144): "Experience [*Erfahrung*], no matter how deeply it may penetrate, discovers only the human in man, only worldliness in the world, only divinity in God. And only God in divinity, only in the world worldliness, and only in man the human." And ibid., p. 118 (*Zweistromland*, p. 145): "To the question of essence there are only tautological answers. God is only divine, man only human, the world only worldly; one can drill shafts into them as deeply as one wants, one always finds the same again." Rosenzweig's understanding of the mystical as an effacing of the autonomy of one of the three basic elements that are in correlation (God, human, or world) was anticipated by Cohen, *Reason and Hope*, p. 84: "But whenever God and man, or God and nature are equated, mysticism inevitably ensues. It turns the moral into the supernatural, and the supernatural into the natural."

25. Rosenzweig, *Star of Redemption*, p. 48; *Stern der Erlösung*, p. 43.

26. Kierkegaard, *Either/Or*, 2: 241–242: "The mystic has chosen himself absolutely, and consequently according to his freedom, and consequently is *eo ipso* acting, but his action is internal action. The mystic chooses himself in his perfect isolation; for him the whole world is dead and exterminated, and the wearied soul chooses God or himself. . . . Already here you will perceive how little the mystic's life is ethically structured, since the supreme expression of repentance is to repent that he did not choose God earlier . . . For the mystic the whole world is dead; he has fallen in love with God. . . . Just as there are lovers who have a certain resemblance to each other . . . so the mystic is absorbed in contemplation of the divine, whose image is reflected more and more in his loving soul, and thus the mystic renews and revives the lost image of God in humankind. The more he contemplates, the more clearly this image is reflected in him, the more he himself comes to resemble this image. " See ibid., pp. 244–245: "Finally, a mystic's life is displeasing to me because I regard it as a deception of the world in which he lives, a deception of the persons to whom he is bound or with whom he could establish a relationship if it had not pleased him to become a mystic. . . . The person who devotes himself one-sidedly to a mystical life eventually becomes so alienated from all people that every relationship,

even the tenderest and most intimate, becomes a matter of indifference to him." The similarity between Kierkegaard and Rosenzweig in their criticism of the mystical for its ethical shortcomings was already noted in Elliot R. Wolfson, *Venturing Beyond: Law and Morality in Kabbalistic Mysticism* (Oxford: Oxford University Press, 2006), pp. 9–11. On the intellectual kinship between Kierkegaard and Rosenzweig, see below, nn. 90, 174, and 356. One can surmise that the influence of Kierkegaard on Rosenzweig is part of a larger trend in German philosophy in the early part of the twentieth century, largely due to the translation of Diedrichs. See Hans Georg-Gadamer, *Philosophical Hermeneutics*, translated and edited by David E. Linge (Berkeley: University of California Press, 1976), p. 214, and David S. Groiser, "Repetition and Renewal: Kierkegaard, Rosenzweig and the German-Jewish Renaissance," in *Die Gegenwärtigkeit der deutsch-jüdischen Denkens*, edited by Julia Matveev and Ashraf Noor (Munich: Wilhelm Fink, 2011), pp. 265–301.

27. Rosenzweig, *Star of Redemption*, pp. 223–224; *Stern der Erlösung*, pp. 231–232.

28. Rosenzweig, *Star of Redemption*, p. 224; *Stern der Erlösung*, p. 232.

29. Rosenzweig, "The New Thinking," p. 116; *Zweistromland*, p. 143. In that context, the mystic is described as the "associate" of the pantheist, who affirms the subsumption of everything into divinity, and the atheist is associated with the materialist, who maintains that the human is a product of nature and God "nothing but its reflection." By contrast, in the beginning of the first book of the *Star*, Rosenzweig links the mystic and the atheist (see below at n. 291).

30. Franz Rosenzweig, *Understanding the Sick and the Healthy: A View of World, Man, and God*, translated and with an introduction by Nahum Glatzer, and with an introduction by Hilary Putnam (Cambridge, MA: Harvard University Press, 1999), p. 68.

31. Rosenzweig, *Star of Redemption*, p. 414; *Stern der Erlösung*, p. 435.

32. Ibid. On the role of liturgy in the shaping of Rosenzweig's thinking, see Hans Martin Dober, "Franz Rosenzweigs *Der Stern der Erlösung* als liturgietheoretische Konzeption," in *Faith, Truth, and Reason*, pp. 185–201.

33. Rosenzweig, "'Urzelle' to the *Star of Redemption*," in *Philosophical and Theological Writings*, p. 71. See also the curious and, to my knowledge, somewhat neglected comments of Rosenzweig, op. cit., pp. 69–70. The two base points of the triangle of the sciences are identified as faith and unfaith, or as theology and philosophy. The *salto mortale*, that is, the life-risking leap (a phrase made famous by Jacobi, as the editors remark on p. 69 n. 49), on the triangle's summit is linked to theosophy. Despite Rosenzweig's self-acknowledged bewilderment and resistance to the pinnacle of the sciences, it seems to me that his own thinking in the *Star* occupies the same place as theosophy, that is, the midpoint positioned between the two bases of philosophy and theology. It is not inconsequential that he voices his interest in pursuing Steinerian theosophy in a more serious manner (pp. 71–72).

34. Rosenzweig, *Star of Redemption*, p. 116; *Stern der Erlösung*, p. 118. It is of interest to recall here the following description of the relationship of scholasticism and mysticism in medieval Christian philosophy offered by Martin Heidegger, "Supplements to *The Doctrine of Categories and Meaning in Duns Scotus*," in *Becoming Heidegger: On the Trail*

of His Early Occasional Writings, 1910–1927, edited by Theodore Kisiel and Thomas Sheehan (Evanston: Northwestern University Press, 2007), p. 85: "Philosophy as a rationalistic structure, detached from life, is *powerless*; mysticism as irrational experience is *aimless*" (emphasis in original).

35. Rosenzweig, "The New Thinking," p. 129; *Zweistromland*, p. 153.

36. Rosenzweig, "The New Thinking," p. 110; *Zweistromland*, p. 140. On Rosenzweig's notion of a mythological as opposed to a rational-logical system based on Schelling's later philosophy, see Schwarcz, "Atheism," pp. 130–131, 143–149. For other discussions of the element of system in Rosenzweig's thought, see Emil L. Fackenheim, *To Mend the World: Foundations of Post-Holocaust Jewish Theology* (New York: Schocken, 1989), pp. 4–9; Green, "Notion of Truth," pp. 297–298; Mosès, *System and Revelation*, pp. 36–45; Rose, *Judaism and Modernity*, pp. 113–114; and the elaborate analysis in Pollock, *Franz Rosenzweig*, pp. 14–65; idem, "Franz Rosenzweig's 'Oldest System-Program,'" *New German Critique* 111 (2010): 59–95. A valuable collection of essays that provides something of the historical and ideational background for Rosenzweig is found in *System and Context: Early Romantic and Early Idealistic Constellations*, edited by Rolf Ahlers (Lewiston: Edwin Mellen Press, 2004), and see Paul Franks, *All or Nothing: Systematicity, Transcendental Arguments, and Skepticism in German Idealism* (Cambridge, MA: Harvard University Press, 2005).

37. Rosenzweig, "The New Thinking," p. 131; *Zweistromland*, p. 155. On the question of the "Jewishness" of the "new philosophy," see the letter of Rosenzweig to Rudolf Hallo, written on February 4, 1923, in Rosenzweig, *Briefe und Tagebücher*, vol. 2, pp. 888–890, partially translated in Stahmer, "'Speech-Letters' and 'Speech-Thinking,'" p. 64. For discussion of Rosenzweig's objection to branding the *Star* as a "Jewish book," see Gordon, "Rosenzweig Redux," pp. 15–17; idem, *Rosenzweig and Heidegger*, pp. 3–4; and the critique of Gordon's position in Cass Fisher, *Contemplative Nation: A Philosophical Account of Jewish Language* (Stanford: Stanford University Press, 2012), pp. 165–168.

38. Jean-Luc Nancy, *Being Singular Plural*, translated by Robert D. Richardson and Anne E. O'Byrne (Stanford: Stanford University Press, 2000), p. 3 (emphasis in original).

39. The position I have taken with respect to Rosenzweig corresponds to the larger claim concerning the task of modern Jewish thinkers to respond to the messianic philosophically offered by Goetschel, *The Discipline of Philosophy*, pp. 15–16: "Jewish philosophy argues for an intimate link with philosophy once it is no longer conceived as the exclusionary narrative of a West that limits its roots to an Athens it imagined in splendid isolation from anything 'East' of it. Against such a limited vision, which has informed the dominant narrative of philosophy as 'Greek,' Jewish philosophy insists on highlighting the cross-border traffic with Jewish and other legacies on which philosophy has continually relied, if often oddly in denial. As a reminder of a universalism not yet realized and therefore still to come, the messianic serves as the critical marker to reclaim the promise of the vision of universalism that philosophy otherwise remains tempted to exclude. As a continuous thread, the issue at the heart of the projects of modern Jewish philosophers weaves through their thought and makes it universal just where critics often

are tempted to diagnose them as most particular. Yet the critical force of their universalism consists precisely in the incessant reclaiming of the particular so pointedly shared by the philosophical projects that this book revisits, with an eye on their particular Jewish accent."

40. Rosenzweig, *Star of Redemption*, pp. 144–145; *Stern der Erlösung*, pp. 147–148.

41. Levinas, *Difficult Freedom*, p. 182.

42. Rosenzweig, "The New Thinking," pp. 111–112; *Zweistromland*, p. 141.

43. Franz Rosenzweig, *Der Mensch und sein Werk: Gesammelte Schriften I. Briefe und Tagebücher*, edited by Rachel Rosenzweig and Edith Rosenzweig-Scheinmann, with the participation of Bernhard Casper, vol. 1: *1900–1918* (The Hague: Martinus Nijhoff, 1979), pp. 484–485 (emphasis in original). An English translation is found in Rosenzweig, *Philosophical and Theological Writings*, pp. 51–52 n. 11.

44. Elliot R. Wolfson, *Alef, Mem, Tau: Kabbalistic Musings on Time, Truth, and Death* (Berkeley: University of California Press, 2005), pp. 50–52. See also Löwith, "F. Rosenzweig and M. Heidegger"; Mosès, *System and Revelation*, pp.150–173; and Gordon, *Rosenzweig and Heidegger*, pp. 185–205, esp. 123, where the author suggests that some readers may find in the literary configuration of the *Star* "a touch of wizardry . . . a Kabbalistic symbol-mongering that a philosopher of greater prudence, though perhaps less imagination, might have thought best to avoid. . . . Intended or not, Rosenzweig's claims to systematicity lapse occasionally into parody—at times, one suspects that he is out to explode the ideal of a self-grounding structure from within."

45. On Rosenzweig's positioning his new thinking in the interstitial space between philosophy and theology, see Cohen, *The Natural and the Supernatural Jew*, pp. 126–132; Eric L. Santner, "Miracles Happen: Benjamin, Rosenzweig, Freud, and the Matter of the Neighbor," in Slavoj Žižek, Eric L. Santner, and Kenneth Reinhard, *The Neighbor: Three Inquiries in Political Theology* (Chicago: University of Chicago Press, 2005), p. 82. See also Leora Batnitzky, "The New Thinking: Philosophy or Religion?" in *Franz Rosenzweigs »neues Denken«*, pp. 79–89.

46. Rosenzweig, "The New Thinking," p. 118; *Zweistromland*, p. 145.

47. Rosenzweig, *Star of Redemption*, p. 441; *Stern der Erlösung*, p. 465. The passage is cited below at n. 288.

48. *Die "Gritli"-Briefe*, pp. 159–160, cited in Pollock, *Franz Rosenzweig*, pp. 258–259.

49. Rosenzweig, "The New Thinking," p. 114; *Zweistromland*, p. 142.

50. Rosenzweig, "The New Thinking," p. 136; *Zweistromland*, p. 160.

51. Hartwig Wiedebach, "Rosenzweigs Konnektionismus: Der *Stern der Erlösung* als Tatsächlichkeits-System," in *Franz Rosenzweigs »neues Denken«*, pp. 371–392.

52. Rosenzweig, *Star of Redemption*, p. 312; *Stern der Erlösung*, p. 327.

53. Babylonian Talmud, Berakhot 17a. See Zachary Braiterman, "'Into Life'? Franz Rosenzweig and the Figure of Death," *AJS Review* 23 (1998): 203–221; idem, *The Shape of Revelation*, pp. 118–119. For a different approach, see Heinz-Jürgen Görtz, "'Ins Leben': Zum 'theologischen Interesse' des 'Neuen Denkens' Franz Rosenzweigs," *Revista Portuguesa de Filosofia* 62 (2006): 567–590. For a learned discussion of the impact of the

rabbinic traditions on the divine light and their influence on Rosenzweig, see Ottfried
Fraisse, "Das Licht des Geistes und das Licht der Erlösung: Ein Beitrag zum Verhältnis
von Idealismus und rabbinischer Tradition in Franz Rosenzweigs *Stern der Erlösung*," in
Faith, Truth, and Reason, pp. 203–222, esp. 210–214.

54. Rosenzweig, *Star of Redemption*, p. 271; *Stern der Erlösung*, p. 282.

55. Rosenzweig, *Star of Redemption*, p. 280; *Stern der Erlösung*, p. 291.

56. On the notion of "absolute empiricism," see Cohen, *The Natural and the Supernatural Jew*, pp. 129–130; Schindler, *Zeit, Geschichte, Ewigkeit*, pp. 114–123.

57. For instance, consider the statement in the 1949 introduction to "What Is Metaphysics?" in Heidegger, *Pathmarks*, pp. 287–288 (*Wegmarken*, p. 379): "According to its
essence, metaphysics is at the same time both ontology in the narrower sense, and
theology. This ontotheological essence of philosophy proper . . . must indeed be
grounded in the way in which the ὄν opens up in it, namely, as ὄν. Thus the theological
character of ontology is not merely due to the fact that Greek metaphysics was later
taken up and transformed by the ecclesiastic theology of Christianity. Rather it is due to
the manner in which beings as beings have revealed themselves from early on. It was this
unconcealedness [*Unverborgenheit*] of beings that first provided the possibility for
Christian theology to take possession of Greek philosophy." A proper analysis of this text
will have to be pursued elsewhere, but it is interesting to take stock of the fact that, for
Heidegger, the theological aspect of ontology is related to the manner in which beings
were disclosed, a form of disclosure in the nature of being that allowed for the subsequent appropriation of Greek philosophy on the part of Christian theology. Heidegger
concludes by saying that theologians will have to decide whether this appropriation is a
good or bad thing based on their experience of what is Christian, an inquiry informed by
Paul's statement "Has not God let the wisdom of this world become foolishness?" (1
Corinthians 1:20). From the continuation (1 Corinthians 1:22), it is obvious that the
wisdom of the world corresponds to Greek philosophy. In a provocative tone, Heidegger
muses, "Will Christian theology one day resolve to take seriously the word of the apostle
and thus also the conception of philosophy as foolishness?" Here, too, I detect an affinity
with Rosenzweig's critique of the old philosophy, although, as I have argued in the body
of this chapter, I do not think he was able to overcome the ontotheological in the way
that Heidegger suggested.

58. Laurens ten Kate, "The Gift of Loss: A Study of the Fugitive God in Bataille's
Atheology, with References to Jean-Luc Nancy," in *Flight of the Gods: Philosophical
Perspectives on Negative Theology*, edited by Ilse N. Bulhof and Laurens ten Kate (New
York: Fordham University Press, 2000), p. 277. See also John Peacocke, "Heidegger and
the Problem of Onto-Theology," in *Post-Secular Philosophy: Between Philosophy and
Theology*, edited by Phillip Blond (London: Routledge, 1998), pp. 177–194; Iain Thomson,
"Ontotheology," in *Interpreting Heidegger: Critical Essays*, edited by Daniel O. Dahlstrom (Cambridge: Cambridge University Press, 2011), pp. 106–131. On the concept of
philosophical theology in Rosenzweig and his sources, see Bernhard Casper, "Die
Gründung einer philosophischen Theologie im Ereignis," *Dialegesthai* 2003, available at

http://mondodomani.org/dialegesthai/bco1.htm. In spite of Heidegger's critique of onto-theology, there is a point of resemblance between him and Rosenzweig on the need to translate the philosophical into the theological and the theological into the philosophical. See Löwith, "F. Rosenzweig and M. Heidegger," p. 56, and idem, *Nature, History, and Existentialism*, p. 55. Löwith correctly notes, however, that "Heidegger's attitude towards Christianity is an estrangement and Rosenzweig's attitude towards Judaism a return." And see the elaboration on the opposed goals of the two thinkers in Löwith, "F. Rosenzweig and M. Heidegger," pp. 61–75; idem, *Nature, History, and Existentialism*, pp. 60–76.

59. I have accepted the rendering in Franz Rosenzweig, *The Star of Redemption*, translated by William Hallo (New York: Holt, Rinehart, and Winston, 1970), p. 17 [*Stern der Erlösung*, p. 19]. Galli, *Star of Redemption*, p. 24, translates: "his essence by nature, his essence that is there."

60. Ricoeur, *Figuring the Sacred*, p. 105, astutely observed that Rosenzweig "uses the weapons of his adversary and gets caught in the snares of metalogic, metaethics and metaphysics. Parting is not painless for a way of thinking whose strength is to have designated God, the world, and humanity as the primordial 'elements,' the wombs of the real." For analysis of Ricoeur's discussion of Rosenzweig, see W. David Hall, *Paul Ricoeur and the Poetic Imperative: The Creative Tension between Love and Justice* (Albany: State University of New York Press, 2007), pp. 11, 68, 71–72, 114–115, 131, 140–142, 150–151, 153, 156–158.

61. On this dimension of the ontotheological, see Jean-Luc Marion, "Thomas Aquinas and Onto-theo-logy," in *Mystics: Presence and Aporia*, edited by Michael Kessler and Christian Sheppard (Chicago: University of Chicago Press, 2003), pp. 38–74, esp. 39–40.

62. My approach is thus quite different from the Wittgensteinian reading of Rosenzweig's alleged critique of the notion of essence and the implied "absurdity of metaphysics" proffered by Hilary Putnam. See references to Putnam and Franks cited in Ch. 1 n. 120, and compare Gordon, "Rosenzweig Redux," pp. 29–30.

63. Rosenzweig, "Atheistic Theology," p. 17.

64. Rosenzweig, "The New Thinking," p. 115; *Zweistromland*, p. 143. See also idem, *Understanding the Sick*, p. 66: "The world is appearance, illusion. However, it does appear to me; this is more than mere illusion. This is 'essence,' and it is concluded that the 'ego' is the essence of the world. All the wisdom of philosophy can be summed up in this sentence." It is precisely this reductionism that Rosenzweig opposes as the inevitable outcome of the "fallacious enterprise" of philosophical speculation: "And so the 'ego' is thwarted in its attempt to become the essence of the world; it turns out to be nothing. It is neither 'subject' nor 'object'—nothing. To justify its claims it must be nothing. The result: the essence of the world is 'nothing'; nothing is at the core of the 'world of appearance.' . . . This much philosophy understood correctly—the world must be something other than it appears to be. But this something cannot be identified with the Self" (p. 67).

65. Mary-Jane Rubenstein, "Unknow Thyself: Apophaticism, Deconstruction, and Theology After Ontotheology," *Modern Theology* 19 (2003): 387–417. See also David

Tracy, "The Post-Modern Re-Naming of God as Incomprehensible and Hidden," *Cross Currents* 50 (2000): 240–247; Merold Westphal, *Overcoming Onto-Theology: Toward a Postmodern Christian Faith* (New York: Fordham University Press, 2001); and the very rich analysis of ontotheology and the presencing of the invisible in Joeri Schrijvers, *Ontotheological Turnings: The Decentering of the Modern Subject in Recent French Phenomenology* (Albany: State University of New York Press, 2011).

66. The following assessment of Michael P. Steinberg, *Judaism Musical and Unmusical* (Chicago: University of Chicago Press, 2007), p. 201, can be considered a succinct formulation of the prevailing approach to Rosenzweig: "*The Star of Redemption* attracts devotion more because of the work's renowned difficulty and esotericism than despite of these qualities. The work can be described, I would hazard, as an existential argument for the resacralization of Jewish life. In this respect, it parallels Rosenzweig's own biographical trajectory from his near conversion to Protestantism in 1913 through a rigorously deliberate agenda of reinvestiture in Jewish practice and ritual. It parallels also the desire for resacralization among present-day readers." I do not know why the author thinks his view is risky, since what he articulates confirms the standard understanding of Rosenzweig that has prevailed in the field. Compare the discussion of the "hagiographic impulse" in scholarship on Rosenzweig and the emphasis placed on his "return" to Judaism as a motivating force in the Weimar-era Jewish renaissance in Gordon, "Rosenzweig Redux," pp. 4–17. I do not agree with Gordon's assessment that "the hagiographic 'aura' that once illuminated Rosenzweig's memory has now decayed, yielding scholarship less responsive to social needs but also—for that very reason perhaps—more balanced in appraisal" (p. 24).

67. Ricoeur, *Figuring the Sacred*, p. 97.

68. Rosenzweig introduced the notion of "pure factuality" (*reine Tatsächlichkeit*) in the "Urzelle," p. 67. See the lengthy philological-textual discussion in n. 45 *ad locum*, and ibid., p. 69, where the "pure factuality" is described further as "something for itself," a "philosophical *salto mortale*" (see above, n. 33). See also Rosenzweig, "The New Thinking," p. 135: "What was put into the *Star of Redemption* was, at the beginning, the experience of factuality prior to all of actual experience's matters of fact. [The experience] of factuality that forces upon thinking, instead of its favorite word 'really,' the little word 'and,' the basic word of all experience, to which its tongue is unaccustomed." See Freund, *Franz Rosenzweig's Philosophy of Existence*, pp. 86–87; Benjamin Pollock, " 'Erst die Tatsache ist sicher vor dem Rückfall ins Nichts': Rosenzweig's Concept of Factuality," in *Franz Rosenzweigs »neues Denken«*, pp. 359–370.

69. Rosenzweig, *Star of Redemption*, p. 313; *Stern der Erlösung*, p. 328.

70. Rosenzweig, *Star of Redemption*, p. 404; *Stern der Erlösung*, p. 424.

71. Gordon, *Rosenzweig and Heidegger*, pp. 175–177.

72. Batnitzky, *Idolatry*, p. 66. On the hermeneutic of reading backward in Rosenzweig, see also Wolfson, *Alef, Mem, Tau*, p. 59. An attempt at a "backward reading" of the "metaphorical system" of the *Star* is offered by Ricoeur, *Figuring the Sacred*, pp. 93–107. For a criticism of this approach and preference for a linear hermeneutic, see Yehoyada

Amir, "'Liqra't meqor ḥayyei emet'—The Encounter of Franz Rosenzweig with the Poems of Judah Halevi," in *The Commentaries of Franz Rosenzweig*, p. 19.

73. Rosenzweig, "The New Thinking," p. 113. This comment is also referenced by Batnitzky, *Idolatry*, p. 64.

74. Rosenzweig, "The New Thinking," p. 134.

75. Zachary Braiterman, "Cyclical Motions and the Force of Repetition in the Thought of Franz Rosenzweig," in *Beginning/Again: Toward a Hermeneutics of Jewish Texts*, edited by Aryeh Cohen and Shaul Magid (New York: Seven Bridges Press, 2002), pp. 215–238; idem, *Shape of Revelation*, pp. 135–165.

76. On the expression "theopoetic," see Ch. 1 n. 1.

77. For the background of this way of conceiving temporality, see Bruckstein, "On Jewish Hermeneutics."

78. Commenting on Rosenzweig's notion of temporality, Ricoeur, *Figuring the Sacred*, pp. 102–103, writes: "For we cannot set the past of creation, the present of revelation, and the future of redemption on one line. It is a question, rather, of three levels of temporalization, of three layers with a different temporal quality, each of which, in its own way, contains a past, a present, and a future moment in the sense of linear succession. . . . We move beyond all narrative linearity; or, if we can still speak of narration, this would be a narration that will have broken with all chronology."

79. Rosenzweig, *Understanding the Sick*, p. 36.

80. Text cited in Horwitz, "From Hegelianism," p. 41.

81. For an attempt to contrast the kabbalistic and Rosenzweigian approaches to time, see Wolfson, *Alef, Mem, Tau*, pp. 176–177.

82. Scholem, "Franz Rosenzweig and His Book," p. 35; Idel, *Old Worlds*, p. 288 n. 24.

83. Batnitzky, *Idolatry*, p. 70.

84. Green, "Notion of Truth," pp. 301–302.

85. The point is well summarized in the description of Rosenstock's "philosophy of speech," which had a great impact on Rosenzweig, by Alexander Altmann, "About the Correspondence," in *Judaism Despite Christianity: The "Letters on Christianity and Judaism" between Eugen Rosenstock-Huessy and Franz Rosenzweig*, edited by Eugen Rosenstock-Huessy (University, Alabama: University of Alabama Press, 1969), p. 30: "According to it, truth is revealed through speech as expressing the intercommunication of one mind with another. It is not the formal truths of logic in their timeless, abstract, systematic character that are really vital and relevant, but rather the truths that are brought out in the relationships of human beings with God and with one another— truths that spring from the presentness of time and yet reach into the eternal." See Galli, *Franz Rosenzweig and Jehuda Halevi*, pp. 340–341.

86. The point, which has been noted by various scholars, is well expressed by Claudia Welz, *Love's Transcendence and the Problem of Theodicy* (Tübingen: Mohr Siebeck, 2008), pp. 189–190: "Rosenzweig's project does not aim at a 'true' essence of God which had so far been misunderstood; even more radically, it aims at the abolition of all essentialism and of the ontology of substance that is usually linked to it. . . . Accordingly, 'the truth'

does . . . not denote the correct cognizable information about what God, man, and the world 'is.' Rather, it denotes the right relationship between God, man, and the world."

87. Rosenzweig, *Star of Redemption*, p. 439; *Stern der Erlösung*, pp. 462–463.

88. Rosenzweig, *Star of Redemption*, p. 441; *Stern der Erlösung*, p. 465. On the different dimensions of the concept of the *Gestalt* in Rosenzweig, see Schwartz, *Metaphor und Offenbarung*, pp. 193–215.

89. I am here reworking my comments in the introduction to Galli's translation of the *Star of Redemption*, pp. xvii–xviii.

90. Rosenzweig, *Star of Redemption*, p. 13 (*Stern der Erlösung*, pp. 7–8), refers to Kierkegaard as one who resisted Hegel's integration of revelation into the knowable All. See also *Star of Redemption*, p. 25; *Stern der Erlösung*, p. 20. The affinities between Kierkegaard and Rosenzweig have been noted by a number of scholars. See Michael Oppenheim, "Søren Kierkegaard and Franz Rosenzweig: The Movement from Philosophy to Religion," Ph.D. dissertation, University of California, Santa Barbara, 1976; Welz, *Love's Transcendence*, pp. 88–276; idem, "Selbstwerdung im Angesicht des Anderen: Vertrauen und Selbstverwandlung bei Kierkegaard und Rosenzweig," in *Wir und die Anderen/We and the Others* [*Rosenzweig Jahrbuch* 5], edited by Martin Brasser and Hans Martin Dober (Freiburg im Breisgau: Karl Alber, 2010), pp. 68–83; idem, "Franz Rosenzweig: A Kindred Spirit in Alignment with Kierkegaard," in *Kierkegaard and Existentialism*, edited by Jon Stewart (Burlington: Ashgate, 2011), pp. 299–321 (Rosenzweig's explicit references to Kierkegaard are listed on pp. 299–301). On p. 319, Welz delineates several desiderata for future research, and the first of them is "to inquire into the topic of 'truth' in Kierkegaard and Rosenzweig, in a comparison of the *Concluding Unscientific Postscript* and the *Star of Redemption*. Both authors thematize the problem of the objectivity or subjectivity of truth and see human existence proceeding on a path that leads from a state of untruth to a participation in divine truth without ever 'having' it on one's own." See below, n. 174.

91. Søren Kierkegaard, *Philosophical Fragments; Johannes Climacus*, edited and translated with introduction and notes by Howard V. Hong and Edna H. Hong (Princeton: Princeton University Press, 1987), p. 167. The text is cited and analyzed in Wolfson, *A Dream*, pp. 47–48. See also Søren Kierkegaard, *Concluding Unscientific Postscript to Philosophical Fragments*, edited and translated, with introduction and notes, by Howard V. Hong and Edna H. Hong. 2 vols. (Princeton: Princeton University Press, 1992), 1: 207: "So, then, subjectivity, inwardness, is truth. Is there *a more inward* expression for it? Yes, if the discussion about 'Subjectivity, inwardness, is truth' begins in this way: 'Subjectivity is untruth.' . . . Viewed Socratically, subjectivity is untruth if it refuses to comprehend that subjectivity is truth but wants, for example, to be objective. Here, on the other hand, in wanting to begin to become truth by becoming subjective, subjectivity is in the predicament of being untruth" (emphasis in original). See ibid., p. 213: "It cannot be expressed more inwardly that subjectivity is truth than when subjectivity is at first untruth, and yet subjectivity is truth." On the art of genius "to deceive people into the truth," see Søren Kierkegaard, *The Book on Adler*, edited and translated, with introduction

and notes, by Howard V. Hong and Edna H. Hong (Princeton: Princeton University Press, 1998), p. 171. Compare the analysis of deception, truth, and metaphorical communication in Jamie Lorentzen, *Kierkegaard's Metaphors* (Macon: Mercer University Press, 2001), pp. 27–67.

92. Rosenzweig, *Star of Redemption*, pp. 408–409; *Stern der Erlösung*, p. 429.

93. Cohen, *Religion of Reason*, p. 414; *Religion der Vernunft*, p. 480.

94. Galli, *Franz Rosenzweig and Jehuda Halevi*, p. 199; Rosenzweig, *Jehuda Halevi. Fünfundneunzig Hymnen und Gedichte*, p. 54. Compare Rosenzweig, *Ninety-Two Poems*, p. 37; Rosenzweig, *The Commentaries of Franz Rosenzweig*, p. 79.

95. Babylonian Talmud, Shabbat 55a; Yoma 69b; Sanhedrin 64a.

96. Rosenzweig, *Star of Redemption*, p. 403; *Stern der Erlösung*, p. 423.

97. Rosenzweig, *Star of Redemption*, p. 408; *Stern der Erlösung*, p. 428.

98. Rosenzweig, *Star of Redemption*, p. 403; *Stern der Erlösung*, p. 423.

99. Rosenzweig, *Star of Redemption*, p. 409; *Stern der Erlösung*, p. 429.

100. Rosenzweig, *Star of Redemption*, pp. 410–411; *Stern der Erlösung*, pp. 431–432.

101. Rosenzweig, *Star of Redemption*, p. 411; *Stern der Erlösung*, p. 432.

102. Rosenzweig, *Star of Redemption*, p. 412; *Stern der Erlösung*, p. 433.

103. Rosenzweig, *Star of Redemption*, p. 446; *Stern der Erlösung*, p. 471.

104. Rosenzweig, *Star of Redemption*, p. 441; *Stern der Erlösung*, p. 465.

105. Rosenzweig, *Star of Redemption*, p. 410; *Stern der Erlösung*, p. 431.

106. Heidegger, *Pathmarks*, p. 148; *Wegmarken*, p. 193. The comparison of the understanding of revelation (*Offenbarung*) as unhiddenness in Rosenzweig and Buber, on the one hand, and the notion of truth (*alētheia*) as disclosure (*Entdeckung*) in Heidegger, on the other hand, is briefly noted by Gordon, *Rosenzweig and Heidegger*, pp. 268–269. Heidegger's notion of truth as unconcealment or disclosedness has been the focus of many studies, of which I will here mention a few representative examples: Marvin Farber, "Heidegger on the Essence of Truth," *Philosophy and Phenomenological Research* 18 (1958): 523–532; John M. Anderson, "Truth, Process, and Creature in Heidegger's Thought," in *Heidegger and the Quest for Truth*, edited with an introduction by Manfred S. Frings (Chicago: Quadrangle Books, 1968), pp. 28–61; Joan Stambaugh, *The Finitude of Being* (Albany: State University of New York Press, 1992), pp. 13–30; Ernst Tugendhat, *Der Wahrheitsbegriff bei Husserl und Heidegger* (Berlin: Walter de Gruyter, 1967), pp. 389–393, 396–399, 402–403; idem, "Heidegger's Idea of Truth," in *The Heidegger Controversy: A Critical Reader*, edited by Richard Wolin (Cambridge, MA: MIT Press, 1993), pp. 245–263, and the discussion in Santiago Zabala, *The Hermeneutic Nature of Analytic Philosophy: A Study of Ernst Tugendhat*, foreword by Gianni Vattimo (New York: Columbia University Press, 2008), pp. 25–44; Daniel O. Dahlstrom, *Heidegger's Concept of Truth* (Cambridge: Cambridge University Press, 1994), pp. 182, 214, 223–231, 238–240, 291–292, 300–301, 314–315, 322–325, 389–392, 397–407, 431–432; Frederick A. Olafson, "Being, Truth, and Presence in Heidegger's Thought," *Inquiry* 41 (1998): 45–64; Miguel de Beistegui, *Truth and Genesis: Philosophy as Differential Ontology* (Bloomington: Indiana University Press, 2004), pp. 122–130, 142–146, 153–154; Mark A. Wrathall,

"Heidegger, Truth, and Reference," *Inquiry* 45 (2002): 217–228; idem, "Heidegger on Plato, Truth, and Unconcealment: The 1931–32 Lecture on *The Essence of Truth*," *Inquiry* 47 (2004): 443–463; idem, *Heidegger and Unconcealment: Truth, Language, and History* (Cambridge: Cambridge University Press, 2011), pp. 11–39; Francisco J. Gonzalez, *Plato and Heidegger: A Question of Dialogue* (University Park: Pennsylvania State University Press, 2009), pp. 225–255; Louis P. Blond, *Heidegger and Nietzsche: Overcoming Metaphysics* (New York: Continuum, 2010), pp. 79–98. See additional studies cited below in nn. 128 and 339.

107. Hans-Georg Gadamer, *Truth and Method*, second, revised edition, translation revised by Joel Weinsheimer and Donald G. Marshall (New York: Continuum, 2011), p. 524.

108. Martin Heidegger, *Being and Time: A Translation of Sein und Zeit*, translated by Joan Stambaugh (Albany: State University of New York Press, 1996), § 44, pp. 198–201; *Sein und Zeit* (Tübingen: Max Niemeyer, 1993), pp. 214–219.

109. Heidegger, *Being and Time*, § 44, pp. 201–202, 208; *Sein und Zeit*, pp. 219–220, 226.

110. Heidegger, *Being and Time*, § 44, p. 202; *Sein und Zeit*, p. 220.

111. Heidegger, *Being and Time*, § 44, p. 203 (emphasis in original); *Sein und Zeit*, pp. 220–221.

112. Heidegger, *Being and Time*, § 44, p. 203; *Sein und Zeit*, p. 221.

113. Heidegger, *Being and Time*, § 44, p. 204; *Sein und Zeit*, p. 221.

114. Heidegger, *Being and Time*, § 44, p. 208; *Sein und Zeit*, p. 227.

115. Friedrich Nietzsche, *Writings from the Late Notebooks*, edited by Rüdiger Bittner, translated by Kate Sturge (Cambridge: Cambridge University Press, 2003), p. 161.

116. Ibid., p. 212.

117. Ibid., p. 154.

118. Martin Heidegger, *Nietzsche, Volume I: The Will to Power as Art*, translated with notes and an analysis by David Farrell Krell (New York: Harper & Row, 1979), p. 215; Martin Heidegger, *Nietzsche: Der Wille zur Macht als Kunst* [GA 43] (Frankfurt am Main: Vittorio Klostermann, 1985), pp. 267–268. Compare the discussion of the question concerning truth in Nietzsche's thought in Martin Heidegger, *Contributions to Philosophy (Of the Event)*, translated by Richard Rojcewicz and Daniela Vallega-Neu Maly (Bloomington: Indiana University Press, 2012), § 234, pp. 285–289; *Beiträge zur Philosophie (Vom Ereignis)* [GA 65] (Frankfurt am Main: Vittorio Klostermann, 1989), pp. 361–365.

119. Heidegger, *Being and Time*, § 44, pp. 204–205 (emphasis in original); *Sein und Zeit*, pp. 222–223.

120. On concealing and revealing in Heidegger's thought, see Loy M. Vail, *Heidegger and Ontological Difference* (University Park: Pennsylvania State University Press, 1972), pp. 25–46; Carlo Sini, *Images of Truth: From Sign to Symbol*, translated by Massimo Verdicchio (Atlantic Highlands: Humanities Press, 1993), pp. 63–68; Gert-Jan van der Heiden, *The Truth (and Untruth) of Language: Heidegger, Ricoeur, and Derrida on Disclosure and Displacement* (Pittsburgh: Duquesne University Press, 2010), pp. 38–45.

121. Heidegger, *Pathmarks*, p. 150; *Wegmarken*, pp. 196–197. See William J. Richardson, S.J., *Heidegger Through Phenomenology to Thought*, preface by Martin Heidegger, third edition (The Hague: Martinus Nijhoff, 1974), p. 96. Compare Levinas's discussion of this Heideggerian theme in Ch. 3 at nn. 325–326.

122. Heidegger, *Being and Time*, § 44, p. 207 (emphasis in original); *Sein und Zeit*, p. 226.

123. For a nuanced discussion of the *Kehre*, see Van Buren, *The Young Heidegger*, pp. 240–245.

124. Bernasconi, *The Question of Language*, pp. 15–27, and esp. p. 87: "What conceals itself in *aletheia*, as a trace, is *lethe*, concealment. *Lethe* is the heart of *aletheia* . . . A-letheia* says 'unconcealment,' but at the same time says this pervasive concealment."

125. Martin Heidegger, *The Essence of Truth: On Plato's Cave Allegory and Theaetetus*, translated by Ted Sadler (New York: Continuum, 2002), pp. 65–66, 104; *Vom Wesen der Wahrheit: Zu Platons Höhlengleichnis und Theätet* [GA 34] (Frankfurt am Main: Vittorio Klostermann, 1988), pp. 90, 145.

126. Heidegger, *Poetry, Language, Thought*, p. 53; *Holzwege* [GA 5] (Frankfurt am Main: Vittorio Klostermann, 2003), p. 40. For an alternative translation, see Martin Heidegger, *Off the Beaten Track*, edited and translated by Julian Young and Kenneth Haynes (Cambridge: Cambridge University Press, 2002), p. 30. I have used the older translation because, in my opinion, it offers a more precise rendering of the German original.

127. Heidegger, *Poetry, Language, Thought*, p. 54; *Holzwege*, pp. 40–41. Compare idem, *Off the Beaten Track*, pp. 30–31.

128. Heidegger, *Contributions*, § 228, p. 281; *Beiträge*, p. 356. See John Sallis, "Interrupting Truth," in *Heidegger toward the Turn: Essays on the Work of the 1930s*, edited by James Risser (Albany: State University of New York Press, 1999), pp. 19–30.

129. Kathleen Freeman, *Ancilla to the Pre-Socratic Philosophers* (Cambridge, MA: Harvard University Press, 1978), p. 33; Charles H. Kahn, *The Art and Thought of Heraclitus: An Edition of the Fragments with Translation and Commentary* (Cambridge: Cambridge University Press, 1979), pp. 32–33, 105. Compare Heidegger, *The Essence of Truth*, pp. 9–11 (*Vom Wesen der Wahrheit*, pp. 13–15); idem, *Introduction to Metaphysics*, new translation by Gregory Fried and Richard Polt (New Haven: Yale University Press, 2000), pp. 120–121 (*Einführung in die Metaphysik* [GA 40] [Frankfurt am Main: Vittorio Klostermann, 1983], p. 122); idem, *Pathmarks*, pp. 229–230 (*Wegmarken*, pp. 300–301). For discussion of Heidegger's interpretation of the Heraclitean saying and the self-concealing of nature, see Charles E. Scott, "Appearing to Remember Heraclitus," in *The Presocratics after Heidegger*, edited by David C. Jacobs (Albany: State University of New York Press, 1999), pp. 249–261, esp. 252–257; Daniel O. Dahlstrom, "Being at the Beginning: Heidegger's Interpretation of Heraclitus," in *Interpreting Heidegger: Critical Essays*, pp. 135–155. The interpretive history of the aphorism of Heraclitus is traced by Pierre Hadot, *The Veil of Isis: An Essay on the History of the Idea of Nature*, translated by

Michael Chase (Cambridge, MA: Harvard University Press, 2006), pp. 39–87. Heidegger's specific explication thereof is discussed on pp. 303–307.

130. Martin Heidegger, *The Principle of Reason*, translated by Reginald Lilly (Bloomington: Indiana University Press, 1992), p. 70; *Der Satz vom Grund* [GA 10] (Frankfurt am Main: Vittorio Klostermann, 1997), p. 104.

131. Martin Heidegger, *Country Path Conversations*, translated by Bret W. Davis (Bloomington: Indiana University Press, 2010), p. 25; *Feldweg-Gespräche* [GA 77] (Frankfurt am Main: Vittorio Klostermann, 1995), p. 39; idem, *Identity and Difference*, p. 29 (German text: p. 92); idem, *Pathmarks*, p. 309; *Wegmarken*, p. 409. See Astghik Simonyan, "Poetics of the Same: A Philosophical Poetic Recourse into Sameness," Ph.D. dissertation, University of London, 2010, pp. 170–175.

132. Heidegger, *Pathmarks*, p. 230; *Wegmarken*, p. 301.

133. Hannah Arendt, "Martin Heidegger at Eighty," in *Heidegger and Modern Philosophy: Critical Essays*, edited by Michael Murray (New Haven: Yale University Press, 1978), p. 300. The English translation of the essay by Albert Hofstadter first appeared in the *New York Review of Books* 17, no. 6 (October 21, 1971) based on the German radio address recorded in New York on September 25, 1969, and then printed as "Martin Heidegger ist achtzig Jahre alt" in *Merkur* 23 (1969): 893–902, and later in Hannah Arendt, *Menschen in finsteren Zeiten*, edited and translated by Ursula Ludz (Munich: Piper, 1989), pp. 172–184. Arendt sent a written version of the address to Heidegger on his eightieth birthday, September 26, 1969. See *Letters 1925–1975: Hannah Arendt and Martin Heidegger*, edited by Ursula Ludz, translated by Andrew Shields (Orlando: Harcourt, 2004), pp. 148–162. It is of interest to note the following remark of Heidegger in a letter to Arendt, dated November 27, 1969, expressing his gratitude to her for this commemoration: "More than anyone, you have touched the inner movement of my thought and of my work as a teacher, which has remained since the *Sophist* lecture" (*Letters 1925–1975*, p. 163). The passage I have cited amply attests to the veracity of Heidegger's praise of Arendt.

134. Heidegger, *Poetry, Language, Thought*, p. 54; *Holzwege*, p. 41. Compare idem, *Off the Beaten Track*, p. 31.

135. Welz, *Love's Transcendence*, pp. 188–189.

136. The critical difference was expressed in another terminological register by Löwith, "F. Rosenzweig and M. Heidegger," pp. 75–76: "In contradistinction to Heidegger, Rosenzweig, owing to his actual inheritance, his Judaism . . . was in the happy position of being able to hold up David's star of eternal truth in the midst of time. . . . 'God is the truth' . . . even if one day everything by which he made known his eternity in time . . . terminated where the eternal also finds its end: in eternity." See also Gibbs, *Correlations*, pp. 110–111.

137. Rosenzweig, *Star of Redemption*, p. 413; *Stern der Erlösung*, p. 434.

138. Cass Fisher, "Divine Perfections at the Center of the Star: Reassessing Rosenzweig's Theological Language," *Modern Judaism* 31 (2011): 189–190. Fisher repeats his view in the chapter on Rosenzweig in *Contemplative Nation*, pp. 153–206, esp. 201–203, although in that context he decided not to discuss the matter of apophasis in detail, and

hence my work is not engaged directly. See, however, Cass Fisher, "Speaking Metaphysically of a Metaphysical God: Rosenzweig, Schelling, and the Metaphysical Divide," in *German-Jewish Thought Between Religion and Politics*, pp. 151–166, esp. 162. To my ear, Fisher states the obvious and fails to challenge Rosenzweig in the way that the dialogical dimension of his new thinking would have demanded, to think, in Heideggerian terms, the unthought and to say the unsaid. For a more nuanced understanding of my thesis, see Virginia Burrus, "Seeing God in Bodies: Wolfson, Rosenzweig, Augustine," in *Reading the Church Fathers*, edited by Scot Douglass and Morwenna Ludlow (London: T & T Clark, 2011), pp. 44–59, esp. 50–52.

139. I have here followed Hallo's translation of *The Star*, p. 390 (*Stern der Erlösung*, p. 434). In particular, Galli's translation of *wesenlosen* as incorporeal (p. 413) is misleading and obscures the intent of this admittedly difficult passage.

140. For a different approach, see Welz, *Love's Transcendence*, pp. 189–191.

141. Galli, *Franz Rosenzweig and Jehuda Halevi*, p. 204; Rosenzweig, *Jehuda Halevi. Fünfundneunzig Hymnen und Gedichte*, pp. 69–70. See also Rosenzweig, *Ninety-Two Poems*, p. 53; Rosenzweig, *The Commentaries of Franz Rosenzweig*, p. 101.

142. Galli, *Franz Rosenzweig and Jehuda Halevi*, p. 204; Rosenzweig, *Jehuda Halevi. Fünfundneunzig Hymnen und Gedichte*, p. 70; Rosenzweig, *Ninety-Two Poems*, p. 53; Rosenzweig, *The Commentaries of Franz Rosenzweig*, p. 101. Concerning Rosenzweig's own attraction to a more gnostic or dualistic orientation in the early phase of his thinking, see Benjamin Pollock, "On the Road to Marcionism: Franz Rosenzweig's Early Theology," *Jewish Quarterly Review* 102 (2012): 224–255. The comment of Rosenzweig on Halevi's *yah anah emṣa'akha* is mentioned by Pollock, op. cit., p. 228 n. 12. It is of interest to compare the Rosenzweig of this phase to the Marcionite dimension of the young Heidegger's reading of the Pauline faith as a declarative enactment discussed in Simon Critchley, *The Faith of the Faithless: Experiments in Political Theology* (London: Verso, 2012), pp. 201–202.

143. Galli, *Franz Rosenzweig and Jehuda Halevi*, p. 205; Rosenzweig, *Jehuda Halevi. Fünfundneunzig Hymnen und Gedichte*, pp. 70–71. See also Rosenzweig, *Ninety-Two Poems*, pp. 53–55; Rosenzweig, *The Commentaries of Franz Rosenzweig*, p. 102.

144. Galli, *Franz Rosenzweig and Jehuda Halevi*, p. 206; Rosenzweig, *Jehuda Halevi. Fünfundneunzig Hymnen und Gedichte*, p. 71. See also Rosenzweig, *Ninety-Two Poems*, p. 57; Rosenzweig, *The Commentaries of Franz Rosenzweig*, pp. 102–103.

145. See reference below at n. 333.

146. See Elliot R. Wolfson, "Divine Suffering and the Hermeneutics of Reading: Philosophical Reflections on Lurianic Mythology," in *Suffering Religion*, edited by Robert Gibbs and Elliot R. Wolfson (London: Routledge, 2002), pp. 101–162, esp. 110–115.

147. Rosenzweig, *Star of Redemption*, p. 412; *Stern der Erlösung*, pp. 433–434.

148. Rosenzweig, "The New Thinking," p. 117; *Zweistromland*, p. 144. See Reiner Wiehl, "Experience in Rosenzweig's New Thinking," in *The Philosophy of Franz Rosenzweig*, pp. 42–68; Mate, *Memory of the West*, pp. 107–142.

149. Scholem, *Messianic Idea*, pp. 282–303.

150. Ibid., p. 284.

151. Ibid., p. 286.

152. Ibid., pp. 287–288 (emphasis in original).

153. Ibid., p. 289 (emphasis in original).

154. Ibid., pp. 289–290.

155. Ibid., p. 292.

156. Ibid., p. 297.

157. Ibid. p. 296 (emphasis added).

158. Shigenori Nagatomo, "The Logic of the *Diamond Sutra*: A Is Not A, Therefore It Is A," *Asian Philosophy* 10 (2000): 213–244.

159. Palestinian Talmud, Berakhot 1:3, 3b; Babylonian Talmud, Eruvin 13b, Giṭṭin 6b. In the former two contexts, these words, it will be recalled, are attributed to the *bat qol*, the heavenly voice.

160. Wolfson, *Alef, Mem, Tau*, p. 60.

161. Ibid., pp. 64–65.

162. Scholem, *Messianic Idea*, p. 303.

163. Rosenzweig, "The New Thinking," p. 123; *Zweistromland*, p. 149. On Rosenzweig's relationship to Goethe, especially his aesthetics, see Ephraim Meir, "Goethe's Place in Rosenzweig's *Star of Redemption*," *Da'at* 48 (2002): 97–107 (Hebrew).

164. Rosenzweig, "The New Thinking," p. 131; *Zweistromland*, p. 155. See Cohen, *The Natural and the Supernatural Jew*, pp. 130–131, 137–143; Wolfson, *Alef, Mem, Tau*, pp. 50–51; and Schindler, *Zeit, Geschichte, Ewigkeit*, pp. 81–87.

165. Rosenzweig, *Star of Redemption*, p. 177; *Stern der Erlösung*, p. 183.

166. Rosenzweig, *Star of Redemption*, pp. 191, 200; *Stern der Erlösung*, pp. 197, 207.

167. Rosenzweig, *Star of Redemption*, p. 211; *Stern der Erlösung*, p. 219.

168. On the contrast between the space of the plastic arts and the time of music, see Rosenzweig, *Star of Redemption*, p. 263; *Stern der Erlösung*, p. 273.

169. Rosenzweig, *Star of Redemption*, p. 212; *Stern der Erlösung*, p. 220.

170. Rosenzweig, *Star of Redemption*, p. 307; *Stern der Erlösung*, p. 322.

171. Rosenzweig, *Star of Redemption*, pp. 307–308; *Stern der Erlösung*, pp. 322–323.

172. Rosenzweig, *Star of Redemption*, p. 306; *Stern der Erlösung*, p. 320.

173. Mosès, *System and Revelation*, p. 170 (emphasis in original). A similar position was taken by Manfred H. Vogel, *Rosenzweig on Profane/Secular History* (Atlanta: Scholars Press, 1996), p. 12: "Now, according to Rosenzweig, Judaism proffers this prefiguration, presentiment, of eternity in the liturgical calendar which it instates. Namely, Rosenzweig contends that in the Jewish calendar of holy, sacred, days . . . a prefiguration of the state of eternity reflects itself. For in ever-repeating itself, year in and year out, in a prescribed order . . . the Jewish liturgical calendar transforms the linear progression of temporality into a cyclical progression; and with regard to a cyclical progression of temporality a good case can be made that it (in contra-distinction to a linear progression) can provide us with an intimation, a prefiguration, of eternity. . . . Cyclical progression is the closest

that one can come to the abrogation of progression, i.e., to eternity, while still being within the progression and this clearly should allow us to conclude that Judaism in appropriating a cyclical progression in its liturgical calendar is providing us with a prefiguration of the state of Eternity." See also Glatzer, *Franz Rosenzweig*, p. xxv; Catherine Chalier, "Franz Rosenzweig: Temps liturgique et temps historique," *Le Nouveaux Cahiers* 72 (1983): 28–31; Bernhard Casper, "Zeit—Erfahrung—Erlösung. Zur Bedeutung Rosenzweigs angesichts des Denkens des 20. Jahrhunderts," in *Der Philosoph Franz Rosenzweig*, pp. 553–566; Hagai Dagan, "Hatramah and Deḥikat ha-Keṣ in F. Rosenzweig's Concept of Redemption," *Da'at* 50–52 (2003): 391–407, esp. 405–406 (Hebrew); Dana Hollander, "On the Significance of the Messianic Idea in Rosenzweig," *Cross Currents* 53 (2004): 555–565, esp. 559–561. For an alternative approach, which emphasizes a tension in Rosenzweig's messianic idea between the temporal and the eternal, the this-worldly and the other-worldly, see Gregory Kaplan, "In the End Shall Christians Become Jews and Jews, Christians? On Franz Rosenzweig's Apocalyptic Eschatology," *Cross Currents* 53 (2004): 511–529. See also Agata Bielik-Robson, "Tarrying with the Apocalypse: The Wary Messianism of Rosenzweig and Levinas," in *The Messianic Now: Philosophy, Religion, Culture*, edited by Arthur Bradley and Paul Fletcher (London: Routledge, 2011), pp. 69–86. The author proposes that Rosenzweig and Levinas transform the "revelatory energy" of apocalyptic messianism into a "redemptive ethical force" and thereby change the "plane of the messianic concern from the ontological to the strictly moral" (p. 84). For both, moreover, albeit in distinctive ways, the messianic is harnessed to the nomian, but in such a manner that the law is transposed dialectically into an antinomian "form of apocalyptic fire" (p. 85). The discrepancy between the Jewish and the Christian paths to redemption lends partial support to the thesis of Leora Batnitzky, "Dialogue as Judgment, Not Mutual Affirmation: A New Look at Franz Rosenzweig's Dialogical Philosophy," *Journal of Religion* 79 (1999): 523–544, that for Rosenzweig, dialogue is an asymmetrical relation of self-judgment predicated on exposing real differences between the parties engaged in the dialogical encounter. Common sense dictates that the possibility of any genuine conversation between the two faith communities, let alone any meaningful reconciliation, is dependent on accepting irreducible disparities. As Batnitzky concludes, "love requires and generates judgment. The possibility of love is predicated on an overwhelming and infinite self-judgment, on the substitution of the other's judgment for the self. It is precisely this substitution that Rosenzweig argues Judaism and Christianity are incapable of in regard to each other" (pp. 543–544). I would propose, however, that this presentation fails to take seriously that there can be complementarity in the face of irresolvable difference. Indeed, it strikes me that the very heart of dialogical thinking is determined by the indeterminacy that arises from just such a correlativity within diversity.

174. With regard to the "eternal moment," there is a conceptual affinity between Rosenzweig and both Kierkegaard and Nietzsche, as was already noted by Löwith, "F. Rosenzweig and M. Heidegger," pp. 76–77; idem, *Nature, History, and Existentialism*, pp. 77–78. See also Oppenheim, "Søren Kierkegaard and Franz Rosenzweig," pp. 165–

171, esp. 170; idem, "Taking Time Seriously: An Inquiry into the Methods of Communication of Søren Kierkegaard and Franz Rosenzweig," *Studies in Religion/Sciences Religieuses* 7 (1978): 53–60; Galli, *Franz Rosenzweig and Jehuda Halevi*, p. 305. The possible similarity between Rosenzweig's conception of the *Augenblick* and the Kierke-gaardian sense of the moment or the instant is also noted by Ricoeur, *Figuring the Sacred*, p. 103. The notion of temporality in Kierkegaard and Nietzsche has been examined by many scholars. For representative studies, see Karl Löwith, *Nietzsche's Philosophy of the Eternal Recurrence of the Same*, translated by J. Harvey Lomax, foreword by Bernd Magnus (Berkeley: University of California Press, 1997) and David J. Kangas, *Kierke-gaard's Instant: On Beginnings* (Bloomington: Indiana University Press, 2007).

175. Rosenzweig, *Star of Redemption*, p. 307; *Stern der Erlösung*, p. 322.

176. Galli, *Franz Rosenzweig and Jehuda Halevi*, pp. 222–223; Rosenzweig, *Jehuda Halevi. Fünfundneunzig Hymnen und Gedichte*, pp. 110–111. See also Rosenzweig, *Ninety-Two Poems*, p. 113; Rosenzweig, *The Commentaries of Franz Rosenzweig*, p. 162. On the relation of eternity and time, see Galli's discussion, *Franz Rosenzweig and Jehuda Halevi*, pp. 462–463.

177. The affinity between Rosenzweig and Heschel with regard to their views on time was briefly noted by Galli, *Franz Rosenzweig and Jehuda Halevi*, p. 356.

178. Wolfson, *Alef, Mem, Tau*, pp. 204–205 n. 361, 205 n. 3. Particularly important to assess Heschel's phenomenology of time are descriptions of temporality in Hasidism, a topic too vast and intricate to be dealt with in this note. I will mention one emblematic passage from Menaḥem Mendel of Viṭebsk, *Peri ha-Areṣ al ha-Torah im Be'ur Ṭa'am ha-Peri*, 3 vols. (Jerusalem: Makhon Peri ha-Areṣ, 2011), 1: 107–108: "This is the matter of man's worshipping his Creator all the days of his life: none of the times [*ha-ittim*] are the same—'a time to love and a time to hate' (Ecclesiastes 3:8). For this is the whole of man, that he changes every moment and every second . . . and this is the matter: he takes off a form and puts on a form [*posheṭ ṣurah we-lovesh ṣurah*] . . . The matter of a man's variation in his worship of God is also called garments [*malbushim*]—the clothes one wears in the morning are not what one wears in the evening." It strikes me that the idea that the texture of time is determined by the liturgical demand of each moment is critical for understanding the notions of temporality proffered by Rosenzweig and Heschel. With regard to the former, it is also important to recall the remark of Judah Halevi, *Sefer ha-Kuzari*, translated by Yehuda Even-Shmuel (Tel-Aviv: Dvir, 1972), III.5, p. 101, that for the pious individual (*ḥasid*) the moment of prayer is "the seed of time and its fruition," and all other times are "like paths that lead him to this moment . . . for by means of it he is likened to the spiritual substances and he is distanced from the animals." Just as the three times of prayer on the weekdays are the fulfillment of time, so the Sabbath is the "fruit of the week" because that day is "summoned for the conjunction to the divine matter." Time, in its essence, marks the moment of transfiguration for the Jew, the angelic overcoming of his animality, a process that is realized most fully on the Sabbath, a day set aside for the spiritual union with the *amr ilāhī* (*inyan elohi*), the term used to designate the effluence of God that materializes in the physical universe but

which is perceived uniquely by the people of Israel; of all ethnicities, only the Jews are accorded the potentiality of being conjoined to this effluence, whence derives their prophetic-angelic status. Halevi's perspective resonates as well with the words of Abraham Joshua Heschel, *The Sabbath: Its Meaning for Modern Man* (New York: Farrar, Straus & Young, 1951), p. 99: "Time, however, is beyond our reach, beyond our power. It is both near and far, intrinsic to all experience and transcending all experience. It belongs exclusively to God. Time, then, is *otherness*, a mystery that hovers above all categories." See below, n. 184. Heschel's statement that time belongs exclusively to God brings to mind Rosenzweig's characterization of the Sabbath in the section of the *Star* entitled "God's time." See below, nn. 207, 278, 280, 281.

179. Heschel, *Man Is Not Alone*, p. 200 (emphasis in original).

180. Ibid., p. 201.

181. Ibid., p. 202.

182. Ibid., pp. 202, 204.

183. Ibid., pp. 205–206 (emphasis in original).

184. Abraham Joshua Heschel, *The Earth Is the Lord's: The Inner Life of the Jew in East Europe* (New York: Henry Schuman, 1950), p. 15: "The Jews in Eastern Europe lived more in time than in space. It was as if their soul was always on the way, as if the secret of their heart had no affinity with things." And see Abraham Joshua Heschel, *The Insecurity of Freedom: Essays on Human Existence* (New York: Farrar, Straus & Giroux, 1959), p. 20: "Judaism claims that the way to nobility of the soul is the art of sanctifying time. Moral dedications, acts of worship, intellectual pursuits are means in the art of sanctification of time." See ibid., p. 82: "the chief task of man is to sanctify time. All it takes to sanctify time is *God, a soul*, and a *moment*" (emphasis in original). Abraham Joshua Heschel, *Israel: An Echo of Eternity* (New York: Farrar, Straus & Giroux, 1969), p. 14: "Where is God to be found? God is no less here than there. It is the sacred moment in which His presence is disclosed. We meet God in time rather than space, in moments of faith rather than in a piece of space." Compare Heschel, *God in Search of Man*, p. 200: "Judaism is *a religion of history, a religion of time*. The God of Israel was not found primarily in the facts of nature. He spoke through events of history" (emphasis in original). And ibid., pp. 204–206: "Judaism does not seek to subordinate philosophy to events, timeless verities to a particular history. It tries to point to a level of reality where the events are the manifestations of divine norms, where history is understood as the fulfillment of truth. . . . Judaism claims that time is exceedingly relevant. Elusive as it may be, it is pregnant with the seeds of eternity. Significant to God and decisive for the destiny of man are the things that happen in time, in history. Biblical history is the triumph of time over space."

185. Heschel, *The Insecurity of Freedom*, pp. 81–82.

186. Heschel, *The Sabbath*, p. 8 (emphasis in original). This dimension of Heschel's phenomenology of the Sabbath experience has been duly noted by Edward K. Kaplan, *Holiness in Words: Abraham Joshua Heschel's Poetics of Piety* (Albany: State University of New York Press, 1996), p. 85; idem, *Spiritual Radical: Abraham Joshua Heschel in America*,

1940–1972 (New Haven: Yale University Press, 2007), pp. 126–127. For a nuanced approach to this topic, see Ken Koltun-Fromm, "Vision and Authenticity in Heschel's *The Sabbath*," *Modern Judaism* 31 (2011): 142–165. On the depiction of Sabbath as entering into the holiness of time, see also Heschel, *Israel: An Echo of Eternity*, p. 28, and ibid., p. 32, where the connection between the Sabbath and Jerusalem is underscored by the description of the latter as the physical locality wherein space becomes time.

187. Heschel, *The Sabbath*, p. 10.

188. Ibid., p. 6.

189. Ibid., p. 48.

190. Heschel, *Israel: An Echo of Eternity*, pp. 128–129: "Time is not an empty dimension. It can be a palace of meaning if we know how to build it with precious deeds. Our imperishable homeland is in God's time. We enter God's time though the gate of sacred deeds. The deeds, acts of sanctifying time, are the old ancestral ground where we meet Him again and again. . . . Genuine history occurs when the events of the present disclose the meaning of the past and offer an anticipation of the promise of the future." See John C. Merkle, *The Genesis of Faith: The Depth Theology of Abraham Joshua Heschel* (New York: Macmillan, 1985), pp. 193–194, 198; Arnold Eisen, "Re-Reading Heschel on the Commandments," *Modern Judaism* 9 (1989): 22–23; Kaplan, *Holiness in Words*, pp. 23–24, 175 n. 11.

191. Heschel, *God in Search of Man*, pp. 201–202, emphasizes the nature of revelation as an unprecedented, singular experience that occurs at a unique moment of time. It is precisely this singularity that secures the ongoing possibility of revelation as the recurrent retrieval of prophecy as a linguistic event. See Kavka, "The Meaning of That Hour," pp. 123–126. See also Perlman, *Abraham Heschel's Idea of Revelation*, pp. 77–90, 103–117; Edward Kaplan, "Heschel as Philosopher: Phenomenology and the Rhetoric of Revelation," *Modern Judaism* 21 (2001): 1–14.

192. The affinity between Heschel and Rosenzweig with respect to this issue of partaking of eternity without stepping out of time was already noted by Eisen, "Re-Reading Heschel," p. 22, and see ibid., pp. 16 and 24. For an attempt to demarcate the difference between the idea of revelation in Rosenzweig and Buber, on one hand, and that of Heschel, on the other, see Held, "Reciprocity and Responsiveness," pp. 191–192, 194–198.

193. Lévinas, "Foreword," in Mosès, *System and Revelation*, p. 21. Compare the discussion of Rosenzweig's conception of time and eternity in Biemann, *Inventing New Beginnings*, pp. 213–217.

194. Emmanuel Levinas, *Is It Righteous to Be? Interviews with Emmanuel Levinas*, edited by Jill Robbins (Stanford: Stanford University Press, 2001), pp. 178–179. On Levinas's reading of Rosenzweig's opposition to totality, see Susan A. Handelman, *Fragments of Redemption: Jewish Thought and Literary Theory in Benjamin, Scholem, and Levinas* (Bloomington: Indiana University Press, 1991), pp. 181–187; Batnitzky, *Leo Strauss and Emmanuel Levinas*, pp. 59–62.

195. Levinas, *Is It Righteous to Be?* p. 179.

196. Françoise Dastur, "The Ekstatico-Horizonal Constitution of Temporality," in *Critical Heidegger*, edited by Christopher Macann (London: Routledge, 1996), pp. 158–168, esp. 162–163; idem, *Heidegger and the Question of Time*, translated by François Raffoul and David Pettigrew (Atlantic Highlands: Humanities Press, 1998), pp. 34–38. Compare the texts of Heidegger cited in Wolfson, *Language, Eros, Being*, p. 417 n. 192, and my brief comments in *Alef, Mem, Tau*, p. 61. The reading of Rosenzweig's theological categories of creation, revelation, and redemption in light of a Heideggerian theory of temporality was suggested by Tina Chanter, *Time, Death, and the Feminine: Levinas with Heidegger* (Stanford: Stanford University Press, 2001), pp. 193–197. On the affinity between Levinas's notion of diachrony and Heidegger's ekstasis, see Ch. 3 n. 187.

197. See Stahmer, "'Speech-Letters' and 'Speech-Thinking,'" pp. 63–65.

198. Rosenzweig, "The New Thinking," pp. 126–127; *Zweistromland*, pp. 151–152.

199. Rosenzweig, *Understanding the Sick*, p. 79.

200. Ibid., p. 80: "Once again it is language which erects the visible bridge from man to that which is no man, to the 'other.' A person's name, his first name, is so external [*äusserlich*] to him that it is sufficient witness to the fact that there is something exterior to man, a 'without' [*Aussen*] surrounding him."

201. Lévinas, "Foreword," p. 22 (emphasis in original).

202. The essays included in *Le temps et l'autre* were lectures delivered in 1946–47 at the Collège Philosophique and then published in the 1948 collection *Le Choix—Le Monde—L'Existence*. They were reissued with a preface by Levinas under the new title in 1979. See Emmanuel Levinas, *Time and the Other*, translation by Richard A. Cohen (Pittsburgh: Duquesne University Press, 1987), pp. 29–30.

203. Levinas, *Time and the Other*, pp. 31–32 (emphasis in original).

204. The relation of Levinas to Husserl is a matter that has been engaged by numerous scholars from varied methodological perspectives. Here I mention two especially insightful essays by Edith Wyschogrod, "Intending Transcendence: Desiring God" and "Corporeality and the Glory of the Infinite in the Philosophy of Levinas," both included in *Crossover Queries*, pp. 13–44. See other references cited in Ch. 3 n. 135.

205. On the relation of diachrony, alterity, and transcendence, see Levinas, *Time and the Other*, pp. 105–109, 133–138. The number of scholars who have discussed the theme of time in the thought of Levinas is too sizable to delineate in this note. For a brief analysis of the specific nexus between temporality and alterity in Rosenzweig and Levinas, see Wolfson, *Alef, Mem, Tau*, pp. 49–54.

206. Levinas, *Time and the Other*, p. 137.

207. One of the boldest expositions of eternity in terms of the temporal inversion of beginning and end, emblematized more concretely by the symbol and ritual of Sabbath, is offered by Rosenzweig in a section in the last part of the *Star of Redemption*, pp. 442–443 (*Stern der Erlösung*, p. 467), which was given the title "God's time" (*Gottes Zeit*). For analysis of this passage, see Wolfson, "Facing the Effaced," pp. 56–57; idem, *Alef, Mem, Tau*, pp. 176–177. Part of the text is cited below at n. 281.

208. For a slightly different formulation of this point, see Michael Fishbane, *The Garments of Torah: Essays in Biblical Hermeneutics* (Bloomington: Indiana University Press, 1989), p. 145 n. 15.

209. Rosenzweig, *Star of Redemption*, p. 306 (*Stern der Erlösung*, p. 321): "Eternity . . . must be hastened, it must always be capable of coming as early as 'today'; only through it is it eternity." And ibid., p. 307 (*Stern der Erlösung*, pp. 321–322): "But more is to be demanded of it . . . to hasten the future, to make eternity into the very nearest thing, into the today." Compare Levinas, *Time and the Other*, p. 122: "What is new is what is present—or on the point of presenting itself. The elements of experience and those of dispositions are old to the extent that they withdraw from presence, which constitutes the zero point in the scale of time: the point where what is comes to be—or is the point of being produced. The present is the future making itself present." From one perspective, the possibility of actualizing tomorrow today neutralizes the utopian dimension of the messianic spirit focused on the endpoint of history, but from another perspective, this possibility is precisely what undergirds the horizon of the utopian hope, a time that is both not yet and already present, the facet of the telos that speaks by remaining unspoken. See Bloch, *The Principle of Hope*, pp. 1373–1375: "The Authentic or essence is that *which is not yet, which in the core of things drives towards itself, which awaits its genesis in the tendency-latency of process*; it is itself only now founded, objective-real—hope. . . . The tomorrow in today is alive, people are always asking about it. The faces which turned in the utopian direction have of course been different in every age, just like that which in each individual case they believed they saw. Whereas the *direction* here is always related, indeed in its still concealed goal it is the same; it appears as the only unchanging thing in history. Happiness, freedom, non-alienation, Golden Age, Land of Milk and Honey, the Eternally-Female, the trumpet signal in Fidelio and the Christ-likeness of the Day of Resurrection which follows it: these are so many witnesses and images of such differing value, but all are set up around that which speaks for itself by still remaining silent" (emphasis in original). Compare Tom Moylan, "Bloch against Bloch: The Theological Reception of *Das Prinzip Hoffnung* and the Liberation of the Utopian Function," in *Not Yet: Reconsidering Ernst Bloch*, edited by Jamie Owen Daniel and Tom Moylan (London: Verso, 1997), pp. 96–121, esp. 112: "There is, then, in Bloch's *Principle of Hope* a dialogic tension between a historically entrenched orthodox Marxism with its strong belief in the linear progression toward the communist telos of history and an unorthodox understanding of the fragmentary and disruptive play of utopia throughout human existence. The major methodological difficulty in Bloch's philosophy of hope lies in his overemphasis of the traditional Western category of the telos, the apparently powerful omega point at the end of history that pulls human emancipation forward. To the extent that Bloch privileges this totalizing telos in the name of communism's triumph he dilutes the subversive power of the utopian function as it wends its way through the cracks of everyday life." See also Paul Mendes-Flohr, " 'To Brush History against the Grain': The Eschatology of the Frankfurt School and Ernst Bloch," *Journal of the American Academy of Religion* 51 (1983): 631–650, esp. 636–644; Catherine Keller, *Apocalypse Now and Then:*

A Feminist Guide to the End of the World (Boston: Beacon Press, 1996), p. 122, and Ch. 3 n. 245.

210. Rosenzweig, *Star of Redemption*, p. 213; *Stern der Erlösung*, p. 221.

211. Rosenzweig, "Urzelle," pp. 63, 65 (emphasis in original); *Zweistromland*, pp. 133–134.

212. See Rosenzweig, "The New Thinking," p. 115 (*Zweistromland*, p. 143): "All philosophy asked about 'essence.' It is by this question that it distinguishes itself from the unphilosophical thinking of healthy human understanding." The use of the term *Ereignis* in Rosenzweig calls to mind the same term in the thought of Heidegger. See the brief remark of Ricoeur, *Figuring the Sacred*, p. 104: "It looks as though there is a comparison to be made of Rosenzweig's 'glance,' not just with Kierkegaard's instant, but also with Heidegger's *Ereignis*. But I am deliberately abstaining here from all such comparisons." The theme is mentioned briefly by Casper, *Das dialogische Denken*, p. 130, and in more detail in Bernhard Casper, "'Ereignis': Bemerkungen zu Franz Rosenzweig und Martin Heidegger," in *Jüdisches Denken in einer Welt ohne Gott: Festschrift für Stéphane Mosès*, edited by Jens Mattern, Gabriel Motzkin, and Shimon Sandbank (Berlin: Verlag Vorwerk 8, 2000), pp. 67–77, reprinted in Bernhard Casper, *Religion der Erfahrung. Einführung in das Denken Franz Rosenzweigs* (Paderborn: Schöningh, 2004), pp. 85–100.

213. Rosenzweig, *Understanding the Sick*, pp. 41–42. On Rosenzweig's critique of philosophical essentialism, see Franks, "Everyday Speech," pp. 25–27.

214. Rosenzweig, "The New Thinking," p. 125; *Zweistromland*, p. 150.

215. Levinas, *Time and the Other*, p. 119.

216. On the conceptual identity of time and uncertainty, related to a nonlinear mode of thinking, attested especially in poetic writings, see the thoughtful essay by Maria L. Assad, "Time and Uncertainty: A Metaphorical Equation," in *Time and Uncertainty*, edited by Paul Harris and Michael Crawford (Leiden: Brill, 2004), pp. 19–30.

217. Rosenzweig, *Star of Redemption*, pp. 217–218; *Stern der Erlösung*, p. 226.

218. Rosenzweig, *Star of Redemption*, p. 121; *Stern der Erlösung*, p. 123. See the passage from "The New Thinking" cited above at n. 49.

219. Galli, *Franz Rosenzweig and Jehuda Halevi*, pp. 20–21; Rosenzweig, *Jehuda Halevi. Fünfundneunzig Hymnen und Gedichte*, p. 28; Rosenzweig, *Ninety-Two Poems*, p. 12; Rosenzweig, *The Commentaries of Franz Rosenzweig*, pp. 41–42. For discussion of Halevi's poem, see Wolfson, *Through a Speculum*, pp. 174–175; Raymond P. Scheindlin, *The Song of the Distant Dove: Judah Halevi's Pilgrimage* (Oxford: Oxford University Press, 2008), p. 72.

220. Galli, *Franz Rosenzweig and Jehuda Halevi*, p. 187; Rosenzweig, *Jehuda Halevi. Fünfundneunzig Hymnen und Gedichte*, p. 28; Rosenzweig, *Ninety-Two Poems*, p. 13; Rosenzweig, *The Commentaries of Franz Rosenzweig*, p. 42.

221. *Timaeus* 52b–c. See Jacques Derrida, *Dissemination*, translated, with an introduction and additional notes, by Barbara Johnson (Chicago: University of Chicago Press, 1981), p. 161; John Sallis, *Chorology: On Beginning in Plato's Timaeus* (Bloomington: Indiana University Press, 1999), pp. 118–24; Wolfson, *A Dream*, p. 100.

222. Jacques Derrida, "Tense," in *The Path of Archaic Thinking: Unfolding the Work of John Sallis*, edited by Kenneth Maly (Albany: State University of New York Press, 1995), pp. 50–51. For an explication and expansion of Derrida's essay, see John Sallis, *Platonic Legacies* (Albany: State University of New York Press, 2004), pp. 47–60.

223. On the oneiric undoing of time, see the analysis in Wolfson, *A Dream*, pp. 219–274.

224. Galli, *Franz Rosenzweig and Jehuda Halevi*, p. 187; Rosenzweig, *Jehuda Halevi. Fünfundneunzig Hymnen und Gedichte*, p. 28. For alternative translations, see Rosenzweig, *Ninety-Two Poems*, p. 13; Rosenzweig, *The Commentaries of Franz Rosenzweig*, p. 42.

225. Myriam Bienenstock, "Recalling the Past in Rosenzweig's *Star of Redemption*," *Modern Judaism* 23 (2003): 235, notes that Rosenzweig "understood the meaning of Schelling's identity thesis—the thesis of identity between thought and being, between the *ideal* and the *real*," and consequently, "he could develop a conception of myth very close to Schelling's 'tautegory,' a conception according to which mythical representations are ideal, internal to consciousness, as well as real, external to it. A reading of the first part of *The Star of Redemption* shows that for Rosenzweig, too, as for Schelling, mythical representations are experienced in consciousness but also have at their basis an objectively real theogony, the history of real gods." As I argue below, it is not clear to me that Rosenzweig was ultimately able to affirm this sense of reality external to consciousness.

226. Rosenzweig, *Understanding the Sick*, p. 72.

227. Fishbane, *Garments of Torah*, p. 106.

228. I have here reworked with slight emendation a section of my "Introduction," in Galli's translation of the *Star*, p. xix. The subject of time and interpretation has been the focus of many hermeneutical studies. See, for instance, David Wood, *The Deconstruction of Time* (Evanston: Northwestern University Press, 2001), pp. 319–334.

229. On the role of language in Rosenzweig's *sprachdenken*, see Rivka Horwitz, "Franz Rosenzweig on Language," *Judaism* 13 (1964): 393–406; Nahum N. Glatzer, "The Concept of Language in the Thought of Franz Rosenzweig," in *The Philosophy of Franz Rosenzweig*, pp. 172–184; Schwartz, *Metapher und Offenbarung*, pp. 35–74.

230. Rosenzweig, *Star of Redemption*, p. 263; *Stern der Erlösung*, p. 273.

231. Rosenzweig, *Star of Redemption*, pp. 104–105; *Stern der Erlösung*, p. 105. See Batnitzky, *Idolatry*, pp. 40–54, esp. 42; Santner, "Miracles Happen," pp. 83–88; Schwartz, *Metapher und Offenbarung*, pp. 83–91. On Rosenzweig's understanding of "miracle" as a boundary concept in philosophy, see Wiehl, "Experience," pp. 62–68.

232. Rosenzweig, *Star of Redemption*, pp. 120–121; *Stern der Erlösung*, p. 123. On Rosenzweig's understanding of language—and particularly the language of the Hebrew Bible—as an enactment of revelation as the coming-to-speech of God, see Bruce Rosenstock, *Philosophy and the Jewish Question: Mendelssohn, Rosenzweig, and Beyond* (New York: Fordham University Press, 2010), pp. 128–133.

233. Martin Buber and Franz Rosenzweig, *Scripture and Translation*, translated by Lawrence Rosenwald and Everett Fox (Bloomington: Indiana University Press, 1994), p. 47; Rosenzweig, *Zweistromland*, p. 749. For a far-reaching analysis of Rosenzweig's

328 NOTES TO PAGE 64

philosophy of translation, see Galli, *Franz Rosenzweig and Jehuda Halevi*, pp. 322–359. See also the discussion of Rosenzweig's hermeneutics as a "proliferating translatability" in Wolfgang Iser, *The Range of Interpretation* (New York: Columbia University Press, 2000), pp. 113–144; and further discussions in Dana Hollander, "Franz Rosenzweig on Nation, Translation, and Judaism," *Philosophy Today* 38 (1994): 380–389; Hans-Christoph Askani, *Das Problem der Übersetzung, dargestellt an Franz Rosenzweig* (Tübingen: Mohr Siebeck, 1997); Paul Ricoeur, *On Translation*, translated by Eileen Brennan, with an introduction by Richard Kearney (London: Routledge, 2006), pp. 22–23; Leora Batnitzky, *Idolatry*, pp. 105–141; idem, "Franz Rosenzweig on Translation and Exile," *Jewish Studies Quarterly* 14 (2007): 131–143; Mara H. Benjamin, *Rosenzweig's Bible: Reinventing Scripture for Jewish Modernity* (Cambridge: Cambridge University Press, 2009), pp. 103–134.

234. See, for instance, Martin Heidegger, *Early Greek Thinking*, translated by David Farrell Krell and Frank A. Capuzzi (New York: Harper & Row, 1975), pp. 18–19; *Holzwege*, pp. 328–329. See also Martin Heidegger, *Parmenides*, translated by André Schuwer and Richard Rojcewicz (Bloomington: Indiana University Press, 1992), pp. 12–13; *Parmenides* [GA 54] (Frankfurt am Main: Vittorio Klostermann, 1992), pp. 16–17; and compare the wide-ranging discussion on hermeneutics and the philosophy of translation in Miles Groth, *Translating Heidegger* (Amherst: Humanity Books, 2004), pp. 115–163. See also Frank Schalow, "Attunement and Translation," in *Heidegger, Translation, and the Task of Thinking*, pp. 291–311; Parvis Emad, *Translation and Interpretation: Learning from* Beiträge (Bucharest: Zeta Books, 2012), pp. 60–86. The affinity between Heidegger and Rosenzweig on this point has been noted by Horwitz, "Franz Rosenzweig on Language," pp. 402–403. See also Gordon, "Rosenzweig and Heidegger," and idem, *Rosenzweig and Heidegger*, pp. 273–274.

235. Gadamer, *Truth and Method*, pp. 385–391, and the study of John Sallis, "The Hermeneutics of Translation," in *Language and Linguisticality in Gadamer's Hermeneutics*, edited by Lawrence K. Schmidt (Lanham: Lexington Books, 2000), pp. 67–76. On interpretation as a mode of translation, see also Iser, *The Range of Interpretation*, pp. 5–12. Batnitzky, "Rosenzweig on Translation," pp. 141–142, contrasts the relation between speech and translation in Rosenzweig and Gadamer. According to Batnitzky, Gadamer privileges speech, whereas Rosenzweig makes translation primary. See idem, *Idolatry*, pp. 108–109. Gordon, *Rosenzweig and Heidegger*, p. 183, argues that Rosenzweig's hermeneutic "shares with Heidegger the existential and eminently *practical* dimension that is noticeably lacking in Gadamer" (emphasis in original). For a criticism of Gordon's position, see Fisher, *Contemplative Nation*, p. 182. In my assessment, Gadamer (and Heidegger as well) would have agreed with Rosenzweig's sense that all speech is "dialogic speaking and thus—translation" (*Scripture and Translation*, p. 47), the very assumption that makes translation both impossible and necessary. See Rosenzweig's "Afterword" (in the original 1927 edition, although subsequently printed as the Preface) to the translation of Halevi's poems in Galli, *Franz Rosenzweig and Jehuda Halevi*, p. 170 (Rosenzweig, *Jehuda Halevi. Fünfundneunzig Hymnen und Gedichte*, pp. 2–3): "Will this not be asking

something impossible of language with this task to reflect the foreign tone in its foreignness [*den fremden Ton in seiner Fremdheit wiederzugeben*]: not to Germanize what is foreign, but rather to make foreign what is German [*also nicht das Fremde einzudeutschen, sondern das Deutsche umzufremden*]? Not the impossible, but rather the requisite, and the requisite not merely in translating. The creative achievement of translating can lie nowhere else than where the creative achievement of speaking itself lies." See also Rosenzweig, *Ninety-Two Poems*, p. xlv; Rosenzweig, *The Commentaries of Franz Rosenzweig*, p. 383.

236. Rosenzweig, "Die Schrift und das Wort: Zur neuen Bibelübersetzung," in *Zweistromland*, p. 777; *Scripture and Translation*, p. 40.

237. Rosenzweig, "Neuhebräisch? Anläßlich der Übersetzung von Spinozas Ethik," in *Zweistromland*, p. 724, translation in Glatzer, *Franz Rosenzweig*, p. 264. Rosenzweig applies these words specifically to Jacob Klatzkin's Hebrew translation of Spinoza's *Ethics*, but I have taken the liberty of extending them to the phenomenon of translating revelatory speech more generally.

238. Rosenzweig's view is in accord with Gadamer's assertion, *Truth and Method*, p. 480, that the "hermeneutical experience" is also "the event of a genuine experience." The affinities and differences between Gadamer's hermeneutical approach and Rosenzweig are explored further by Batnitzky, *Idolatry*, pp. 44–46, 69, and 71. Rosenzweig's study "Das älteste Systemprogram des deutschen Idealismus" is alluded to in *Truth and Method*, p. 76, and cited explicitly on p. 99 n. 168, to substantiate Gadamer's discussion of the "romantic demand for a new mythology."

239. Rosenzweig, *Star of Redemption*, p. 213; *Stern der Erlösung*, pp. 221–222.

240. The transfiguration of the erotic imagery of the Song in later midrashic and poetic texts is explored by Michael Fishbane, "The Song of Songs and Ancient Jewish Religiosity: Between Eros and History," in *Von Enoch bis Kafka: Festschrift für Karl E. Grözinger zum 60. Geburtstag*, edited by Manfred Voigts (Wiesbaden: Harrassowitz Verlag, 2002), pp. 69–81.

241. Wolfson, *Language, Eros, Being*, p. 336.

242. Rosenzweig, *Star of Redemption*, p. 217; *Stern der Erlösung*, p. 225. I have modified Galli's translation "the essential book of Revelation." The meaning is not substantially altered. For an alternative rendering, see Hallo's translation of *The Star*, p. 202: "the focal book of revelation." And see Inken Rühle, "Das Hohelied—ein weltliches Liebeslied als Kernbuch der Offenbarung? Zur Bedeutung der Auslegungsgeschichte von *Schir haSchirim* im *Stern der Erlösung*," in *Rosenzweig als Leser: Kontextuelle Kommentare zum "Stern der Erlösung,"* edited by Martin Brasser (Tübingen: Max Niemeyer Verlag, 2004), pp. 453–479.

243. Rosenzweig, *Star of Redemption*, pp. 144–145; *Stern der Erlösung*, pp. 147–148 (cited above at n. 40). With regard to the understanding of system and the interconnectivity of all concrete singularities, there is an interesting affinity between Rosenzweig and the process thought of Whitehead. See Katrin Jona Kirchner, "Experience, the Principle of Relativity and the Function of Language in the Conceptions of Franz Rosenzweig and Alfred N. Whitehead," in *Faith, Truth, and Reason*, pp. 333–354.

244. Wolfson, "Facing the Effaced," pp. 77–78. In that study, I focused on the same passage of the *Star* that I interpret again in this context. To me, it is the crucial statement to understand Rosenzweig's theopoetics. The position I have taken is intermediate between the perspective of Mosès, *System and Revelation*, pp. 102–103, and that of Moyn, *Origins of the Other*, p. 150. According to the former, Rosenzweig's portrayal of love as a metaphor for revelation implies that the analysis of God's love for the human being is "only anthropomorphic in appearance," whereas, according to the latter, the reverse is true, and hence "human love is metaphorical of divine love." For an elaboration of his thesis, see Samuel Moyn, "Divine and Human Love: Franz Rosenzweig's History of the Song of Songs," *Jewish Studies Quarterly* 12 (2005): 194–212. See also Paul Mendes-Flohr, "Between Sensual and Heavenly Love: Franz Rosenzweig's Reading of the Song of Songs," in *Scriptural Exegesis—The Shapes of Culture and the Religious Imagination: Essays in Honour of Michael Fishbane*, edited by Deborah A. Green and Laura S. Lieber (Oxford: Oxford University Press, 2009), pp. 310–318; Simon, *Art and Responsibility*, pp. 104–107; Hanoch Ben-Pazi, "Love Discourse: Rosenzweig vs. Plato. The *Banquet*: *Song of Songs*, the *Symposium* and the *Star of Redemption*," in *Faith, Truth, and Reason*, pp. 105–124. On the comparison of Rosenzweig's use of the term *Gleichnis* in his interpretation of the Song of Songs to Scholem's understanding of the kabbalistic symbol as the expression of the inexpressible, see Benjamin, *Rosenzweig's Bible*, pp. 60–61. Unfortunately, she makes no mention of my previous discussions of this matter in "Facing the Effaced" or in the study cited below in n. 248.

245. Rosenzweig, *Star of Redemption*, p. 216 (translation modified); *Stern der Erlösung*, p. 224. Rosenzweig uses the expression *sinnlich-übersinnliche* to characterize the love of God in his commentary on Halevi's poem translated as *Der Wahre*; see Ch. 1 n. 16.

246. Rosenzweig, *Star of Redemption*, p. 216; *Stern der Erlösung*, p. 224.

247. Rosenzweig, *Star of Redemption*, p. 216; *Stern der Erlösung*, p. 224.

248. See Elliot R. Wolfson, "Suffering Eros and Textual Incarnation: A Kristevan Reading of Kabbalistic Poetics," in *Toward a Theology of Eros: Transfiguring Passion at the Limits of Discipline*, edited by Virginia Burrus and Catherine Keller (New York: Fordham University Press, 2006), pp. 342–343, 346–353. See as well Rühle, "Das Hohelied," pp. 472–478. Worthy of recollection here is the discussion of lyric poetry as the most suitable expression of the human love of God, in Cohen, *Religion of Reason*, pp. 373–374; *Religion der Vernunft*, pp. 433–434. It is reasonable to assume that the reading of the erotic metaphors in the Song proffered by Rosenzweig reflects the discussion of Cohen, though the matter requires a more sustained reflection. See the discussion of lyric poetry and prayer in Poma, *Yearning for Form*, pp. 227–241. Finally, I would add that Rosenzweig's perspective, if I have understood it properly, seems to me proximate to the observation of Gadamer regarding the reformation of intuition through metaphor in his essay "Intuition and Vividness," translated by Dan Tate, in Hans-Georg Gadamer, *The Relevance of the Beautiful and Other Essays*, edited with an introduction by Robert Bernasconi (Cambridge: Cambridge University Press, 1986), pp. 169–170: "For the theory of metaphor, Kant's remark in Section 59 [of the *Critique of Judgment*] seems to me most

profound: that metaphor at bottom makes no comparison of content, but rather undertakes the 'transference of reflection upon an object of intuition to a quite different concept to which perhaps an intuition can never directly correspond.' Does not the poet do that with every word? The poet suspends every direct correspondence and thereby awakens intuition." See below, n. 261.

249. Consider Rosenzweig's comment in "Scripture and Word: On the New Bible Translation" (1925), in Buber and Rosenzweig, *Scripture and Translation*, p. 45: "For poetry is indeed the mother tongue of the human race; we need not reject here the insights of Hamann and Herder." On the similarities between the theories of language in Hamann and Rosenzweig, see Rivka Horwitz, "Hamann and Rosenzweig on Language—The Revival of Myth," *Da'at* 38 (1997): v–xxviii. See also Galli, *Franz Rosenzweig and Jehuda Halevi*, p. 380. Some of the affinities between Rosenzweig and Heidegger with regard to their respective discussions of language might be explicable on the basis of a shared indebtedness to the linguistic turn in German philosophy exemplified by figures such as Hamann, Herder, and Humboldt. See Cristina Lafont, *Heidegger, Language, and World-Disclosure*, translated by Graham Harman (Cambridge: Cambridge University Press, 2000), pp. 1–7, 11, 35, 41, 51, 67–68, 76, 81–82, 90–91, 102–104, 155; Knut M. Stünkel, "Die Sprache bei Hamann und Heidegger," *Neue Zeitschrift für systematische Theologie und Religionsphilosophe* 46 (2004): 26–55; Robert Alan Sparling, *Johann Georg Hamann and the Enlightenment Project* (Toronto: University of Toronto Press, 2011), pp. 216–219. On the role of poetry in Judah Halevi and Rosenzweig as the "language of existence," see Cohen, *The Natural and the Supernatural Jew*, pp. 146–148.

250. Rosenzweig, *Zweistromland*, pp. 3–44, esp. 22–27; and compare Ernest Rubinstein, *An Episode of Jewish Romanticism: Franz Rosenzweig's The Star of Redemption* (Albany: State University of New York Press, 1999), pp. 221–222; Gordon, *Rosenzweig and Heidegger*, pp. 126–129. For discussion of the intellectual background of Schelling on this point, see Theodore D. George, "A Monstrous Absolute: Schelling, Kant, and the Poetic Turn in Philosophy," in *Schelling Now: Contemporary Readings*, edited by Jason M. Wirth (Bloomington: Indiana University Press, 2005), pp. 135–146. Many have discussed Rosenzweig's indebtedness to Schelling, and here I offer a highly select enumeration: Moshe Schwarcz, *From Myth to Revelation* (Tel-Aviv: Hakibbutz Hameuchad, 1978), pp. 238–242 (Hebrew); idem, "Atheism," pp. 130–131, 143–149; Freund, *Franz Rosenzweig's Philosophy of Existence*; Wolfdietrich Schmied-Kowarzik, "Vom Totalexperiment des Glaubens. Kritisches zur positive Philosophie Schellings und Rosenzweigs," in *Der Philosoph Franz Rosenzweig*, pp. 771–799; idem, "Einführende Bemerkungen zu Schelling und Rosenzweig," in *Kabbala und Romantik*, edited by Eveline Goodman-Thau, Gert Mattenklott, and Christoph Schulte (Tübingen: Max Niemeyer Verlag, 1994), pp. 59–68, reprinted in Schmied-Kowarzik, *Rosenzweig im Gespräch*, pp. 46–59; Robert Gibbs, "The Limits of Thought: Rosenzweig, Schelling, and Cohen," *Zeitschrift für Philosophische Forschung* 43 (1989): 618–640; Rubinstein, *An Episode of Jewish Romanticism*; Benny Lévy, "Philosophie de la Révélation? Schelling, Rosenzweig, Levinas," *Cahiers d'Études Lévinassinnes* 2 (2003): 283–383; John R. Betz, "Schelling in Rosenzweigs *Stern der*

Erlösung," *Neue Zeitschrift für Systematische Theologie und Religionsphilosophie* 45 (2003): 208–226; Bienenstock, "Recalling the Past," pp. 234–237; idem, "Auf Schellings Spuren im Stern der Erlösung," in *Rosenzweig als Leser*, pp. 273–290; Schindler, *Zeit, Geschichte, Ewigkeit*, pp. 229–246; Fisher, "Divine Perfections," pp. 201–205; idem, *Contemplative Nation*, pp. 192–195.

251. Rosenzweig, *Star of Redemption*, pp. 348–349; *Stern der Erlösung*, p. 365. See analysis in William Kluback, "Time and History: The Conflict Between Hermann Cohen and Franz Rosenzweig," in *Der Philosoph Franz Rosenzweig*, pp. 801–813, reprinted in William Kluback, *The Legacy of Hermann Cohen* (Atlanta: Scholars Press, 1989), pp. 43–56; Von Ulrich Hortian, "Zeit und Geschichte bei Franz Rosenzweig und Walter Benjamin," in *Der Philosoph Franz Rosenzweig*, pp. 815–827, esp. 819–820; Wolfson, "Facing the Effaced," pp. 60–61.

252. Rosenzweig, *Star of Redemption*, p. 206; *Stern der Erlösung*, p. 213. Here it is also useful to recall Rosenzweig's description in the outline for a series of lectures at the Berlin Lehrhaus (delivered January–March 1921) on the ritual life of Judaism as "wholly artwork" (*ganz Kuntswerk*), cited by Batnitzky, "Rosenzweig on Translation," p. 137. On Rosenzweig's aesthetics, see also Angel E. Garrido-Maturano, "Die Erfüllung der Kunst im Schweigen: Bemerkungen zu Franz Rosenzweigs Theorie der Kunst," in *Théologie négative*, pp. 695–720, esp. 706–709; Simon, *Art and Responsibility*, pp. 49–51, 65, 99–104, 111–151; Wayne Cristaudo, *Religion, Redemption, and Revolution: The New Speech Thinking of Franz Rosenzweig and Eugen Rosenstock-Huessy* (Toronto: University of Toronto Press, 2012), pp. 310–324. See also Luc Anckaert, "Language, Ethics, and the Other between Athens and Jerusalem: A Comparative Study of Plato and Rosenzweig," *Philosophy East and West* 45 (1995): 545–567, esp. 555–560.

253. Rosenzweig, *Star of Redemption*, p. 263; *Stern der Erlösung*, p. 273. On the link between the Jewish national spirit, the art of music, and the sense of time, see the comments of Martin Buber in his 1911 essay "Renewal of Judaism," in *On Judaism*, edited by Nahum N. Glatzer (New York: Schocken Books, 1967), p. 49.

254. On the notion of Jewish *Unheimlichkeit* in Rosenzweig's thinking, see Leora Batnitzky, "Rosenzweig's Aesthetic Theory and Jewish Unheimlichkeit," *New German Critique* 77 (1999): 87–122; idem, "Rosenzweig on Translation," pp. 138–141; idem, *Idolatry*, pp. 83–104. For an analysis of the broader cultural context of this image, see Susan Shapiro, "The Uncanny Jew: A Brief History of an Image," *Judaism* 46 (1997): 63–78. Santner, *On the Psychotheology of Everyday Life*, pp. 5–8, 23–24, discusses the matter of *Unheimlichkeit* in Rosenzweig in more general terms with respect to the sense of the uncanny, the impenetrability of the other, that is internal to any construction of identity. Gordon, *Rosenzweig and Heidegger*, p. 227, argues that the insight into the "uncanny" quality of the human condition in the world is what perhaps "most unites the philosophies of Rosenzweig and Heidegger. In sum, both *The Star of Redemption* and *Being and Time* are in part meditations upon the ungroundedness of human meaning. Rosenzweig interprets this ungroundedness as the truth of Jewish exile; Heidegger speaks of all human being as grounded in the 'un-ground' of nothingness." My own

analysis of homelessness in Rosenzweig closely parallels that of Louis P. Blond, "Franz Rosenzweig: Homelessness in Time," *New German Critique* 37 (2010): 27–58, an essay that appeared after the original version of this chapter was published.

255. Rosenzweig, *Star of Redemption*, p. 319; *Stern der Erlösung*, p. 333.

256. Alexander Altmann, "Franz Rosenzweig on History," in *The Philosophy of Franz Rosenzweig*, pp. 124–137. See also Glatzer, *Franz Rosenzweig*, p. xxv; Paul Mendes-Flohr, "Franz Rosenzweig and the Crisis of Historicism," in *The Philosophy of Franz Rosenzweig*, pp. 138–161; Steven T. Katz, "On Historicism and Eternity: Reflections on the 100th Birthday of Franz Rosenzweig," in *Der Philosoph Franz Rosenzweig*, pp. 745–769; Amos Funkenstein, "An Escape from History: Rosenzweig on the Destiny of Judaism," *History and Memory* 2 (1990): 117–135; Vogel, *Rosenzweig on Profane/Secular History*; Wolfson, "Facing the Effaced," pp. 55–63; Gordon, "Rosenzweig Redux," p. 18; David N. Myers, *Resisting History: Historicism and Its Discontents in German-Jewish Thought* (Princeton: Princeton University Press, 2003), pp. 68–101.

257. Galli, *Franz Rosenzweig and Jehuda Halevi*, p. 177; Rosenzweig, *Jehuda Halevi. Fünfundneunzig Hymnen und Gedichte*, p. 10. See also Rosenzweig, *Ninety-Two Poems*, p. lii; Rosenzweig, *The Commentaries of Franz Rosenzweig*, p. 390.

258. Rosenzweig, *Star of Redemption*, pp. 320–321; *Stern der Erlösung*, pp. 334–335. On the holiness of the Hebrew language, see also Rosenzweig, "Neuhebräisch?," in *Zweistromland*, pp. 725–728, translation in Glatzer, *Franz Rosenzweig*, pp. 265–269. In that context, Rosenzweig reiterates his view that there is both an eternal and a temporal component of Hebrew. The former concerns its status as a holy language, the "language of God" (*Sprache Gottes*) that cannot be made profane, whereas the latter relates to the fact that this language is always unfolding and changing in time as the "spoken language" (*gesprochenen Sprache*) of lived Jewish communities. The eternal dimension is referred to as the "naked truth" (*nackte Wahrheit*), and the temporal as the "naked untruth" (*nackte Unwahrheit*). Neither has the power to survive unless it is "clothed," but once clothed they appear to be like one another (*Zweistromland*, p. 725, translation in Glatzer, *Franz Rosenzweig*, p. 265). See William Cutter, "Ghostly Hebrew, Ghastly Speech: Scholem to Rosenzweig, 1926," *Prooftexts* 10 (1990): 413–433, esp. 424–427.

259. Rosenzweig, *Star of Redemption*, p. 321 (translation modified); *Stern der Erlösung*, pp. 335–336. On silence and gesture in Rosenzweig, see Düttmann, *The Gift of Language*, pp. 23–26.

260. Galli, *Franz Rosenzweig and Jehuda Halevi*, p. 177; Rosenzweig, *Jehuda Halevi. Fünfundneunzig Hymnen und Gedichte*, p. 10. See also Rosenzweig, *Ninety-Two Poems*, pp. lii–liii; Rosenzweig, *The Commentaries of Franz Rosenzweig*, p. 391.

261. Heidegger, *Early Greek Thinking*, p. 19; *Holzwege*, p. 328. The bibliography on Heidegger's poetics is enormous. Here I mention only a modest number of applicable studies: Walter Biemel, "Poetry and Language in Heidegger," in *On Heidegger and Language*, edited and translated by Joseph J. Kockelmans (Evanston: Northwestern University Press, 1972), pp. 65–105; and in the same volume the essays by Henri Birault,

"Thinking and Poeticizing in Heidegger," pp. 147–168, and Werner Marx, "The World Is Another Beginning: Poetic Dwelling and the Role of the Poet," pp. 235–259; David A. White, *Heidegger and the Language of Poetry* (Lincoln: University of Nebraska Press, 1978); Véronique M. Fóti, *Heidegger and the Poets: Poiēsis/Sophia/Technē* (Atlantic Highlands: Humanities Press,1992); Ziarek, *Inflected Language*, pp. 21–42; Marc Froment-Meurice, *That Is to Say: Heidegger's Poetics*, translated by Jan Plu (Stanford: Stanford University Press, 1998); Jennifer Anna Gosetti-Ferencei, *Heidegger, Hölderlin, and the Subject of Poetic Language: Towards a New Poetics of Dasein* (New York: Fordham University Press, 2004); Philippe Lacoue-Labarthe, *Heidegger and the Politics of Poetry*, translated and with an introduction by Jeff Fort (Urbana: University of Illinois Press, 2007); Pol Vandevelde, *Heidegger and the Romantics: The Literary Invention of Meaning* (New York: Routledge, 2012), pp. 77–171; and see my own discussion in *Language, Eros, Being*, pp. 17–25, and the accompanying notes on pp. 412–419. Rosenzweig's views on poetry can also be compared effectively to the reflections of Gadamer on this matter. For a helpful analysis of the latter, see Gerald L. Bruns, "The Remembrance of Language: An Introduction to Gadamer's Poetics," in Hans-Georg Gadamer, *Gadamer on Celan: "Who Am I and Who Are You?" and Other Essays*, translated and edited by Richard Heinemann and Bruce Krajewski (Albany: State University of New York Press, 1997), pp. 1–51. See also James Risser, "Poetic Dwelling in Gadamer's Hermeneutics," *Philosophy Today* 38 (1994): 369–379.

262. Gordon, *Rosenzweig and Heidegger*, pp. 130–131. On the affinity between Greece and Germany in Heidegger's poetical thinking, see Babette E. Babich, *Words in Blood, Like Flowers: Philosophy and Poetry, Music and Eros in Hölderlin, Nietzsche, and Heidegger* (Albany: State University of New York Press, 2006), pp. 227–241.

263. As is well known, in a brief note dictated from his deathbed, which was occasioned by the publication of the second edition of Cohen's *Religion der Vernunft aus den Quellen des Judentums* but which also included his reflections on the confrontation that took place in Davos, Switzerland, between Ernst Cassirer and Martin Heidegger (based on the report by Hermann Herrigel in the *Frankfurter Zeitung* of April 22, 1929), Rosenzweig noted some similarities between Heidegger's thought and Cohen's theory of correlation as well as his own new thinking. The text, "Vertauschte Fronten," written in May 1929, was first published in *Der Morgen* 6, 6 (April 1930): 85–87, reprinted several times, including in *Zweistromland*, pp. 323–326. An English translation, "Transposed Fronts," appears in *Philosophical and Theological Writings*, pp. 146–152. Concerning this episode, see Gordon, *Rosenzweig and Heidegger*, pp. 284–294; idem, "Continental Divide: Ernst Cassirer and Martin Heidegger at Davos, 1929—An Allegory of Intellectual History," *Modern Intellectual History* 1 (2004): 219–248; idem, *Continental Divide: Heidegger, Cassirer, Davos* (Cambridge, MA: Harvard University Press, 2010); and the recent analysis in William H. F. Altman, *Martin Heidegger and the First World War: Being and Time as Funeral Oration* (Lanham: Lexington Books, 2012), pp. 47–78. For further discussion of Rosenzweig's assessment of the event, see Freund, *Franz Rosenzweig's Philosophy of Existence*, p. 78; Schwarzschild, "Franz Rosenzweig and Martin

Heidegger," pp. 887–889; Mosès, *System and Revelation*, pp. 290–291; Gordon, "Rosen-zweig and Heidegger," pp. 113–114; idem, *Rosenzweig and Heidegger*, pp. 275–304; Moyn, *Origins of the Other*, pp. 114–115. It appears from an anecdote related by Strauss, "An Introduction to Heideggerian Existentialism," p. 28, that he was the one to inform Rosenzweig of the preeminence of Heidegger as a thinker. In the same context, Strauss briefly recounts the aforementioned debate at Davos. On Heidegger's relationship to Cassirer, see the nuanced discussion in Kluback, *The Idea of Humanity*, pp. 117–130.

264. For discussion of this Heideggerian theme, with citation of relevant sources, see Wolfson, *Alef, Mem, Tau*, pp. 42–46. It is worthwhile considering the following com-ment of Rosenzweig, *Understanding the Sick*, p. 74, in light of the Heideggerian orienta-tion toward language, being, and human existence: "The world is real only insofar as it enters into this process, a process which brings all of it within the context of the human word and God's sentence. The world as such does not exist. To speak of the world is to speak of a world which is ours and God's. It becomes the world as it becomes man's and God's world. Every word spoken within its confines furthers this end. This is the ultimate secret of the world. Or rather, this would be its ultimate secret, if there were anything secret. But common sense blurts out this secret every day. . . . We face the world each day innocently and fearlessly, considering it as the ultimate that it is; we confront all of its reality, willing to submit to each name. We are certain that our names are the names of things and that the name we bestow will be confirmed by God." Heidegger would have rejected the ontotheological tenor of Rosenzweig's account, but there is a correspondence between the two thinkers with regard to the positing of a world that is independent of and yet only realized through the human act of naming. On the affinities between Rosenzweig and Heidegger related to the poetic nature of thought and its inflection in language, see Glatzer, *Franz Rosenzweig*, p. xxvi; Yudit Kornberg Greenberg, "Martin Heidegger and Franz Rosenzweig on the Limits of Language and Poetry," *History of European Ideas* 20 (1993): 791–800; idem, *Better Than Wine*, pp. 52–56. With respect to the nexus between language and being, we can detect a similarity in the *sprachdenken* affirmed respectively by Heidegger and Rosenzweig, on the one hand, and the kabbalah, on the other hand. See Habermas, *Philosophical-Political Profiles*, p. 24; Wolfson, *Language, Eros, Being*, pp. 10–25; Bouretz, *Witnesses for the Future*, p. 160. Compare Johanna Junk, *Metapher und Sprachmagie, Heidegger und die Kabbala: Eine philosophische Untersuchung* (Bodenheim: Syndikat Buchgesellschaft, 1998). Even though the author does not engage the kabbalistic texts independently, many of the conclusions she reached, as well her interpretive strategies (including a comparative analysis of Heidegger and Wittgenstein), are corroborated by my own work. For scholarly analyses of the thought of these two thinkers, see the sources cited in Wolfson, *Language, Eros, Being*, p. 410 nn. 127–129, to which I would now add Gianni Vattimo, *The Adventure of Difference: Philosophy after Nietzsche and Heidegger*, translated by Cyprian Blamires with the assistance of Thomas Harrison (Baltimore: Johns Hopkins University Press, 1993), pp. 110–112, 124, and Lee Braver, *Groundless Grounds: A Study of Wittgenstein and Heidegger* (Cambridge, MA: MIT Press, 2012). Finally, it is of interest to recall here the

observation of Scholem, "Franz Rosenzweig and His Book," p. 35, that "in his comments both on language and on time-bound thought, Rosenzweig is in very close agreement with the disdained Kabbalah." See above at n. 82.

265. See, for instance, Heidegger, *Poetry, Language, Thought*, p. 92 (*Holzwege*, pp. 269–270): "The word for abyss—*Abgrund*—originally means the soil and ground toward which, because it is undermost, a thing tends downward. But in what follows we shall think of the *Ab-* as the complete absence of the ground [*das völlige Abwesen des Grundes*]." For an alternate translation, see Heidegger, *Off the Beaten Track*, p. 200.

266. See the comprehensive analysis in Robert Mugerauer, *Heidegger and Homecoming: The Leitmotif in the Later Writings* (Toronto: University of Toronto Press, 2008), pp. 93–136. See also Brendan O'Donoghue, *A Poetics of Homecoming: Heidegger, Homelessness and the Homecoming Venture* (Newcastle: Cambridge Scholars, 2011). On Heidegger's engagement with Hölderlin, see Holger Helting, *Heideggers Auslegung von Hölderlins Dichtung des Heiligen: Ein Beitrag zur Grundlagenforschung der Daseinanalyse* (Berlin: Duncker & Humblot, 1999), and Gosetti-Ferencei, *Heidegger, Hölderlin, and the Subject of Poetic Language*, pp. 61–98. For Rosenzweig's engagement with Hölderlin's *Patmos*, see Rosenstock, *Philosophy and the Jewish Question*, pp. 140–142. Interestingly, in his 1930 memorial address to Rosenzweig, Scholem began with a citation from *Patmos*. See Scholem, "Franz Rosenzweig and His Book," pp. 20–21.

267. Martin Heidegger, *On the Way to Language*, translated by Peter D. Hertz (San Francisco: Harper & Row, 1971), p. 123; *Unterwegs zur Sprache* [GA 12] (Frankfurt am Main: Vittorio Klostermann, 1985), p. 242. See analysis and citation of other sources in Wolfson, *Language, Eros, Being*, pp. 14–17. Especially relevant is the aphorism on "Poetizing and thinking in their relation to the word" in Martin Heidegger, *The Event*, translated by Richard Rojcewicz (Bloomington: Indiana University Press, 2013), § 374, p. 289; *Das Ereignis* [GA 71] (Frankfurt am Main: Vittorio Klostermann, 2009), p. 333. After stating that the "word" does not belong to or arise from either poeticizing (*Dichten*) or thinking (*Denken*), Heidegger notes, "The difference between poetry and thinking is also not that the former is granted the imagistic word [*bildhafte Wort*] and the latter is compelled to imagelessness [*bildlose*]; or that the poetic word is sensuous and intuitional, the word of thinking conceptual. These are distinctions deriving from metaphysics and therefore are essentially unsuited for clarifying the essence of the word and the essence of the relation of poetizing and thinking to the word." To get beyond metaphysics to a true understanding of the essence of the word, which will facilitate an understanding of the relation of poetry to thought, the distinction between the verbal and the visual must be dismantled.

268. Rosenzweig, *Star of Redemption*, p. 263; *Stern der Erlösung*, p. 273. On the imagistic dimension of language in Rosenzweig, see Schwartz, *Metapher und Offenbarung*, pp. 75–102. I note, finally, that a similar view to Rosenzweig's notion of the poetic as the language that exceeds language, the nonphenomenal form that takes shape beyond the phenomenal limits of the metaphoric— an unbridgeable gap traversed by a verbal leap from the visible to the invisible—was articulated by Celan, *The Meridian*, p. 74 (*Der*

Meridian, p. 74): "The poem is the place where all synonymy ends; where all tropes and everything improper is led ad absurdum; the poem has, I believe, even there where it is most graphic, an anti-metaphorical character [*antimetaphorischen Charakter*]; the image has a phenomenal trait, intuitively recognizable.—What separates you from it, you will not bridge; you have to make up your mind to jump [*du mußt dich zum Sprung entschließen*]." Compare Celan, *The Meridian*, pp. 104–105 (*Der Meridian*, pp. 104–105): "The poem is inscribed as the figure of the complete language [*Figur der ganzen Sprache*]; but language remains invisible [*aber die Sprache bleibt unsichtbar*]; that which actualizes itself—language—takes steps, as soon as that has happened, back into the realm of the possible. 'Le Poème', writes Valéry, est du langage à l'état naissant; language in statu nascendi, thus language in the process of liberation [*freiwerdende Sprache*]. . . . The poem comes into being through intercourse with something that remains invisible to us: through intercourse with language." See the analysis in Pajari Räsänen, "Counter-figures—An Essay on Antimetaphoric Resistance: Paul Celan's Poetry and Poetics at the Limits of Figurality," Ph.D. dissertation, University of Helsinki, 2007, pp. 173–182. On the poetic leap, see as well Celan, *The Meridian*, p. 133 (*Der Meridian*, p. 133): "Leap—as entrance into the poem [*Sprung—als Eintritt ins Gedicht*]" and "Leap (O. Becker). creat. Leap of the poet [*Sprung des Dichters*], creat. Leap of the reader [*Sprung des Lesers*] (you)—prerequisite (not guarantee!) is the being-turned-toward-each-other [*das Einanderzugewendetsein*]." See the discussion of these marginal notes in Räsänen, "Counter-figures," p. 172 n. 348. See also the language of Levinas describing Celan cited in Ch. 3 at n. 157.

269. Rosenzweig, *Star of Redemption*, p. 263; *Stern der Erlösung*, p. 273.

270. Galli, *Franz Rosenzweig and Jehuda Halevi*, p. 340: "Only through the creative spirit can and do past, present, and future find for themselves a certain mutuality. Eternity *and* time, that is, the oneness of eternality and the plurality of the tenses, interconnect and are bridged by the creative spirit" (emphasis in original). See above, n. 78.

271. Rosenzweig, *Star of Redemption*, p. 263; *Stern der Erlösung*, p. 273.

272. Rosenzweig, *Star of Redemption*, p. 313; *Stern der Erlösung*, p. 328.

273. Rosenzweig, *Star of Redemption*, p. 313; *Stern der Erlösung*, p. 328.

274. This obvious point was made explicitly by Cohen, *Religion of Reason*, pp. 73–74; *Religion der Vernunft*, pp. 85–86. See also the more extensive discussion of religion as idolatry and negative theology in the fourth chapter of Cohen, *Ethics of Maimonides*, pp. 77–105.

275. Rosenzweig offers a terse summary of his view of the messianic future in the commentary to Judah Halevi's poem *yashen we-libbo er*, which he renders as *Auf*, "No longer a dialogue . . . but only one is still speaking, the One. Thus no longer present tense, but rather future, no longer drama, but rather vision" (Galli, *Franz Rosenzweig and Jehuda Halevi*, p. 258; Rosenzweig, *Jehuda Halevi. Fünfundneunzig Hymnen und Gedichte*, p. 201. See also Rosenzweig, *Ninety-Two Poems*, p. 215; Rosenzweig, *The Commentaries of Franz Rosenzweig*, p. 300). It is of interest to compare Rosenzweig's

eschatological vision with the following account of Heidegger offered by Hannah
Arendt, *The Life of the Mind*, 2 vols. (New York: Harcourt Brace Jovanovich, 1978), 1:122,
"in Heidegger the moment of illumination is understood as 'lightning' (*Blitz*), and
finally replaced by an altogether different metaphor, *das Geläut der Stille*, 'the ringing
sound of silence.' In terms of the tradition, the latter metaphor is the closest approxima-
tion to the illumination arrived at in speechless contemplation." For Heidegger, the
culmination of thinking involves a shift from the ocular to the auditory, whereas for
Rosenzweig, the end is marked by the ocular overcoming the auditory. It would seem,
then, that Rosenzweig was not able to overturn the predominance of sight in the history
of Western philosophy. I would argue nonetheless that there is a shared sense in both
thinkers related to the presumption that the final stage of the contemplative path is an
illumination of silent listening, a mental state of pure receptivity, which is expressed
either as a hearing without words or as a seeing without object.

276. Rosenzweig, *Star of Redemption*, p. 440; *Stern der Erlösung*, p. 464.

277. Rosenzweig, *Star of Redemption*, pp. 330–332; *Stern der Erlösung*, pp. 346–347.

278. Rosenzweig, *Star of Redemption*, p. 333; *Stern der Erlösung*, p. 348.

279. The allusion is to Isaiah 58:13.

280. Rosenzweig, *Star of Redemption*, p. 333; *Stern der Erlösung*, pp. 348–349. The
silence associated with Sabbath as a prolepsis of redemption was noted by Glatzer, "The
Concept of Language," pp. 181–182.

281. Rosenzweig, *Star of Redemption*, p. 443; *Stern der Erlösung*, p. 467.

282. I have here reworked my formulation in *Alef, Mem, Tau*, pp. 176–177.

283. Rosenzweig, *Star of Redemption*, p. 440; *Stern der Erlösung*, p. 464.

284. Rosenzweig, *Star of Redemption*, pp. 123–124; *Stern der Erlösung*, pp. 124–125. See
Luca Bertolino, "'Schöpfung aus Nichts' in Franz Rosenzweigs Stern der Erlösung,"
Jewish Studies Quarterly 13 (2006): 247–264, esp. 260–262; Schindler, *Zeit, Geschichte,
Ewigkeit*, pp. 154–161, esp. 157–158.

285. Rosenzweig, *Star of Redemption*, p. 196; *Stern der Erlösung*, p. 203.

286. Mosès, *System and Revelation*, p. 285; Richard A. Cohen, *Elevations: The Height of
the Good in Rosenzweig and Levinas* (Chicago: University of Chicago Press, 1994),
pp. 241–273; Kornberg Greenberg, *Better Than Wine*, pp. 113–118; Wolfson, "Facing the
Effaced," pp. 74–76; Horwitz, "From Hegelianism," pp. 45–46.

287. Rosenzweig, "The New Thinking," pp. 136–137; *Zweistromland*, p. 160.

288. Rosenzweig, *Star of Redemption*, p. 441; *Stern der Erlösung*, p. 465.

289. Rosenzweig, *Star of Redemption*, p. 441; *Stern der Erlösung*, p. 465.

290. Rosenzweig, "The New Thinking," p. 136; *Zweistromland*, p. 159.

291. Rosenzweig, *Star of Redemption*, p. 31; *Stern der Erlösung*, p. 25.

292. In this regard, it is of interest to note the view of Arthur H. Armstrong, *Plotinian
and Christian Studies* (London: Variorum Reprints, 1970), pp. 185–188, that apophatic
theology and moderate skepticism were two closely aligned trends of thinking that
emerged from Platonism. For citation and analysis of some of the appropriate texts, see
John P. Kenney, "The Critical Value of Negative Theology," *Harvard Theological Review*

86 (1993): 441–443. On the link between atheism and apophasis in Late Antiquity, see D. W. Palmer, "Atheism, Apologetic, and Negative Theology in the Greek Apologists of the Second Century," *Vigiliae Christianae* 37 (1983): 234–259.

293. Rosenzweig, *Star of Redemption*, p. 196; *Stern der Erlösung*, p. 202.

294. Regarding this subject, see Shlomo Pines, "Islam According to *The Star of Redemption*: Toward a Study of Franz Rosenzweig's Sources and Biases," *Bar-Ilan Yearbook* 22–23 (1987–88): 303–314 (Hebrew), and the German version, "Der Islam im 'Stern der Erlösung.' Eine Untersuchung zu Tendenzen und Quellen Franz Rosenzweigs," *Hebräische Beiträge zur Wissenschaft des Judentums* 3–5 (1987–89): 138–148; Matthias Lehmann, "Franz Rosenzweigs Kritik des Islam im 'Stern der Erlösung,'" *Jewish Studies Quarterly* 1 (1993/94): 340–361; Rose, *Judaism and Modernity*, pp. 137, 142–143; Gil Anidjar, *The Jew, the Arab: A History of the Enemy* (Stanford: Stanford University Press, 2003), pp. 87–98 (for a critique of Anidjar, see Cristaudo, *Religion, Redemption, and Revolution*, pp. 138–140); Yossef Schwartz, "Die Entfremdete Nähe: Rosenzweigs Blick auf den Islam," in *Franz Rosenzweig "Innerlich Bleibt die Welt Eine": Ausgewählte zum Islam*, edited by Gesine Palmer and Yossef Schwartz (Berlin: Philo, 2003), pp. 113–147; Wayne Cristaudo, "Franz Rosenzweig's 'Troubling' Critique of Islam," *Rosenzweig Yearbook* 2 (2007): 43–86; idem, *Religion, Redemption, and Revolution*, pp. 401–415.

295. Jacques Derrida, *On the Name*, edited by Thomas Dutoit, translated by David Wood, John P. Leavey Jr., and Ian McLeod (Stanford: Stanford University Press, 1995), p. 36; *Sauf le nom* (Paris: Galilée, 1993), p. 16. See also "How to Avoid Speaking: Denials," in Jacques Derrida, *Psyche: Inventions of the Other, Volume II*, edited by Peggy Kamuf and Elizabeth Rottenberg (Stanford: Stanford University Press, 2008), pp. 143–195. The bibliography on Derridean deconstruction and the apophatic orientation is quite substantial. I will mention here only a sampling of available scholarly treatments: Kevin Hart, *The Trespass of the Sign: Deconstruction, Theology and Philosophy* (Cambridge: Cambridge University Press, 1989), pp. 183–194; Toby A. Foshay, "Denegation, Nonduality, and Language in Derrida and Dōgen," *Philosophy East and West* 44 (1994): 543–558; idem, "Introduction: Denegation and Resentment," in *Derrida and Negative Theology*, edited by Howard Coward and Toby Foshay (Albany: State University of New York Press, 1992), pp. 1–24; David E. Klemm, "Open Secrets: Derrida and Negative Theology," in *Negation and Theology*, edited by Robert P. Scharlemann (Charlottesville: University Press of Virginia, 1992), pp. 8–24; Mark C. Taylor, "Non-Negative Negative Atheology," *Diacritics* 20 (1990): 2–16; idem, "nO nOt nO," in *Derrida and Negative Theology*, pp. 167–198, reprinted in idem, *Nots* (Chicago: University of Chicago Press, 1993), pp. 29–54; Martin C. Srajek, *In the Margins of Deconstruction: Jewish Conceptions of Ethics in Emmanuel Levinas and Jacques Derrida* (Dordrecht: Kluwer Academic Publishers, 1997), pp. 214–233, 255–257; Thomas Ryba, "Derrida, Negative Theology and the Trespass of the Sign," *Religion* 27 (1997): 107–115; John D. Caputo, *The Prayers and Tears of Jacques Derrida: Religion without Religion* (Bloomington: Indiana University Press, 1997), pp. 1–68; idem, "Shedding Tears Beyond Being: Derrida's Experience of Prayer," in

Théologie négative, pp. 861–880; Shira Wolosky, "An 'Other' Negative Theology: On Derrida's 'How to Avoid Speaking: Denials,'" *Poetics Today* 19 (1998): 261–280; Marion, "In the Name," pp. 20–53; Robyn Horner, "Derrida and God: Opening a Conversation," *Pacifica* 12 (1999): 12–26, esp. 17–21; Hent de Vries, *Philosophy and the Turn to Religion* (Baltimore: John Hopkins University Press, 1999), pp. 305–358; idem, "The Theology of the Sign and the Sign of Theology: The Apophatics of Deconstruction," in *Flight of the Gods*, pp. 166–194, reprinted in idem, *Minimal Theologies*, pp. 631–657; Ilse N. Bulhof, "Being Open as a Form of Negative Theology: On Nominalism, Negative Theology, and Derrida's Performative Interpretation of Khôra," in *Flight of the Gods*, pp. 195–222; Rubenstein, "Unknow Thyself"; Hugh Rayment-Pickard, *Impossible God: Derrida's Theology* (Burlington: Ashgate, 2003), pp. 123–134; Arthur Bradley, "Without Negative Theology: Deconstruction and the Politics of Negative Theology," *Heythrop Journal* 42 (2001): 133–147; idem, *Negative Theology and Modern French Philosophy* (London: Routledge, 2004), pp. 11–46; Dirk Westerkamp, *Via Negativa: Sprache und Methode der negativen Theologie* (Munich: Wilhelm Fink Verlag, 2006), pp. 200–209; idem, "Naming and Tetragrammatology: Medieval Apophatic Philosophy and Its Double Helix," in *Jewish Lifeworlds and Jewish Thought: Festschrift Presented to Karl E. Grözinger on the Occasion of his 70th Birthday*, edited by Nathanael Riemer (Wiesbaden: Harrassowitz Verlag, 2012), pp. 121–122; William Franke, "Apophasis and the Turn of Philosophy to Religion: From Neoplatonic Negative Theology to Postmodern Negation of Theology," *International Journal for Philosophy of Religion* 60 (2006): 61–76; Min, "Naming the Unnameable God"; Steven Shakespeare, *Derrida and Theology* (New York: Continuum, 2009), pp. 100–123; David Newheiser, "Time and the Responsibilities of Reading: Revisiting Derrida and Dionysius," in *Reading the Church Fathers*, pp. 23–43. For critical assessments of the endeavor to construct a negative atheology on the basis of Derridean deconstruction, see Robert S. Gall, "Of/From Theology and Deconstruction," *Journal of the American Academy of Religion* 58 (1990): 413–437; Clayton Crockett, "Post-Modernism and Its Secrets: Religion without Religion," *Cross Currents* 52 (2003): 499–515; Siebren Miedema and Gert J. J. Biesta, "Jacques Derrida's Religion without Religion and the Im/Possibility of Religious Education," *Religious Education* 99 (2004): 23–37; Martin Hägglund, *Radical Atheism: Derrida and the Time of Life* (Stanford: Stanford University Press, 2008), pp. 116–120, 144–145; Christopher J. Knight, *Omissions Are Not Accidents: Modern Apophaticism From Henry James to Jacques Derrida* (Toronto: University of Toronto Press, 2010), pp. 91–99. See also the reservations expressed by Rodolphe Gasché, *Inventions of Difference: On Jacques Derrida* (Cambridge, MA: Harvard University Press, 1994), pp. 160–167. Finally, mention should be made of Marion's remark, "In the Name," p. 40, that one can "make a favorable comparison between 'negative theology' and atheism or establish a rivalry between it and deconstruction" if one focuses in on the "second way" of apophasis, which is predicated in Husserlian terms on the insufficiency of intuition to grasp the intentional object. By contrast, with respect to the "third way," which relates to the gesture of de-nomination between affirmation and negation, the comparison of atheism and negative theology is no longer relevant because the "excess of intuition overcomes, submerges, in short saturates, the measure of each and every concept. What is given disqualifies every concept." My own understanding is such that the denominated notion of the saturated phenomenon still leads to the atheistic overcoming of theism. The theistic structure dissolves in the excess of being that is neither something that is not nor nothing that is, the Ein Sof of the kabbalistic tradition according to my interpretation. See Elliot R. Wolfson, "Nihilating Nonground and the Temporal Sway of Becoming: Kabbalistically Envisioning Nothing Beyond Nothing," *Angelaki* 17 (2012): 31–45, parts of which are reworked in the section "Polysemy, Atheism, and the Apophatic Overcoming of Ontotheology" in Ch. 4.

296. I have reproduced the translation in Derrida, *On the Name*, p. 36; *Sauf le nom*, pp. 16–17. The letter of Leibniz is cited by Heidegger, *The Principle of Reason*, p. 35; *Der Satz vom Grund*, pp. 53–54. See the passages from Heidegger cited in Ch. 6 at nn. 80–81.

297. Derrida, *On the Name*, p. 36; *Sauf le nom*, p. 18. See analysis in Wyschogrod, *Crossover Queries*, pp. 22–23, and Kearney, *Anatheism*, p. 63. A similar argument has been made by Arthur Bradley, " 'Mystic Atheism': Julia Kristeva's Negative Theology," *Theology & Sexuality* 14 (2008): 279–292. Consider the summation of Bradley's argument: "If Kristeva's work could profitably be described as an *attempt* to write a 'religion without religion', however—which could then be compared to that of Heidegger, Levinas, Marion and perhaps even Derrida himself—the question of whether she manages to strike the right balance between repetition and difference, orthodoxy and heterodoxy, fidelity and rupture signified by that ambiguous preposition 'with/out' still remains open to question. The possibility I want to raise here will be that her attempt to offer a *nondogmatic* repetition of religious dogma in the form of psychoanalysis runs the risk of illicitly *dogmatizing* or *mythologizing* the psychoanalytic project itself. There is an important sense in which her psychoanalytic critique of Christianity remains—both wittingly and unwittingly—complicit with the Judaeo-Christian theology she is attempting to question. This will lead us to the conclusion that Kristeva's so called 'mystic atheism' might best be understood as a contemporary *manifestation* of negative theology that, as we will see, offers a *via negativa* of the *subject* as opposed to *god*" (p. 287, emphasis in original). For discussion of Kristeva's view of negative theology and the technological nature of the sacred, see Bradley, *Negative Theology*, pp. 150–185. On the notion of mystical atheism in Simone Weil, see below, n. 300, and the extension of her category to the existential philosophy of Jean-Paul Sartre in Altizer, *Mircea Eliade*, pp. 130–139.

298. Derrida, *Dissemination*, p. 344.

299. Edward Baring, *The Young Derrida and French Philosophy, 1945–1968* (Cambridge: Cambridge University Press, 2011), p. 63.

300. Taubes, "The Absent God," p. 6 (emphasis in original). On Weil's mystical atheism, see Preface n. 38.

301. Hägglund, *Radical Atheism*, p. 145.

302. Rosenzweig, *Star of Redemption*, pp. 314–315; *Stern der Erlösung*, pp. 329–330.

303. I would like to take this opportunity to acknowledge a mistake in the transcription of this passage in Elliot R. Wolfson, *Open Secret: Postmessianic Messianism and the*

Mystical Revision of Menaḥem Mendel Schneerson (New York: Columbia University Press, 2009), p. 266. Unfortunately, in the process of copyediting, the words "those who have the strength of faith to be deceived" were omitted. I thank David Aaron for calling this error to my attention. The matter has been corrected in the second edition of the book, published in 2012.

304. Galli, *Franz Rosenzweig and Jehuda Halevi*, p. 259; Rosenzweig, *Jehuda Halevi. Fünfundneunzig Hymnen und Gedichte*, pp. 202–203. See also Rosenzweig, *Ninety-Two Poems*, p. 217; Rosenzweig, *The Commentaries of Franz Rosenzweig*, p. 302.

305. Derrida, *Psyche: Inventions of the Other, Volume II*, pp. 234–236.

306. Rosenzweig, *Star of Redemption*, p. 31; *Stern der Erlösung*, p. 25.

307. Rosenzweig, *Star of Redemption*, p. 31; *Stern der Erlösung*, pp. 25–26.

308. Rosenzweig, *Zweistromland*, p. 100.

309. Cohen, *Ethics of Maimonides*, p. 83; "Charakteristik," p. 207. The passage is cited in Ch. 1 at n. 20.

310. Ibid., p. 85. See also *Reason and Hope*, p. 178, and discussion in Zank, *The Idea of Atonement*, pp. 354–355.

311. Cohen, *Ethics of Maimonides*, pp. 85–86: "Nicholas of Cusa could afford to play with the ambiguities of pantheism in a daring and meaningful fashion since he could use them to expound the mystery of the trinity. In contrast, Maimonides guards himself against the serpent of pantheism, although he is not disinclined toward the enchantment of neo-Platonism." And see Cohen's summation on pp. 98–99: "As a result of all these reflections, we may conclude that the negative attributes, of which Maimonides could avail himself, must inevitably take as their premise and prerequisite the privative attributes, in so far as we relate them to God. . . . Instead of saying that Maimonides advocates the doctrine of negative attributes, we ought to say that he admits only those negative attributes that imply the negation of a privative attribute. Maimonides proposes by no means merely a *docta ignorantia*. . . . He is not even ultimately concerned only with the unknowability of God's essence. Rather, by multiplying negations, Maimonides promotes the true, seminal (ethical) cognition of God. . . . Jewish philosophy prior to Maimonides had followed the path indicated by the neo-Platonists who had advocated the doctrine of negative attributes. . . . Maimonides' criticism, however, expresses itself more pointedly and more radically. He puts forward his critique even at the risk of exposing himself to the suspicion of dispensing with the knowledge of God and of depriving it of all content. Why does he commit himself to this course and why did he feel impelled to do so? We know the focus of his thinking: it lies in ethics. Consequently, he has to negate, concerning the content of Knowing God, anything based upon privation . . . in that it creates a link between God and something else by analogy or through any other relationship. . . . Maimonides relates God exclusively to ethics. Hence the only admissible divine attributes are attributes of action." Although I appreciate the motivation for Cohen to forge an intrinsic connection between the Maimonidean *via negativa* and ethics, such that the grounding of the ethical rests on a lack of knowledge of the divine that facilitates the functioning of goodness as the transcendental limit

(ibid., p. 102), I am not convinced of the soundness or accuracy of this interpretation, either textually or conceptually, but this is a matter that cannot be pursued here. On the approach of Maimonides to the problem of negative attribution, see Cohen, *Religion of Reason*, pp. 61–66; *Religion der Vernunft*, pp. 71–76.

312. On Rosenzweig's indebtedness to Cohen in this matter of the nothing and the principle of the origin (*Ursprung*), see the comments of Bruckstein in Cohen, *Ethics of Maimonides*, pp. 88–89, 102. See, however, Rubinstein, *An Episode of Jewish Romanticism*, p. 186. The author notes the influence of Cohen on Rosenzweig's attempt to philosophize anew from the standpoint of the particular Naught, but he also emphasizes that the deduction of reality from nothing is not the latter's own project. See Westerkamp, *Via Negativa*, pp. 188–191; and, more recently, Luca Bertolino, "Die frage ‚Was ist?' bei Hermann Cohen und Franz Rosenzweig," *Journal of Jewish Thought and Philosophy* 21 (2013): 57–71.Bertolino notes that in response to the primary philosophical question "what is?" (τί ἐστι), Cohen and Rosenzweig offer diverse approaches but they both oppose an ontological reductionism predicated on the identity of being and thought.

313. Rosenzweig, *Star of Redemption*, pp. 31–32; *Stern der Erlösung*, p. 26.

314. Rosenzweig, *Star of Redemption*, p. 32; *Stern der Erlösung*, p. 26.

315. Consider the observation of Armstrong, *Plotinian and Christian Studies*, p. 185, that negative theology consists "in a critical negation of all affirmations which one can make about God, followed by an equally critical negation of our negations." The comment is cited by Kenney, "Critical Value," p. 440. My interpretation of Rosenzweig should be compared to William Franke, "Franz Rosenzweig and the Emergence of a Postsecular Philosophy of the Unsayable," *International Journal for Philosophy of Religion* 58 (2005): 161–180. Even though we approach the subject from different angles, there is a fundamental agreement with regard to Rosenzweig's embrace of an apophatic logic or grammar (p. 169), according to which any form of discourse is a linguistic delimitation of an infinitely unsayable ground. My own thesis accords with the following observations of Franke: "Because language remains conversant with the nothing of its elements, a linguistic thinking is able to keep in view, peripherally at least, the Nothing underlying every revelation, every articulation of being and essence. From beyond all manner of verbal determinations, in which our experience consists, language can recall and call forth the unrepresentable, unsayable sea of Nothing on which it surfs and skims. Only this skipping and skidding of language demarcates temporally the eternal abyss of nothing—that is, nothing sayable—which is otherwise imperceptible, giving it positive inflections by delimitation and qualification. . . . To know nothing of God is a way of being in relation to the whole of life and existence as infinite and unknowable . . . This unknowing is far more vital and potent than any positive knowing—in fact, all positive knowing is contained proleptically therein and can only be a working out and an articulating of a relation to some virtual wholeness that is as such unsayable . . . For Rosenzweig, knowledge and its articulation in language, the whole intricate network of mutual relations and disclosure of things, is a veiling of the separate, unspeakable reality of each of his elements—God, World, Man—which are *not* as such, all one, *not* any All. In the relations of Creation,

Revelation, and Redemption, these elements are disclosed and articulated in relation to one another, but in themselves they remain pure enigma, each an ineffable mystery that no concept can grasp" (pp. 170–172, emphasis in original). I comply as well with Franke's conclusion that Rosenzweig "effectively gives a philosophical rationale for the sorts of theosophies that have traditionally been overtly apophatic in purport and intent," though I would, however, respectfully disagree with the statement that "Rosenzweig does not present his philosophy expressly as apophatic" (p. 177). I have argued, to the contrary, that apophasis is the key to understanding how Rosenzweig presented his thought. In consonance with this philosophical orientation, the explicit articulation is concomitantly a saying and an unsaying. Consider the judicious comment of Cohen, *The Natural and the Supernatural Jew*, p. 132: "God begins with the Nothing and moves to infinite fullness. With impassioned language reminiscent of the seventeenth-century German Protestant mystic Jacob Boehme, Rosenzweig sees God passing through the anguish of the *Mysterium Magnum*; the small spark catches fire and burns, the *ungrund* locates its *grund*, the No of the Nothing is denied and out of denial God affirms Himself."

316. Rosenzweig, *Star of Redemption*, p. 32; *Stern der Erlösung*, p. 26.

317. Gibbs, *Correlations*, pp. 48–52; Peter E. Gordon, "Science, Finitude, and Infinity: Neo-Kantianism and the Birth of Existentialism," *Jewish Social Studies* 6 (1999): 30–53; idem, *Rosenzweig and Heidegger*, pp. 47–51, 169; Moyn, *Origins of the Other*, p. 145; Schindler, *Zeit, Geschichte, Ewigkeit*, pp. 132–135; Pierfrancesco Fiorato and Hartwig Wiedebach, "Hermann Cohen im Stern der Erlösung," in *Rosenzweig als Leser*, pp. 317–331.

318. See Helmut Holzhey, "Heidegger und Cohen. Negativität im Denken des Ursprungs," in *In Erscheinung treten. Heinrich Barths Philosophie des Ästhetischen*, edited by Günther Hauff, Hans Rudolf Schweizer, and Armin Wildermuth (Basel: Schwabe, 1990), pp. 97–114; Adelmann, *Einheit des Bewusstseins*, pp. 276–289; Biemann, *Inventing New Beginnings*, pp. 60–61, 90. On the relationship between these two thinkers, see also William Kluback, "Hermann Cohen und Martin Heidegger: Meinungsverschiedenheit oder Entstellung?" *Zeitschrift für philosophische Forschung* 40 (1986): 283–287; idem, *The Idea of Humanity*, pp. 118–119. And compare Christoph von Wolzogen, "Negation und Alterität: Der 'Abgrund der Vernunft' bei Cohen, Heidegger und Levinas," in *Verneinung, Andersheit und Unendlichkeit im Neukantianismus*, pp. 93–106 (reprinted from Wolzogen, *Emmanuel Levinas*, pp. 190–204).

319. Cohen, *Religion of Reason*, p. 66; *Religion der Vernunft*, p 76.

320. Rosenzweig, *Star of Redemption*, pp. 27–28; *Stern der Erlösung*, p. 23. On the influence of Cohen's discussion of the mathematical differential on Rosenzweig's idea of the determinate nothing, see Pollock, *Franz Rosenzweig*, pp. 151–152.

321. Rosenzweig, *Star of Redemption*, p. 28; *Stern der Erlösung*, p. 23.

322. John H. Smith, "The Infinitesimal as Theological Principle: Representing the Paradoxes of God and Nothing in Cohen, Rosenzweig, Scholem, and Barth," *Modern Language Notes* 127 (2012): 571.

323. Kavka, *Jewish Messianism*, pp. 135–136. On the infinitesimal in Cohen's thought, see also Gregory B. Moynahan, "Hermann Cohen's *Das Prinzip der Infinitestimalmethod*,

Ernst Cassirer, and the Politics of Science in Wilhelmine Germany," *Perspectives on Science* 11 (2003): 35–75; Weiss, *Paradox and the Prophets*, pp. 181–192; Adelmann, *Einheit des Bewusstseins*, pp. 214–216; Smith, "The Infinitesimal," pp. 562–588. My own sense of the infinitesimal accords with Smith's perspective, which he summarizes on p. 565: "The idea of the infinitesimal, as Deleuze emphasizes in his book on Leibniz and the baroque, sees reality not as discrete objects, parts and wholes, but as an infinite range of degrees in the play of continuity and difference between nothing and something. Since the infinite is not an object of sensual or any other kind of intuition (*Anschauung*), but only a product of thought, i.e., it is a principle of Cohen's 'erkenntniskritischen Idealismus . . . dass die Welt der Dinge auf dem Grunde der Gesetze des Denkens beruht' (*Infinitesimal-Methode* 125)."

324. My thinking here is in agreement with Gibbs, "The Limits of Thought." My conjecture regarding Rosenzweig also has affinity to the hypothesis proffered by Lazier, *God Interrupted*, p. 184, that Scholem translated Cohen's distinction between the "nothing of the zero" and the "negation out of which . . . originary thought could emerge" into the terms *efes* and *ayin* in the "lexicon of the kabbalah" to mark the emanation of *Keter*, the divine nothingness, from Ein Sof, the infinite beyond all manifestation. As Lazier notes, *ad locum*, "Scholem also picked up on another crucial aspect of Cohen's argument, and which Rosenzweig, too, had made his own: the notion of privation." Lazier's surmise regarding Cohen and Scholem is developed further by Smith, "The Infinitesimal," pp. 579–583.

325. As cited in Horwitz, "From Hegelianism," p. 40.

326. Rosenzweig, *Star of Redemption*, p. 34; *Stern der Erlösung*, pp. 28–29.

327. Rosenzweig, *Star of Redemption*, pp. 35–36; *Stern der Erlösung*, pp. 29–30. My interpretation is a response to John Llewelyn, *Emmanuel Levinas: The Genealogy of Ethics* (London: Routledge, 1995), pp. 152–153, who argues that Rosenzweig's discussion of God's infinite essence represents a place of schism between his thinking and Levinas's emphasis on the beyond-essence. In my judgment, Rosenzweig's own words should not be accorded an ontological sense; the divine essence of which he speaks is not an identifiable and knowable substance or a metaphysical presence. It is the not-nothing that precedes both the something and the nothing.

328. Horwitz, "From Hegelianism," p. 40.

329. Pollock, "On the Road to Marcionism," pp. 242–243.

330. See Elliot R. Wolfson, "The Engenderment of Messianic Politics: Symbolic Significance of Sabbatai Ṣevi's Coronation," in *Toward the Millennium: Messianic Expectations from the Bible to Waco*, edited by Peter Schäfer and Mark Cohen (Leiden: Brill, 1998), pp. 212–216. Consider the sagacious observation of Rose, *Judaism and Modernity*, p. 146: "On the one hand, love has *form*—it has the form of commandment . . . On the other hand, consummated love dissolves the boundaries of these forms—it prostrates itself, it *dies* into love, it obliterates heaven, earth, world. The creative violence in effective form which makes possible the free act is always displaced by the destructive violence of this effacing love—this is the *gnostic* moment, at the heart

of *The Star of Redemption*, its grammar of pathos, which makes it so difficult to sustain a politics" (emphasis in original). Rosenzweig's embrace of a messianism borne out of a pessimistic stance regarding the nature of the world and the current political order fits within a larger trend among German-Jews in the first decades of the twentieth century that equally opposed the progressive impulses of both secular rationalism and traditional orthodox eschatology. See Anson Rabinbach, "Between Enlightenment and Apocalypse: Benjamin, Bloch, and Modern Jewish Messianism," *New German Critique* 34 (1985): 78–124, esp. 80–81; Michael Löwy, "Walter Benjamin and Franz Rosenzweig: Messianism against „Progress"," in *Faith, Truth, and Reason*, pp. 373–390. On the complex reactions to the restorative and revolutionary messianism of the nineteenth century in German thinkers between the world wars, see Klaus Schreiner, "Messianism in the Political Culture of the Weimar Republic," in *Toward the Millennium*, pp. 311–361.

331. Rosenzweig, *Star of Redemption*, p. 290; *Stern der Erlösung*, p. 303, and see discussion in Wolfson, "Facing the Effaced," pp. 69–70.

332. Idel, *Old Worlds*, pp. 162–163. Horwitz, "From Hegelianism," pp. 37–38, notes this passage and refers to Idel's work, but she still suggests that Rosenzweig was not familiar with the Lurianic teaching at the time that he composed the *Star*.

333. Rosenzweig, *Philosophical and Theological Writings*, pp. 56–57; *Zweistromland*, p. 128. For discussion of this passage, see Schindler, *Zeit, Geschichte, Ewigkeit*, pp. 232–233. On the affinity between Schelling and the kabbalistic idea of ṣimṣum, see Christoph Schulte, "Zimzum in the Works of Schelling," *Iyyun* 41 (1992): 21–40. See also Wolfson, *Alef, Mem, Tau*, pp. 37–38, and references to other scholars cited on pp. 194–195 n. 233 and p. 197 n. 250.

334. Wolfson, *Alef, Mem, Tau*, pp. 119–122. On Heidegger, Rosenzweig, and the kabbalah, see above, nn. 11 and 20, and the comments in the following two notes.

335. Freund, *Franz Rosenzweig's Philosophy of Existence*, p. 89, asserts that the Nought affirmed by Rosenzweig is "completely different" from "the Nought of which Martin Heidegger speaks . . . Heidegger's Nought also is not a formal one; it signifies an absolute, real Nought, a *nihil absolutum*, that one can also perceive as death. The state of being contained within this Nought is called existence. . . . In the case of Rosenzweig, however, the Nought with which the construction begins comes into action only when the consciousness of being is already well established. It is placed before this being that precedes thought merely hypothetically in order to make possible the conceptual, constructive re-creation of the experienced threefold being. . . . If the Nought of Heidegger is an extra-conceptual, non-rational Nought, then the Nought of Rosenzweig is a conceived Nought that is not purely formal only because of the devaluation of thinking itself." In the case of Rosenzweig, insofar as "thinking is subordinate to the factuality that is prior to thinking," the Nought is conceived as Nought on the basis of something experienced, and it is therefore "differential." Freund does admit, however, that only "when faith negates thinking as a whole, does the Nought of Rosenzweig also assume the features of a real Nought, a 'dark depth,' by which it then moves nearer to the Nought of Heidegger." In my judgment, the concluding sentence is crucial, and I

agree that Rosenzweig ends up in a position that is very close to Heidegger, and both of them can be viewed as creative interpreters of Schelling. See also the perceptive quip of Levinas, *Time and the Other*, p. 49: "One can also find this turning of nothingness into existing in Heidegger. The Heideggerian nothingness still has a sort of activity and being: 'nothingness nothings.' It does not keep still. It affirms itself in this production of nothingness." In the accompanying n. 21, reference is made to Heidegger's 1929 essay "What Is Metaphysics?" where the expression *das Nichts nichtet* appears, and to § 58 of *Being and Time*, "where Heidegger links nothingness and existence." For a lucid analysis of metaphysics and the nothing, see Blond, *Heidegger and Nietzsche*, pp. 31–53.

336. On the comparison of Heidegger's conception of nothingness and the domain of Being's withdrawal to the kabbalistic speculation on the Infinite and the idea of *ṣimṣum*, see Marlène Zarader, *The Unthought Debt: Heidegger and the Hebraic Heritage*, translated by Bettina Bergo (Stanford: Stanford University Press, 2006), pp. 130–138. Zarader's approach, which is similar to my own, forges a new path in seeking tacit affinities between Heidegger and Jewish mysticism. The more typical approach is summarized by Otto Pöggeler, "Heidegger's Topology of Being," in *On Heidegger and Language*, p. 146: "Heidegger sees an unbridgeable cleft between his thought and the tradition of the Old Testament." Also relevant are the comments on Heidegger's discussion of the nothing and Scholem's remarks about the kabbalistic interpretation of *creatio ex nihilo* as *creatio ex Deo* in the essay by Jacob Taubes, "From the Adverb 'Nothing' to the Substantive 'Nothing': Deliberations on Heidegger's Question Concerning Nothing," in *From Cult to Culture: Fragments Toward a Critique of Historical Reason*, edited by Charlotte E. Fonrobert and Amir Engel, with an introduction by Aleida Assmann, Jan Assmann, and Wolf-Daniel Hartwich (Stanford: Stanford University Press, 2010), pp. 124–136, esp. 132–134. I do not concur with Taubes's conclusion that "Heidegger does not sustain the mystic-theological tradition from Johannes Scotus Eriugena to Jakob Böhme and Schelling, but he presumes the revelation of the orthodox phrase *creatio ex nihilo* that persists in the Christian mystic tradition . . . . The expression 'the Nothing' that Heidegger introduces does not mean the nihil of the mystic tradition: it is a 'Nothing of Dasein.'" See my own analysis in Wolfson, "Nihilating Nonground," pp. 31–34, 40–41.

337. Heidegger, *Contributions*, § 90, p. 140; *Beiträge*, p. 178.

338. Heidegger, *Contributions*, § 129, p. 194; *Beiträge*, pp. 246–247.

339. Heidegger, *Contributions*, § 242, pp. 301–302; *Beiträge*, pp. 381–382. On Heidegger's notion of attunement to truth, see Rodolphe Gasché, "Tuned to Accord: On Heidegger's Concept of Truth," in *Heidegger toward the Turn*, pp. 31–49.

340. See Reiner Schürmann, "Ultimate Double Binds," in *Heidegger toward the Turn*, pp. 260–262.

341. Rosenzweig, *Star of Redemption*, p. 27; *Stern der Erlösung*, p. 22.

342. Rosenzweig, *Star of Redemption*, p. 124; *Stern der Erlösung*, p. 125. See Pollock, *Franz Rosenzweig*, pp. 137–138.

343. Rosenzweig, *Star of Redemption*, p. 126; *Stern der Erlösung*, p. 128.

344. Rosenzweig, *Star of Redemption*, pp. 126–127; *Stern der Erlösung*, p. 128.

345. Rosenzweig, *Star of Redemption*, pp. 123–124; *Stern der Erlösung*, pp. 124–125.

346. Wolfson, *Alef, Mem, Tau*, p. 59.

347. My position is in accord with the conclusion reached by Pollock, *Franz Rosenzweig*, p. 140: "In the Idealist account of the original identity of the All as a kind of nothingness we thus find that the Idealist 'one-and-universal Nothing' which Rosenzweig opposes is not merely 'nothing at all' in the superficial sense . . . But neither is the Idealist nothing particular or determined as is Rosenzweig's 'nothing.' Rather, *the opposition between Rosenzweig's nothing and the Idealist nothing proves to be an opposition between a 'nothing' that is 'something' and a 'nothing' that is at once already 'all'*" (emphasis in original).

348. Rosenzweig, *Star of Redemption*, p. 124; *Stern der Erlösung*, p. 125.

349. Rosenzweig, "The New Thinking," pp. 114–115; *Zweistromland*, pp. 142–143.

350. Rosenzweig, *Star of Redemption*, p. 411; *Stern der Erlösung*, p. 432.

351. Rosenzweig, *Star of Redemption*, p. 411; *Stern der Erlösung*, p. 432.

352. Rosenzweig, *Star of Redemption*, p. 411; *Stern der Erlösung*, p. 432.

353. Rosenzweig, *Star of Redemption*, p. 415; *Stern der Erlösung*, p. 436.

354. Rosenzweig, *Star of Redemption*, p. 411; *Stern der Erlösung*, p. 432.

355. It is of interest to note Rosenzweig's rendering of the penultimate line in Halevi's poem that begins *yah shimkha aromimkha we-ṣidqatkha lo akhasseh*, entitled *Gelobt!* The Hebrew reads, *ki tidrosh be-sof u-ve-ro'sh ba-mufle u-va-mekhusseh*, which translates as "If you seek / in the end and in the beginning / in that which is wondrous / and that which is covered." Rosenzweig, *Jehuda Halevi. Fünfundneunzig Hymnen und Gedichte*, p. 24, translates: "Forsch we viel! / Keim ruht und Ziel / in Wunder und / Verborgenheit." See Galli, *Franz Rosenzweig and Jehuda Halevi*, p. 18: "Search and search! / The seed and goal rest / in miracle / and concealment." For an alternative translation, see Rosenzweig, *Ninety-Two Poems*, p. 8.

356. Kierkegaard, *Concluding Unscientific Postscript*, pp. 245–246: "All paganism consists in this, that God is related directly to a human being, as the remarkably striking to the amazed. But the spiritual relationship with God in truth, that is, inwardness, is first conditioned by the actual breakthrough of inward deepening that corresponds to the divine cunning that God has nothing remarkable, nothing at all remarkable, about him—indeed, he is so far from being remarkable that he is invisible, and thus one does not suspect that he is there [*er til*], although his invisibility is in turn his omnipresence. . . . This relation between omnipresence and invisibility is like the relation between mystery and revelation, that the mystery expresses that the revelation is revelation in the stricter sense, that the mystery is the one and only mark by which it can be known. . . . In paganism, the direct relation is idolatry; in Christianity, everyone indeed knows that God cannot manifest himself in this way." The likely influence of Kierkegaard on Rosenzweig's criticism of Hegel's idealism is noted by Ricoeur, *Figuring the Sacred*, p. 105.

357. Rosenzweig, *Star of Redemption*, pp. 411–412; *Stern der Erlösung*, p. 433.

358. Rosenzweig, *Star of Redemption*, p. 414; *Stern der Erlösung*, pp. 435–436.

359. Kavka, *Jewish Messianism*, p. 14, and the elaboration of the argument on pp. 135–157.

360. Rosenzweig, *Star of Redemption*, p. 412; *Stern der Erlösung*, p. 433.

361. Rosenzweig, *Star of Redemption*, p. 412; *Stern der Erlösung*, p. 433.

362. Rosenzweig, *Star of Redemption*, p. 255; *Stern der Erlösung*, p. 265. Aaron W. Hughes, *The Art of Dialogue in Jewish Philosophy* (Bloomington: Indiana University Press, 2008), pp. 173–174, correctly notes that, for Rosenzweig, the dialogic gives way to silence, but that silence, paradoxically, can be glimpsed only from the vantage point of anticipation, which requires speech for its articulation. Instead of thinking of silence and language as binary oppositions, we should think of language that "both speaks and unspeaks, says and unsays." At the "heart of Rosenzweig's thought," therefore, is the "anticipation of language for speaking," which is "a silence that articulates." A similar sentiment was expressed by Kornberg Greenberg, *Better Than Wine*, p. 63, when she noted that, in contrast to Heidegger and Levinas, "for Rosenzweig, silence is a great moment of bliss. This moment is in the realm of linguistic *manifestation* rather than in the sphere of concealment" (emphasis in original). See also Franke, "Franz Rosenzweig," p. 175: "The only articulable, systematizeable knowledge is knowledge of what is *not* man, *not* world, *not* God, for these elements are all in their own nature unknowable. To this extent, everything within the purview of language and revelation is but a reference to what is not . . . every determination in language is but a delimitation of something that exceeds language" (emphasis in original).

363. Rosenzweig, *Star of Redemption*, p. 309; *Stern der Erlösung*, p. 324.

364. Rosenzweig, *Star of Redemption*, p. 412; *Stern der Erlösung*, pp. 433–434.

365. See above, n. 212.

366. Wolfson, *Alef, Mem, Tau*, pp. 74, 76, 92, 93, 108, 109, and the corresponding notes for references to primary sources. For an extended analysis of the name in Rosenzweig, see Nadine Schmahl, *Das Tetragramm als Sprachfigur: Ein Kommentar zu Franz Rosenzweigs letztem Aufsatz* (Tübingen: Mohr Siebeck, 2009).

367. Rosenzweig, "The New Thinking," p. 136; *Zweistromland*, pp. 159–160.

368. Rosenzweig, *Star of Redemption*, pp. 412–413; *Stern der Erlösung*, p. 434.

369. Rosenzweig, *Star of Redemption*, p. 413; *Stern der Erlösung*, p. 434.

370. Rosenzweig, *Star of Redemption*, p. 29; *Stern der Erlösung*, p. 24.

371. Rosenzweig, *Star of Redemption*, p. 413; *Stern der Erlösung*, p. 434.

372. From my poem that Galli included in the "Translator's Acknowledgments" in Rosenzweig, *Star of Redemption*, p. x.

373. For a more hopeful assessment of this possibility, see Ilse N. Bulhof, "Negative Theology as Spirituality: Deep Openness," in *Théologie négative*, pp. 423–441.

374. See, however, Franke, "Franz Rosenzweig," pp. 174–175: "Negative theology claims no positive knowledge of God, but it does so in order to free the relation to God from all the pretences of finite concepts so as to allow the inconceivable *reality or irreality* of divinity to be fully experienced, or at least sensed, in unknowing. This is essentially

what Rosenzweig's whole philosophy does. In positioning himself against a certain narrow formulation of negative theology, Rosenzweig is actually renovating the deeper insight of apophatic thinking in all ages. His thinking opens upon what cannot be said and makes that the basis for all that is in any way affirmed. . . . It is a knowing of the nothingness of our knowledge, but this itself opens to a revelation of the positive relatedness of all things, of their forming an All, after all—albeit an All that cannot be said, one that can be grasped by neither thought nor word" (emphasis added). There is much in this statement that overlaps with my own analysis, but there is one critical difference. Franke does not seem to appreciate the extent to which this apophatic turn challenges the theistic faith that Rosenzweig sought to affirm against the prevalent atheistic theologies of his day. From that standpoint, it is not sufficient to speak of the "inconceivable reality or irreality of divinity to be fully experienced," nor is it satisfactory to depict revelation as an opening to the All that is beyond reason and language. What is lost is the personal God of the Jewish tradition. Rosenzweig's thought does renovate the "deeper insight of apophatic thinking," but it is important to understand how this conflicts with his own stated goal vis-à-vis the liturgical and ritual demands of Judaism.

375. Rosenzweig, "The New Thinking," p. 131; *Zweistromland*, p. 155.

376. Rosenzweig, "The New Thinking," p. 132; *Zweistromland*, pp. 155–156.

377. Derrida, *On the Name*, p. 52; *Sauf le nom*, p. 49.

378. See above, n. 360.

379. François Nault, "Le Discours de la doublure: Nietzsche et la théologie négative," *Religiogiques* 12 (1995): 273–294.

380. Based on Rosenzweig's account of revelation in his commentary to Halevi's poem *ye'iruni be-shimkha ra'ayoni*, which I will cite in full: "God reveals in revelation always only just this—revelation. In other words, he reveals always only Himself to the human, to the human only. The accusative and dative in its union is the peculiar content of revelation. Whatever does not follow immediately from this bond established here between God and human, whatever cannot verify its unmediatedness to this bond, does not belong to it. The problem has not been solved for the seer of the vision, but rather—it moves into the past. The miracle does not astonish him, but rather the vision has given him the courage to bow down before the source of the miracle. Out of the problem of thought has arisen a strength of heart" (Galli, *Franz Rosenzweig and Jehuda Halevi*, pp. 187–188; Rosenzweig, *Jehuda Halevi. Fünfundneunzig Hymnen und Gedichte*, p. 29; see also Rosenzweig, *Ninety-Two Poems*, p. 13; Rosenzweig, *The Commentaries of Franz Rosenzweig*, p. 42). A portion of the passage is cited in Glatzer, *Franz Rosenzweig*, p. 285. See analysis of Franks and Morgan, *Philosophical and Theological Writings*, pp. 87–88, and Franks, "Everyday Speech," p. 30. A similar formulation was used in Rosenzweig's letter to Buber (June 5, 1925), in Rosenzweig, *Briefe und Tagebücher*, vol. 1, p. 1040: *"So ist Offenbarung sicher nicht Gesetzgebung; sie ist überhaupt nur—Offenbarung. Sie hat unmittelbar nur sich selbst zum Inhalt."* The passage is translated in Franz Rosenzweig, *On Jewish Learning*, edited by Nahum N. Glatzer (New York: Schocken, 1955), p. 118: "Thus revelation is certainly not Law-giving. It is only this: Revelation. The primary content of

revelation is revelation itself." See Gershom Scholem, *On the Kabbalah and Its Symbolism*, translated by Ralph Manheim (New York: Schocken Books, 1969), pp. 50–51 n. 3. An almost identical formulation appears in Michel Henry, *The Essence of Manifestation*, translated by Girard Etzkorn (The Hague: Martinus Nijhoff, 1973), § 37, p. 286: "The manner in which the essence originally presents itself to itself, whereby it reveals itself, this is what presents itself originally to itself, what reveals itself in the revelation of the essence and constitutes it. This is why *the content of revelation is revelation itself*, why it is the Parousia itself which makes itself present to itself in the Parousia, because the revelation is in itself, because the Parousia is in its structure, Unity" (emphasis added).

381. Rosenzweig, *Understanding the Sick*, p. 68. Support for my interpretation may be culled from the hitherto unpublished document analyzed in Benjamin Pollock, "'Within Earshot of the Young Hegel': Rosenzweig's Letter to Rudolf Ehrenberg of September 1910," in *German-Jewish Thought Between Religion and Politics*, pp. 185–207, esp. 200–201. Pollock, no doubt, would not agree with my assessment that the Nietzschean death of God and the consequent need for humans to create new values in a world bereft of an absolute persist in Rosenzweig's later theological turn. I read the *Star* as a noble but tragic attempt to find a way beyond his earlier rejection of the Hegelian belief in the presence of God in history and the consequent sense of world-denial (what Pollock has identified as Rosenzweig's Marcionism; see above, n. 142) and the inevitable reduction of the divine to a metaphorical construct of the human imagination.

382. Rosenzweig, *Understanding the Sick*, pp. 45, 53, 55.

383. Rosenzweig, "A Note on Anthropomorphisms," p. 138; *Zweistromland*, p. 737. See Batnitzky, *Idolatry*, p. 21. I am not persuaded by the reading of this passage offered by Franks, "Everyday Speech," pp. 31–32. That is to say, I do not impute to the author a misreading, but I do not think he has pushed Rosenzweig hard enough, and hence he does not interrogate the philosophical tenability of revelatory speech, an interrogation that is justified by Rosenzweig's sway of thinking. See my comments in Ch. 1 n. 131.

384. Rosenzweig, "A Note on Anthropomorphisms," pp. 144–145; *Zweistromland*, p. 741.

385. Rosenzweig, "A Note on Anthropomorphisms," p. 145; *Zweistromland*, p. 741.

386. Wolfson, "*Via Negativa*," pp. 407–415. See, however, Hilary Putnam, "On Negative Theology," *Faith and Philosophy* 14 (1997): 419. Putnam concludes his essay on the *via negativa* in Maimonides by referring to Rosenzweig's insistence (read in a distinctly Wittgensteinian way; see above, n. 62) that it is the "primal right" of human beings "to give names, to create and speak languages—but our language is also the language that we use to speak to God, and that God uses to speak to us in scripture. *That* religious language connects us to God is something one can feel with one's whole being, not something that one can *explain*. *Pace*, Maimonides, it is not the theoretical intellect that connects us to the Divine" (emphasis in original). I do not disagree with the final statement, which does mark an essential difference between Maimonides and Rosenzweig, but Putnam's presentation relates to only a part of the whole story. One cannot ignore Rosenzweig's complex discussion of negative theology at the beginning of

the *Star* and his embrace of silence at the end. The positive affirmation of language has to be examined within the framework of these apophatic bookends. Putnam's position, without explicit reference to Rosenzweig, is reiterated in his "God and the Philosophers," *Midwest Studies in Philosophy* 21 (1997): 175–187.

387. Theo de Boer, "Levinas and Negative Theology," in *Théologie négative*, pp. 849–859. The interpretation of Levinas offered in the concluding paragraph underscores the similarity of his thought to Rosenzweig: "There is a line from negative theology to atheism. What is the relevance of an abstract Being that we cannot know? Negative theology can however also be a first step to a metaphysics of non-indifference. Scepticism regarding the super-essence turns into testimony of a trace left behind by Transcendence in concrete individuals" (p. 859).

388. Lieven Boeve, "The Rediscovery of Negative Theology Today: The Narrow Gulf Between Theology and Philosophy," in *Théologie négative*, pp. 443–459. See idem, "Christus Postmodernus: An Attempt at Apophatic Christology," in *The Myriad Christ: Plurality and the Quest for Unity in Contemporary Christology*, edited by Terrence Merrigan and Jacques Haers (Leuven: Peeters Press, 2000), pp. 577–593; and idem, "Negative Theology and Theological Hermeneutics: The Particularity of Naming God," *Journal of Philosophy and Scripture* 3 (2006): 1–13. For an alternative approach, see Franke, "Apophasis and the Turn of Philosophy."

389. In "The New Thinking," Rosenzweig credits Feuerbach for anticipating the distinctiveness of the I and Thou, the critical component of Cohen's theory of correlation that serves as the basis for his own dialogical philosophy. See "The New Thinking," p. 127; *Zweistromland*, p. 152; Freund, *Franz Rosenzweig's Philosophy of Existence*, pp. 142–143; Kornberg Greenberg, *Better Than Wine*, pp. 5, 22–24; Rosenstock, *Philosophy and the Jewish Question*, p. 125. On anthropomorphism and the need for religious illusion in Feuerbach's thought, see Van A. Harvey, *Feuerbach and the Interpretation of Religion* (Cambridge: Cambridge University Press, 1995), pp. 281–309; and compare the innovative analysis in Jeffrey J. Kripal, *The Serpent's Gift: Gnostic Reflections on the Study of Religion* (Chicago: University of Chicago Press, 2007), pp. 59–89.

390. See discussion of this theme in Eduardo Mendieta, "Modernity's Religion: Habermas and the Linguistification of the Sacred," in *Perspectives on Habermas*, edited by Lewis Edwin Hahn (Chicago: Open Court, 2000), pp. 123–138. Also apposite is the essay by Wendell S. Dietrich, "Is Rosenzweig an Ethical Monotheist? A Debate with the New Francophone Literature," in *Der Philosoph Franz Rosenzweig*, pp. 891–900. The author points out the extent to which Rosenzweig departs from the nineteenth-century portrayal of Judaism as an ethical monotheism, focusing on the eclipse of the ethical. My analysis raises questions about the legitimacy of the term *monotheism*, at least if it is interpreted literally.

391. Ben Vedder, "The Possibility of an A-Theological Ontology: Heidegger's Changing Position," in *Théologie négative*, pp. 757–768. The question of theology and Heidegger's thought is a complex matter that has been investigated by a variety of scholars. Here I will mention a modest sampling of relevant studies: Robert S. Gall, *Beyond Theism and Atheism: Heidegger's Significance for Religious Thinking* (Dordrecht: Martinus

Nijhoff, 1987); Westphal, *Overcoming Onto-Theology*, pp. 29–46; David R. Crownfield, "The Question of God: Thinking after Heidegger," *Philosophy Today* 40 (1996): 47–54; Philippe Capelle, "Phénoménologies, Religion et Théologies chez Martin Heidegger," *Studia Phaenomenologia* 1 (2001): 181–196; Laurence Paul Hemming, *Heidegger's Atheism: The Refusal of a Theological Voice* (Notre Dame: University of Notre Dame Press, 2002); McGrath, *The Early Heidegger*, pp. 25–59; Benjamin D. Crowe, *Heidegger's Religious Origins: Destruction and Authenticity* (Bloomington: Indiana University Press, 2006); idem, *Heidegger's Phenomenology of Religion* (Bloomington: Indiana University Press, 2008); Thomas Kalary, "Heidegger's Thinking of Difference and the God-Question," in *Heidegger, Translation, and the Task of Thinking*, pp. 111–133. See also the collection of essays in *Heidegger et la question de Dieu*, edited by Richard Kearney and Joseph Stephen O'Leary, preface by Jean-Yves Lacoste (Paris: Presses Universitaires de France, 2009). On Heidegger's particular stance on Christianity, see Gianni Vattimo, *After Christianity*, translated by Luca D'Isanto (New York: Columbia University Press, 2002), pp. 123–137; Norbert Fischer and Friedrich-Wilhelm von Hermann, "Die christliche Botschaft und das Denken Heideggers. Durchblick durch das Thema," in *Heidegger und die christliche Tradition*, edited by Norbert Fischer and Friedrich Wilhelm von Hermann (Hamburg: Felix Meiner Verlag, 2007), pp. 9–20; Martina Roesner, "Logos und Anfang: Zur Johanneischen Dimension in Heideggers Denken," in *Heidegger und die christliche Tradition*, pp. 33–54. See additional references in Ch. 3 n. 89 and Ch. 6 n. 31.

392. Rosenzweig, *Understanding the Sick*, p. 57.

393. See reference above at n. 307.

394. Rosenzweig, *Star of Redemption*, p. 153; *Stern der Erlösung*, p. 157. Mack, "Franz Rosenzweig's and Emmanuel Levinas's Critique," p. 60, detects in these words an allusion to Schelling's departure from German transcendental philosophy by his assuming that the divine nature is constituted by chaos and materiality.

395. As I noted in the conclusion of the first chapter, Cohen, *Religion of Reason*, p. 65 (*Religion der Vernunft*, p. 75), wrote that mythology is "overcome through the definition of God." For Rosenzweig, not only is it not the case that the definition of God overcomes mythology, but the former is also impossible without the latter, and the *Star* can be seen as an effort to reclaim the mythologic in a meaningful way.

396. Rosenzweig, *Understanding the Sick*, p. 57.

397. Rosenzweig, "Atheistic Theology," p. 24; *Zweistromland*, p. 696.

398. Rosenzweig, *Star of Redemption*, p. 121 (*Stern der Erlösung*, p. 123): "the word of God is Revelation only because at the same time it is the word of Creation. God said: Let there be light—and what is the light of God? It is man's soul."

399. Rosenzweig, *Star of Redemption*, p. 119; *Stern der Erlösung*, p. 121.

Chapter 3: Echo of the Otherwise and the Lure of Theolatry

1. Wyschogrod, *Crossover Queries*, p. 2.

2. Ibid., p. 4. See Levinas, *Oeuvres 1: Carnets de captivité suivi de Écrits sur la captivité et Notes philosophiques diverses*, edited and annotated by Rodolphe Calin, preface and

explanatory notes by Rodolphe Calin and Catherine Chalier, general preface by Jean-Luc Marion (Paris: Éditions Grasset & Fasquelle, 2009), p. 324.

3. Wyschogrod, *Crossover Queries*, p. 15.

4. Ibid. See discussion in the section "Erotics of Transcendence, Saintly Transgression, and the Impossible Hope" in Ch. 5.

5. Edmund Husserl, *Ideas Pertaining to a Pure Phenomenology and to a Phenomenological Philosophy. First Book: General Introduction to a Pure Phenomenology*, translated by F. Kersten (Dordrecht: Kluwer Academic Publishers, 1983), § 51, p. 116 (emphasis in original).

6. Ibid., p. 117.

7. Ibid., § 58, pp. 133–134 (emphasis in original). See the detailed study of Damian Byers, *Intentionality and Transcendence: Closure and Openness in Husserl's Phenomenology* (Madison: University of Wisconsin Press, 2002), and the discussion of divine transcendence in Husserl's phenomenology in Welz, *Love's Transcendence*, pp. 30–57. See also James G. Hart, "A Précis of an Husserlian Philosophical Theology," in *Essays in Phenomenological Theology*, edited by Steven W. Laycock and James G. Hart (Albany: State University of New York Press, 1986), pp. 89–168, esp. 102–103, 112–124, 134–142; Richard Kearney, "Hermeneutics of the Possible God," in *Givenness and God: Questions of Jean-Luc Marion*, edited by Ian Leask and Eoin Cassidy (New York: Fordham University Press, 2005), pp. 221–224.

8. Emmanuel Levinas, *The Theory of Intuition in Husserl's Phenomenology*, translated by André Orianne (Evanston: Northwestern University Press, 1973), p. 40 (emphasis in original).

9. Husserl, *Ideas Pertaining to a Pure Phenomenology and to a Phenomenological Philosophy. First Book*, § 44, p. 95 (emphasis in original).

10. Ibid., § 57, p. 133.

11. Levinas, *The Theory of Intuition*, p. 41.

12. Ibid., p. 43.

13. Levinas, *Basic Philosophical Writings*, p. 36. On Husserl's contribution to the question of transcendence and phenomenology, compare Emmanuel Levinas, *Of God Who Comes to Mind*, translated by Bettina Bergo (Stanford: Stanford University Press, 1998), pp. 124–125.

14. Levinas, *Totality and Infinity*, p. 27 (emphasis in original); *Totalité et infini*, p. xvi.

15. Levinas, *Totality and Infinity*, p. 44; *Totalité et infini*, p. 15.

16. Levinas, *The Theory of Intuition*, p. 44.

17. Drabinski, *Sensibility and Singularity*, p. 3. See as well the analysis of alterity and transcendence in Natalie Depraz, *Transcendance et incarnation: le statut de l'intersubjectivité comme altérité à soi chez Husserl* (Paris: J. Vrin, 1995), pp. 91–124.

18. Emmanuel Levinas, "Martin Heidegger and Ontology," *Diacritics* 26 (1996): 12, 17. The essay first appeared in *Revue Philosophique* (1932). An abridged and modified version appeared in Emmanuel Levinas, *En découvrant l'existence avec Husserl et Heidegger*, published in 1949. I have consulted the third edition of this collection (Paris: J. Vrin, 2001), pp. 77–109. For a subtle discussion of the different versions of this essay, particu-

larly as how they relate to Levinas's analysis of Heidegger's reflections on the nature of time and human existence, see Chanter, *Time, Death, and the Feminine*, pp. 170–188. Levinas's complex intellectual relation to Heidegger is chronicled in Ethan Kleinberg, *Generation Existential: Heidegger's Philosophy in France, 1927–1961* (Ithaca: Cornell University Press, 2005), pp. 19–45, 245–279. See idem, "Back to Where We've Never Been: Heidegger, Levinas, and Derrida on Tradition and History," *History and Theory* 51 (2012): 114–135, esp. 118–121.

19. Levinas, *The Theory of Intuition*, pp. 42–43.

20. Emmanuel Levinas, *Discovering Existence with Husserl*, translated by Richard A. Cohen and Michael B. Smith (Evanston: Northwestern University Press. 1998), p. 176.

21. For an analysis of this theme, see Nicholas Dewey, "Truth, Method, and Transcendence," in *Consequences of Hermeneutics: Fifty Years after Gadamer's Truth and Method*, edited by Jeff Malpas and Santiago Zabala (Evanston: Northwestern University Press, 2010), pp. 25–44.

22. Wyschogrod, *Crossover Queries*, p. 14.

23. Levinas, *Discovering Existence*, pp. 118–119.

24. Wyschogrod, *Crossover Queries*, pp. 14, 40.

25. Levinas, *Discovering Existence*, p. 97.

26. Levinas, *Basic Philosophical Writings*, p. 67.

27. Levinas, *Totality and Infinity*, p. 42; *Totalité et infini*, p. 13. On narcissism and the primacy of the same, related especially to Heidegger's analysis of Dasein, see Emmanuel Levinas, *Collected Philosophical Papers*, translated by Alphonso Lingis (Dordrecht: Martinus Nijhoff, 1987), pp. 49–53.

28. On the idea of transcendence in Levinas, see references cited in the Introduction, n. 89, to which many other studies could have been added.

29. Emmanuel Levinas, *On Escape*, translated by Bettina Bergo (Stanford: Stanford University Press, 2003), p. 73.

30. Emmanuel Levinas, *Ethics and Infinity: Conversations with Philippe Nemo*, translated by Richard A. Cohen (Pittsburgh: Duquesne University Press, 1985), pp. 42–44.

31. For a nuanced discussion that traces the roots of the problem of intentionality and nongivenness to Husserl and Heidegger, see François-David Sebbah, *Testing the Limit: Derrida, Henry, Levinas, and the Phenomenological Tradition*, translated by Stephen Barker (Stanford: Stanford University Press, 2012), pp. 34–57.

32. John Sallis, "Imagination and the Meaning of Being," in *Heidegger et l'idée de la phénoménologie* (Dordrecht: Kluwer Academic Publishers, 1988), p. 127. Sallis does not draw the comparison between Heidegger and Levinas, but I find his depiction of the former useful. Levinas's indebtedness to the postmetaphysical or nonmetaphysical implications of the hermeneutical turn in Heidegger's *Being and Time*, which provide the ground for a radical interrogation of the philosophical heritage of the West, is duly noted by Fagenblat, *A Covenant of Creatures*. For the influence of Heidegger on Levinas, see ibid., pp. 156–162, and see the comparison of Levinas's *il y a* and Heidegger's notion of

everydayness in Michael Fagenblat, *"Il y a du quotidien*: Levinas and Heidegger on the Self," *Philosophy and Social Criticism* 28 (2002): 578–604, esp. 583–589. See, however, idem, *A Covenant of Creatures*, pp. 79–84. For an attempt to problematize Levinas's reading of Heidegger by showing a common ground in their respective discussions of ontology and Western thought, see Zarader, *The Unthought Debt*, pp. 138–149.

33. Henry, *The Essence of Manifestation*, § 7, p. 39; idem, "Phenomenology of Life," in *Transcendence and Phenomenology*, edited by Conor Cunningham and Peter M. Candler Jr. (London: SCM Press, 2007), p. 242.

34. Dan Zahavi, "Michel Henry and the Phenomenology of the Invisible," *Continental Philosophy Review* 32 (1999): 224. For a more extended discussion of the theme of horizon and the constitution of intersubjectivity related thereto, see Zahavi, *Husserl and Transcendental Intersubjectivity*, pp. 39–52. The prospect of invisibility in Husserl is enhanced from another perspective by his inclusion in the purview of phenomenological inquiry the possibility of phantom phenomena that are ostensibly not visible, for example, the appearance of ghosts. However, as he clearly asserts, the ghostly body is experienced as illusory and not as an actual material thing. Bracketing the technical details of Husserl's account of the perceptibility of the imperceptible specter, we can say that this example indicates that he entertained the tenability of a psychic subject without a material body, even though this phantasm has no objective existence, inasmuch as it fails to comply with the conditions of intersubjectivity. See Husserl, *Ideas Pertaining to a Pure Phenomenology and to a Phenomenological Philosophy. Second Book*, § 21, pp. 100–101, and the comments of Schrijvers, *Ontotheological Turnings*, p. 212.

35. Robert Sokolowski, *Presence and Absence: A Philosophical Investigation of Language and Being* (Bloomington: Indiana University Press, 1978), p. xvi. Sokolowski's monograph is a creative expansion and application of the theme of the empty and filled intentions, which he considers the "predominant concern of Husserl's philosophy."

36. Husserl, *Ideas Pertaining to a Pure Phenomenology and to a Phenomenological Philosophy. Second Book*, § 15, pp. 39–40.

37. Husserl, *Cartesian Meditations*, § 50, p. 109.

38. Ibid., p. 112.

39. Ibid., § 55, p. 122.

40. Husserl, *Ideas Pertaining to a Pure Phenomenology and to a Phenomenological Philosophy. Second Book*, § 56, p. 246.

41. Zahavi, "Michel Henry," pp. 230–231. Compare Henry, *The Essence of Manifestation*, § 7, p. 41.

42. Henry, *The Essence of Manifestation*, § 45, p. 379.

43. Smith, *Speech and Theology*, pp. 22–24, 50–51. For a detailed phenomenological study of the constitution of hiddenness, including the phenomenon of self-hiddenness, see James Richard Mensch, *Hiddenness and Alterity: Philosophical and Literary Sightings of the Unseen* (Pittsburgh: Duquesne University Press, 2005).

44. Heidegger, *Being and Time*, § 7, p. 31 (emphasis in original); *Sein und Zeit*, p. 35.

45. Heidegger, *Being and Time*, § 7, p. 31 (emphasis in original); *Sein und Zeit*, pp. 35–36. See the analysis of Heidegger in Jean-Luc Marion, *Reduction and Givenness*:

Investigations of Husserl, Heidegger, and Phenomenology, translated by Thomas A. Carlson (Evanston: Northwestern University Press, 1998), pp. 56–61.

46. The implications of Heidegger's phenomenological critique of phenomenology with its emphasis on the inapparent influenced a number of other phenomenologists, including Jean-Paul Sartre, Maurice Merleau-Ponty, and Michel Henry. See Dan Zahavi, "Subjectivity and Immanence in Michel Henry," in *Subjectivity and Transcendence*, edited by Arne Grøn, Iben Damgaard, and Søren Overgaard (Tübingen: Mohr Siebeck, 2007), pp. 143–145. Zahavi also notes the reverberation of the Heideggerian phenomenology of the invisible in Derrida and Levinas. Compare Zahavi, "Michel Henry," pp. 223–240; idem, *Self-Awareness and Alterity*, pp. 192–194. One should, of course, add Marion to this list of thinkers for whom the focus of phenomenology is on that which exceeds appearance. On the role of the invisible or the unseen (*l'invu*)—the visible in excess or what he calls the "saturated phenomenon"—in the phenomenological constitution of the visible, see Marion, *In Excess*, pp. 104–113; idem, *The Crossing of the Visible*, translated by James K. A. Smith (Stanford: Stanford University Press, 2004), pp. 1–45. For discussion of Marion's apophatic phenomenology, see Robyn Horner, *Rethinking God as Gift: Marion, Derrida, and the Limits of Theology* (New York: Fordham University Press, 2001), pp. 94–97, 119–120, 160–172; Tamsin Jones, *A Genealogy of Marion's Philosophy of Religion: Apparent Darkness* (Bloomington: Indiana University Press, 2011), pp. 110–118, 130–154. For further references, see Ch. 6 n. 66. Also relevant here is the study of Sebbah, *Testing the Limit*. The author triangulates—in the manner of the Wittgensteinian family resemblance—the thought of Derrida, Henry, and Levinas around the supposition that all three apply an "excessive application of the phenomenological method" in pursuit of a "phenomenology *of* excess" that loses "all sense of proportion and of critical stresses, as it moves toward a description of excess itself; a phenomenology that is the victim of immoderation, since its focus on the originary would lead ineluctably and in perverse ways to its being moved ever closer toward that which *exceeds* the field of appearance; a phenomenology characterized by what may be called an *escalation of the originary*" (p. 3, emphasis in original).

47. Martin Heidegger, *Four Seminars*, translated by Andrew Mitchell and François Raffoul (Bloomington: Indiana University Press, 2003), p. 80. See Marion, *Reduction and Givenness*, p. 60; Schrijvers, *Ontotheological Turnings*, pp. 212–213.

48. Heidegger, *Four Seminars*, p. 79. On Heidegger's "tautological phenomenology," see the analysis in Dominique Janicaud, *Phenomenology "Wide Open": After the French Debate*, translated by Charles N. Cabral (New York: Fordham University Press, 2005), pp. 72–75.

49. Martin Heidegger, *Heidegger: Cahiers de l'Herne* (Paris: L'Herne, 1983), pp. 114–115, cited in Marion, *In Excess*, p. 110.

50. Heidegger, *Contributions*, § 267, p. 371; *Beiträge*, pp. 471–472.

51. Levinas, *Totality and Infinity*, p. 45 (emphasis in original); *Totalité et infini*, pp. 15–16. Compare Levinas's observation in Florian Rötzer, *Conversations with French Philosophers*, foreword by Rainer Rochlitz, translated by Gary E. Aylesworth (Atlantic

Highlands: Humanities Press, 1995), p. 58, "it seems to me that the relation to the other, even in Heidegger, is always present only at a moment of being-in-the-world. This strange relation to other humans as the beginning of new concepts and a new attitude and a new finality of thinking is absent in Heidegger. The purely ethical has always had a bad reputation. It was always disputed by ontology or religion." And the further comments about Heidegger in ibid., p. 62: "Dasein is a being who, in being, is concerned with its own being. Later, in the exchange with Beaufret . . . he says Dasein is a being concerned with the meaning of this being. . . . The whole book *Being and Time* was so out of the ordinary, where this being exposed to being, this being concerned with being, leads to the meaningfulness of everything." For a clear and concise summary of Levinas's reading of Heidegger's alleged ontology, see Kosky, *Levinas and the Philosophy of Religion*, pp. 9–16. See also Bergo, *Levinas*, pp. 47–48.

52. Levinas, *Totality and Infinity*, p. 89; *Totalité et infini*, p. 61. For additional disparaging remarks concerning other aspects of Heidegger's thought, see *Totality and Infinity*, pp. 109, 113, 138, 242, 294; *Totalité et infini*, pp. 81, 85, 111, 220, 270.

53. Levinas, *Basic Philosophical Writings*, p. 5 (emphasis in original).

54. See Levinas, *Ethics and Infinity*, p. 37.

55. Ibid., pp. 38, 41, 43.

56. Levinas, *Is It Righteous to Be?* p. 177.

57. Levinas, *Basic Philosophical Writings*, p. 154 (emphasis in original). See also Levinas, *Of God Who Comes to Mind*, pp. 125–126.

58. On Levinas's misreading of Heidegger's intentions regarding ontology in *Being and Time* and in the later work, see Kosky, *Levinas and the Philosophy of Religion*, p. 200 n. 13. It is worth noting that according to Welz, *Love's Transcendence*, pp. 277–282, the "philosophical background" of Levinas is Heidegger's criticism of the metaphysics of presence. She correctly identifies the Heideggerian challenge of how to elude ontotheology to be Levinas's project.

59. Janicaud, *Phenomenology "Wide Open,"* p. 73. On the phenomenology of the inapparent, see idem, *Chronos: Pour l'intelligence du partage temporel* (Paris: Grasset, 1997), pp. 157–171. See idem, "The Theological Turn of French Phenomenology," in *Phenomenology and the "Theological Turn,"* p. 26, where Heidegger's theme of the "phenomenology of the unapparent" is related to the critique of Husserlian intentionality on the part of Levinas and Merleau-Ponty, on one hand, and reinvented in the thought of Derrida and Henry, on the other. For a more extensive discussion of this dimension of Heidegger's thought, see ibid., pp. 28–31.

60. de Beistegui, *Truth and Genesis*, pp. 115 and 127 (emphasis in original).

61. Marion, *Reduction and Givenness*, p. 60. See also Gérard Guest, "Aux confins de l'inapparent: l'extrême phénoménologie de Heidegger," *Existentia* 12 (2002): 113–141; Richard Polt, *The Emergency of Being: On Heidegger's Contribution to Philosophy* (Ithaca: Cornell University Press, 2006), pp. 102–103. On the depiction of Heidegger's "move from a transcendental-aesthetic to a mythical-poetic figure of imagination" as the

"ab-sence of phenomenology," see Brian Elliott, *Phenomenology and Imagination in Husserl and Heidegger* (London: Routledge, 2005), 137–154, esp. 140–141.

62. Françoise Dastur, "La pensée à venir: une phénoménologie de l'inapparent?" in *L'avenir de la philosophie est-il grec?* edited by Catherine Collobert (Saint-Laurent, Quebec: Fides, 2002), p. 146.

63. Emmanuel Levinas, *Face to Face with Levinas*, edited by Richard A. Cohen (Albany: State University of New York Press, 1986), p. 20.

64. This example, and others that could have been cited, renders questionable the categorical statement of Samuel Moyn, "Judaism against Paganism: Emmanuel Levinas's Response to Heidegger and Nazism in the 1930s," *History and Memory* 10 (1998): 26, that the thought of Levinas vis-à-vis Heidegger is "an independent and unique philosophical stance." It is ludicrous to deny the innovations of Levinas, and surely his own view of his thinking in relation to Heidegger conforms to Moyn's characterization, but careful textual scrutiny of their respective writings might yield a different picture. It is relevant here to recall Levinas's response to a question he received from Philippe Nemo regarding the "absolute novelty" of Heidegger's *Sein und Zeit* when it appeared in 1927: "That is in any case the impression that I have maintained of it. To be sure, in the history of philosophy it happens that after the fact one rediscovers the tendencies which retrospectively seem to announce the great innovations of today; but these consist at least in thematizing something which it was not beforehand. A thematization which requires genius and offers a new language" (Levinas, *Ethics and Infinity*, p. 39). This is a far more nuanced understanding of the novelty of Levinas in relation to Heidegger than the words of Moyn would suggest. On the influence of the later Heidegger's phenomenology of presencing on the phenomenologies of the invisible of Levinas and Marion, see Schrijvers, *Ontotheological Turnings*, pp. 221–224, esp. 223.

65. Wyschogrod, *Emmanuel Levinas*, pp. 123–124. The analogy between Heidegger and Levinas on this point is not drawn by Wyschogrod. A similar theme expressed in a more scientific idiom seems to be implied in the aphorism on invisibility in Hans Blumenberg, *Care Crosses the River*, translated by Paul Fleming (Stanford: Stanford University Press, 2010), p. 95: "In 1930, a budding philosopher writes in his postdoctoral thesis: 'Perhaps no one has correctly understood what I want, unless one sees that the visibility of things is actually to be experienced only against the backdrop of absolute negativity.' It may be that in the year 1930, one couldn't expect readers to understand this. A half a century later, anyone who has even fleetingly glimpsed the sights the earth offers from outer space gets the point. . . . The view from outer space reveals the earth—so to speak—in a sea of negativity: an island in the nothingness. This makes it eminently visible: painfully clear."

66. Maurice Blanchot, *The Space of Literature*, translated, with an introduction, by Ann Smock (Lincoln: University of Nebraska Press, 1982), p. 32. See the analysis of the image in Blanchot's thought in Alain P. Toumayan, *Encountering the Other: The Artwork and the Problem of Difference in Blanchot and Levinas* (Pittsburgh: Duquesne University Press, 2004), pp. 114–143, esp. 124–127.

360 NOTES TO PAGE 99

67. Maurice Merleau-Ponty, *The Invisible and the Visible*, edited by Claude Lefort, translated by Alphonso Lingis (Evanston: Northwestern University Press, 1968), p. 151. See reference to my discussion cited in the Introduction, n. 52.

68. Merleau-Ponty, *The Invisible and the Visible*, p. 215 (emphasis in original).

69. Ibid., p. 216.

70. An exception is Kosky, *Levinas and the Philosophy of Religion*, pp. 42–46, who suggests that an ontotheological constitution of metaphysics is at work in both Heidegger and Levinas. See also Wurgaft, "How to Read Maimonides," p. 382: "While Levinas would explicitly identify Heidegger's ontology as a 'philosophy of power' in the 1961 *Totality and Infinity*, this was not so much a rejection of that ontology as a sign of Levinas' continued need to engage with it and think through its possible consequences." On the reclaiming of a postethical quasiontology on the part of Levinas, see Paul Ricoeur, "Otherwise: A Reading of Emmanuel Levinas's *Otherwise than Being or Beyond Essence*," *Yale French Studies* 104 (2004): 82–99, esp. 97–99. On the comparison of the ontologies of Levinas and Heidegger, see Bergo, *Levinas*, pp. 39–43. Throughout her book, Bergo refers to Levinas's ontology. See esp. p. 111: "In Levinas' ontology, which is structured as the coming to pass (the *se produire*) of incomparable events, the encounter with gendered alterity is both aesthetic and ethical in nature." The poetic configuration of things in Heidegger's later thought is character- ized as a movement toward a "new ontology" by Vandevelde, *Heidegger and the Romantics*, pp. 140–171.

71. Paul Davies, "A Linear Narrative? Blanchot with Heidegger in the Work of Levinas," in *Philosophers' Poets*, edited by David Wood (London: Routledge, 1990), p. 42.

72. On the affinity between the Heideggerian *es gibt* and the Levinasian *il y a*, see Mark C. Taylor, *Altarity* (Chicago: University of Chicago Press, 1987), p. 211: "The *il y a* re-sounding in this voice from *l'autre rive*, echoes Heidegger's *Es gibt*. We have seen that the sending of Being and beings effects a donation, which is a *coup*. The *il y a* of Levinas's *dire*, like the *Es gibt* of Heidegger's *sagen*, inflicts *un coup de don*. There is no necessity attached to this gift; it is contingent—as contingent as the throw of the dice, *le coup de dés*." See as well Mark C. Taylor, "The Uncertainty Principle," in *Saintly Influence*, p. 293 n. 18: "Levinas's account of *il y a* and *le dire* in *Otherwise than Being, or Beyond Essence* approaches Heidegger's analysis of the *es gibt*, through which being is given. The *es gibt* is not formless being but is the event through which being as such emerges. When under- stood in this way, Heidegger's *es gibt* and Levinas's *il y a* anticipate Derrida's *différance*." Needless to say, Levinas himself ardently distinguished his *il y a* from the Heideggerian *es gibt*; see, for example, *Ethics and Infinity*, pp. 47–52. See also Simon Critchley, *Very Little . . . Almost Nothing: Death, Philosophy, Literature* (London: Routledge, 1997), pp. 55–57; Wolzogen, *Emmanuel Levinas*, pp. 22–44; de Vries, *Minimal Theologies*, pp. 394–395; and the reservations expressed in John Sallis, "Levinas and the Elemental," in *Radicalizing Levinas*, edited by Peter Atterton and Matthew Calarco (Albany: State University of New York Press, 2010), pp. 87–94. Consider Heidegger's own attempt to distinguish the expressions *il y a* and *es gibt* in *Pathmarks*, pp. 254–255; *Wegmarken*,

p. 334. Many others have weighed in on this issue. For some additional sources, see Wolfson, *A Dream*, p. 298 n. 62.

73. Santiago Zabala, *The Remnants of Being: Hermeneutic Ontology After Metaphysics* (New York: Columbia University Press, 2009), p. 5–6: "To continue to speak of Being and ontology is not an excessive claim, because, on the one hand, this same Being and ontology have shaped what we call philosophy, and, on the other, one cannot just abandon Being and replace it with something else, since it is the sphere through which we think. . . . The remains of Being is the condition of the ontology of remnants, and these remnants show Being's remains."

74. Heidegger, *Identity and Difference*, pp. 55, 58 (emphasis in original); German text: pp. 121–122, 125.

75. Heidegger, *Identity and Difference*, p. 64; German text: p. 132.

76. Heidegger, *Identity and Difference*, p. 71; German text: pp. 139–140.

77. Martin Heidegger, *The End of Philosophy*, translated by Joan Stambaugh (Chicago: University of Chicago Press, 2003), pp. 84–85 (*Vorträge und Aufsätze*, p. 69): "What does 'overcoming metaphysics' [«*Überwindung der Metaphysik*»] mean? In the thinking of the history of Being, this rubric is used only as an aid for that thinking to be comprehensible at all. . . . Above all, overcoming does not mean thrusting aside [*Wegdrängen*] a discipline from the field of philosophical 'education.' . . . Metaphysics cannot be abolished like an opinion. One can by no means leave it behind as a doctrine no longer believed and represented." Ibid., pp. 91–92 (*Vorträge und Aufsätze*, p. 77): "Overcoming [*Überwindung*] is worthy of thought only when we think about incorporation [*Verwindung*]. This perduring thinking [*inständige Denken*] still thinks at the same time about overcoming. Such remembrance [*Andenken*] experiences the unique Appropriating [*einzige Ereignis*] of the expropriating of beings [*Enteignung des Seienden*], in which the need of the truth of Being [*Wahrheit des Seins*], and thus the origination of truth [*Anfängnis der Wahrheit*], opens up and radiates upon human being in the manner of a parting. Overcoming is the delivering over [*Über-lieferung*] of metaphysics to its truth." Consider as well Heidegger's language in *The Event*, § 139, p. 86 (*Das Ereignis*, p. 102): "How indeed in the truth of historical humans, and in their word (language), *beyng essentially occurs*—even if already for a long time there has been an overcoming [*überwinden*] of being and a twisting free [*verwunden*] of beyng" (emphasis in original).

78. Zabala, *The Remnants of Being*, p. 5 (emphasis in original). See ibid., p. 8: "It is important to understand from the start that metaphysics (Being as presence, objectivism) is not something we can neglect once and for all, because it is not something we can completely overcome, *überwinden*; we can only get over it from within, *verwinden*." Zabala's utilization of the Heideggerian distinction between *Überwindung* and *Verwindung* is indebted to the interpretation of Vattimo. See Gianni Vattimo, "The End of (Hi)story," *Chicago Review* 35 (1987): 20–30, esp. 25–29; idem, " 'Verwindung': Nihilism and the Postmodern in Philosophy," *Substance* 16 (1987): 7–17; idem, *The End of Modernity: Nihilism and Hermeneutics in Postmodern Culture*, translated by Jon R. Snyder (Baltimore: Johns Hopkins University Press, 1988), pp. 164–181; idem, "Metaphysics,

Violence, Secularization," in *Recoding Metaphysics: The New Italian Philosophy*, edited by
Giovanna Borradori (Evanston: Northwestern University Press, 1988), pp. 60–61; idem,
The Adventure of Difference: Philosophy, p. 113; idem, *Beyond Intepretation: The Meaning of
Hermenetutics for Philosophy*, translated by David Webb (Stanford: Stanford University
Press, 1997), pp. 76–77, 88–89; idem, *Nihilism & Emancipation: Ethics, Politics, & Law*,
edited by Santiago Zabala, translated by William McCuaig (New York: Columbia
University Press, 2004), pp. 27–28, 39, 73, 160, 169, 172; Gaetano Chiurazzi, "The
Experiment of Nihilism: Interpretation and Experience of Truth in Gianni Vattimo," in
Between Nihlism and Politics: The Hermeneutics of Gianni Vattimo, edited by Silvia Benso
and Brian Schroeder (Albany: State University of New York Press, 2010), pp. 21–24;
Silivia Benso, "Emancipation and the Future of the Utopian: On Vattimo's Philosophy of
History," in *Between Nihilism and Politics*, pp. 212–217. On the Heideggerian notion of
Verwindung, see below, n. 289.

79. Zabala, *The Remnants of Being*, pp. 19–20.

80. Derrida, *Writing and Difference*, pp. 141–142; *L'écriture et la différence*, pp.
208–209. Compare Derrida's illuminating comment in Richard Kearney, "On the Gift:
A Discussion between Jacques Derrida and Jean-Luc Marion," moderated by Richard
Kearney, in *God, the Gift, and Postmodernism*, p. 75: "When Levinas refers to the excess
of the infinitely other, he says that the other, the face, precisely does not appear as such.
He says many times that he wants to find within phenomenology the injunction to go
beyond phenomenology. There are many places where he says that we have to go
phenomenologically beyond phenomenology. That is what I am trying to do, also. I
remain and I want to remain a rationalist, a phenomenologist." For a different perspective, see Jacques Derrida, *Points . . . Interviews, 1974–1994*, edited by Elisabeth Weber,
translated by Peggy Kamuf and others (Stanford: Stanford University Press, 1995), p. 187.
In an interview with Didier Eribon published in *Le Nouvel Observateur*, November 6–12,
1987, Derrida reacted to Christian Jambet's remark in the preface to Victor Farías,
Heidegger et le nazisme, translated by Myriam Benarroch and Jean-Baptiste Grasset
(Paris: Éditions Verdier, 1986), p. 14, to the effect that Heideggerian ontology culminates
in the methical deconstruction of metaphysics: "And one can no more speak of
'ontology' with regard to the deconstruction that I try to put to work than one can
speak, if one has read a little, of 'Heidegger's ontology' or even 'Heidegger's philosophy.'
And 'deconstruction'—which does not 'culminate'—is certainly not a 'method.' It even
develops a rather complicated discourse on the concept of method that Mr. Jambet
would be well advised to meditate on a little." For an analysis of Derrida's critique of
Levinas, see Smith, *Speech and Theology*, pp. 44–50.

81. Derrida, *Writing and Difference*, p. 144; *L'écriture et la différence*, p. 212.

82. Levinas, *Totality and Infinity*, p. 201; *Totalité et infini*, p. 175.

83. Levinas, *Totality and Infinity*, p. 104; *Totalité et infini*, p. 77. The passage is cited in
Wolfson, "Secrecy," p. 65. See also Charles Mopsik, "La Pensée d'Emmanuel Lévinas et
la Cabale," in *Cahier de l'herne: Emmanuel Levinas*, edited by Catherine Chalier and
Miquel Abensour (Paris: Éditions de l'Herne, 1991), pp. 429–431; Oona Ajzenstat, *Driven*

Back to the Text: The Premodern Sources of Levinas's Postmodernism (Pittsburgh: Duquesne University Press, 2001), p. 178; Meskin, "The Role of Lurianic Kabbalah," pp. 53 and 66. Meskin's study is an attempt—successful in my opinion—to decode Levinas's evocation of the idea of *ṣimṣum* in conjunction with *Totality and Infinity* in response to Wyschogrod's comment that his "theological thinking" is the "reverse of the Parmenidean understanding of being." See *Crossover Queries*, p. 285. On the possible kabbalistic influence on Levinas, see also Cohen, *Elevations*, pp. 241–273; Chalier, *La trace de l'infini*, pp. 77–106, 156–158, 189–201, 208–231.

84. Emmanuel Levinas, *Alterity and Transcendence*, translated by Michael Smith (New York: Columbia University Press, 1999), pp. 62–63, previously cited in Wolfson, "Divine Suffering," p. 151 n. 88; and Emmanuel Levinas, *Beyond the Verse: Talmudic Readings and Lectures*, translated by Gary D. Mole (London: Athlone Press, 1994), p. 166, cited and analyzed in Wolfson, "Secrecy," pp. 66–67. See also David G. Leahy, "Cuspidal Limits of Infinity: Secret of the Incarnate Self in Levinas," in *Rending the Veil: Concealment and Secrecy in the History of Religions*, edited by Elliot R. Wolfson (New York: Seven Bridges Press, 1999), pp. 241–243.

85. Ḥayyim of Volozhyn, *Nefesh ha-Ḥayyim* (Benei Beraq, 1989), 3.7, pp. 162–165. The interpretation of the Lurianic doctrine of *ṣimṣum* advanced by this kabbalist, following the opinion of his teacher, Elijah ben Solomon, known honorifically as the Vilna Gaon, and that of Moses Ḥayyim Luzzatto, treats the matter figuratively rather than literally. The complexity of this issue in the history of kabbalistic and Hasidic literature cannot be pursued here, but for two helpful reviews of the problem with fairly exhaustive citation of previous scholarly discussions, see Yoni Garb, "Rabbi Kook and His Sources: From Kabbalistic Historiosophy to National Mysticism," in *Studies in Modern Religions, Religious Movements and the Bābī-Bahāʾī Faiths* (Leiden: Brill, 2004), pp. 81–82; Raphael B. Schuchat, *A World Hidden in the Dimensions of Time: The Theory of Redemption in the Writings of the Vilna Gaon, Its Sources and Influences on Later Generations* (Ramat-Gan: Bar-Ilan University Press, 2008), pp. 117–122 (Hebrew). I see no reason to assume that the influence of *Nefesh ha-Ḥayyim* on Levinas should be limited to his later thought, culminating in *Otherwise than Being*, as suggested by Jacob Meskin, "Toward a New Understanding of the Work of Emmanuel Levinas," *Modern Judaism* 20 (2000): 78–102, esp. 84–86. Some other scholars who have weighed in on the question of the influence of Ḥayyim of Volozhyn on Levinas include Catherine Chalier, "L'âme de la vie: Lévinas, lecteur de R. Haïm de Volozin," in *Ce Cahier de l'Herne: Emmanuel Levinas*, pp. 442–460; Stéphane Moses, "L'idée de l'infini en nous," in *Répondre d'autrui: Emmanuel Lévinas*, edited by Jean-Christophe Aeschlimann and Paul Ricouer (Boudry-Neuchâtel: À la Baconnière, 1989), pp. 41–51; Martin Kavka, "Religious Experience in Levinas and R. Hayyim of Volozhin," *Philosophy Today* 50 (2006): 69–79, and see the study of Mopsik cited above, n. 83.

86. Heidegger, *Early Greek Thinking*, p. 26; *Holzwege*, pp. 336–337.

87. Heidegger, *Early Greek Thinking*, p. 18; *Holzwege*, p. 327. On the eschatological elements in Heidegger's thought, see Derrida, "On a Newly Arisen," pp. 146–149, 166–167.

88. Martin Heidegger, *The Phenomenology of Religious Life*, translated by Matthias Fritsch and Jennifer Anna Gosetti-Ferencei (Bloomington: Indiana University Press, 2004), pp. 71–72; *Phänomenologie des religiösen Lebens* [GA 60] (Frankfurt am Main: Vittorio Klostermann, 1995), p. 102.

89. Heidegger, *The Phenomenology of Religious Life*, p. 73; *Phänomenologie des religiösen Lebens*, p. 104. Compare Ryan David Coyne, "The End of Care: Augustine and the Development of Heidegger's Philosophy," Ph.D. thesis, University of Chicago, 2008, pp. 66–67; Judith E. Tonning, "'*Hineingehalten in die Nacht*': Heidegger's Early Appropriation of Christian Eschatology," in *Phenomenology and Eschatology: Not Yet in the Now*, edited by Neal DeRoo and John Panteleimon Manoussakis (Burlington: Ashgate, 2009), pp. 142–143. See also Friedrich-Wilhelm von Herrmann, "Faktische Lebenserfahrung und urchristliche Religiosität: Heideggers phänomenologischen Auslegung Paulinischer Briefe," in *Heidegger und die christliche Tradition*, pp. 21–31. The distinction between objective time and temporality as the enactment of life is a continuation of the line of argument employed by Heidegger in the lecture "The Concept of Time in the Science of History," delivered July 17, 1915, at the University of Freiburg as part of the process of his achieving the *Habilitation*. See *Becoming Heidegger*, pp. 60–72. In that lecture, Heidegger distinguishes the concept of time in physics and the concept of time in the science of history. The former is based on a mathematical understanding of time as a homogeneous series of quantitative and interchangeable points, whereas the latter focuses on the qualitative structure of time and the uniqueness and singularity of past events that impact the present and determine the future. Developing Troeltsch's examination of Augustine and the periodization of the history of Christianity, Heidegger adduces the essential element in his concept of time in history: "*Time-periods* [*Zeiten*] *in history are distinguished qualitatively*. . . . Consequently, the concept of time in the science of history has none of the homogeneity characterizing the concept of time in the natural sciences. . . . *The qualitative factor of the historical concept of time is nothing but the congealing—the crystallization—of an objectification of life within history* . . . But when I ask about the 'when' of a *historical* event [*Ereignis*], I am asking not about its quantity but about its place in a *qualitative historical* context" (p. 71, emphasis in original). The reckoning of time in history proceeds on the basis of events to which a given culture assigns value. For a thoughtful analysis of Heidegger's essay against the background of the notions of time proffered by the neo-Kantian schools of Marburg and Heidelberg, see Gillian Rose, *Dialectic of Nihilism: Post-Structuralism and Law* (Oxford: Basil Blackwell, 1984), pp. 50–67, esp. 52–54.

90. See further discussion in Ch. 6 at nn. 31–48. On the question of gnostic elements in Heidegger's thought, see sources cited in Wolfson, *Language, Eros, Being*, p. 472 n. 6.

91. Levinas, *Time and the Other*, p. 39.

92. Ibid., p. 30.

93. Ibid., p. 39.

94. Levinas, *Face to Face with Levinas*, p. 21.

95. Ibid., p. 22.

96. Wyschogrod, *Crossover Queries*, p. 284.

97. For a similar argument regarding deconstruction as essentially a form of skepticism, see Joshua Kates, *Fielding Derrida: Philosophy, Literary Criticism, History, and the Work of Deconstruction* (New York: Fordham University Press, 2008), pp. 11–25. See also the analysis of Simon Critchley, *The Ethics of Deconstruction: Derrida and Levinas* (West Lafayette: Purdue University Press, 1992), pp. 156–169, and Bernard Flynn, "Merleau-Ponty and the Philosophical Position of Skepticism," in *Merleau-Ponty and the Possibilities of Philosophy: Transforming the Tradition*, edited by Bernard Flynn, Wayne J. Froman, and Robert Vallier (Albany: State University of New York Press, 2009), pp. 117–128.

98. Emmanuel Levinas, "Quelques réflexions sur le philosophie de l'Hitlérisme," *Espirit* 2 (1934): 199–208.

99. Emmanuel Levinas, "Reflections on the Philosophy of Hitlerism," *Critical Inquiry* 17 (1990): 69.

100. Ibid., p. 70. See the analysis of this text in Chanter, *Time, Death, and the Feminine*, pp. 173–174, and see also Robert Bernasconi, "Skepticism in the Face of Philosophy," in *Re-Reading Levinas*, edited by Robert Bernasconi and Simon Critchley (Bloomington: Indiana University Press, 1991), pp. 149–161; Michael L. Morgan, *Discovering Levinas* (Cambridge: Cambridge University Press, 2007), pp. 305–320. See references cited below, n. 359, and the citation from Gillian Rose below, n. 407.

101. Levinas, *Totality and Infinity*, pp. 46–47; *Totalité et infini*, p. 17.

102. Levinas, *Collected Philosophical Papers*, pp. 52–53. On the link between Heideggerian paganism and the critique of technology, see Levinas's essay "Heidegger, Gagarin, and Us," in *Difficult Freedom*, pp. 231–234, and see the analysis in David J. Gauthier, *Martin Heidegger, Emmanuel Levinas, and the Politics of Dwelling* (Lanham: Rowman & Littlefield, 2011), pp. 116–120. See also the brief but stirring criticism of Heidegger (dated November 15, 1987) in Emmanuel Levinas, "As If Consenting to Horror," *Critical Inquiry* 15 (1989): 485–488. Levinas praises the philosophical brilliance of *Sein und Zeit*, but he raises the question of whether it can be read without perceiving therein an implicit theorizing of violence that led to the Nazi abominations. See Handelman, *Fragments*, pp. 188–195.

103. Levinas, "Reflections," p. 63.

104. Heidegger, *Being and Time*, § 22, p. 96; *Sein und Zeit*, p. 104.

105. Martin Heidegger, *Hegel's Concept of Experience* (New York: Harper & Row, 1970), p. 65; *Holzwege*, p. 152. My analysis of this passage has benefited from the discussion in Edith Wyschogrod, *An Ethics of Remembering: History, Heterology, and the Nameless Others* (Chicago: University of Chicago Press, 1998), pp. 123–124, 143.

106. Heidegger, *Hegel's Concept of Experience*, p. 66; *Holzwege*, pp. 152–153.

107. Heidegger, *Hegel's Concept of Experience*, pp. 67–68 (translation modified); *Holzwege*, pp. 153–154.

108. Heidegger, *Country Path Conversations*, p. 29; *Feldweg-Gespräche*, p. 45. On skepticism, transcendental philosophy, and Heidegger's analysis of truth as disclosedness, see Dahlstrom, *Heidegger's Concept of Truth*, pp. 407–423.

109. Heidegger, *Pathmarks*, p. 292; *Wegmarken*, p. 387. Compare the comment of Theodor Adorno, *Minima Moralia: Reflections from Damaged Life*, translated by E. F. N. Jephcott (London: Verso, 1978), p. 39: " 'It is even part of my good fortune not to be a house-owner', Nietzsche already wrote in the *Gay Science*. Today we should have to add: it is part of morality not to be at home in one's home."

110. Regarding this theme, see Dermot Moran, "Husserl and Heidegger on the Transcendental 'Homelessness' of Philosophy," in *Epistemology, Archaeology, Ethics: Current Investigations of Husserl's Corpus*, edited by Pol Vandevelde and Sebastian Luft (New York: Continuum, 2010), pp. 169–187. See also the analysis of images of alienation, the constitution of home, and the liminal experience of appropriation in Steinbock, *Home and Beyond*, pp. 178–235; and compare O'Donoghue, *A Poetics of Homecoming*, pp. 21–55.

111. Novalis, *Novalis: Philosophical Writings*, translated and edited by Margaret Mahony Stoljar (Albany: State University of New York Press, 1997), p. 135 (emphasis in original).

112. Jacques Derrida and Maurizio Ferraris, *A Taste for the Secret*, translated by Giacomo Donis, edited by Giacomo Donis and David Webb (Cambridge: Polity Press, 2001), p. 55. See Ch. 4 n. 71.

113. Emmanuel Levinas, *In the Time of the Nations*, translated by Michael B. Smith (London: Athlone Press, 1994), pp. 168–169.

114. Levinas, *Totality and Infinity*, pp. 84–85; *Totalité et infini*, p. 57. On the notion of investiture, see Llewelyn, *Margins of Religion*, pp. 176–182.

115. Levinas, *Totality and Infinity*, p. 85; *Totalité et infini*, p. 58.

116. In this regard, there is a shared sensibility in Kierkegaard (see Ch. 2 n. 90) and Levinas, as noted by J. Aaron Simmons, *God and the Other: Ethics and Politics After the Theological Turn* (Bloomington: Indiana University Press, 2011), p. 124. See also Merold Westphal, "Levinas, Kierkegaard, and the Theological Task," *Modern Theology* 8 (1992): 241–242. Comparing the two thinkers, Westphal writes: "Both are eager to expose the pretensions of philosophical thought as pretentious by confronting it with its ownmost other. . . . Both are willing to talk of absurdity and paradox, recognizing that philosophical thought is normally predicated on the exclusion of what they find to be essential, thus rendering Reason irrational." See also idem, "The Transparent Shadow: Kierkegaard and Levinas in Dialogue," in *Kierkegaard in Post/Modernity*, edited by Martin J. Matuštík and Merold Westphal (Bloomington: Indiana University Press, 1995), pp. 265–281. See below, n. 511.

117. With respect to the matter of the unthought, there is kinship between Heidegger and Levinas. See Martin Heidegger, *What Is Called Thinking?* translated by Fred W. Wieck and J. Glenn Gray, with an introduction by J. Glenn Gray (New York: Harper & Row, 1968), pp. 76–77; *Was heisst Denken?* [GA 8] (Frankfurt am Main: Vittorio Klostermann, 2002), pp. 82–83. See also Heidegger, *Parmenides*, pp. 12–13; *Parmenides*, p. 16; and Heidegger, *The Principle of Reason*, p. 71; *Der Satz vom Grund*, p. 105. Compare Elliot R. Wolfson, "Revealing and Re/veiling Menaḥem Mendel Schneerson's Messianic

Secret," *Kabbalah: Journal for the Study of Jewish Mystical Texts* 26 (2012): 29–43, esp.
33–36. The full force of Heidegger's sense of the unthought can be appreciated if it is
contrasted with the following comment in the preface to Ludwig Wittgenstein, *Tractatus
Logico-Philosophicus*, translated by D. F. Pears and B. F. McGuinness, with an introduction by Bertrand Russell (London: Routledge & Kegan Paul, 1974), p. 3: "Thus the aim
of this book is to draw the limit to thought, or rather—not to thought, but to the
expression of thought: for in order to be able to draw a limit to thought, we should have
to find both sides of the limit thinkable (i.e. we should have to be able to think what
cannot be thought)." In the end, Wittgenstein cannot avoid the paradox of imposing
upon the human mind the directive to think what cannot be thought, but the latter is
positioned on the other side of thinking, whereas for Heidegger, the unthought is not the
limit but the enigma that lies at the center of whatever is thought.

118. Levinas, *Totality and Infinity*, p. 88; *Totalité et infini*, pp. 60–61.

119. Levinas, *Otherwise than Being*, p. 170; *Autrement qu'être*, p. 216.

120. This insight is highlighted in the study of Graham Harman, "Levinas and the
Triple Critique of Heidegger," *Philosophy Today* 53 (2009): 407–413. A consequence
of this anthropocentrism is the radical distinction between human and animal to the
point that subjectivity does not apply to the latter. Let me mention one typical expression of this biased perspective in Martin Heidegger, *The Basic Problems of Phenomenology*,
translation, introduction, and lexicon by Albert Hofstadter (Bloomington: Indiana
University Press, 1982), pp. 190–191 (*Die Grundprobleme der Phänomenologie* [GA 24]
(Frankfurt am Main: Vittorio Klostermann, 1975), pp. 270–271): "We may remark
incidentally that a great difficulty presents itself here, which is how to make out what is
given to animals as living beings and how the given is unveiled for them. Hobbes says
that the given is not given to them as true or false because they cannot speak and make
assertions about what is given to them. But he must surely say that the mirror-image [*das
Spiegelbild*] is given to them *as* similar. The question would already obtrude here as to
how far, in general, something can be given *as* something to animals. We also come here
to the further question whether, in general, anything is given *as a being* [als Seiendes] to
animals. It is yet a problem to establish ontically how something is given to animals. On
closer consideration we see that, speaking cautiously, since we ourselves are not mere
animals, we basically do not have an understanding of the 'world' of the animals. But
since we nevertheless also live as existents [*Existierende*] . . . the possibility is available to
us, by going back from what is given to us as existents, to make out reductively what
could be given to an animal that merely lives but does not exist [*was einem nur lebenden
Tier, das nicht existiert*]" (emphasis in original). And compare Heidegger's observation in
the "Letter on Humanism" in *Pathmarks*, pp. 246–247, to the effect that thinking of the
human as the rational animal is indicative of the metaphysical orientation that has
informed Western philosophy; the new turn in thinking demands to consider the human
being less on the basis of *animalitas* and more in the direction of *humanitas*. See the
comments concerning Heidegger and Levinas on this topic in Jacques Derrida, *Points*,
pp. 268, 277–284, and the more extended discussions in idem, *Of Spirit: Heidegger and*

368 NOTES TO PAGES 105–6

the Question, translated by Geoffrey Bennington and Rachel Bowlby (Chicago: University of Chicago Press, 1989), pp. 47–57, and idem, *The Animal That Therefore I Am*, edited by Marie-Louise Mallet, translated by David Wills (New York: Fordham University Press, 2008), pp. 22–23, 38–39, 89–92, 105–118, 141–160. There is a considerable bibliography on this topic, of which I will here cite a few relevant studies: William McNeill, "Life Beyond the Organism: Animal Being in Heidegger's Freiburg Lectures, 1929–30," in *Animal Others: On Ethics, Ontology, and Animal Life*, edited by H. Peter Steeves, foreword by Tom Regan (Albany: State University of New York Press, 1999), pp. 197–248; Stuart Elden, "Heidegger's Animals," *Continental Philosophy Review* 39 (2006): 273–291; Josh Hayes, "Heidegger's Fundamental Ontology and the Problem of Animal Life," *PhaenEx: Journal of Existential and Phenomenological Theory of Culture* 2 (2007): 42–60; Matthew Calarco, "Heidegger's Zoontology," in *Animal Philosophy: Essential Readings in Continental Thought*, edited by Matthew Calarco and Peter Atterton (New York: Continuum, 2004), pp. 18–30; idem, *Zoographies: The Question of the Animal From Heidegger to Derrida* (New York: Columbia University Press, 2008); idem, "Faced by Animals," in *Radicalizing Levinas*, pp. 113–133; Leonard Lawlor, *This Is Not Sufficient: An Essay on Animality and Human Nature* (New York: Columbia University Press, 2007), pp. 39–70; Brett Buchanan, *Onto-Ethologies: The Animal Environments of Uexküll, Heidegger, Merleau-Ponty, and Deleuze* (Albany: State University of New York Press, 2008), pp. 39–114; Kevin A. Aho, *Heidegger's Neglect of the Body* (Albany: State University of New York Press, 2009), pp. 73–103; Blair McDonald, "To Do What One Ought to Do: Reconsidering Heidegger's Thesis—'The Animal Is Poor in World'," *Colloquy: Text Theory Critique* 21 (2011): 6–24. For a learned analysis of the roots of the anthropocentric bias in Aristotle's view that animals lack reason, see Richard Sorabji, *Animal Minds and Human Morals: The Origins of the Western Debate* (Ithaca: Cornell University Press, 1993).

121. For a discussion of unsaying and the originary saying in Heidegger and Levinas, see Wyschogrod, *Crossover Queries*, pp. 497–499. My own approach narrows the gap that Wyschogrod places between the two with regard to this matter. On the role of language and Levinas's account of the Saying, see also Schrijvers, *Ontotheological Turnings*, pp. 105–135.

122. Levinas, *Totality and Infinity*, p. 150; *Totalité et infini*, p. 124.

123. Levinas, *Totality and Infinity*, pp. 180–181; *Totalité et infini*, p. 156.

124. I concur with the observation of Robert Gibbs, "The Name of God in Levinas's Philosophy," in *Saintly Influence*, p. 111: "It is not, therefore, a matter of a genetic sequence of concepts in Levinas." The specific context of Gibbs's comment is his reflections on the unpronounceable name of God in the Jewish tradition and the philosophical concept of illeity and the effacement of transcendence. See as well the opinion of Blanchot that Levinas's work subsequent to *Totality and Infinity* is a more rigorous reflection of what he said in that book, cited and discussed in Gary D. Mole, *Lévinas, Blanchot, Jabès: Figures of Estrangement* (Gainesville: University Press of Florida, 1997), p. 16.

125. Emmanuel Levinas, *Entre Nous: On Thinking-of-the-Other*, translated by Michael B. Smith and Barbara Harshav (New York: Columbia University Press, 1998), p. 197. See

Salomon Malka, *Emmanuel Levinas: His Life and Legacy*, foreword by Philippe Nemo, translated by Michael Kigel and Sara M. Embree (Pittsburgh: Duquesne University Press, 2006), p. 285.

126. Levinas, *Entre Nous*, pp. 197–198 (emphasis in original).

127. Levinas, *Of God Who Comes to Mind*, p. 82. Concerning this passage, see the remarks of Jacques Derrida, *Adieu to Emmanuel Levinas*, translated by Pascale-Anne Brault and Michael Naas (Stanford: Stanford University Press, 1999), p. 143 n. 62.

128. Levinas, *The Theory of Intuition*, p. xxxiv.

129. For a concise account of Heidegger's view, see Jean Wahl, *A Short History of Existentialism*, translated by Forrest Williams and Stanley Maron (New York: Philosophical Library, 1949), p. 15: "Heidegger observes the word 'transcendence' ought to denote the end towards which we are going; properly speaking, to transcend is to rise towards. Thus, a being such as God could never be a transcendent being. Only man can transcend." In the continuation of his analysis, Wahl delineates five "movements of transcendence" in Heidegger's thought: (1) transcendence towards the world; (2) transcendence towards other human beings; (3) transcendence towards the future; (4) transcendence towards Being; and (5) transcendence out of Nothingness (pp. 15–17). See also Silvia Benso, *The Face of Things: A Different Side of Ethics* (Albany: State University of New York Press, 2000), pp. 88–90.

130. Levinas, *Collected Philosophical Papers*, pp. 52–53: "Heideggerian philosophy precisely marks the apogee of a thought in which the finite does not refer to the infinite (prolonging certain tendencies of Kantian philosophy: the separation between the understanding and reason, diverse themes of transcendental dialectics), in which every deficiency is but weakness and every fault committed against oneself—the outcome of a long tradition of pride, heroism, domination, and cruelty. Heideggerian ontology subordinates the relation with the other to the relation with the neuter, Being, and it thus continues to exalt the will to power, whose legitimacy the other alone can unsettle, troubling good conscience. . . . Heidegger does not only sum up a whole evolution of Western philosophy. He exalts it by showing in the most pathetic way its anti-religious essence become a religion in reverse. . . . In Heidegger atheism is a paganism, the presocratic texts anti-Scriptures. Heidegger shows in what intoxication the lucid sobriety of philosophers is steeped." In spite of Levinas's critique of Heidegger's atheism, there is a similar emphasis in his own thinking on the interplay of faith and doubt, and the soul's moving in between atheism and belief as an expression of the "original mode of the presence of God." See Levinas, *Entre Nous*, p. 56, and the discussion in Joeri Schrijvers, "'And There Shall Be No More Boredom': Problems with Overcoming Metaphysics in Heidegger, Levinas and Marion," in *Transcendence and Phenomenology*, pp. 50–83, esp. 79–82.

131. Levinas, "Martin Heidegger and Ontology," pp. 12–13.

132. Ibid., p. 13 (emphasis in original).

133. Ibid., p. 13 n. 5 (emphasis in original).

134. There are numerous studies on the dimension of time in Levinas's thought, of which I will here mention a few representative examples: Jacques Derrida, "At This Very

Moment in This Work Here I Am," in *Re-Reading Levinas*, pp. 11–48; Cohen, *Elevations*,
pp. 133–161; Shaun Gallagher, *The Inordinance of Time* (Evanston: Northwestern University Press, 1998), pp. 108–126; Wyschogrod, *Emmanuel Levinas*, pp. 113–140; Rudolf
Bernet, "L'autre du temps," in *Emmanuel Lévinas: Positivité et transcendance*, edited by
Jean-Luc Marion (Paris: Presses Universitaires de France, 2000), pp. 143–163; Chanter,
Time, Death, and the Feminine; idem, "Conditions: The Politics of Ontology and the
Temporality of the Feminine," in *Addressing Levinas*, edited by Eric Sean Nelson, Antje
Kapust, and Kent Still (Evanston: Northwestern University Press, 2005), pp. 310–337;
Wolfson, *Alef, Mem, Tau*, pp. 51–53.

135. Levinas, *Time and the Other*, p. 90. See Rudolf Bernet, "Levinas's Critique of
Husserl," in *The Cambridge Companion to Levinas*, edited by Simon Critchley and Robert
Bernasconi (Cambridge: Cambridge University Press, 2002), pp. 82–99, esp. 86–89. On
the relationship of Husserl and Levinas, see also Jacques Colette, "Lévinas et la phénoménologie husserlienne," in *Le cahiers de la nuit surveillée: Emmanuel Lévinas*, edited by
Jacques Rolland (Lagrasse: Verdier, 1984), pp. 19–36; Smith, *Speech and Theology*,
pp. 27–32.

136. Levinas, "Martin Heidegger and Ontology," p. 13 (emphasis in original).

137. Ibid., p. 14.

138. Ibid., pp. 16–17.

139. Ibid., p. 22. Compare the essay "L'ontologie dans le temporal" in Levinas, *En
découvrant l'existence avec Husserl et Heidegger*, pp. 111–128, esp. 116–119.

140. Levinas, *On Escape*, pp. 54–56. See Bernasconi, "No Exit," pp. 102–106; Allen,
The Philosophical Sense of Transcendence, p. 56; Stefanos Geroulanos, *An Atheism That Is
Not Humanist Emerges in French Thought* (Stanford: Stanford University Press, 2010),
pp. 175, 177, 194–200.

141. Levinas, *On Escape*, p. 70.

142. See the comments on the text of *De l'évasion* in the interview with François
Poirié published in Levinas, *Is It Righteous to Be?* p. 39. See also the remarks on the
"Jewish condition" in the 1966 address "Honneur sans Drapeau," rendered into English
as "Nameless," in Emmanuel Levinas, *Proper Names*, translated by Michael B. Smith
(Stanford: Stanford University Press, 1996), pp. 122–123: "The Jews are a people like all
other peoples . . . But by a strange election, they are a people conditioned and situated
among the nations in such a way (is this metaphysics or sociology?) that it is liable to find
itself, overnight and without forewarning, in the wretchedness of its exile, its desert,
ghetto or concentration camp—all the splendors of life swept away like tinsel, the
Temple in flames, the prophets without vision, reduced to an inner morality that is
belied by the universe." On the question of Jewish universalism in Levinas, see Sarah
Hammerschlag, *The Figural Jew: Politics and Identity in Postwar French Thought* (Chicago: University of Chicago Press, 2010), pp. 117–165, esp. 144–154; and the unfavorable
appraisal of Judith Butler, *Parting Ways: Jewishness and the Critique of Zionism* (New
York: Columbia University Press, 2012), pp. 38–53, esp. 43–48. For additional references,
see below n. 350 and Ch. 5 n. 9.

143. Levinas, *Proper Names*, p. 132. See Levinas, *Totality and Infinity*, p. 235 (*Totalité et infini*, pp. 211–212): "Death is a menace that approaches me as a mystery; its secrecy determines it—it approaches without being able to be assumed, such that the time that separates me from my death dwindles and dwindles without end, involves a sort of last interval which my consciousness cannot traverse, and where a leap will somehow be produced from death to me. . . . It is a relation with an instant whose exceptional character is due not to the fact that it is at the threshold of nothingness or of a rebirth, but to the fact that, in life, it is the impossibility of every possibility [*l'impossibilité de toute possibilité*], the stroke of a total passivity alongside of which the passivity of the sensibility, which moves into activity, is but a distant imitation. Thus the fear for my being which is my relation with death is not the fear of nothingness, but the fear of violence—and thus it extends into fear of the Other, of the absolutely unforeseeable." Compare Levinas, *Time and the Other*, pp. 70–71: "Death in Heidegger is an event of freedom, whereas for me the subject seems to reach the limit of the possible in suffering. It finds itself enchained, overwhelmed, and in some way passive. . . . This is why death is never a present." For a nuanced discussion of the similarities and differences between Heidegger and Levinas on the role of death as the impossible possibility in the constitution of human subjectivity, see Kosky, *Levinas and the Phenomenology of Religion*, pp. 119–123, 126–128, and idem, " 'Love Strong as Death': Levinas and Heidegger," in *The Exorbitant*, pp. 108–129. See also the remark on "the gift of death" in Marion, *Being Given*, p. 246 (*Étant donné*, p. 341): "It is not merely a matter of giving the impossibility of being [*l'impossibilité de l'étant*], but giving impossibility itself as directly nonbeing [*l'impossibilité elle-même comme directement non-étant*]." Mention should be made here of the argument proffered by Kleinberg, *Generation Existential*, p. 254, that the view that there is no escape from the *il y a* "must be read in the historical context of Levinas's own experience in the POW camp, the persecution of his family in France, and the tragic fate of his family in Lithuania and of the Jewish people in Europe. Levinas transfers his own sense of unease, insecurity, and persecution to the philosophical fear that there is no escape from anonymous being, which continues with or without individual beings."

144. Maurice Blanchot, *The Gaze of Orpheus and Other Literary Essays*, preface by Geoffrey Hartman, translated by Lydia Davis, edited with an afterword by P. Adams Sitney (Barrytown: Station Hill Press, 1981), p. 55. On the possibility of dying (*le mourir*) and the impossibility of death (*la mort*) in Blanchot, see Simon Critchley, "*Il y a*—A Dying Stronger than Death (Blanchot with Levinas)," *Oxford Literary Review* 15 (1993): 81–131. See also John Gregg, *Maurice Blanchot and the Literature of Transgression* (Princeton: Princeton University Press, 1994), pp. 35–45, 121–125, 160–161; Gerald L. Bruns, *Maurice Blanchot: The Refusal of Philosophy* (Baltimore: Johns Hopkins University Press, 1997), pp. 66–70; Leslie Hill, *Blanchot: Extreme Contemporary* (London: Routledge, 1997), pp. 112–114; Toumayan, *Encountering the Other*, pp. 27, 155. On the related discussion of poetry as the politics of the impossible, see Bruns, *Maurice Blanchot*, pp. 34–55.

145. Levinas, "Reflections," p. 69.

146. Ibid., p. 65.

147. Levinas, *Totality and Infinity*, p. 54 (emphasis in original); *Totalité et infini*, p. 25.

148. Levinas, "Reflections," p. 65.

149. Ibid. For an elaboration of Levinas's views, see Edith Wyschogrod, "Repentance and Forgiveness: The Undoing of Time," *International Journal for Philosophy of Religion* 60 (2006): 157–168.

150. Numerous scholars have discussed the Platonic and Neoplatonic influence on the apophatic dimensions of Levinas's thought. For example, see Jean-Marc Narbonne, *Levinas and the Greek Heritage* (Leuven: Peeters, 2006); John Izzi, "Proximity in Distance: Levinas and Plotinus," in *Levinas and the Ancients*, edited by Brian Schroeder and Silvia Benso (Bloomington: Indiana University Press, 2008), pp. 196–209; Brian Schroeder, "A Trace of the Eternal Return? Levinas and Neoplatonism," in *Levinas and the Ancients*, pp. 210–229; Allen, *The Philosophical Sense of Transcendence*; Tanja Staehler, *Plato and Levinas: The Ambiguous Out-Side of Ethics* (New York: Routledge, 2010). For a critique of the Levinasian attempt to deploy phenomenology in the service of retrieving the Platonic metaphysics of transcendence, see Stella Sandford, *The Metaphysics of Love: Gender and Transcendence in Levinas* (London: Athlone Press, 2000), pp. 1–32.

151. Emmanuel Levinas, *Existence and Existents*, translated by Alphonso Lingis, foreword by Robert Bernasconi (Pittsburgh: Duquesne University Press, 2001), p. xxvii. See Bernasconi, "No Exit," pp. 106–107.

152. Levinas, *Existence and Existents*, pp. 81–82.

153. Ibid., p. 82.

154. Ibid., p. 77. In *Otherwise than Being*, pp. 34–35 (*Autrement qu'être*, p. 44), Levinas expands on the essential connection of the verb and the temporalization of time, inspired most likely by the German word for verb, *Zeitwort*, literally, time-word: "Essence, temporalization, is the verbalness of a verb [*la verbalité du verbe*]. To suggest the difference between Being [*l'être*] and entities [*l'étant*], and the strange temporal itch, a modification without change, one resorts to metaphors taken from the temporal and not from time [*l'on recourt à des métaphores empruntées au temporel et non pas au temps*]. . . . But being is the verb itself. Temporalization is the verb form to be [*le verbe de l'être*]. Language issued from the verbalness of a verb would then not only consist in making being understood, but also in making its essence vibrate." The attentive ear will discern an implicit critique of Heidegger here.

155. Levinas, *Proper Names*, p. 63 (in that context, Levinas is describing Jabès, but his words can be applied to the nature of the poet as such).

156. Edith Wyschogrod, "Language and Alterity in the Thought of Levinas," in *The Cambridge Companion to Levinas*, pp. 200–201.

157. Levinas, *Proper Names*, pp. 41–43. Compare Gerald L. Bruns, "The Concepts of Art and Poetry in Emmanuel Levinas's Writings," in *The Cambridge Companion to Levinas*, pp. 216–220, and the analysis of both the poetic style of Levinas and his views on poetry in Megan Craig, *Levinas and James: Toward a Pragmatic Phenomenology*

(Bloomington: Indiana University Press, 2010), pp. 130–159. On the image of the leap in Celan's poetics, see Ch. 2 n. 268.

158. Many scholars have discussed the account of *il y a* in Blanchot and Levinas. For a representative list, see Critchley, "*Il y a*—A Dying Stronger than Death," pp. 110–116; idem, "*Il y a*—Holding Levinas's Hand to Blanchot's Fire," in *Maurice Blanchot: The Demand of Writing*, edited by Carolyn Bailey Gill (London: Routledge, 1996), pp. 108–122; Davies, "A Linear Narrative?" pp. 42–58; Bruns, *Maurice Blanchot*, pp. 58–61; Hill, *Blanchot*, pp. 62–63, 110–112, 115–117; Toumayan, *Encountering the Other*, pp. 148–155.

159. Levinas, *Proper Names*, pp. 131–132.

160. Ibid., p. 134.

161. Ibid.

162. Ibid., p. 137.

163. This aspect of the Levinasian account of transcendence has been emphasized by Westphal, "Levinas, Kierkegaard, and the Theological Task," p. 243: "The criterion of genuine otherness or transcendence is self-transcendence, the journey from the false self that wills to be the center to the true self that welcomes the Other." See idem, *Transcendence and Self-Transcendence: On God and the Soul* (Bloomington: Indiana University Press, 2004), pp. 177–200.

164. Levinas, *Proper Names*, p. 43.

165. Levinas, *Otherwise than Being*, pp. 169–170; *Autrement qu'être*, pp. 215–216.

166. Levinas, *Otherwise than Being*, p. 108; *Autrement qu'être*, p. 137.

167. Taylor, *Altarity*, p. 215. On the interweaving of the Jewish tradition concerning the unsayable name and the philosophical concept of the infinite transcendent, see Gibbs, "The Name of God," pp. 97–112, and below, n. 402.

168. Levinas, *Existence and Existents*, p. 61 (emphasis in original).

169. William James, *The Principles of Psychology* (Cambridge, MA: Harvard University Press, 1981), p. 462. To date, the most extensive attempt to read Levinas through the lens of James is offered by Craig, *Levinas and James*. However, she does not discuss the Levinasian *il y a* in light of James's "blooming, buzzing confusion."

170. Levinas, *Existence and Existents*, p. 61.

171. Levinas, *Ethics and Infinity*, p. 49, thus summarized this discussion in *Existence and Existents* in the interview with Nemo: "Other experiences, all close to the 'there is,' are described in this book, notably that of insomnia. In insomnia one can and one cannot say that there is an 'I' which cannot manage to fall asleep. The impossibility of escaping wakefulness is something 'objective,' independent of my initiative. This impersonality absorbs my consciousness; consciousness is depersonalized. I do not stay awake: 'it' stays awake." Compare the analysis of insomnia in Craig, *Levinas and James*, pp. 1–31, esp. 16–18, and see Bergo, *Levinas*, p. 60; Critchley, *Very Little . . . Almost Nothing*, pp. 57–58.

172. Levinas, *Existence and Existents*, p. 62.

173. Levinas, *Collected Philosophical Papers*, p. 4.

174. Wolfson, *A Dream*, pp. 74–90. The position I took in my analysis and what I think Levinas is also articulating was expressed in a different way by Paul Kugler, *The Alchemy of Discourse: An Archetypal Approach to Language* (Lewisburg: Bucknell University Press, 1982), p. 94: "The traditional approach to language and dreams has been to imagine the word or dream-image as a piece of paper. On one side is the image (acoustic or oneiric) and on the other side is the meaning. . . . We have attempted to reimagine the sheet of paper as a Möbius strip, a strip of paper with only one side, thus doing away with the nominalist-realist split. By sticking to the image and pushing it far enough . . . we suddenly find ourselves on the meaning side, the other side, and yet we never left the image or the phenomenal world. Image has become meaning has become image has become meaning." See also the brief but incisive analysis of the dream in Jean-Yves Lacoste, "The Appearing and the Irreducible," in *Words of Life: New Theological Turns in French Phenomenology*, edited by Bruce Ellis Benson and Norman Wirzba (New York: Fordham University Press, 2010), pp. 45–46, 61–62. I regret that at the time of writing my book on dreams I was unaware of Jerry J. Valberg, *Dream, Death, and the Self* (Princeton: Princeton University Press, 2007). In a manner analogous to my own analysis, Valberg presumes that the phenomenological distinction between dream and reality must be deconstructed, and that at the center of the dream is a "personal horizon" that culminates with death. The experience of nothingness imposed by the "solipsistic impossibility" of death—the termination of the sense of "mineness" of the subject matter that will cease to be—casts light on the nature of the self that both constructs and is constructed by the dream. See especially Valberg, op. cit., p. 180: "Facts of presence . . . hold only from within this subject matter, only from within the horizon. So if there were no horizon, there would be no such facts. There would be a sheer absence of presence. What would that be like? . . . It is a big zero, an unimaginable blank. An unimaginable nothingness: NOTHINGNESS. If there were no horizon, nothing would be present, and if nothing were present, there would be NOTHING. The world, we may assume, would still be there, just as it is. But it would not be present, or appear in any way. There would be NOTHING. . . . If there were NOTHING, there would be no such thing as THIS."

175. Levinas, *Existence and Existents*, p. 57. Compare the discussion of nightmares and dreams in Llewelyn, *Margins of Religion*, pp. 186–193. See also the analysis of Macbeth's final words in Levinas, *Time and the Other*, pp. 72–73, which concludes that "*Hamlet* is precisely a lengthy testimony to this impossibility of assuming death. Nothingness is impossible. . . . 'To be or not to be' is a sudden awareness of this impossibility of annihilating oneself."

176. Luce Irigaray, *Elemental Passions*, translated by Joanne Collie and Judith Still (New York: Routledge, 1992), p. 38.

177. Jean-Luc Nancy, *The Fall of Sleep*, translated by Charlotte Mandell (New York: Fordham University Press, 2009), pp. 13–15 (emphasis in original). I regret not having cited Nancy's work in my own analysis of a similar theme (see reference in n. 174). For a critical response to Nancy, see Nicolas de Warren, "The Inner Night: Towards a Phe-

nomenology of (Dreamless) Sleep," in *On Time—New Contributions to the Husserlian Phenomenology of Time*, edited by Dieter Lohmar and Ichiro Yamaguchi (Dordrecht: Springer, 2010), pp. 273–294. It is instructive to compare and contrast the view of Nancy with the following statement of Eugen Fink, inspired by the Heraclitean saying "In the night, a man kindles a light because his sight is quenched; while living, he approximates to a dead man during sleep; while awake, he approximates to one who sleeps" (Freeman, *Ancilla*, p. 26), in Martin Heidegger and Eugen Fink, *Heraclitus Seminar 1966/67*, translated by Charles H. Seibert (University, Alabama: University of Alabama Press, 1979), p. 137: "In dreaming, we must distinguish the one who dreams and the dreamed I. . . . The sleeper, or the sleeping I, is also the dreaming I, who is not the I of the dream world who is awake and sees in the dreams. In the dream world, the I of the dream world behaves similarly to the wakeful I. While the dreaming I sleeps, the dreamed I of the dream world finds itself in a condition of wakefulness. . . . A phenomenological analysis of the dream indicates that not the sleeping, but the dreamed I kindles a light. Although the sleeper does not see, still, as a dreamer, he has a dreamed I that has encounters. . . . Dreaming is a mode of the real I, while being awake in the dream world is the mode of an intentional I. . . . Only because we customarily do not make the distinction between the sleeping-dreaming I and the I of the dream world, can one say that the sleeper kindles a light in the dream. Seen phenomenologically, however, that is not correct. The I of the dream world, and not the sleeping I, kindles a light."

178. Bergo, *Levinas*, p. 59.

179. Levinas, *Existence and Existents*, p. 83. Compare the comments of Levinas included in Wahl, *A Short History of Existentialism*, p. 50: "Well, I think that the new philosophical 'twist' originated by Heidegger consists in distinguishing between *Being* and *being* (thing or person), and in giving to *Being* the relation, the movement, the efficacy which until then resided in the existent. Existentialism is to experience and think existence—the verb 'to be'—as event, an event which neither produces that which exists, nor is the action of what exists upon another object. It is the pure fact of existing which is event" (emphasis in original). See, however, Levinas, *Time and the Other*, p. 44. After rendering Heidegger's distinction between *Sein* and *Seiendes* respectively as "existing" and "existent," Levinas notes that he does not intend to ascribe a "specifically existentialist meaning to these terms."

180. Levinas, *Existence and Existents*, p. 59.

181. Ibid., pp. 59–60 (emphasis in original).

182. Levinas, *Time and the Other*, p. 46.

183. Ibid., pp. 47–50. Tellingly, Levinas invokes the teaching of Heraclitus offered by Cratylus—reality may be compared to the river in which one cannot bathe even once—as an analogue to his conception of the there is, which lacks any "fixity of unity" (p. 49), a radical notion of becoming that undermines the idea of being affirmed by the Parmenidean monism. Compare Levinas, *Totality and Infinity*, p. 60; *Totalité et infini*, p. 31.

184. Levinas, *Existence and Existents*, p. 35.

185. Ibid., pp. 88–89.

186. Ibid., p. 90 (emphasis in original).

187. In my opinion, the reflections of Heidegger on the ecstatic character of time as the temporalizing transcendence, which is dependent on the futural dimension of human existence as the being-there (*Dasein*) that is essentially a movement of self-surpassing, have more in common with Levinas's own notion of diachrony than he acknowledged. See Ch. 2 n. 196. On the similarity between the Levinasian diachrony and Heideggerian ekstasis, see Françoise Dastur, "Phenomenology of the Event: Waiting and Surprise," *Hypatia* 15 (2000): 182. For a dissenting view, see Patrick L. Bourgeois, "Ricoeur between Levinas and Heidegger: Another's Further Alterity," *Journal of French and Francophone Philosophy* 11 (2010): 36–37.

188. Levinas, *Time and the Other*, p. 39.

189. Ibid., pp. 30–31.

190. Ibid., p. 31.

191. Ibid., p. 32 (emphasis in original).

192. Ibid.

193. On the ethical relation and time, see Levinas, *Totality and Infinity*, pp. 220–247; *Totalité et infini*, pp. 195–225.

194. Levinas, *Totality and Infinity*, p. 269; *Totalité et infini*, p. 247.

195. Levinas, *Time and the Other*, p. 75.

196. Ibid., p. 76. Even with regard to this matter, it is of interest to compare Levinas's view of eros with Heidegger, *Nietzsche, Volume I*, p. 194 (*Nietzsche: Der Wille zur Macht als Kunst*, pp. 239–240): "As soon as man lets himself be bound by Being in his view upon it, he is cast beyond himself [*wird er über sich hinaus entrückt*], so that he is stretched, as it were, between himself and Being and is outside himself [*außer sich ist*]. Such elevation beyond oneself [*Über-sich-hinweg-gehoben*] and such being drawn toward Being itself [*vom Sein selbst Angezogen-werden*] is *erōs*. Only to the extent that Being is able to elicit 'erotic' power in its relation to man is man capable of thinking about Being and overcoming oblivion of Being [*Seinsvergessenheit*]." The forgetfulness of Being, also referred to as Being concealing itself, comes about when human beings fall prey to mere appearance and to the prevailing opinions concerning beings. The state of the conceal-ment of Being is so severe that human beings no longer know that the appearances are mere appearances, for if they were to possess such knowledge, they would at least catch a glimpse of Being peering through the fleeting appearances and would thereby be rescued from the oblivion. When, however, one is bound to the otherness of Being, then one is transformed ecstatically, standing outside of oneself, an ascension to Being that Hei-degger names *eros*. It goes without saying that I am not suggesting that Heidegger's treatment of eros in any way equals Levinas, but I do think it is important to point out some elements of commonality if for no other reason than to underscore that even with regard to this topic Levinas was responding to Heidegger. On Heidegger's discussion of eros in conjunction with his notion of striving for being (*Seinserstrebnis*), see Gonzalez, *Plato and Heidegger*, pp. 189–192. Levinas's dialogue with Heidegger on the subject of

eros is discussed extensively by Drew M. Dalton, *Longing for the Other: Levinas and Metaphysical Desire* (Pittsburgh: Duquesne University Press, 2009), pp. 67–110. I concur with Dalton's assertion that "on closer investigation we discover, that at least in terms of his conception of human longing, Levinas is profoundly indebted to Heidegger for providing a framework upon which to build his understanding of metaphysical desire, and for providing a system with which Levinas can disagree in the attempt to enunciate more fully his own understanding of the phenomenon" (p. 68). For a valuable discussion of eros in Levinas's thought, see Bergo, *Levinas*, pp. 111–119.

197. Levinas, *Time and the Other*, p. 87.

198. Ibid., p. 32. The themes of eros, femininity, mystery, and modesty are explored in more detail in Levinas, *Totality and Infinity*, pp. 256–266; *Totalité et infini*, pp. 233–244. See Wolfson, "Secrecy, Modesty, and the Feminine." For a more contemporary articulation that parallels Levinas's understanding of the diachronic temporality of the deferred present and the impossible possibility of waiting for a future that is already past when it arrives, see Claude Romano, "Awaiting," in *Phenomenology and Eschatology*, pp. 35–52, esp. 46–47.

199. For a fuller discussion of this theme, see Wolfson, *Open Secret*, pp. 265–300.

200. Levinas, *Time and the Other*, p. 54.

201. Levinas, *Totality and Infinity*, pp. 22–23 (emphasis in original); *Totalité et infini*, p. xi.

202. Levinas, *Totality and Infinity*, p. 23 (emphasis in original); *Totalité et infini*, pp. xi-xii. See the analysis of this passage in Ajzenstat, *Driven Back*, pp. 68–71. And see the concise presentation of Levinas's view in Calvin O. Schrag, *God as Otherwise Than Being: Towards a Semantics of the Gift* (Evanston: Northwestern University Press, 2002), p. 113: "The eschatology of Levinas draws its inspiration from a philosophy of difference, in which the Kingdom of God is always deferred, yet to come, to unfold in the fullness of time that is never that of a present." The ostensibly apolitical and ahistorical implications of Levinas's position are noted in Butler, *Parting Ways*, pp. 40–42: "For Levinas, then, messianism seems linked with this fact, that judgment does not and cannot occur in history. The order of morality is not evinced in any historically unfolding sequence of events, and we cannot regard historical events, no matter how terrible or felicitous, as enacting or revealing moral judgments of some kind. . . . One is called upon to respond ethically, and this call is the effective action of the messianic upon human life. If messianism is engaged in a form of waiting, a waiting for the Messiah and, indeed a waiting for justice, it also is precisely a kind of waiting that cannot be fulfilled in historical time. Messianism is distinguished from eschatology. If one waits for judgment within time, one waits for that which time itself can *never* deliver. If there is a sense to the messianic, it will consist of the interruption of historical time by something outside it. . . . Messianism, for Levinas, establishes a perspective by which both history and politics are considered arbitrary, unjustified, even absurd: if we cannot feel the absurd element in history, a part of our messianic sensibility is lost" (emphasis in original). I concur that Levinas promotes a messianism that is divorced from eschatology and thus affirms a waiting that can never be consummated by the arrival of the one for whom one

is waiting, but I do not accept Butler's assertion that his perspective rendered history and politics arbitrary, unjustified, and absurd. The conception of temporality implied by this harboring of a messianic belief that cannot be realized in time is precisely what renders the historical and the political meaningful, justified, and sensible. In this regard, Levinas's position conforms to Neusner's contention that the messianism promulgated by the rabbinic sages of the Mishnah was an ahistorical force, a teleology without an eschatology. This posture was meant to lead the Jewish people away from the belief that redemption could be achieved politically, that the end of time could be reached only by rising above time. The ahistorical, therefore, is not capricious and meaningless; on the contrary, it bespeaks the enduring patterns that promote and inculcate the metahistorical task of sanctification, as opposed to salvation, which was imposed upon Israel as part of its sacred mission. See Jacob Neusner, *Messiah in Context: Israel's History and Destiny in Formative Judaism* (Philadelphia: Fortress Press, 1984), pp. 12–16, 18–20; idem, *Death and Birth of Judaism: The Impact of Christianity, Secularism, and the Holocaust on Jewish Faith* (New York: Basic Books, 1987), pp. 56–57; idem, *Theological and Philosophical Premises of Judaism* (Boston: Academic Studies Press, 2008), pp. 55–58. A full appreciation of Neusner's interpretation of rabbinic messianism would require an exploration of the atemporal temporality that he elicits from the sources. See Jacob Neusner, "Paradigmatic Versus Historical Thinking: The Case of Rabbinic Judaism," *History and Theory* 36 (1997): 353–377, esp. 354–355; idem, *The Presence of the Past, The Pastness of the Present: History, Time, and Paradigm in Rabbinic Judaism* (Bethesda: CDL Press, 1999); idem, *The Theology of the Oral Torah: Revealing the Justice of God* (Montreal: McGill-Queen's University Press, 1999), pp. 241–279; idem, *Handbook of Rabbinic Theology: Language, System, Structure* (Leiden: Brill, 2002), pp. 179–198; idem, *The Idea of History in Rabbinic Judaism* (Leiden: Brill, 2004), pp. 45–68, 193–230; idem, *Theological and Philosophical Premises of Judaism*, pp. 35–58. I hope one day to write a full analysis of Neusner's reflections on time in rabbinic thought, but for the time being, see my brief remarks in *Alef, Mem, Tau*, p. 208 n. 21. See also Kevin P. Edgecomb, "An Appreciation and Précis of Jacob Neusner's *Theology of the Oral Torah: Revealing the Justice of God*," in *The Documentary History of Judaism and Its Recent Interpreters*, edited by Jacob Neusner (Lanham: University Press of America, 2010), pp. 71–82.

203. One would do well to recall Derrida's observation about Levinas in *Writing and Difference*, p. 83 (*L'écriture et la différence*, pp. 123–124): "If the messianic eschatology from which Levinas draws inspiration seeks neither to assimilate itself into what is called a philosophical truism, nor even to 'complete'. . . philosophical truisms, nevertheless it is developed in its discourse neither as a theology, nor as a Jewish mysticism (it can even be understood as the trial of theology and mysticism); neither as a dogmatics, nor as *a* religion, nor as *a* morality. . . . Truthfully, messianic eschatology is never mentioned literally: it is but a question of designating a space or a hollow within naked experience where this eschatology can be understood and where it must resonate" (emphasis in original). The first part of the final sentence needs to be modified, but the main drift of Derrida's comments is compatible with my own analysis. See Ch. 6 n. 215.

204. Levinas, *Totality and Infinity*, p. 280; *Totalité et infini*, p. 257.

205. Levinas, *Totality and Infinity*, p. 285; *Totalité et infini*, p. 261. See Howard Caygill, *Levinas and the Political* (London: Routledge, 2002), pp. 97–98; Welz, *Love's Transcendence*, pp. 302–303.

206. Maurice Blanchot, *The Writing of Disaster*, translated by Ann Smock (Lincoln: University of Nebraska Press, 1986), pp. 141–142.

207. Walter Benjamin, *Selected Writings, Volume 4: 1938–1940*, translated by Edmund Jephcott and others, edited by Howard Eiland and Michael W. Jennings (Cambridge, MA: Harvard University Press, 2003), p. 396.

208. Ibid., p. 397.

209. Ibid. See Werner Hamacher, " 'Now': Walter Benjamin on Historical Time," in *Walter Benjamin and History*, edited by Andrew Benjamin (London: Continuum, 2005), pp. 38–68. Another crucial aspect of Benjamin's eschatological speculation relates to his speculation on the "pure" or "originary" language as the symbolic expression of the noncommunicable. Concerning this theme, see Marc de Launay, "Messianisme et philologie du langage," *Modern Language Notes* 127 (2012): 645–664.

210. Walter Benjamin, *Selected Writings, Volume 3: 1935–1938*, translated by Edmund Jephcott, Howard Eiland, and others, edited by Howard Eiland and Michael W. Jennings (Cambridge, MA: Harvard University Press, 2002), p. 305. On the pessimistic implications of Benjamin's messianism, which "promises neither realization nor redemption" on the stage of world politics, see Rose, *Judaism and Modernity*, p. 189.

211. Kluback, *The Idea of Humanity*, pp. 25–26; Kenneth Seeskin, "Maimonides and Hermann Cohen on Messianism," *Maimonidean Studies* 5 (2008): 380; idem, "Judaism and the Idea of Future," in *Judaic Sources and Western Thought: Jerusalem's Enduring Presence*, edited by Jonathan A. Jacobs (Oxford: Oxford University Press, 2011), pp. 60–61, 65–66; Weiss, *Paradox and the Prophets*, pp. 180–214. See also Wendell S. Dietrich, "The Function of the Idea of Messianic Mankind in Hermann Cohen's Later Thought," *Journal of the American Academy of Religion* 48 (1980): 245–258; Robert Gibbs, "Hermann Cohen's Messianism: The History of the Future," in *"Religion der Vernunft aus den Quellen des Judentums,"* pp. 331–349; Pierfrancesco Fiorato, "Notes on Future and History in Hermann Cohen's Anti-Eschatological Messianism," in *Hermann Cohen's Critical Idealism*, pp. 133–160; Andrea Poma, "Suffering and Non-Eschatological Messianism in Hermann Cohen," in *Hermann Cohen's Critical Idealism*, pp. 413–428; Myriam Bienenstock, "Hermann Cohen on the Concept of History: An Invention of Prophetism?" *Journal of Jewish Thought and Philosophy* 20 (2012): 55–70. For the influence of Cohen's ethical idealism, rejection of the mythological, and the emphasis on the future in Cassirer's thought, see Kluback, *The Idea of Humanity*, pp. 102–103, 216.

212. Schwarzschild, *The Pursuit of the Ideal*, pp. 209–211. Compare the comment of Martin Buber cited from Ernst Simon, "Martin Buber: His Way between Thought and Deed," *Jewish Frontier* 15 (1948): 26, in Maurice S. Friedman, *Martin Buber: The Life of Dialogue*, 4th edition (New York: Routledge, 2002), p. 332: "There are no knots in the mighty cable of our Messianic belief, which, fastened to a rock on Sinai, stretches to a

380 NOTES TO PAGE 116

still invisible peg anchored in the foundations of the world. In our view, redemption occurs forever, and none has yet occurred. Standing, bound and shackled, in the pillory of mankind, we demonstrate with the bloody body of our people the unredeemedness of the world." The lack of eschatological finality precludes the possibility of Jews accepting the Christian belief that Jesus was the actual Messiah, although Buber maintained that Jews would eventually come to accept the vital role accorded to Jesus in the messianic drama of history. See Arthur A. Cohen, *The Myth of the Judeo-Christian Tradition and Other Dissenting Essays* (New York: Harper & Row, 1970), p. 31. On the messianic role and the in-between status of the Jew as being "neither committed nor aloof, neither rooted nor alien, neither of this world nor of any other," see Cohen, *The Natural and the Supernatural Jew*, pp. 306–311, esp. 309. And compare the analogous Levinasian view in Altizer, *Living the Death of God*, p. 62: "There is certainly a deep aniconic ground in the Jew which is alien to the Christian, a ground precluding any possibility of incarnation, and just as the Jewish Messiah is deeply different from the Christian Messiah, a Messiah who could never be the Son of God, the Jewish apocalypse is radically different from the Christian apocalypse, and is so if only because it could never actually be envisioned, and all too significantly rabbinic Judaism was only truly born with a full negation of apocalyptic Judaism."

213. The similarity between Cohen and Levinas is noted by Schwarzschild, *The Pursuit of the Ideal*, pp. 312–313 n. 76. For discussion of the messianic idea of the infinite in Cohen and Levinas, see Wyschogrod, *Crossover Queries*, pp. 419–422. For other studies that discuss the affinities between Cohen and Levinas, see Introduction n. 65.

214. Many scholars have discussed the messianic in Levinas's thought. Here I list a sampling of some of the relevant studies: Handelman, *Fragments*, pp. 306–336; Graham Ward, "On Time and Salvation: The Eschatology of Emmanuel Levinas," in *Facing the Other: The Ethics of Emmanuel Levinas*, edited by Seán Hand (Surrey: Curzon, 1996), pp. 153–172; Robert Bernasconi, "Different Styles of Eschatology: Derrida's Take on Levinas' Political Messianism," *Research in Phenomenology* 28 (1998): 3–19; Wyschogrod, *Emmanuel Levinas*, pp. 194–207; Caygill, *Levinas and the Political*, pp. 166–172; Ajzenstat, *Driven Back*, pp. 247–275; Elias Bongmba, "Eschatology: Levinasian Hints in a Preface," in *Levinas and Biblical Studies*, edited by Tamara Cohn Eskenazi, Gary A. Phillips, and David Jobling (Atlanta: Society of Biblical Literature, 2003), pp. 75–90; Kavka, *Jewish Messianism*, pp. 129–192; Catherine Chalier, "The Messianic Utopia," in *Emmanuel Levinas: Critical Assessments of Leading Philosophers*, vol. 3: *Levinas, Judaism, and the Philosophy of Religion*, edited by Claire Elise Katz (New York: Routledge, 2005), pp. 44–58; idem, *La trace de l'infini*, pp. 168–169; Morgan, *Discovering Levinas*, pp. 208–227; Bergo, *Levinas*, pp. 148–168; idem, "The Time and Language of Messianism: Levinas and Saint Paul," in *Levinas and the Ancients*, pp. 178–195; idem, "Levinas's Weak Messianism in Time and Flesh, or the Insistence of Messiah Ben David," in *The Messianic Now*, pp. 45–68; Ephraim Meir, *Levinas's Jewish Thought: Between Jerusalem and Athens* (Jerusalem: Magnes Press, 2008), pp. 116–119, 201–204; Fagenblat, *A Covenant of Creatures*, pp. 94–96; Bouretz, *Witness for the Future*, pp. 647–719; Dana

Hollander, " 'A Thought in Which Everything Has Been Thought': On the Messianic Idea in Levinas," in *Symposium: Canadian Journal of Continental Philosophy/Revue canadienne de philosophie continentale* 14 (2010): 133–159; Del Nevo, "The Kabbalistic Heart of Levinas," pp. 188–191; Bielik-Robson, "Tarrying with the Apocalypse," pp. 69–86, esp. 74–79. See also the intermittent comments on the subject of messianism in the conversation between David Kangas and Martin Kavka, "Hearing, Patiently: Time and Salvation in Kierkegaard and Levinas," in *Kierkegaard and Levinas: Ethics, Politics, and Religion*, edited by J. Aaron Simmons and David Wood (Bloomington: Indiana University Press, 2008), pp. 125–152.

215. Levinas, *Difficult Freedom*, p. 59.

216. Ibid., p. 84 (emphasis in original).

217. In response to Kearney's question about the possibility of an "eschatology of noncoincidence wherein man and God could coexist eternally without fusing into oneness," Levinas responded: "But why eschatology? Why should we wish to reduce time to eternity? Time is the most profound relationship that man can have with God, precisely as a going towards God. . . . To be in time is to be for God (*être à Dieu*), a perpetual leave taking (*adieu*)" (*Face to Face with Levinas*, p. 23). See ibid., p. 31, where Levinas affirms the sense of the messianic "according to the Talmudic maxim that 'the doctors of the law will never have peace, neither in this world nor in the next; they go from meeting to meeting, discussing always—for there is always more to be discussed.' I could not accept a form of messianism that would terminate the need for discussion, that would end our watchfulness." See Ajzenstat, *Driven Back*, pp. 81–83.

218. Levinas, *Difficult Freedom*, p. 88.

219. On the ethical language of sacrifice in Levinas, see Dennis King Keenan, *The Question of Sacrifice* (Bloomington: Indiana University Press, 2005), pp. 74–88. See also the interesting observation of Edith Wyschogrod, "Introduction," in *The Enigma of Gift and Sacrifice*, edited by Edith Wyschogrod, Jean-Joseph Goux, and Eric Boynton (New York: Fordham University Press, 2002), p. 8, that the concern with sacrificing another in the thought of Levinas bears traces of Maimonides's wariness of sacrificial cults due to their rootedness in the polytheism of the ancient world. In particular, Wyschogrod discerns the vestige of Maimonides's suspicion in Levinas's treatment of the sacrifice of Abraham.

220. Babylonian Talmud, Sanhedrin 98b. In her analysis of Levinas's reading of this rabbinic text, Wyschogrod, *Emmanuel Levinas*, pp. 204–206, notes the similarity of Levinas's interpretation and the response of Jesus (Luke 17:20–21) to the query of the Pharisees regarding the coming of the kingdom of God to the effect that it is not an observable phenomenon on the historical plane but an internal shift within each person. See also Handelman, *Fragments*, p. 332; Ajzenstat, *Driven Back*, p. 265.

221. Levinas, *Difficult Freedom*, p. 89.

222. Ibid., p. 90. Compare the discussion of this passage in Butler, *Parting Ways*, pp. 40–41.

223. Levinas, *Time and the Other*, p. 33.

224. Ibid., p. 42. For an analysis that complements the Levinasian perspective, see John D. Caputo, "Temporal Transcendence: The Very Idea of *à venir* in Derrida," in *Transcendence and Beyond*, pp. 188–203. See also Joanna Hodge, *Derrida On Time* (London: Routledge, 2007), pp. 196–214.

225. Levinas, *Time and the Other*, p. 61.

226. On the "messianic naturalism" in Maimonides and Levinas, see Fagenblat, *A Covenant of Creatures*, pp. 94–96, 225 n. 60. For discussion of the Maimonidean depiction of the messianic era, see Aviezer Ravitzky, *History and Faith: Studies in Jewish Philosophy* (Amsterdam: J. C. Gieben, 1996), pp. 73–112.

227. Levinas, *Beyond the Verse*, p. 181.

228. Ibid., p. 150.

229. Levinas, *Time and the Other*, p. 94.

230. Compare Levinas, *Oeuvres 1: Carnets*, p. 173: "*Le messianisme est plus qu'une 'creation' parfaite. Et il n'y aurait pas de Messie sans temps. Temps condition de la 'consommation.'*"

231. Levinas, *Beyond the Verse*, p. 143. Levinas's views can be profitably compared to Yeshayahu Leibowitz's rejection of a literal understanding of the messianic redeemer, but this is a matter that lies beyond the scope of this chapter. See the preliminary remarks of Adam Zachary Newton, *The Fence and the Neighbor: Emmanuel Levinas, Yeshayahu Leibowitz, and Israel among the Nations* (Albany: State University of New York Press, 2001), pp. 95–96; Michael Fagenblat, "Lacking All Interest: Levinas, Leibowitz, and the Pure Practice of Religion," *Harvard Theological Review* 97 (2004): 7 n. 18. See below, n. 396.

232. Emmanuel Levinas, *God, Death, and Time*, translated by Bettina Bergo (Stanford: Stanford University Press, 2000), p. 139.

233. Maurice Blanchot, *Awaiting Oblivion*, translated by John Gregg (Lincoln: University of Nebraska Press, 1997), pp. 24–25.

234. Levinas, *Of God Who Comes to Mind*, p. 51 (emphasis in original).

235. Levinas, *Beyond the Verse*, p. 122.

236. Wolfson, "Secrecy," pp. 70–71.

237. Levinas, *Beyond the Verse*, pp. 215–216 n. 10.

238. Ibid., p. 216 n. 10.

239. Emmanuel Levinas, *The Levinas Reader*, edited by Seán Hand (Oxford: Blackwell, 1989), p. 149.

240. Ibid., pp. 232–233.

241. Levinas, *God, Death, and Time*, p. 17 (emphasis in original).

242. Ibid., p. 29.

243. Ibid., p. 15.

244. Levinas, *Totality and Infinity*, p. 264 (emphasis in original); *Totalité et infini*, p. 242. Compare *Totality and Infinity*, p. 247 (*Totalité et infini*, p. 225): "Hence truth requires as its ultimate condition an infinite time, the condition for both goodness and the transcendence of the face. . . . But for this condition to be realized, it is not enough

that an infinite time be given. It is necessary to go back to the primary phenomenon of time in which the phenomenon of the 'not yet' is rooted. It is necessary to go back to paternity, without which time is but the image of eternity. Without it the time necessary for the manifestation of truth beyond visible history (but which remains time—that is, is temporalized relative to a present situated in itself and identifiable) would be impossible."

245. Levinas, *Totality and Infinity*, p. 232; *Totalité et infini*, p. 208. See also Levinas, *Of God Who Comes to Mind*, pp. 37–38, where the contrast is drawn between Heidegger's privileging the ecstasy of the future in his notion of being-toward-death and the nothingness of the future in the Marxist utopianism of Bloch: "The nothingness of the utopia is not the nothingness of death, and hope is not anguish. . . . But it is not death that, in Bloch, opens the authentic future, and it is relative to the future of utopia that death itself must be understood. The future of utopia is the hope of realizing that which is not yet." See Bouretz, *Witness for the Future*, pp. 461–462. Compare the discussion of the temporality of consciousness and the time of death in Bergo, *Levinas*, pp. 96–100.

246. Levinas, *Totality and Infinity*, p. 234; *Totalité et infini*, pp. 210–211.

247. Levinas, *Totality and Infinity*, p. 235; *Totalité et infini*, p. 211.

248. Levinas, *Discovering Existence*, p. 148; see Bernet, "Levinas's Critique," p. 92. And compare Levinas, *Basic Philosophical Writings*, p. 155. Commenting on Bergson's notion of *durée* as "pure change" and the "bursting forth of incessant novelty," Levinas writes: "Does not temporality itself announce itself here as a transcendence, as a thinking under which, independently of any experience, the alterity of absolute novelty, the absolute in the etymological sense of the term, would burst forth?"

249. Branko Klun, "Transcendence and Time: Levinas's Criticism of Heidegger," *Gregorianum* 88 (2007): 587–603.

250. Levinas, *Time and the Other*, pp. 71–72.

251. Levinas, *God, Death, and Time*, p. 50.

252. Ibid., p. 52 (emphasis in original).

253. The expression appears in the 1982 essay "Diachrony and Representation," in Levinas, *Time and the Other*, p. 114.

254. Levinas, *Totality and Infinity*, p. 282; *Totalité et infini*, p. 258.

255. Levinas, *God, Death, and Time*, p. 33.

256. Levinas, *Totality and Infinity*, p. 267; *Totalité et infini*, p. 245.

257. Levinas, *Totality and Infinity*, p. 284; *Totalité et infini*, p. 260.

258. Levinas, *Totality and Infinity*, p. 275; *Totalité et infini*, p. 252. See Yael Lin, "Finding Time for a Fecund Feminine in Levinas's Thought," *Philosophy Today* 53 (2009): 179–190.

259. Levinas, *Discovering Existence*, p. 148.

260. Levinas, *Otherwise than Being*, p. 32 (emphasis in original); *Autrement qu'être*, pp. 40–41. Compare the critique of Husserl's privileging of presence, the present, and representation, and the consequent interpretation of the diachrony of time as a privation of synchrony, in Levinas, *Entre Nous*, pp. 125–126.

261. Levinas, *Totality and Infinity*, pp. 283–284; *Totalité et infini*, p. 260. See the discussion of Bergson and Heidegger in Levinas, *God, Death, and Time*, pp. 54–56; the brief remarks in the interview with Poirié in Levinas, *Is It Righteous to Be?* pp. 30–31; and compare the passage from *Basic Philosophical Writings* cited above, n. 248.

262. Emmanuel Levinas, *Transcendance et intelligibilité: Suivi d'un entretien* (Geneva: Labor et Fides, 1996), pp. 35–36.

263. Levinas, *Totality and Infinity*, p. 284; *Totalité et infini*, p 261.

264. See Dastur, "Phenomenology of the Event," p. 182.

265. Levinas, *Totality and Infinity*, p. 284; *Totalité et infini*, p. 261.

266. Levinas, *Totality and Infinity*, pp. 284–285; *Totalité et infini*, p. 261.

267. See Levinas's critique of Heidegger on this point in *En découvrant*, p. 127. Compare my summation of Levinas's view in Wolfson, *Alef, Mem, Tau*, p. 158: "The sign at the end signifies that which (properly speaking) cannot be signified, the transcendent alterity opening time to eternity, not to be rendered in the Platonic sense of an immutable realm that stands over and against the temporal, but rather in the apprehension of the eternality of time and the temporality of eternity, a middle way that renders the traditional binary between evanescence and permanence obsolete."

268. Levinas, *Otherwise than Being*, p. 52; *Autrement qu'être*, p. 67.

269. Levinas, *Totality and Infinity*, p. 171; *Totalité et infini*, p. 146.

270. Levinas, *Totality and Infinity*, pp. 192–193; *Totalité et infini*, pp. 166–167.

271. Levinas, *Totality and Infinity*, p. 295; *Totalité et infini*, p. 271.

272. Levinas, *Totality and Infinity*, pp. 27–28; *Totalité et infini*, p. xvi.

273. Wyschogrod, *Emmanuel Levinas*, p. xxii. Emanuel Levinas, *Nine Talmudic Readings*, translated and with an introduction by Annette Aronowicz (Bloomington: Indiana University Press, 1990), p. 176, identifies idolatry with the politics of the state and as the intellectual temptation of the relative and the exotic. On the thematic link between idolatry and the metaphysics of presence, see Catherine Chalier, "L'idolatrie de l'être à travers le pensée d'Emmanuel Lévinas," in *Idoles: Données et débats. Actes du 24ᵉ Colloque des intellectuels juifs de langue française*, edited by Jean Halpérin et Georges Lévitte (Paris: Denoël, 1985), pp. 89–102. And see the more recent analysis in Annabel Herzog, "Levinas and the Unnamed Balaam: On Ontology and Idolatry," *Journal of Jewish Thought and Philosophy* 19 (2011): 131–146.

274. Levinas, *Totality and Infinity*, p. 195; *Totalité et infini*, p. 169.

275. Levinas, *Totality and Infinity*, p. 195; *Totalité et infini*, p. 169.

276. Levinas, *Totality and Infinity*, p. 196; *Totalité et infini*, p. 170.

277. Levinas, *Otherwise than Being*, pp. 37–38; *Autrement qu'être*, pp. 47–48. See Handelman, *Fragments*, pp. 250–259; Bernhard Waldenfels, "Levinas on the Saying and the Said," in *Addressing Levinas*, pp. 86–97; and the insightful analysis in David Michael Kleinberg-Levin, *Before the Voice of Reason: Echoes of Responsibility in Merleau-Ponty's Ecology and Levinas's Ethics* (Albany: State University of New York Press, 2008), pp. 147–180.

278. Levinas, *Otherwise than Being*, p. 181; *Autrement qu'être*, p. 228.

279. Levinas, *Otherwise than Being*, p. 183; *Autrement qu'être*, p. 230.

280. Levinas, *Face to Face with Levinas*, p. 29 (emphasis in original).

281. Levinas, *Totality and Infinity*, pp. 197–198; *Totalité et infini*, p. 172.

282. Levinas, *Ethics and Infinity*, p. 42. Responding to Nemo's question whether language had the same "originary importance" for him as it did for Heidegger, Levinas said, "In fact, for me, the said [*le dit*] does not count as much as the saying [*le dire*] itself. The latter is important for me less through its information contents than by the fact that it is addressed to an interlocutor." The affinity between Levinas's notion of the Saying and Heidegger's characterization of the "genuine greeting" (*echte Gruß*) is noted by Kleinberg-Levin, *Before the Voice of Reason*, pp. 167–168. On the proximity and distance between the Heideggerian *Sage* and the Levinasian *le dire*, see Ziarek, *Inflected Language*, pp. 86–89, and the comments of Derrida cited below at n. 344.

283. Heidegger, *On the Way to Language*, p. 107; *Unterwegs zur Sprache*, p. 202.

284. Heidegger, *Pathmarks*, pp. 58–59; *Wegmarken*, p. 74. The passage is from the appendix (dated March 11, 1964) to the lecture "Phenomenology and Theology," given on March 9, 1927, in Tübingen and then again on February 14, 1928, in Marburg. The appendix is based on a letter in which Heidegger outlined some of the key issues (*Hauptgesichtspunkte*) pertaining to the discussion on "The Problem of a Nonobjectifying Thinking and Speaking in Today's Theology," which took place at Drew University on April 9–11, 1964.

285. Heidegger, *On the Way to Language*, p. 126; *Unterwegs zur Sprache*, pp. 245–246.

286. I have modified Hertz's translation, "it can only be experienced as the abiding gift yielded by Saying." Rendering *das Gewährende* as the "abiding gift" has implications beyond what Heidegger intended, since he has explicitly stated that the "giving yield" (*Er-gebnis*) of the event of appropriation (*Ereignis*) is not the outcome (*Ergebnis*) of any cause; that is, there is no agency. I trust the word "imparting" will be viewed as more neutral and surely less theologically charged.

287. I have amended Hertz's translation of *reichendes Geben* as the "giving reach."

288. Heidegger, *On the Way to Language*, p. 127; *Unterwegs zur Sprache*, pp. 246–247.

289. Heidegger, *Contributions*, § 21, pp. 45–46; *Beiträge*, p. 56. See idem, *The Event*, § 92, p. 54 (*Das Ereignis*, p. 67): "*The first beginning* ἀλήθεια as the first emergence of the departing essence of being [*abschiedlichen Wesens des Seins*] qua event-related beginning [*ereignishaften Anfangs*]. What is first—it rests on the fact that in general the 'clearing' ['*Lichtung*'] emerges as disconcealment [*Entbergung*]. But at the same time the essence is concealed and receives its determination from beings and the uniqueness of being" (emphasis in original). And compare *The Event*, § 304, p. 240 (*Das Ereignis*, p. 276): "*The first step of inceptual thinking* [*anfänglichen Denkens*] is to ground the 'there'—as opening (in interrogation) the conjunction of the truth of beyng—on the experience of the twisting free of beyng [*die Erfahrung der Verwindung des Seyns*], an experience which itself, as the appropriating event [*Er-eignis*], is the inceptuality of the beginning [*die Anfängnis des Anfangs*]" (emphasis in original). It seems to me that what Heidegger here names the "twisting free" (*Verwindung*) of being (see above, nn. 77–78) corresponds to

the self-concealing or withdrawing of being that transpires in the clearing through which the truth of being in the being of truth is manifest. See *The Event*, § 305, p. 240 (*Das Ereignis*, p. 276): "*The knowledge of thinking* is proficiency in beyng and in its twisting free toward the beginning [*seiner Verwindung in den Anfang*]; this twisting free brings into the clear the inceptuality in the mode of the event, and the foreignness of Da-sein is appropriated out of this clearing" (emphasis in original).

290. For discussion of Heidegger's critique of metaphysical presence, see Chanter, *Time, Death, and the Feminine*, pp. 123–139.

291. Heidegger, *Pathmarks*, p. 241 note b; *Wegmarken*, p. 316 note a.

292. Llewelyn, *Emmanuel Levinas*, pp. 46, 50, and 72. But see idem, *Appositions of Jacques Derrida and Emmanuel Levinas* (Bloomington: Indiana University Press, 2001), p. 108, where a distinction is made between Heidegger's use of *Ereignis* in *Being and Time* and the Levinasian *événement*.

293. Heidegger, *Pathmarks*, p. 240 note a; *Wegmarken*, p. 315 note a.

294. Martin Heidegger, *On Time and Being*, translated by Joan Stambaugh (New York: Harper & Row, 1972), pp. 40–41; *Zur Sache des Denkens* [GA 14] (Frankfurt am Main: Vittorio Klostermann, 2007), pp. 49–50.

295. I have altered Stambaugh's translation of *Seinsprägungen* as the "formations of Being" to the "imprints of Being," which seems to better convey the agency of the swaying-ground of the event of *Ereignis*.

296. Heidegger, *On Time and Being*, p. 41; *Zur Sache des Denkens*, p. 50. See the discussion of appropriation and concealment in Stambaugh, *The Finitude of Being*, pp. 75–82.

297. Thomas Sheehan, "Facticity and *Ereignis*," in *Interpreting Heidegger*, p. 42.

298. Levinas, *Ethics and Infinity*, p. 41.

299. Levinas, *Is It Righteous to Be?* p. 176. For a similar portrayal of the "last Heidegger," especially as it relates to affinities with Blanchot, see Levinas, *Proper Names*, pp. 128–129.

300. Levinas, *Entre Nous*, pp. 207–217. The French text of "Mourir pour . . ." was first published in *Heidegger. Questions ouvertes*, edited by Eliane Escoubas (Paris: Éditions Osiris, 1988), pp. 255–264. The Levinasian critique of the alleged link between violence and ontology in Heidegger has been very influential and has, in my judgment, blinded numerous scholars from seeing the extent to which many of the themes affirmed by Levinas can be found in Heidegger. A clear example of this trend is the analysis of Richard A. Cohen, *Ethics, Exegesis and Philosophy: Interpretation After Levinas* (Cambridge: Cambridge University Press, 2001), pp. 120–142. For a more sophisticated analysis, see Vattimo, "Metaphysics, Violence, Secularization," pp. 53–59.

301. For instance, see the explicit references to *Holzwege* in Levinas, *Oeuvres 1: Carnets*, pp. 350, 362, 375. See also the note of the editors, p. 485 n. 33, where they discern an allusion in the remarks of Levinas, p. 295, to the definition of the human as the "shepherd of being" in Heidegger's "Letter on Humanism." For another reference to Heidegger's *Holzwege*, see *Is It Righteous to Be?* p. 177.

302. Levinas, *Totality and Infinity*, pp. 275–276; *Totalité et infini*, pp. 252–253.

303. Levinas, *Oeuvres 1: Carnets*, p. 350: *"Contre les sarcasmes qui s'attachent au fait qu'après le départ glorieux de* Sein und Zeit *à la découverte de l'être, Heidegger se trouve sur les* Holzwege *où il erre après les longues recherches de l'Être."*

304. Ibid., p. 375: *"Chez Heidegger la parole suppose certes déjà la coprésence et le rapport préalable avec autrui et d'autrui avec le monde même que vise la parole de celui qui parle— mais l'essentiel de la parole est dans la signification, dans le* 'etwas als etwas' *(voir surtout* Holzwege *et interprétation de Hölderlin). La parole ne joue donc pas—en tant que invoca- tion—de rôle dans le rapport même avec le monde."*

305. See the note of the editors, ibid., pp. 497–498 n. 20.

306. Heidegger, *Being and Time*, § 33, p. 149; *Sein und Zeit*, p. 159.

307. Levinas, *Oeuvres 1: Carnets*, p. 376. The correct source for the expression *etwas als etwas* was already noted by the editors, ibid., p. 498 n. 20.

308. Rötzer, *Conversations with French Philosophers*, p. 57.

309. Levinas, *Is It Righteous to Be?* p. 33. See ibid., p. 35, where Levinas praises the early Heidegger (attested in *Being and Time*, his lectures at Freiburg, and the debate with Cassirer in Davos) for offering a "new way, a radicalization of philosophical interroga- tion, a priority with respect to reflections on physic-mathematical sciences. . . . A new outcome of Greek thinking which no longer appeared uniquely as the dawn of modern science but as the awakening of the question of being, but perhaps also as the place of its first covering up. But these deviations also always attest to itineraries in their necessary ways, in their ambiguity, in their necessary and dramatic erring. Never simple errors or detours, a new pathos of thinking."

310. Levinas, *Otherwise than Being*, pp. 182–183; *Autrement qu'être*, p. 230.

311. Levinas, *Otherwise than Being*, p. 182; *Autrement qu'être*, p. 230. Levinas com- bined Ecclesiastes 1:2 and 9.

312. Heidegger, *Pathmarks*, p. 243; *Wegmarken*, p. 318.

313. A similar argument has been proffered by Adam Konopka, "The 'Inversions' of Intentionality in Levinas and the Later Heidegger," *PhaenEx: Journal of Existential and Phenomenological Theory of Culture* 4 (2009): 146–162.

314. Heidegger, *Identity and Difference*, pp. 64–65; German text: pp. 132–133.

315. Heidegger, *Pathmarks*, p. 208; *Wegmarken*, p. 272.

316. Heidegger, *Pathmarks*, pp. 310–311; *Wegmarken*, pp. 410–411. Gibbs, "The Name of God," p. III, impressionistically notes that Heidegger's "efforts to cross out Being seem almost simplistic" when compared to the impact of the Jewish tradition of the ineffable name of God and the notion of illeity in Levinas's thought. I am of the opinion that the issue is more complex and that Levinas's philosophical translation of the Jewish liturgical practice concerning the name has greater affinity to Heidegger's later thought. See the comment of Derrida cited in Ch. 4 at n. 117.

317. Heidegger, *Pathmarks*, p. 312; *Wegmarken*, p. 413.

318. Jacques Derrida, *Of Grammatology*, translated by Gayatri Chakravorty Spivak, corrected edition (Baltimore: Johns Hopkins University Press, 1997), p. 60. For a

comparative analysis of *sous rature* in Heidegger and Derrida, see *Of Grammatology*, "Translator's Preface," pp. xvii–xviii.

319. Derrida, *Of Grammatology*, p. 23. Compare idem, *Psyche: Inventions of the Other, Volume II*, pp. 189–190, and idem, *Dissemination*, p. 354, where a passage about the crossing out of Being and the fourfold of the quadrangle (*das Geviert*) is mentioned without explicit reference to Heidegger. It is of interest that Derrida mentions the Heideggerian notion of the fourfold in conjunction with the "sacred quaternary" of the Pythagorean tradition as well as the "four cardinal points of the Kabbalah" and the "Great Quaternary of Eckartshausen" (p. 353). In the same context, Derrida displays a discriminating understanding of kabbalistic symbolism when he writes about the *squaring of the circle* as the "uniting of the masculine sex and the feminine sex into a whole, just as it is possible to unite into a single figure the framed circle of the circled square." The image of squaring the circle is also linked to the alchemical philosopher's stone. The text of Derrida and some relevant passages in the oeuvre of Jung are cited in Wolfson, *Language, Eros, Being*, p. 512 n. 291. I hope to return to this passage in a work on Heidegger and the kabbalah.

320. Heidegger, *The Event*, § 98, pp. 56–57; *Das Ereignis*, p. 69.

321. Heidegger, *Pathmarks*, p. 148; *Wegmarken*, pp. 193–194.

322. Heidegger, *On the Way to Language*, p. 76; *Unterwegs zur Sprache*, p. 170.

323. Heidegger, *On the Way to Language*, p. 81; *Unterwegs zur Sprache*, p. 175.

324. Heidegger, *On the Way to Language*, pp. 120–122; *Unterwegs zur Sprache*, pp. 240–242. See Gerald L. Bruns, "Disappeared: Heidegger and the Emancipation of Language," in *Languages of the Unsayable: The Play of Negativity in Literature and Literary Theory*, edited by Sanford Budick and Wolfgang Iser (New York: Columbia University Press, 1989), pp. 124–127, and compare the brief but incisive discussion on language, being, and God exhibited in the various phases of Heidegger's thought in Schrag, *God as Otherwise Than Being*, pp. 26–31.

325. Levinas, *Proper Names*, p. 134.

326. Ibid., p. 136.

327. Ibid., p. 137.

328. See Gershon Greenberg, "Amalek during the Shoa: Jewish Orthodox Thought," *Jerusalem Studies in Jewish Thought* 19 (2005): 891–913 (Hebrew). For a more contemporary application of this symbolism, see Henry F. Knight, "Coming to Terms with Amalek: Testing the Limits of Hospitality," in *Confronting Genocide: Judaism, Christianity, Islam*, edited by Steven Leonard Jacobs (Lanham: Lexington Books, 2009), pp. 223–237.

329. Levinas, *Proper Names*, p. 139 (emphasis in original). Concerning this Levinasian passage and the parallel treatment of Amalek in Blanchot as the personification of evil, see Mole, *Lévinas, Blanchot, Jabès*, p. 18; Hill, *Blanchot*, pp. 162 and 258 n. 5.

330. Levinas, *In the Time of the Nations*, p. 18, designates Amalek as the "symbol of absolute evil." On Amalek as the cause of Jewish suffering, see ibid., pp. 19–20, 46, 75, 131; Newton, *The Fence and the Neighbor*, p. 216 n. 98; Naomi Seidman, *Faithful Render-*

ings: Jewish-Christian Difference and the Politics of Translation (Chicago: University of Chicago Press, 2006), pp. 28–29.

331. The key verse is "The hand upon the throne of the Lord [*kes yah*], the Lord will be at war with Amaleq through the ages" (Exodus 17:16), which is interpreted to mean that as long as the seed of Amalek, the archenemy of Israel, exists in the world, both the name (*YHWH*) and the throne (*kisse*) are in a diminished state, but when that seed is destroyed, both the name and the throne will be perfected. Compare *Pesiqta de-Rav Kahana*, edited by Bernard Mandelbaum (New York: Jewish Theological Seminary of America, 1962), 3:16, p. 53; *Pesiqta Rabbati: A Synoptic Edition of Pesiqta Rabbati Based upon All Extant Manuscripts and the Editio Princeps*, edited by Rivka Ulmer (Atlanta: Scholars Press, 1997), 12:21, p. 187; *Midrash Tehillim*, edited by Solomon Buber (Vilna: Rom, 1891), 9:10, pp. 86–87; *Midrash Tanḥuma* (Jerusalem: Eshkol, 1972), Ki Teṣe 11, p. 919. For a useful study that catalogs the formation of the symbol of Amalek as Israel's main foe in biblical and postbiblical sources from Late Antiquity, see Louis H. Feldman, *"Remember Amalek!": Vengeance, Zealotry, and Group Destruction in the Bible According to Philo, Pseudo-Philo, and Josephus* (Cincinnati: Hebrew Union College Press, 2004). The rabbinic material is summarized briefly on pp. 46–53.

332. Levinas, *In the Time of the Nations*, p. 46.

333. Hill, *Blanchot*, pp. 125–126. The passage from Levinas (see above, n. 326) is cited by Hill, op. cit., pp. 249–250 n. 12.

334. See ibid., p. 140, where Hill attempts to distinguish Blanchot and Heidegger in the following way: "No longer synonymous—unlike the *il y a*—with the unity of being, the neutre is necessarily irreducible to the truth of Being in its Heideggerian sense; indeed, from the very outset . . . the neutre is affirmed by Blanchot as that which is indifferent to the movement of concealment and unconcealment, veiling and unveiling, that is constitutive of Heideggerian *aletheia*. The neutre has nothing to do with being or non-being; it signifies without concealing or unveiling, and it does not belong to the realm of the visible or the invisible." In my opinion, these words can be read as an apt description of Heidegger's efforts to get beyond the metaphysical binary of being and nonbeing, visible and invisible. That is precisely the point of his repeated assertions that untruth belongs to the essence of truth.

335. Ibid., p. 99.

336. Martin Heidegger, *Die Geschichte des Seyns* [GA 69] (Frankfurt am Main: Vittorio Klostermann, 1998), p. 168. See Richard Polt, "The Question of Nothing," in *A Companion to Heidegger's Introduction to Metaphysics*, edited by Richard Polt and Gregory Fried (New Haven: Yale University Press, 2001), pp. 57–82, esp. 73.

337. Martin Heidegger, *Sojourns: The Journey to Greece*, translated by John Panteleimon Manoussakis, foreword by John Sallis (Albany: State University of New York Press, 2005), p. 45.

338. Heidegger, *On the Way to Language*, p. 126; *Unterwegs zur Sprache*, pp. 245–246.

339. Heidegger, *Poetry, Language, Thought*, p. 170 (*Vorträge und Aufsätze*, p. 172): "The thingness of the thing remains concealed, forgotten. The nature of the thing never comes to light [*Vorschein*], that is, it never gets a hearing [*Sprache*]."

340. Rötzer, *Conversations with French Philosophers*, p. 61: "The relation to the face of the other, seeing the face of the other . . . means I come closer to the other, so that his face takes on meaning for me. What's meaningful in the face is the command to responsibility. Now I'm talking like Heidegger. If Heidegger taught us things like knives, forks, for example, even the street, 'fall into' my 'hand,' are ready-to-hand for me before I objectify them, then this possibility isn't based upon a knowing. It also can't be grounded on a meaning, for here meaning is grounded in the hand."

341. Levinas, *Oeuvres 1: Carnets*, p. 376: "*Ce qui est simplement* Zuhandenheit *chez Heidegger—devient corps chez Merleau-Ponty—pas instrument, mais corps, incarnation de la pensée.*"

342. Levinas, *Time and the Other*, p. 109 (emphasis in original).

343. Consider Levinas's characterization of the implication of the ontological difference between being and beings affirmed by Heidegger in Rötzer, *Conversations with French Philosophers*, p. 57: "The return to being as *Verbum.*"

344. Derrida, *Writing and Difference*, p. 149; *L'écriture et la différence*, p. 221.

345. Heidegger, *Being and Time*, § 34, p. 153; *Sein und Zeit*, p. 163.

346. Compare Levinas, *Oeuvres 1: Carnets*, p. 359: "*Toute pensée est langage. Penser = exprimer une pensée et la question de celui écoute fait partie de l'expression de celui qui parle et de celui qui pense.*"

347. Wyschogrod, *Crossover Queries*, p. 35.

348. Ibid., p. 37.

349. Ibid., pp. 25–26.

350. Ibid., pp. 311–312, 363. See Edith Wyschogrod, "Crucifixion and Alterity: Pathways to Glory on the Thought of Altizer and Levinas," in *Thinking Through the Death of God*, pp. 96–99. Wyschogrod's approach is confirmed by the recent analysis of the Levinasian "ethical negative theology" in light of the Maimonidean *via negativa* in Fagenblat, *A Covenant of Creatures*, pp. 111–139. For reservation regarding Wyschogrod's conjecture regarding the Maimonidean influence on Levinas, see Kavka, "Religious Experience," p. 70. Levinas also appealed to Maimonides as one who synthesized the particularism of Jewish revelation and the universalism of Greek philosophy, indeed, as someone who understood the particular vocation of the Jew as an articulation of a universalistic ideal, an orientation that he understood as inherently against paganism. See Emmanuel Levinas, "L'actualité de Maïmonide," *Paix et Droit* 15, no. 4 (1935): 6–7, and the analyses in Moyn, *Origins of the Other*, pp. 190–191; Francesca Albertini, "Emmanuel Levinas' Theological-Political Interpretation of Moses Maimonides," in *Moses Maimonides (1138–1204): His Religious, Scientific and Philosophical Wirkungsgeschichte in Different Cultural Contexts*, edited by Görge K. Hasselhoff and Otfried Fraisse (Würzburg: Ergon Verlag, 2004), pp. 573–585; Wurgaft, "How to Read Maimonides," pp. 370–375. See also Levinas, *Difficult Freedom*, p. 15, and Wolfson "Secrecy," pp. 53–54. On the relationship of Scripture to philosophy, Levinas does not deny the "radical difference in spirit," even as he insists on their "*essential* connection in human civilization" (*In the Time of Nations*, p. 169). For an alternate take on Levinas's respective relationship to Halevi

and to Maimonides, see Martin Kavka, "Screening the Canon: Levinas and Medieval Jewish Philosophy," in *New Directions in Jewish Philosophy*, edited by Aaron W. Hughes and Elliot R. Wolfson (Bloomington: Indiana University Press, 2010), pp. 19–51. On the relationship of Judaism and philosophy in Levinas, see above, n. 142 and Ch. 5 n. 9.

351. Maimonides, *The Guide*, 1.37, p. 86.

352. Ibid., 2.35, p. 368.

353. Wyschogrod, *Crossover Queries*, p. 32.

354. Levinas, *Otherwise than Being*, p. 3 (emphasis in original); *Autrement qu'être*, pp. 3–4. The apophatic implications of the "face" give me pause to accept the conclusion of Westphal, "Levinas, Kierkegaard, and the Theological Task," p. 246, that, for Levinas, the face-to-face encounter with the human Other is attainable, whereas, for Kierkegaard, the face-to-face encounter with the divine Other is not possible in the present. Levinas insisted repeatedly that one can never experience the totality of the other, and hence Westphal's distinction is not entirely accurate.

355. Levinas, *Otherwise than Being*, pp. 44, 46 (emphasis in original); *Autrement qu'être*, pp. 57, 59.

356. Levinas, *Basic Philosophical Writings*, p. 76.

357. Levinas, *Time and the Other*, p. 65.

358. Levinas, *Basic Philosophical Writings*, p. 76.

359. On the matter of skepticism, see Levinas, *Otherwise than Being*, pp. 165–171 (*Autrement qu'être*, pp. 210–218), and the analysis of Jan de Greef, "Skepticism and Reason," in Levinas, *Face to Face with Levinas*, pp. 159–179. See also Handelman, *Fragments*, pp. 233–235; Dennis King Keenan, *Death and Responsibility: The "Work" of Levinas* (Albany: State University of New York Press, 1999), pp. 19–31, and the exchange between Levinas and Wyschogrod in *Crossover Queries*, pp. 291–292. For a different perspective that alleges Levinas's denial of skepticism, see Batnitzky, *Leo Strauss and Emmanuel Levinas*, pp. 129–132.

360. Levinas, *Discovering Existence*, pp. 167–168.

361. Levinas, *Otherwise than Being*, p. 152; *Autrement qu'être*, p. 194.

362. Wyschogrod, *Crossover Queries*, p. 292.

363. For an extensive analysis of this theme, see Renée D. N. van Riessen, *Man as a Place of God: Levinas' Hermeneutics of Kenosis* (Dordrecht: Springer, 2007).

364. Levinas, *Discovering Existence*, p. 179 (emphasis in original).

365. Ibid.

366. It is of interest to recall Levinas's comment to Françoise Armengaud: "Perhaps Jewish texts have always been understood as constantly accompanied by a layer of symbolic meaning, apologues, new interpretations to be discovered: in short, always lined with *midrash*. And the language of philosophy does not mean that an intellectual wind has torn the reader loose from all literalness, all particularity, all features that are 'just so,' and as such reduced to insignificance" (*In the Time of the Nations*, p. 168).

367. Wyschogrod, *Crossover Queries*, p. 296. See also Levinas, *Otherwise than Being*, pp. 24–25 (*Autrement qu'être*, p. 31); idem, *Basic Philosophical Writings*, p. 75.

368. Emmanuel Levinas, "The Jewish Understanding of Scripture," *Cross Currents* 44 (1994): 497. For a different rendering, see Levinas, *Beyond the Verse*, p. 110.

369. As noted by Derrida, *Writing and Difference*, p. 99; *L'écriture et la différence*, p. 147.

370. For a more extended discussion of Levinas's critique of the Christian doctrine of incarnation, see Wolfson, "Secrecy," pp. 57–60, and Robert Gibbs, "The Disincarnation of the Word: The Trace of God in Reading Scripture," in *The Exorbitant*, pp. 32–51. See also the reservation expressed by Robyn Horner, "On Levinas's Gifts to Christian Theology," in *The Exorbitant*, pp. 130–149, esp. 139: "Immediately, we can see one of the main difficulties that the adoption of the thought of Levinas would entail. To the extent that Christian theology is articulated within a horizon of being, it would fall under Levinas's critique of being as totalizing. . . . A second issue, however, arises from a more deconstructive impulse. This is the question of whether Christian attempts to think the possibility of God remain trapped in the dead-end of language that simply cannot go beyond itself, save through the illusory positioning of a transcendental signifier."

371. Levinas, *The Levinas Reader*, p. 148. Passages such as this one would seem to challenge the conclusion of Leora Batnitzky, "Levinas Between German Metaphysics and Christian Theology," in *The Exorbitant*, p. 29: "Incarnation, for Levinas, is the way in which I am for the other. As the ethical relation, incarnation fuses the human with the divine. The trace of the other is divine, and the only meaning the divine trace can have, for Levinas, is an ethical meaning. In this important sense, ethics, Levinas's main theme, is the fusing of divine and human nature. Incarnation is my spiritual rebirth, but this rebirth is at one and the same time secular in that it can and does concern only human relations." I agree that Levinas appropriates the term *incarnation* to name the ethical relation that one subject must assume in relation to the other, and I also agree that we cannot speak of this relation in the absence of the wholly other, which is God, but I do not agree that there is a "fusing" of the human and the divine. Levinas's use of this Christological expression is meant to undermine precisely the possibility of such a fusion. I thus concur with the observation of Gibbs, "The Disincarnation," p. 33: "Levinas does not view the other person, particularly his face, as an incarnation of God or of the infinite. His account of the face portrays how it disrupts the reification that our judgments impose both on the other person and on God." And see the reference in the following note.

372. Levinas, *Totality and Infinity*, pp. 78–79; *Totalité et infini*, pp. 50–51. See the interpretation of this passage in Gibbs, "The Disincarnation," p. 36: "For whatever reason, readers tend to see the infinite relation with the other as one in which God becomes incarnate in the other's face—not a mere image, but a dwelling or presence of God. Levinas rejects this emphatically because he finds that the other person becomes disincarnate, loses his sheer immanence in facing me, becomes something other than the dwelling of God within human form. . . . The radical transcendence of God exceeds incarnation and is made manifest in the face of the other person—a facing where my cognition of the other person is exceeded and called into question."

373. Levinas, *Otherwise than Being*, p. 94; *Autrement qu'être*, p. 120.

374. Levinas, *Of God Who Comes to Mind*, p. 118 (emphasis in original). Regarding this passage, see Charles P. Bigger, *Between Chora and the Good: Metaphor's Metaphysical Neighborhood* (New York: Fordham University Press, 2005), p. 101, and concerning Levinas's rejection of the incarnation, see p. 264.

375. See above, n. 72, and the account of Heidegger in Levinas, *Proper Names*, p. 128: "In Heidegger, being, in the verbal sense he gives it, to distinguish it from beings . . . is the measure of all things, and of man. Man answers, or does not answer, its call. But a call that does not come from anyone. It comes from Being, which is not a being—from a phosphorescence of Nothingness, or, more precisely, from a luminosity in which the ebb and flow of Nothingness and Being continue on. Subjectivity's meaning does not come from itself, but from that phosphorescence, from the truth of being." In my judgment, Levinas's *il y a* can be described in these precise terms, a Being that is not any particular being but the luminescence that sustains the general ebb and flow of Nothingness and Being.

376. Levinas, *Ethics and Infinity*, pp. 47–48.

377. In the published text (see the following note), the word appears as "its," an obvious typographical error that I have taken the liberty of correcting.

378. Levinas, *Ethics and Infinity*, pp. 48–49.

379. Levinas, *Of God Who Comes to Mind*, p. 124.

380. Levinas, *Existence and Existents*, p. 52.

381. Ibid.

382. Ibid., pp. 55–56 (emphasis in original).

383. Ibid., pp. 57–58 (emphasis in original).

384. Levinas, *Ethics and Infinity*, p. 49. See above, n. 171.

385. Derrida, *Writing and Difference*, pp. 141–142; *L'écriture et la différence*, pp. 208–209. For an assessment of Derrida's relationship to Levinas relevant to this point, see Kosky, *Levinas and the Philosophy of Religion*, pp. 33–36; Kas Saghafi, *Apparitions—Of Derrida's Other* (New York: Fordham University Press, 2010), pp. 7–28. On Levinas's critique of ontotheology, see Schrijvers, *Ontotheological Turnings*, pp. 198–207.

386. Derrida, *Writing and Difference*, p. 146; *L'écriture et la différence*, p. 217. On the "ontological wager of hyperessentiality" at work in Pseudo-Dionysius the Areopagite and Meister Eckhart, see also Derrida, *Psyche: Inventions of the Other, Volume II*, pp. 147–148.

387. Derrida, *Writing and Difference*, p. 141; *L'écriture et la différence*, p. 208.

388. Levinas, *In the Time of the Nations*, p. 171.

389. Ibid., p. 172. See recent analysis of this passage in Fagenblat, *A Covenant of Creatures*, pp. 111–112.

390. Wyschogrod, *Crossover Queries*, p. 288.

391. Maimonides, *The Guide*, I.60, p. 145. For a contemporary approach that resonates with the Maimonidean perspective, see Johnston, *Saving God*, pp. 29, 39–30, 51. See also Kenneth Seeskin, *No Other Gods: The Modern Struggle Against Idolatry* (West Orange: Behrman House, 1995), and idem, *Searching for a Distant God*, pp. 53–55.

392. On the meontological dimensions of Levinas, see Kavka, *Jewish Messianism*, pp. 20–29.

393. Wyschogrod, *Crossover Queries*, p. 29.

394. Levinas, *Totality and Infinity*, pp. 77–79; *Totalité et infini*, pp. 49–52.

395. See Preface n. 20.

396. Levinas, *Totality and Infinity*, p. 77; *Totalité et Infini*, p. 50. See Kosky, *Levinas and the Philosophy of Religion*, pp. 26–27. For discussion of the atheistic tendencies in Levinas and Leibowitz, related to a "radicalized Maimonidean negative theology," see Fagenblat, *A Covenant of Creatures*, p. 142, and in more detail, idem, "Lacking All Interest," pp. 5–9.

397. Levinas, *Difficult Freedom*, pp. 14–15 (emphasis in original). The implicit critique of Rudolph Otto's idea of the numinous is evident in this passage. Concerning Levinas's appeal to the beyond being and its relationship to Otto's conception of the *mysterium* as the wholly other, see Dalton, *Longing for the Other*, pp. 229–245.

398. Levinas, *Totality and Infinity*, p. 77 (my emphasis); *Totalité et infini*, p. 50.

399. Levinas, *Totality and Infinity*, p. 53; *Totalité et infini*, pp. 23–24.

400. Levinas, *Totality and Infinity*, pp. 77–78; *Totalité et infini*, p. 50.

401. Levinas, *Totality and Infinity*, p. 181; *Totalité et infini*, p. 156.

402. Levinas, *Beyond the Verse*, pp. 120–121. See above nn. 124, 167, 238, and below n. 476.

403. Levinas, *Existence and Existents*, p. 56.

404. Levinas, *Totality and Infinity*, pp. 88–89; *Totalité et infini*, p. 61. Compare Levinas, *Otherwise than Being*, p. 105 (*Autrement qu'être*, p. 133): "The oneself is a creature, but an orphan by birth or an atheist no doubt ignorant of its Creator." On the Levinasian notion of the atheistic self, see Kosky, *Levinas and the Philosophy of Religion*, pp. 186–188; Nick Mansfield, *The God Who Deconstructs Himself: Sovereignty and Subjectivity Between Freud, Bataille, and Derrida* (New York: Fordham University Press, 2010), pp. 70–71.

405. Levinas, *Totality and Infinity*, pp. 88–89; *Totalité et infini*, pp. 60–61.

406. Levinas, *Totality and Infinity*, p. 78; *Totalité et infini*, pp. 50–51.

407. Wyschogrod, *Crossover Queries*, p. 42. Compare Levinas, *Time and the Other*, pp. 93–94; idem, *Otherwise than Being*, pp. 12–13 (*Autrement qu'être*, pp. 15–16); idem, *Collected Philosophical Papers*, pp. 106–110; idem, "Martin Buber and the Theory of Knowledge," in *The Philosophy of Martin Buber*, edited by Paul A. Schilpp and Maurice Friedman (La Salle: Open Court, 1967), pp. 133–150, retranslated in Levinas, *Proper Names*, pp. 17–35; idem, *Outside the Subject*, translated by Michael B. Smith (Stanford: Stanford University Press, 1993), pp. 4–48. On the relationship of Buber and Levinas, see Wyschogrod, *Emmanuel Levinas*, pp. 142–145; Cohen, *Elevations*, pp. 90–111; Bergo, *Levinas*, pp. 87–89; the essays included in *Levinas and Buber: Dialogue and Difference*, edited by Peter Atterton, Matthew Calarco, and Maurice Friedman (Pittsburgh: Duquesne University Press, 2004); Gregory Kaplan, "Ethics as First Philosophy and the Other's Ambiguity in the Dialogue of Buber and Levinas," *Philosophy Today* 50 (2006):

40–57; Meir, *Levinas's Jewish Thought*, pp. 94–124. For a strong contrast drawn between Levinas and Buber, see Butler, *Parting Ways*, p. 38: "Indeed, the Levinasian position, taken seriously, would defeat Buber's philosophical notion of dialogue, despite the superficial resonances between them." According to Butler, Levinas's affirmation of a heterogeneity that is prior to the being of the self "constantly decenters the autonomous subject I appear to be" and hence "permanently complicates the question of location," interrupting the possibility of multiculturalism predicated on the assumption that "cultures are constituted autonomous domains whose task it is to establish dialogue with other cultures." For a more evenhanded discussion of the relationship between ethics and politics in Levinas, but one that likewise is attentive to the fact that the dialogic breaks in the middle under the burden of the gap between world and God and the need to transition from the nonethical to the ethical, see Gillian Rose, *The Broken Middle: Out of Our Ancient Society* (Oxford: Blackwell, 1992), pp. 247–277. For a summation of Rose's argument, see pp. 259–260: "In Levinas, there is neither the simultaneity of suspending the ethical, nor the radicality of transforming the political, but there resounds the brutal sincerity . . . of judgement which has itself fixed what it deplores. For, according to its own metaphysic, this authorship can have no aesthetic—no mask or pseudonym—nor any humour of the religious; even less can it draw the silk curtains of facetiousness which would be to expiate the authority that authorship arrogates. The ambivalence and equivocation of 'the saying' and 'the said' are reintroduced in the guise of perennial philosophical scepticism which punctuates reason, and, in this way, the author appeals over the top of his own text to his 'interlocutor' beyond its totalizing discourse." Rose, pp. 267–271, notes the influence of the third book of Rosenzweig's *Star of Redemption* on Levinas's opposition to a political methodology.

408. Levinas, *Totality and Infinity*, p. 78; *Totalité et infini*, p. 51.

409. Moyn, *Origins of the Other*, p. 186. See also the discussion of the posttheistic and posthumanistic strands of Levinas's thought in Llewelyn, *Margins of Religion*, pp. 144–147, and the chapter "Levinas and the Final À-Dieu to Theology" in Raschke, *Postmodernism*, pp. 108–140.

410. Levinas, *Discovering Existence*, p. 178.

411. Ibid., p. 179.

412. Levinas, *Basic Philosophical Writings*, p. 159.

413. Wyschogrod, *Crossover Queries*, p. 286.

414. Levinas, *Totality and Infinity*, p. 77; *Totalité et infini*, p. 49.

415. Levinas, *Totality and Infinity*, p. 297; *Totalité et infini*, p. 273.

416. Wyschogrod, *Crossover Queries*, p. 34.

417. Levinas, *In the Time of the Nations*, p. 171. For analysis of the nonphenomenality of the trace in Levinas, see Wyschogrod, *Emmanuel Levinas*, pp. 158–164, 224.

418. Levinas, *Totality and Infinity*, p. 66; *Totalité et infini*, pp. 37–38.

419. Wyschogrod, *Crossover Queries*, p. 291, and see also the comment of Levinas on p. 283, and compare Levinas, *Oeuvres 1: Carnets*, p. 328: "*Au* Liegen *heideggérien s'oppose la création: l'idée de fondement est inversée—le commencement qui n'est pas un fondement,*

mais une parole." That Heidegger himself was concerned that his own approach to language could border on the mystical is attested in the interesting aside in *Being and Time*, § 44, p. 202 (*Sein und Zeit*, p. 220): after discussing the philological import of the term *alētheia* as unconcealment, he remarked "In citing such evidence we must guard against uninhibited word-mysticism [*Wort-mystik*]."

420. Levinas, *Discovering Existence*, p. 179.

421. Levinas, *Oeuvres 1: Carnets*, p. 172.

422. Ibid., p. 175: "*Pour le romantisme le symbole vaut comme l'inconnu stimulant une histoire qui vaut indépendamment du symbol. Pour moi l'accomplissement du symbole ne saurait se séparer de l'historie qui y mène. C'est par {elle que} l'accomplissement est créa- tion. . . . Symbole—préfiguration de l'accomplissement et non pas image de l'être voilé.*" The implementation or fulfillment (*l'accomplissement*) is identified as the Messiah in another passage on p. 176.

423. Ibid., p. 176: "*La notion de temps et de sa fécondité miraculeuse—l'essentiel du symbole.*"

424. Ibid., pp. 167–168.

425. Wyschogrod, *Crossover Queries*, p. 284.

426. Levinas, *Otherwise than Being*, p. 19 (*Autrement qu'être*, p. 23), and see p. 95 (*Autrement qu'être*, p. 121).

427. Wyschogrod, *Crossover Queries*, p. 292.

428. Levinas, *Otherwise than Being*, p. 88; *Autrement qu'être*, p. 112.

429. Levinas, *Otherwise than Being*, pp. 89–90; *Autrement qu'être*, pp. 113–114.

430. Wyschogrod, *Crossover Queries*, p. 29.

431. Levinas, *Otherwise than Being*, p. 55; *Autrement qu'être*, p. 70.

432. Levinas, *Otherwise than Being*, p. 103; *Autrement qu'être*, p. 130. On the incarna- tion of the self in Levinas, see the innovative analysis in Leahy, "Cuspidal Limits."

433. Levinas, *Otherwise than Being*, pp. 103–104; *Autrement qu'être*, pp. 131–132.

434. Levinas, *Otherwise than Being*, p. 104; *Autrement qu'être*, p. 132.

435. Levinas, *Otherwise than Being*, p. 50; *Autrement qu'être*, pp. 64–65.

436. Levinas, *Otherwise than Being*, p. 104; *Autrement qu'être*, p. 132.

437. Levinas, *Otherwise than Being*, p. 108; *Autrement qu'être*, p. 138.

438. Levinas, *Otherwise than Being*, p. 109; *Autrement qu'être*, p. 139.

439. Levinas, *Otherwise than Being*, p. 79 (emphasis in original); *Autrement qu'être*, p. 100.

440. Wyschogrod, *Crossover Queries*, p. 30.

441. Levinas, *Totality and Infinity*, p. 23; *Totalité et infini*, p. xii.

442. Levinas, *Otherwise than Being*, p. 187 n. 5; *Autrement qu'être*, p. 8 n. 4.

443. Levinas, *Otherwise than Being*, p. 12; *Autrement qu'être*, p. 15.

444. Wyschogrod, *Crossover Queries*, p. 293.

445. For a similar argument regarding the persistence of images in Levinas, see Phillipe Crignon, "Figuration: Emmanuel Levinas and the Image," *Yale French Studies* 104 (2004): 100–125, esp. 122–124.

446. Levinas, *Oeuvres 1: Carnets*, p. 229: "*La métaphore se détache de la représentation sensible pour dégager les significations que les objects incarnent. Certes cette incarnation est autre chose que la réalisation d'un concept dans l'individu, puisque cette signification ne se laisse pas définir comme le concept en dehors de la représentation qui l'incarne. Significations innombrables. Abstraction poétique.*" See ibid., p. 232: "*Toute signification—en tant que signification—est métaphorique, elle mène vers là-haut.*"

447. Ibid., p. 329: "*Métaphore: Le fait du langage qui mène au-delà de l'expérience—n'est pas une preuve de l'existence de Dieu. Certes. Mais c'est que 'être avec Dieu' ou 'monter,' ou 's'élever'—ou 'religion' ou 'langage'—ou 'relation avec l'Autre' conditionnent seulement la recherche de l'existence.*"

448. Ibid., pp. 351–352: "*La métaphore comme sens figuré qui s'ajoute au prétendu sens littéral—c'est le sens qu'un terme prend dans un contexte humain: là où l'objet par le langage est offert à Autrui . . . Les objects reçoivent des significations du fait de se placer dans la transcendance d'Autrui: orientation vers Dieu.*" See ibid., p. 267: "*Le pouvoir métaphorique des mots comme 'au-delà,' 'transcendant,' 'à l'infini,' Dieu.*"

449. Emmanuel Levinas, *Oeuvres 2: Parole et silence et autres conferences inédites au Collège philosophique*, edited by Rodolphe Calin, preface and explanatory notes by Rodolphe Calin and Catherine Chalier (Paris: Éditions Grasset & Fasquelle, 2009), p. 325.

450. Levinas, *Oeuvres 1: Carnets*, pp. 241–242.

451. Ibid., p. 229: "*La métaphore, essence du langage, résiderait dans cette poussée à l'extrême dans ce superlatif toujours plus superlatif qu'est la transcendance.*"

452. Ibid., pp. 232–233: "*Parole dit l'être—parole est métaphore. . . . . Toute significa-tion—en tant que signification—est métaphorique, elle mène vers là-haut. . . . Mener vers là-haut, est un mouvement irréductible, le fond de la spiritualité humaine—de l'être qui parle. . . . La signification comme signification est dans cet au-delà. Cet au-delà est-il l'infini de l'Autre?*" See ibid., p. 234: "*La métaphore est un au-delà, la transcendance.*"

453. Ibid., p. 233.

454. Ibid., pp. 236–237: "*La métaphore par excellence est Dieu. . . . Termes méta-phoriques par excellence—dont le contenu même est métaphore: Dieu, Absolu, au-delà de l'Être, au-delà.*" Compare Levinas, *Oeuvres 2: Parole et silence*, p. 328: "*Certains termes philosophiques comme transcendance, comme au-dessus de l'être, peut-être Dieu—ce sont des métaphores par excellence.*"

455. Levinas, *Oeuvres 1: Carnets*, p. 240: "*La métaphore des métaphores—Dieu.*" And Levinas, *Oeuvres 2: Parole et silence*, p. 346: "*La métaphore = idée de l'infini = Dieu est la métaphore des métaphores et qui apporte le 'transport' nécessaire pour poser 'absolument' les significations.*"

456. The point was captured succinctly by Jill Robbins, *Altered Reading: Levinas and Literature* (Chicago: University of Chicago Press, 1999), pp. 37–38: "God *is* not, apart from trace. The trace *of* God means the trace that is God" (emphasis in original).

457. Levinas, *Of God Who Comes to Mind*, p. 50.

458. Levinas, *Basic Philosophical Writings*, p. 36 (emphasis in original).

459. Ibid., p. 64. On Levinas's idea of God's transcendence as absent presence or (non)presence, see Welz, *Love's Transcendence*, pp. 293–297.

460. Levinas, *Oeuvres 1: Carnets*, p. 242: "*Penser—mouvement qui a un term. Idée de l'infini: dans le term pensé, refuse du terme. Métaphore.*"

461. Ibid., p. 235.

462. Ibid., p. 331.

463. Ibid., p. 241: "*De sorte que dans le langage il y a ce mouvement vers l'infini et il n'existe pas de langage sans ce mouvement. Et ce mouvement vient de l'autre, en tant que le langage est réponse à un autre et dépassement de ce qui est dit. [Cette dernière chose n'est pas sûre. Le dépassement de la métaphore ne vient-il pas de la trace?]*"

464. Levinas, *Oeuvres 2: Parole et silence*, p. 326.

465. Heidegger, *The Principle of Reason*, p. 48; *Der Satz vom Grund*, p. 72. Compare Heidegger, *On the Way to Language*, p. 100; *Unterwegs zur Sprache*, p. 195.

466. On the two possible meanings implied in this subtitle, see Jacques Derrida, *Margins of Philosophy*, translated, with additional notes by Alan Bass (Chicago: University of Chicago Press, 1982), p. 258 n. 61.

467. See the comprehensive analysis of Giuseppe Stellardi, *Heidegger and Derrida on Philosophy and Metaphor: Imperfect Thought* (Amherst: Humanity Books, 2000). Llewelyn, *Emmanuel Levinas*, pp. 163–179, also compares Levinas's view on metaphor with Derrida and Heidegger but reaches a conclusion different from my own. Llewelyn surmises that Levinas is caught in the predicament that to deny metaphoricity he must think it, and by thinking it, he must also think of being again, and thus he seems "unable to evade the Parmenidean-Heideggerian thesis that being and thinking are one." I concur that Levinas is still trapped in the snare of ontology, but it is not because he denies metaphoricity. On the contrary, it is due to his affirming the metaphorical as the linguistic mode of signification by which one can approach the unapproachable and speak the unspeakable.

468. On the alleged collusion between metaphor and metaphysics in Heidegger and Derrida, see Paul Ricoeur, *The Rule of Metaphor: Multi-Disciplinary Studies of the Creation of Meaning in Language*, translated by Robert Czerny with Kathleen McLaughlin and John Costello, SJ (Toronto: University of Toronto Press, 1977), pp. 280–295; Stellardi, *Heidegger and Derrida*, pp. 83–84, 130–132. For an extensive analysis of the debate between Derrida and Ricoeur on the status of metaphor, see Leonard Lawlor, *Imagination and Change: The Difference between the Thought of Ricoeur and Derrida* (Albany: State University of New York Press, 1992), pp. 11–50.

469. Levinas, *Totality and Infinity*, p. 207 (emphasis in original); *Totalité et infini*, pp. 181–182.

470. Levinas, *Otherwise than Being*, p. 53; *Autrement qu'être*, p. 69.

471. Levinas, *Otherwise than Being*, p. 94; *Autrement qu'être*, p. 119.

472. Levinas, *Otherwise than Being*, p. 178; *Autrement qu'être*, p. 224.

473. Levinas, *Otherwise than Being*, p. 178; *Autrement qu'être*, p. 224. On the Levinasian semantics of proximity and the notion of "non-indifference," see the extended discussion in Ziarek, *Inflected Language*, pp. 65–102.

474. Levinas, *Otherwise than Being*, p. 94; *Autrement qu'être*, pp. 119–120.

475. Levinas, *Otherwise than Being*, p. 12; *Autrement qu'être*, p. 15.

476. Levinas, *Otherwise than Being*, p. 12; *Autrement qu'être*, p. 15. Levinas, *Beyond the Verse*, p. 124, adduces this philosophic point from the Jewish custom of not pronouncing the Tetragrammaton as it is written: "Does not this transcendence of the Name of God, in comparison to all thematization, become effacement, and is not this effacement the very commandment that obligates me to the other man? . . . The transcendence of God is his actual effacement, but this obligates us to men." And ibid., p. 127: "A configuration of purely ontological notions turns here into ethical relations. As in the Talmud: the absolution of the Ab-solute, the effacement of God, is positively the obligation to make peace in the world." See above, n. 402.

477. Levinas, *God, Death, and Time*, p. 197 (emphasis in original).

478. Vries, *Minimal Theologies*, pp. 533–534. See ibid., pp. 23–24, 33–36, 347–348.

479. Ibid., 351.

480. Ibid., p. 533.

481. Ibid., p. 480 (emphasis in original). For another attempt to diminish the opposition between transcendence and immanence in Levinas, see Benso, *The Face of Things*, p. 141. I do concur with Benso that, for Levinas, we would do well to avoid rendering the difference as dichotomous or antinomical.

482. Levinas, *Oeuvres 1: Carnets*, p. 236.

483. Ibid., p. 358.

484. Levinas, *Of God Who Comes to Mind*, p. 146.

485. Levinas, *Otherwise than Being*, p. 11: "The non-present here is invisible, separated (or sacred) and thus a non-origin, an-archical. The Good cannot become present or enter into a representation." It is worth noting that the English translation omits the following comment that appears after the first sentence in the original French: "L'impossibilité de thématiser peut tenir à la bonté du diachronique" (*Autrement qu'être*, p. 13), which may be rendered as "The impossibility of thematizing may reflect the goodness of the diachronic."

486. Levinas, *Otherwise than Being*, p. 8; *Autrement qu'être*, p. 10.

487. Levinas, *Otherwise than Being*, p. 100; *Autrement qu'être*, p. 126.

488. Edith Wyschogrod, "Trends in Postmodern Jewish Philosophy: Contexts of a Conversation," in *Reasoning After Revelation*, p. 131.

489. Levinas, *Otherwise than Being*, p. 152; *Autrement qu'être*, p. 194. See Wyschogrod, "Crucifixion and Alterity," pp. 99–101, and Ch. 5 at n. 58. A similar point in different terminology was already made in Levinas, *Totality and Infinity*, p. 23 (*Totalité et infini*, p. xi): "This 'beyond' the totality and objective experience is, however, not to be described in a purely negative fashion. It is reflected *within* the totality and history, *within* experience. The eschatological, as the 'beyond' of history, draws beings out of the jurisdiction of history and the future; it arouses them in and calls them forth to their full responsibility" (emphasis in original).

490. Levinas, *Otherwise than Being*, p. 140; *Autrement qu'être*, p. 179.

491. Janicaud, "The Theological Turn," pp. 26–27.

492. Ibid., p. 27.

493. Fagenblat, *A Covenant of Creatures*, pp. 101–106.

494. Levinas, *Totality and Infinity*, p. 301; *Totalité et infini*, p. 278.

495. Levinas, *Totality and Infinity*, pp. 301–302; *Totalité et infini*, p. 278.

496. Levinas, *Totality and Infinity*, p. 33; *Totalité et infini*, p. 3. For an elaborate analysis of metaphysical desire in Levinas's thought, see Dalton, *Longing for the Other*.

497. Levinas, *Totality and Infinity*, p. 302; *Totalité et infini*, p. 278.

498. See above at nn. 370–372.

499. Levinas, *The Levinas Reader*, p. 186.

500. Levinas, *Discovering Existence*, p. 97.

501. Levinas, *Otherwise than Being*, p. 5; *Autrement qu'être*, p. 6. See the provocative characterization of Levinas's discussion of illeity in *Otherwise than Being* as a "secular apophasis" in Fagenblat, *A Covenant of Creatures*, pp. 106–110.

502. Levinas, *God, Death, and Time*, p. 207.

503. Levinas, *Totality and Infinity*, p. 79 (emphasis in original); *Totalité et infini*, pp. 51–52. See Llewelyn, *The HypoCritical Imagination*, pp. 6–7, 121–138.

504. Levinas, *Entre Nous*, p. 153.

505. Levinas, *Otherwise than Being*, pp. 11–12; *Autrement qu'être*, p. 14. For discussions of Levinas and negative theology, see sources cited in Introduction, n. 74.

506. Levinas, *Oeuvres 1: Carnets*, p. 334: "*Les attributs négatifs ne sont pas simplement limitatifs. Force méta-phorique de la négation.*"

507. Levinas, *In the Time of the Nations*, p. 151; idem, *Ethics and Infinity*, pp. 75–76, and the oft-cited comment in the preface to *Totality and Infinity*, p. 28 (*Totalité et infini*, p. xvi), "We were impressed by the opposition to the idea of totality in Franz Rosenzweig's *Stern der Erlösung*, a work too often present in this book to be cited." Compare the study of Luc A. Anckaert, *A Critique of Infinity: Rosenzweig and Levinas* (Leuven: Peeters, 2006); and idem, "The Transcendental Possibility of Experience in Rosenzweig and Levinas," in *Faith, Truth, and Reason*, pp. 61–81.

508. Levinas, *Of God Who Comes to Mind*, p. 139.

509. Ibid., p. 100.

510. Levinas, *Basic Philosophical Writings*, p. 155.

511. See Levinas, *Totality and Infinity*, p. 35; *Totalité et infini*, p. 5. The author appropriates the term *transascendence* from Wahl to designate the "metaphysical movement" toward the transcendent, and as he openly acknowledges in n. 2, *ad locum*, he has "drawn much inspiration from the themes evoked" in *Existence humaine et transcendance*. Wahl is referred to as well in *Totality and Infinity*, p. 61 n. 6; *Totalité et infini*, p. 32 n. 1. It is worth recalling that Levinas dedicated this work to Marcelle and Jean Wahl. The friendship between Levinas and Wahl is discussed by Malka, *Emmanuel Levinas*, pp. 149–151, 153–155, 158–160, 191–192. See also Levinas, *Collected Philosophical Papers*, p. 8; "Jean Wahl et le sentiment," *Cahiers du Sud* 42 (1955): 453–459, English version in

Levinas, *Proper Names*, pp. 110–118, and the paper given by Levinas subsequent to Wahl's death, "Jean Wahl: Sans avoir ni être," in *Jean Wahl et Gabriel Marcel*, edited by Jeanne Hersch (Paris: Éditions Beauchesne, 1976), pp. 13–31, English version in Levinas, *Outside the Subject*, pp. 67–83. See also the brief comments about Wahl in Levinas, *Ethics and Infinity*, p. 55. For discussion of transcendence in Levinas, see Forthomme, *Une philosophie de la transcendance*, pp. 31–93. Levinas's indebtedness to Wahl's idea of transcendence and the quest for the "theological other" is discussed by Samuel Moyn, "Transcendence, Morality, and History: Emmanuel Levinas and the Discovery of Søren Kierkegaard in France," *Yale French Studies* 104 (2004): 37–46; idem, *Origins of the Other*, pp. 177–186. Obviously central to Moyn's argument is the impact of and reaction to Kierkegaard in Wahl, Levinas, and other French intellectuals. Levinas's engagement with Kierkegaard has been the subject of other studies as well. Most important for the theme of this chapter is J. Aaron Simmons, "Existential Appropriations: The Influence of Jean Wahl on Levinas's Reading of Kierkegaard," in *Kierkegaard and Levinas*, pp. 41–66. On the theme of transcendence in these two thinkers, see also the following studies of Merold Westphal: "Commanded Love and Divine Transcendence in Levinas and Kierkegaard," in *The Face of the Other and the Trace of God: Essays on the Philosophy of Emmanuel Levinas*, edited by Jeffrey Bloechl (New York: Fordham University Press, 2000), pp. 200–233; "The Trauma of Transcendence as Heteronomous Intersubjectivity," in *Intersubjectivité et théologie philosophique*, edited by Marco M. Olivetti (Padua: CEDAM, 2001), pp. 87–110; "Transcendence, Heteronomy, and the Birth of the Responsible Self," in *Calvin O. Schrag and the Task of Philosophy after Postmodernity*, edited by Martin J. Matuštík and William L. McBride (Evanston: Northwestern University Press, 2002), pp. 201–225; "Intentionality and Transcendence," in *Subjectivity and Transcendence*, pp. 71–93. The essays have been reprinted in Merold Westphal, *Levinas and Kierkegaard in Dialogue* (Bloomington: Indiana University Press, 2008). See also Claudia Welz, "The Presence of the Transcendent—Transcending the Present? Kierkegaard and Levinas on Subjectivity and the Ambiguity of God's Transcendence," in *Subjectivity and Transcendence*, pp. 149–176; and compare the analysis of Levinas and Kierkegaard in Simmons, *God and the Other*, pp. 35–131; Bettina Bergo, "Anxious Responsibility and Responsible Anxiety: Kierkegaard and Levinas on Ethics and Religion," in *Rethinking Philosophy of Religion: Approaches From Continental Philosophy*, edited by Philip Goodchild (New York: Fordham University Press, 2002), pp. 94–122; Llewelyn, *Margins of Religion*, pp. 98–99, 139–142; Wyschogrod, *Crossover Queries*, pp. 182–183. See also the collection of essays in *Despite Oneself: Subjectivity and Its Secret in Kierkegaard and Levinas*, edited by Claudia Welz and Karl Verstrynge (London: Turnshare Ltd., 2008).

512. Jean Wahl, *Existence humaine et transcendance* (Neuchatel: Éditions de la Baconnière, 1944), p. 38.

513. Jean Wahl, "Realism, Dialectic, and the Transcendent," *Philosophy and Phenomenological Research* 4 (1944): 498–500; idem, *Existence humaine*, pp. 10–11.

514. See Keller, "Rumors of Transcendence," pp. 140–141.

515. Levinas, *Ethics and Infinity*, p. 77.

516. Levinas, *Difficult Freedom*, pp. 178–179.

517. Levinas, *Basic Philosophical Writings*, p. 156.

518. Ibid., p. 75.

519. Levinas, *Beyond the Verse*, pp. 127–128.

520. It is of interest to recall the words of Levinas, *Totality and Infinity*, p. 198 (*Totalité et infini*, p. 172): "The face, still a thing among things, breaks through the form that nevertheless delimits it. . . . The permanent openness of the contours of its form in expression imprisons this openness which breaks up form in a caricature. The face at the limit of holiness and caricature is thus still in a sense exposed to powers." And compare the interpretation of this passage in Edith Wyschogrod, "Doing before Hearing: On the Primacy of Touch," in *Textes pour Emmanuel Lévinas*, edited by François Laruelle (Paris: Collections Surfaces, 1980), p. 184: "The equivocacy of the Face is evident for its alterity remains founded upon exteriority rather than the converse. Therefore Levinas is forced to describe the Face as hovering between 'sanctity and caricature,' as breaking the form that delimits it, as a metaphor for the idea of the infinite which is always too constricting for its content, etc. The Face as form must be presented as a fractured image. As epiphany it establishes the parameters of ethical life and attests the vulnerability of flesh but must remain a mask since the ethical cannot appear; as *imago* it shares the limits of the represented and loses the otherness of interiority." Wyschogrod's observation that, for Levinas, *the face must remain a mask* anticipates my own view.

521. Wyschogrod, *Crossover Queries*, p. 284.

522. Gordon, *Rosenzweig and Heidegger*, p. 230.

523. Blanchot, *The Writing of Disaster*, p. 143: "Jewish messianic thought . . . suggests the relation between the event and its nonoccurrence. . . . Both future and past . . . his coming does not correspond to any presence at all. . . . And if it happens that to the question 'When will you come?' the Messiah answers, 'Today,' the answer is certainly impressive: so, it is today! It is now and always now. There is no need to wait, although to wait is an obligation. And when is it now? When is the now which does not belong to ordinary time, which necessarily overturns it, does not maintain but destabilizes it? . . . Every just act . . . makes of its day the last day or—as Kafka said—the very last: a day no longer situated in the ordinary succession of days but one that makes of the most commonplace ordinary, the extraordinary." In light of this embrace of Kafka, read through a Levinasian lens, it is of interest to recall Blanchot's comment in a letter to Salomon Malka, published in *L'Arche* (1988), that his "proximity" to Judaism might be expressed "not in the time to come [*l'avenir*], but perhaps in the future," cited in Sarah Hammerschlag, "Literary Unrest: Blanchot, Lévinas, and the Proximity of Judaism," *Critical Inquiry* 36 (2010): 652.

524. Franz Kafka, *Parables and Paradoxes* (New York: Schocken, 1971), p. 81. See Wolfson, *Open Secret*, p. 268. The thematic affinity between Kafka and Levinas's messianism as an interruption of history rather than an eschatological fulfillment thereof is noted briefly by Butler, *Parting Ways*, p. 40.

Chapter 4: Secrecy of the Gift and the Gift of Secrecy

1. The expression is borrowed from William E. Connolly, *A World of Becoming* (Durham: Duke University Press, 2011), p. 38.

2. Rötzer, *Conversations with French Philosophers*, p. 47. The German transcript of the interview is found in Florian Rötzer, *Französische Philosophen im Gespräch* (Munich: Klaus Boer Verlag, 1986), pp. 67–87; the relevant passage occurs on p. 74. Part of the text is cited in Sanford L. Drob, *Kabbalah and Postmodernism: A Dialogue* (New York: Peter Lang, 2009), p. 4. See also Peter Sloterdijk, *Derrida, an Egyptian: On the Problem of the Jewish Pyramid*, translated by Wieland Hoban (Cambridge: Polity Press, 2009), p. xii.

3. Jürgen Habermas, *The Philosophical Discourse of Modernity: Twelve Lectures*, translated by Frederick Lawrence (Cambridge, MA: MIT Press, 1987), pp. 182–183.

4. To be precise, Habermas, *The Philosophical Discourse*, pp. 406–407 n. 46, does not refer to a "book" by Susan Handelman but rather her essay "Jacques Derrida and the Heretic Hermeneutic," in *Displacement: Derrida and After*, edited by Mark Krupnick (Bloomington: Indiana University Press, 1983), pp. 98–129. The suggestion regarding Derrida and kabbalah is discussed, albeit in less detail, in Susan A. Handelman, *The Slayers of Moses: The Emergence of Rabbinic Interpretation in Modern Literary Theory* (Albany: State University of New York Press, 1982), pp. 196, 218–219. In both contexts, Handelman is explicating the comparison of Derrida and kabbalah found in Harold Bloom.

5. Habermas, *The Philosophical Discourse*, p. 181.

6. Ibid., p. 182.

7. Ibid. On Levinas's alleged characterization of Derrida as a "heretical cabbalist," see the anecdote recounted by J. Hillis Miller, *For Derrida* (New York: Fordham University Press, 2009), p. 304. See also Drob, *Kabbalah and Postmodernism*, p. 3, and see the further clarification offered in the email message from Miller cited by Drob, ibid., pp. 265–266 n. 7.

8. Habermas, *The Philosophical Discourse*, p. 183 (emphasis in original).

9. Handelman, "Jacques Derrida," p. 111. Here it is apposite to recall the application of the adjective "rabbinical" to Derrida made by Jean-Luc Nancy, *Noli me tangere: On the Raising of the Body*, translated by Sarah Clift, Pascale-Anne Brault, and Michael Naas (New York: Fordham University Press, 2008), p. 110 n. 19, and see Jacques Derrida, *On Touching—Jean-Luc Nancy*, translated by Christine Irizarry (Stanford: Stanford University Press, 2005), p. 59, and compare the comments on this matter in Miller, *For Derrida*, pp. 302–304.

10. Habermas, *The Philosophical Discourse*, pp. 406–407 n. 46 (emphasis in original). It is of interest to note that in spite of Derrida's harsh reaction to Habermas's contextualization of his thought, the Jewish framing is reiterated in the conclusion of the short piece that Habermas wrote after Derrida's death, "Ein lezter Gruss: Derridas klärende Wirkung," published in the *Frankfurter Rundschau*, October 11, 2004. An English translation, "A Last Farewell: Derrida's Enlightening Impact," appears in *The Derrida-Habermas Reader*, edited by Lasse Thomassen (Chicago: University of Chicago Press,

2006), pp. 307–308. In the last paragraph, Habermas compares Derrida to Adorno: "Their Jewish roots are the common factor that links them. While Gershom Scholem remained a challenge for Adorno, Emmanuel Levinas became an authority for Derrida. So it is that his œuvre can also have an enlightening impact in Germany, because Derrida appropriated the themes of the later Heidegger without committing any neo-pagan betrayal of his own Mosaic roots." See Martin Beck Matuštik, "Between Hope and Terror: Habermas and Derrida Plead for the Im/Possible," in *The Derrida-Habermas Reader*, p. 289.

11. See Dana Hollander, "Is Deconstruction a Jewish Science? Reflections on 'Jewish Philosophy' in Light of Jacques Derrida's *Judéïtés*," *Philosophy Today* 50 (2006): 128–138.

12. Jacques Derrida, "An Interview with Derrida," in *Derrida and Différance*, edited by David Wood and Robert Bernasconi (Evanston: Northwestern University Press, 1988), p. 75.

13. David Shapiro, Michal Govrin, and Jacques Derrida, *Body of Prayer* (New York: Cooper Union for the Advancement of Science and Art, 2001), p. 59. On Derrida's sense of alienation from French, which he identifies as his "only mother tongue," see Jacques Derrida and Maurizio Ferraris, *A Taste for the Secret*, translated by Giacomo Donis, edited by Giacomo Donis and David Webb (Cambridge: Polity Press, 2001), p. 38. See below at n. 71.

14. See Ch. 3 at n. 112.

15. See Derrida and Ferraris, *A Taste for the Secret*, p. 59.

16. Jacques Derrida, *The Gift of Death*, translated by David Wills (Chicago: University of Chicago Press, 1995), p. 92; *Donner la mort* (Paris: Éditions Galilée, 1999), p. 127. Obviously, Freud was an important source for Derrida's observations on the phenomenon of *Unheimlichkeit*. See Jacques Derrida, *Specters of Marx: The State of the Debt, the Work of Mourning, and the New International*, translated by Peggy Kamuf, introduction by Bernd Magnus and Stephen Cullenberg (New York: Routledge, 1994), pp. 172–174. Many have opined on the link between Jewishness and the uncanny in Freud. For two representative treatments, see Diane Jonte-Pace, *Speaking the Unspeakable: Religion, Misogyny, and the Uncanny Mother in Freud's Cultural Texts* (Berkeley: University of California Press, 2001), pp. 74–98; Jay Geller, *On Freud's Jewish Body: Mitigating Circumcisions* (New York: Fordham University Press, 2007), pp. 43–62.

17. Jacques Derrida, *Of Hospitality: Ann Dufourmantelle Invites Jacques Derrida to Respond*, translated by Rachel Bowlby (Stanford: Stanford University Press, 2000), p. 89. It is of interest to note that Derrida ends this lecture with an exegesis of Genesis 19:1–9 and Judges 19:23–30 in an effort to elucidate the possibility of placing the law of hospitality above morality or ethics (pp. 151–155). This does not, however, have any bearing on the question of the author's ethnic identity.

18. Drob, *Kabbalah and Postmodernism*, pp. 43–45, compares the postmodern sense of exile as the condition of human existence to the kabbalah, specifically as enunciated in the Lurianic doctrines of withdrawal (*ṣimṣum*) and breaking the vessels (*shevirat ha-kelim*). I agree with this comparison only partially, since for the kabbalists the sense of

exile for both God and human is still determined from the Archimedean point of the Infinite. In the postmodern sensibility and in Derridean deconstruction, there is no such point, and the homelessness of the human situation in the world can never be rectified.

19. Hélène Cixous, *Portrait of Jacques Derrida as a Young Jewish Saint*, translated by Beverley Bie Brahic (New York: Columbia University Press, 2004), p. 65.

20. Robert Smith, *Derrida and Autobiography* (Cambridge: Cambridge University Press, 1995), p. 78, astutely comments on this aspect of Derrida's thought when he notes, "What cuts also closes; what closes also cuts. It cuts both ways. The *annulment* creates the circle of '*anneau,*' the ring."

21. Geoffrey Bennington and Jacques Derrida, *Jacques Derrida*, translated by Geoffrey Bennington (Chicago: University of Chicago Press, 1993), p. 154 (emphasis in original); Geoffrey Bennington and Jacques Derrida, *Derrida* (Paris: Éditions du Seuil, 2008), p. 133. See Gérard Bensussan, "The Last, the Remnant . . . (Derrida and Rosenzweig)," in *Judeities: Questions for Jacques Derrida*, edited by Bettina Bergo, Joseph Cohen, and Raphael Zagury-Orly, translated by Bettina Bergo and Michael B. Smith (New York: Fordham University Press, 2007), pp. 36–51; Hammerschlag, *The Figural Jew*, pp. 241–252; Cixous, *Portrait of Jacques Derrida*, pp. 77, 82, 85–86; Miller, *For Derrida*, pp. 169–170.

22. For discussion of circumcision in Derrida, culminating in the observation that circumcision is "another name for deconstruction," see Caputo, *The Prayers and Tears*, 250–263. See also the rich and playful exposition of this theme, presented for the most part as a midrashic exposition of Derridean texts, in Cixous, *Portrait of Jacques Derrida*, pp. 67–87.

23. Jacques Derrida, *Glas*, translated by John P. Leavey Jr. and Richard Rand (Lincoln: University of Nebraska Press, 1986), p. 41.

24. Bennington and Derrida, *Jacques Derrida*, pp. 170–171; Bennington and Derrida, *Derrida*, pp. 145–146.

25. Cixous, *Portrait of Jacques Derrida*, p. 86.

26. Ibid., p. 75, where Cixous describes her own family as consisting of "true false Jews. It's true we're not really Jewish but it doesn't suffice to say it. It suffices to say it for it to become false. If you don't say it, it becomes false as well. One can't however not. We say we're Jewish so as not to say the contrary. But we don't say we are not so as not to offend the religion that we respect and don't have. We have an idea of the thing we've never had."

27. Bennington and Derrida, *Jacques Derrida*, pp. 302–303; Bennington and Derrida, *Derrida*, pp. 250–251.

28. The double role of Elijah as the messianic prophet and as the one who holds the infant at the rite of circumcision is duly noted in Jacques Derrida, "Shibboleth for Paul Celan," in *Word Traces: Readings of Paul Celan*, edited by Aris Fioretos (Baltimore: Johns Hopkins University Press, 1994), p. 62.

29. Derrida, "On a Newly Arisen," p. 167. See Caputo, *The Prayers and Tears*, pp. 99–100; Catherine Keller, *God and Power: Counter-Apocalyptic Journeys* (Minneapolis: Fortress Press, 2005), pp. 88–91; O'Regan, *Theology and the Spaces of Apocalyptic*, pp. 92–93.

30. Derrida, *Specters of Mark*, p. 59. Compare Caputo, "Apostles," p. 186: "Deconstruction is (like) a deep desire for a Messiah who never shows (up), a subtle spirit or elusive specter that would be extinguished by the harsh hands of presence and actuality. The very idea of a Messiah who is never to show and whom we accordingly desire all the more is the very paradigm of deconstruction." Caputo, as is well known, theologizes Derridean deconstruction and thus renders the openness of the future in Derrida's thought as a matter of "faith and hope in something impossible. Here the gift of faith means a faith in the gift, where faith means that we *lack* the eyes to see and must feel in the dark" (emphasis in original). A less theologically biased reading of Derrida could lead one to the conclusion that the impossible is predicated on the denial of faith—whether construed as the gift of faith or as faith in the gift—and the consequent acceptance that we do not lack eyes to see but rather have the astute vision to see that there is nothing to see.

31. Jacques Derrida and Gianni Vattimo, *Religion* (Stanford: Stanford University Press, 1998), pp. 17–18. See Jacques Derrida, ". . . and pomegranates," in *Violence, Identity, and Self-Determination*, edited by Hent de Vries and Samuel Weber (Stanford: Stanford University Press, 1997), p. 326: "Not to-come without some sort of messianic memory and promise, of a messianicity older than all religion, more originary than all messianism." On the "double bind" of the messianic posture, which embraces the concomitant belief in the coming and deferral of the future, see Jacques Derrida, *Politics of Friendship*, translated by George Collins (London: Verso, 1997), pp. 173–174. Derrida's apocalyptic and messianic speculation has been the focus of many studies. See, for instance, Critchley, *The Ethics of Deconstruction*, pp. 79–82; Werner Hamacher, "Lingua Amissa: The Messianism of Commodity-Language and Derrida's *Specters of Marx*," in *Futures of Jacques Derrida*, edited by Richard Rand (Stanford: Stanford University Press, 2001), pp. 130–178; Gary Banham, "Derrida, the Messianic, and Eschatology," in *Rethinking Philosophy of Religion*, pp. 123–135; Shakespeare, *Derrida and Theology*, pp. 124–148; Clayton Crockett, *Radical Political Theology: Religion and Politics After Liberalism* (New York: Columbia University Press, 2011), pp. 145–159; and reference to Caputo, below, n. 38. A more comprehensive assessment of the messianic dimension of Derrida's thought would require a detailed analysis of other twentieth-century Jewish thinkers influenced by and responding to modes of philosophical eschatology. For representative studies, see Robert Gibbs, "Lines, Circles, Points: Messianic Epistemology in Cohen, Rosenzweig and Benjamin," in *Toward the Millennium*, pp. 363–382; idem, "Messianic Epistemology," in *Derrida and Religion: Other Testaments*, edited by Yvonne Sherwood and Kevin Hart (New York: Routledge, 2005), pp. 119–129, esp. 121–122; and the comprehensive study of Bouretz, *Witnesses for the Future*. Compare the additional studies cited in Ch. 3 n. 214.

32. Derrida and Vattimo, *Religion*, p. 17.

33. Ibid., p. 47.

34. Ibid., *Religion*, p. 51.

35. Derrida, *Adieu to Emmanuel Levinas*, p. 67.

36. Derrida, *Specters of Marx*, p. 37 (emphasis in original). See Wolfson, *Open Secret*, pp. 269–272, and Ch. 3 n. 523.

37. Derrida and Ferraris, *A Taste for the Secret*, p. 31.

38. Derrida, "On a Newly Arisen," p. 164. See Caputo, *The Prayers and Tears*, pp. 77–81, 95–99, 147–151; idem, "Apostles," pp. 199–200.

39. Jacques Derrida, *Archive Fever: A Freudian Impression*, translated by Eric Prenowitz (Chicago: University of Chicago Press, 1996), p. 68.

40. Derrida, *Specters of Marx*, p. 168.

41. Ibid., p. 161.

42. Ibid., p. 163 (emphasis in original). For an innovative engagement with the image of ghost in Derrida's writings as a mode of conversing with the ghost of Derrida, see David Appelbaum, *Jacques Derrida's Ghost: A Conjuration* (Albany: State University of New York Press, 2009).

43. On the relationship of "Greek" and "Jewish" in the philosophy of Levinas, see the extensive discussion in Ze'ev Levy, *Otherness and Responsibility: A Study of Emmanuel Levinas' Philosophy* (Jerusalem: Magnes Press, 1997), pp. 156–178. Levy deals specifically with Derrida's perspective on this question on pp. 170–171.

44. Derrida, *Writing and Difference*, p. 82; *L'écriture et la différence*, p. 122.

45. Derrida, *Writing and Difference*, p. 83; *L'écriture et la différence*, pp. 123–124.

46. Alan Roughley, *Reading Derrida Reading Joyce* (Gainesville: University Press of Florida, 1999), pp. 9–19, esp. 19. For a comparative analysis of the statement "Jewgreek is greekjew" in Derrida and Joyce, see Richard Kearney, *Navigations: Collected Irish Essays 1976–2006* (Syracuse: Syracuse University Press, 2006), pp. 114–118.

47. Derrida, *Writing and Difference*, p. 153; *L'écriture et la différence*, pp. 227–228. See the discussion of Derrida's essay, with special focus on the hybrid terms "jewgreek" and "greekjew," in Llewelyn, *Appositions*, pp. 143–155. See also Handelman, *Fragments*, pp. 263–264.

48. Derrida, *Psyche: Inventions of the Other, Volume II*, p. 116.

49. Geoffrey Bennington, "Mosaic Fragment: If Derrida Were an Egyptian . . . ," in *Derrida: A Critical Reader*, edited by David Wood (Oxford: Blackwell, 1992), pp. 97–119. See also Handelman, "Jacques Derrida," pp. 124–125; Caputo, *The Prayers and Tears*, p. 25; Gil Anidjar, "Introduction: 'Once More, Once More:' Derrida, the Arab, the Jew," in Derrida, *Acts of Religion*, pp. 32–33.

50. Bennington, "Mosaic Fragment," pp. 97 and 104.

51. Sloterdijk, *Derrida, an Egyptian*, p. 27.

52. Derrida, *Writing and Difference*, p. 152; *L'écriture et la différence*, p. 226. See Geoffrey Bennington, "Derridabase," in Bennington and Derrida, *Jacques Derrida*, pp. 303–304; Gideon Ofrat, *The Jewish Derrida*, translated by Peretz Kidron (Syracuse: Syracuse University Press, 2001), p. 138.

53. Derrida, *Writing and Difference*, p. 153 (emphasis added); *L'écriture et la différence*, p. 227. See the analysis of this passage in Dana Hollander, *Exemplarity and Chosenness: Rosenzweig and Derrida on the Nation of Philosophy* (Stanford: Stanford University Press,

2008), pp. 71–72. Derrida displayed particular interest in the hybridity of the Jewish-German symbiotic identity, as is attested in his essay "Interpretations at War: Kant, the Jew, the German," in *Acts of Religion*, pp. 137–188. See also Jacques Derrida, "A Testimony Given . . . ," in *Questioning Judaism: Interviews by Elisabeth Weber*, translated by Rachel Bowlby (Stanford: Stanford University Press, 2004), pp. 45–47, and compare Hollander, *Exemplarity and Chosenness*, pp. 126–129.

54. This expression was introduced in Elisabeth Weber's opening remark to Derrida that in many of his writings, he had been "meditating on circumcision, turning around it." See Derrida, "A Testimony Given . . . ," p. 39. It is possible that Derrida playfully imparted to this expression the Jewish concept of *teshuvah*, "repentance," which etymologically derives from a root that literally means to "turn around." If this is correct, then he seems to be saying that even the wound of circumcision, which is related to writing or the wound of language, cannot foster a return to the tradition. It is relevant to recall here the somewhat enigmatic reflections on Yom Kippur, the Day of Atonement, associated with the acts of confession and repentance, in Derrida, "Circumfession," in *Jacques Derrida*, p. 202: "I had begun again, at the Hotel Martinique, to write 'for myself'—follow the New York thread, from trip to trip, up to this one, the Kippours of N.Y., the cut with Kippour, the noncircumcision of the sons—up to that year when, coming out of a restaurant near the MOMA I enter a 'reformed' synagogue . . . circumcision remains the threat of what is making me write here, even if what hangs on it only hangs by a thread and threatens to be lost." Regarding this passage and the Jewish concept of *teshuvah*, see David Dault, "Rosenzweig and Derrida at Yom Kippur," in *Derrida and Religion*, pp. 98–99. Consider the passing reference in Derrida, *The Animal That Therefore I Am*, p. 38, "in 'Circumfession,' where I also bring back on stage certain white hens sacrificed in the *Pardès* on the Day of Atonement of my Algerian childhood." And compare the comments about the Day of Atonement and the etymology of the word *kippur* in Hélène Cixous and Jacques Derrida, *Veils*, translated by Geoffrey Bennington (Stanford: Stanford University Press, 2001), p. 45 (see below, n. 155).

55. Derrida, "A Testimony Given . . . ," p. 40.

56. Compare Jacques Derrida, *Acts of Literature*, edited by Derek Attridge (New York: Routledge, 1992), p. 285.

57. On the figurative meaning of circumcision, the *circumfigure*, see Cixous, *Portrait of Jacques Derrida*, pp. 77–78. See ibid., p. 8, where she notes that Derrida's "actual" circumcision on July 23, 1930, the date of his mother's birthday, was "literal" and not merely an "example" or a "figure." However, even in that first circumcision he was "circumcised at least twice . . . literally and figuratively, in his flesh and forever, and circumcised like all poets, like all men circumcised by language or with an inclination to circumcise language."

58. Derrida, "Shibboleth," p. 64; Cixous and Derrida, *Veils*, pp. 75–76.

59. Paul's privileging the circumcision of the heart over the literal circumcision is addressed in Cixous and Derrida, *Veils*, p. 76. The affinity between Derrida and Paul on

this matter is duly noted by Caputo, *The Prayers and Tears*, pp. 233, 250, and 262. On the penchant for the Christian emphasis on inwardness and the consequent rejection of Pharisaic literalness, see Jacques Derrida, *Monolingualism of the Other; or, the Prosthesis of Origin*, translated by Patrick Mensah (Stanford: Stanford University Press, 1998), p. 54. See also idem, *On Touching*, pp. 267–268, 367 n. 9. In that extensive note, Derrida characterizes Muslims as the "hyperbolic heirs" of the "endless contradiction" between the literal and the spiritual, the touchable and the untouchable, which is the "contradiction of the very Infinite itself."

60. Romans 2:28–29: "For he is not a real Jew who is one outwardly, nor is true circumcision something external and physical. He is a Jew who is one inwardly, and real circumcision is a matter of the heart, spiritual and not literal."

61. See Derrida, "A Testimony Given . . . ," p. 43. Derrida explains that it is his lack of knowledge of Hebrew, Jewish history, and texts of Jewish culture that allows him "to move about in the metaphorical, rhetorical, allegorical dimension of Judaism." The specific example he gives to illustrate the point is circumcision: "Perhaps it's because of my ignorance and the fact of my not belonging in Jewish culture that I come to consider that, basically, circumcision is there where there isn't any and that what it marks, namely belonging to a community, alliance, wounding, the relationship to the father, the symbolic, etc., is something that happens in all cultures, in all languages: the straightforward fact of speaking establishes us from the outset in the alliance of circumcision, in general. It's the paradox of 'All poets are Jews.'" Concerning the final statement, which is attributed to Marina Tsvétayeva, see below at n. 206.

62. On the overcoming of the binary in Jesus, see also Galatians 5:6, "For in Christ Jesus neither circumcision nor uncircumcision is of any avail, but faith working through love." It is of interest to consider the assessment of Derrida's view in Cixous, *Portrait of Jacques Derrida*, pp. 68–69: "For men circumcision for women, I emphasize, noncircumcision, or perhaps circumcision-by-alliance. Therefore I cannot discuss circumcision, I cannot discuss it, with all due circumspection, I can talk about it from the sidelines as sister and daughter of sometimes-circumcised sometimes-not Jews and right away there's the question, up it pops with its scissors ready to separate the foreskin from the glans, Jewish-Jew from Non-Jewish Jew, circumcised-Jew from non-circumcised Jew all the same or maybe not, it all depends on the question, where you draw the line that sorts them out, yes, the minute I want to start talking about circumcision I find myself cut off, barred, stopped, tortured with questions." And see ibid., pp. 73–74, where Cixous notes the obvious oddity that the Jewish identity of the male infant, which necessitates circumcision, is dependent on the mother, who is excluded from the ritual: "the Jewish wife has no place in the Jewish circle, and yet there can be no true circumcision if the excluded mother is not known to be the daughter of a Jewish woman. She is not Jewish, she has no bar mitzvah and no tallith, she is not among the Jews in the synagogue, she is off to the side, she is apart, she is parked in the balcony, she is there to look at him—her son her brother her spouse her lover her father, she is the overlooked essential, the witness excluded for millennia who is nonetheless bizarrely necessary, from far away and right

under your nose." Even if one were to argue that the view expressed by Cixous reflects the Orthodox perspective and not the other denominations where the participation of women active in synagogal practices has been augmented, the problem of circumcision remains, since it excludes all Jewish women irrespective of their affiliation.

63. Derrida, "A Testimony Given . . . ," p. 41. See Hollander, *Exemplarity and Chosenness*, pp. 51–57, 132–134; Hammerschlag, *The Figural Jew*, pp. 228–241. See also Irene E. Harvey, *Labyrinths of Exemplarity: At the Limits of Deconstruction* (Albany: State University of New York Press, 2002), pp. 179–205. Although Harvey is not interested in the specific question of Derrida's Jewishness or his more general attitude toward Judaism, her analysis of the Derridean reading of Rousseau sheds light on the tension between the universal and the particular as exemplified in the nonmetaphysical function of the example to thematize what must remain unthematized. Commenting on Derrida's explication (*Of Grammatology*, p. 109) of a passage from chapter six in Lévi-Strauss's *The Savage Mind*, entitled "Universalization and Particularization," Harvey, op. cit., pp. 187–188, writes: "Thus the metaphysical matrix of universal/particular, and essential necessity versus determined contingent, is in place surrounding the usage of 'example' here so that its function—going without saying—becomes a particular of an essential necessity, a determined ulterior, continuing addition or articulation. What authorizes this frame? What necessity governs this usage? Only the metaphysics that Derrida would deconstruct, and again we should note that by not thematizing example here Derrida is not thereby found guilty of anything. Rather, we aim here only to locate *the space of exemplarity* within his discourse, which his own usage—within metaphysics—cannot account for. Again . . . the universal/particular matrix is itself a concealment of a plurality of structures. In this way, then, Derrida's usage of example contributes to the concealment, especially since it remains, for the most part, 'unnoticed,' unsaid, unmentioned, unremarked" (emphasis in original).

64. Jacques Derrida, "Abraham, the Other," in *Judeities*, p. 12. The affinity between exemplarity and the Levinasian ethics as first philosophy is noted by Derrida, op. cit., p. 23. On the relationship between exemplarity and the law, see Harvey, *Labyrinths*, pp. 173–176.

65. Derrida, "A Testimony Given . . . ," p. 41 (emphasis added).

66. See above, n. 21.

67. Derrida, "A Testimony Given . . . ," p. 42.

68. Ibid., p. 43.

69. Derrida, "Abraham, the Other," pp. 29–30.

70. Ibid., p. 33. For a sensitive discussion of the larger context of this question, see Hollander, "Is Deconstruction a Jewish Science?"

71. Derrida and Ferraris, *A Taste for the Secret*, pp. 27–28. See ibid., pp. 38–39: "The first few months after my expulsion was a very bad time . . . And, paradoxically, the feeling of not belonging came to affect my relationship with the Jewish community and

with the Jewish children who, like me, had been grouped together in the Jewish school. I hated that school. . . . In that period an obscure feeling arose in me that has, I think, remained to this day—a trauma that caused me not only to cultivate a sort of not-belonging to French culture and to France in general, but also, in some way, to reject my belonging to Judaism." On the intrinsic connection of the secret and not-belonging, see above, n. 16. On the status of the Jew and the quality of *Unheimlichkeit*, the sense of "what is at once at home and not at home, intimate and strange, domestic and foreign," see Derrida, "Abraham, the Other," p. 22.

72. Derrida, "Shibboleth," p. 54.

73. Compare Derrida's admission in *Monolingualism*, pp. 49–50: "Believe me, although I measure the absurdity and presumptuousness of these infantile allegations (such as the 'I am the last Jew' in *Circonfession*), I risk them in order to be honest with my interlocutors and myself, with this someone in me who feels things in that way. In that way and no other. Since I always tell the truth, you can believe me."

74. In Derrida, "Abraham, the Other," p. 17, the critical statement *je suis le dernier des Juifs* is translated as "I am the last and the least of the Jews."

75. Ibid., p. 35.

76. Derrida, "Shibboleth," p. 56. Jean-Luc Nancy, "The Judeo-Christian," in *Judeities*, pp. 214–233, explores the "historical" question of whether the "last of the Jews" should not be considered the "first of the Christians."

77. Derrida, "Abraham, the Other," pp. 6–7.

78. Derrida, *Writing and Difference*, p. 75; *L'écriture et la différence*, p. 112. See Joseph G. Kronick, "Edmond Jabès and the Poetry of the Jewish Unhappy Consciousness," *Modern Language Notes* 106 (1991): 975.

79. Caputo, *The Prayers and Tears*, p. 230.

80. Caputo, "Apostles," p. 200.

81. Cixous, *Portrait of Jacques Derrida*, p. 80.

82. Bennington and Derrida, *Jacques Derrida*, pp. 190–191; Bennington and Derrida, *Derrida*, p. 162.

83. Derrida, *Monolingualism*, p. 53.

84. Ibid., p. 54.

85. For an extended discussion of the hypernomian dimension of kabbalistic piety, see Wolfson, *Venturing Beyond*, pp. 186–285.

86. See Jacques Derrida, "To Forgive: The Unforgivable and the Imprescriptible," in *Questioning God*, edited by John D. Caputo, Mark Dooley, and Michael J. Scanlon (Bloomington: Indiana University Press, 2001), pp. 25–26, 48; idem, *On Cosmopolitanism and Forgiveness*, translated by Mark Dooley and Michael Hughes, with a preface by Simon Critchley and Richard Kearney (London: Routledge, 2001), pp. 33, 59–60; and discussion in Wolfson, *A Dream*, p. 241.

87. Bennington and Derrida, *Jacques Derrida*, p. 194 (emphasis in original); Bennington and Derrida, *Derrida*, p. 164.

88. Jacques Derrida, *Signéponge/Signsponge*, translated by Richard Rand (New York: Columbia University Press, 1984), pp. 14–15. For a sophisticated analysis of writing and the law in Derrida, see Rose, *Dialectic of Nihilism*, pp. 131–170.

89. Derrida, *Signéponge/Signsponge*, pp. 14–17.

90. For discussion of Derrida and negative theology, see the studies cited in Ch. 2 n. 295.

91. For a critical assessment of the Jewish dimension of Derrida's philosophical writings, see Ofrat, *The Jewish Derrida*. The possible influence of kabbalah is noted on pp. 13–14. For additional studies that explore this influence, see Idel, *Old Worlds*, pp. 176–192; Drob, *Kabbalah and Postmodernism*.

92. Derrida, *Dissemination*, pp. 342–345. Idel, *Old Worlds*, pp. 245–247, has duly noted the influence of Levi Isaac of Berditchev on Derrida, as mediated through the interpretation of Scholem, *On the Kabbalah*, pp. 81–82. See below, n. 168. The utilization of the motif of ṣimṣum by Derrida is noted briefly by Thomas J. J. Altizer, "History as Apocalypse," in *Deconstruction and Theology* (New York: Crossroad, 1982), pp. 148–149 (cited below at n. 141), and Hart, *The Trespass of the Sign*, p. 62; and compare the more extended discussion in Drob, *Kabbalah and Postmodernism*, pp. 65–90. See also Shakespeare, *Derrida and Theology*, pp. 126–127.

93. Derrida, *Dissemination*, p. 344.

94. Ibid., p. 342. On the history of the term *ein sof*, see Gershom Scholem, *Origins of the Kabbalah*, edited by R. J. Zwi Werblowsky, translated by Allan Arkush (Princeton: Princeton University Press, 1987), pp. 265–270; Isaiah Tishby, *The Wisdom of the Zohar: An Anthology of Texts*, translated by David Goldstein (Oxford: Oxford University Press, 1989), pp. 229–255. See also the recent comprehensive study of Sandra Valabregue-Perry, *Concealed and Revealed: "Ein Sof" in Theosophic Kabbalah* (Los Angeles: Cherub Press, 2010) (Hebrew), and idem, "The Concept of Infinity (*Eyn-sof*) and the Rise of Theosophical Kabbalah," *Jewish Quarterly Review* 102 (2012): 405–430.

95. See Terence R. Wright, "Midrash and Intertextuality: Ancient Rabbinic Exegesis and Postmodern Reading of the Bible," in *Divine Aporia: Postmodern Conversations about the Other*, edited by John C. Hawley (Lewisburg: Bucknell University Press, 2000), pp. 97–119.

96. Derrida, *Dissemination*, pp. 344–345. On the nexus of numerology, mystical illumination, and theophanic vision, see Derrida, "On a Newly Arisen," p. 135.

97. Moshe Idel, "Infinities of Torah in Kabbalah," in *Midrash and Literature*, edited by Geoffrey H. Hartman and Sanford Budick (New Haven: Yale University Press, 1986), p. 149. Idel's suggestion is accepted by Ofrat, *The Jewish Derrida*, p. 14.

98. Derrida, *Dissemination*, p. 55.

99. Ibid., p. 344. The kabbalistic influence of the "endless interpretability of a text," which is linked more specifically to Luria, was suggested en passant by Hart, *The Trespass of the Sign*, p. 44.

100. The expression was coined by Martin Hägglund, "The Necessity of Discrimination: Disjoining Derrida and Levinas," *Diacritics* 34 (2004): 55, on the basis of the comment of Jacques Derrida, *Speech and Phenomena and Other Essays on Husserl's Theory of Signs*,

translated, with an introduction, by David B. Allison, preface by Newton Garver (Evanston: Northwestern University Press, 1973), p. 102: "The appearing of the infinite *différance* is itself finite. Consequently, *différance*, which does not occur outside this relation, becomes the finitude of life as an essential relation with oneself and one's death. *The infinite différance is finite*" (emphasis in original). See also Hägglund, *Radical Atheism*, p. 146.

101. Derrida, *Dissemination*, p. 344.

102. Idel, *Old Worlds*, p. 245. See idem, *Absorbing Perfections: Kabbalah and Interpretation* (New Haven: Yale University Press, 2002), p. 77.

103. Umberto Eco, *Semiotics and the Philosophy of Language* (Bloomington: Indiana University Press, 1984), pp. 154–155.

104. Ibid., p. 156.

105. Elliot R. Wolfson, "Structure, Innovation, and Diremptive Temporality: The Use of Models to Study Continuity and Discontinuity in Kabbalistic Tradition," *Journal for the Study of Religions and Ideologies* 6 (2007): 149–154. For a similar contrast between the kabbalistic conception of the Torah comprising the infinity of the divine and the deconstructionist claim that there is nothing outside the text, see Idel, *Absorbing Perfections*, pp. 124–128. For a contrast of the kabbalistic and Derridean conceptions of the trace, see the reference to Bloom cited below, n. 147.

106. See Preface n. 49.

107. Moshe Idel, *Kabbalah and Eros* (New Haven: Yale University Press, 2005), p. 129.

108. Eve Tavor Bannet, *Structuralism and the Logic of Dissent* (London: Macmillan, 1989), pp. 198–190. For a criticism of Bannet, see Shakespeare, *Derrida and Theology*, p. 177.

109. Derrida, *Margins*, p. 65.

110. Derrida, *Writing and Difference*, p. 146; *L'écriture et la différence*, p. 217. See idem, *Margins*, pp. 33–34 n. 6, and the analysis of John D. Caputo, "Mysticism and Transgression: Derrida and Meister Eckhart," in *Derrida and Deconstruction*, edited by Hugh Silverman (New York: Routledge, 1989), pp. 24–39. See also Caputo, *The Mystical Element*, p. 130, where Eckhart's mystical atheism—the desire to be liberated from God—is interpreted as akin to Heidegger's demand to free thought from the ontotheological conception of God. For other attempts to read Eckhart in a manner that is more conducive to the Derridean hermeneutic, see Reiner Schürmann, "Neoplatonic Henology as an Overcoming of Metaphysics," *Research in Phenomenology* 13 (1983): 25–41; Niklaus Largier, "Repräsentation und Negativität: Meister Eckharts Kritik als Dekonstruktion," in *Contemplata aliis trader: Studien zum Verhältnis von Literatur und Spiritualität*, edited by Claudia Brinker, Urs Herzog, Niklaus Largier, and Paul Michel (Bern: Peter Lang, 1995), pp. 371–390; Amy Hollywood, "Preaching as Social Practice in Meister Eckhart," in *Mysticism and Social Transformation*, edited by Janet K. Ruffing, with a foreword by Robert J. Egan (Syracuse: Syracuse University Press, 2001), pp. 76–90; David Newheiser, "Eckhart, Derrida, and the Gift of Love," *Heythrop Journal* (2012), published online http://onlinelibrary.wiley.com/doi/10.1111/j.1468-2265.2012.00754.x/pdf.

111. This information is supplied in the version of "How to Avoid Speaking: Denials" included in Derrida, *Psyche: Inventions of the Other, Volume II*, p. 143.

112. Ibid., p. 158 (emphasis in original).

113. Ibid., p. 147.

114. Ibid., p. 148 (emphasis in original). See Marion, "In the Name," pp. 21–23; Caputo, "Apostles," pp. 187–189.

115. Alain Badiou, *Being and Event*, translated by Oliver Feltham (New York: Continuum, 2005), p. 26, remarked that the Platonic depiction of the Good as the supreme being that is "beyond substance" (*epekeina tēs ousias*) is a path of thought that is "found in negative theologies, for which the exteriority-to-situation of being is revealed in its heterogeneity to any presentation and to any predication . . . an alterity which institutes the One of being, torn from the multiple, and nameable exclusively as absolute Other. From the point of view of *experience*, this path consecrates itself to mystical annihilation; an annihilation in which, on the basis of an interruption of all presentative situations, and at the end of a negative spiritual exercise, a Presence is gained, a presence which is exactly that of the being of the One as non-being" (emphasis in original).

116. Heidegger, *Pathmarks*, p. 243; *Wegmarken*, p. 319.

117. Derrida, *Writing and Difference*, p. 137; *L'écriture et la différence*, p. 201.

118. Dermot Moran, *The Philosophy of John Scottus Eriugena: A Study of Idealism in the Middle Ages* (Cambridge: Cambridge University Press, 1989), p. 101. For a similar critique of Derrida's interpretation of Dionysius, see Westerkamp, "Naming and Tetragrammatology," p. 114.

119. Michael A. Sells, *Mystical Languages of Unsaying* (Chicago: University of Chicago Press, 1994), p. 12.

120. Derrida, *On the Name*, p. 54; *Sauf le nom*, p. 53.

121. Sells, *Mystical Languages*, p. 20.

122. Ibid., pp. 12–13.

123. Ibid., p. 3.

124. Derrida, *Psyche: Inventions of the Other, Volume II*, p. 145.

125. Wolfson, *Language, Eros, Being*, p. 215. And see ibid., pp. 217–218, where I briefly discuss the commingling of the apophatic and the kataphatic in Pseudo-Dionysius.

126. Ibid., p. 219, and see p. 343. See also Elliot R. Wolfson, "Negative Theology and Positive Assertion in the Early Kabbalah," *Da'at* 32–33 (1994): v–xxii.

127. Gershom Scholem, "The Traditions of R. Jacob and R. Isaac ben R. Jacob ha-Kohen," *Madda'ei ha-Yahadut* 2 (1927): 227 (Hebrew). For very similar language, see the anonymous text cited from a manuscript in Wolfson, *Through a Speculum*, p. 289, and compare the formulation of Nicholas of Cusa's *De Deo Abscondito*, "God is beyond nothing and something" (*Deus est supra nihil et aliquid*), in Jasper Hopkins, *Complete Philosophical and Theological Treatises of Nicholas of Cusa* (Minneapolis: Arthur J. Banning Press, 2001), p. 303.

128. David S. Ariel, "Shem Tob Ibn Shem Tob's Kabbalistic Critique of Jewish Philosophy in the 'Commentary on the Sefirot': Study and Text," Ph.D. dissertation, Brandeis University, 1982, p. 42.

129. Meir Ibn Gabbai, *Derekh Emunah*, in Moshe Schatz, *Ma'yan Moshe* (Jerusalem, 2011), pp. 117–122: "The Ein Sof has no name in itself, for even the name *ein sof* should not be attributed to it in truth . . . Thought does not grasp the Cause of Causes and neither something nor nothing should be said about it."

130. Ḥayyim Vital, *Sha'arei Qedushah*, edited by Amnon Gross (Jerusalem, 2005), 3:1, p. 91.

131. Derrida, *Acts of Religion*, pp. 213–214.

132. Cixous and Derrida, *Veils*, pp. 43–44 (emphasis in original). On the veil, secrecy, and transparency, see the extensive analysis in Ginette Michaud, *Battements du secret littéraire: Lire Jacques Derrida et Hélène Cixous*, vol. one (Paris: Hermann Éditeurs, 2010), pp. 41–145.

133. Scholem, *On the Kabbalah*, pp. 53–61; Tishby, *The Wisdom of the Zohar*, pp. 1085, 1091–1092; Albert van der Heide, "Pardes: Methodological Reflections on the Theory of the Four Senses," *Journal of Jewish Studies* 34 (1983): 147–159; Frank Talmage, "Apples of Gold: The Inner Meaning of Sacred Texts in Medieval Judaism," in *Jewish Spirituality: From the Bible through the Middle Ages*, edited by Arthur Green (New York: Crossroad, 1987), pp. 319–321; Moshe Idel, "PaRDeS: Some Reflections on Kabbalistic Hermeneutics," in *Death, Ecstasy, and Other Worldly Journeys*, edited by John J. Collins and Michael Fishbane (Albany: State University of New York Press, 1995), pp. 249–268.

134. Bennington and Derrida, *Jacques Derrida*, pp. 110–111 (emphasis in original); Bennington and Derrida, *Derrida*, pp. 98–100. In a second passage from this work, Derrida utilizes the kabbalistic acronym again: "A circumcision is my size, it takes my body, it turns round me to envelop me in its blade strokes, they pull upward, a spiral raises and hardens me, I am erect in my circumcision for centuries like the petrified memory . . . we have just enough breath left to ask for pardon, for the Great Pardon, in the languages of the PaRDeS, for all the evil that my writing is drawn, withdrawn and drawn out from, an eternal skin above not you, but me dreaming of him who dreams of the place of God" (Bennington and Derrida, *Jacques Derrida*, pp. 242–243; Bennington and Derrida, *Derrida*, p. 203; see also Bennington and Derrida, *Jacques Derrida*, pp. 246, 247–248, 312; Bennington and Derrida, *Derrida*, pp. 206, 207, 258).

135. Scholem, *On the Kabbalah*, pp. 48–49; Idel, "Infinites of the Torah," pp. 141–157.

136. Derrida, *Dissemination*, p. 343.

137. It is of interest to note, by contrast, that Derrida, *On the Name*, pp. 25–26, insists that the notion of the secret in which he is interested is not mystical in nature, related either to the negative theology in Christian tradition or to an esoteric doctrine in the Pythagorean, Platonic, or Neoplatonic community.

138. Derrida , *Writing and Difference*, p. 74; *L'écriture et la différence*, p. 112.

139. Shira Wolosky, "Derrida, Jabès, Levinas: Sign-Theory as Ethical Discourse," *Prooftexts* 2 (1982): 292. A similar conclusion is reached in Shakespeare, *Derrida and Theology*, pp. 96–99.

140. Derrida, *Writing and Difference*, p. 75; *L'écriture et la différence*, p. 113.

141. Altizer, "History as Apocalypse," pp. 148–149.

142. Derrida, *Writing and Difference*, p. 67; *L'écriture et la différence*, p. 103.

143. Altizer, "History as Apocalypse," p. 149. See the discussion of Altizer's kabbalistic reading of Derrida as the foundation for the death-of-God theology in Shakespeare, *Derrida and Theology*, pp. 176–177.

144. For an elaboration of Derrida's claim, see Mole, *Lévinas, Blanchot, Jabès*, pp. 87, 116–117. On the resemblance between Jabès and kabbalistic notions of textuality and writing, see the brief remarks in Wolfson, "Divine Suffering," pp. 138–139.

145. See above, n. 92.

146. Harold Bloom, *A Map of Misreading* (Oxford: Oxford University Press, 1975), p. 43.

147. Harold Bloom, *Kabbalah and Criticism* (New York: Seabury Press, 1975), pp. 52–53 (emphasis in original). The distinction between the trace of traditional metaphysics and the Derridean trace is stated concisely by Zahavi, *Self-Awareness and Alterity*, p. 264 n. 68.

148. Harold Bloom, "The Breaking of Form," in *Deconstruction and Criticism*, edited by Harold Bloom (New York: Seabury Press, 1979), p. 4 (emphasis in original).

149. Derrida, *Psyche: Inventions of the Other, Volume II*, p. 167.

150. For discussion of this Derridean theme, see Taylor, *Nots*, pp. 36–37; Foshay, "Introduction: Denegation and Resentment."

151. Derrida, *Psyche: Inventions of the Other, Volume II*, p. 189 (emphasis in original).

152. Taylor, *Nots*, p. 53.

153. Consider the interpretation of Jerusalem in Derrida, *Adieu to Levinas*, pp. 101–114.

154. Derrida, *Psyche: Inventions of the Other, Volume II*, p. 309 n. 13.

155. The hybrid cultural identification is illumined by the following remark Derrida made about his youth in an interview in April 1989 conducted by Derek Attridge: "Racism was everywhere in Algeria at that time, it was running wild in all directions. Being Jewish and a victim of anti-semitism didn't spare one the anti-Arab racism I felt everywhere around me, in manifest or latent form" (Derrida, *Acts of Literature*, p. 39). Perhaps the thread linking Jew and Arab in Derrida's mind is the shared sense of being persecuted. See Derrida's musing on the memory of being blessed on Yom Kippur, the "Day of Atonement," in Cixous and Derrida, *Veils*, p. 45, "I can still see this father, but I could not see him, by definition, by situation, he blessed his two sons one day bigger than he, lifting with both arms his tallith stretched above the two heads. Bigger than he, and one bigger than the other, the sons are stifling a little under the solemn protection, under the roof of that temple so close, during the interminable prayer, in what was called the 'great temple,' an old mosque right in the middle of an Arab district, anciently judeo-arab, a mosque in the Spanish style since become a mosque again." For an extended discussion of this destabilizing cultural marker of self-identity, see Anidjar, "Introduction," in Derrida, *Acts of Religion*, pp. 1–39, and idem, *The Jew, the Arab*, pp. 40–60. See Ch. 5 n. 3.

156. See Ch. 5 n. 4. In this connection, it is of interest to recall the comment in Derrida, *On the Name*, p. 63 (*Sauf le nom*, p. 70): "Whatever the translations, analogies, transpositions, transferences, metaphors, never has any discourse expressly given itself this title (negative theology, apophatic method, *via negativa*) in the thoughts of Jewish, Muslim, Buddhist culture." It is possible to contest Derrida's claim on historical and textual grounds, but what is important is his assumption that negative theology shows exclusive affinity with Christian philosophy.

157. For a different interpretation of Derrida's statement in "How to Avoid Speaking: Denials," see Toby Foshay, "Resentment and Apophasis: The Trace of the Other in Levinas, Derrida and Gans," in *Shadow of Spirit: Postmodernism and Religion*, edited by Philippa Berry and Andrew Wernick (London: Routledge, 1992), p. 84. According to Foshay, Derrida's silence regarding apophasis in Jewish and Islamic thought "is an inherent function of the need to avoid speaking of essences, identities and 'things in themselves.' In other words, Derrida can allow himself to speak of the Platonic and Neoplatonic heritage of negative theology, but not of the Jewish or Islamic, which are closest to him and, as it were, identical with him. He cannot altogether avoid speaking of the analogy and isomorphism of apophaticism and deconstruction, but he can defer mere personal and 'attitudinal' questions of identity."

158. Handelman, *The Slayers of Moses*, p. 163.

159. Ibid., p. 165.

160. Ibid., 165–166.

161. Wolosky, "Derrida, Jabès, Levinas," pp. 290–291.

162. Handelman, *The Slayers of Moses*, pp. 205–206; idem, "Jacques Derrida," pp. 118–122.

163. Wolosky, "Derrida, Jabès, Levinas," pp. 285–287.

164. Derrida, *Of Grammatology*, p. 13.

165. Derrida and Vattimo, *Religion*, pp. 66 and 47.

166. Derrida, *The Gift of Death*, pp. 89–90; *Donner la mort*, pp. 124–125.

167. Derrida, *Glas*, pp. 49–50.

168. This is precisely how Derrida, *Dissemination*, pp. 344–345, interprets the dictum of Levi Isaac of Berditchev concerning the messianic Torah, which is composed of the white spaces in which the letters are invisible: "the blanks will never be anything but provisionally filled in, one surface or square always remaining empty, open to the play of permutations, blanks barely glimpsed as blanks, (almost) pure spacing, going on forever and not in the expectation of any Messianic fulfillment. It is a spacing that is merely attended. For there exists a whole interpretation of spacing, of textual generation and polysemy, of course, revolving around the Torah. Polysemy is the possibility of a 'new Torah' capable of arising out of the other ('Torah will issue out of me')." See above, n. 92.

169. Derrida, *Dissemination*, p. 26 (emphasis in original).

170. Jacques Derrida, *Literature in Secret: An Impossible Filiation*, in *The Gift of Death*, translated by David Wills, second edition (Chicago: University of Chicago Press, 2008),

pp. 122–123; *Donner la mort*, p. 165. On the secret in Derrida's deconstruction, see Caputo, *The Prayers and Tears*, pp. 101–112.

171. Jacques Derrida, *Geneses, Genealogies, Genres, and Genius: The Secrets of the Archive*, translated by Beverley Bie Brahic (New York: Columbia University Press, 2006), p. 32.

172. Derrida, *On the Name*, p. 24.

173. Smith, *Derrida and Autobiography*, pp. 41–42, 77–78, 82–83.

174. Elliot R. Wolfson, "Circumcision, Vision of God, and Textual Interpretation: From Midrashic Trope to Mystical Symbol," *History of Religions* 27 (1987): 189–215; idem, *Through a Speculum*, pp. 330–331, 342–343, 357–358.

175. Sacha Stern, *Jewish Identity in Early Rabbinic Writings* (Leiden: E. J. Brill, 1994), pp. 229–231.

176. Elliot R. Wolfson, "Occultation of the Feminine and the Body of Secrecy in Medieval Kabbalah," in *Rending the Veil*, pp. 135–148; revised version in Elliot R. Wolfson, *Luminal Darkness: Imaginal Gleanings from Zoharic Literature* (Oxford: Oneworld Publications, 2007), pp. 272–282. For a more explicit Lacanian analysis, see Elliot R. Wolfson, "Circumcision, Secrecy, and the Veiling of the Veil: Phallomorphic Exposure and Kabbalistic Esotericism," in *The Covenant of Circumcision: New Perspectives on an Ancient Jewish Rite*, edited by Elizabeth W. Mark (Hanover: Brandeis University Press, 2003), pp. 58–70, and the slightly modified version in Wolfson, *Language, Eros, Being*, pp. 128–141.

177. Derrida, *Glas*, p. 42. On p. 41 Derrida refers to circumcision as the "symbolic castration." By contrast, see Derrida, *Archive Fever*, p. 42, where the irreducibility of circumcision to castration is emphasized in opposition to the Freudian view that circumcision is a symbolic substitute for the castration of the son by the primitive father. See also Derrida, "On a Newly Arisen," pp. 139–140. The change in Derrida's perspective has been noted by Caputo, *The Prayer and Tears*, pp. 234, 240, 259, 262, 306–307. On Derrida's presentation of circumcision in *Archive Fever* as a response to Freud, especially as read by Yerushalmi, see Geller, *On Freud's Jewish Body*, pp. 29–31.

178. Wolfson, *Through a Speculum*, pp. 336–345.

179. Derrida, *Points*, p. 96. See Drucilla Cornell, "Where Love Begins: Sexual Difference and the Limit of the Masculine Symbolic," in *Derrida and Feminism: Recasting the Question of Woman*, edited by Ellen K. Feder, Mary C. Rawlinson, and Emily Zakin (New York: Routledge, 1997), pp. 194–197; Gayatri Chakravorty Spivak, "Displacement and the Discourse of Woman," in *Feminist Interpretations of Jacques Derrida*, edited by Nancy J. Holland (University Park: Pennsylvania State University Press, 2001), pp. 60–68.

180. Derrida, *Acts of Literature*, p. 58.

181. Derrida, *Writing and Difference*, pp. 76–77; *L'écriture et la différence*, p. 114.

182. It is this logical conundrum that underlies Derrida's notion of "iterability," which presumes a convergence of sameness and difference such that there is genuine reiteration of the "wholly other," *tout autre*, in every moment. The distinctiveness of each moment

necessitates that what is experienced in the present is utterly new, but the present can be new only to the extent that it is old. Innovation is possible against the backdrop of replication. See, for example, Derrida's remark in Derrida and Ferraris, *A Taste for the Secret*, p. 47, "Every time I write something, I have the impression of making a beginning—but in fact that which is the same in texture is ceaselessly exposed to a singularity which is that of the other (another text, someone else, another word of the language). Everything appears anew: which means newness and repetition together. . . . In the actual writing, of course, I'm well aware of the fact that at bottom it all unfolds according to the same law that commands these always different things. . . . I can only hope that what I say about philosophy, literature, the event, the signature, the iterability (altering-altered repetition) is consistent with our encountering this ever renewed singularity." For a similar description of prayer in terms of the paradox of being concurrently old and new, see the comments of Derrida in *Body of Prayer*, pp. 65–67. Also relevant is the following comment in "An Interview with Derrida," in Wood and Bernasconi, *Derrida and Différance*, pp. 73–74: "What I write resembles, by my account, a dotted outline of a book to be written, in what I call—at least for me—the 'old new language,' the most archaic and the newest, unheard of, and thereby at present unreadable. You know that the oldest synagogue in Prague is called the Old-New?"

183. Jacques Derrida, "Point de folie—Maintenant l'architecture," in *Architecture Theory Since 1968*, edited by K. Michael Hays (Cambridge, MA: MIT Press 1998), p. 580 (emphasis in original).

184. Jacques Derrida, *Positions*, translated and annotated by Alan Bass (Chicago: University of Chicago Press, 1981), p. 14.

185. Derrida, *Writing and Difference*, p. 67; *L'écriture et la différence*, p. 102. On the symbolic nexus of exile and writing, which includes a brief discussion of Derrida, see Ofrat, *The Jewish Derrida*, pp. 160–164.

186. Jacques Derrida, "Des Tours de Babel," in *Difference in Translation*, edited with and introduction by Joseph F. Graham (Ithaca: Cornell University Press, 1985), p. 170.

187. Ibid., p. 174.

188. On the link between "alterity," "singularity," and an "essential and abyssal equivocality" that cannot be rendered in translation, see Derrida, *The Gift of Death*, pp. 87–88; *Donner la mort*, pp. 121–122.

189. On the "double bind" that the name YHWH imposes on the recipient as something that necessarily must be translated but which is impossible to translate, see Jacques Derrida, *The Ear of the Other: Otiobiography, Transference, Translation*, edited by Christie McDonald, translated by Peggy Kamuf (Lincoln: University of Nebraska Press, 1998), pp. 102–103; idem, "On a Newly Arisen," p. 117.

190. This formulation is used by Derrida in his response to Marion, "In the Name," p. 45.

191. On the depiction of deconstruction in terms of the conditions of the translatability and untranslatability of language, see Caputo, *The Prayers and Tears*, p. 53.

192. Derrida's language in Marion, "In the Name," p. 44.

193. Derrida, *Psyche: Inventions of the Other, Volume II*, p. 146. I agree with Westerkamp, "Naming and Tetragrammatology," p. 122, that the "unnameable *différance*" of
Derrida should not be mistaken for the "ineffable being" of the Jewish tradition, but I
would question his conclusion that "Derrida's Grammatology does not invoke any kind
of Tetragrammatology." In my mind, in light of Derrida's comments about the relationship of the name and what he calls *dénomination*, the matter is more complex. There is a
way to construe grammatology as a creative translation of the more traditional
Tetragrammatology.

194. I have here taken the liberty of repeating my comments in Elliot R. Wolfson,
"From Sealed Book to Open Text: Time, Memory, and Narrativity in Kabbalistic
Hermeneutics," in *Interpreting Judaism in a Postmodern Age*, edited by Steven Kepnes
(New York: New York University Press, 1996), p. 145. See also Drob, *Kabbalah and
Postmodernism*, p. 52, who refers to this part of my analysis.

195. Derrida, *Of Grammatology*, p. 158; *De la grammatologie* (Paris: Éditions de
Minuit, 1967), p. 227. See ibid., p. 163 (*De la grammatologie*, p. 233), where in a slightly
different formulation Derrida refers to the "axial proposition" of the essay as "that there
is nothing outside the text" (*qu'il n'y a rien hors du texte*). For an attempt to trace
Derrida's expressions to a passage in Georges Vajda's translation of Scholem's essay "The
Meaning of Torah in Jewish Mysticism," see Idel, *Absorbing Perfections*, pp. 122–123.

196. Derrida, *Archive Fever*, p. 42.

197. Derrida, "Shibboleth," p. 59.

198. Caputo, *The Prayers and Tears*, p. 233.

199. Bennington and Derrida, *Jacques Derrida*, pp. 70–71 (emphasis in original);
Bennington and Derrida, *Derrida*, pp. 68–69.

200. Derrida, "Shibboleth," p. 68.

201. Derrida, *Psyche: Inventions of the Other, Volume II*, p. 161.

202. Derrida, "Shibboleth," p. 67.

203. Ibid., p. 54.

204. Ibid., p. 55.

205. Ibid., p. 59.

206. Ibid., p. 54, and see analysis in Hammerschlag, *The Figural Jew*, pp. 217–226;
Cixous, *Portrait of Jacques Derrida*, pp. 83–84; John Felstiner, " 'All Poets Are Yids': The
Voice of the 'Other' in Paul Celan," in *Demonizing the Other: Antisemitism, Racism and
Xenophobia*, edited by Robert S. Wistrich (London: Routledge, 1999), pp. 244–256; Eric
Kligerman, *Sites of the Uncanny: Paul Celan, Specularity and the Visual Arts* (Berlin:
Walter de Gruyter, 2007), pp. 10–17. See also Shakespeare, *Derrida and Theology*,
pp. 127–130, and above, n. 61. On the intimate connection of the poet and the Jew, see
Derrida's essay on Jabès in *Writing and Difference*, pp. 64–78; *L'écriture et la différence*,
pp. 99–116.

207. Blake, *The Complete Poetry and Prose*, p. 39. Although Derrida does not mention
the comment of Blake in this passage, it is of interest to note that later in the essay
("Shibboleth," p. 63), he does observe that "Blake's *Jerusalem*, that great poem of

circumcision, regularly associates these three turns of speech, these three revolutions: *circumcision, circumscription,* and *circumference*" (emphasis in original).

208. Derrida, *Archive Fever*, p. 42.

209. Derrida, "Shibboleth," p. 67.

210. Ibid., p. 68.

211. Ibid., p. 67.

212. Derrida, *Writing and Difference*, p. 67; *L'écriture et la différence*, p. 102.

213. Derrida, *Writing and Difference*, p. 67; *L'écriture et la différence*, pp. 102–103.

214. Derrida, *Writing and Difference*, p. 65; *L'écriture et la différence*, p. 100.

215. See Elliot R. Wolfson, "Beyond Good and Evil: Hypernomianism, Transmorality and Kabbalistic Ethics," in *Crossing Boundaries: Essays on the Ethical Status of Mysticism*, edited by Jeffrey J. Kripal and G. William Barnard (New York: Seven Bridges Press, 2002), pp. 103–156, and the revised version in Wolfson, *Venturing Beyond*, pp. 186–285. See also Elliot R. Wolfson, *Abraham Abulafia—Kabbalist and Prophet: Hermeneutics, Theosophy, Theurgy* (Los Angeles: Cherub Press, 2000), pp. 36–37, 204–228; idem, *Open Secret*, pp. 55–58, 161–199.

216. Derrida reiterates this point in a number of writings. For example, see Jacques Derrida, "Devant la Loi," in *Kafka and the Contemporary Critical Performance: Centenary Readings*, edited by Alan Udoff (Bloomington: Indiana University Press, 1987), p. 131; idem, "Sending: On Representation," in *Transforming the Hermeneutic Context: From Nietzsche to Nancy*, edited by Gayle L. Ormiston and Alan D. Schrift (Albany: State University of New York Press, 1990), p. 137; idem, *Of Hospitality*, p. 81.

217. Derrida, *Acts of Religion*, p. 43: "A transgression should always know what it transgresses, which always makes the transgression impure, and compromised in advance with what it transgresses."

218. Derrida, *On the Name*, p. 36; *Sauf le nom*, p. 17.

219. Derrida, "Shibboleth," p. 54.

220. Derrida, "On a Newly Arisen," p. 121.

221. Elliot R. Wolfson, "Hebraic and Hellenic Conceptions of Wisdom in *Sefer ha-Bahir*," *Poetics Today* 19 (1998): 156–163. The material here is a reworking of that analysis, and especially the expanded version in Wolfson, *Language, Eros, Being*, pp. 146–167.

222. *The Book Bahir: An Edition Based on the Earliest Manuscripts*, edited by Daniel Abrams, with an introduction by Moshe Idel (Los Angeles: Cherub Press, 1994), sec. 3, p. 119 (Hebrew).

223. Jacques Derrida, *Given Time: I. Counterfeit Money*, translated by Peggy Kamuf (Chicago: University of Chicago Press, 1992), p. 7; *Donner le temps: I. La fausse monnaie* (Paris: Éditions Galilée, 1991), pp. 18–19. It is on account of this feature of generosity, giving without any thought of return, that Cixous associates the realm of the gift with the feminine in contrast to the masculine, which is linked with the realm of the proper. See Toril Moi, *Sexual/Textual Politics: Feminist Literary Theory* (London: Routledge,

1985), pp. 110–113. It should be noted that Derrida's view that reciprocity is antithetical to the nature of the gift cannot be applied to every culture as anthropological studies have shown. Even the claim that reciprocity is always symmetrical is questionable in light of the phenomenon of asymmetrical exchange and gift giving in some societies. See Marcel Mauss, *The Gift: The Form and Reason for Exchange in Archaic Societies*, translated by Wilfred Douglas Halls, foreword by Mary Douglas (New York: W. W. Norton, 1990), pp. 39–43, 146–147 n. 61; Yunxiang Yan, *The Flow of Gifts: Reciprocity and Social Networks in a Chinese Village* (Stanford: Stanford University Press, 1996), pp. 4–13; Aafke E. Komter, *Social Solidarity and the Gift* (Cambridge: Cambridge University Press, 2005), pp. 67–75, 86–95, 108–112, 201–205. For a critique of Mauss, see Derrida, *Given Time*, pp. 24–26; *Donner le temps*, pp. 41–42.

224. Derrida, *Given Time*, p. 7 (emphasis in original); *Donner le temps*, pp. 18–19. For an analysis of gift giving in terms of sacred objects that are not exchangeable, see Maurice Godelier, *The Enigma of the Gift*, translated by Nora Scott (Chicago: University of Chicago Press, 1999).

225. See Ian Leask, "Husserl, Givenness, and the Priority of the Self," *International Journal of Philosophical Studies* 11 (2003): 141–156.

226. Derrida's remark is found in Kearney, "On the Gift," p. 59. Compare Wyschogrod's analysis of this aspect of Derrida's phenomenology of the gift discussed in Ch. 5 at nn. 75–79. Needless to say, many scholars have weighed in on the nature of the gift in Derrida and Marion. For instance, see Caputo, "Apostles," pp. 200–215; Thomas A. Carlson, *Indiscretion: Finitude and the Naming of God* (Chicago: University of Chicago Press, 1999), pp. 190–236; Horner, *Rethinking God as Gift*, pp. 123–137; Christina M. Gschwandtner, *Reading Jean-Luc Marion: Exceeding Metaphysics* (Bloomington: Indiana University Press, 2007), pp. 72–76; Welz, *Love's Transcendence*, pp. 362–364; Ian James, *The New French Philosophy* (Cambridge: Polity Press, 2012), pp. 26–29.

227. Derrida in Kearney, "On the Gift," pp. 59 and 63. The thematic link between the gift and the impossible has been discussed by a number of scholars. See, for instance, Caputo, *The Prayers and Tears*, pp. 169–173, Rayment-Pickard, *Impossible God*, pp. 107–114; Shakespeare, *Derrida and Theology*, pp. 149–174. For a critique of this notion, see Adriaan Peperzak, "Giving," in *The Enigma of Gift and Sacrifice*, pp. 161–175, esp. 162–163.

228. Derrida, *Given Time*, p. 16; *Donner le temps*, p. 29.

229. Marion, *Being Given*, pp. 74–78 (*Étant donné*, pp. 108–114); idem, *The Visible and the Revealed*, translated by Christina M. Gschwandtner and others (New York: Fordham University Press, 2008), pp. 81–88; Sebbah, *Testing the Limit*, pp. 98–101. For a slightly different, but obviously related, account of the "paradox inscribed in the logic of the gift," see Jean-Yves Lacoste, *Experience and the Absolute: Disputed Questions on the Humanity of Man*, translated by Mark Raftery-Skehan (New York: Fordham University Press, 2004), pp. 158–159. Lacoste focuses on the fact that since "the gift (the thing given) is what the giver relinquishes, the giving (the act of giving) carries within itself the conditions of its forgetting." This is not to deny the fact that the gift can, and indeed at

times does retain "a trace of the giving" and thus bears "witness to the giver," but it is possible and often is the case that the gift runs "the risk of being effaced because the gift is no longer perceived as such, but as a possession." Inasmuch as "the giver has no right over what he has given," it follows that "the destiny of the gift lies in the hands of whoever has received it." The forgetfulness of the giving can lead, therefore, to a state of ingratitude. Lacoste goes on to say that the "global structure of experience," that is, our sense of the world, entails that the gift of Being, the "gift par excellence," invariably escapes our notice. "A reality entirely different from creation, the world must—here—be defined as the denial that Being is a gift; and insofar as being-in-the-world defines the initial logic [*logique initiale*] of existence, this denial is a judgment man has always already made, an a priori. . . . Atheism or paganism, whether existential or thematized, can neither kill God nor give underived existence [*aséité*] to the world. But in their transcendental or existential forms, they clearly and distinctly manifest that one can only know [*connaître*] Being as a gift (experientially and theoretically) by undertaking the critique of the world." Compare Jean-Yves Lacoste, "De la donation comme promesse," *Revista Portuguesa de Filosofia* 65 (2009): 841–856, esp. 847–851, printed as well in Jean-Yves Lacoste, *La phénoménalité de dieu: Neuf études* (Paris: Cerf, 2008), pp. 159–177, esp. 166–171; and analysis in Joeri Schrijvers, *An Introduction to Jean-Yves Lacoste* (Surrey: Ashgate, 2012), pp. 73–75, 84–92.

230. Derrida, *Given Time*, pp. 79–81 (emphasis in original); *Donner le temps*, pp. 105–107. Compare Gasché, *Inventions of Difference*, pp. 191–198.

231. For a criticism of my Derridean reading of the bahiric parable, see Peter Schäfer, *Mirror of His Beauty: Feminine Images of God from the Bible to the Early Kabbalah* (Princeton: Princeton University Press, 2002), p. 285 n. 47, and my rejoinder in *Language, Eros, Being*, pp. 499–500 n. 111.

232. Babylonian Talmud, Ḥagigah 11b.

233. David Stern, *Parables in Midrash: Narrative and Exegesis in Rabbinic Literature* (Cambridge, MA: Harvard University Press, 1991), p. 222.

234. Derrida , *Given Time*, p. 9; *Donner le temps*, p. 21.

235. Derrida, *Given Time*, p. 147 (emphasis in original); *Donner le temps*, p. 187.

236. Derrida, *The Gift of Death*, pp. 29–30; *Donner la mort*, p. 50.

237. Derrida, *On the Name*, p. 25.

238. Ibid., p. 59.

239. Ibid., pp. 26–27. On the impossibility of testifying to a secret, see Jacques Derrida, *Demeure: Fiction and Testimony*, translated by Elizabeth Rottenberg (Stanford: Stanford University Press, 2000), pp. 30–31.

240. Derrida, *The Gift of Death*, p. 100; *Donner la mort*, p. 137.

241. Søren Kierkegaard, *Fear and Trembling*, edited and translated with notes and introduction by Howard V. Hong and Edna H. Hong (Princeton: Princeton University Press, 1983), pp. 112–120.

242. Derrida, *The Gift of Death*, p. 59; *Donner la mort*, p. 87. See the analysis in Keenan, *The Question of Sacrifice*, pp. 149–154; Llewelyn, *Margins of Religion*, pp. 42–43,

67–69. On Abraham's keeping silent about the secret, see Derrida, *Literature in Secret*, pp. 121–122; *Donner la mort*, pp. 163–164.

243. I have articulated this insight on kabbalistic esotericism in many of my studies, and here I will mention a few salient examples: Wolfson, "Occultation," pp. 113–124 (*Luminal Darkness*, pp. 258–264); *Abraham Abulafia*, pp. 9–93, esp. 21–38; "Divine Suffering," pp. 110–115; *Language, Eros, Being*, pp. 9–10, 16–21, 25–27, 128–141, 220–221, 384.

244. Derrida, "On a Newly Arisen," p. 118 (emphasis in original).

245. Derrida, *Psyche: Inventions of the Other, Volume II*, p. 162 (emphasis in original).

246. Caputo, *The Prayers and Tears*, p. 33.

247. Derrida, "On a Newly Arisen," p. 118 (emphasis in original). On the double bind of translation, see Jacques Derrida, "Living On: Border Lines," in *Deconstruction and Criticism*, edited by Harold Bloom (New York: Seabury Press, 1979), pp. 76–79.

248. Caputo, *The Mystical Element*, pp. 99–100, 118–127, 173–183; Schürmann, *Meister Eckhart: Mystic and Philosopher*, pp. 16–17, 111–121, 192–213.

249. Derrida, *On the Name*, p. 84; *Sauf le nom*, p. 111.

250. Derrida, *On the Name*, pp. 84–85; *Sauf le nom*, p. 112. It is of interest to note that this paragraph does not appear in the first version of the study, which was published originally in English translation as "Post-Scriptum: Aporias, Ways and Voices," translated by John Leavey Jr., in *Derrida and Negative Theology*, pp. 283–323.

251. These comments of Derrida are taken from Shapiro et al., *Body of Prayer*, pp. 61–63. Compare Derrida, *The Gift of Death*, p. 67 (*Donner la mort*, p. 96): "And this name which must always be singular is here none other than the name of God as completely other, the nameless name of God [*le nom sans nom de Dieu*], the unpronounceable name of God as other to which I am bound by an absolute, unconditional obligation, by an incomparable, nonnegotiable duty. The other as absolute other, namely, God, must remain transcendent, hidden, secret, jealous of the love, requests, and commands that he gives and that he asks to be kept secret. Secrecy is essential to the exercise of this absolute responsibility as sacrificial responsibility."

252. See above, n. 243.

253. Derrida, *The Gift of Death*, p. 87; *Donner la mort*, p. 121.

254. Derrida, *On the Name*, p. 56; *Sauf le nom*, p. 56.

255. Derrida, *On the Name*, p. 85; *Sauf le nom*, p. 112.

256. My language here is indebted to Carlson, *Indiscretion*, pp. 157–158 n. 15.

257. Derrida, *The Gift of Death*, p. 49 (emphasis in original); *Donner la mort*, p. 75.

258. Shapiro et al., *Body of Prayer*, p. 63. See the criticism of my claim in Drob, *Kabbalah and Postmodernism*, pp. 52–53. His suggestion that I am unaware of an atheistic element in traditional kabbalah is unwarranted. The issue for me is that in the kabbalistic sources the atheistic is dialectically bound with the theistic, whereas Derrida's reading of the atheism implicit in the kabbalah amputates it from its theistic skeleton.

259. Bennington and Derrida, *Jacques Derrida*, pp. 155–156; Bennington and Derrida, *Derrida*, p. 134.

260. Caputo, *The Prayers and Tears*, pp. 288–289. For a criticism of Caputo, see Hägglund, *Radical Atheism*, pp. 227–228 n. 61.

261. The characterization of Derridean atheism proceeding from his conception of time is indebted to the innovative analysis of Hägglund, *Radical Atheism*.

262. Derrida, *Speech and Phenomena*, pp. 127–128 n. 14.

263. Heidegger, *Holzwege*, p. 336. For a different translation of the critical passage, see Heidegger, *Early Greek Thinking*, pp. 50–51.

264. Derrida, *Speech and Phenomena*, p. 156. For an alternative translation, see Derrida, *Margins*, p. 24. See the parallel formulation in the text cited below, n. 271.

265. Derrida, *Of Grammatology*, p. 61.

266. Derrida, *Margins*, p. 65.

267. Ibid.

268. The play on the words *trait, re-trait*, and *retrait* is basic to the analysis in Jacques Derrida, *Memories of the Blind: The Self-Portrait and Other Ruins*, translated by Pascale-Anne Brault and Michael Naas (Chicago: University of Chicago Press, 1993). Of particular interest to this chapter is the following remark, ibid., p. 54: "Is it by chance that in order to speak of the trait we are falling back upon the language of negative theology or of those discourses concerned with naming the withdrawal [*retrait*] of the invisible or hidden god? The withdrawal of the One whom one must not look in the face, or represent, or adore, that is, idolize under the traits or guise of the icon? The One whom it is even dangerous to name by one or the other of his proper names? The end of iconography."

269. Derrida, *Margins*, p. 65.

270. Derrida, *Of Grammatology*, p. 163.

271. Derrida, *Margins*, pp. 66–67: "But at the same time, this erasure of the trace must have been traced in the metaphysical text. Presence, then, far from being, as is commonly thought, *what* the sign signifies, what a trace refers to, presence, then, is the trace of the trace, the trace of the erasure of the trace. Such is, for us, the text of metaphysics, and such is, for us, the language we speak. Only on this condition can metaphysics and our language signal in the direction of their own transgression. And this is why it is not contradictory to think *together* the *erased* and the *traced* of the trace. And also why there is no contradiction between the absolute erasure of the 'early trace' of difference and that which maintains it as trace, sheltered and visible in presence. . . . The trace of the trace which (is) difference above all could not appear or be named *as such*, that is, in its presence. It is the 'as such' which precisely, and as such, evades us forever. . . . Beyond Being and beings, this difference, ceaselessly differing and deferring (itself), would trace (itself) (by itself)—this *différance* would be the first or last trace if we still could speak, here, of origin or end. Such a *différance* would at once, again, give us to think a writing without presence and without absence, without history, without cause, without *archia*, without *telos*, a writing that absolutely upsets all dialectics, all theology, all teleology, all ontology. A writing exceeding everything that the history of metaphysics has comprehended in the form of the Aristotelian *gramme*, in its point, in its

line, in its circle, in its time, and in its space" (emphasis in original). This crucial articulation of Derrida's notion of trace and *différance* emerges from an engaged reading of Heidegger's reference to the "early trace" (*die frühe Spur*) of the difference between Being and beings that has been forgotten in the "oblivion of Being." For a comprehensive study of this topic, see Douglas L. Donkel, *The Understanding of Difference in Heidegger and Derrida* (New York: Peter Lang, 1992), and compare the discussion of the Derridean trace against the background of Heidegger's thinking in Paola Marrati, *Genesis and Trace: Derrida Reading Husserl and Heidegger* (Stanford: Stanford University Press, 2005), pp. 87–176. On the notion of the trace and arche-writing, see also the nuanced discussions in Tom Conley, "A Trace of Style," in *Displacement: Derrida and After*, pp. 74–92; Gasché, *The Tain of the Mirror*, pp. 157, 186–194, 277–278, 289–293; idem, *Inventions of Difference*, pp. 25, 40–42, 44–49, 158, 160–170; Caputo, *The Prayers and Tears*, pp. 57–61, 319–320; Howells, *Derrida*, pp. 50–52, 74, 134–135; Geoffrey Bennington, *Interrupting Derrida* (London: Routledge, 2000), pp. 12, 15, 28, 35, 169–171, 178, 196; Irene E. Harvey, *Derrida and the Economy of Différance* (Bloomington: Indiana University Press, 1986), pp. 153–181.

272. Derrida, *Speech and Phenomena*, p. 146.

273. Derrida, *Of Grammatology*, p. 203.

274. This is not to deny that Derrida himself affirms the fusion of the ocular and the verbal (see, for example, *Memories*, p. 4), but he does so in a manner that is quite distant from the kabbalistic understanding of synesthesia.

275. Pseudo-Dionysius, *The Divine Names*, 980A, in *Pseudo-Dionysius: The Complete Works*, translation by Colm Luibheid, foreword, notes, and translation collaboration by Paul Rorem, preface by René Roques, introductions by Jaroslav Pelikan, Jean Leclercq, and Karlfried Froehlich (New York: Paulist Press, 1987), p. 128.

276. Heidegger, *Introduction to Metaphysics*, p. 121; *Einführung in die Metaphysik*, p. 122.

277. Wolfson, *Language, Eros, Being*, pp. 96–97, and, more recently, *A Dream*, p. 247.

278. Heidegger, *Contributions*, § 188, p. 244; *Beiträge*, p. 308.

279. On the "inner connection" of being and seeming, see Heidegger, *Introduction to Metaphysics*, pp. 106–107; *Einführung in die Metaphysik*, p. 108. See Charles Guignon, "Being as Appearing: Retrieving the Greek Experience of *Phusis*," in *A Companion to Heidegger's Introduction to Metaphysics*, pp. 34–56, esp. 38–41; Susan Schoenbaum, "Heidegger's Interpretation of *Phusis* in *Introduction to Metaphysics*," in *A Companion to Heidegger's Introduction to Metaphysics*, p. 154; and my own discussion in *Language, Eros, Being*, pp. 14–16.

280. Keiji Nishitani, "Ontology and Utterance," *Philosophy East and West* 31 (1981): 40.

281. Robert E. Carter, *The Nothingness Beyond God: An Introduction to the Philosophy of Nishida Kitarō* (New York: Paragon House, 1997), p. 59.

282. See Masao Abe, "Non-Being and Mu: The Metaphysical Nature of Negativity in the East and the West," *Religious Studies* 11 (1975): 181–192; Carter, *The Nothingness*

Beyond God, pp. 81–99; idem, *The Kyoto School: An Introduction*, with a foreword by Thomas P. Kasulis (Albany: State University of New York Press, 2013), pp. 35–40; James W. Heisig, *Philosophers of Nothingness: An Essay on the Kyoto School* (Honolulu: University of Hawai'i Press, 2001), pp. 61–64; Robert J. J. Wargo, *The Logic of Nothingness: A Study of Nishida Kitarō* (Honolulu: University of Hawai'i Press, 2005), pp. 75–88, 112–113.

283. Eric S. Nelson, "Language and Emptiness in Chan Buddhism and the Early Heidegger," *Journal of Chinese Philosophy* 37 (2010): 472–492, esp. 483–484.

284. See Wolfson, *Open Secret*, pp. 109–111, and the sources I mentioned in that book on p. 345 n. 235, as well as additional sources in Wolfson, *A Dream*, pp. 287–288 n. 30 and p. 295 n. 53. On the comparison of Derridean deconstruction and the Mahāyāna tradition, see Wolfson, *Open Secret*, p. 345 n. 237.

285. Christopher Johnson, *System and Writing in the Philosophy of Jacques Derrida* (Cambridge: Cambridge University Press, 1993), p. 44.

286. Jacques Derrida, *Psyche: Inventions of the Other, Volume I*, edited by Peggy Kamuf and Elizabeth Rottenberg (Stanford: Stanford University Press, 2007), p. 284.

287. Jacques Derrida, *Learning to Live Finally: An Interview with Jean Birnbaum*, translated by Pascale-Anne Brault and Michael Naas, with a bibliography by Peter Krapp (Hoboken: Melville House Publishing, 2007), p. 31.

288. Derrida, *Acts of Literature*, p. 187. For further discussion of the Kafka passage, see Wolfson, *Venturing Beyond*, pp. 257–259.

289. Derrida, *Dissemination*, p. 123.

290. Derrida, *On the Name*, p. 44; *Sauf le nom*, pp. 33–34.

291. Derrida, *On the Name*, p. 43; *Sauf le nom*, pp. 31–32. On the application of Derrida's account of the impossible possibility to theology, see Rayment-Pickard, *Impossible God*, pp. 59–63, 123–155, and the summary on p. 128: "His possibility of 'theology,' in so far as we can speak of such a thing, is the articulation of the possibility of theology which is also its impossibility: the crossroads at which a theology becomes both possible and impossible."

292. Paul Celan, *Poems of Paul Celan*, translated by Michael Hamburger (New York: Persea Books, 1972), pp. 196–199.

293. Jacques Derrida, *Sovereignties in Question: The Poetics of Paul Celan*, edited by Thomas Dutoit and Outi Pasanen (New York: Fordham University Press, 2005), p. 3.

294. Derrida, *On the Name*, p. 35; *Sauf le nom*, p. 15.

295. Derrida, *Writing and Difference*, p. 201; *L'écriture et la différence*, p. 299.

296. Derrida, *Speech and Phenomena*, p. 146.

297. See above, n. 92.

298. Hent de Vries, "The Shibboleth Effect: On Reading Paul Celan," in *Judeities*, pp. 175–213, esp. 205–209.

299. Derrida, *Points*, p. 83 (emphasis in original). See Ch. 5 n. 82.

300. Derrida, *Points*, p. 82.

301. Johnson, *System and Writing*, p. 19.

Chapter 5: Immanent Atheology and the Trace of Transcendence

1. Edith Wyschogrod, "Crossover Dreams," *Journal of the American Academy of Religion* 54 (1986): 543, 545, and 547. The expression "immanent theology" occurs on p. 546, in the context of discussing the "second limen in biblical theology," but it seems to me that this is a typographical error.

2. Derrida, *Psyche: Inventions of the Other, Volume II*, p. 167.

3. Ibid., p. 309 n. 13. On the hybrid expression "the Jew, the Arab," see Ch. 4 n. 155. The proximity to Arabic as the "other that is the nearest neighbor," the *Unheimlich*, is noted by Derrida, *Monolingualism*, p. 37. On the role of autobiographical writing in Derrida, see Smith, *Derrida and Autobiography*; Jill Robbins, "Circumcising Confession: Derrida, Autobiography, Judaism," *Diacritics* 25 (1995): 20–38; Joseph G. Kronick, "Philosophy as Autobiography: The Confessions of Jacques Derrida," *Modern Language Notes* 115 (2000): 997–1018.

4. Wyschogrod, *Crossover Queries*, p. 21. See also idem, "How to Say No in French: Derrida and Negation in Recent French Philosophy," in *Negation and Theology*, edited by Robert P. Scharlemann (Charlottesville: University Press of Virginia, 1992), p. 41; and compare the comments of Knight, *Omissions*, pp. 197–198.

5. Levinas, *In the Time of the Nations*, p. 144.

6. Levinas, *Otherwise than Being*, p. 108; *Autrement qu'être*, p. 137.

7. Levinas, *Beyond the Verse*, p. 199.

8. On occasion Levinas does distinguish the two genres. See, for example, his comment in the interview with Richard Kearney in Levinas, *Face to Face with Levinas*, p. 18: "I always make a clear distinction in what I write, between philosophical and confessional texts. . . . I would never, for example, introduce a talmudic or biblical verse into one of my philosophical texts to try to prove or justify a phenomenological argument."

9. In the main, I concur with the position of Gibbs and Bergo that Levinas's philosophical work should not be radically separated from his Jewish thinking. According to Gibbs, Levinas thinks as a Jew in his philosophical texts even as his Jewish texts communicate an inherent desire for philosophy; according to Bergo, the philosophy of Levinas arises from the Jewish "biblical experience." See Gibbs, *Correlations*, pp. 155–175; Bergo, *Levinas*, p. 293. Due to the surfeit of studies that address this dimension of Levinas's thought, I will offer a modest list that presents perspectives varying in method and substance: Handelman, *Fragments*, pp. 187–188, 263–305; Cohen, *Elevations*, pp. 173–194; idem, *Levinasian Meditations: Ethics, Philosophy, and Religion* (Pittsburgh: Duquesne University Press, 2010), pp. 207–272; Ze'ev Levy, "Emmanuel Lévinas as a Jewish Philosopher," in *Ḥazon Naḥum: Studies in Jewish Law, Thought, and History Presented to Dr. Norman Lamm on the Occasion of His Seventieth Birthday*, edited by Yaakov Elman and Jeffrey S. Gurock (New York: Yeshiva University Press, 1997), pp. 577–597; Tamra Wright, *The Twilight of Jewish Philosophy: Emmanuel Levinas' Ethical Hermeneutics* (Amsterdam: Harwood Academic Publishers, 1999), pp. 141–172; Newton, *The Fence and the Neighbor*, pp. 85–99; Ajzenstat, *Driven*

Back, pp. 64–83; Moyn, *Origins of the Other*, pp. 195–237; Morgan, *Discovering Levinas*, pp. 336–347, 402–403, 412–413; Shmuel Trigano, "Levinas and the Project of Jewish Philosophy," *Jewish Studies Quarterly* 8 (2001): 279–307; Leora Batnitzky, "Jewish Philosophy After Metaphysics," in *Religion After Metaphysics*, edited by Mark A. Wrathall (Cambridge: Cambridge University Press, 2003), pp. 146–165; Meir, *Levinas's Jewish Thought*; idem, "Judaism and Philosophy: Each Other's Other in Levinas," *Modern Judaism* 30 (2010): 348–362; Fagenblat, *A Covenant of Creatures*, pp. 1–32; Hammerschlag, *The Figural Jew*, pp. 117–165. See Ch. 3 n. 142.

10. Levinas, *In the Time of the Nations*, pp. 167–168.

11. Ibid., p. 169. See Ch. 3 n. 350.

12. Robbins, "Circumcising Confession," p. 23. For a more extended discussion on the relationship between Levinas's philosophical and nonphilosophical writings, see Jill Robbins, *Prodigal Son/Elder Brother: Interpretation and Alterity in Augustine, Petrarch, Kafka, Levinas* (Baltimore: Johns Hopkins University Press, 1991), pp. 100–132. Consider as well Derrida's description of Levinas's work in the speech he gave at the latter's funeral on December 27, 1995, in Derrida, *Adieu to Emmanuel Levinas*, p. 12, as "something different from, a simple dialogue between Jewish thought and its others, the philosophies of Greek origin or, in the tradition of a certain 'Here I am,' the other Abrahamic monotheisms."

13. Wyschogrod, *Crossover Queries*, p. 62. Compare the formulation in Wyschogrod, "Trends," p. 126: "For Levinas, ethics is Hebrew in its moral vision and Greek in the conceptual transposition of that vision."

14. Levinas, *Difficult Freedom*, p. 15.

15. Edith Wyschogrod, "Religion as Life and Text: Postmodern Re-figurations," in *The Craft of Religious Studies*, edited by Jon R. Stone (New York: St. Martin's Press, 1998), pp. 240–241.

16. Ibid., p. 244.

17. Edith Wyschogrod, "Hasidism, Hellenism, Holocaust: A Postmodern View," in *Interpreting Judaism in a Postmodern Age*, edited by Steven Kepnes (New York: New York University Press, 1996), pp. 302–303.

18. Ibid., p. 303. The passage of Derrida that she cites is from *Writing and Difference*, p. 259; *L'écriture et la différence*, p. 381.

19. Wyschogrod, *Crossover Queries*, p. 2. For a nuanced discussion of Wyschogrod's complex engagement with Hegel, see Martin Kavka, "Should Levinasians Also Be Hegelians? On Wyschogrod's Levinasianism," *Philosophy Today* 55 (2011): 372–385.

20. Wyschogrod, *Crossover Queries*, p. 1.

21. Georg Wilhelm Friedrich Hegel, *Phenomenology of Spirit*, translated by Arnold V. Miller (Oxford: Oxford University Press, 1977), p. 19, cited by Wyschogrod, *Crossover Queries*, p. 3.

22. Wyschogrod, *Crossover Queries*, pp. 3–4.

23. Edith Wyschogrod, *Spirit in Ashes: Hegel, Heidegger, and Man-Made Mass Death* (New Haven: Yale University Press, 1985), pp. 144–145.

24. Ibid., pp. 93–94.

25. On *différance* and Hegelian negation, see Marian Hobson, *Jacques Derrida: Opening Lines* (London: Routledge, 1998), pp. 154–161.

26. Wyschogrod, *Crossover Queries*, p. 6.

27. Adorno, *Negative Dialectics*, p. 158.

28. Ibid., pp. 159–160.

29. Ibid., pp. 160–161.

30. Wyschogrod, *Spirit in Ashes*, p. 212.

31. Wyschogrod, "Trends," pp. 133–134.

32. Wyschogrod, *Spirit in Ashes*, p. 94 (emphasis in original).

33. Ibid., pp. 15–16.

34. Wyschogrod, *Crossover Queries*, p. 77.

35. Ibid., p. 311.

36. Ibid., pp. 372–373. Wyschogrod cites the passage from Derrida, *Dissemination*, p. 351, where the distinction between "discursive polysemy" and "textual dissemination" is made.

37. Wyschogrod, "Trends," p. 127 (emphasis in original).

38. Ibid., p. 128.

39. On apophaticism and Derridean deconstruction, see references cited in Ch. 2 n. 295.

40. See the informative remarks in Derrida, *Margins*, pp. 33–34 n. 6.

41. Wyschogrod, "Religion as Life and Text," p. 248. Compare idem, "How to Say No in French," pp. 46–54.

42. Wyschogrod, "Hasidism, Hellenism, Holocaust," p. 312.

43. Wyschogrod, "How to Say No in French," p. 40. The expression of Derrida, "apophatics of denial," is cited by Wyschogrod in that context.

44. Wyschogrod, *An Ethics of Remembering*, p. 240.

45. Edith Wyschogrod, "Doing before Hearing: On the Primacy of Touch," in *Textes pour Emmanuel Lévinas*, edited by François Laruelle (Paris: Collections Surfaces, 1980), p. 187.

46. Wyschogrod, *An Ethics of Remembering*, p. 14.

47. Derrida, *Psyche: Inventions of the Other, Volume II*, pp. 162–163. A section of this passage is cited in Ch. 4 at n. 245, and see discussion in Wyschogrod, *Crossover Queries*, pp. 20–21.

48. Wyschogrod, *Crossover Queries*, pp. 21–22.

49. See Ch. 4 n. 131.

50. Wyschogrod, *Crossover Queries*, p. 22.

51. Ibid., p. 23.

52. Levinas, *Entre Nous*, p. 221, cited by Wyschogrod, *Crossover Queries*, p. 28. See also Levinas, *Basic Philosophical Writings*, p. 158.

53. Wyschogrod, *Crossover Queries*, p. 14. For an analysis of this subject, see Marina Paola Banchetti-Robino, "Husserl's Theory of Language as Calculus Ratiocinator," *Synthese* 112 (1997): 303–321. The author's thesis is summarized as follows: "The language

with which to express these semantical relations and the notion of truth as correspondence is a metalanguage which is itself the product of the Husserlian transcendental reduction. In this reduction, language is stripped of the ontological commitments of the natural attitude, is reinterpreted, and is used to describe the results of phenomenological investigation into the essence and origin of meaning and meaning relations. Thus, one sees in Husserl a commitment to the notion that reality as such can be reached by subtracting the influence of the language of the natural attitude with all of its ontological commitments, and a commitment to the notion that language is a reinterpretable calculus which can be used in phenomenological investigation" (p. 304).

54. Levinas, *Totality and Infinity*, p. 192; *Totalité et infini*, p. 166. For citation of this passage, see Ch. 3 at n. 270.

55. Levinas, *Proper Names*, p. 130.

56. Levinas, *Of God Who Comes to Mind*, p. 124.

57. Levinas, *Entre Nous*, p. 219.

58. Wyschogrod, *Emmanuel Levinas*, p. 162.

59. Levinas, *Basic Philosophical Writings*, p. 155, cited in Ch. 3 at n. 510.

60. Levinas, *Otherwise than Being*, p. 152; *Autrement qu'être*, p. 194. On incarnation and the glory of the infinite, see Wyschogrod, *Crossover Queries*, pp. 43–44.

61. Levinas, *Totality and Infinity*, pp. 78–79; *Totalité et infini*, pp. 50–51, cited in Ch. 3 at n. 372. See Wyschogrod, *Emmanuel Levinas*, pp. 142–143.

62. Wyschogrod, *Crossover Queries*, p. 15, cited in Ch. 3 at n. 3.

63. Thomas J. J. Altizer, "The Impossible Possibility of Ethics," in *Saintly Influence*, p. 32. Compare idem, *Living the Death of God*, pp. 60–61.

64. Wyschogrod, *Crossover Queries*, p. 349.

65. Wyschogrod, "Trends," p. 132. Daniel W. Smith, *Essays on Deleuze* (Edinburgh: Edinburgh University Press, 2012), pp. 271–286, develops Agamben's taxonomy and contrasts the transcendence of Derrida and the immanence of Deleuze. I am not convinced that Derrida should be considered a philosopher of transcendence. On the notion of univocity and the Deleuzian ontology of immanence, see Smith, op. cit., pp. 27–42.

66. Wyschogrod, *Crossover Queries*, pp. 268–269 (emphasis added).

67. Smith, *Essays on Deleuze*, pp. 175–188.

68. The drift of my position accords with the Deleuzian reading of Wyschogrod offered by Karmen MacKendrick, "Eros, Ethics, Explosion: The Loss of Deixis in Recurrence," *Philosophy Today* 55 (2011): 361–371.

69. Wyschogrod, *Crossover Queries*, p. 5 (emphasis in original).

70. Ibid., p. 19.

71. Wyschogrod, *An Ethics of Remembering*, p. 242.

72. Ibid., p. xvi.

73. Ibid., p. 241.

74. Ibid., p. 219.

75. Ibid., pp. 219–220 (citing Derrida, *Given Time*, p. 122), 242 (citing Derrida, *Points*, p. 83), 244 (citing Derrida, *Given Time*, p. 30).

76. Ibid., pp. 243–244.

77. Ibid., p. 243. The homonymy is repeated in Wyschogrod, "Introduction," in *The Enigma of Gift and Sacrifice*, p. 6.

78. The precise statement cited by Wyschogrod is from Derrida, *Given Time*, p. 30 (*Donner le temps*, p. 47): "*Know* still what giving *wants to say, know how to give*, know what you want and want to say when you give, know what you intend to give, know how the gift annuls itself, commit yourself [*engage-toi*] even if commitment is the destruction of the gift by the gift, give economy its chance" (emphasis in original). For a similar formulation, see the passage of Derrida cited in Ch. 4 at n. 224.

79. Wyschogrod, *An Ethics of Remembering*, p. 244.

80. See Bettina Bergo, "The Historian and the Messianic 'Now': Reading Edith Wyschogrod's *An Ethics of Remembering*," in *Saintly Influence*, pp. 202–218, esp. 212–216. Although Bergo emphasizes the similarity between Wyschogrod and Benjamin in contrast to my emphasis on Derrida, our analyses are in basic agreement.

81. Wyschogrod, *Crossover Queries*, p. 262.

82. Wyschogrod, *An Ethics of Remembering*, p. 242. Wyschogrod quotes the following passage from Derrida, *Points*, p. 83: "How could the desire for presence let itself be destroyed? It is desire itself. But what gives it . . . breath and necessity—what there is and what remains to be thought—is that which in the presence of the present does not present itself." The continuation of Derrida's remarks are cited in Ch. 4 at n. 299.

83. Wyschogrod, *An Ethics of Remembering*, p. 242.

84. Derrida, *Specters of Marx*, p. 168.

85. Caputo, *The Prayers and Tears*, pp. xix, 56–57, 70–71, 95–101; idem, "Temporal Transcendence." But see Hägglund, *Radical Atheism*, pp. 132–141. The author criticizes Caputo's theological misreading of the Derridean conception of the impossible that is central to his notion of the messianic without messianism.

86. Derrida, *Specters of Marx*, p. 65. Wyschogrod refers to this edition, but her quotation does not correspond exactly to the text she cites. I have taken the liberty of restoring the passage as it appears in the original, including the italics.

87. Wyschogrod, *Crossover Queries*, p. 374.

88. Edith Wyschogrod, *Saints and Postmodernism: Revisioning Moral Philosophy* (Chicago: University of Chicago Press, 1990), pp. 141–146, esp. 142.

89. Ibid., p. 161.

90. Wyschogrod, *Crossover Queries*, p. 5.

91. This dimension of Levinas's engagement with sanctity and the saintly life, as well as Wyschogrod's transformation thereof into a more robust hagiographical ethics that celebrates the excessive desire of the saint, is explored incisively by Virginia Burrus, "A Saint of One's Own: Emmanuel Levinas, Eliezer ben Hyrcanus, and Eulalia of Mérida," *L'Espirit Créateur* 50 (2010): 6–20. See also Peter Ochs, "Saints and the Heterological Historian," in *Saintly Life*, pp. 219–237.

92. Wyschogrod, *Crossover Queries*, p. 9.

93. Wyschogrod, *Saints and Postmodernism*, p. 191.

94. Altizer, "The Impossible Possibility," pp. 34–36.

95. See Ch. 3 n. 150.

96. Altizer, "The Impossible Possibility," p. 43.

97. Ibid., p. 46.

98. Wyschogrod, *Crossover Queries*, p. 299.

99. Ibid., p. 311.

100. Ibid., p. 363.

101. Ibid.

102. Ibid., p. 303.

103. Wyschogrod, *Emmanuel Levinas*, p. 159.

104. Wyschogrod elaborates on Buber's interpretation of Hasidism in "Hasidism, Hellenism, Holocaust," pp. 304–311.

105. Wyschogrod, *Crossover Queries*, pp. 303–304 (emphasis added).

106. Ibid., p. 305.

107. Ibid., p. 306.

108. Gilles Deleuze, "Active and Reactive," in *The New Nietzsche: Contemporary Styles of Interpretation*, edited and introduced by David B. Allison (New York: Delta Books, 1977), p. 86; idem, *Nietzsche and Philosophy*, translated by Hugh Tomlinson (London: Athlone Press, 1983), pp. 39–72; idem, *Difference and Repetition*, pp. 41–42, 242–243; idem, *Pure Immanence: Essays on a Life*, with an introduction by John Rajchman, translated by Anne Boyman (New York: Zone Books, 2001), p. 87 (emphasis in original). I have previously discussed some of these passages in "Kenotic Overflow," pp. 114–116. Compare the attempt to relate the Deleuzian interpretation of Nietzsche's eternal return to Kant's idea of the split subjectivity, that is, the belief that the subject encounters itself as an appearance in time, in Levi R. Bryant, *Difference and Givenness: Deleuze's Transcendental Empiricism and the Ontology of Immanence* (Evanston: Northwestern University Press, 2008), pp. 182–183, 188–190, 194–195.

109. Wyschogrod, *An Ethics of Remembering*, pp. 155–159. Deleuze is mentioned explicitly on p. 155.

110. Bryant, *Difference and Givenness*, p. 188.

111. Wyschogrod, *Crossover Queries*, p. 58.

112. Wyschogrod, *Saints and Postmodernism*, p. 64 (emphasis in original).

113. Ibid.

114. Wyschogrod, *Crossover Queries*, p. 58.

115. Wyschogrod, *Saints and Postmodernism*, p. xxiii.

116. Ibid., pp. 6–7.

117. For discussion of the mystical dimension of Teresa of Avila, especially what she identifies as the third stage of contemplative prayer, see Wyschogrod, *Saints and Postmodernism*, pp. 36–37; idem, *Crossover Queries*, pp. 271–272.

118. Wyschogrod, *Crossover Queries*, p. 306.

119. Wyschogrod, *Saints and Postmodernism*, p. 83. The passage is part of the section of Wyschogrod's book entitled "Thinking, Animality, and the Saintly Hand," in which she

engages Derrida's critique of Heidegger. For a nuanced analysis, see Virginia Burrus, "Wyschogrod's Hand: Saints, Animality, and the Labor of Love," *Philosophy Today* 55 (2011): 412–421.

120. Wyschogrod, *Saints and Postmodernism*, p. 113. In that context, Wyschogrod refers to Teresa of Avila.

121. See Ch. 3 nn. 101–102.

122. Levinas, *Proper Names*, pp. 137–138.

123. Wyschogrod, *Saints and Postmodernism*, p. 211. For discussion of the Deleuzian conception of the virtual image, see Keith Ansell Pearson, "The Reality of the Virtual: Bergson and Deleuze," *Modern Language Notes* 129 (2005): 1112–1127, esp. 1120–1126.

124. Wyschogrod, *Crossover Queries*, p. 315.

125. Ibid., pp. 307–308.

126. Ibid., p. 315.

127. Ibid., p. 48.

128. Ibid.

129. Ibid., p. 315.

130. Ibid., p. 54.

131. Ibid., pp. 54–55.

132. Ibid., p. 55.

133. Ibid., p. 56.

134. Wyschogrod, *Saints and Postmodernism*, p. xxiii.

135. Wyschogrod, *Crossover Queries*, p. 57.

136. Ibid.

137. See the discussion in Wyschogrod, *Saints and Postmodernism*, pp. 141–146.

138. Wyschogrod, *Crossover Queries*, pp. 58–59.

139. Ibid., p. 59.

140. Ibid., pp. 46–47.

141. Ibid., p. 53.

142. Wyschogrod, "Crossover Dreams," p. 544.

143. Wyschogrod, *Saints and Postmodernism*, p. 25.

144. Consider the concluding paragraph in John D. Caputo, "Hearing the Voices of the Dead: Wyschogrod, Megill, and the Heterological Historian," in *Saintly Influence*, p. 174: "Objectivity is not an illusory but a local phenomenon. Objectivity is a second-order, higher-level stratum of objectifying constitution, and objectification is constituted by rule keeping. . . . Wyschogrod makes it clear that the heterological historian knows these rules as well as anyone else, and she knows that to ignore or break them would be her ruin as a professional historian. But the rules are not why she is in this game rather than another, and they do not give a deep account of what her professional life as an historian is finally about. She is there because she is haunted, because she hears voices, because she hears the call of the dead and has been called upon to respond, and because, like Derrida, she is dreaming of being a historian."

145. Wyschogrod, "Crossover Dreams," p. 544.

146. Ibid.

147. Wyschogrod, *Saints and Postmodernism*, p. 34. See idem, *Crossover Queries*, p. 270.

148. Wyschogrod, "Crossover Dreams," p. 545.

149. Wyschogrod, "Hasidism, Hellenism, Holocaust," p. 310.

150. For an exploration of this theme, see Wolfson, "Divine Suffering," pp. 135–139.

151. Wyschogrod, "Crossover Dreams," p. 545.

152. Ibid., pp. 545–546. Compare the analysis of hospitality, alterity, and justice in Edith Wyschogrod, "Autochthony and Welcome: Discourses of Exile in Lévinas and Derrida," in *Derrida and Religion*, pp. 53–61, esp. 54: "The home is a site that allows for self-enclosure, the shutting in of oneself that constitutes individuation, yet is also open to the other. To be sure, the home founds possession or ownership but is not itself owned in the same way as are moveable goods; it is possessed because 'it already . . . is hospitable for its proprietor' [Levinas, *Totality and Infinity*, p. 157]. Yet the home is 'the very opposite of a root. It indicates a disengagement, a wandering that has made it possible' [ibid., p. 172]. Is Abraham, the biblical paradigm of hospitality, not described as "A wandering Aramean'? (Deuteronomy 26:5)." Even though the essay was reprinted in Wyschogrod, *Crossover Queries*, pp. 423–431, I have cited the version in *Derrida and Religion* because the last sentence in the text from *Crossover Queries* (p. 424) reads incorrectly "Did Abraham, the biblical paradigm of hospitality, not claim, 'A wandering Aramean was my father'?" Contextually, Abraham is not the one who utters this statement but each Israelite when the priest sets down the offering of the first fruits on the altar as a sacrifice to God on his behalf. The erroneous sentence appears as well in the first published version of the essay in the *Journal of Philosophy and Scripture* 1 (2003): 36. I am not sure whether the author or an editor made the correction, but it seems reasonable to conclude that, in preparing her anthology, Wyschogrod made use of a text that matched the original publication.

153. Wyschogrod, "Crossover Dreams," p. 546.

154. Ibid. Wyschogrod's analysis seems to be patterned on the discussion of Hegel's view on the point, line, and plane, in Derrida, *Margins*, pp. 40–46.

155. Wyschogrod, *Spirit in Ashes*, p. 95.

156. Wyschogrod, "Crossover Dreams," p. 546.

157. Ibid.

158. Ibid., p. 547.

159. Gilles Deleuze, "Nomad Thought," in *The New Nietzsche*, pp. 142–149, and see the analysis in Wyschogrod, *Saints and Postmodernism*, pp. 205–208. On the Deleuzian nomadology, see Raschke, *Postmodernism*, pp. 141–164.

160. Wyschogrod, "Hasidism, Hellenism, Holocaust," p. 312.

161. Ibid. To be specific, Wyschogrod proposes that the "philosophy of deep negation" together with the Hasidic tale "constitute an atheoretical mode of writing Jewish theology in a post-Holocaust age."

162. The passage referred to is from the Babylonian Talmud, Shabbat 88a.

163. Wyschogrod, "Doing before Hearing," p. 191.

164. Ibid., p. 192.

165. Wyschogrod, "Trends," p. 130.

166. Wyschogrod, *Crossover Queries*, p. 54.

167. Wyschogrod, "Hasidism, Hellenism, Holocaust," p. 318. The use of "neo-kabbalistic" relates to the "deep negation" of the abyss or the nonground.

Chapter 6: Undoing (K)not of Apophaticism: A Heideggerian Afterthought

1. See references cited in Ch. 2 n. 295.

2. Derrida, *The Gift of Death*, p. 49; *Donner la mort*, p. 75.

3. Janicaud, "The Theological Turn," pp. 16–103.

4. Wolfson, *A Dream*, p. 30. I have taken the liberty of reworking some of that discussion in this context.

5. Corbin, *Creative Imagination*, pp. 268–269. See also idem, *Le paradoxe du mono-théisme* (Paris: Éditions de L'Herne, 2003), pp. 24–27.

6. Paul Ricoeur, *Freud and Philosophy: An Essay on Interpretation*, translated by Denis Savage (New Haven: Yale University Press, 1970), p. 27.

7. Catherine Keller, "The Apophasis of Gender: A Fourfold Unsaying of Feminist Theology," *Journal of the American Academy of Religion* 76 (2008): 912.

8. Ibid.

9. A typical example of this position is articulated by Pamela Sue Anderson, "Ineffable Knowledge and Gender," in *Rethinking Philosophy of Religion*, pp. 162–183. Consider also the related but distinct link between women's spiritual quest and the experience of nothingness explored by feminist theologians like Mary Daly. For an analysis of this theme, see Carol P. Christ, "Nothingness, Awakening, Insight, New Naming," in *Experience of the Sacred: Readings in the Phenomenology of Religion*, edited by Summer B. Twiss and Walter H. Conser Jr. (Hanover: University Press of New England, 1992), pp. 121–128.

10. Keller, "The Apophasis of Gender," p. 913.

11. See Wolfson, *Language, Eros, Being*, pp. 130–131.

12. Derrida, *Glas*, p. 188.

13. Keller, "The Apophasis of Gender," p. 914.

14. Ibid., p. 916.

15. Ibid., p. 918 (emphasis in original).

16. A similar critique may be leveled against Ann-Marie Priest, "Woman as God, God as Woman: Mysticism, Negative Theology, and Luce Irigaray," *Journal of Religion* 83 (2003): 1–23.

17. Catherine Keller, "Returning God: The Gift of Feminist Theology," in *Feminism, Sexuality, and the Return of Religion*, edited by Linda Martin Alcoff and John D. Caputo (Bloomington: Indiana University Press, 2011), p. 59 (emphasis in original).

18. Ibid., pp. 61–62.

19. Ibid., p. 67.

20. Ibid., p. 68 (emphasis in original).

21. Ibid., pp. 68–69.

22. For a good summary of this conceptual framing, see the introduction in *Polydoxy: Theology of Multiplicity and Relation*, edited by Catherine Keller and Laurel C. Schneider (London: Routledge, 2011), pp. 1–15.

23. Ibid., p. 4.

24. For reference, see Ch. 2 n. 38.

25. Henry, *The Essence of Manifestation*, § 7, p. 41. On the dimension of invisibility in Henry's phenomenology, see Zahavi, "Michel Henry"; Jean-Luc Marion, *Figures de phénoménologie: Husserl, Heidegger, Levinas, Henry, Derrida* (Paris: J. Vrin, 2012), pp. 95–115.

26. Kearney, *Anatheism*, p. xiv.

27. Laurel C. Schneider, *Beyond Monotheism: A Theology of Multiplicity* (London: Routledge, 2008).

28. Heidegger, *The Phenomenology of Religious Life*, p. 77; *Phänomenologie des religiösen Lebens*, p. 109.

29. Heidegger, *The Phenomenology of Religious Life*, p. 78; *Phänomenologie des religiösen Lebens*, p. 110. For discussion of this passage, see Marta Zaccagnini, *Christentum der Endlichkeit: Heideggers Vorlesungen "Einleitung in die Phänomenologie der Religion"* (Münster: LIT Verlag, 2003), pp. 57–58; Coyne, "The End of Care," pp. 81–82.

30. See Ch. 2 at n. 302.

31. Heidegger, *The Phenomenology of Religious Life*, pp. 73–74; *Phänomenologie des religiösen Lebens*, p. 105. See the rich analysis of this dimension of Heidegger's thought in Tonning, "'Hineingehalten in die Nacht.'" On the Pauline nature of Heidegger's early attempt to uncover the primal Christianity (*Urchristentum*) as a reformation of thinking, see the analysis of Critchley, *The Faith of the Faithless*, pp. 166–194.

32. Heidegger, *The Phenomenology of Religious Life*, p. 81; *Phänomenologie des religiösen Lebens*, p. 114.

33. Coyne, "The End of Care," pp. 67–68.

34. Heidegger, *The Phenomenology of Religious Life*, p. 66; *Phänomenologie des religiösen Lebens*, p. 95. Critchley, *The Faith of the Faithless*, pp. 174–175, notes that Heidegger's discussion of the *parousia* is a foreshadowing of his notion of ecstatic temporality developed in *Being and Time*. See Ch. 2 n. 196.

35. Heidegger, *The Phenomenology of Religious Life*, p. 69; *Phänomenologie des religiösen Lebens*, p. 98. Compare also Radloff, "Preliminary Notes," pp. 167–168: "As an object the image of the divine is in fact an idol. Temporally it is determined in terms of the Now of its being-present. This Now is an event 'in' time. The incarnation of Christ is a past event 'in' time and his second coming in an anticipated event 'at' a future time—the event that ends time. Taking a clue from Heidegger's lectures on St. Paul we can see that what is at stake here are two different understandings of the παρουσία. The original sense of the παρουσία signifies that Christian factical life lives historicity itself in the enactment of one's having-become called to Christ. The enactment of the 'past' *and* the 'future' as

promise, in the Now of serving (δουλεύειν) and waiting (ἀναμένειν), signifies the comportment of a turning-away from the idols of the world toward God . . . The παρουσία, therefore, is not understood as an expected end-time, but is the Now of witnessing the presence of the Messiah through one's comportment. One does not make God an object of speculation in terms of expectation of an event 'in' objective-historical time" (emphasis in original). On the distinction between kairotic time, which is not measurable chronoscopically, and historical time in Heidegger, see also Bradley H. McLean, *Biblical Interpretation and Philosophical Hermeneutics* (Cambridge: Cambridge University Press, 2012), pp. 130–132.

36. Heidegger, *The Phenomenology of Religious Life*, p. 57; *Phänomenologie des religiösen Lebens*, p. 82.

37. Heidegger, *The Phenomenology of Religious Life*, p. 73; *Phänomenologie des religiösen Lebens*, p. 104.

38. Heidegger, *The Phenomenology of Religious Life*, p. 73; *Phänomenologie des religiösen Lebens*, p. 104.

39. Heidegger, *The Phenomenology of Religious Life*, p. 73; *Phänomenologie des religiösen Lebens*, p. 105.

40. Heidegger, *The Phenomenology of Religious Life*, p. 81; *Phänomenologie des religiösen Lebens*, p. 114.

41. Biemann, *Inventing New Beginnings*, pp. 45–46.

42. See Wolfson, *A Dream*, p. 254, where I argue that the "kabbalistic understanding of temporality" involves the "an-archical infinity actualized, time after time, in the *purely present future*, the future that is already present as the present that is always future—a chiastic paradox that is at the heart of Jewish messianism." Compare as well my account of the messianic dimension of Ḥabad in Wolfson, *Open Secret*, pp. 265–300, esp. 280–281: "The absolute nonbeing of the event, accordingly, demands instantaneous action, since at any point in time it is pertinent to speak of bringing about the coming of the Messiah. . . . The paradox 'in time though not in time,' *bi-zeman akh eino bi-zeman*, indicates that this moment . . . cannot be measured temporally, no matter how refined our tools of analytic computation, and hence, mathematically, there is no way to think of its occurrence but as the occurrence of what cannot occur save in the nonoccurrence of its occurrence. . . . The nonoccurrence in no way effects the belief in the possibility of the advent of the future; on the contrary, insofar as that advent is not an event that can materialize in time, the nonoccurrence is, strictly speaking, what guarantees its occurrence. . . . the time of redemption is this timeless moment, which cannot transpire temporally and therefore must always be capable of occurring (in)temporally."

43. Critchley, *The Faith of the Faithless*, p. 175.

44. Heidegger, *The Phenomenology of Religious Life*, pp. 67–69; *Phänomenologie des religiösen Lebens*, p. 98.

45. Heidegger, *The Phenomenology of Religious Life*, pp. 73–74; *Phänomenologie des religiösen Lebens*, p. 105.

46. Heidegger, *The Phenomenology of Religious Life*, p. 80; *Phänomenologie des religiösen Lebens*, p. 113.

47. Heidegger, *The Phenomenology of Religious Life*, p. 80; *Phänomenologie des religiösen Lebens*, p. 113.

48. Heidegger, *The Phenomenology of Religious Life*, pp. 81–82; *Phänomenologie des religiösen Lebens*, p. 115. See Critchley, *The Faith of the Faithless*, pp. 175–176.

49. Heidegger, *Introduction to Metaphysics*, p. 8; *Einführung in die Metaphysik*, p. 9.

50. Heidegger, *The Metaphysical Foundations of Logic*, p. 165 n. 9; *Metaphysische Anfangsgründe der Logik*, p. 211 n. 3.

51. Heidegger, *Elucidations*, pp. 46–47; *Erläuterungen*, p. 28. Compare Gall, *Beyond Theism*, pp. 31–32.

52. Martin Heidegger, *Mindfulness*, translated by Parvis Emad and Thomas Kalary (New York: Continuum, 2006), pp. 210–212; *Besinnung* [GA 66] (Frankfurt am Main: Vittorio Klostermann, 1997), pp. 237–239. See the analysis of part of this passage in Emad, *Translation and Interpretation*, pp. 112–113.

53. Heidegger, *Mindfulness*, p. 213; *Besinnung*, pp. 240–241.

54. For a well-argued defense of such a position, see Mayra Rivera, *The Touch of Transcendence: A Postcolonial Theology* (Louisville: Westminster John Knox Press, 2007).

55. Richard Kearney, "In Place of a Response," in *After God: Richard Kearney and the Religious Turn in Continental Philosophy*, edited by John Panteleimon Manoussakis (New York: Fordham University Press, 2006), p. 375. The construal of the divine or the infinite as possibility has been a recurrent theme in Kearney's publications. See, for example, Kearney, "Hermeneutics of the Possible God" and *The God Who May Be: A Hermeneutics of Religion* (Bloomington: Indiana University Press, 2001).

56. Richard Kearney, "Sacramental Imagination and Eschatology," in *Phenomenology and Eschatology*, p. 56. See the criticism of representing the givenness of being as a divine gift in Wolfson, *A Dream*, pp. 32–33.

57. John D. Caputo, "Spectral Hermeneutics: On the Weakness of God and the Theology of the Event," in John D. Caputo and Gianni Vattimo, *After the Death of God*, edited by Jeffrey W. Robbins, with an afterword by Gabriel Vahanian (New York: Columbia University Press, 2007), p. 49.

58. I am equally suspicious of Caputo's claim that the experience of God as the impossible is based on a "phenomenological ground" that comes "after onto-theology." See John D. Caputo, "The Experience of God and the Axiology of the Impossible," in *Religion After Metaphysics*, pp. 123–145. Apart from the very debatable use of the Derridean notion of the impossible, Caputo's phenomenology is the handmaiden to his theological presuppositions. His enterprise, therefore, is an exercise in the more traditional phenomenology of religion, that is, the application of a phenomenological method to explicate a particular form of religious experience; the latter is in no way grounded in the former. Proverbially speaking, Caputo has placed the cart before the horse.

59. Caputo, "Spectral Hermeneutics," p. 49.

60. Ibid., p. 51.

61. John D. Caputo, *The Weakness of God: A Theology of the Event* (Bloomington: Indiana University Press, 2006), p. 4.

62. Ibid., p. 2.

63. Bernard McGinn, "The God beyond God: Theology and Mysticism in the Thought of Meister Eckhart," *Journal of Religion* 61 (1981): 1–19.

64. The expression "God without God" appears in two letters that Husserl wrote, one to Adelgundis Jaegerschmidt and the other to Edith Stein. The former is cited in Steven W. Laycock, "Introduction: Toward an Overview of Phenomenological Theology," in *Essays in Phenomenological Theology*, pp. 1–2, and the second in Steven W. Laycock, "The Intersubjective Dimension of Husserl's Thought," op. cit., p. 169.

65. Keith Ansell Pearson, "Pure Reserve: Deleuze, Philosophy, and Immanence," in *Deleuze and Religion*, pp. 141–155, esp. 149–153.

66. Marion, "The Saturated Phenomenon"; idem, *The Visible and the Revealed*, pp. 18–48, 119–144; idem, *In Excess*, pp. 158–162; idem, *Being Given*, pp. 199–221 (*Étant donné*, pp. 280–296); and the critical evaluations by Robyn Horner, "The Betrayal of Transcendence," in *Transcendence: Philosophy, Literature, and Theology Approach the Beyond*, edited by Regina Schwartz (New York: Routledge, 2004), pp. 61–79, esp. 70–76; Christina M. Gschwandtner, *Reading Jean-Luc Marion: Exceeding Metaphysics* (Bloomington: Indiana University Press, 2007), pp. 59–86, 150–155, 233–242; Shane Mackinlay, "Exceeding Truth: Jean-Luc Marion's Saturated Phenomena," *Pacifica* 20 (2007): 40–51, and the fuller treatment in idem, *Interpreting Excess: Jean-Luc Marion, Saturated Phenomenon, and Hermeneutics* (New York: Fordham University Press, 2009); Smith, *Speech and Theology*, pp. 32–41. For other references, see Ch. 3 n. 46.

67. Marion, *Being Given*, p. 36; *Étant donné*, p. 57. See idem, *Reduction and Givenness*, p. 64.

68. Angelus Silesius, *The Cherubinic Wanderer*, p. 88; *Angelus Silesius*, p. 92.

69. Derrida, *On the Name*. p. 56 (emphasis in original); *Sauf le nom*, pp. 56–57. I have modified the translation slightly.

70. Derrida, *Psyche: Inventions of the Other, Volume II*, p. 173.

71. Heidegger, *Poetry, Language, Thought*, p. 172; *Vorträge und Aufsätze*, pp. 173–174.

72. Heidegger's view is described correctly in these terms by Marion, *God Without Being*, p. 104.

73. Heidegger, *The Principle of Reason*, p. 68; *Der Satz vom Grund*, p. 101.

74. Freeman, *Ancilla*, p. 28; Kahn, *The Art and Thought of Heraclitus*, pp. 70–71, and analysis on pp. 227–229.

75. The more technical term for release often used by Heidegger is *Gelassenheit*. Many have opined on this critical expression, noting especially the affinity between Heidegger and Meister Eckhart. For a representative study, see Bret W. Davis, *Heidegger and the Will: On the Way to Gelassenheit* (Evanston: Northwestern University Press, 2007).

76. Heidegger, *Poetry, Language, Thought*, p. 101; *Holzwege*, p. 279.

77. Heidegger, *Poetry, Language, Thought*, p. 102; *Holzwege*, p. 280.

78. Heidegger, *The Principle of Reason*, p. 113 (emphasis in original); *Der Satz vom Grund*, p. 169.

79. Heidegger, *The Principle of Reason*, p. 35; *Der Satz vom Grund*, p. 53. See the discussion of this principle in Blond, *Heidegger and Nietzsche*, pp. 54–78.

80. Heidegger, *The Principle of Reason*, p. 37; *Der Satz vom Grund*, p. 56.

81. Heidegger, *The Principle of Reason*, p. 41; *Der Satz vom Grund*, p. 61.

82. Heidegger, *The Principle of Reason*, p. 43; *Der Satz vom Grund*, p. 63.

83. Heidegger, *The Principle of Reason*, p. 49; *Der Satz vom Grund*, p. 73.

84. Heidegger, *Being and Time*, § 7, pp. 31–32; *Sein und Zeit*, pp. 35–36.

85. Heidegger, *On Time and Being*, p. 6 (emphasis in original); *Zur Sache des Denkens*, p. 10. See the analysis in Vattimo, *The Adventure of Difference*, pp. 110–120.

86. Heidegger, *The Basic Problems of Phenomenology*, p. 10 (emphasis in original; translation modified); *Die Grundprobleme der Phänomenologie*, pp. 13–14.

87. Heidegger, *The Basic Problems of Phenomenology*, p. 260; *Die Grundprobleme der Phänomenologie*, p. 367.

88. Heidegger, *The Basic Problems of Phenomenology*, p. 281; *Die Grundprobleme der Phänomenologie*, p. 398.

89. Heidegger (see reference in following note) writes "as Plato says somewhere." The source is the *Theaetetus* 201e. See Wolfson, *A Dream*, pp. 97 and 347 n. 261.

90. Heidegger, *The Basic Problems of Phenomenology*, pp. 52–53; *Die Grundprobleme der Phänomenologie*, pp. 72–73.

91. Heidegger, *Pathmarks*, pp. 254–255; *Wegmarken*, pp. 334–335.

92. See references in Ch. 3 n. 117.

93. See passage cited in Ch. 3 at n. 288.

94. Heidegger, *Pathmarks*, pp. 239, 254; *Wegmarken*, pp. 313, 333.

95. Heidegger, *Introduction to Metaphysics*, p. 15; *Einführung in die Metaphysik*, p. 11.

96. Heidegger, *Contributions*, § 276, p. 391; *Beiträge*, p. 497.

97. Heidegger, *Contributions*, § 276, p. 391; *Beiträge*, p. 497.

98. Heidegger, *Contributions*, § 276, p. 393; *Beiträge*, pp. 499–500.

99. Heidegger, *Contributions*, § 276, pp. 393–394; *Beiträge*, p. 500.

100. Heidegger, *Contributions*, § 281, p. 401; *Beiträge*, p. 510.

101. Heidegger, *Contributions*, § 36, p. 62; *Beiträge*, p. 78.

102. Heidegger, *Contributions*, § 37, pp. 62–63; *Beiträge*, pp. 78–79.

103. Pöggeler, "Heidegger's Topology of Being," pp. 114–115, 127; Wilhelm S. Wurzer, "Heidegger's Turn to *Germanien*—A Sigetic Venture," in *Heidegger toward the Turn*, pp. 199–204.

104. Heidegger, *Contributions*, § 129, p. 194; *Beiträge*, p. 246.

105. Compare Heidegger, *Mindfulness*, pp. 278–279 (*Besinnung*, pp. 312–313): "For ab-ground is the swaying of refusal as the swaying of en-ownment of gifting [*Denn Ab-grund ist Wesung der Verweigerung als der Er-eignung der Verschenkung*]. . . . The be-ing historical inquiry does not experience 'nothingness' [*das Nichts*] merely as the 'nihilating' [*Nichtiges*], but, insofar as this thinking inquires into be-ing itself in the

fullness of its swaying, this thinking experiences 'nothingness' as the en-ownment" (emphasis in original).

106. Heidegger, *Contributions*, § 242, p. 300 (emphasis in original); *Beiträge*, p. 380. For discussion of this passage, see Emad, *Translation and Interpretation*, pp. 104–105.

107. Heidegger, *Contributions*, § 131, p. 196; *Beiträge*, p. 249.

108. Martin Heidegger, *Nietzsche, Volume II: The Eternal Recurrence of the Same*, translated with notes and an analysis by David Farrell Krell (New York: Harper & Row, 1984), p. 57; *Nietzsches metaphysische Grundstellung im abendländischen Denken: Die ewige Wiederkehr des Gleichen* [GA 44] (Frankfurt am Main: Vittorio Klostermann, 1986), p. 60. Compare Heidegger, *Nietzsche, Volume II*, p. 182 (*Nietzsches metaphysische Grundstellung*, p. 203), where thinking in terms of the moment—the thought that conquers nihilism—is depicted as the transposition to "independent action and decision, glancing ahead at what is assigned us as our task and back at what is given us as our endowment." The concurrence of past endowment and future task conveys Nietzsche's view that the temporality of the moment is expressive of the curvature of eternity, and thus it embraces everything in itself at once, an insight that is linked to Zarathustra's "downgoing" (*Untergang*). See Heidegger, *Nietzsche, Volume II*, p. 59; *Nietzsches metaphysische Grundstellung*, p. 63.

109. Heidegger, *Contributions*, § 238, p. 293 (emphasis in original); *Beiträge*, p. 371.

110. Hans Blumenberg, *Work on Myth*, translated by Robert M. Wallace (Cambridge, MA: MIT Press, 1985), p. 247.

111. Heidegger, *Nietzsche, Volume II*, p. 7; *Nietzsches metaphysische Grundstellung*, p. 4.

112. Deleuze, *Difference and Repetition*, p. 66. See also idem, *Nietzsche and Philosophy*, p. 220 n. 31; and the critical assessment in Crockett, *Radical Political Theology*, pp. 134–135. For Heidegger's critique of Nietzsche's doctrine, see Blond, *Heidegger and Nietzsche*, pp. 130–136.

113. Deleuze, *Difference and Repetition*, p. 41. Compare idem, *Nietzsche and Philosophy*, p. 48: "*Returning is the being of that which becomes*. . . . The present must coexist with itself as past and yet to come. . . . The eternal return is thus an answer to the problem of *passage*. And in this sense it must not be interpreted as the return of something that is, that is 'one' or the 'same.' We misinterpret the expression 'eternal return' if we understand it as 'return of the same.' It is not being that returns but rather the returning itself that constitutes being insofar as it is affirmed of becoming and of that which passes. It is not some one thing which returns but rather returning itself is the one thing which is affirmed of diversity or multiplicity" (emphasis in original).

114. Heidegger, *Contributions*, § 33, p. 58 (emphasis in original); *Beiträge*, p. 73.

115. Regarding this Heideggerian motif, see Heidegger, *Identity and Difference*, p. 45 (German text: p. 111); and other sources mentioned in Ch. 2 n. 131.

116. Heidegger, *Introduction to Metaphysics*, p. 41; *Einführung in die Metaphysik*, p. 42. On the paradox of the repetition of the origin in Heidegger, see Marrati, *Genesis and Trace*, pp. 109–113. See also Miguel de Beistegui, *Thinking with Heidegger: Displacements* (Bloomington: Indiana University Press, 2003), pp. 49–60; Calvin O. Schrag, "Hei-

degger on Repetition and Historical Understanding," *Philosophy East and West* 20 (1970): 287–295; David Wood, *Thinking after Heidegger* (Cambridge: Polity Press 2002), pp. 61–77; William S. Allen, *Ellipsis: Of Poetry and the Experience of Language after Heidegger, Hölderlin, and Blanchot* (Albany: State University of New York Press, 2007), pp. 25–57; Biemann, *Inventing New Beginnings*, pp. 90–91.

117. Concerning this comportment of the moment, see Wolfson, *Alef, Mem, Tau*, pp. 71–72; idem, *A Dream*, p. 228.

118. Heidegger, *Contributions*, § 38, p. 64 (emphasis in original); *Beiträge*, p. 80.

119. Heidegger, *Contributions*, § 242, p. 303; *Beiträge*, p. 384. On "the remembering expectation of the event" (*die erinnernde Erwartung des Ereignisses*), see also Heidegger, *Contributions*, § 31, p. 55; *Beiträge*, p. 69.

120. Heidegger, *On Time and Being*, p. 15; *Zur Sache des Denkens*, p. 20.

121. Heidegger, *On Time and Being*, p. 16; *Zur Sache des Denkens*, p. 20.

122. Heidegger, *On Time and Being*, p. 17; *Zur Sache des Denkens*, p. 22.

123. Heidegger, *On Time and Being*, p. 18; *Zur Sache des Denkens*, p. 23.

124. Heidegger, *On Time and Being*, p. 19; *Zur Sache des Denkens*, p. 24.

125. Heidegger, *On Time and Being*, pp. 19–22; *Zur Sache des Denkens*, pp. 24–27. See the comments on this passage in Derrida, *Margins*, p. 26 n. 26.

126. Heidegger, *On Time and Being*, p. 21; *Zur Sache des Denkens*, p. 27.

127. Heidegger, *Contributions*, § 242, p. 303; *Beiträge*, p. 384.

128. Marion, *The Reason of the Gift*, p. 20.

129. Heidegger, *On Time and Being*, p. 22; *Zur Sache des Denkens*, p. 27.

130. Marion, *Being Given*, p. 37; *Étant donné*, p. 57.

131. Marion, *Being Given*, p. 38; *Étant donné*, p. 59. See the discussion of Marion's reading of Heidegger in Gschwandtner, *Reading Jean-Luc Marion*, pp. 62–65, 263 n. 28; and Brian Elliott, "Reduced Phenomena and Unreserved Debts in Marion's Reading of Heidegger," in *Givenness and God*, pp. 91–92.

132. Jean-Luc Marion, "The 'End of Metaphysics' as a Possibility," in *Religion After Metaphysics*, pp. 181–182.

133. Ibid., p. 182.

134. Ibid., pp. 182–183.

135. For a different attempt to interpret Heidegger's *Ereignis* in apocalyptic terms as the "absolute event" that is "the final actualization of the Godhead itself," see Altizer, *Godhead and the Nothing*, p. 124. See also Altizer, *The New Gospel of Christian Atheism*, pp. 75–76, 135–136, and more fully in "Heidegger: *Ereignis* and the Nothing," in Thomas J. J. Altizer, *The Call to Radical Theology*, edited and with an introduction by Lissa McCullough, foreword by David E. Klemm (Albany: State University of New York Press, 2012), pp. 67–77.

136. See Ch. 3 n. 199.

137. Marion, *God Without Being*, pp. 101–102.

138. Ibid., pp. 103–104.

139. Ibid., pp. 104–105.

140. See Ch. 3 nn. 316–319. Compare Jean-Luc Marion, "La double idolâtrie. Remarques sur la différence ontologique et la pensée de Dieu," in *Heidegger et la question de Dieu*, pp. 88–89.

141. Marion, *God Without Being*, p. 105.

142. Marion's discussion of givenness is set against the backdrop of Heidegger's phenomenology of the inapparent in Janicaud, "The Theological Turn," pp. 28–32, 59–62.

143. On the phenomenon of the gift in Derrida and Marion, see Ch. 4 n. 226.

144. Jean-Luc Marion, *The Idol and Distance: Five Studies*, translated and with an introduction by Thomas A. Carlson (New York: Fordham University Press, 2001), p. 142 (emphasis in original). Compare Marion, "In the Name," p. 38: "The Name does not name God as an essence; it designates what passes beyond every name. The name designates what is not named and says what is not named. There is nothing surprising then in the fact that in Judaism the term 'Name' replaces the Tetragrammaton which should not and can never be pronounced as a proper name, nor that, amounting to the same thing, in Christianity it names the fortunate and necessary 'absence of divine names' (Hölderlin)." I note, finally, that Marion's view of the gift and the name brings to mind this passage on baptism in *The Gospel of Philip* 64:22–31 in *The Nag Hammadi Scriptures*, edited by Marvin Meyer, introduction by Elaine H. Pagels (New York: HarperCollins, 2007), p. 171: "Anyone who goes down into the water and comes up without receiving anything and says, 'I am a Christian,' has borrowed the name. But one who receives the Holy Spirit has the name as a gift. A gift does not have to be paid back, but what is borrowed must be paid. This is how it is with us, when one of us experiences a mystery."

145. Jean-Luc Marion, "The Reason of the Gift," in *Givenness and God*, pp. 104–105. See the analysis of this passage in Joseph S. O'Leary, "The Gift: A Trojan Horse in the Citadel of Phenomenology?" in *Givenness and God*, p. 152. On the agreement between Marion and Derrida on the need to remove the gift from the horizon of economy, see Marion's remark in Kearney, "On the Gift," p. 62.

146. Jean-Luc Marion, *The Reason of the Gift*, translated and with an introduction by Stephen E. Lewis (Charlottesville: University of Virginia Press, 2011), p. 76.

147. Marion, *Being Given*, p. 25 (emphasis in original); *Étant donné*, p. 39.

148. Marion, *Being Given*, p. 26; *Étant donné*, p. 40. See the analysis in Gschwandtner, *Reading Jean-Luc Marion*, pp. 67–72; Schrijvers, *Ontotheological Turnings*, pp. 51–80; and the critique of Florian Forestier, "The Phenomenon and the Transcendental: Jean-Luc Marion, Marc Richir, and the Issue of Phenomenalization," *Continental Philosophy Review* 45 (2012): 381–402, esp. 387–393.

149. Marion, *Being Given*, p. 70; *Étant donné*, p. 102.

150. Marion, *Being Given*, pp. 73–74; *Étant donné*, p. 107.

151. Marion, *The Reason of the Gift*, p. 20.

152. Ibid., p. 77.

153. Marion, *Being Given*, p. 77; *Étant donné*, p. 113.

154. Marion, *Being Given*, p. 78; *Étant donné*, p. 114.

155. Jean-Luc Marion, "The Recognition of the Gift," in *Philosophical Concepts and Religious Metaphors: New Perspectives on Phenomenology and Theology*, edited by Cristian Ciocan (Bucharest: Zeta Books, 2009), p. 16.

156. In *The Reason of the Gift*, pp. 80–81, Marion links his own discussion of the disappearance of the gift with Heidegger's idea of beings appearing in such a way that they remain concealed in their unconcealment.

157. Ibid., pp. 78–79.

158. Marion, *Being Given*, p. 227; *Étant donné*, p. 316.

159. Marion, *Being Given*, p. 225; *Étant donné*, p. 315. I have modified the translation of *la visée*.

160. Marion, *Being Given*, p. 199; *Étant donné*, p. 280.

161. Marion, *Being Given*, p. 226; *Étant donné*, p. 316.

162. Marion, *Being Given*, p. 319; *Étant donné*, p. 437. For an analysis of this motif, see Thomas A. Carlson, "Blindness and the Decision to See: On Revelation and Reception in Jean-Luc Marion," in *Counter-Experiences: Reading Jean-Luc Marion*, edited by Kevin Hart (Notre Dame: University of Notre Dame Press, 2007), pp. 153–179, esp. 158–159.

163. Marion, "The Saturated Phenomenon," p. 208.

164. Ibid., p. 212. See Manoussakis, *God after Metaphysics*, pp. 13–19.

165. Marion, "The Saturated Phenomenon," p. 208.

166. As noted by Welz, *Love's Transcendence*, p. 353.

167. Marion, *The Visible and the Revealed*, p. 62.

168. Ibid., p. 63. On the visibility of the invisible in the sacrament of the mystery of Christ as the phenomenality of the abandoned, see Jean-Luc Marion, "The Phenomenality of the Sacrament—Being and Givenness," in *Words of Life*, pp. 89–102.

169. Marion, *Being Given*, p. 71; *Étant donné*, p. 103.

170. Marion, *Being Given*, p. 80 (emphasis in original); *Étant donné*, p. 116.

171. See Caputo, "Apostles," p. 202. Marion has been criticized on these grounds by a number of thinkers, including especially Janicaud and Derrida. See the discussion in Horner, *Rethinking God as Gift*, pp. 102–108; Welz, *Love's Transcendence*, pp. 357–360; James, *The New French Philosophy*, pp. 27–31. Compare Lacoste, "De la donation comme promesse," pp. 853–856; idem, *La phénoménalité de dieu*, pp. 173–177.

172. Caputo, "Apostles," p. 202.

173. Marion, *God Without Being*, pp. 25–52.

174. Jean-Luc Marion, *The Erotic Phenomenon*, translated by Stephen E. Lewis (Chicago: University of Chicago Press, 2007), p. 103.

175. Marion, *The Reason of the Gift*, pp. 69–90.

176. We can speak of a double self-negation of the sacrifice insofar as it occasions both a theosis of the human and an anthropomorphosis of the divine. See the analysis of the primordial sacrifice in Altizer, *Godhead and the Nothing*, pp. 15–30, and the summary in Ray L. Hart, "Godhead and God," in *Thinking Through the Death of God*, p. 63 n. 3.

177. Marion, *Being Given*, p. 246; *Étant donné*, p. 341.

178. Compare the earlier analysis of the gift of a presence in Jean-Luc Marion, *Prolegomena to Charity*, translated by Stephen E. Lewis (New York: Fordham University Press, 2002), pp. 124–152. See also the discussion of the Eucharist as the hermeneutic site of theology in Marion, *God Without Being*, pp. 139–158, and see Gschwandtner, *Reading Jean-Luc Marion*, pp. 92–95, 148–149; Philipp W. Rosemann, "Postmodern Philosophy and Jean-Luc Marion's Eucharistic Realism," in *Transcendence and Phenomenology*, pp. 84–110, esp. 101–107.

179. Marion, *God Without Being*, pp. 165–167.

180. Marion, *Prolegomena*, p. 152.

181. Marion, *God Without Being*, p. 168.

182. Ibid., p. 171.

183. Ibid., p. 176. Compare Lacoste, *Experience and the Absolute*, p. 82: "Theology knows and declares that, if the world is interposed between God and us, and that if there exists no clear alternative between a chiaroscuro omnipresence and the Parousia, it is because the world shelters a third presence by which the Absolute participates in the logic of inherence, namely, what Christology and the theology of the sacraments teach. And yet even the gift of the Eucharist, in which the Absolute occupies a place here and now, is made to us only on condition that the world interposes itself, and that a so-called 'real' presence does not render it diaphanous and theophanic. This interposition is ontically the most tenuous there is: the breadth and tenuity of the Eucharistic species, of bread and wine. But these tenuous realities bear within themselves all the ontological density of the world; and if they are the place of a presence that constitutes the joy of believing, they also constitute for him a constant reminder of his historiality. That is why this presence does not absolve us of the duty to be patient." See also Lacoste, "The Appearing," pp. 60–67.

184. Marion, *God Without Being*, p. 169. For a more extended discussion of the theme of distance, see Marion, *The Idol and Distance*, pp. 198–253, and see the analysis of Westphal, *Overcoming Onto-Theology*, pp. 266–271.

185. Marion, *God Without Being*, pp. 171–172.

186. Ibid., p. 174.

187. Ibid., p. 175.

188. Ibid., pp. 175–176.

189. Ibid., p. 176 (emphasis in original). Compare Marion, *Prolegomena*, p. 150: "Henceforth Christ comes to the disciples in each moment, because he comes to them from beyond time—from whence likewise he can come at the end of this same time. Alpha and Omega, because preceding time from the very heart of the Trinity."

190. Marion, *The Erotic Phenomenon*, pp. 34–35 (emphasis in original).

191. A similar methodology is pursued in Marion, *The Visible and the Revealed*, pp. 97–98. Compare Jean-Luc Marion, *In the Self's Place: The Approach of Saint Augustine*, translated by Jeffrey L. Kosky (Stanford: Stanford University Press, 2012), p. 115. Giving witness to the nature of truth as the saturated phenomenon is epitomized in the words ascribed to Jesus, "I am the way, the truth, and the life" (John 14:6), whence Marion educes the following conclusion: "Hatred (and love) of the truth can be addressed

only to he who claims to incarnate the truth. It proves therefore epistemologically Christological, therefore theological. For it alone can both advise me and itself constitute the advice, verify and say what it verifies." On occasion Marion speaks of both Jewish and Christian revelation under the rubric of the saturated phenomenon. See *In Excess*, pp. 52–53. Even so, the preponderance of evidence indicates that, according to Marion, the exemplary expression of the saturated phenomenon is the incarnation of the Word, and hence the phenomenological, theological, and Christological are virtually synonymous.

192. Janicaud, "The Theological Turn," p. 67.

193. Smith, "Liberating Religion," p. 18. Compare Smith, *Speech and Theology*, p. 98: "Marion's religious phenomenon is in the end collapsed into a very particular *theological* phenomenon; correlatively, his (albeit im/possible) phenomenology of religion slides toward a very possible, and very particular, theology. The result of this rather insidious movement is two-fold: first, this conception of a phenomenology of religion *reduces* religion to theology; that is, it effects a leveling of the plurivocity of (global) religious experience and forces it into a rather theistic, or at least theophanic, mold. Religion, for Marion, turns out to be very narrowly defined and, in a sense, reduced to its theological sedimentation. Second, and as a result of this, Marion *particularizes* religion and the religious phenomenon as quite Christian—at best, monotheistic, and at worst, downright Catholic. . . . This *particularization* is yet another kind of *reduction*: a reduction which reduces the size of the kingdom, which keeps the walls close to Rome and makes it impossible for any who are different to enter" (emphasis in original). For an elaboration on the ethical shortcomings of Marion's thought, see Elliot R. Wolfson, "Givenness and the Disappearance of the Gift: Ethics and the Invisible in Marion's Christocentric Phenomenology," to appear in *Ethics of In-Visibility: Imago Dei, Memory, and Human Dignity*, edited by Claudia Welz (Tübingen: Mohr Siebeck, 2014). Portions of that study are reproduced here.

194. Smith, "Liberating Religion," pp. 23–24 (emphasis in original).

195. Ibid., pp. 27–28 (emphasis in original). It behooves me to note that while I am sympathetic to Smith's critique of Marion, I was disappointed to see that the thesis he puts forward in *Speech and Theology* betrays a similar logical flaw. Let me cite his own summation of the argument: "against the criticisms of Levinas and Marion, I mean to show that the transcendent phenomenon is not reduced to the sphere of ownness; rather, within Husserl's account of the appearance of the Other, we see an appearing which is at the same time a withholding, such that the Other is both present and absent. I will describe this as 'incarnational' insofar as it bears analogy to the appearance of God within humanity, such that the Other appears within the sphere of immanence without giving up its transcendence. . . . By describing my account as 'incarnational,' I mean to invoke the analogy of the Incarnation, of the appearance of God within humanity in the person of the God-man, Jesus of Nazareth. . . . This is an instance of the transcendent appearing within the immanent, without sacrificing transcendence. In the Incarnation, the Infinite shows up within the finite, nevertheless without loss. My task, however, in no way involves the defense of a Christology, though it perhaps presupposes one. I invoke the Incarnation as a metaphor, bracketing strictly christological questions, but nevertheless

pursuing a question about the philosophical possibility of theology itself" (p. 10). I accept that Smith's book is not an apologia for Christology, but his choice of the specifically Christian dogma to illustrate his idea of an incarnational phenomenology (pp. 55–56) makes him vulnerable to his own vilification of Marion for subjugating phenomenology to revealed theology (p. 61 n. 67).

196. Marion, "In the Name," p. 39, and references to other essays on pp. 52–53 n. 66.

197. Marion, "The Saturated Phenomenon," p. 177. Compare Marion, *In Excess*, p. 53.

198. I thus take issue with the criticism of Janicaud's critique in Zahavi, *Self-Awareness and Alterity*, pp. 264–265 n. 69; idem, "Michel Henry," pp. 234–237. The position I have taken is closer to Brian Harding, "What Is Minimalist Phenomenology?" *Alea* 6 (2007): 163–181, esp. 163–167.

199. Kearney, "On the Gift," p. 56.

200. Ibid. See the critical assessment by James K. A. Smith, "Respect and Donation: A Critique of Marion's Critique of Husserl," *American Catholic Philosophical Quarterly* 71 (1997): 523–538; idem, *Speech and Theology*, pp. 32–41.

201. Kearney, "On the Gift," p. 57.

202. It is of interest to note Derrida's response to Kearney's question about the possibility of a theological donation or a saturated phenomenon, "Contrary to Jean-Luc, I am interested in Christianity and in the gift in the Christian sense, and I would be interested in drawing conclusions in this respect" (Kearney, "On the Gift," p. 57). I suspect the comment was uttered with a touch of irony, but its main rhetorical force seems to have been to compel Marion to acknowledge the Christological underpinnings of his position. To that end, Derrida reminds his interlocutor of his own sustained interest in the economy of the gift in Christian texts (see ibid., pp. 59–60).

203. Kearney, "On the Gift," p. 63.

204. Ibid., pp. 63–64.

205. Marion, "The Recognition of the Gift," pp. 17–18.

206. Ibid., pp. 18–19.

207. Ibid., p. 26 (emphasis in original).

208. Marion, *God Without Being*, p. 139.

209. Ibid., pp. 139–140.

210. Ibid., p. 140.

211. Ibid., p. 142.

212. Ibid., p. 143. See, by contrast, the interpretation of Levinas in Marion, *In the Self's Place*, p. 137. Utilizing Levinas's claim regarding the priority of the saying to anything said, Marion elicits confirmation of the notion that truth—or, to be more precise, what he calls the third-order truth—is neither a "predication about things" nor the "manifestation of the thing" but the "event of an evidence, which shows itself only inasmuch as I tolerate its excess. And I can do so only inasmuch as I love it." Truth, in other words, is not a matter of noematic correspondence or unveiling but the witnessing that ensues from speaking the truth, a matter of veracity or sincerity that is expressed in the vocal attestation of saying without anything being said.

213. Marion, *Being Given*, p. 243; *Étant donné*, p. 337.

214. Marion, *Being Given*, p. 243; *Étant donné*, p. 337.

215. For a critique of Marion along these lines, see Kathryn Tanner, "Theology and the Limits of Phenomenology," in *Counter-Experiences*, pp. 201–231. See also the extended discussion of phenomenology and God in Gschwandtner, *Reading Jean-Luc Marion*, pp. 150–177. Derrida, *Writing and Difference*, p. 83 (*L'écriture et la différence*, p. 123), addressing the same question with respect to Levinas, maintained that his messianic eschatology "never bases its authority on Hebraic theses or texts. It seeks to be understood within a *recourse to experience itself*. Experience itself and that which is most irreducible within experience: the passage and departure toward the other; the other itself as what is most irreducibly other within it: Others" (emphasis in original). For citation of more of this passage, see Ch. 3 n. 203. A different criticism of Marion's Christological phenomenology based on emphasizing the ethical-prophetic dimensions of Christian faith is offered by Brian Robinette, "A Gift to Theology? Jean-Luc Marion's 'Saturated Phenomenon' in Christological Perspective," *Heythrop Journal* 48 (2007): 86–108, and the rejoinder by Joseph M. Rivera, "The Call and the Gifted in Christological Perspective: A Consideration of Brian Robinette's Critique of Jean-Luc Marion," *Heythrop Journal* 51 (2010): 1053–1060. See the criticism of Anthony J. Steinbock, "The Poor Phenomenon: Marion and the Problem of Givenness," in *Words of Life*, pp. 120–131.

216. Marion, *Being Given*, p. 241; *Étant donné*, p. 335. For an analysis of Marion's view on the icon, the face, the idol, and his phenomenology of givenness, see Manoussakis, *God after Metaphysics*, pp. 20–24, 40–45. Manoussakis suggests a fourth reduction that builds upon the three reductions delineated by Marion. He refers to this as the "prosopic reduction," a conception of personhood that evolves out of Marion's identification of the icon (*eikon*) as the face (*prosopon*). See also John Panteleimon Manoussakis, "Toward a Fourth Reduction?" in *After God: Richard Kearney*, pp. 21–33, and Smith, *Speech and Theology*, pp. 92–94.

217. Marion, *God Without Being*, pp. 17–18. Marion applies the Pauline depiction of Christ (Colossians 1:15) to all icons. See Welz, *Love's Transcendence*, pp. 354–355 n. 81.

218. A similar criticism against Marion is leveled by Schrag, *God as Otherwise than Being*, pp. 64, 89–92. For an even more strident critique of Marion's nonmetaphysical transcendence and the positing of a God without being, see Puntel, *Being and God*, pp. 302–408.

219. Kearney, "On the Gift," p. 58. See ibid., p. 60: "So Marion would try to account phenomenologically for the gift (which, again, I distinguish from *Gegebenheit*). But I doubt that there is a possibility of a phenomenology of the gift." The debate between Marion and Derrida on the gift and the phenomenology of the unapparent is analyzed by Caputo, "Apostles," pp. 203–208.

220. Kearney, "On the Gift," p. 66. See ibid., p. 71, where Derrida again challenges Marion's equation of *Gegebenheit* and the gift. My siding with Derrida against Marion has affinity with the position taken by Llewelyn, *Margins of Religion*, pp. 397–398.

221. The coinage is used by Derrida in Kearney, "On the Gift," p. 67.

222. Ibid., p. 70.

223. Ibid. A similar critique applies to Manoussakis, *God after Metaphysics*, p. 5: "It is this original revelation of beings in the epochal history of Being that compels us today to think and rethink God *after* Metaphysics through *aesthesis*. What is at stake, in other words, is an effort to disengage God from His metaphysical commitment to the sphere of transcendence (*epekeina*) by learning to recognize the ways He touches our immanence (*entautha*)—an Incarnational approach through and through" (emphasis in original). Appeal to an immanence rooted in the Christian doctrine of incarnation makes it unfeasible to argue that we can avoid the metaphysical commitment to transcendence. Manoussakis clarifies his position by citing Heidegger's observation that the dictum of Heraclitus (recorded by Aristotle in *De partibus animalium*, A 5, 645a 17) "For here too the gods are present" (*einai gar kai entautha theous*) implies that "the gods come to presence" (*daß Götter anwesen*) even "in the sphere of the familiar" (Heidegger, *Pathmarks*, pp. 269–270; *Wegmarken*, pp. 355–356). Manoussakis's reading obscures a fundamental difference between the Christological view he is promulgating and the mythopoeic idea expressed by Heidegger. According to Heidegger, the human can be said to dwell in the nearness of the gods—the precise term employed by Heidegger is *daimon*, based on the Heraclitean fragment he is exegeting, *ethos anthropoi daimon*; see Freeman, *Ancilla*, p. 32: "Character for man is destiny"; Kahn, *The Art and Thought of Heraclitus*, pp. 80–81, 260: "Man's character is his fate") because there is no transcendence but only immanence, and hence the gods are found "even here" (*kai entautha*), that is, in the commonplace, whereas according to Manoussakis, the belief in the Word made flesh transfigures the ordinary into the extraordinary, and hence there is no immanence that is not the instantiation of transcendence. Consider the statement of Manoussakis, *God after Metaphysics*, p. 121: "In the Incarnation it is the Creator who creates Himself anew in the creature's fashion—if in the Creation God gave the first man spirit, in the Incarnation man gives Him a body. It is the Incarnation that complements and completes the Creation." It seems to me that immanence is here perceived as subordinate to transcendence, and thus the logocentrism of the Platonic hierarchy is reified.

224. Caputo, "Apostles," p. 202, cites the image of the blossoming of the rose without why as one of several examples to illustrate Marion's idea of the gift without giver or recipient or the even more paradoxical notion of "a gift without a gift itself, where the gift now appears to be taken in the positivistic and reified sense which is precisely excluded by the reduction *to* donation. Giving without a gift is found where the lover gives his invisible love without a visible token, without a ring. The lover gives his love but he does not give a *thing*, something *present*" (emphasis in original). For Marion's own words to which Caputo is referring, see the comment in Kearney, "On the Gift," p. 65. Compare Caputo, "Apostles," p. 221 n. 29, where he supports his contention that "Marion depends heavily upon the later Heidegger" by concluding that Marion's conception of the gift "looks a lot like the mystical rose that blossoms without why, free from the principle of sufficient reason and all causality, that Heidegger comments upon in *The Principle of Reason*."

225. Connolly, *A World of Becoming*, p. 39.

226. See Tim Maudlin, *The Metaphysics Within Physics* (Oxford: Oxford University Press, 2007), pp. 78–103.

227. Connolly, *A World of Becoming*, p. 39.

228. Ibid., p. 74.

229. Ibid., p. 75.

230. Levinas, *God, Death, and Time*, p. 165.

231. Mark C. Taylor, "Refiguring Postmodern Times," in *Consciousness and Reality: Studies in Memory of Toshihiko Izutsu*, edited by Sayyid Jalāl al-Dīn Āshtiyānī, Hideichi Matsubara, Takashi Iwami, and Akiro Matsumoto (Leiden: Brill, 2000), p. 172. Compare Taylor, *Nots*, p. 54, and see the critical evaluation in Raschke, *Postmodernism*, pp. 43–45.

232. Derrida, *Writing and Difference*, p. 129; *L'écriture et la différence*, p. 190.

233. Derrida, *Writing and Difference*, p. 128; *L'écriture et la différence*, p. 188.

234. Schrag, *God as Otherwise than Being*, p. 72.

235. Ibid., p. 53.

236. Ibid., p. 73.

237. Ibid., p. 112.

238. Ibid., p. 113.

239. Ibid., p. 131.

240. Ibid., pp. 142–143.

241. Kearney, *The God Who May Be*, p. 10. On the role of the imagination in Kearney's theological enterprise, see B. Keith Putt, "Theopoetics of the Possible," in *After God: Richard Kearney*, pp. 241–269, esp. 242–250.

242. In many of my studies, I have emphasized that epistemologically there is no naked truth to behold but only truth exposed in the mantle of truth, which is to say, the veil of untruth. The view I have expressed can be profitably compared to the discussion on the metaphorics of the naked truth in Hans Blumenberg, *Paradigms for a Metaphorology*, translated with an afterword by Robert Savage (Ithaca: Cornell University Press, 2010), pp. 40–51, esp. 41: "The reader will surely agree that it is tautologous to speak of the 'naked truth' . . . But this metaphor does not mean to bring anything into the *concept* of truth; it projects conjectures and evaluations of a very complex kind over the top of the concept, as it were. The metaphor is intimately linked with the import and importance of *clothing*, considered as guise or disguise, in relation to which nakedness likewise splits into unmasking, into the uncovering of a deception, on the one hand, and shameless unveiling, the violation of a sacred mystery, on the other" (emphasis in original). See the discussion of Blumenberg's approach to truth and the overcoming of epistemological resignation in Elizabeth Brient, *The Immanence of the Infinite: Hans Blumenberg and the Threshold to Modernity* (Washington, DC: Catholic University Press, 2002), pp. 133–138.

243. Derrida, "On a Newly Arisen," p. 167 (emphasis in original).

BIBLIOGRAPHY

Aaron, David H. *Biblical Ambiguities: Metaphor, Semantics, and Divine Imagery*. Leiden: Brill, 2001.

Abe, Masao. "Non-Being and Mu: The Metaphysical Nature of Negativity in the East and the West," *Religious Studies* 11 (1975): 181–192.

Abrams, Daniel, ed. *The Book Bahir: An Edition Based on the Earliest Manuscripts*, with an introduction by Moshe Idel. Los Angeles: Cherub Press, 1994 (Hebrew).

Adelmann, Dieter. *Einheit des Bewusstseins als Grundproblem der Philosophie Hermann Cohens: Vorbereitende Untersuchung für eine historisch-verifizierende Konfrontation der Fundamentalontologie Martin Heideggers mit Hermann Cohens "System der Philosophie."* Potsdam: Universitätsverlag Potsdam, 2012.

Adorno, Theodor W. *Minima Moralia: Reflections from Damaged Life*, translated by E. F. N. Jephcott. London: Verso, 1978.

———. *Negative Dialectics*, translated by E. B. Ashton. New York: Seabury Press, 1979.

Adriannse, H. J. "After Theism," in *Religion: Beyond a Concept*, edited by Hent de Vries, 392–412. New York: Fordham University Press, 2008.

Aho, Kevin A. *Heidegger's Neglect of the Body*. Albany: State University of New York Press, 2009.

Ajzenstat, Oona. *Driven Back to the Text: The Premodern Sources of Levinas's Postmodernism*. Pittsburgh: Duquesne University Press, 2001.

Albertini, Francesca. *Das Verständnis des Seins bei Hermann Cohen: Von Neukantianismus zu einer jüdischen Religionsphilosophie*. Würzburg: Königshausen & Neumann, 2003.

———. "Emmanuel Levinas' Theological-Political Interpretation of Moses Maimonides," in *Moses Maimonides (1138–1204): His Religious, Scientific and Philosophical Wirkungsgeschichte in Different Cultural Contexts*, edited by Görge K. Hasselhoff and Otfried Fraisse, 573–585. Würzburg: Ergon Verlag, 2004.

Allen, Sarah. *The Philosophical Sense of Transcendence: Levinas and Plato on Loving Beyond Being*. Pittsburgh: Duquesne University Press, 2009.

Allen, William S. *Ellipsis: Of Poetry and the Experience of Language after Heidegger, Hölderlin, and Blanchot*. Albany: State University of New York Press, 2007.

Altizer, Thomas J. J. *The Call to Radical Theology*, edited and with an introduction by Lissa McCullough, foreword by David E. Klemm. Albany: State University of New York Press, 2012.

———. *The Contemporary Jesus*. Albany: State University of New York Press, 1997.

———. "Emptiness and God," in *The Religious Philosophy of Nishitani Keiji*, edited by Taitetsu Unno, 70–81. Berkeley: Asian Humanities Press, 1989.

———. *Genesis and Apocalypse: A Theological Voyage Toward Authentic Christianity*. Louisville: Westminster/John Knox Press, 1990.

———. *The Genesis of God: A Theological Genealogy*. Louisville: Westminster/John Knox Press, 1993.

———. *Godhead and the Nothing*. Albany: State University of New York Press, 2003.

———. "History as Apocalypse," in *Deconstruction and Theology*, 147–177. New York: Crossroad, 1982.

———. "The Impossible Possibility of Ethics," in *Saintly Influence: Edith Wyschogrod and the Possibilities of Philosophy of Religion*, edited by Eric Boynton and Martin Kavka, 31–47. New York: Fordham University Press, 2009.

———. *Living the Death of God: A Theological Memoir*. Albany: State University of New York Press, 2006.

———. *Mircea Eliade and the Dialectic of the Sacred*. Philadelphia: Westminster Press, 1963.

———. *The New Apocalypse: The Radical Christian Vision of William Blake*. Aurora: Davies Group Publishers, 2000.

———. *The New Gospel of Christian Atheism*. Aurora: Davies Group Publishers, 2002.

———. *Oriental Mysticism and Biblical Eschatology*. Philadelphia: Westminster Press, 1961.

———. *The Self-Embodiment of God*. New York: Harper & Row, 1977.

———. *Total Presence: The Language of Jesus and the Language of Today*. New York: Seabury Press, 1980.

———, and William Hamilton. *Radical Theology and the Death of God*. Indianapolis: Bobbs-Merrill, 1966.

Altman, William H. F. *Martin Heidegger and the First World War*: Being and Time *as Funeral Oration*. Lanham: Lexington Books, 2012.

Altmann, Alexander. "Franz Rosenzweig on History," in *The Philosophy of Franz Rosenzweig*, edited by Paul Mendes-Flohr, 124–137. Hanover: University Press of New England, 1988.

———. "The God of Religion, the God of Metaphysics and Wittgenstein's 'Language-Games,' " *Zeitschrift für Religions- und Geistesgeschichte* 39 (1987): 289–306.

———. "Hermann Cohens Begriff der Korrelation," in *In zwei Welten: Siegfried Moses zum fünfundsiebzigsten Geburtstag*, edited by Hans Tramer, 377–399. Tel-Aviv: Verlag Bitaon, 1962.

———. *The Meaning of Jewish Existence: Theological Essays 1930–1939*, edited by Alfred L. Ivry, introduction by Paul Mendes-Flohr, translated by Edith Ehrlich and Leonard H. Ehrlich. Hanover: University Press of New England, 1991.

———. *Von der mittelalterlichen zu modernen Aufklärung: Studien zu jüdischen Geistesgeschichte.* Tübingen: J. C. B. Mohr, 1987.

Amir, Yehoyada. " 'Liqra't meqor ḥayyei emet'—The Encounter of Franz Rosenzweig with the Poems of Judah Halevi," in *The Commentaries of Franz Rosenzweig to Ninety-Five Poems of Judah Halevi,* translated and annotated by Michael Swartz, 1–28. Jerusalem: Magnes Press, 2011 (Hebrew).

———. "Particularism and Universalism in the Religious Philosophy of Hermann Cohen," *Jerusalem Studies in Jewish Thought* 19 (2005): 643–675 (Hebrew).

Anckaert, Luc A. *A Critique of Infinity: Rosenzweig and Levinas.* Leuven: Peeters, 2006.

———. "Language, Ethics, and the Other between Athens and Jerusalem: A Comparative Study of Plato and Rosenzweig," *Philosophy East and West* 45 (1995): 545–567.

———. "The Transcendental Possibility of Experience in Rosenzweig and Levinas," in *Faith, Truth, and Reason: New Perspectives on Franz Rosenzweig's »Star of Redemption«,* edited by Yehoyada Amir, Yossi Turner, and Martin Brasser, 61–81. Munich: Verlag Karl Alber, 2012.

Anderson, John M. "Truth, Process, and Creature in Heidegger's Thought," in *Heidegger and the Quest for Truth,* edited with an introduction by Manfred S. Frings, 28–61. Chicago: Quadrangle Books, 1968.

Anderson, Pamela Sue. "Ineffable Knowledge and Gender," in *Rethinking Philosophy of Religion: Approaches from Continental Philosophy,* edited by Philip Goodchild, 162–183. New York: Fordham University Press, 2002.

Angelus Silesius, text selection and commentary by Gerhard Wehr. Wiesbaden: Marixverlag, 2011.

Anidjar, Gil. "Introduction: 'Once More, Once More': Derrida, the Arab, the Jew," in Jacques Derrida, *Acts of Religion,* edited, with an introduction, by Gil Anidjar, 1–39. New York: Routledge, 2002.

———. *The Jew, the Arab: A History of the Enemy.* Stanford: Stanford University Press, 2003.

Appelbaum, David. *Jacques Derrida's Ghost: A Conjuration.* Albany: State University of New York Press, 2009.

Arendt, Hannah. *The Life of the Mind.* 2 vols. New York: Harcourt Brace Jovanovich, 1978.

———. "Martin Heidegger at Eighty," in *Heidegger and Modern Philosophy: Critical Essays,* edited by Michael Murray, 293–303. New Haven: Yale University Press, 1978.

———. "Martin Heidegger ist achtzig Jahre alt," *Merkur* 23 (1969): 893–902.

———. *Menschen in finsteren Zeiten,* edited and translated by Ursula Ludz. Munich: Piper, 1989.

Ariel, David S. "Shem Tob Ibn Shem Tob's Kabbalistic Critique of Jewish Philosophy in the 'Commentary on the Sefirot': Study and Text," Ph.D. dissertation, Brandeis University, 1982.

Armstrong, Arthur H. *Plotinian and Christian Studies*. London: Variorum Reprints, 1970.

Askani, Hans-Christoph. *Das Problem der Übersetzung, dargestellt an Franz Rosenzweig*. Tübingen: Mohr Siebeck, 1997.

Assad, Maria L. "Time and Uncertainty: A Metaphorical Equation," in *Time and Uncertainty*, edited by Paul Harris and Michael Crawford, 19–30. Leiden: Brill, 2004.

Assmann, Jan. *Of God and Gods: Egypt, Israel, and the Rise of Monotheism*. Madison: University of Wisconsin Press, 2008.

———. *The Price of Monotheism*, translated by Robert Savage. Stanford: Stanford University Press, 2010.

Atlan, Henri. *The Sparks of Randomness*, vol. 2: *The Atheism of Scripture*, translated by Lenn J. Schramm. Stanford: Stanford University Press, 2013.

Babich, Babette E. *Words in Blood, Like Flowers: Philosophy and Poetry, Music and Eros in Hölderlin, Nietzsche, and Heidegger*. Albany: State University of New York Press, 2006.

Bahrani, Zainab. *The Graven Image: Representation in Babylonia and Assyria*. Philadelphia: University of Pennsylvania Press, 2003.

Banchetti-Robino, Marina Paola. "Husserl's Theory of Language as Calculus Ratiocinator," *Synthese* 112 (1997): 303–321.

Banham, Gary. "Derrida, the Messianic, and Eschatology," in *Rethinking Philosophy of Religion: Approaches from Continental Philosophy*, edited by Philip Goodchild, 123–135. New York: Fordham University Press, 2002.

Bannet, Eve Tavor. *Structuralism and the Logic of Dissent*. London: Macmillan, 1989.

Barak, Uriel. "Rabbi A. I. Kook on the Nature of Franz Rosenzweig's Connection to Kabbalah," *Da'at* 67 (2009): 97–116 (Hebrew).

Baring, Edward. *The Young Derrida and French Philosophy, 1945–1968*. Cambridge: Cambridge University Press, 2011.

Batnitzky, Leora. "Dialogue as Judgment, Not Mutual Affirmation: A New Look at Franz Rosenzweig's Dialogical Philosophy," *Journal of Religion* 79 (1999): 523–544.

———. "Franz Rosenzweig on Translation and Exile," *Jewish Studies Quarterly* 14 (2007): 131–143.

———. "Hermann Cohen and Leo Strauss," in *Hermann Cohen's Ethics*, edited by Robert Gibbs, 187–212. Leiden: Brill, 2006.

———. *Idolatry and Representation: The Philosophy of Franz Rosenzweig Reconsidered*. Princeton: Princeton University Press, 2000.

———. "Jewish Philosophy After Metaphysics," in *Religion After Metaphysics*, edited by Mark A. Wrathall, 146–165. Cambridge: Cambridge University Press, 2003.

———. *Leo Strauss and Emmanuel Levinas: Philosophy and the Politics of Revelation*. Cambridge: Cambridge University Press, 2006.

———. "Levinas Between German Metaphysics and Christian Theology," in *The Exorbitant: Emmanuel Levinas Between Jews and Christians*, edited by Kevin Hart and Michael A. Signer, 17–31. New York: Fordham University Press, 2010.

———. "The New Thinking: Philosophy or Religion?" in *Franz Rosenzweigs "neues Denken": Internationaler Kongreß-Kassel 2004*, edited by Wolfdietrich Schmied-Kowarzik, 2 vols., 79–89. Freiburg: Verlag Karl Alber, 2006.

———. "Rosenzweig's Aesthetic Theory and Jewish Unheimlichkeit," *New German Critique* 77 (1999): 87–122.

Benjamin, Mara H. *Rosenzweig's Bible: Reinventing Scripture for Jewish Modernity.* Cambridge: Cambridge University Press, 2009.

Benjamin, Walter. *Selected Writings, Volume 3: 1935–1938*, translated by Edmund Jephcott, Howard Eiland, and others, edited by Howard Eiland and Michael W. Jennings. Cambridge, MA: Harvard University Press, 2002.

———. *Selected Writings, Volume 4: 1938–1940*, translated by Edmund Jephcott and others, edited by Howard Eiland and Michael W. Jennings. Cambridge, MA: Harvard University Press, 2003.

Bennington, Geoffrey. *Interrupting Derrida.* London: Routledge, 2000.

———. "Mosaic Fragment: If Derrida Were an Egyptian . . . ," in *Derrida: A Critical Reader*, edited by David Wood, 97–119. Oxford: Blackwell, 1992.

———, and Jacques Derrida. *Derrida.* Paris: Éditions du Seuil, 2008.

———. *Jacques Derrida*, translated by Geoffrey Bennington. Chicago: University of Chicago Press, 1993.

Ben-Pazi, Hanoch. "Love Discourse: Rosenzweig vs. Plato. The *Banquet: Song of Songs*, the *Symposium* and the *Star of Redemption*," in *Faith, Truth, and Reason: New Perspectives on Franz Rosenzweig's »Star of Redemption«*, edited by Yehoyada Amir, Yossi Turner, and Martin Brasser, 105–124. Munich: Verlag Karl Alber, 2012.

Benso, Silvia. "Emancipation and the Future of the Utopian: On Vattimo's Philosophy of History," in *Between Nihlism and Politics: The Hermeneutics of Gianni Vattimo*, edited by Silvia Benso and Brian Schroeder, 203–219. Albany: State University of New York Press, 2010.

———. *The Face of Things: A Different Side of Ethics.* Albany: State University of New York Press, 2000.

Bensussan, Gérard. "The Last, the Remnant . . . (Derrida and Rosenzweig)," in *Judeities: Questions for Jacques Derrida*, edited by Bettina Bergo, Joseph Cohen, and Raphael Zagury-Orly, translated by Bettina Bergo and Michael B. Smith, 36–51. New York: Fordham University Press, 2007.

Bergo, Bettina. "Anxious Responsibility and Responsible Anxiety: Kierkegaard and Levinas on Ethics and Religion," in *Rethinking Philosophy of Religion: Approaches from Continental Philosophy*, edited by Philip Goodchild, 94–122. New York: Fordham University Press, 2002.

———. "The Historian and the Messianic 'Now': Reading Edith Wyschogrod's *An Ethics of Remembering*," in *Saintly Influence: Edith Wyschogrod and the Possibilities of Philosophy of Religion*, edited by Eric Boynton and Martin Kavka, 202–218. New York: Fordham University Press, 2009.

————. *Levinas Between Ethics and Politics: For the Beauty that Adorns the Earth.* Pittsburgh: Duquesne University Press, 2003.

————. "Levinas's Weak Messianism in Time and Flesh, or the Insistence of Messiah Ben David," in *The Messianic Now: Philosophy, Religion, Culture,* edited by Arthur Bradley and Paul Fletcher, 45–68. London: Routledge, 2011.

————. "Ontology, Transcendence, and Immanence in Emmanuel Levinas' Philosophy," *Research in Phenomenology* 35 (2005): 141–177.

————. "The Time and Language of Messianism: Levinas and Saint Paul," in *Levinas and the Ancients,* edited by Brian Schroeder and Silvia Benso, 178–195. Bloomington: Indiana University Press, 2008.

Bernasconi, Robert. "Different Styles of Eschatology: Derrida's Take on Levinas' Political Messianism," *Research in Phenomenology* 28 (1998): 3–19.

————. "No Exit: Levinas' Aporetic Account of Transcendence," *Research in Phenomenology* 35 (2005): 101–117.

————. *The Question of Language in Heidegger's History of Being.* Atlantic Highlands: Humanities Press, 1985.

————. "Skepticism in the Face of Philosophy," in *Re-Reading Levinas,* edited by Robert Bernasconi and Simon Critchley, 149–161. Bloomington: Indiana University Press, 1991.

Bernet, Rudolf. "L'autre du temps," in *Emmanuel Lévinas: Positivité et transcendance,* edited by Jean-Luc Marion, 143–163. Paris: Presses Universitaires de France, 2000.

————. "Levinas's Critique of Husserl," in *The Cambridge Companion to Levinas,* edited by Simon Critchley and Robert Bernasconi, 82–99. Cambridge: Cambridge University Press, 2002.

Bertolino, Luca. "Die frage ,Was ist?' bei Hermann Cohen und Franz Rosenzweig," *Journal of Jewish Thought and Philosophy* 21 (2013): 57–71.

————. "'Schöpfung aus Nichts' in Franz Rosenzweigs Stern der Erlösung," *Jewish Studies Quarterly* 13 (2006): 247–264.

Betz, John R. "Schelling in Rosenzweigs *Stern der Erlösung,*" *Neue Zeitschrift für Systematische Theologie und Religionsphilosophie* 45 (2003): 208–226.

Bielik-Robson, Agata. "Tarrying with the Apocalypse: The Wary Messianism of Rosenzweig and Levinas," in *The Messianic Now: Philosophy, Religion, Culture,* edited by Arthur Bradley and Paul Fletcher, 69–86. London: Routledge, 2011.

Biemann, Asher D. *Inventing New Beginnings: On the Idea of Renaissance in Modern Judaism.* Stanford: Stanford University Press, 2009.

Biemel, Walter. "Poetry and Language in Heidegger," in *On Heidegger and Language,* edited and translated by Joseph J. Kockelmans, 65–105. Evanston: Northwestern University Press, 1972.

Bienenstock, Myriam. "Auf Schellings Spuren im *Stern der Erlösung,*" in *Rosenzweig als Leser: Kontextuelle Kommentare zum "Stern der Erlösung,"* edited by Martin Brasser, 273–290. Tübingen: Max Niemeyer Verlag, 2004.

———. "Hermann Cohen on the Concept of History: An Invention of Prophetism?" *Journal of Jewish Thought and Philosophy* 20 (2012): 55–70.

———. "Hermann Cohen über Freiheit und Selbstbestimmung," in *Religious Apologetics—Philosophical Argumentation*, edited by Yossef Schwartz and Volkhard Krech, 509–529. Tübingen: Mohr Siebeck, 2004.

———. "Recalling the Past in Rosenzweig's *Star of Redemption*," *Modern Judaism* 23 (2003): 226–242.

Bigger, Charles P. *Between Chora and the Good: Metaphor's Metaphysical Neighborhood*. New York: Fordham University Press, 2005.

Birault, Henri. "Thinking and Poeticizing in Heidegger," in *On Heidegger and Language*, edited and translated by Joseph J. Kockelmans, 147–168. Evanston: Northwestern University Press, 1972.

Blake, William. *The Complete Poetry and Prose of William Blake*, newly revised edition, edited by David V. Erdman, commentary by Harold Bloom. Berkeley: University of California Press, 1982.

Blanchot, Maurice. *Awaiting Oblivion*, translated by John Gregg. Lincoln: University of Nebraska Press, 1997.

———. *The Gaze of Orpheus and Other Literary Essays*, preface by Geoffrey Hartman, translated by Lydia Davis, edited with an afterword by P. Adams Sitney. Barrytown: Station Hill Press, 1981.

———. *The Infinite Conversation*, translation and foreword by Susan Hanson. Minneapolis: University of Minnesota Press, 1993.

———. *The Space of Literature*, translated, with an introduction, by Ann Smock. Lincoln: University of Nebraska Press, 1982.

———. *The Writing of Disaster*, translated by Ann Smock. Lincoln: University of Nebraska Press, 1986.

Bloch, Ernst. *The Principle of Hope*, translated by Neville Plaice, Stephen Plaice, and Paul Knight, 3 vols. Cambridge, MA: MIT Press, 1986.

Blond, Louis P. "Franz Rosenzweig: Homelessness in Time," *New German Critique* 37 (2010): 27–58.

———. *Heidegger and Nietzsche: Overcoming Metaphysics*. New York: Continuum, 2010.

Bloom, Harold. "The Breaking of Form," in *Deconstruction and Criticism*, edited by Harold Bloom, 1–37. New York: Seabury Press, 1979.

———. *Kabbalah and Criticism*. New York: Seabury Press, 1975.

———. *A Map of Misreading*. Oxford: Oxford University Press, 1975.

Blumenberg, Hans. *Care Crosses the River*, translated by Paul Fleming. Stanford: Stanford University Press, 2010.

———. *Paradigms for a Metaphorology*, translated with an afterword by Robert Savage. Ithaca: Cornell University Press, 2010.

———. *Work on Myth*, translated by Robert M. Wallace. Cambridge, MA: MIT Press, 1985.

Boeve, Lieven. "Christus Postmodernus: An Attempt at Apophatic Christology," in
    The Myriad Christ: Plurality and the Quest for Unity in Contemporary Christology,
    edited by Terrence Merrigan and Jacques Haers, 577–593. Leuven: Peeters Press,
    2000.

———. "Negative Theology and Theological Hermeneutics: The Particularity of
    Naming God," *Journal of Philosophy and Scripture* 3 (2006): 1–13.

———. "The Rediscovery of Negative Theology Today: The Narrow Gulf Between
    Theology and Philosophy," in *Théologie négative*, edited by Marco M. Olivetti,
    443–459. Milan: CEDAM, 2002.

Bongmba, Elias. "Eschatology: Levinasian Hints in a Preface," in *Levinas and Biblical
    Studies*, edited by Tamara Cohn Eskenazi, Gary A. Phillips, and David Jobling,
    75–90. Atlanta: Society of Biblical Literature, 2003.

Bouretz, Pierre. *Witnesses for the Future: Philosophy and Messianism*, translated by
    Michael Smith. Baltimore: Johns Hopkins University Press, 2010.

Bourgeois, Patrick L. "Ricoeur between Levinas and Heidegger: Another's Further
    Alterity," *Journal of French and Francophone Philosophy* 11 (2010): 32–51.

Bradley, Arthur. "'Mystic Atheism': Julia Kristeva's Negative Theology," *Theology &
    Sexuality* 14 (2008): 279–292.

———. *Negative Theology and Modern French Philosophy*. London: Routledge, 2004.

———. "Without Negative Theology: Deconstruction and the Politics of Negative
    Theology," *Heythrop Journal* 42 (2001): 133–147.

Braiterman, Zachary. "Cyclical Motions and the Force of Repetition in the Thought of
    Franz Rosenzweig," in *Beginning/Again: Toward a Hermeneutics of Jewish Texts*,
    edited by Aryeh Cohen and Shaul Magid, 215–238. New York: Seven Bridges Press,
    2002.

———. "'Into Life'? Franz Rosenzweig and the Figure of Death," *AJS Review* 23 (1998):
    203–221.

———. *The Shape of Revelation: Aesthetics and Modern Jewish Thought*. Stanford:
    Stanford University Press, 2007.

Brann, Eva T. H. *The World of the Imagination: Sum and Substance*. Boston: Rowman &
    Littlefield, 1991.

Brasser, Martin. "Die verändernde Kraft des Wörtchens 'ist': Heideggers Kasseler
    Vorträge und Rosenzweigs neues Denken," in *Franz Rosenzweigs "neues Denken":
    Internationaler Kongreß-Kassel 2004*, edited by Wolfdietrich Schmied-Kowarzik, 2
    vols., 216–227. Freiburg: Verlag Karl Alber, 2006.

Braver, Lee. *Groundless Grounds: A Study of Wittgenstein and Heidegger*. Cambridge, MA:
    MIT Press, 2012.

Brient, Elizabeth. *The Immanence of the Infinite: Hans Blumenberg and the Threshold to
    Modernity*. Washington, DC: Catholic University Press, 2002.

Bruckstein, Almut Sh. "Hermann Cohen. *Ethics of Maimonides*: Residues of Jewish
    Philosophy—Traumatized," in *Hermann Cohen's Ethics*, edited by Robert Gibbs,
    115–125. Leiden: Brill, 2006.

————. "Joining the Narrators: A Philosophy of Talmudic Hermeneutics," in Steven Kepnes, Peter Ochs, and Robert Gibbs, *Reasoning After Revelation: Dialogues in Postmodern Jewish Philosophy*, 105–121. Boulder: Westview Press, 1998.

————. "On Jewish Hermeneutics: Maimonides and Bachya as Vectors in Cohen's Philosophy of Origin," in *Hermann Cohen's Philosophy of Religion: International Conference in Jerusalem 1996*, edited by Stéphane Moses and Hartwig Wiedebach, 35–50. Hildesheim: Georg Olms Verlag, 1997.

Bruns, Gerald L. "The Concepts of Art and Poetry in Emmanuel Levinas's Writings," in *The Cambridge Companion to Levinas*, edited by Simon Critchley and Robert Bernasconi, 206–233. Cambridge: Cambridge University Press, 2002.

————. "Disappeared: Heidegger and the Emancipation of Language," in *Languages of the Unsayable: The Play of Negativity in Literature and Literary Theory*, edited by Sanford Budick and Wolfgang Iser, 117–139. New York: Columbia University Press, 1989.

————. *Maurice Blanchot: The Refusal of Philosophy*. Baltimore: Johns Hopkins University Press, 1997.

————. "The Remembrance of Language: An Introduction to Gadamer's Poetics," in Hans-Georg Gadamer, *Gadamer on Celan: "Who Am I and Who Are You?" and Other Essays*, translated and edited by Richard Heinemann and Bruce Krajewski, 1–51. Albany: State University of New York Press, 1997.

Bryant, Levi R. *Difference and Givenness: Deleuze's Transcendental Empiricism and the Ontology of Immanence*. Evanston: Northwestern University Press, 2008.

Buber, Martin. *Eclipse of God: Studies in the Relation Between Religion and Philosophy*. New York: Harper & Row, 1952.

————. *Good and Evil: Two Interpretations*. New York: Charles Scribner's Sons, 1952.

————. *I and Thou*, a new translation, with a prologue and notes by Walter Kaufmann. New York: Charles Scribner's Sons, 1970.

————. *Ich und Du*. Heidelberg: Verlag Lambert Schneider, 1974.

————. *Kingship of God*, third edition, translated by Richard Scheimann. Amherst: Humanity Books, 1990.

————. *The Knowledge of Man: A Philosophy of the Interhuman*, edited with an introductory essay by Maurice Friedman, translated by Maurice Friedman and Ronald Gregor Smith. New York: Harper & Row, 1965.

————. *Moses: The Revelation and the Covenant*, with an introduction by Michael Fishbane. Amherst: Humanity Books, 1998.

————. *On Judaism*, edited by Nahum N. Glatzer. New York: Schocken Books, 1967.

————. *The Origin and Meaning of Hasidism*. New York: Horizon Press, 1960.

————. *Two Types of Faith: A Study of the Interpretation of Judaism and Christianity*, translated by Norman P. Goldhawk. New York: Macmillan, 1951.

————, and Franz Rosenzweig. *Scripture and Translation*, translated by Lawrence Rosenwald and Everett Fox. Bloomington: Indiana University Press, 1994.

Buchanan, Brett. *Onto-Ethologies: The Animal Environments of Uexküll, Heidegger, Merleau-Ponty, and Deleuze*. Albany: State University of New York Press, 2008.

Bulhof, Ilse N. "Being Open as a Form of Negative Theology: On Nominalism, Negative Theology, and Derrida's Performative Interpretation of Khôra," in *Flight of the Gods: Philosophical Perspectives on Negative Theology*, edited by Ilse N. Bulhof and Laurens ten Kate, 195–222. New York: Fordham University Press, 2000.

———. "Negative Theology as Spirituality: Deep Openness," in *Théologie négative*, edited by Marco M. Olivetti, 423–441. Milan: CEDAM, 2002.

Burrus, Virginia. "A Saint of One's Own: Emmanuel Levinas, Eliezer ben Hyrcanus, and Eulalia of Mérida," *L'Espirit Créateur* 50 (2010): 6–20.

———. "Seeing God in Bodies: Wolfson, Rosenzweig, Augustine," in *Reading the Church Fathers*, edited by Scot Douglass and Morwenna Ludlow, 44–59. London: T & T Clark, 2011.

———. "Wyschogrod's Hand: Saints, Animality, and the Labor of Love," *Philosophy Today* 55 (2011): 412–421.

Butler, Judith. *Parting Ways: Jewishness and the Critique of Zionism*. New York: Columbia University Press, 2012.

Byers, Damian. *Intentionality and Transcendence: Closure and Openness in Husserl's Phenomenology*. Madison: University of Wisconsin Press, 2002.

Calarco, Matthew. "Faced by Animals," in *Radicalizing Levinas*, edited by Peter Atterton and Matthew Calarco, 113–133. Albany: State University of New York Press, 2010.

———. "Heidegger's Zoontology," in *Animal Philosophy: Essential Readings in Continental Thought*, edited by Matthew Calarco and Peter Atterton, 18–30. New York: Continuum, 2004.

———. *Zoographies: The Question of the Animal from Heidegger to Derrida*. New York: Columbia University Press, 2008.

Capelle, Philippe. "Phénoménologies, Religion et Théologies chez Martin Heidegger," *Studia Phaenomenologica* 1 (2001): 181–196.

Caputo, John D. "Apostles of the Impossible: On God and the Gift in Derrida and Marion," in *God, the Gift, and Postmodernism*, edited by John D. Caputo and Michael J. Scanlon, 185–222. Bloomington: Indiana University Press, 1999.

———. "The Experience of God and the Axiology of the Impossible," in *Religion After Metaphysics*, edited by Mark A. Wrathall, 123–145. Cambridge: Cambridge University Press, 2003.

———. "Hearing the Voices of the Dead: Wyschogrod, Megill, and the Heterological Historian," in *Saintly Influence: Edith Wyschogrod and the Possibilities of Philosophy of Religion*, edited by Eric Boynton and Martin Kavka, 161–174. New York: Fordham University Press, 2009.

———. "Mysticism and Transgression: Derrida and Meister Eckhart," in *Derrida and Deconstruction*, edited by Hugh Silverman, 24–39. New York: Routledge, 1989.

———. *The Prayers and Tears of Jacques Derrida: Religion without Religion*. Bloomington: Indiana University Press, 1997.

———. "Shedding Tears Beyond Being: Derrida's Experience of Prayer," in *Théologie négative*, edited by Marco M. Olivetti, 861–880. Milan: CEDAM, 2002.

———. "Temporal Transcendence: The Very Idea of *à venir* in Derrida," in *Transcendence and Beyond: A Postmodern Inquiry*, edited by John D. Caputo and Michael J. Scanlon, 188–203. Bloomington: Indiana University Press, 2007.

———, and Gianni Vattimo. *After the Death of God*, edited by Jeffrey W. Robbins, with an afterword by Gabriel Vahanian. New York: Columbia University Press, 2007.

Carlson, Thomas A. "Blindness and the Decision to See: On Revelation and Reception in Jean-Luc Marion," in *Counter-Experiences: Reading Jean-Luc Marion*, edited by Kevin Hart, 153–179. Notre Dame: University of Notre Dame Press, 2007.

———. *Indiscretion: Finitude and the Naming of God*. Chicago: University of Chicago Press, 1999.

Carter, Robert E. *The Kyoto School: An Introduction*, with a foreword by Thomas P. Kasulis. Albany: State University of New York Press, 2013.

———. *The Nothingness Beyond God: An Introduction to the Philosophy of Nishida Kitarō*. New York: Paragon House, 1997.

Casper, Bernhard. *Das dialogische Denken: Eine Untersuchung der religionsphilosophischen Bedeutung Franz Rosenzweigs, Ferdinand Ebners und Martin Bubers*. Freiburg: Verlag Karl Alber, 2002.

———. "Die Gründung einer philosophischen Theologie im Ereignis," *Dialegesthai* 2003, available at http://mondodomani.org/dialegesthai/bc01.htm.

———. "'Ereignis': Bemerkungen zu Franz Rosenzweig und Martin Heidegger," in *Jüdisches Denken in einer Welt ohne Gott: Festschrift für Stéphane Mosès*, edited by Jens Mattern, Gabriel Motzkin, and Shimon Sandbank, 66–77. Berlin: Verlag Vorwerk 8, 2000.

———. *Religion der Erfahrung. Einführung in das Denken Franz Rosenzweigs*. Paderborn: Schöningh, 2004.

———. "Zeit—Erfahrung—Erlösung. Zur Bedeutung Rosenzweigs angesichts des Denkens des 20. Jahrhunderts," in *Der Philosoph Franz Rosenzweig (1886–1929): Internationaler Kongreß-Kassel 1986*, edited by Wolfdietrich Schmied-Kowarzik, 2 vols., 553–566. Freiburg: Verlag Karl Alber, 1988.

Caygill, Howard. *Levinas and the Political*. London: Routledge, 2002.

Celan, Paul. *Der Meridian: Endfassung—Entwürfe—Materialien*, edited by Bernhard Böschenstein and Heino Schmull with assistance from Michael Schwarzkopf and Christiane Wittkop. Frankfurt am Main: Suhrkamp Verlag, 1999.

———. *The Meridian: Final Version—Drafts—Materials*, edited by Bernhard Böschenstein and Heino Schmull with assistance from Michael Schwarzkopf and Christiane Wittkop, translated and with a preface by Pierre Joris. Stanford: Stanford University Press, 2011.

———. *Poems of Paul Celan*, translated by Michael Hamburger. New York: Persea Books, 1972.

Chacón, Rodrigo. "German Sokrates: Heidegger, Arendt, Strauss," Ph.D. dissertation, New School for Social Research, 2009.

Chalier, Catherine. "Franz Rosenzweig: Temps liturgique et temps historique," *Le Nouveaux Cahiers* 72 (1983): 28–31.

———. "L'âme de la vie: Lévinas, lecteur de R. Haïm de Volozin," in *Ce Cahier de l'Herne: Emmanuel Levinas*, edited by Catherine Chalier and Miguel Abensour, 442–460. Paris: Éditions de l'Herne, 1991.

———. "L'idolâtrie de l'être à travers le pensée d'Emmanuel Lévinas," in *Idoles: Données et débats. Actes du 24ᵉ Colloque des intellectuels juifs de langue française*, edited by Jean Halpérin et Georges Lévitte, 89–102. Paris: Denoël, 1985.

———. *La trace de l'infini: Emmanuel Levinas et la source hébraïque*. Paris: Cerf, 2002.

———. "The Messianic Utopia," in *Emmanuel Levinas: Critical Assessments of Leading Philosophers*, vol. 3: *Levinas, Judaism, and the Philosophy of Religion*, edited by Claire Elise Katz, 44–58. New York: Routledge, 2005.

Chanter, Tina. "Conditions: The Politics of Ontology and the Temporality of the Feminine," in *Addressing Levinas*, edited by Eric Sean Nelson, Antje Kapust, and Kent Still, 310–337. Evanston: Northwestern University Press, 2005.

———. *Time, Death, and the Feminine: Levinas with Heidegger*. Stanford: Stanford University Press, 2001.

Cheetham, Tom. *Green Man, Earth Angel: The Prophetic Tradition and the Battle for the Soul of the World*, foreword by Robert Sardello. Albany: State University of New York Press, 2005.

———. *The World Turned Inside Out: Henry Corbin and Islamic Mysticism*. Woodstock: Spring Journal Books, 2003.

The Cherubinic Wanderer, translation and foreword by Maria Shrady, introduction and notes by Josef Schmidt, preface by E. J. Furcha. New York: Paulist Press, 1986.

Chiurazzi, Gaetano. "The Experiment of Nihilism: Interpretation and Experience of Truth in Gianni Vattimo," in *Between Nihlism and Politics: The Hermeneutics of Gianni Vattimo*, edited by Silvia Benso and Brian Schroeder, 15–32. Albany: State University of New York Press, 2010.

Christ, Carol P. "Nothingness, Awakening, Insight, New Naming," in *Experience of the Sacred: Readings in the Phenomenology of Religion*, edited by Summer B. Twiss and Walter H. Conser Jr., 121–128. Hanover: University Press of New England, 1992.

Chroust, Anton-Hermann. *Aristotle: Protrepticus—A Reconstruction*. Notre Dame: University of Notre Dame Press, 1964.

Cixous, Hélène. *Portrait of Jacques Derrida as a Young Jewish Saint*, translated by Beverley Bie Brahic. New York: Columbia University Press, 2004.

———, and Jacques Derrida. *Veils*, translated by Geoffrey Bennington. Stanford: Stanford University Press, 2001.

Cohen, Arthur A. *The Myth of the Judeo-Christian Tradition and Other Dissenting Essays*. New York: Harper & Row, 1970.

———. *The Natural and the Supernatural Jew*. New York: Pantheon Books, 1962.

Cohen, Hermann. *Das Prinzip der Infinitesimal-Methode und seine Geschichte*, introduction by Peter Schulthess [*Werke* 5]. Hildesheim: Georg Olms Verlag, 2005.

————. *Der Begriff der Religion im System der Philosophie*, introduction by Andrea Poma, second, revised edition [*Werke* 10]. Hildesheim: Georg Olms Verlag, 2002.

————. *Ethics of Maimonides*, translated with commentary by Almut Sh. Bruckstein, foreword by Robert Gibbs. Madison: University of Wisconsin Press, 2004.

————. *Ethik des reinen Willens*, with an introduction by Peter A. Schmid [*Werke* 7]. Hildesheim: Georg Olms Verlag, 2008.

————. *Kleinere Schriften IV, 1907–1912*, edited and introduced by Hartwig Wiedebach [*Werke* 15]. Hildesheim: Georg Olms Verlag, 2009.

————. *Kleinere Schriften V, 1913–1915*, edited and introduced by Hartwig Wiederbach [*Werke* 16]. Hildesheim: Georg Olms Verlag, 1997.

————. *Kleinere Schriften VI, 1916–1918*, edited and introduced by Hartwig Wiedebach [*Werke* 17]. Hildesheim: Georg Olms Verlag, 2002.

————. *Reason and Hope: Selections from the Jewish Writings of Hermann Cohen*, translated by Eva Jospe. New York: W. W. Norton, 1971.

————. *Religion der Vernunft aus den Quellen des Judentums*, second edition. Frankfurt am Main: J. Kaufmann Verlag, 1929.

————. *Religion of Reason Out of the Sources of Judaism*, translated, with an introduction by Simon Kaplan, introductory essay by Leo Strauss, and introductory essays for the second edition by Steven S. Schwarzschild and Kenneth Seeskin. Atlanta: Scholars Press, 1995.

Cohen, Richard A. "Against Theology, or 'The Devotion of a Theology Without Theodicy': Levinas on Religion," in *The Exorbitant: Emmanuel Levinas Between Jews and Christians*, edited by Kevin Hart and Michael A. Signer, 74–89. New York: Fordham University Press, 2010.

————. "Authentic Selfhood in Heidegger and Rosenzweig," *Human Studies* 16 (1993): 111–128.

————. *Elevations: The Height of the Good in Rosenzweig and Levinas*. Chicago: University of Chicago Press, 1994.

————. *Ethics, Exegesis and Philosophy: Interpretation After Levinas*. Cambridge: Cambridge University Press, 2001.

————. *Levinasian Meditations: Ethics, Philosophy, and Religion*. Pittsburgh: Duquesne University Press, 2010.

Coleridge, Samuel Taylor. *Biographia Literaria or Biographical Sketches of My Literary Life and Opinions*, vol. 7 of *The Collected Works of Samuel Taylor Coleridge*, edited by James Engell and W. Jackson Bate. Princeton: Princeton University Press, 1983.

Colette, Jacques. "Lévinas et la phénoménologie husserlienne," in *Le cahiers de la nuit surveillée: Emmanuel Lévinas*, edited by Jacques Rolland, 19–36. Lagrasse: Verdier, 1984.

Come, Arnold B. *Kierkegaard as Humanist: Discovering My Self*. Montreal: McGill-Queen's University Press, 1995.

The Complete Mystical Works of Meister Eckhart, translated and edited by Maurice O'Connell Walshe, revised with a foreword by Bernard McGinn. New York: Crossroad, 2009.

Conley, Tom. "A Trace of Style," in *Displacement: Derrida and After*, edited by Mark
    Krupnick, 74–92. Bloomington: Indiana University Press, 1983.
Connolly, William E. *A World of Becoming*. Durham: Duke University Press, 2011.
Corbin, Henry. *Creative Imagination in the Ṣūfism of Ibn ʿArabī*, translated by Ralph
    Manheim. Princeton: Princeton University Press, 1969.
———. *Le paradoxe du monothéisme*. Paris: Éditions de L'Herne, 2003.
Cornell, Drucilla. "Where Love Begins: Sexual Difference and the Limit of the Mascu-
    line Symbolic," in *Derrida and Feminism: Recasting the Question of Woman*, edited
    by Ellen K. Feder, Mary C. Rawlinson, and Emily Zakin, 161–206. New York:
    Routledge, 1997.
Coyne, Ryan David. "The End of Care: Augustine and the Development of Heidegger's
    Philosophy," Ph.D. thesis, University of Chicago, 2008.
Craig, Megan. *Levinas and James: Toward a Pragmatic Phenomenology*. Bloomington:
    Indiana University Press, 2010.
Crignon, Philippe. "Figuration: Emmanuel Levinas and the Image," *Yale French Studies*
    104 (2004): 100–125.
Cristaudo, Wayne. "Franz Rosenzweig's 'Troubling' Critique of Islam," *Rosenzweig
    Yearbook* 2 (2007): 43–86.
———. *Religion, Redemption, and Revolution: The New Speech Thinking of Franz
    Rosenzweig and Eugen Rosenstock-Huessy*. Toronto: University of Toronto Press,
    2012.
Critchley, Simon. *The Ethics of Deconstruction: Derrida and Levinas*. West Lafayette:
    Purdue University Press, 1992.
———. *The Faith of the Faithless: Experiments in Political Theology*. London: Verso, 2012.
———. "*Il y a*—A Dying Stronger than Death (Blanchot with Levinas)," *Oxford
    Literary Review* 15 (1993): 81–131.
———. "*Il y a*—Holding Levinas's Hand to Blanchot's Fire," in *Maurice Blanchot: The
    Demand of Writing*, edited by Carolyn Bailey Gill, 108–122. London: Routledge, 1996.
———. *Very Little . . . Almost Nothing: Death, Philosophy, Literature*. London: Rout-
    ledge, 1997.
Crockett, Clayton. "Post-Modernism and Its Secrets: Religion without Religion," *Cross
    Currents* 52 (2003): 499–515.
———. *Radical Political Theology: Religion and Politics After Liberalism*. New York:
    Columbia University Press, 2011.
Crowe, Benjamin D. *Heidegger's Phenomenology of Religion*. Bloomington: Indiana
    University Press, 2008.
———. *Heidegger's Religious Origins: Destruction and Authenticity*. Bloomington:
    Indiana University Press, 2006.
Crownfield, David R. "The Question of God: Thinking after Heidegger," *Philosophy
    Today* 40 (1996): 47–54.
Cutter, William. "Ghostly Hebrew, Ghastly Speech: Scholem to Rosenzweig, 1926,"
    Prooftexts 10 (1990): 413–433.

Dagan, Hagai. "Hatramah and Deḥikat ha-Keṣ in F. Rosenzweig's Concept of Redemption," *Da'at* 50–52 (2003): 391–407 (Hebrew).

Dahlstrom, Daniel O. "Being at the Beginning: Heidegger's Interpretation of Heraclitus," in *Interpreting Heidegger: Critical Essays*, edited by Daniel O. Dahlstrom, 135–155. Cambridge: Cambridge University Press, 2011.

———. *Heidegger's Concept of Truth*. Cambridge: Cambridge University Press, 1994.

Dalton, Drew M. *Longing for the Other: Levinas and Metaphysical Desire*. Pittsburgh: Duquesne University Press, 2009.

Dastur, Françoise. "The Ekstatico-Horizonal Constitution of Temporality," in *Critical Heidegger*, edited by Christopher Macann, 158–168. London: Routledge, 1996.

———. *Heidegger and the Question of Time*, translated by François Raffoul and David Pettigrew. Atlantic Highlands: Humanities Press, 1998.

———. "La pensée à venir: une phénoménologie de l'inapparent?" in *L'avenir de la philosophie est-il grec?* edited by Catherine Collobert, 135–148. Saint-Laurent, Quebec: Fides, 2002.

———. "Phenomenology of the Event: Waiting and Surprise," *Hypatia* 15 (2000): 178–189.

Dault, David. "Rosenzweig and Derrida at Yom Kippur," in *Derrida and Religion: Other Testaments*, edited by Yvonne Sherwood and Kevin Hart, 97–109. New York: Routledge, 2005.

Davies, Paul. "A Linear Narrative? Blanchot with Heidegger in the Work of Levinas," in *Philosophers' Poets*, edited by David Wood, 37–69. London: Routledge, 1990.

Davis, Bret W. *Heidegger and the Will: On the Way to Gelassenheit*. Evanston: Northwestern University Press, 2007.

de Beistegui, Miguel. *Immanence: Deleuze and Philosophy*. Edinburgh: Edinburgh University Press, 2010.

———. *Thinking with Heidegger: Displacements*. Bloomington: Indiana University Press, 2003.

———. *Truth and Genesis: Philosophy as Differential Ontology*. Bloomington: Indiana University Press, 2004.

de Boer, Theodore. "Levinas and Negative Theology," in *Théologie négative*, edited by Marco M. Olivetti, 849–859. Milan: CEDAM, 2002.

———. *The Rationality of Transcendence: Studies in the Philosophy of Emmanuel Levinas*. Amsterdam: J. C. Gieben, 1997.

de Greef, Jan. "Skepticism and Reason," in Levinas, *Face to Face with Levinas*, edited by Richard A. Cohen, 159–179. Albany: State University of New York Press, 1986.

de Launay, Marc. "Messianisme et philologie du langage," *Modern Language Notes* 127 (2012): 645–664.

de Vries, Hent. *Minimal Theologies: Critiques of Secular Reason in Adorno and Levinas*, translated by Geoffrey Hale. Baltimore: Johns Hopkins University Press, 2005.

———. *Philosophy and the Turn to Religion*. Baltimore: John Hopkins University Press, 1999.

———. "The Shibboleth Effect: On Reading Paul Celan," in *Judeities: Questions for Jacques Derrida*, edited by Bettina Bergo, Joseph Cohen, and Raphael Zagury-Orly, translated by Bettina Bergo and Michael B. Smith, 175–213. New York: Fordham University Press, 2007.

——. "The Theology of the Sign and the Sign of Theology: The Apophatics of Deconstruction," in *Flight of the Gods: Philosophical Perspectives on Negative Theology*, edited by Ilse N. Bulhof and Laurens ten Kate, 166–194. New York: Fordham University Press, 2000.

de Warren, Nicolas. "The Inner Night: Towards a Phenomenology of (Dreamless) Sleep," in *On Time—New Contributions to the Husserlian Phenomenology of Time*, edited by Dieter Lohmar and Ichiro Yamaguchi, 273–294. Dordrecht: Springer, 2010.

Del Nevo, Matthew. "The Kabbalistic Heart of Levinas," *Culture, Theory and Critique* 52 (2011): 183–198.

Deleuze, Gilles. "Active and Reactive," in *The New Nietzsche: Contemporary Styles of Interpretation*, edited and introduced by David B. Allison, 80–106. New York: Delta Books, 1977.

——. *Difference and Repetition*, translated by Paul Patton. New York: Columbia University Press, 1994.

——. *Nietzsche and Philosophy*, translated by Hugh Tomlinson. London: Athlone Press, 1983.

——. "Nomad Thought," in *The New Nietzsche: Contemporary Styles of Interpretation*, edited by David B. Allison, 142–149. New York: Delta Books, 1977.

——. *Pure Immanence: Essays on a Life*, with an introduction by John Rajchman, translated by Anne Boyman. New York: Zone Books, 2001.

Depraz, Natalie. *Transcendance et incarnation: le statut de l'intersubjectivité comme altérité à soi chez Husserl*. Paris: J. Vrin, 1995.

Derrida, Jacques. "Abraham, the Other," in *Judeities: Questions for Jacques Derrida*, edited by Bettina Bergo, Joseph Cohen, and Raphael Zagury-Orly, translated by Bettina Bergo and Michael B. Smith, 1–35. New York: Fordham University Press, 2007.

——. *Acts of Religion*, edited, with an introduction, by Gil Anidjar. New York: Routledge, 2002.

——. *Adieu to Emmanuel Levinas*, translated by Pascale-Anne Brault and Michael Naas. Stanford: Stanford University Press, 1999.

——. ". . . and pomegranates," in *Violence, Identity, and Self-Determination*, edited by Hent de Vries and Samuel Weber, 326–344. Stanford: Stanford University Press, 1997.

——. *The Animal That Therefore I Am*, edited by Marie-Louise Mallet, translated by David Wills. New York: Fordham University Press, 2008.

——. *Archive Fever: A Freudian Impression*, translated by Eric Prenowitz. Chicago: University of Chicago Press, 1996.

——. "At This Very Moment in This Work Here I Am," in *Re-Reading Levinas*, edited by Robert Bernasconi and Simon Critchley, 11–48. Bloomington: Indiana University Press, 1991.

————. *De la grammatologie.* Paris: Éditions de Minuit, 1967.

————. *Demeure: Fiction and Testimony*, translated by Elizabeth Rottenberg. Stanford: Stanford University Press, 2000.

————. "Des Tours de Babel," in *Difference in Translation*, edited with an introduction by Joseph F. Graham, 165–207. Ithaca: Cornell University Press, 1985.

————. "Devant la Loi," in *Kafka and the Contemporary Critical Performance: Centenary Readings*, edited by Alan Udoff, 128–149. Bloomington: Indiana University Press, 1987.

————. *Dissemination*, translated, with an introduction and additional notes, by Barbara Johnson. Chicago: University of Chicago Press, 1981.

————. *Donner la mort.* Paris: Éditions Galilée, 1999.

————. *Donner le temps: I. La fausse monnaie.* Paris: Éditions Galilée, 1991.

————. *The Ear of the Other: Otiobiography, Transference, Translation*, edited by Christie McDonald, translated by Peggy Kamuf. Lincoln: University of Nebraska Press, 1998.

————. *L'écriture et la différence.* Paris: Éditions du Seuil, 1967.

————. *Eyes of the University: Right to Philosophy 2*, translated by Jan Plug and others. Stanford: Stanford University Press, 2004.

————. *Geneses, Genealogies, Genres, and Genius: The Secrets of the Archive*, translated by Beverley Bie Brahic. New York: Columbia University Press, 2006.

————. *The Gift of Death*, translated by David Wills. Chicago: University of Chicago Press, 1995.

————. *Given Time: I. Counterfeit Money*, translated by Peggy Kamuf. Chicago: University of Chicago Press, 1992.

————. *Glas*, translated by John P. Leavey Jr. and Richard Rand. Lincoln: University of Nebraska Press, 1986.

————. "An Interview with Derrida," in *Derrida and Différance*, edited by David Wood and Robert Bernasconi, 71–82. Evanston: Northwestern University Press, 1988.

————. *Learning to Live Finally: An Interview with Jean Birnbaum*, translated by Pascale-Anne Brault and Michael Naas, with a bibliography by Peter Krapp. Hoboken: Melville House, 2007.

————. *Literature in Secret: An Impossible Filiation*, in *The Gift of Death*, translated by David Wills, second edition, 117–158. Chicago: University of Chicago Press, 2008.

————. "Living On: Border Lines," in *Deconstruction and Criticism*, edited by Harold Bloom, 75–176. New York: Seabury Press, 1979.

————. *Margins of Philosophy*, translated, with additional notes by Alan Bass. Chicago: University of Chicago Press, 1982.

————. *Memories of the Blind: The Self-Portrait and Other Ruins*, translated by Pascale-Anne Brault and Michael Naas. Chicago: University of Chicago Press, 1993.

————. *Monolingualism of the Other; or, The Prosthesis of Origin*, translated by Patrick Mensah. Stanford: Stanford University Press, 1998.

————. *Of Grammatology*, translated by Gayatri Chakravorty Spivak, corrected edition. Baltimore: Johns Hopkins University Press, 1977.

————. *Of Hospitality: Ann Dufourmantelle Invites Jacques Derrida to Respond*, translated by Rachel Bowlby. Stanford: Stanford University Press, 2000.

————. "On a Newly Arisen Apocalyptic Tone in Philosophy," in *Raising the Tone of Philosophy: Late Essays by Immanuel Kant, Transformative Critique by Jacques Derrida*, edited by Peter Fenves, 117–171. Baltimore: Johns Hopkins University Press, 1993.

————. *On Cosmopolitanism and Forgiveness*, translated by Mark Dooley and Michael Hughes, with a preface by Simon Critchley and Richard Kearney. London: Routledge, 2001.

————. *On the Name*, edited by Thomas Dutoit, translated by David Wood, John P. Leavey Jr., and Ian McLeod. Stanford: Stanford University Press, 1995.

————. *On Touching—Jean-Luc Nancy*, translated by Christine Irizarry. Stanford: Stanford University Press, 2005.

————. "Point de folie—Maintenant l'architecture," in *Architecture Theory Since 1968*, edited by K. Michael Hays, 566–581. Cambridge, MA: MIT Press, 1998.

————. *Points . . . Interviews, 1974–1994*, edited by Elisabeth Weber, translated by Peggy Kamuf and others. Stanford: Stanford University Press, 1995.

————. *Politics of Friendship*, translated by George Collins. London: Verso, 1997.

————. *Positions*, translated and annotated by Alan Bass. Chicago: University of Chicago Press, 1981.

————. "Post-Scriptum: Aporias, Ways and Voices," translated by John Leavey Jr., in *Derrida and Negative Theology*, edited by Howard Coward and Toby Foshay, 283–323. Albany: State University of New York Press, 1992.

————. *Psyche: Inventions of the Other, Volume I*, edited by Peggy Kamuf and Elizabeth Rottenberg. Stanford: Stanford University Press, 2007.

————. *Psyche: Inventions of the Other, Volume II*, edited by Peggy Kamuf and Elizabeth Rottenberg. Stanford: Stanford University Press, 2008.

————. *Sauf le nom*. Paris: Galilée, 1993.

————. "Sending: On Representation," in *Transforming the Hermeneutic Context: From Nietzsche to Nancy*, edited by Gayle L. Ormiston and Alan D. Schrift, 107–138. Albany: State University of New York Press, 1990.

————. "Shibboleth for Paul Celan," in *Word Traces: Readings of Paul Celan*, edited by Aris Fioretos, 3–72. Baltimore: Johns Hopkins University Press, 1994.

————. *Signéponge/Signsponge*, translated by Richard Rand. New York: Columbia University Press, 1984.

————. *Sovereignties in Question: The Poetics of Paul Celan*, edited by Thomas Dutoit and Outi Pasanen. New York: Fordham University Press, 2005.

————. *Specters of Marx: The State of the Debt, the Work of Mourning, and the New International*, translated by Peggy Kamuf, introduction by Bernd Magnus and Stephen Cullenberg. New York: Routledge, 1994.

————. *Speech and Phenomena and Other Essays on Husserl's Theory of Signs*, translated, with an introduction, by David B. Allison, preface by Newton Garver. Evanston: Northwestern University Press, 1973.

————. "Tense," in *The Path of Archaic Thinking: Unfolding the Work of John Sallis*, edited by Kenneth Maly, 49–74. Albany: State University of New York Press, 1995.

————. "A Testimony Given . . . ," in *Questioning Judaism: Interviews by Elisabeth Weber*, translated by Rachel Bowlby, 39–58. Stanford: Stanford University Press, 2004.

————. "To Forgive: The Unforgivable and the Imprescriptible," in *Questioning God*, edited by John D. Caputo, Mark Dooley, and Michael J. Scanlon, 21–51. Bloomington: Indiana University Press, 2001.

————. *Writing and Difference*, translated, with an introduction and additional notes, by Alan Bass. Chicago: University of Chicago Press, 1978.

————, and Gianni Vattimo, *Religion*. Stanford: Stanford University Press, 1998.

Derrida Jacques, and Maurizio Ferraris. *A Taste for the Secret*, translated by Giacomo Donis, edited by Giacomo Donis and David Webb. Cambridge: Polity Press, 2001.

Despite Oneself: Subjectivity and Its Secret in Kierkegaard and Levinas, edited by Claudia Welz and Karl Verstrynge. London: Turnshare, 2008.

Dewey, Nicholas. "Truth, Method, and Transcendence," in *Consequences of Hermeneutics: Fifty Years after Gadamer's Truth and Method*, edited by Jeff Malpas and Santiago Zabala, 25–44. Evanston: Northwestern University Press, 2010.

Diamond, Cora. "Wittgenstein on Religious Belief: The Gulf Between Us," in *Religion and Wittgenstein's Legacy*, edited by Dewi Z. Phillips and Mario von der Ruhr, 99–138. Burlington: Ashgate, 2004.

Diamond, James. "Exegetical Idealization: Hermann Cohen's Religion of Reason out of the Sources of Maimonides," *Journal of Jewish Thought and Philosophy* 18 (2010): 49–73.

Dietrich, Wendell S. "The Function of the Idea of Messianic Mankind in Hermann Cohen's Later Thought," *Journal of the American Academy of Religion* 48 (1980): 245–258.

————. "Is Rosenzweig an Ethical Monotheist? A Debate with the New Francophone Literature," in *Der Philosoph Franz Rosenzweig (1886–1929): Internationaler Kongreß-Kassel 1986*, edited by Wolfdietrich Schmied-Kowarzik, 2 vols., 891–900. Freiburg: Verlag Karl Alber, 1988.

Dober, Hans Martin. "Franz Rosenzweigs *Der Stern der Erlösung* als liturgietheoretische Konzeption," in *Faith, Truth, and Reason: New Perspectives on Franz Rosenzweig's »Star of Redemption«*, edited by Yehoyada Amir, Yossi Turner, and Martin Brasser, 185–201. Munich: Verlag Karl Alber, 2012.

Doneson, Daniel. "Beginning at the Beginning: On the Starting Point of Reflection," in *Heidegger's Jewish Followers: Essays on Hannah Arendt, Leo Strauss, Hans Jonas, and Emmanuel Levinas*, edited by Samuel Fleischacker, 106–130. Pittsburgh: Duquesne University Press, 2008.

Donkel, Douglas L. *The Understanding of Difference in Heidegger and Derrida*. New York: Peter Lang, 1992.

Drabinski, John E. *Sensibility and Singularity: The Problem of Phenomenology in Levinas*. Albany: State University of New York Press, 2001.

Drob, Sanford L. *Kabbalah and Postmodernism: A Dialogue*. New York: Peter Lang, 2009.

Düring, Ingemar. *Aristotle's Protrepticus: An Attempt at Reconstruction*. Gothenburg: Acta Universitatis Gothoburgensis, 1961.

Düttmann, Alexander García. *The Gift of Language: Memory and Promise in Adorno, Benjamin, Heidegger, and Rosenzweig*, translated by Arline Lyons. Syracuse: Syracuse University Press, 2000.

Eco, Umberto. *Semiotics and the Philosophy of Language*. Bloomington: Indiana University Press, 1984.

Edgecomb, Kevin P. "An Appreciation and Précis of Jacob Neusner's *Theology of the Oral Torah: Revealing the Justice of God*," in *The Documentary History of Judaism and Its Recent Interpreters*, edited by Jacob Neusner, 53–156. Lanham: University Press of America, 2010.

Eisen, Arnold. "Re-Reading Heschel on the Commandments," *Modern Judaism* 9 (1989): 1–33.

Elden, Stuart. "Heidegger's Animals," *Continental Philosophy Review* 39 (2006): 273–291.

Elliott, Brian. *Phenomenology and Imagination in Husserl and Heidegger*. London: Routledge, 2005.

———. "Reduced Phenomena and Unreserved Debts in Marion's Reading of Heidegger," in *Givenness and God: Questions of Jean-Luc Marion*, edited by Ian Leask and Eoin Cassidy, 87–97. New York: Fordham University Press, 2005.

Emad, Parvis. *Translation and Interpretation: Learning from* Beiträge, edited, with an introduction, by Frank Schalow. Bucharest: Zeta Books, 2012.

Erlewine, Robert. "Hermann Cohen and the Humane Intolerance of Ethical Monotheism," *Jewish Studies Quarterly* 15 (2008): 148–173.

———. *Monotheism and Tolerance: Recovering a Religion of Reason*. Bloomington: Indiana University Press, 2010.

———. "Rediscovering Heschel: Theocentrism, Secularism, and Porous Thinking," *Modern Judaism* 32 (2012): 174–194.

Fackenheim, Emil L. *To Mend the World: Foundations of Post-Holocaust Jewish Theology*. New York: Schocken, 1989.

Fagenblat, Michael. *A Covenant of Creatures: Levinas's Philosophy of Judaism*. Stanford: Stanford University Press, 2010.

———. "*Il y a du quotidien*: Levinas and Heidegger on the Self," *Philosophy and Social Criticism* 28 (2002): 578–604.

———. "Lacking All Interest: Levinas, Leibowitz, and the Pure Practice of Religion," *Harvard Theological Review* 97 (2004): 1–32.

Farber, Marvin. "Heidegger on the Essence of Truth," *Philosophy and Phenomenological Research* 18 (1958): 523–532.

Farías, Victor. *Heidegger et le nazisme*, translated by Myriam Benarroch and Jean-Baptiste Grasset. Paris: Éditions Verdier, 1986.

Feldman, Louis H. *"Remember Amalek!": Vengeance, Zealotry, and Group Destruction in the Bible According to Philo, Pseudo-Philo, and Josephus.* Cincinnati: Hebrew Union College Press, 2004.

Felstiner, John. "'All Poets Are Yids': The Voice of the 'Other' in Paul Celan," in *Demonizing the Other: Antisemitism, Racism and Xenophobia*, edited by Robert S. Wistrich, 244–256. London: Routledge, 1999.

Fenton, Paul B. "Henry Corbin et la mystique juive," in *Henry Corbin: Philosophies et sagesses des religions du livre: Actes du Colloque "Henry Corbin," Sorbonne, les 6–8 Novembre 2003*, edited by Mohammad Ali Amir-Moezzi, Christian Jambet, and Pierre Lory, 151–164. Turnhout: Brepols Publishers, 2005.

Feron, Etienne. *De l'idée de transcendance à la question du langage: l'itinéraire philosophique de Levinas.* Grenoble: J. Millon, 1982.

Fichte, Johann Gottlieb. *Foundations of Transcendental Philosophy (Wissenschaftslehre) nova methodo (1796/99)*, translated and edited by Daniel Breazeale. Ithaca: Cornell University Press, 1992.

———. *Science of Knowledge with the First and Second Introductions*, edited and translated by Peter Heath and John Lachs. Cambridge: Cambridge University Press, 1982.

Finch, Henry Leroy. *Simone Weil and the Intellect of Grace*, edited by Martin Andic, foreword by Annie Finch. New York: Continuum, 1999.

Finlayson, James Gordon. "On Not Being Silent in the Darkness: Adorno's Singular Apophaticism," *Harvard Theological Review* 105 (2012): 1–32.

Fiorato, Pierfrancesco. *Geschichtliche Ewigkeit: Ursprung und Zeitlichkeit in der Philosophie Hermann Cohens.* Würzburg: Königshausen & Neumann, 1993.

———. "Notes on Future and History in Hermann Cohen's Anti-Eschatological Messianism," in *Hermann Cohen's Critical Idealism*, edited by Reinier Munk, 133–160. Dordrecht: Springer, 2005.

———, and Hartwig Wiedebach. "Hermann Cohen im Stern der Erlösung," in *Rosenzweig als Leser: Kontextuelle Kommentare zum "Stern der Erlösung,"* edited by Martin Brasser, 305–355. Tübingen: Max Niemeyer Verlag, 2004.

Fischer, Norbert, and Friedrich-Wilhelm von Hermann. "Die christliche Botschaft und das Denken Heideggers. Durchblick durch das Thema," in *Heidegger und die christliche Tradition*, edited by Norbert Fischer and Friedrich Wilhelm von Hermann, 9–20. Hamburg: Felix Meiner Verlag, 2007.

Fishbane, Michael. *Biblical Myth and Rabbinic Mythmaking.* Oxford: Oxford University Press, 2003.

———. *The Garments of Torah: Essays in Biblical Hermeneutics.* Bloomington: Indiana University Press, 1989.

———. "The Song of Songs and Ancient Jewish Religiosity: Between Eros and History," in *Von Enoch bis Kafka: Festschrift für Karl E. Grözinger zum 60. Geburtstag*, edited by Manfred Voigts, 69–81. Wiesbaden: Harrassowitz Verlag, 2002.

Fisher, Cass. *Contemplative Nation: A Philosophical Account of Jewish Language*. Stanford: Stanford University Press, 2012.

———. "Divine Perfections at the Center of the Star: Reassessing Rosenzweig's Theological Language," *Modern Judaism* 31 (2011): 188–212.

———. "Speaking Metaphysically of a Metaphysical God: Rosenzweig, Schelling, and the Metaphysical Divide," in *German-Jewish Thought Between Religion and Politics: Festschrift in Honor of Paul Mendes-Flohr on the Occasion of His Seventieth Birthday*, edited by Christian Wiese and Martina Urban, 151–166. Berlin: Walter de Gruyter, 2012.

Flynn, Bernard. "Merleau-Ponty and the Philosophical Position of Skepticism," in *Merleau-Ponty and the Possibilities of Philosophy: Transforming the Tradition*, edited by Bernard Flynn, Wayne J. Froman, and Robert Vallier, 117–128. Albany: State University of New York Press, 2009.

Forestier, Florian. "The Phenomenon and the Transcendental: Jean-Luc Marion, Marc Richir, and the Issue of Phenomenalization," *Continental Philosophy Review* 45 (2012): 381–402.

Forthomme, Bernard. *Une philosophie de la transcendance: La métaphysique d'Emmanuel Lévinas*. Paris: J. Vrin, 1979.

Foshay, Toby A. "Denegation, Nonduality, and Language in Derrida and Dōgen," *Philosophy East and West* 44 (1994): 543–558.

———. "Introduction: Denegation and Resentment," in *Derrida and Negative Theology*, edited by Howard Coward and Toby Foshay, 1–24. Albany: State University of New York Press, 1992.

———. "Resentment and Apophasis: The Trace of the Other in Levinas, Derrida and Gans," in *Shadow of Spirit: Postmodernism and Religion*, edited by Philippa Berry and Andrew Wernick, 81–92. London: Routledge, 1992.

Fóti, Véronique M. *Heidegger and the Poets: Poiēsis/Sophia/Technē*. Atlantic Highlands: Humanities Press, 1992.

Fraisse, Ottfried. "Das Licht des Geistes und das Licht der Erlösung: Ein Beitrag zum Verhältnis von Idealismus und rabbinischer Tradition in Franz Rosenzweigs *Stern der Erlösung*," in *Faith, Truth, and Reason: New Perspectives on Franz Rosenzweig's »Star of Redemption«*, edited by Yehoyada Amir, Yossi Turner, and Martin Brasser, 203–222. Munich: Verlag Karl Alber, 2012.

Franke, William. "Apophasis and the Turn of Philosophy to Religion: From Neoplatonic Negative Theology to Postmodern Negation of Theology," *International Journal for Philosophy of Religion* 60 (2006): 61–76.

———. "Franz Rosenzweig and the Emergence of a Postsecular Philosophy of the Unsayable," *International Journal for Philosophy of Religion* 58 (2005): 161–180.

———. *On What Cannot Be Said: Apophatic Discourses in Philosophy, Religion, Literature, and the Arts*, vol. 2: *Modern and Contemporary Transformations*, edited with theoretical and critical essays by William Franke. Notre Dame: University of Notre Dame Press, 2007.

Franks, Paul. *All or Nothing: Systematicity, Transcendental Arguments, and Skepticism in German Idealism*. Cambridge, MA: Harvard University Press, 2005.

——. "Everyday Speech and Revelatory Speech in Rosenzweig and Wittgenstein," *Philosophy Today* 50 (2006): 24–39.

——. "Talking of Eyebrows: Religion and the Space of Reasons after Wittgenstein, Rosenzweig, and Diamond," in *Religion and Wittgenstein's Legacy*, edited by Dewi Z. Phillips and Mario von der Ruhr, 139–160. Burlington: Ashgate, 2004.

Freeman, Kathleen. *Ancilla to the Pre-Socratic Philosophers*. Cambridge, MA: Harvard University Press, 1978.

Freudenthal, Gideon. *No Religion without Idolatry: Mendelssohn's Jewish Enlightenment*. Notre Dame: University of Notre Dame Press, 2012.

Freund, Else-Rahel. *Franz Rosenzweig's Philosophy of Existence: An Analysis of* The Star of Redemption. The Hague: Martinus Nijhoff, 1979.

Freund, Richard A. "La tradition mystique juive et Simone Weil," *Cahiers Simone Weil* 10 (1987): 289–295.

Friedman, Maurice S. *Martin Buber: The Life of Dialogue*, fourth edition. New York: Routledge, 2002.

Froman, Wayne J. "Rosenzweig and Heidegger on 'the Moment' ('der Augenblick')," in *Franz Rosenzweigs "neues Denken": Internationaler Kongreß-Kassel 2004*, edited by Wolfdietrich Schmied-Kowarzik, 2 vols., 228–246. Freiburg: Verlag Karl Alber, 2006.

Froment-Meurice, Marc. *That Is to Say: Heidegger's Poetics*, translated by Jan Plu. Stanford: Stanford University Press, 1998.

Frunză, Sandu. "Aspects of the Connection Between Judaism and Christianity in Franz Rosenzweig's Philosophy," in *Essays in Honor of Moshe Idel*, edited by Sandu Frunză and Mihaela Frunză, 200–227. Cluj-Napoca: Provo Press, 2008.

Funkenstein, Amos. "An Escape from History: Rosenzweig on the Destiny of Judaism," *History and Memory* 2 (1990): 117–135.

Gadamer, Hans-Georg. *Gadamer on Celan: "Who Am I and Who Are You?" and Other Essays*, translated and edited by Richard Heinemann and Bruce Krajewski. Albany: State University of New York Press, 1997.

——. *Philosophical Hermeneutics*, translated and edited by David E. Linge. Berkeley: University of California Press, 1976.

——. *The Relevance of the Beautiful and Other Essays*, edited with an introduction by Robert Bernasconi. Cambridge: Cambridge University Press, 1986.

——. *Truth and Method*, second, revised edition, translation revised by Joel Weinsheimer and Donald G. Marshall. New York: Continuum, 2011.

Gall, Robert S. *Beyond Theism and Atheism: Heidegger's Significance for Religious Thinking*. Dordrecht: Martinus Nijhoff, 1987.

——. "Of/From Theology and Deconstruction," *Journal of the American Academy of Religion* 58 (1990): 413–437.

Gallagher, Shaun. *The Inordinance of Time*. Evanston: Northwestern University Press, 1998.

Galli, Barbara. *Franz Rosenzweig and Jehuda Halevi: Translating, Translations, and Translators*, foreword by Paul Mendes-Flohr. Montreal: McGill-Queen's University Press, 1995.

———. "Franz Rosenzweig's Theory of Translation Through Kabbalistic Motifs," in *The Legacy of Franz Rosenzweig: Collected Essays*, edited by Luc Anckaert, Martin Brasser, and Norbert Samuelson, 189–197. Leuven: Leuven University Press, 2004.

———. *On Wings of Moonlight: Elliot R. Wolfson's Poetry in the Path of Rosenzweig and Celan*. Montreal: McGill Queens University Press, 2007.

———. "Poetics of Time in Rosenzweig and Kafka," in *Faith, Truth, and Reason: New Perspectives on Franz Rosenzweig's »Star of Redemption«*, edited by Yehoyada Amir, Yossi Turner, and Martin Brasser, 259–275. Munich: Verlag Karl Alber, 2012.

———. "Rosenzweig Speaking of Meanings and Monotheism in Biblical Anthropomorphisms," *Journal of Jewish Thought and Philosophy* 2 (1993): 157–184.

———. "Rosenzweig's All, Kabbalistically Reflected," in *Franz Rosenzweigs "neues Denken": Internationaler Kongreß-Kassel 2004*, edited by Wolfdietrich Schmied-Kowarzik, 2 vols., 713–724. Freiburg: Verlag Karl Alber, 2006.

Garb, Jonathan. "Rabbi Kook and His Sources: From Kabbalistic Historiosophy to National Mysticism," in *Studies in Modern Religions, Religious Movements and the Bābī-Bahā'ī Faiths*, 77–96. Leiden: Brill, 2004.

Garrido-Maturano, Angel E. "Die Erfüllung der Kunst im Schweigen: Bemerkungen zu Franz Rosenzweigs Theorie der Kunst," in *Théologie négative*, edited by Marco M. Olivetti, 695–720. Milan: CEDAM, 2002.

Gasché, Rodolphe. *Inventions of Difference: On Jacques Derrida*. Cambridge, MA: Harvard University Press, 1994.

———. *The Tain of the Mirror: Derrida and the Philosophy of Reflection*. Cambridge, MA: Harvard University Press, 1986.

———. "Tuned to Accord: On Heidegger's Concept of Truth," in *Heidegger Toward the Turn: Essays on the Work of the 1930s*, edited by James Risser, 31–49. Albany: State University of New York Press, 1999.

Gauthier, David J. *Martin Heidegger, Emmanuel Levinas, and the Politics of Dwelling*. Lanham: Rowman & Littlefield, 2011.

Geller, Jay. *On Freud's Jewish Body: Mitigating Circumcisions*. New York: Fordham University Press, 2007.

George, Theodore D. "A Monstrous Absolute: Schelling, Kant, and the Poetic Turn in Philosophy," in *Schelling Now: Contemporary Readings*, edited by Jason M. Wirth, 135–146. Bloomington: Indiana University Press, 2005.

Geroulanos, Stefanos. *An Atheism That Is Not Humanist Emerges in French Thought*. Stanford: Stanford University Press, 2010.

Gibbons, Sarah L. *Kant's Theory of Imagination: Bridging Gaps in Judgment and Experience*. Oxford: Oxford University Press, 1994.

Gibbs, Robert. *Correlations in Rosenzweig and Levinas*. Princeton: Princeton University Press, 1992.

———. "The Disincarnation of the Word: The Trace of God in Reading Scripture," in *The Exorbitant: Emmanuel Levinas Between Jews and Christians*, edited by Kevin Hart and Michael A. Signer, 32–51. New York: Fordham University Press, 2010.

———. "Hermann Cohen's Messianism: The History of the Future," in *"Religion der Vernunft aus den Quellen des Judentums": Tradition und Ursprungsdenken in Hermann Cohens Spätwerk Internationale Konferenz in Zürich 1998*, edited by Helmut Holzhey, Gabriel Motzkin, and Hartwig Wiedebach, 331–349. Hildesheim: Georg Olms Verlag, 2000.

———. "The Limits of Thought: Rosenzweig, Schelling, and Cohen," *Zeitschrift für Philosophische Forschung* 43 (1989): 618–640.

———. "Lines, Circles, Points: Messianic Epistemology in Cohen, Rosenzweig and Benjamin," in *Toward the Millennium: Messianic Expectations from the Bible to Waco*, edited by Peter Schäfer and Mark R. Cohen, 363–382. Leiden: Brill, 1997.

———. "Messianic Epistemology," in *Derrida and Religion: Other Testaments*, edited by Yvonne Sherwood and Kevin Hart, 119–129. New York: Routledge, 2005.

———. "The Name of God in Levinas's Philosophy," in *Saintly Influence: Edith Wyschogrod and the Possibilities of Philosophy of Religion*, edited by Eric Boynton and Martin Kavka, 97–112. New York: Fordham University Press, 2009.

Givsan, Hassan. "Rosenzweig und Heidegger," in *Franz Rosenzweigs "neues Denken": Internationaler Kongreß-Kassel 2004*, edited by Wolfdietrich Schmied-Kowarzik, 2 vols., 179–202. Freiburg: Verlag Karl Alber, 2006.

Glatzer, Nahum N. "The Concept of Language in the Thought of Franz Rosenzweig," in *The Philosophy of Franz Rosenzweig*, edited by Paul Mendes-Flohr, 172–184. Hanover: University Press of New England, 1988.

———. *Franz Rosenzweig: His Life and Thought*. Philadelphia: Jewish Publication Society of America, 1953.

———. "Was Franz Rosenzweig a Mystic?" in *Studies in Jewish Religious and Intellectual History Presented to Alexander Altmann on the Occasion of His Seventieth Birthday*, edited by Siegfried Stein and Raphael Loewe, 121–132. University, Alabama: University of Alabama Press, 1979.

Godelier, Maurice. *The Enigma of the Gift*, translated by Nora Scott. Chicago: University of Chicago Press, 1999.

Goetschel, Roland. "Le paradigme Maimonidien chez Hermann Cohen," in *The Thought of Maimonides: Philosophical and Legal Studies*, edited by Ira Robinson, Lawrence Kaplan, and Julien Bauer, 384–403. Lewiston: Edwin Mellen Press, 1990.

Goetschel, Willi. *The Discipline of Philosophy and the Invention of Modern Jewish Thought*. New York: Fordham University Press, 2013.

Gonzalez, Francisco J. *Plato and Heidegger: A Question of Dialogue*. University Park: Pennsylvania State University Press, 2009.

Goodchild, Philip. "Why Is Philosophy So Compromised with God?" in *Deleuze and Religion*, edited by Mary Bryden, 156–166. New York: Routledge, 2001.

Goodman, Lenn E. *God of Abraham*. New York: Oxford University, 1996.

Goodman-Thau, Eveline. *Aufstand der Wassen: Jüdische Hermeneutik zwischen Tradition und Moderne*. Berlin: Philo Verlagsgesellschaft, 2002.

Gordon, Peter E. "Continental Divide: Ernst Cassirer and Martin Heidegger at Davos, 1929—An Allegory of Intellectual History," *Modern Intellectual History* 1 (2004): 219–248.

———. *Continental Divide: Heidegger, Cassirer, Davos*. Cambridge, MA: Harvard University Press, 2010.

———. "Franz Rosenzweig and the Philosophy of Jewish Existence," in *The Cambridge Companion to Modern Jewish Philosophy*, edited by Michael L. Morgan and Peter Eli Gordon, 122–146. Cambridge: Cambridge University Press, 2007.

———. "Redemption in the World: Authenticity and Existence in Rosenzweig and Heidegger," in *Franz Rosenzweigs "neues Denken": Internationaler Kongreß-Kassel 2004*, edited by Wolfdietrich Schmied-Kowarzik, 2 vols., 203–215. Freiburg: Verlag Karl Alber, 2006.

———. *Rosenzweig and Heidegger: Between Judaism and German Philosophy*. Berkeley: University of California Press, 2003.

———. "Rosenzweig and Heidegger: Translation, Ontology, and the Anxiety of Affiliation," *New German Critique* 77 (1999): 113–148.

———. "Rosenzweig Redux: The Reception of German-Jewish Thought," *Jewish Social Studies* 8 (2001): 1–57.

———. "Science, Finitude, and Infinity: Neo-Kantianism and the Birth of Existentialism," *Jewish Social Studies* 6 (1999): 30–53.

Görtz, Heinz-Jürgen. " 'Ins Leben': Zum 'theologischen Interesse' des 'Neuen Denkens' Franz Rosenzweigs," *Revista Portuguesa de Filosofia* 62 (2006): 567–590.

Gosetti-Ferencei, Jennifer Anna. *Heidegger, Hölderlin, and the Subject of Poetic Language: Towards a New Poetics of Dasein*. New York: Fordham University Press, 2004.

Gottlieb, Michah. *Faith and Freedom: Moses Mendelssohn's Political Thought*. Oxford: Oxford University Press, 2011.

Green, Kenneth Hart. "Editor's Introduction: Leo Strauss as a Modern Jewish Thinker," in *Jewish Philosophy and the Crisis of Modernity: Essays and Lectures in Modern Jewish Thought*, edited with an introduction by Kenneth Hart Green, 1–84. Albany: State University of New York Press, 1997.

———. *Jew and Philosopher: The Return to Maimonides in the Jewish Thought of Leo Strauss*. Albany: State of New York University Press, 1993.

———. *Leo Strauss and the Recovery of Maimonides*. Chicago: University of Chicago Press, 2013.

———. "The Notion of Truth in Franz Rosenzweig's *The Star of Redemption*: A Philosophical Enquiry," *Modern Judaism* 7 (1987): 297–323.

Greenberg, Gershon. "Amalek during the Shoa: Jewish Orthodox Thought," *Jerusalem Studies in Jewish Thought* 19 (2005): 891–913 (Hebrew).

Greenberg, Yudit Kornberg. *Better Than Wine: Love, Poetry, and Prayer in the Thought of Franz Rosenzweig*. Atlanta: Scholars Press, 1996.

————. "Martin Heidegger and Franz Rosenzweig on the Limits of Language and Poetry," *History of European Ideas* 20 (1993): 791–800.

Gregg, John. *Maurice Blanchot and the Literature of Transgression*. Princeton: Princeton University Press, 1994.

Groiser, David S. "Repetition and Renewal: Kierkegaard, Rosenzweig and the German-Jewish Renaissance," in *Die Gegenwärtigkeit der deutsch-jüdischen Denkens*, edited by Julia Matveev and Ashraf Noor, 265–301. Munich: Wilhelm Fink, 2011.

Groth, Miles. *Translating Heidegger*. Amherst: Humanity Books, 2004.

Gschwandtner, Christina M. *Reading Jean-Luc Marion: Exceeding Metaphysics*. Bloomington: Indiana University Press, 2007.

Guest, Gérard. "Aux confins de l'inapparent: l'extrême phénoménologie de Heidegger," *Existentia* 12 (2002): 113–141.

Guibal, Francis. "La transcendance," in *Emmanuel Lévinas: Positivité et transcendance*, edited by Jean-Luc Marion, 209–238. Paris: Presses Universitaires de France, 2000.

Guignon, Charles. "Being as Appearing: Retrieving the Greek Experience of *Phusis*," in *A Companion to Heidegger's Introduction to Metaphysics*, edited by Richard Polt and Gregory Fried, 34–56. New Haven: Yale University Press, 2001.

Gur-Ze'ev, Ilan. "Adorno and Horkheimer: Diasporic Philosophy, Negative Theology, and Counter-Education," *Educational Theory* 55 (2005): 343–365.

Guttmann, Julius. *Philosophies of Judaism: The History of Jewish Philosophy from Biblical Times to Franz Rosenzweig*, introduction by R. J. Zwi Werblowsky, translated by David W. Silverman. New York: Holt, Rinehart, and Winston, 1964.

Gyatso, Janet. "Compassion at the Millennium: A Buddhist Salvo for the Ethics of the Apocalypse," in *Thinking Through the Death of God: A Critical Companion to Thomas J. J. Altizer*, edited by Lissa McCullough and Brian Schroeder, 147–167. Albany: State University of New York Press, 2004.

Habermas, Jürgen. "A Last Farewell: Derrida's Enlightening Impact," in *The Derrida-Habermas Reader*, edited by Lasse Thomassen, 307–308. Chicago: University of Chicago Press, 2006.

————. *The Philosophical Discourse of Modernity: Twelve Lectures*, translated by Frederick Lawrence. Cambridge, MA: MIT Press, 1987.

————. *Philosophical-Political Profiles*, translated by Frederick G. Lawrence. London: Heinemann, 1983.

Hadot, Pierre. *The Veil of Isis: An Essay on the History of the Idea of Nature*, translated by Michael Chase. Cambridge, MA: Harvard University Press, 2006.

Hägglund, Martin. "The Necessity of Discrimination: Disjoining Derrida and Levinas," *Diacritics* 34 (2004): 40–71.

————. *Radical Atheism: Derrida and the Time of Life*. Stanford: Stanford University Press, 2008.

Halbertal, Moshe, and Avishai Margalit. *Idolatry*, translated by Naomi Goldblum. Cambridge, MA: Harvard University Press, 1992.

Halevi, Judah. *Sefer ha-Kuzari*, translated by Yehuda Even-Shmuel. Tel-Aviv: Dvir, 1972.

Hall, W. David. *Paul Ricoeur and the Poetic Imperative: The Creative Tension between Love and Justice*. Albany: State University of New York Press, 2007.

Hamacher, Werner. "Lingua Amissa: The Messianism of Commodity-Language and Derrida's *Specters of Marx*," in *Futures of Jacques Derrida*, edited by Richard Rand, 130–178. Stanford: Stanford University Press, 2001.

———. "'Now': Walter Benjamin on Historical Time," in *Walter Benjamin and History*, edited by Andrew Benjamin, 38–68. London: Continuum, 2005.

Hammerschlag, Sarah. *The Figural Jew: Politics and Identity in Postwar French Thought*. Chicago: University of Chicago Press, 2010.

———. "Literary Unrest: Blanchot, Lévinas, and the Proximity of Judaism," *Critical Inquiry* 36 (2010): 652–672.

Handelman, Susan A. *Fragments of Redemption: Jewish Thought and Literary Theory in Benjamin, Scholem, and Levinas*. Bloomington: Indiana University Press, 1991.

———. "Jacques Derrida and the Heretic Hermeneutic," in *Displacement: Derrida and After*, edited by Mark Krupnick, 98–129. Bloomington: Indiana University Press, 1983.

———. *The Slayers of Moses: The Emergence of Rabbinic Interpretation in Modern Literary Theory*. Albany: State University of New York Press, 1982.

Harding, Brian. "What Is Minimalist Phenomenology?" *Alea* 6 (2007): 163–181.

Harman, Graham. "Levinas and the Triple Critique of Heidegger," *Philosophy Today* 53 (2009): 407–413.

Hart, James G. "A Précis of an Husserlian Philosophical Theology," in *Essays in Phenomenological Theology*, edited by Steven W. Laycock and James G. Hart, 89–168. Albany: State University of New York Press, 1986.

Hart, Kevin. *The Trespass of the Sign: Deconstruction, Theology and Philosophy*. Cambridge: Cambridge University Press, 1989.

Hart, Ray L. "Godhead and God," in *Thinking Through the Death of God: A Critical Companion to Thomas J. J. Altizer*, edited by Lissa McCullough and Brian Schroeder, 47–63. Albany: State University of New York Press, 2004.

Harvey, Irene E. *Derrida and the Economy of Différance*. Bloomington: Indiana University Press, 1986.

———. *Labyrinths of Exemplarity: At the Limits of Deconstruction*. Albany: State University of New York Press, 2002.

Harvey, Van A. *Feuerbach and the Interpretation of Religion*. Cambridge: Cambridge University Press, 1995.

Harvey, Warren Zev. "How Much Kabbalah in *The Star of Redemption*?" *Immanuel* 1 (1987): 128–134.

———. "Why Philosophers Quote Kabbalah: The Cases of Mendelssohn and Rosenzweig," *Studia Judaica* 16 (2008): 118–125.

Hayes, Josh. "Heidegger's Fundamental Ontology and the Problem of Animal Life," *PhaenEx: Journal of Existential and Phenomenological Theory of Culture* 2 (2007): 42–60.

Ḥayyim of Volozhyn. *Nefesh ha-Ḥayyim.* Benei Beraq, 1989.

Hector, Kevin W. *Theology without Metaphysics: God, Language, and the Spirit of Recognition.* Cambridge: Cambridge University Press, 2011.

Hegel, Georg Wilhelm Friedrich. *Phenomenology of Spirit,* translated by Arnold V. Miller. Oxford: Oxford University Press, 1977.

Heide, Albert van der. "Pardes: Methodological Reflections on the Theory of the Four Senses," *Journal of Jewish Studies* 34 (1983): 147–159.

Heidegger, Martin. *Aus der Erfahrung des Denkens* [GA 13]. Frankfurt am Main: Vittorio Klostermann, 2002.

———. *The Basic Problems of Phenomenology,* translation, introduction, and lexicon by Albert Hofstadter. Bloomington: Indiana University Press, 1982.

———. *Becoming Heidegger: On the Trail of His Early Occasional Writings, 1910–1927,* edited by Theodore Kisiel and Thomas Sheehan. Evanston: Northwestern University Press, 2007.

———. *Being and Time: A Translation of Sein und Zeit,* translated by Joan Stambaugh. Albany: State University of New York Press, 1996.

———. *Beiträge zur Philosophie (Vom Ereignis)* [GA 65]. Frankfurt am Main: Vittorio Klostermann, 1989.

———. *Besinnung* [GA 66]. Frankfurt am Main: Vittorio Klostermann, 1997.

———. *Contributions to Philosophy (Of the Event),* translated by Richard Rojcewicz and Daniela Vallega-Neu Maly. Bloomington: Indiana University Press, 2012.

———. *Country Path Conversations,* translated by Bret W. Davis. Bloomington: Indiana University Press, 2010.

———. *Das Ereignis* [GA 71]. Frankfurt am Main: Vittorio Klostermann, 2009.

———. *Der Satz vom Grund* [GA 10]. Frankfurt am Main: Vittorio Klostermann, 1997.

———. *Die Geschichte des Seyns* [GA 69]. Frankfurt am Main: Vittorio Klostermann, 1998.

———. *Die Grundprobleme der Phänomenologie* [GA 24]. Frankfurt am Main: Vittorio Klostermann, 1975.

———. *Early Greek Thinking,* translated by David Farrell Krell and Frank A. Capuzzi. New York: Harper & Row, 1975.

———. *Einführung in die Metaphysik* [GA 40]. Frankfurt am Main: Vittorio Klostermann, 1983.

———. *The End of Philosophy,* translated by Joan Stambaugh. Chicago: University of Chicago Press, 2003.

———. *Elucidations of Hölderlin's Poetry,* translated by Keith Hoeller. Amherst: Humanity Books, 2000.

———. *Erläuterungen zu Hölderlins Dichtung* [GA 4]. Frankfurt am Main: Vittorio Klostermann, 1996.

———. *The Essence of Truth: On Plato's Cave Allegory and Theaetetus,* translated by Ted Sadler. New York: Continuum, 2002.

———. *The Event,* translated by Richard Rojcewicz. Bloomington: Indiana University Press, 2013.

————. *Feldweg-Gespräche* [GA 77]. Frankfurt am Main: Vittorio Klostermann, 1995.

————. *Four Seminars*, translated by Andrew Mitchell and François Raffoul. Bloomington: Indiana University Press, 2003.

————. *Hegel's Concept of Experience*. New York: Harper & Row, 1970.

————. *Heidegger: Cahiers de l'Herne*. Paris: L'Herne, 1983.

————. *Holzwege* [GA 5]. Frankfurt am Main: Vittorio Klostermann, 2003.

————. *Identity and Difference*, translated and with an introduction by Joan Stambaugh. New York: Harper & Row, 1969.

————. *Introduction to Metaphysics*, new translation by Gregory Fried and Richard Polt. New Haven: Yale University Press, 2000.

————. *The Metaphysical Foundations of Logic*, translated by Michael Heim. Bloomington: Indiana University Press, 1984.

————. *Metaphysische Anfangsgründe der Logik im Ausgang von Leibniz* [GA 26]. Frankfurt am Main: Vittorio Klostermann, 1978.

————. *Mindfulness*, translated by Parvis Emad and Thomas Kalary. New York: Continuum, 2006.

————. *Nietzsche: Der Wille zur Macht als Kunst* [GA 43]. Frankfurt am Main: Vittorio Klostermann, 1985.

————. *Nietzsche, Volume I: The Will to Power as Art*, translated with notes and an analysis by David Farrell Krell. New York: Harper & Row, 1979.

————. *Nietzsche, Volume II: The Eternal Recurrence of the Same*, translated with notes and an analysis by David Farrell Krell. New York: Harper & Row, 1984.

————. *Nietzsches metaphysische Grundstellung im abendländischen Denken: Die ewige Wiederkehr des Gleichen* [GA 44]. Frankfurt am Main: Vittorio Klostermann, 1986.

————. *Off the Beaten Track*, edited and translated by Julian Young and Kenneth Haynes. Cambridge: Cambridge University Press, 2002.

————. *On the Way to Language*, translated by Peter D. Hertz. San Francisco: Harper & Row, 1971.

————. *On Time and Being*, translated by Joan Stambaugh. New York: Harper & Row, 1972.

————. *Parmenides* [GA 54]. Frankfurt am Main: Vittorio Klostermann, 1992.

————. *Parmenides*, translated by André Schuwer and Richard Rojcewicz. Bloomington: Indiana University Press, 1992.

————. *Pathmarks*, edited by William McNeill. Cambridge: Cambridge University Press, 1998.

————. *Phänomenologie des religiösen Lebens* [GA 60]. Frankfurt am Main: Vittorio Klostermann, 1995.

————. *The Phenomenology of Religious Life*, translated by Matthias Fritsch and Jennifer Anna Gosetti-Ferencei. Bloomington: Indiana University Press, 2004.

————. *Poetry, Language, Thought*, translation and introduction by Albert Hofstadter. New York: Harper & Row, 1971.

———. *The Principle of Reason*, translated by Reginald Lilly. Bloomington: Indiana University Press, 1992.

———. *Sein und Zeit*. Tübingen: Max Niemeyer, 1993.

———. *Sojourns: The Journey to Greece*, translated by John Panteleimon Manoussakis, foreword by John Sallis. Albany: State University of New York Press, 2005.

———. *Unterwegs zur Sprache* [GA 12]. Frankfurt am Main: Vittorio Klostermann, 1985.

———. *Vom Wesen der Wahrheit: Zu Platons Höhlengleichnis und Theätet* [GA 34]. Frankfurt am Main: Vittorio Klostermann, 1988.

———. *Vorträge und Aufsätze* [GA 7]. Frankfurt am Main: Vittorio Klostermann, 2000.

———. *Was heisst Denken?* [GA 8]. Frankfurt am Main: Vittorio Klostermann, 2002.

———. *Wegmarken* [GA 9]. Frankfurt am Main: Vittorio Klostermann, 1996.

———. *What Is Called Thinking?* translated by Fred W. Wieck and J. Glenn Gray, with an introduction by J. Glenn Gray. New York: Harper & Row, 1968.

———. *Zur Sache des Denkens* [GA 14]. Frankfurt am Main: Vittorio Klostermann, 2007.

———, and Eugen Fink. *Heraclitus Seminar 1966/67*, translated by Charles H. Seibert. University, Alabama: University of Alabama Press, 1979.

Heiden, Gert-Jan van der. *The Truth (and Untruth) of Language: Heidegger, Ricoeur, and Derrida on Disclosure and Displacement*. Pittsburgh: Duquesne University Press, 2010.

Held, Shai. "Reciprocity and Responsiveness: Self-Transcendence and the Dynamics of Covenant in the Theology and Spirituality of Abraham Joshua Heschel," Ph.D. dissertation, Harvard University, 2010.

Helting, Holger. *Heideggers Auslegung von Hölderlins Dichtung des Heiligen: Ein Beitrag zur Grundlagenforschung der Daseinanalyse*. Berlin: Duncker & Humblot, 1999.

Hemming, Laurence Paul. *Heidegger's Atheism: The Refusal of a Theological Voice*. Notre Dame: University of Notre Dame Press, 2002.

Henry, Michel. *The Essence of Manifestation*, translated by Girard Etzkorn. The Hague: Martinus Nijhoff, 1973.

———. "Phenomenology of Life," in *Transcendence and Phenomenology*, edited by Conor Cunningham and Peter M. Candler Jr., 241–259. London: SCM Press, 2007.

Herrmann, Friedrich-Wilhelm von. "Faktische Lebenserfahrung und urchristliche Religiosität: Heideggers phänomenologischen Auslegung Paulinischer Briefe," in *Heidegger und die christliche Tradition*, edited by Norbert Fischer and Friedrich-Wilhelm von Hermann, 21–31. Hamburg: Felix Meiner Verlag, 2007.

Herzog, Annabel. "Levinas and the Unnamed Balaam: On Ontology and Idolatry," *Journal of Jewish Thought and Philosophy* 19 (2011): 131–146.

Heschel, Abraham Joshua. *The Earth Is the Lord's: The Inner Life of the Jew in East Europe*. New York: Henry Schuman, 1950.

———. *God in Search of Man: A Philosophy of Judaism*. New York: Farrar, Straus & Cudahy, 1955.

———. "The Holy Dimension," *Journal of Religion* 23 (1943): 117–124.

———. *The Insecurity of Freedom: Essays on Human Existence.* New York: Farrar, Straus & Giroux, 1959.

———. *Israel: An Echo of Eternity.* New York: Farrar, Straus & Giroux, 1969.

———. *Man Is Not Alone: A Philosophy of Religion.* New York: Farrar, Straus & Young, 1951.

———. *Man's Quest for God: Studies in Prayer and Symbolism.* New York: Scribner, 1954.

———. *Moral Grandeur and Spiritual Audacity,* edited by Susannah Heschel. New York: Farrar, Strauss, Giroux, 1996.

———. *The Prophets.* New York: Harper & Row, 1962.

———. *The Sabbath: Its Meaning for Modern Man.* New York: Farrar, Straus & Young, 1951.

———. *Who Is Man?* Stanford: Stanford University Press, 1965.

Hill, Leslie. *Blanchot: Extreme Contemporary.* London: Routledge, 1997.

Hobson, Marian. *Jacques Derrida: Opening Lines.* London: Routledge, 1998.

Hodge, Joanna. *Derrida on Time.* London: Routledge, 2007.

Hollander, Dana. *Exemplarity and Chosenness: Rosenzweig and Derrida on the Nation of Philosophy.* Stanford: Stanford University Press, 2008.

———. "Franz Rosenzweig on Nation, Translation, and Judaism," *Philosophy Today* 38 (1994): 380–389.

———. "Is Deconstruction a Jewish Science? Reflections on 'Jewish Philosophy' in Light of Jacques Derrida's *Judéités,*" *Philosophy Today* 50 (2006): 128–138.

———. "Is the Other My Neighbor? Reading Levinas Alongside Hermann Cohen," in *The Exorbitant: Emmanuel Levinas Between Jews and Christians,* edited by Kevin Hart and Michael A. Signer, 90–107. New York: Fordham University Press, 2010.

———. "On the Significance of the Messianic Idea in Rosenzweig," *Cross Currents* 53 (2004): 555–565.

———. "'A Thought in Which Everything Has Been Thought': On the Messianic Idea in Levinas," in *Symposium: Canadian Journal of Continental Philosophy/Revue canadienne de philosophie continentale* 14 (2010): 133–159.

Hollywood, Amy. "Preaching as Social Practice in Meister Eckhart," in *Mysticism and Social Transformation,* edited by Janet K. Ruffing, with a foreword by Robert J. Egan, 76–90. Syracuse: Syracuse University Press, 2001.

Holzhey, Helmut. "Heidegger und Cohen. Negativität im Denken des Ursprungs," in *In Erscheinung treten. Heinrich Barths Philosophie des Ästhetischen,* edited by Günther Hauff, Hans Rudolf Schweizer, and Armin Wildermuth, 97–114. Basel: Schwabe, 1990.

Hopkins, Jasper. *Complete Philosophical and Theological Treatises of Nicholas of Cusa.* Minneapolis: Arthur J. Banning Press, 2001.

Hopper, Stanley R. "Introduction," in *Interpretation: The Poetry of Meaning,* edited by Stanley R. Hopper and David L. Miller, ix–xxii. New York: Harcourt, Brace and World, 1967.

Horkheimer, Max, and Theodor W. Adorno, *Dialectic of Enlightenment: Philosophical Fragments*, edited by Gunzelin Schmid Noerr, translated by Edmund Jephcott. Stanford: Stanford University Press, 2002.

Horner, Robyn. "The Betrayal of Transcendence," in *Transcendence: Philosophy, Literature, and Theology Approach the Beyond*, edited by Regina Schwartz, 61–79. New York: Routledge, 2004.

———. "Derrida and God: Opening a Conversation," *Pacifica* 12 (1999): 12–26.

———. "On Levinas's Gifts to Christian Theology," in *The Exorbitant: Emmanuel Levinas Between Jews and Christians*, edited by Kevin Hart and Michael A. Signer, 130–149. New York: Fordham University Press, 2010.

———. *Rethinking God as Gift: Marion, Derrida, and the Limits of Theology*. New York: Fordham University Press, 2001.

Horowitz, Isaiah. *Shenei Luḥot ha-Berit ha-Shalem*, edited by Meyer Katz. Haifa: Yad Ramah Institute, 2006.

Hortian, Von Ulrich. "Zeit und Geschichte bei Franz Rosenzweig und Walter Benjamin," in *Der Philosoph Franz Rosenzweig (1886–1929): Internationaler Kongreß-Kassel 1986*, edited by Wolfdietrich Schmied-Kowarzik, 2 vols., 815–827. Freiburg: Verlag Karl Alber, 1988.

Horwitz, Rivka. *Buber's Way to "I and Thou": An Historical Analysis and the First Publication of Martin Buber's Lectures "Religion als Gegenwart."* Heidelberg: Verlag Lambert Schneider, 1978.

———. "Franz Rosenzweig on Language," *Judaism* 13 (1964): 393–406.

———. "From Hegelianism to a Revolutionary Understanding of Judaism: Franz Rosenzweig's Attitude Toward Kabbala and Myth," *Modern Judaism* 26 (2006): 31–54.

———. "Hamann and Rosenzweig on Language—The Revival of Myth," *Da'at* 38 (1997): v–xxviii.

———. "A Revolutionary Understanding of Judaism: Franz Rosenzweig's Attitude to Kabbalah and Myth," in *Franz Rosenzweigs "neues Denken": Internationaler Kongreß-Kassel 2004*, edited by Wolfdietrich Schmied-Kowarzik, 2 vols., 689–712. Freiburg: Verlag Karl Alber, 2006. Hebrew version in *Judaism, Topics, Fragments, Faces, Identities: Jubilee Volume in Honor of Professor Rivka Horwitz*, edited by Haviva Pedaya and Ephraim Meir, 43–71. Beer-Sheva: Ben-Gurion University of the Negev Press, 2007.

———. "Two Models of Atonement in Cohen's 'Religion of Reason': One According to Ezekiel, the Other 'Joyful in Sufferings' According to Job," in *„Religion der Vernunft aus den Quellen des Judentums": Tradition und Ursprungsdenken in Hermann Cohens Spätwerk Internationale Konferenz in Zürich 1998*, edited by Helmut Holzhey, Gabriel Motzkin, and Hartwig Wiedebach, 175–190. Hildesheim: Georg Olms Verlag, 2000.

Howells, Christina. *Derrida: Deconstruction from Phenomenology to Ethics*. Cambridge: Polity Press, 1999.

Hughes, Aaron W. *The Art of Dialogue in Jewish Philosophy*. Bloomington: Indiana University Press, 2008.

———. "Maimonides and the Pre-Maimonidean Jewish Philosophical Tradition According to Hermann Cohen," *Journal of Jewish Thought and Philosophy* 18 (2010): 1–26.

Husserl, Edmund. *Cartesian Meditations: An Introduction to Phenomenology*, translated by Dorion Cairns. The Hague: Martinus Nijhoff, 1977.

———. *Ideas Pertaining to a Pure Phenomenology and to a Phenomenological Philosophy. First Book: General Introduction to a Pure Phenomenology*, translated by F. Kersten. Dordrecht: Kluwer Academic Publishers, 1983.

———. *Ideas Pertaining to a Pure Phenomenology and to a Phenomenological Philosophy. Second Book: Studies in the Phenomenology of Constitution*, translated by Richard Rojcewicz and André Schuwer. Dordrecht: Kluwer Academic Publishers, 1989.

Hyman, Arthur. "Maimonidean Elements in Hermann Cohen's Philosophy of Religion," in *Hermann Cohen's Critical Idealism*, edited by Reinier Munk, 357–370. Dordrecht: Springer, 2005.

Ibn Gabbai, Meir. *Derekh Emunah*, in Moshe Schatz, *Ma'yan Moshe*, 99–181. Jerusalem, 2011.

Idel, Moshe. *Absorbing Perfections: Kabbalah and Interpretation*. New Haven: Yale University Press, 2002.

———. "Infinities of Torah in Kabbalah," in *Midrash and Literature*, edited by Geoffrey H. Hartman and Sanford Budick, 141–157. New Haven: Yale University Press, 1986.

———. *Kabbalah and Eros*. New Haven: Yale University Press, 2005.

———. *Old Worlds, New Mirrors: On Jewish Mysticism and Twentieth-Century Thought*. Philadelphia: University of Pennsylvania Press, 2010.

———. "PaRDeS: Some Reflections on Kabbalistic Hermeneutics," in *Death, Ecstasy, and Other Worldly Journeys*, edited by John J. Collins and Michael Fishbane, 249–268. Albany: State University of New York Press, 1995.

———. "Rosenzweig and the Kabbalah," in *The Philosophy of Franz Rosenzweig*, edited by Paul Mendes-Flohr, 162–171. Hanover: University Press of New England, 1988.

Irigaray, Luce. *Elemental Passions*, translated by Joanne Collie and Judith Still. New York: Routledge, 1992.

Isaac the Blind. *Perush Sefer Yeṣirah*, in Gershom Scholem, *The Kabbalah in Provence*, edited by Rivka Schatz, Appendix. Jerusalem: Akadamon, 1970 (Hebrew).

Iser, Wolfgang. *The Range of Interpretation*. New York: Columbia University Press, 2000.

Ivry, Alfred L. "Hermann Cohen, Leo Strauss, Alexander Altmann: Maimonides in Germany," in *The Trias of Maimonides: Jewish, Arabic, and Ancient Culture of Knowledge*, edited by Georges Tamer, 175–183. Berlin: Walter de Gruyter, 2005.

Izzi, John. "Proximity in Distance: Levinas and Plotinus," in *Levinas and the Ancients*, edited by Brian Schroeder and Silvia Benso, 196–209. Bloomington: Indiana University Press, 2008.

Jacoby, Russell. *Picture Imperfect: Utopian Thought for an Anti-Utopian Age*. New York: Columbia University Press, 2005.

Jambet, Christian. *Le caché et l'apparent*. Paris: Éditions de l'Herne, 2003.

James, Ian. *The New French Philosophy*. Cambridge: Polity Press, 2012.

James, William. *The Principles of Psychology*. Cambridge, MA: Harvard University Press, 1981.

Janicaud, Dominique. *Chronos: Pour l'intelligence du partage temporel*. Paris: Grasset, 1997.

———. *Phenomenology "Wide Open": After the French Debate*, translated by Charles N. Cabral. New York: Fordham University Press, 2005.

———. "The Theological Turn of French Phenomenology," in *Phenomenology and the "Theological Turn": The French Debate*, 16–103. New York: Fordham University Press, 2000.

Janssens, David. *Between Athens and Jerusalem: Philosophy, Prophecy, and Politics in Leo Strauss's Early Thought*. Albany: State University of New York Press, 2008.

Jasper, David. "In the Wasteland: Apocalypse, Theology, and the Poets," in *Thinking Through the Death of God: A Critical Companion to Thomas J. J. Altizer*, edited by Lissa McCullough and Brian Schroeder, 185–195. Albany: State University of New York Press, 2004.

Johnson, Christopher. *System and Writing in the Philosophy of Jacques Derrida*. Cambridge: Cambridge University Press, 1993.

Johnston, Mark. *Saving God: Religion after Idolatry*. Princeton: Princeton University Press, 2009.

Jones, Tamsin. *A Genealogy of Marion's Philosophy of Religion: Apparent Darkness*. Bloomington: Indiana University Press, 2011.

Jonte-Pace, Diane. *Speaking the Unspeakable: Religion, Misogyny, and the Uncanny Mother in Freud's Cultural Texts*. Berkeley: University of California Press, 2001.

Judah Loewe of Prague. *Derekh Ḥayyim*, edited by Joshua David Hartman, vol. 3. Jerusalem: Makhon Yerushalayim, 2007.

Junk, Johanna. *Metapher und Sprachmagie, Heidegger und die Kabbala: Eine philosophische Untersuchung*. Bodenheim: Syndikat Buchgesellschaft, 1998.

Kafka, Franz. *Parables and Paradoxes*. New York: Schocken, 1971.

Kahn, Charles H. *The Art and Thought of Heraclitus: An Edition of the Fragments with Translation and Commentary*. Cambridge: Cambridge University Press, 1979.

Kalary, Thomas. "Heidegger's Thinking of Difference and the God-Question," in *Heidegger, Translation, and the Task of Thinking: Essays in Honor of Parvis Emad*, edited by Frank Schalow, 111–133. Dordrecht: Springer, 2011.

Kangas, David J. *Kierkegaard's Instant: On Beginnings*. Bloomington: Indiana University Press, 2007.

————, and Martin Kavka. "Hearing, Patiently: Time and Salvation in Kierkegaard and Levinas," in *Kierkegaard and Levinas: Ethics, Politics, and Religion*, edited by J. Aaron Simmons and David Wood, 125–152. Bloomington: Indiana University Press, 2008.

Kant, Immanuel. *Critique of Pure Reason*, translated and edited by Paul Guyer and Allen Wood. Cambridge: Cambridge University Press, 1999.

————. *Lectures on Metaphysics*, translated and edited by Karl Ameriks and Steve Naragon. Cambridge: Cambridge University Press, 1997.

————. "On a Newly Arisen Superior Tone in Philosophy," in *Raising the Tone of Philosophy: Late Essays by Immanuel Kant, Transformative Critique by Jacques Derrida*, edited by Peter Fenves, 51–81. Baltimore: Johns Hopkins University Press, 1993.

————. *Prolegomena to Any Future Metaphysics That Will Be Able to Present Itself as Science*, edited by Günter Zöller, translated by Peter G. Lucas and Günter Zöller. Oxford: Oxford University Press, 2004.

Kaplan, Edward K. "Heschel as Philosopher: Phenomenology and the Rhetoric of Revelation," *Modern Judaism* 21 (2001): 1–14.

————. *Holiness in Words: Abraham Joshua Heschel's Poetics of Piety*. Albany: State University of New York Press, 1996.

————. "Sacred versus Symbolic Religion: Abraham Joshua Heschel and Martin Buber," *Modern Judaism* 14 (1994): 213–231.

————. *Spiritual Radical: Abraham Joshua Heschel in America, 1940–1972*. New Haven: Yale University Press, 2007.

————, and Samuel H. Dresner. *Abraham Joshua Heschel: Prophetic Witness*. New Haven: Yale University Press, 1998.

Kaplan, Gregory. "Ethics as First Philosophy and the Other's Ambiguity in the Dialogue of Buber and Levinas," *Philosophy Today* 50 (2006): 40–57.

————. "In the End Shall Christians Become Jews and Jews, Christians? On Franz Rosenzweig's Apocalyptic Eschatology," *Cross Currents* 53 (2004): 511–529.

Kaplowitz, Mark. "'The Gravest Obstacle and Thus a Great Misfortune': Hermann Cohen's Interpretation of Spinoza," Ph.D. dissertation, New York University, 2010.

Kate, Laurens ten. "The Gift of Loss: A Study of the Fugitive God in Bataille's Atheology, with References to Jean-Luc Nancy," in *Flight of the Gods: Philosophical Perspectives on Negative Theology*, edited by Ilse N. Bulhof and Laurens ten Kate, 250–292. New York: Fordham University Press, 2000.

Kates, Joshua. *Fielding Derrida: Philosophy, Literary Criticism, History, and the Work of Deconstruction*. New York: Fordham University Press, 2008.

Katz, Claire. "'Before the Face of God One Must Not Go with Empty Hands': Transcendence and Levinas' Prophetic Consciousness," *Philosophy Today* 50 (2006): 58–68.

Katz, Steven T. "On Historicism and Eternity: Reflections on the 100th Birthday of Franz Rosenzweig," in *Der Philosoph Franz Rosenzweig (1886–1929): Internationaler Kongreß-Kassel 1986*, edited by Wolfdietrich Schmied-Kowarzik, 2 vols., 745–769. Freiburg: Verlag Karl Alber, 1988.

Kavka, Martin. *Jewish Messianism and the History of Philosophy*. Cambridge: Cambridge University Press, 2004.

———. "The Meaning of That Hour: Prophecy, Phenomenology, and the Public Sphere in the Early Writings of Abraham Joshua Heschel," in *Religion and Violence in a Secular World*, edited by Clayton Crockett, 108–136. Charlottesville: University of Virginia Press, 2006.

———. "Religious Experience in Levinas and R. Hayyim of Volozhin," *Philosophy Today* 50 (2006): 69–79.

———. "Screening the Canon: Levinas and Medieval Jewish Philosophy," in *New Directions in Jewish Philosophy*, edited by Aaron W. Hughes and Elliot R. Wolfson, 19–51. Bloomington: Indiana University Press, 2010.

———. "Should Levinasians Also Be Hegelians? On Wyschogrod's Levinasianism," *Philosophy Today* 55 (2011): 372–385.

———. "Verification (*Bewährung*) in Franz Rosenzweig," in *German-Jewish Thought Between Religion and Politics: Festschrift in Honor of Paul Mendes-Flohr on the Occasion of His Seventieth Birthday*, edited by Christian Wiese and Martina Urban, 167–183. Berlin: Walter de Gruyter, 2012.

Kearney, Richard. *Anatheism: Returning to God After God*. New York: Columbia University Press, 2010.

———. *The God Who May Be: A Hermeneutics of Religion*. Bloomington: Indiana University Press, 2001.

———. "Hermeneutics of the Possible God," in *Givenness and God: Questions of Jean-Luc Marion*, edited by Ian Leask and Eoin Cassidy, 220–242. New York: Fordham University Press, 2005.

———. "In Place of a Response," in *After God: Richard Kearney and the Religious Turn in Continental Philosophy*, edited by John Panteleimon Manoussakis, 365–387. New York: Fordham University Press, 2006.

———. *Navigations: Collected Irish Essays 1976–2006*. Syracuse: Syracuse University Press, 2006.

———. "On the Gift: A Discussion between Jacques Derrida and Jean-Luc Marion," moderated by Richard Kearney, in *God, the Gift, and Postmodernism*, edited by John D. Caputo and Michael J. Scanlon, 54–78. Bloomington: Indiana University Press, 1999.

———. "Sacramental Imagination and Eschatology," in *Phenomenology and Eschatology: Not Yet in the Now*, edited by Neal DeRoo and John Panteleimon Manoussakis, 55–67. Burlington: Ashgate, 2009.

———. *The Wake of Imagination: Toward a Postmodern Culture*. Minneapolis: University of Minnesota Press, 1988.

———, and Joseph Stephen O'Leary, eds. *Heidegger et la question de Dieu*, preface by Jean-Yves Lacoste. Paris: Presses Universitaires de France, 2009.

Keenan, Dennis King. *Death and Responsibility: The "Work" of Levinas*. Albany: State University of New York Press, 1999.

———. *The Question of Sacrifice*. Bloomington: Indiana University Press, 2005.

Keller, Catherine. *Apocalypse Now and Then: A Feminist Guide to the End of the World*. Boston: Beacon Press, 1996.

———. "The Apophasis of Gender: A Fourfold Unsaying of Feminist Theology," *Journal of the American Academy of Religion* 76 (2008): 905–933.

———. *God and Power: Counter-Apocalyptic Journeys*. Minneapolis: Fortress Press, 2005.

———. "Returning God: The Gift of Feminist Theology," in *Feminism, Sexuality, and the Return of Religion*, edited by Linda Martin Alcoff and John D. Caputo, 55–76. Bloomington: Indiana University Press, 2011.

———. "Rumors of Transcendence: The Movement, State, and Sex of 'Beyond,'" in *Transcendence and Beyond: A Postmodern Inquiry*, edited by John D. Caputo and Michael J. Scanlon, 129–150. Bloomington: Indiana University Press, 2007.

Kenney, John P. "The Critical Value of Negative Theology," *Harvard Theological Review* 86 (1993): 439–453.

Kierkegaard, Søren. *The Book on Adler*, edited and translated, with introduction and notes, by Howard V. Hong and Edna H. Hong. Princeton: Princeton University Press, 1998.

———. *Concluding Unscientific Postscript to Philosophical Fragments*, edited and translated, with introduction and notes, by Howard V. Hong and Edna H. Hong. 2 vols. Princeton: Princeton University Press, 1992.

———. *Either/Or*, edited and translated, with introduction and notes, by Howard V. Hong and Edna H. Hong. 2 vols. Princeton: Princeton University Press, 1987.

———. *Fear and Trembling*, edited and translated with notes and introduction by Howard V. Hong and Edna H. Hong. Princeton: Princeton University Press, 1983.

———. *Philosophical Fragments: Johannes Climacus*, edited and translated with introduction and notes by Howard V. Hong and Edna H. Hong. Princeton: Princeton University Press, 1987.

———. *The Sickness Unto Death: A Christian Psychological Exposition for Upbuilding and Awakening*, edited and translated, with introduction and notes, by Howard V. Hong and Edna H. Hong. Princeton: Princeton University Press, 1980.

Kinkel, Walter. "Das Urteil des Ursprungs: Ein Kapitel aus einem Kommentar zu Hermann Cohens Logik der reinen Erkenntnis," *Kantstudien* 17 (1912): 274–382.

Kirchner, Katrin Jona. "Experience, the Principle of Relativity and the Function of Language in the Conceptions of Franz Rosenzweig and Alfred N. Whitehead," in *Faith, Truth, and Reason: New Perspectives on Franz Rosenzweig's »Star of Redemption«*, edited by Yehoyada Amir, Yossi Turner, and Martin Brasser, 333–354. Freiburg: Verlag Karl Alber, 2012.

Kleinberg, Ethan. "Back to Where We've Never Been: Heidegger, Levinas, and Derrida on Tradition and History," *History and Theory* 51 (2012): 114–135.

———. *Generation Existential: Heidegger's Philosophy in France, 1927–1961*. Ithaca: Cornell University Press, 2005.

Kleinberg-Levin, David Michael. *Before the Voice of Reason: Echoes of Responsibility in Merleau-Ponty's Ecology and Levinas's Ethics*. Albany: State University of New York Press, 2008.

Klemm, David E. "Open Secrets: Derrida and Negative Theology," in *Negation and Theology*, edited by Robert P. Scharlemann, 8–24. Charlottesville: University Press of Virginia, 1992.

Kligerman, Eric. *Sites of the Uncanny: Paul Celan, Specularity and the Visual Arts*. Berlin: Walter de Gruyter, 2007.

Kluback, William. *Hermann Cohen: The Challenge of a Religion of Reason*. Chico: Scholar's Press, 1984.

———. "Hermann Cohen und Martin Heidegger: Meinungsverschiedenheit oder Entstellung?" *Zeitschrift für philosophische Forschung* 40 (1986): 283–287.

———. *The Idea of Humanity: Hermann Cohen's Legacy to Philosophy and Theology*. Lanham: University Press of America, 1987.

———. *The Legacy of Hermann Cohen*. Atlanta: Scholars Press, 1989.

———. "Time and History: The Conflict Between Hermann Cohen and Franz Rosenzweig," in *Der Philosoph Franz Rosenzweig (1886–1929): Internationaler Kongreß-Kassel 1986*, edited by Wolfdietrich Schmied-Kowarzik, 2 vols., 801–813. Freiburg: Verlag Karl Alber, 1988.

Klun, Branko. "Transcendence and Time: Levinas's Criticism of Heidegger," *Gregorianum* 88 (2007): 587–603.

Kneller, Jane. *Kant and the Power of Imagination*. Cambridge: Cambridge University Press, 2007.

Knight, Christopher J. *Omissions Are Not Accidents: Modern Apophaticism from Henry James to Jacques Derrida*. Toronto: University of Toronto Press, 2010.

Knight, Henry F. "Coming to Terms with Amalek: Testing the Limits of Hospitality," in *Confronting Genocide: Judaism, Christianity, Islam*, edited by Steven Leonard Jacobs, 223–237. Lanham: Lexington Books, 2009.

Koltun-Fromm, Ken. "Vision and Authenticity in Heschel's *The Sabbath*," *Modern Judaism* 31 (2011): 142–165.

Komter, Aafke E. *Social Solidarity and the Gift*. Cambridge: Cambridge University Press, 2005.

Konopka, Adam. "The 'Inversions' of Intentionality in Levinas and the Later Heidegger," *PhaenEx: Journal of Existential and Phenomenological Theory of Culture* 4 (2009): 146–162.

Koren, Israel. *The Mystery of the Earth: Mysticism and Hasidism in the Thought of Martin Buber*. Leiden: Brill, 2010.

Kosky, Jeffrey L. "Contemporary Encounters with Apophatic Theology: The Case of Emmanuel Levinas," *Journal for Cultural and Religious Theory* 1 (2000), available at www.jcrt.org.

———. *Levinas and the Philosophy of Religion*. Bloomington: Indiana University Press, 2001.

————. "'Love Strong as Death': Levinas and Heidegger," in *The Exorbitant: Emmanuel Levinas Between Jews and Christians*, edited by Kevin Hart and Michael Signer, 108–129. New York: Fordham University Press, 2010.

Kreisel, Howard. *Prophecy: The History of an Idea in Medieval Jewish Philosophy*. Dordrecht: Kluwer Academic Publishers, 2001.

Kripal, Jeffrey J. *The Serpent's Gift: Gnostic Reflections on the Study of Religion*. Chicago: University of Chicago Press, 2007.

Kronick, Joseph G. "Edmond Jabès and the Poetry of the Jewish Unhappy Consciousness," *Modern Language Notes* 106 (1991): 967–996.

————. "Philosophy as Autobiography: The Confessions of Jacques Derrida," *Modern Language Notes* 115 (2000): 997–1018.

Kugler, Paul. *The Alchemy of Discourse: An Archetypal Approach to Language*. Lewisburg: Bucknell University Press, 1982.

Lacoste, Jean-Yves. "The Appearing and the Irreducible," in *Words of Life: New Theological Turns in French Phenomenology*, edited by Bruce Ellis Benson and Norman Wirzba, 42–67. New York: Fordham University Press, 2010.

————. "De la donation comme promesse," *Revista Portuguesa de Filosofia* 65 (2009): 841–856.

————. *Experience and the Absolute: Disputed Questions on the Humanity of Man*, translated by Mark Raftery-Skehan. New York: Fordham University Press, 2004.

————. *La phénoménalité de dieu: Neuf études*. Paris: Cerf, 2008.

Lacoue-Labarthe, Philippe. *Heidegger and the Politics of Poetry*, translated and with an introduction by Jeff Fort. Urbana: University of Illinois Press, 2007.

Lafont, Cristina. *Heidegger, Language, and World-Disclosure*, translated by Graham Harman. Cambridge: Cambridge University Press, 2000.

Largier, Niklaus. "Repräsentation und Negativität: Meister Eckharts Kritik als Dekonstruktion," in *Contemplata aliis trader: Studien zum Verhältnis von Literatur und Spiritualität*, edited by Claudia Brinker, Urs Herzog, Niklaus Largier, and Paul Michel, 371–390. Bern: Peter Lang, 1995.

Lawlor, Leonard. *Imagination and Change: The Difference between the Thought of Ricoeur and Derrida*. Albany: State University of New York Press, 1992.

————. *This Is Not Sufficient: An Essay on Animality and Human Nature*. New York: Columbia University Press, 2007.

Laycock, Steven W. "The Intersubjective Dimension of Husserl's Thought," in *Essays in Phenomenological Theology*, edited by Steven W. Laycock and James G. Hart, 169–186. Albany: State University of New York Press, 1986.

————. "Introduction: Toward an Overview of Phenomenological Theology," in *Essays in Phenomenological Theology*, edited by Steven W. Laycock and James G. Hart, 1–22. Albany: State University of New York Press, 1986.

Lazier, Benjamin. *God Interrupted: Heresy and the European Imagination Between the World Wars*. Princeton: Princeton University Press, 2008.

Leahy, David G. "Cuspidal Limits of Infinity: Secret of the Incarnate Self in Levinas," in *Rending the Veil: Concealment and Secrecy in the History of Religions*, edited by Elliot R. Wolfson, 209–248. New York: Seven Bridges Press, 1999.

Leask, Ian. "Husserl, Givenness, and the Priority of the Self," *International Journal of Philosophical Studies* 11 (2003): 141–156.

Lehmann, Matthias. "Franz Rosenzweigs Kritik des Islam im 'Stern der Erlösung,'" *Jewish Studies Quarterly* 1 (1993/94): 340–361.

Letters 1925–1975: Hannah Arendt and Martin Heidegger, edited by Ursula Ludz, translated by Andrew Shields. Orlando: Harcourt, 2004.

Levinas, Emmanuel. "L'actualité de Maïmonide," *Paix et Droit* 15, no. 4 (1935): 6–7.

———. "As If Consenting to Horror," *Critical Inquiry* 15 (1989): 485–488.

———. *Autrement qu'être ou au-delà de l'essence*. Dordrecht: Kluwer Academic Publishers, 1974.

———. *Basic Philosophical Writings*, edited by Adriaan T. Peperzak, Simon Critchley, and Robert Bernasconi, translated by Alphonso Lingis and Richard A. Cohen. Bloomington: Indiana University Press, 1996.

———. *Beyond the Verse: Talmudic Readings and Lectures*, translated by Gary D. Mole. London: Athlone Press, 1994.

———. *Collected Philosophical Papers*, translated by Alphonso Lingis. Dordrecht: Martinus Nijhoff, 1987.

———. *Difficult Freedom: Essays on Judaism*, translated by Seán Hand. Baltimore: Johns Hopkins University Press, 1990.

———. *Discovering Existence with Husserl*, translated by Richard A. Cohen and Michael B. Smith. Evanston: Northwestern University Press, 1998.

———. *En découvrant l'existence avec Husserl et Heidegger*, third edition. Paris: J. Vrin, 2001.

———. *Entre Nous: On Thinking-of-the-Other*, translated by Michael B. Smith and Barbara Harshav. New York: Columbia University Press, 1998.

———. *Ethics and Infinity: Conversations with Philippe Nemo*, translated by Richard A. Cohen. Pittsburgh: Duquesne University Press, 1985.

———. *Existence and Existents*, translated by Alphonso Lingis, foreword by Robert Bernasconi. Pittsburgh: Duquesne University Press, 2001.

———. *Face to Face with Levinas*, edited by Richard A. Cohen. Albany: State University of New York Press, 1986.

———. "God and Philosophy," in *The Levinas Reader*, edited by Seán Hand, 166–189. Oxford: Blackwell, 1989.

———. *God, Death, and Time*, translated by Bettina Bergo. Stanford: Stanford University Press, 2000.

———. *In the Time of the Nations*, translated by Michael B. Smith. London: Athlone Press, 1994.

———. *Is It Righteous to Be? Interviews with Emmanuel Levinas*, edited by Jill Robbins. Stanford: Stanford University Press, 2001.

————. "Jean Wahl et le sentiment," *Cahiers du Sud* 42 (1955): 453–459.

————. "Jean Wahl: Sans avoir ni être," in *Jean Wahl et Gabriel Marcel*, edited by Jeanne Hersch, 13–31. Paris: Éditions Beauchesne, 1976.

————. "The Jewish Understanding of Scripture," *Cross Currents* 44 (1994): 488–505.

————. *The Levinas Reader*, edited by Seán Hand. Oxford: Blackwell, 1989.

————. "Martin Buber and the Theory of Knowledge," in *The Philosophy of Martin Buber*, edited by Paul A. Schilpp and Maurice Friedman, 133–150. La Salle: Open Court, 1967.

————. "Martin Heidegger and Ontology," *Diacritics* 26 (1996): 11–32.

————. "Mourir pour . . ." in *Heidegger: Questions ouvertes*, edited by Eliane Escoubas, 255–264. Paris: Éditions Osiris, 1988.

————. *Nine Talmudic Readings*, translated and with an introduction by Annette Aronowicz. Bloomington: Indiana University Press, 1990.

————. *Oeuvres 1: Carnets de captivité suivi de Écrits sur la captivité et Notes philosophiques diverses*, edited and annotated by Rodolphe Calin, preface and explanatory notes by Rodolphe Calin and Catherine Chalier, general preface by Jean-Luc Marion. Paris: Éditions Grasset & Fasquelle, 2009.

————. *Oeuvres 2: Parole et silence et autres conferences inédites au Collège philosophique*, edited by Rodolphe Calin, preface and explanatory notes by Rodolphe Calin and Catherine Chalier. Paris: Éditions Grasset & Fasquelle, 2009.

————. *Of God Who Comes to Mind*, translated by Bettina Bergo. Stanford: Stanford University Press, 1998.

————. *On Escape*, translated by Bettina Bergo. Stanford: Stanford University Press, 2003.

————. *Otherwise than Being or Beyond Essence*, translated by Alphonso Lingis. Dordrecht: Kluwer Academic Publishers, 1991.

————. *Outside the Subject*, translated by Michael B. Smith. Stanford: Stanford University Press, 1993.

————. *Proper Names*, translated by Michael B. Smith. Stanford: Stanford University Press, 1996.

————. "Quelques réflexions sur le philosophie de l'Hitlérisme," *Espirit* 2 (1934): 199–208.

————. "Reflections on the Philosophy of Hitlerism," *Critical Inquiry* 17 (1990): 63–71.

————. *The Theory of Intuition in Husserl's Phenomenology*, translated by André Orianne. Evanston: Northwestern University Press, 1973.

————. *Time and the Other*, translated by Richard A. Cohen. Pittsburgh: Duquesne University Press, 1987.

————. *Totalité et infini: Essai sur l'extériorité*. The Hague: Martinus Nijhoff, 1961.

————. *Totality and Infinity: An Essay on Exteriority*, translated by Alphonso Lingis. Dordrecht: Kluwer Academic Publishers, 1969.

————. "The Trace of the Other," translated by Alphonso Lingis, in *Deconstruction in Context*, edited by Mark C. Taylor, 345–359. Chicago: University of Chicago Press, 1986.

————. *Transcendance et intelligibilité: Suivi d'un entretien*. Geneva: Labor et Fides, 1996.

Levinas and Buber: Dialogue and Difference, edited by Peter Atterton, Matthew Calarco, and Maurice Friedman. Pittsburgh: Duquesne University Press, 2004.

Lévy, Benny. "Philosophie de la Révélation? Schelling, Rosenzweig, Levinas," *Cahiers d'Études Lévinassinnes* 2 (2003): 283–383.

Levy, Ze'ev. *Between Yafeth and Shem: On the Relationship between Jewish and General Philosophy*. New York: Peter Lang, 1987.

————. "Emmanuel Lévinas as a Jewish Philosopher," in *Ḥazon Naḥum: Studies in Jewish Law, Thought, and History Presented to Dr. Norman Lamm on the Occasion of His Seventieth Birthday*, edited by Yaakov Elman and Jeffrey S. Gurock, 577–597. New York: Yeshiva University Press, 1997.

————. "Hermann Cohen and Emmanuel Lévinas," in *Hermann Cohen's Philosophy of Religion: International Conference in Jerusalem 1996*, edited by Stéphane Moses and Hartwig Wiedebach, 133–143. Hildesheim: Georg Olms, 1997.

————. *Otherness and Responsibility: A Study of Emmanuel Levinas' Philosophy*. Jerusalem: Magnes Press, 1997.

Lin, Yael. "Finding Time for a Fecund Feminine in Levinas's Thought," *Philosophy Today* 53 (2009): 179–190.

Llewelyn, John. "Am I Obsessed by Bobby? (Humanism of the Other Animal)," in *Re-Reading Levinas*, edited by Robert Bernasconi and Simon Critchley, 234–245. Bloomington: Indiana University Press, 1991.

————. *Appositions of Jacques Derrida and Emmanuel Levinas*. Bloomington: Indiana University Press, 2001.

————. *Emmanuel Levinas: The Genealogy of Ethics*. London: Routledge, 1995.

————. *Margins of Religion: Between Kierkegaard and Derrida*. Bloomington: Indiana University Press, 2009.

————. *The HypoCritical Imagination: Between Kant and Levinas*. London: Routledge, 2000.

Lorentzen, Jamie. *Kierkegaard's Metaphors*. Macon: Mercer University Press, 2001.

Löwith, Karl. "F. Rosenzweig and M. Heidegger on Temporality and Eternity," *Philosophy and Phenomenological Research* 3 (1942): 53–77.

————. "M. Heidegger und F. Rosenzweig. Ein Nachtrag zu 'Sein und Zeit,'" *Zeitschrift für philosophische Forschung* 12 (1958): 161–187.

————. *Nature, History, and Existentialism*, edited by Arnold Levison. Evanston: Northwestern University Press, 1966.

————. *Nietzsche's Philosophy of the Eternal Recurrence of the Same*, translated by J. Harvey Lomax, foreword by Bernd Magnus. Berkeley: University of California Press, 1997.

Löwy, Michael. "Walter Benjamin and Franz Rosenzweig: Messianism against „Progress"," in *Faith, Truth, and Reason: New Perspectives on Franz Rosenzweig's »Star of Redemption«*, edited by Yehoyada Amir, Yossi Turner, and Martin Brasser, 373–390. Munich: Verlag Karl Alber, 2012.

Mack, Michael. "Franz Rosenzweig's and Emmanuel Levinas's Critique of German Idealism's Pseudotheology," *Journal of Religion* 83 (2003): 56–78.

MacKendrick, Karmen. "Eros, Ethics, Explosion: The Loss of Deixis in Recurrence," *Philosophy Today* 55 (2011): 361–371.

Mackinlay, Shane. "Exceeding Truth: Jean-Luc Marion's Saturated Phenomena," *Pacifica* 20 (2007): 40–51.

———. *Interpreting Excess: Jean-Luc Marion, Saturated Phenomenon, and Hermeneutics.* New York: Fordham University Press, 2009.

Maimonides, Moses. *The Guide of the Perplexed*, translated with an introduction and notes by Shlomo Pines, with an introductory essay by Leo Strauss. Chicago: University of Chicago Press, 1963.

Makkreel, Rudolf A. *Imagination and Interpretation in Kant: The Hermeneutical Import of the Critique of Judgment.* Chicago: University of Chicago Press, 1990.

Malka, Salomon. *Emmanuel Levinas: His Life and Legacy*, foreword by Philippe Nemo, translated by Michael Kigel and Sara M. Embree. Pittsburgh: Duquesne University Press, 2006.

Manoussakis, John Panteleimon. *God after Metaphysics: A Theological Aesthetic.* Bloomington: Indiana University Press, 2007.

———. "Toward a Fourth Reduction?" in *After God: Richard Kearney and the Religious Turn in Continental Philosophy*, edited by John Panteleimon Manoussakis, 21–33. New York: Fordham University Press, 2006.

Mansfield, Nick. *The God Who Deconstructs Himself: Sovereignty and Subjectivity Between Freud, Bataille, and Derrida.* New York: Fordham University Press, 2010.

Marion, Jean-Luc. *Being Given: Toward a Phenomenology of Givenness*, translated by Jeffrey L. Kosky. Stanford: Stanford University Press, 2002.

———. *The Crossing of the Visible*, translated by James K. A. Smith. Stanford: Stanford University Press, 2004.

———. "The 'End of Metaphysics' as a Possibility," in *Religion After Metaphysics*, edited by Mark A. Wrathall, 166–189. Cambridge: Cambridge University Press, 2003.

———. *The Erotic Phenomenon*, translated by Stephen E. Lewis. Chicago: University of Chicago Press, 2007.

———. *Étant donné: Essai d'une phénoménologie de la donation.* Paris: Presses Universitaires de France, 1997.

———. *Figures de phénoménologie: Husserl, Heidegger, Levinas, Henry, Derrida.* Paris: J. Vrin, 2012.

———. *God Without Being: Hors-Texte*, translated by Thomas A. Carlson, with a foreword by David Tracy. Chicago: University of Chicago Press, 1991.

———. *In Excess: Studies of Saturated Phenomena*, translated by Robyn Horner and Vincent Berraud. New York: Fordham University Press, 2002.

———. "In the Name: How to Avoid Speaking of 'Negative Theology,'" in *God, the Gift, and Postmodernism*, edited by John D. Caputo and Michael J. Scanlon, 20–53. Bloomington: Indiana University Press, 1999.

———. *In the Self's Place: The Approach of Saint Augustine*, translated by Jeffrey L. Kosky. Stanford: Stanford University Press, 2012.

———. "La double idolâtrie: Remarques sur la différence ontologique et la pensée de Dieu," in *Heidegger et la question de Dieu*, edited by Richard Kearney and Joseph Stephen O'Leary, preface by Jean-Yves Lacoste, 67–94. Paris: Presses Universitaires de France, 2009.

———. "The Phenomenality of the Sacrament—Being and Givenness," in *Words of Life: New Theological Turns in French Phenomenology*, edited by Bruce Ellis Benson and Norman Wirzba, 89–102. New York: Fordham University Press, 2010.

———. *Prolegomena to Charity*, translated by Stephen E. Lewis. New York: Fordham University Press, 2002.

———. "The Reason of the Gift," in *Givenness and God: Questions of Jean-Luc Marion*, edited by Ian Leask and Eoin Cassidy, 101–134. New York: Fordham University Press, 2005.

———. *The Reason of the Gift*, translated and with an introduction by Stephen E. Lewis. Charlottesville: University of Virginia Press, 2011.

———. "The Recognition of the Gift," in *Philosophical Concepts and Religious Metaphors: New Perspectives on Phenomenology and Theology*, edited by Cristian Ciocan, 15–28. Bucharest: Zeta Books, 2009.

———. *Reduction and Givenness: Investigations of Husserl, Heidegger, and Phenomenology*, translated by Thomas A. Carlson. Evanston: Northwestern University Press, 1998.

———. "The Saturated Phenomenon," in *Phenomenology and the "Theological Turn": The French Debate*, 176–216. New York: Fordham University Press, 2000.

———. "Thomas Aquinas and Onto-theo-logy," in *Mystics: Presence and Aporia*, edited by Michael Kessler and Christian Sheppard, 38–74. Chicago: University of Chicago Press, 2003.

———. *The Visible and the Revealed*, translated by Christina M. Gschwandtner and others. New York: Fordham University Press, 2008.

Marrati, Paola. *Genesis and Trace: Derrida Reading Husserl and Heidegger*. Stanford: Stanford University Press, 2005.

Marx, Werner. "The World Is Another Beginning: Poetic Dwelling and the Role of the Poet," in *On Heidegger and Language*, edited and translated by Joseph J. Kockelmans, 235–259. Evanston: Northwestern University Press, 1972.

Mate, Reyes. *Memory of the West: The Contemporaneity of Forgotten Jewish Thinkers*, translated by Anne Day Dewey, edited by John R. Welch. Amsterdam: Rodopi, 2004.

Matuštik, Martin Beck. "Between Hope and Terror: Habermas and Derrida Plead for the Im/Possible," in *The Derrida-Habermas Reader*, edited by Lasse Thomassen, 278–296. Chicago: University of Chicago Press, 2006.

Maudlin, Tim. *The Metaphysics Within Physics*. Oxford: Oxford University Press, 2007.

Mauss, Marcel. *The Gift: The Form and Reason for Exchange in Archaic Societies*, translated by Wilfred Douglas Halls, foreword by Mary Douglas. New York: W. W. Norton, 1990.

McCullough, Lissa. "Simone Weil's God: A Radical Christianity for the Secular World," Ph.D. dissertation, University of Chicago, 1999.

———. "The Void: Simone Weil's Naming of Evil," in *Wrestling with God and with Evil: Philosophical Reflections*, edited by Hendrik M. Vroom, 25–41. Amsterdam: Rodopi, 2007.

McDonald, Blair. "To Do What One Ought to Do: Reconsidering Heidegger's Thesis— 'The Animal Is Poor in World,'" *Colloquy: Text Theory Critique* 21 (2011): 6–24.

McGinn, Bernard. "The God beyond God: Theology and Mysticism in the Thought of Meister Eckhart," *Journal of Religion* 61 (1981): 1–19.

McGrath, Sean J. *The Early Heidegger and Medieval Philosophy: Phenomenology for the Godforsaken*. Washington, DC: Catholic University of America Press, 2006.

McLean, Bradley H. *Biblical Interpretation and Philosophical Hermeneutics*. Cambridge: Cambridge University Press, 2012.

McLellan, David. *Utopian Pessimist: The Life and Thought of Simone Weil*. New York: Poseidon Press, 1990.

McNeill, William. "Life Beyond the Organism: Animal Being in Heidegger's Freiburg Lectures, 1929–30," in *Animal Others: On Ethics, Ontology, and Animal Life*, edited by H. Peter Steeves, foreword by Tom Regan, 197–248. Albany: State University of New York Press, 1999.

Meier, Heinrich. *Leo Strauss and the Theologico-Political Problem*, translated by Marcus Brainard. New York: Cambridge University Press, 2006.

Meir, Ephraim. "Goethe's Place in Rosenzweig's *Star of Redemption*," *Da'at* 48 (2002): 97–107 (Hebrew).

———. "Judaism and Philosophy: Each Other's Other in Levinas," *Modern Judaism* 30 (2010): 348–362.

———. *Levinas's Jewish Thought: Between Jerusalem and Athens*. Jerusalem: Magnes Press, 2008.

Melber, Jehuda. *Hermann Cohen's Philosophy of Judaism*. New York: Jonathan David, 1968.

Menaḥem Mendel of Viṭebsk. *Peri ha-Areṣ al ha-Torah im Be'ur Ṭa'am ha-Peri*, 3 vols. Jerusalem: Makhon Peri ha-Areṣ, 2011.

Mendes-Flohr, Paul. "Between Sensual and Heavenly Love: Franz Rosenzweig's Reading of the Song of Songs," in *Scriptural Exegesis—The Shapes of Culture and the Religious Imagination: Essays in Honour of Michael Fishbane*, edited by Deborah A. Green and Laura S. Lieber, 310–318. Oxford: Oxford University Press, 2009.

———. "Franz Rosenzweig and the Crisis of Historicism," in *The Philosophy of Franz Rosenzweig*, edited by Paul Mendes-Flohr, 138–161. Hanover: University Press of New England, 1988.

————. *From Mysticism to Dialogue: Martin Buber's Transformation of German Social Thought*. Detroit: Wayne State University Press, 1989.

————. "'To Brush History against the Grain': The Eschatology of the Frankfurt School and Ernst Bloch," *Journal of the American Academy of Religion* 51 (1983): 631–650.

Mendieta, Eduardo. "Modernity's Religion: Habermas and the Linguistification of the Sacred," in *Perspectives on Habermas*, edited by Lewis Edwin Hahn, 123–138. Chicago: Open Court, 2000.

Mensch, James Richard. *After Modernity: Husserlian Reflections on a Philosophical Tradition*. Albany: State University of New York Press, 1996.

————. *Hiddenness and Alterity: Philosophical and Literary Sightings of the Unseen*. Pittsburgh: Duquesne University Press, 2005.

————. *Intersubjectivity and Transcendental Idealism*. Albany: State University of New York Press, 1988.

Merkle, John C. *The Genesis of Faith: The Depth Theology of Abraham Joshua Heschel*. New York: Macmillan, 1985.

Merleau-Ponty, Maurice. *The Invisible and the Visible*, edited by Claude Lefort, translated by Alphonso Lingis. Evanston: Northwestern University Press, 1968.

Meskin, Jacob. "The Role of Lurianic Kabbalah in the Early Philosophy of Emmanuel Levinas," in *Levinas Studies: An Annual Review*, vol. 2, edited by Jeffrey Bloechl, 49–77. Pittsburgh: Duquesne University Press, 2007.

————. "Toward a New Understanding of the Work of Emmanuel Levinas," *Modern Judaism* 20 (2000): 78–102.

Meyer, Thomas. *Zwischen Philosophie und Gesetz: Jüdische Philosophie und Theologie von 1933 bis 1938*. Leiden: Brill, 2009.

Michaud, Ginette. *Battements du secret littéraire: Lire Jacques Derrida et Hélène Cixous*, vol. 1. Paris: Hermann Éditeurs, 2010.

Midrash Tanhuma. Jerusalem: Eshkol, 1972.

Midrash Tehillim, edited by Solomon Buber. Vilna: Rom, 1891.

Miedema, Siebren, and Gert J. J. Biesta, "Jacques Derrida's Religion without Religion and the Im/Possibility of Religious Education," *Religious Education* 99 (2004): 23–37.

Miller, David L. *Christs: Meditations on Archetypal Images in Christian Theology*. New Orleans: Spring Journal Books, 2005.

————. *Hells and Holy Ghosts: A Theopoetics of Christian Belief*. Nashville: Abingdon Press, 1989.

————. "Theopoiesis," in Stanley R. Hopper, *Why Permissions and Other Poems: Transformations of Theology in Poetry*, 1–12. Atlanta: Scholars Press, 1987.

Miller, J. Hillis. *For Derrida*. New York: Fordham University Press, 2009.

Min, Anselm K. "Naming the Unnameable God: Levinas, Derrida, and Marion," *International Journal of the Philosophy of Religion* 60 (2006): 99–116.

Mittelman, Alan. "'The Jew in Christian Culture' by Hermann Cohen: An Introduction and Translation," *Modern Judaism* 23 (2003): 51–73.

Moi, Toril. *Sexual/Textual Politics: Feminist Literary Theory*. London: Routledge, 1985.

Mole, Gary D. *Lévinas, Blanchot, Jabès: Figures of Estrangement*. Gainesville: University Press of Florida, 1997.

Mooij, Jan Johann Albinn. *Fictional Realities: The Uses of Literary Imagination*. Amsterdam: John Benjamins, 1993.

Mopsik, Charles. "La pensée d'Emmanuel Lévinas et la Cabale," in *Cahier de l'Herne: Emmanuel Levinas*, edited by Catherine Chalier and Miguel Abensour, 428–441. Paris: Éditions de l'Herne, 1991.

Moran, Dermot. "Husserl and Heidegger on the Transcendental 'Homelessness' of Philosophy," in *Epistemology, Archaeology, Ethics: Current Investigations of Husserl's Corpus*, edited by Pol Vandevelde and Sebastian Luft, 169–187. New York: Continuum, 2010.

———. *The Philosophy of John Scottus Eriugena: A Study of Idealism in the Middle Ages*. Cambridge: Cambridge University Press, 1989.

Morgan, Michael L. *Discovering Levinas*. Cambridge: Cambridge University Press, 2007.

Mosès, Stéphane. "Franz Rosenzweig in Perspective: Reflections on His Last Diaries," in *The Philosophy of Franz Rosenzweig*, edited by Paul Mendes-Flohr, 185–201. Hanover: University Press of New England, 1988.

———. "L'idée de l'infini en nous," in *Répondre d'autrui: Emmanuel Lévinas*, edited by Jean-Christophe Aeschlimann and Paul Ricouer, 41–51. Boudry-Neuchâtel: À la Baconnière, 1989.

———. *System and Revelation: The Philosophy of Franz Rosenzweig*, foreword by Emmanuel Lévinas, translated by Catherine Tihanyi. Detroit: Wayne State University Press, 1992.

Moylan, Tom. "Bloch against Bloch: The Theological Reception of *Das Prinzip Hoffnung* and the Liberation of the Utopian Function," in *Not Yet: Reconsidering Ernst Bloch*, edited by Jamie Owen Daniel and Tom Moylan, 96–121. London: Verso, 1997.

Moyn, Samuel. "Divine and Human Love: Franz Rosenzweig's History of the Song of Songs," *Jewish Studies Quarterly* 12 (2005): 194–212.

———. "Judaism against Paganism: Emmanuel Levinas's Response to Heidegger and Nazism in the 1930s," *History and Memory* 10 (1998): 25–58.

———. *Origins of the Other: Emmanuel Levinas Between Revelation and Ethics*. Ithaca: Cornell University Press, 2005.

———. "Transcendence, Morality, and History: Emmanuel Levinas and the Discovery of Søren Kierkegaard in France," *Yale French Studies* 104 (2004): 37–46.

Moynahan, Gregory B. "Hermann Cohen's *Das Prinzip der Infinitesimalmethod*, Ernst Cassirer, and the Politics of Science in Wilhelmine Germany," *Perspectives on Science* 11 (2003): 35–75.

Muffs, Yochanan. *The Personhood of God: Biblical Theology, Human Faith and the Divine Image*. Woodstock: Jewish Lights, 2005.

Mugerauer, Robert. *Heidegger and Homecoming: The Leitmotif in the Later Writings*. Toronto: University of Toronto Press, 2008.

Munk, Reiner. *The Rationale of Halakhic Man: Joseph B. Soloveitchik's Conception of Jewish Thought*. Amsterdam: J. C. Gieben, 1996.

Myers, David N. *Resisting History: Historicism and Its Discontents in German-Jewish Thought*. Princeton: Princeton University Press, 2003.

The Nag Hammadi Scriptures, edited by Marvin Meyer, introduction by Elaine H. Pagels. New York: HarperCollins, 2007.

Nagatomo, Shigenori. "The Logic of the *Diamond Sutra*: A Is Not A, Therefore It Is A," *Asian Philosophy* 10 (2000): 213–244.

Nancy, Jean-Luc. *Being Singular Plural*, translated by Robert D. Richardson and Anne E. O'Byrne. Stanford: Stanford University Press, 2000.

———. *The Creation of the World or Globalization*, translated and with an introduction by François Raffoul and David Pettigrew. Albany: State University of New York Press, 2007.

———. "A Deconstruction of Monotheism," in *Religion: Beyond a Concept*, edited by Hent de Vries, 380–391. New York: Fordham University Press, 2008.

———. *Dis-Enclosure: The Deconstruction of Christianity*, translated by Bettina Bergo, Gabriel Malenfant, and Michael B. Smith. New York: Fordham University Press, 2008.

———. *The Fall of Sleep*, translated by Charlotte Mandell. New York: Fordham University Press, 2009.

———. *The Ground of the Image*, translated by Jeff Fort. New York: Fordham University Press, 2005.

———. *The Inoperative Community*, edited by Peter Connor, foreword by Christopher Fynsk. Minneapolis: University of Minnesota Press, 1990.

———. *Noli me tangere: On the Raising of the Body*, translated by Sarah Clift, Pascale-Anne Brault, and Michael Naas. New York: Fordham University Press, 2008.

———. "On Dis-enclosure and Its Gesture, Adoration: A Concluding Dialogue with Jean-Luc Nancy," in *Re-treating Religion: Deconstructing Christianity with Jean-Luc Nancy*, edited by Alena Alexandrova, Ignaas Devisch, Laurens ten Kate, and Aukje van Rooden, 304–343. New York: Fordham University Press, 2012.

———. "Preamble: In the Midst of the World; or, Why Deconstruct Christianity?" in *Re-treating Religion: Deconstructing Christianity with Jean-Luc Nancy*, edited by Alena Alexandrova, Ignaas Devisch, Laurens ten Kate, and Aukje van Rooden, 1–21. New York: Fordham University Press, 2012.

Narbonne, Jean-Marc. *Levinas and the Greek Heritage*. Leuven: Peeters, 2006.

Nauen, Franz. "Hermann Cohen's Perceptions of Spinoza: A Reappraisal," *AJS Review* 4 (1979): 111–124.

Nault, François. "Le discours de la doublure: Nietzsche et la théologie négative," *Religiogiques* 12 (1995): 273–294.

Nelson, Eric S. "Language and Emptiness in Chan Buddhism and the Early Heidegger," *Journal of Chinese Philosophy* 37 (2010): 472–492.

Neusner, Jacob. *Death and Birth of Judaism: The Impact of Christianity, Secularism, and the Holocaust on Jewish Faith*. New York: Basic Books, 1987.

————. *Handbook of Rabbinic Theology: Language, System, Structure*. Leiden: Brill, 2002.

————. *The Idea of History in Rabbinic Judaism*. Leiden: Brill, 2004.

————. *Messiah in Context: Israel's History and Destiny in Formative Judaism*. Philadelphia: Fortress Press, 1984.

————. "Paradigmatic Versus Historical Thinking: The Case of Rabbinic Judaism," *History and Theory* 36 (1997): 353–377.

————. *The Presence of the Past, the Pastness of the Present: History, Time, and Paradigm in Rabbinic Judaism*. Bethesda: CDL Press, 1999.

————. *Theological and Philosophical Premises of Judaism*. Boston: Academic Studies Press, 2008.

————. *The Theology of the Oral Torah: Revealing the Justice of God*. Montreal: McGill-Queen's University Press, 1999.

Nevin, Thomas R. *Simone Weil: Portrait of a Self-Exiled Jew*. Chapel Hill: University of North Carolina Press, 1991.

Newheiser, David. "Eckhart, Derrida, and the Gift of Love," *Heythrop Journal* (2012), published online http://onlinelibrary.wiley.com/doi/10.1111/j.1468–2265.2012.00754.x/pdf.

————. "Time and the Responsibilities of Reading: Revisiting Derrida and Dionysius," in *Reading the Church Fathers*, edited by Scot Douglass and Morwenna Ludlow, 23–43. London: T&T Clark, 2011.

Newton, Adam Zachary. *The Fence and the Neighbor: Emmanuel Levinas, Yeshayahu Leibowitz, and Israel among the Nations*. Albany: State University of New York Press, 2001.

Nietzsche, Friedrich. *Writings from the Late Notebooks*, edited by Rüdiger Bittner, translated by Kate Sturge. Cambridge: Cambridge University Press, 2003.

Nishitani, Keiji. "Ontology and Utterance," *Philosophy East and West* 31 (1981): 29–43.

Nordmann, Sophie. *Du singulier à l'universel: Essai sur la philosophie religieuse de Hermann Cohen*. Paris: J. Vrin, 2007.

Novalis. *Novalis: Philosophical Writings*, translated and edited by Margaret Mahony Stoljar. Albany: State University of New York Press, 1997.

Ochs, Peter. "Saints and the Heterological Historian," in *Saintly Influence: Edith Wyschogrod and the Possibilities of Philosophy of Religion*, edited by Eric Boynton and Martin Kavka, 219–237. New York: Fordham University Press, 2009.

O'Donoghue, Brendan. *A Poetics of Homecoming: Heidegger, Homelessness and the Homecoming Venture*. Newcastle: Cambridge Scholars, 2011.

Ofrat, Gideon. *The Jewish Derrida*, translated by Peretz Kidron. Syracuse: Syracuse University Press, 2001.

Olafson, Frederick A. "Being, Truth, and Presence in Heidegger's Thought," *Inquiry* 41 (1998): 45–64.

O'Leary, Joseph S. "The Gift: A Trojan Horse in the Citadel of Phenomenology?" in *Givenness and God: Questions of Jean-Luc Marion*, edited by Ian Leask and Eoin Cassidy, 135–166. New York: Fordham University Press, 2005.

Oppenheim, Michael. "Foreword," in Franz Rosenzweig, *God, Man, and the World: Lectures and Essays*, edited and translated by Barbara E. Galli, xi–xxxiv. Syracuse: Syracuse University Press, 1998.

———. *Mutual Upholding: Fashioning Jewish Philosophy Through Letters*. New York: Peter Lang, 1992.

———. "Søren Kierkegaard and Franz Rosenzweig: The Movement from Philosophy to Religion," Ph.D. dissertation, University of California, Santa Barbara, 1976.

———. *Speaking/Writing of God: Jewish Reflections on the Life with Others*. Albany: State University of New York Press, 1997.

———. "Taking Time Seriously: An Inquiry into the Methods of Communication of Søren Kierkegaard and Franz Rosenzweig," *Studies in Religion/Sciences Religieuses* 7 (1978): 53–60.

O'Regan, Cyril. *Gnostic Return in Modernity*. Albany: State University of New York Press, 2001.

———. *Theology and the Spaces of Apocalyptic*. Milwaukee: Marquette University Press, 2009.

Palmer, D. W. "Atheism, Apologetic, and Negative Theology in the Greek Apologists of the Second Century," *Vigiliae Christianae* 37 (1983): 234–259.

Peacocke, John. "Heidegger and the Problem of Onto-Theology," in *Post-Secular Philosophy: Between Philosophy and Theology*, edited by Phillip Blond, 177–194. London: Routledge, 1998.

Pearson, Keith Ansell. "Pure Reserve: Deleuze, Philosophy, and Immanence," in *Deleuze and Religion*, edited by Mary Bryden, 141–155. New York: Routledge, 2001.

———. "The Reality of the Virtual: Bergson and Deleuze," *Modern Language Notes* 129 (2005): 1112–1127.

Peperzak, Adriaan T. *Beyond: The Philosophy of Emmanuel Levinas*. Evanston: Northwestern University Press, 1997.

———. "Giving," in *The Enigma of Gift and Sacrifice*, edited by Edith Wyschogrod, Jean-Joseph Goux, and Eric Boynton, 161–175. New York: Fordham University Press, 2002.

Perlman, Lawrence. *Abraham Heschel's Idea of Revelation*. Atlanta: Scholars Press, 1989.

Pesiqta de-Rav Kahana, edited by Bernard Mandelbaum. New York: Jewish Theological Seminary of America, 1962.

Pesiqta Rabbati: A Synoptic Edition of Pesiqta Rabbati Based upon All Extant Manuscripts and the Editio Princeps, edited by Rivka Ulmer. Atlanta: Scholars Press, 1997.

Pezze, Barbara Dalle. *Martin Heidegger and Meister Eckhart: A Path Towards Gelassenheit*, with a foreword by Timothy O'Leary. Lewiston: Edwin Mellen Press, 2008.

Pines, Shlomo. "Der Islam im 'Stern der Erlösung.' Eine Untersuchung zu Tendenzen und Quellen Franz Rosenzweigs," *Hebräische Beiträge zur Wissenschaft des Judentums* 3–5 (1987–89): 138–148.

———. "Islam According to *The Star of Redemption*: Toward a Study of Franz Rosenzweig's Sources and Biases," *Bar-Ilan Yearbook* 22–23 (1987–88): 303–314 (Hebrew).

Podmore, Simon D. *Kierkegaard and the Self Before God: Anatomy of the Abyss.* Bloomington: Indiana University Press, 2011.

Pöggeler, Otto. "Heidegger's Topology of Being," in *On Heidegger and Language*, edited and translated by Joseph J. Kockelmans, 107–146. Evanston: Northwestern University Press, 1972.

Pollock, Benjamin. "'Erst die Tatsache ist sicher vor dem Rückfall ins Nichts': Rosenzweig's Concept of Factuality," in *Franz Rosenzweigs "neues Denken": Internationaler Kongreß-Kassel 2004*, edited by Wolfdietrich Schmied-Kowarzik, 2 vols., 359–370. Freiburg: Verlag Karl Alber, 2006.

———. *Franz Rosenzweig and the Systematic Task of Philosophy.* Cambridge: Cambridge University Press, 2009.

———. "Franz Rosenzweig's 'Oldest System-Program,'" *New German Critique* 111 (2010): 59–95.

———. "On the Road to Marcionism: Franz Rosenzweig's Early Theology," *Jewish Quarterly Review* 102 (2012): 224–255.

———. "'Within Earshot of the Young Hegel': Rosenzweig's Letter to Rudolf Ehrenberg of September 1910," in *German-Jewish Thought Between Religion and Politics: Festschrift in Honor of Paul Mendes-Flohr on the Occasion of His Seventieth Birthday*, edited by Christian Wiese and Martina Urban, 185–207. Berlin: Walter de Gruyter, 2012.

Polt, Richard. *The Emergency of Being: On Heidegger's Contribution to Philosophy.* Ithaca: Cornell University Press, 2006.

———. "The Question of Nothing," in *A Companion to Heidegger's Introduction to Metaphysics*, edited by Richard Polt and Gregory Fried, 57–82. New Haven: Yale University Press, 2001.

Polydoxy: Theology of Multiplicity and Relation, edited by Catherine Keller and Laurel C. Schneider. London: Routledge, 2011.

Poma, Andrea. *The Critical Philosophy of Hermann Cohen*, translated by John Denton. Albany: State University of New York Press, 1997.

———. "Suffering and Non-Eschatological Messianism in Hermann Cohen," in *Hermann Cohen's Critical Idealism*, edited by Reinier Munk, 413–442. Dordrecht: Springer, 2005.

———. *Yearning for Form and Other Essays on Hermann Cohen's Thought.* Dordrecht: Springer, 2006.

Priest, Ann-Marie. "Woman as God, God as Woman: Mysticism, Negative Theology, and Luce Irigaray," *Journal of Religion* 83 (2003): 1–23.

Pseudo-Dionysius: The Complete Works, translated by Colm Luibheid, foreword, notes, and translation collaboration by Paul Rorem, preface by René Roques, introductions by Jaroslav Pelikan, Jean Leclercq, and Karlfried Froehlich. New York: Paulist Press, 1987.

Puntel, Lorenz B. *Being and God: A Systematic Approach in Confrontation with Martin Heidegger, Emmanuel Levinas, and Jean-Luc Marion*, translated by and in collaboration with Alan White. Evanston: Northwestern University Press, 2011.

Putnam, Hilary. "God and the Philosophers," *Midwest Studies in Philosophy* 21 (1997): 175–187.

———. "Introduction," in Franz Rosenzweig, *Understanding the Sick and the Healthy: A View of World, Man, and God*, translated and with an introduction by Nahum Glatzer, 3–9. Cambridge, MA: Harvard University Press, 1999.

———. *Jewish Philosophy as a Guide to Life: Rosenzweig, Buber, Levinas, Wittgenstein*. Bloomington: Indiana University Press, 2008.

———. "On Negative Theology," *Faith and Philosophy* 14 (1997): 407–422.

Putt, B. Keith. "Theopoetics of the Possible," in *After God: Richard Kearney and the Religious Turn in Continental Philosophy*, edited by John Panteleimon Manoussakis, 241–269. New York: Fordham University Press, 2006.

Rabi, Wladimir. "La conception weilienne de la création: Rencontre avec la kabbale juive," in *Simone Weil: Philosophe, historienne et mystique*, edited by Gilbert Kahn, 141–160. Paris: Éditions Aubier Montaigne, 1978.

Rabinbach, Anson. "Between Enlightenment and Apocalypse: Benjamin, Bloch, and Modern Jewish Messianism," *New German Critique* 34 (1985): 78–124.

Radloff, Bernhard. "Preliminary Notes on Divine Images in the Light of Being-Historical Thinking," in *Heidegger, Translation, and the Task of Thinking: Essays in Honor of Parvis Emad*, edited by Frank Schalow, 145–171. Dordrecht: Springer, 2011.

Räsänen, Pajari. "Counter-figures—An Essay on Antimetaphoric Resistance: Paul Celan's Poetry and Poetics at the Limits of Figurality," Ph.D. dissertation, University of Helsinki, 2007.

Raschke, Carl. *Postmodernism and the Revolution in Religious Theory: Toward a Semiotics of the Event*. Charlottesville: University of Virginia Press, 2012.

Rashkover, Randi. "Justifying Philosophy and Restoring Revelation: Assessing Strauss's Medieval Return," in *Encountering the Medieval in Modern Jewish Thought*, edited by James A. Diamond and Aaron W. Hughes, 229–257. Leiden: Brill, 2012.

———. *Revelation and Theopolitics: Barth, Rosenzweig, and the Politics of Praise*. London: T & T Clark International, 2005.

Ravitzky, Aviezer. *History and Faith: Studies in Jewish Philosophy*. Amsterdam: J. C. Gieben, 1996.

Rayment-Pickard, Hugh. *Impossible God: Derrida's Theology*. Burlington: Ashgate, 2003.

Richardson, SJ, William J. *Heidegger Through Phenomenology to Thought*, preface by Martin Heidegger, third edition. The Hague: Martinus Nijhoff, 1974.

Ricoeur, Paul. *Figuring the Sacred: Religion, Narrative, and Imagination*, translated by David Pellauer, edited by Mark I. Wallace. Minneapolis: Fortress Press, 1995.

———. *Freud and Philosophy: An Essay on Interpretation*, translated by Denis Savage. New Haven: Yale University Press, 1970.

———. *On Translation*, translated by Eileen Brennan, with an introduction by Richard Kearney. London: Routledge, 2006.

———. "Otherwise: A Reading of Emmanuel Levinas's *Otherwise than Being or Beyond Essence*," *Yale French Studies* 104 (2004): 82–99.

———. *The Rule of Metaphor: Multi-Disciplinary Studies of the Creation of Meaning in Language*, translated by Robert Czerny with Kathleen McLaughlin and John Costello, SJ. Toronto: University of Toronto Press, 1977.

Risser, James. "Poetic Dwelling in Gadamer's Hermeneutics," *Philosophy Today* 38 (1994): 369–379.

Rivera, Joseph M. "The Call and the Gifted in Christological Perspective: A Consideration of Brian Robinette's Critique of Jean-Luc Marion," *Heythrop Journal* 51 (2010): 1053–1060.

Rivera, Mayra. *The Touch of Transcendence: A Postcolonial Theology*. Louisville: Westminster John Knox Press, 2007.

Robbins, Jill. *Altered Reading: Levinas and Literature*. Chicago: University of Chicago Press, 1999.

———. "Circumcising Confession: Derrida, Autobiography, Judaism," *Diacritics* 25 (1995): 20–38.

———. *Prodigal Son/Elder Brother: Interpretation and Alterity in Augustine, Petrarch, Kafka, Levinas*. Baltimore: Johns Hopkins University Press, 1991.

Robert, William. "A Mystical Impulse: From Apophatics to Decreation in Pseudo-Dionysius, Meister Eckhart and Simone Weil," *Medieval Mystical Theology* 21 (2012): 113–132.

Robinette, Brian. "A Gift to Theology? Jean-Luc Marion's 'Saturated Phenomenon' in Christological Perspective," *Heythrop Journal* 48 (2007): 86–108.

Roesner, Martina. "Logos und Anfang: Zur Johanneischen Dimension in Heideggers Denken," in *Heidegger und die christliche Tradition*, edited by Norbert Fischer and Friedrich Wilhelm von Hermann, 33–54. Hamburg: Felix Meiner Verlag, 2007.

Rollins, Peter. *The Fidelity of Betrayal: Towards a Church Beyond Belief*. London: Society for Promoting Christian Knowledge, 2008.

———. *How (Not) to Speak of God*. London: Paraclete Press, 2006.

———. *Insurrection*. New York: Howard Books, 2011.

Romano, Claude. "Awaiting," in *Phenomenology and Eschatology: Not Yet in the Now*, edited by Neal DeRoo and John Panteleimon Manoussakis, 35–52. Burlington: Ashgate, 2009.

Rose, Gillian. *The Broken Middle: Out of Our Ancient Society*. Oxford: Blackwell, 1992.

———. *Dialectic of Nihilism: Post-Structuralism and Law*. Oxford: Basil Blackwell, 1984.

———. *Judaism and Modernity: Philosophical Essays*. Oxford: Blackwell, 1993.

Rosemann, Philipp W. "Postmodern Philosophy and Jean-Luc Marion's Eucharistic Realism," in *Transcendence and Phenomenology*, edited by Conor Cunningham and Peter M. Candler Jr., 84–110. London: SCM Press, 2007.

Rosenstock, Bruce. *Philosophy and the Jewish Question: Mendelssohn, Rosenzweig, and Beyond*. New York: Fordham University Press, 2010.

Rosenstock-Huessy, Eugen, ed. *Judaism Despite Christianity: The "Letters on Christianity and Judaism" between Eugen Rosenstock-Huessy and Franz Rosenzweig*. University, Alabama: University of Alabama Press, 1969.

Rosenzweig, Franz. *The Commentaries of Franz Rosenzweig to Ninety-Five Poems of Judah Halevi*, translated and annotated by Michael Swartz. Jerusalem: Magnes Press, 2011 (Hebrew).

———. *Der Mensch und sein Werk: Gesammelte Schriften I. Briefe und Tagebücher*, edited by Rachel Rosenzweig and Edith Rosenzweig-Scheinmann, with the participation of Bernhard Casper, vol. 1: *1900–1918*. The Hague: Martinus Nijhoff, 1979.

———. *Der Mensch und sein Werk: Gesammelte Schriften I. Briefe und Tagebücher*, edited by Rachel Rosenzweig and Edith Rosenzweig-Scheinmann, with the participation of Bernhard Casper, vol. 2: *1918–1929*. The Hague: Martinus Nijhoff, 1979.

———. *Der Mensch und sein Werk: Gesammelte Schriften II. Der Stern der Erlösung*, with an introduction by Reinhold Mayer. The Hague: Martinus Nijhoff, 1976.

———. *Der Mensch und sein Werk: Gesammelte Schriften III. Zweistromland: Kleinere Schriften zu Glauben und Denken*, edited by Reinhold Mayer and Annemarie Mayer. Dordrecht: Martinus Nijhoff, 1984.

———. *Der Mensch und sein Werk: Gesammelte Schriften IV. Sprachdenken im Übersetzen, 1 Band: Jehuda Halevi. Fünfundneunzig Hymnen und Gedichte*, edited by Reinhold Mayer and Annemarie Mayer. Dordrecht: Martinus Nijhoff, 1984.

———. *Die "Gritli"-Briefe. Briefe an Margrit Rosenstock-Huessy*, edited by Inken Rühle and Reinhold Mayer, with a preface by Rafael Rosenzweig. Tübingen: Bilam Verlag, 2002.

———. "Einleitung," in Hermann Cohen, *Jüdische Schriften*, vol. 1, xiii–lxiv. Berlin: C. A. Schwetschke & Sohn, 1924.

———. *God, Man, and the World: Lectures and Essays*, edited and translated by Barbara E. Galli, with a foreword by Michael Oppenheim. Syracuse: Syracuse University Press, 1998.

———. *Kleinere Schriften*. Berlin: Schocken Verlag, 1937.

———. *Ninety-Two Poems and Hymns of Yehuda Halevi*, translated by Thomas Kovach, Eva Jospe, and Gilya Gerda Schmidt, edited and with an introduction by Richard A. Cohen. Albany: State University of New York Press, 2000.

———. *On Jewish Learning*, edited by Nahum N. Glatzer. New York: Schocken, 1955.

————. *Philosophical and Theological Writings*, translated and edited, with notes and commentary, by Paul W. Franks and Michael L. Morgan. Indianapolis: Hackett, 2000.

————. *The Star of Redemption*, translated by William Hallo. New York: Holt, Rinehart, and Winston, 1970.

————. *The Star of Redemption*, translated by Barbara Galli. Madison: University of Wisconsin Press, 2005.

————. *Understanding the Sick and the Healthy: A View of World, Man, and God*, translated and with an introduction by Nahum Glatzer, and with an introduction by Hilary Putnam. Cambridge, MA: Harvard University Press, 1999.

Rötzer, Florian. *Conversations with French Philosophers*, foreword by Rainer Rochlitz, translated by Gary E. Aylesworth. Atlantic Highlands: Humanities Press, 1995.

————. *Französische Philosophen im Gespräch*. Munich: Klaus Boer Verlag, 1986.

Roughley, Alan. *Reading Derrida Reading Joyce*. Gainesville: University Press of Florida, 1999.

Rubenstein, Mary-Jane. "Unknow Thyself: Apophaticism, Deconstruction, and Theology After Ontotheology," *Modern Theology* 19 (2003): 387–417.

Rubinstein, Ernest. *An Episode of Jewish Romanticism: Franz Rosenzweig's The Star of Redemption*. Albany: State University of New York Press, 1999.

Rühle, Inken. "Das Hohelied—ein weltliches Liebeslied als Kernbuch der Offenbarung? Zur Bedeutung der Auslegungsgeschichte von *Schir haSchirim* im *Stern der Erlösung*," in *Rosenzweig als Leser: Kontextuelle Kommentare zum "Stern der Erlösung*," edited by Martin Brasser, 453–479. Tübingen: Max Niemeyer Verlag, 2004.

Ryba, Thomas. "Derrida, Negative Theology and the Trespass of the Sign," *Religion* 27 (1997): 107–115.

Safranski, Rüdiger. *Martin Heidegger: Between Good and Evil*, translated by Ewald Osers. Cambridge, MA: Harvard University Press, 1998.

Saghafi, Kas. *Apparitions—Of Derrida's Other*. New York: Fordham University Press, 2010.

Sallis, John. *Chorology: On Beginning in Plato's Timaeus*. Bloomington: Indiana University Press, 1999.

————. *Delimitations: Phenomenology and the End of Metaphysics*. Bloomington: Indiana University Press, 1986.

————. *Force of Imagination: The Sense of the Elemental*. Bloomington: Indiana University Press, 2000.

————. "The Hermeneutics of Translation," in *Language and Linguisticality in Gadamer's Hermeneutics*, edited by Lawrence K. Schmidt, 67–76. Lanham: Lexington Books, 2000.

————. "Imagination and the Meaning of Being," in *Heidegger et l'idée de la phénoménologie*, 127–144. Dordrecht: Kluwer Academic Publishers, 1988.

————. "Interrupting Truth," in *Heidegger toward the Turn: Essays on the Work of the 1930s*, edited by James Risser, 19–30. Albany: State University of New York Press, 1999.

———. "Levinas and the Elemental," in *Radicalizing Levinas*, edited by Peter Atterton and Matthew Calarco, 87–94. Albany: State University of New York Press, 2010.

———. *Platonic Legacies*. Albany: State University of New York Press, 2004.

Samuelson, Norbert. "The Concept of 'Nichts' in Rosenzweig's *Star of Redemption*," in *Der Philosoph Franz Rosenzweig (1886–1929): Internationaler Kongreß-Kassel 1986*, edited by Wolfdietrich Schmied-Kowarzik, 2 vols., 643–656. Freiburg: Verlag Karl Alber, 1988.

Sandford, Stella. *The Metaphysics of Love: Gender and Transcendence in Levinas*. London: Athlone Press, 2000.

Santner, Eric L. "Miracles Happen: Benjamin, Rosenzweig, Freud, and the Matter of the Neighbor," in Slavoj Žižek, Eric L. Santner, and Kenneth Reinhard, *The Neighbor: Three Inquiries in Political Theology*, 76–133. Chicago: University of Chicago Press, 2005.

———. *On the Psychotheology of Everyday Life: Reflections on Freud and Rosenzweig*. Chicago: University of Chicago Press, 2001.

Sax, Benjamin Elliot. "Language and Jewish Renewal: Franz Rosenzweig's Hermeneutic of Citation," Ph.D. dissertation, University of Chicago, 2008.

Schäfer, Peter. *Mirror of His Beauty: Feminine Images of God from the Bible to the Early Kabbalah*. Princeton: Princeton University Press, 2002.

Schalow, Frank. "Attunement and Translation," in *Heidegger, Translation, and the Task of Thinking: Essays in Honor of Parvis Emad*, edited by Frank Schalow, 291–311. Dordrecht: Springer, 2011.

Scheindlin, Raymond P. *The Song of the Distant Dove: Judah Halevi's Pilgrimage*. Oxford: Oxford University Press, 2008.

Schindler, Renate. *Zeit, Geschichte, Ewigkeit in Franz Rosenzweig's Stern der Erlösung*. Berlin: Parerga Verlag, 2007.

Schmahl, Nadine. *Das Tetragramm als Sprachfigur: Ein Kommentar zu Franz Rosenzweigs letztem Aufsatz*. Tübingen: Mohr Siebeck, 2009.

Schmied-Kowarzik, Wolfdietrich. "Dasein als 'je meines' oder Existenz als Aufgerufensein. Zur Differenz existenzphilosophischer Grundlegungen bei Martin Heidegger und Franz Rosenzweig," in *Die Jemeinigkeit des Mitseins. Die Daseinsanalytik Martin Heideggers und die Kritik der soziologischen Vernunft*, edited by Johannes Weiss, 197–217. Konstanz: UVK, 2001.

———. "Einführende Bemerkungen zu Schelling und Rosenzweig," in *Kabbala und Romantik*, edited by Eveline Goodman-Thau, Gert Mattenklott, and Christoph Schulte, 59–68. Tübingen: Max Niemeyer Verlag, 1994.

———. "Rosenzweig als Vorläufer von Heidegger und ihrer beider Nachfolge Schellings," *Philosophische Rundschau* 52 (2005): 222–233.

———. *Rosenzweig im Gespräch mit Ehrenberg, Cohen und Buber*. Freiburg: Verlag Karl Alber, 2006.

————. "Vom Totalexperiment des Glaubens. Kritisches zur positive Philosophie Schellings und Rosenzweigs," in *Der Philosoph Franz Rosenzweig (1886–1929): Internationaler Kongreß-Kassel 1986*, edited by Wolfdietrich Schmied-Kowarzik, 2 vols., 771–799. Freiburg: Verlag Karl Alber, 1988.

Schneider, Laurel C. *Beyond Monotheism: A Theology of Multiplicity*. London: Routledge, 2008.

Schoenbaum, Susan. "Heidegger's Interpretation of *Phusis* in *Introduction to Metaphysics*," in *A Companion to Heidegger's Introduction to Metaphysics*, edited by Richard Polt and Gregory Fried, 143–160. New Haven: Yale University Press, 2001.

Scholem, Gershom. "Franz Rosenzweig and His Book *The Star of Redemption*," in *The Philosophy of Franz Rosenzweig*, edited by Paul Mendes-Flohr, 20–41. Hanover: University Press of New England, 1988.

————. *Major Trends in Jewish Mysticism*. New York: Schocken, 1954.

————. *The Messianic Idea in Judaism and Other Essays in Jewish Spirituality*. New York: Schocken Books, 1971.

————. *On the Kabbalah and Its Symbolism*, translated by Ralph Manheim. New York: Schocken Books, 1969.

————. *Origins of the Kabbalah*, edited by R. J. Zwi Werblowsky, translated by Allan Arkush. Princeton: Princeton University Press, 1987.

————. "The Traditions of R. Jacob and R. Isaac ben R. Jacob ha-Kohen," *Madda'ei ha-Yahadut* 2 (1927): 165–293 (Hebrew).

Schrag, Calvin O. *God as Otherwise than Being: Towards a Semantics of the Gift*. Evanston: Northwestern University Press, 2002.

————. "Heidegger on Repetition and Historical Understanding," *Philosophy East and West* 20 (1970): 287–295.

Schreiner, Klaus. "Messianism in the Political Culture of the Weimar Republic," in *Toward the Millennium: Messianic Expectations from the Bible to Waco*, edited by Peter Schäfer and Mark Cohen, 311–361. Leiden: Brill, 1998.

Schrijvers, Joeri. " 'And There Shall Be No More Boredom': Problems with Overcoming Metaphysics in Heidegger, Levinas and Marion," in *Transcendence and Phenomenology*, edited by Conor Cunningham and Peter M. Candler Jr., 50–83. London: SCM Press, 2007.

————. *An Introduction to Jean-Yves Lacoste*. Surrey: Ashgate, 2012.

————. *Ontotheological Turnings: The Decentering of the Modern Subject in Recent French Phenomenology*. Albany: State University of New York Press, 2011.

Schroeder, Brian. "A Trace of the Eternal Return? Levinas and Neoplatonism," in *Levinas and the Ancients*, edited by Brian Schroeder and Silvia Benso, 210–229. Bloomington: Indiana University Press, 2008.

Schuchat, Raphael B. *A World Hidden in the Dimensions of Time: The Theory of Redemption in the Writings of the Vilna Gaon, Its Sources and Influences on Later Generations*. Ramat-Gan: Bar-Ilan University Press, 2008 (Hebrew).

Schulte, Christoph. "Zimzum in the Works of Schelling." *Iyyun* 41 (1992): 21–40.

Schürmann, Reiner. *Meister Eckhart: Mystic and Philosopher.* Bloomington: Indiana University Press, 1978.

———. "Neoplatonic Henology as an Overcoming of Metaphysics," *Research in Phenomenology* 13 (1983): 25–41.

———. "Trois penseurs du délaissement: Maître Eckhart, Heidegger, Suzuki: Part One," *Journal of the History of Philosophy* 12 (1974): 455–477.

———. "Trois penseurs du délaissement: Maître Eckhart, Heidegger, Suzuki: Part Two," *Journal of the History of Philosophy* 13 (1975): 56–60.

———. "Ultimate Double Binds," in *Heidegger toward the Turn: Essays on the Work of the 1930s,* edited by James Risser, 243–267. Albany: State University of New York Press, 1999.

Schwarcz, Moshe. "Atheism and Modern Jewish Thought," *Proceedings of the American Academy for Jewish Research* 44 (1971): 127–150.

———. *From Myth to Revelation.* Tel-Aviv: Hakibbutz Hameuchad, 1978 (Hebrew).

Schwartz, Michal. *Metapher und Offenbarung: Zur Sprache von Franz Rosenzweigs Stern der Erlösung.* Berlin: Philo, 2003.

Schwartz, Regina M. *The Curse of Cain: The Violent Legacy of Monotheism.* Chicago: University of Chicago Press, 1997.

Schwartz, Yossef. "Die Entfremdete Nähe: Rosenzweigs Blick auf den Islam," in *Franz Rosenzweig "Innerlich Bleibt die Welt Eine": Ausgewählte zum Islam,* edited by Gesine Palmer and Yossef Schwartz, 113–147. Berlin: Philo, 2003.

Schwarzschild, Steven S. "Franz Rosenzweig and Martin Heidegger: The German and the Jewish Turn to Ethnicism," in *Der Philosoph Franz Rosenzweig (1886–1929): Internationaler Kongreß-Kassel 1986,* edited by Wolfdietrich Schmied-Kowarzik, 2 vols., 887–889. Freiburg: Verlag Karl Alber, 1988.

———. *The Pursuit of the Ideal: Jewish Writings of Steven Schwarzschild,* edited by Menachem Kellner. Albany: State University of New York Press, 1990.

Scott, Charles E. "Appearing to Remember Heraclitus," in *The Presocratics after Heidegger,* edited by David C. Jacobs, 249–261. Albany: State University of New York Press, 1999.

Sebbah, François-David. *Testing the Limit: Derrida, Henry, Levinas, and the Phenomenological Tradition,* translated by Stephen Barker. Stanford: Stanford University Press, 2012.

Seeskin, Kenneth. "Hermann Cohen on Idol Worship," in *„Religion der Vernunft aus den Quellen des Judentums": Tradition und Ursprungsdenken in Hermann Cohens Spätwerk Internationale Konferenz in Zürich 1998,* edited by Helmut Holzhey, Gabriel Motzkin, and Hartwig Wiedebach, 107–116. Hildesheim: Georg Olms Verlag, 2000.

———. "Judaism and the Idea of Future," in *Judaic Sources and Western Thought: Jerusalem's Enduring Presence,* edited by Jonathan A. Jacobs, 49–70. Oxford: Oxford University Press, 2011.

———. "Maimonides and Hermann Cohen on Messianism," *Maimonidean Studies* 5 (2008): 375–392.

———. *No Other Gods: The Modern Struggle Against Idolatry.* West Orange: Behrman House, 1995.

———. *Searching for a Distant God: The Legacy of Maimonides.* Oxford: Oxford University Press, 2000.

Seidman, Naomi. *Faithful Renderings: Jewish-Christian Difference and the Politics of Translation.* Chicago: University of Chicago Press, 2006.

Sellars, Wilfrid. "The Role of Imagination in Kant's Theory of Experience," in *Categories: A Colloquium*, edited by Henry W. Johnstone, 231–245. University Park: Pennsylvania State University Press, 1978.

Sells, Michael A. *Mystical Languages of Unsaying.* Chicago: University of Chicago Press, 1994.

Shakespeare, Steven. *Derrida and Theology.* New York: Continuum, 2009.

Shapiro, David, Michal Govrin, and Jacques Derrida. *Body of Prayer.* New York: Cooper Union for the Advancement of Science and Art, 2001.

Shapiro, Susan. "The Uncanny Jew: A Brief History of an Image," *Judaism* 46 (1997): 63–78.

Sheehan, Thomas. "Facticity and *Ereignis*," in *Interpreting Heidegger: Critical Essays*, edited by Daniel O. Dahlstrom, 42–68. Cambridge: Cambridge University Press, 2011.

Sheppard, Eugene R. *Leo Strauss and the Politics of Exile: The Making of a Political Philosopher.* Waltham: Brandeis University Press, 2006.

Sherratt, Yvonne. *Hitler's Philosophers.* New Haven: Yale University Press, 2013.

Sikka, Sonya. *Forms of Transcendence: Heidegger and Medieval Mystical Theology.* Albany: State University of New York Press, 1997.

Simmons, J. Aaron. "Existential Appropriations: The Influence of Jean Wahl on Levinas's Reading of Kierkegaard," in *Kierkegaard and Levinas: Ethics, Politics, and Religion*, edited by J. Aaron Simmons and David Wood, 41–66. Bloomington: Indiana University Press, 2008.

———. *God and the Other: Ethics and Politics After the Theological Turn.* Bloomington: Indiana University Press, 2011.

Simon, Ernst. "Martin Buber: His Way between Thought and Deed," *Jewish Frontier* 15 (1948): 25–28.

Simon, Jules. *Art and Responsibility: A Phenomenology of the Diverging Paths of Rosenzweig and Heidegger.* New York: Continuum, 2011.

Simonyan, Astghik. "Poetics of the Same: A Philosophical Poetic Recourse into Sameness," Ph.D. dissertation, University of London, 2010.

Sini, Carlo. *Images of Truth: From Sign to Symbol*, translated by Massimo Verdicchio. Atlantic Highlands: Humanities Press, 1993.

Sloterdijk, Peter. *Derrida, an Egyptian: On the Problem of the Jewish Pyramid*, translated by Wieland Hoban. Cambridge: Polity Press, 2009.

Smith, Daniel W. *Essays on Deleuze*. Edinburgh: Edinburgh University Press, 2012.

Smith, James K. A. "Liberating Religion from Theology: Marion and Heidegger on the Possibility of a Phenomenology of Religion," *International Journal for Philosophy of Religion* 46 (1999): 17–33.

———. "Respect and Donation: A Critique of Marion's Critique of Husserl," *American Catholic Philosophical Quarterly* 71 (1997): 523–538.

———. *Speech and Theology: Language and the Logic of Incarnation*. New York: Routledge, 2002.

Smith, John H. "The Infinitesimal as Theological Principle: Representing the Paradoxes of God and Nothing in Cohen, Rosenzweig, Scholem, and Barth," *Modern Language Notes* 127 (2012): 562–588.

Smith, Robert. *Derrida and Autobiography*. Cambridge: Cambridge University Press, 1995.

Smith, Steven B. "'Destruktion' or Recovery? Leo Strauss's Critique of Heidegger," *Review* of *Metaphysics* 51 (1997): 345–377.

Sokolowski, Robert. *Presence and Absence: A Philosophical Investigation of Language and Being*. Bloomington: Indiana University Press, 1978.

Solomon, Norman. "Cohen on Atonement, Purification and Repentance," in *Hermann Cohen's Critical Idealism*, edited by Reinier Munk, 395–411. Dordrecht: Springer, 2005.

Solowiejczyk, Josef. "Das reine Denken und die Seinskonstituierung bei Hermann Cohen," Ph.D. dissertation, Friedrich-Wilhelms-Universität zu Berlin, 1932.

Sommer, Benjamin D. *The Bodies of God and the World of Ancient Israel*. Cambridge: Cambridge University Press, 2009.

Sorabji, Richard. *Animal Minds and Human Morals: The Origins of the Western Debate*. Ithaca: Cornell University Press, 1993.

Sparling, Robert Alan. *Johann Georg Hamann and the Enlightenment Project*. Toronto: University of Toronto Press, 2011.

Spivak, Gayatri Chakravorty. "Displacement and the Discourse of Woman," in *Feminist Interpretations of Jacques Derrida*, edited by Nancy J. Holland, 43–71. University Park: Pennsylvania State University Press, 2001.

Srajek, Martin C. *In the Margins of Deconstruction: Jewish Conceptions of Ethics in Emmanuel Levinas and Jacques Derrida*. Dordrecht: Kluwer Academic Publishers, 1997.

Staehler, Tanja. *Plato and Levinas: The Ambiguous Out-Side of Ethics*. New York: Routledge, 2010.

Stahmer, Harold M. "'Speech-Letters' and 'Speech-Thinking': Franz Rosenzweig and Eugen Rosenstock-Huessy," *Modern Judaism* 4 (1984): 57–81.

Stambaugh, Joan. *The Finitude of Being*. Albany: State University of New York Press, 1992.

Steinberg, Michael P. *Judaism Musical and Unmusical*. Chicago: University of Chicago Press, 2007.

Steinbock, Anthony J. *Home and Beyond: Generative Phenomenology after Husserl*. Evanston: Northwestern University Press, 1995.

———. "The Poor Phenomenon: Marion and the Problem of Givenness," in *Words of Life: New Theological Turns in French Phenomenology*, edited by Bruce Ellis Benson and Norman Wirzba, 120–131. New York: Fordham University Press, 2010.

Stellardi, Giuseppe. *Heidegger and Derrida on Philosophy and Metaphor: Imperfect Thought*. Amherst: Humanity Books, 2000.

Stern, David. *Parables in Midrash: Narrative and Exegesis in Rabbinic Literature*. Cambridge, MA: Harvard University Press, 1991.

Stern, Sacha. *Jewish Identity in Early Rabbinic Writings*. Leiden: Brill, 1994.

Strauss, Leo. "Cohen's Analysis of Spinoza's Biblical Science (1924)," in *Leo Strauss: The Early Writings (1921–1932)*, translated and edited by Michael Zank, 140–172. Albany: State University of New York Press, 2002.

———. "How to Begin to Study Medieval Philosophy," in *The Rebirth of Classical Political Rationalism: An Introduction to the Thought of Leo Strauss—Essays and Lectures by Leo Strauss*, selected and introduced by Thomas L. Pangle, 207–226. Chicago: University of Chicago Press, 1989.

———. "An Introduction to Heideggerian Existentialism," in *The Rebirth of Classical Political Rationalism: An Introduction to the Thought of Leo Strauss—Essays and Lectures by Leo Strauss*, selected and introduced by Thomas L. Pangle, 27–46. Chicago: University of Chicago Press, 1989.

———. *Jewish Philosophy and the Crisis of Modernity: Essays and Lectures in Modern Jewish Thought*, edited with an introduction by Kenneth Green. Albany: State University of New York Press, 1997.

———. *Leo Strauss on Maimonides: The Complete Writings*, edited with an introduction by Kenneth Hart Green. Chicago: University of Chicago Press, 2013.

———. *Philosophy and Law: Contributions to the Understanding of Maimonides and His Predecessors*, translated with an introduction by Eve Adler. Albany: State University of New York Press, 1995.

———. *Spinoza's Critique of Religion*. New York: Schocken Books, 1965.

Ströker, Elisabeth. *Husserl's Transcendental Phenomenology*, translated by Lee Hardy. Stanford: Stanford University Press, 1993.

Stroumsa, Guy G. "A Nameless God: Judaeo-Christian and Gnostic 'Theologies of the Name,'" in *The Image of the Judaeo-Christian in Ancient Jewish and Christian Literature*, edited by Peter J. Tomson and Doris Lambers-Petry, 230–243. Tübingen: Mohr Siebeck, 2003.

Stünkel, Knut M. "Die Sprache bei Hamann und Heidegger," *Neue Zeitschrift für systematische Theologie und Religionsphilosophe* 46 (2004): 26–55.

System and Context: Early Romantic and Early Idealistic Constellations, edited by Rolf Ahlers. Lewiston: Edwin Mellen Press, 2004.

Talmage, Frank. "Apples of Gold: The Inner Meaning of Sacred Texts in Medieval Judaism," in *Jewish Spirituality: From the Bible through the Middle Ages*, edited by Arthur Green, 313–355. New York: Crossroad, 1987.

Tanner, Kathryn. "Theology and the Limits of Phenomenology," in *Counter-Experiences: Reading Jean-Luc Marion*, edited by Kevin Hart, 201–231. Notre Dame: University of Notre Dame Press, 2007.

Taubes, Jacob. *From Cult to Culture: Fragments Toward a Critique of Historical Reason*, edited by Charlotte E. Fonrobert and Amir Engel, with an introduction by Aleida Assmann, Jan Assmann, and Wolf-Daniel Hartwich. Stanford: Stanford University Press, 2010.

Taubes, Susan A. "The Absent God," *Journal of Religion* 35 (1955): 6–16.

Taylor, Mark C. *After God*. Chicago: University of Chicago Press, 2007.

———. *Altarity*. Chicago: University of Chicago Press, 1987.

———. "Altizer's Originality: A Review Essay," *Journal of the American Academy of Religion* 52 (1984): 569–584.

———. "Betraying Altizer," in *Thinking Through the Death of God: A Critical Companion to Thomas J. J. Altizer*, edited by Lissa McCullough and Brian Schroeder, 11–28. Albany: State University of New York Press, 2004.

———. "Foreword: The Last Theologian," in Thomas J. J. Altizer, *Living the Death of God: A Theological Memoir*, xi–xviii. Albany: State University of New York Press, 2006.

———. "nO nOt nO," in *Derrida and Negative Theology*, edited by Howard Coward and Toby Foshay, 167–198. Albany: State University of New York Press, 1992.

———. "Non-Negative Negative Atheology," *Diacritics* 20 (1990): 2–16.

———. *Nots*. Chicago: University of Chicago Press, 1993.

———. "Refiguring Postmodern Times," in *Consciousness and Reality: Studies in Memory of Toshihiko Izutsu*, edited by Sayyid Jalāl al-Dīn Āshtiyānī, Hideichi Matsubara, Takashi Iwami, and Akiro Matsumoto, 149–173. Leiden: Brill, 2000.

———. "The Uncertainty Principle," in *Saintly Influence: Edith Wyschogrod and the Possibilities of Philosophy of Religion*, edited by Eric Boynton and Martin Kavka, 16–28. New York: Fordham University Press, 2009.

Thomson, Iain. "Ontotheology," in *Interpreting Heidegger: Critical Essays*, edited by Daniel O. Dahlstrom, 106–131. Cambridge: Cambridge University Press, 2011.

Tishby, Isaiah. *The Wisdom of the Zohar: An Anthology of Texts*, translated by David Goldstein. Oxford: Oxford University Press, 1989.

Tonning, Judith E. "'*Hineingehalten in die Nacht*': Heidegger's Early Appropriation of Christian Eschatology," in *Phenomenology and Eschatology: Not Yet in the Now*, edited by Neal DeRoo and John Panteleimon Manoussakis, 133–151. Burlington: Ashgate, 2009.

Toumayan, Alain P. *Encountering the Other: The Artwork and the Problem of Difference in Blanchot and Levinas*. Pittsburgh: Duquesne University Press, 2004.

Tracy, David. "The Post-Modern Re-Naming of God as Incomprehensible and Hidden," *Cross Currents* 50 (2000): 240–247.

Trigano, Shmuel. "Levinas and the Project of Jewish Philosophy," *Jewish Studies Quarterly* 8 (2001): 279–307.

Tugendhat, Ernst. *Der Wahrheitsbegriff bei Husserl und Heidegger*. Berlin: Walter de Gruyter, 1967.

——. "Heidegger's Idea of Truth," in *The Heidegger Controversy: A Critical Reader*, edited by Richard Wolin, 245–263. Cambridge, MA: MIT Press, 1993.

Turner, Donald L., and Ford Turrell. "The Non-Existent God: Transcendence, Humanity, and Ethics in the Philosophy of Emmanuel Levinas," *Philosophia* 35 (2007): 375–382.

Udoff, Alan. "Rosenzweig's Heidegger Reception and the re-Origination of Jewish Thinking," in *Der Philosoph Franz Rosenzweig (1886–1929): Internationaler Kongreß-Kassel 1986*, edited by Wolfdietrich Schmied-Kowarzik, 2 vols., 923–950. Freiburg: Verlag Karl Alber, 1988.

Urban, Martina. *Aesthetics of Renewal: Martin Buber's Early Representation of Hasidism as Kulturkritik*. Chicago: University of Chicago Press, 2008.

——. "Persecution and the Art of Representation: Schocken's Maimonides Anthologies of the 1930s," in *Maimonides and His Heritage*, edited by Idit Dobbs-Weinstein, Lenn E. Goodman, and James A. Grady, 153–179. Albany: State University of New York Press, 2009.

Vail, Loy M. *Heidegger and Ontological Difference*. University Park: Pennsylvania State University Press, 1972.

Valabregue-Perry, Sandra. *Concealed and Revealed: "Ein Sof" in Theosophic Kabbalah*. Los Angeles: Cherub Press, 2010 (Hebrew).

——. "The Concept of Infinity (*Eyn-sof*) and the Rise of Theosophical Kabbalah," *Jewish Quarterly Review* 102 (2012): 405–430.

Valberg, Jerry J. *Dream, Death, and the Self*. Princeton: Princeton University Press, 2007.

Van Buren, John. *The Young Heidegger: Rumor of the Hidden King*. Bloomington: Indiana University Press, 1994.

Van Riessen, Renée D. N. *Man as a Place of God: Levinas' Hermeneutics of Kenosis*. Dordrecht: Springer, 2007.

Vandevelde, Pol. *Heidegger and the Romantics: The Literary Invention of Meaning*. New York: Routledge, 2012.

Vater, Michael G. "F. W. J. Schelling: Further Presentations from the System of Philosophy (1802)," *Philosophical Forum* 32 (2001): 373–397.

——. "Schelling's Neoplatonic System-Notion: 'Ineinsbildung' and Temporal Unfolding," in *The Significance of Neoplatonism*, edited by R. Baine Harris, 275–299. Albany: State University of New York Press, 1976.

Vattimo, Gianni. *The Adventure of Difference: Philosophy after Nietzsche and Heidegger*, translated by Cyprian Blamires with the assistance of Thomas Harrison. Baltimore: Johns Hopkins University Press, 1993.

——. *After Christianity*, translated by Luca D'Isanto. New York: Columbia University Press, 2002.

——. *Beyond Intepretation: The Meaning of Hermenetutics for Philosophy*, translated by David Webb. Stanford: Stanford University Press, 1997.

———. "The End of (Hi)story," *Chicago Review* 35 (1987): 20–30.

———. *The End of Modernity: Nihilism and Hermeneutics in Postmodern Culture*, translated by Jon R. Snyder. Baltimore: Johns Hopkins University Press, 1988.

———. "Metaphysics, Violence, Secularization," in *Recoding Metaphysics: The New Italian Philosophy*, edited by Giovanna Borradori, 45–61. Evanston: Northwestern University Press, 1988.

———. *Nihilism & Emancipation: Ethics, Politics, & Law*, edited by Santiago Zabala, translated by William McCuaig. New York: Columbia University Press, 2004.

———. " 'Verwindung': Nihilism and the Postmodern in Philosophy," *Substance* 16 (1987): 7–17.

Vedder, Ben. "The Possibility of an A-Theological Ontology: Heidegger's Changing Position," in *Théologie négative*, edited by Marco M. Olivetti, 757–768. Milan: CEDAM, 2002.

Velkley, Richard L. *Heidegger, Strauss, and the Premises of Philosophy: On Original Forgetting*. Chicago: University of Chicago Press, 2011.

———. "On the Roots of Rationalism: Strauss's Natural Right and History as Response to Heidegger," *Review of Politics* 70 (2008): 247–259.

Visker, Rudi. *Truth and Singularity: Taking Foucault into Phenomenology*. Dordrecht: Kluwer Academic Publishers, 1999.

Vital, Ḥayyim. *Sha'arei Qedushah*, edited by Amnon Gross. Jerusalem, 2005.

Vogel, Lawrence. "Overcoming Heidegger's Nihilism: Leo Strauss and Hans Jonas," in *Heidegger's Jewish Followers: Essays on Hannah Arendt, Leo Strauss, Hans Jonas, and Emmanuel Levinas*, edited by Samuel Fleischacker, 131–150. Pittsburgh: Duquesne University Press, 2008.

Vogel, Manfred H. *Rosenzweig on Profane/Secular History*. Atlanta: Scholars Press, 1996.

Wahl, Jean. *Existence humaine et transcendance*. Neuchâtel: Éditions de la Baconnière, 1944.

———. "Realism, Dialectic, and the Transcendent," *Philosophy and Phenomenological Research* 4 (1944): 496–506.

———. *A Short History of Existentialism*, translated by Forrest Williams and Stanley Maron. New York: Philosophical Library, 1949.

Waldenfels, Bernhard. "Levinas on the Saying and the Said," in *Addressing Levinas*, edited by Eric Sean Nelson, Antje Kapust, and Kent Still, 86–97. Evanston: Northwestern University Press, 2005.

Ward, Graham. "On Time and Salvation: The Eschatology of Emmanuel Levinas," in *Facing the Other: The Ethics of Emmanuel Levinas*, edited by Seán Hand, 153–172. Surrey: Curzon, 1996.

Ward, James F. "Political Philosophy and History: The Links between Strauss and Heidegger," *Polity* 20 (1987): 273–295.

Wargo, Robert J. J. *The Logic of Nothingness: A Study of Nishida Kitarō*. Honolulu: University of Hawai'i Press, 2005.

Wasserstrom, Steven. "Melancholy Jouissance and the Study of Kabbalah: A Review Essay of Elliot R. Wolfson, *Alef, Mem, Tau*," *AJS Review* 32 (2008): 389–396.

Weil, Simone. *Awaiting God: A New Translation of* Attente de Dieu *and* Lettre à un religieux, translated by Bradley Jersak, introduction by Sylvie Weil. Abbotsford, BC: Fresh Wind Press, 2012.

———. *First and Last Notebooks*, translated by Richard Rees. London: Oxford University Press, 1970.

———. *Gravity and Grace*, introduction and postscript by Gustave Thibon, translated by Emma Crawford and Mario von der Ruhr. London: Routledge, 2002.

———. *Intimations of Christianity Among the Ancient Greeks*. London: Routledge, 1998.

———. *Lettre à un religieux*. Paris: Éditions Gallimard, 1951.

———. *The Need for Roots: Prelude to a Declaration of Duties Towards Mankind*, translated by Arthur Wills, with a preface by T. S. Eliot. London: Routledge, 2002.

———. *The Notebooks*, translated by Arthur Wills. London: Routledge, 2004.

Weiss, Daniel H. *Paradox and the Prophets: Hermann Cohen and the Indirect Communication of Religion*. Oxford: Oxford University Press, 2012.

Welz, Claudia. "Franz Rosenzweig: A Kindred Spirit in Alignment with Kierkegaard," in *Kierkegaard and Existentialism*, edited by Jon Stewart, 299–321. Burlington: Ashgate, 2011.

———. *Love's Transcendence and the Problem of Theodicy*. Tübingen: Mohr Siebeck, 2008.

———. "Selbstwerdung im Angesicht des Anderen: Vertrauen und Selbstverwandlung bei Kierkegaard und Rosenzweig," in *Wir und die Anderen/We and the Others* [*Rosenzweig Jahrbuch* 5], edited by Martin Brasser and Hans Martin Dober, 68–83. Freiburg im Breisgau: Karl Alber, 2010.

Westerkamp, Dirk. "Naming and Tetragrammatology: Medieval Apophatic Philosophy and Its Double Helix," in *Jewish Lifeworlds and Jewish Thought: Festschrift Presented to Karl E. Grözinger on the Occasion of His 70th Birthday*, edited by Nathanael Riemer, 111–123. Wiesbaden: Harrassowitz Verlag, 2012.

———. *Via Negativa: Sprache und Methode der negativen Theologie*. Munich: Wilhelm Fink Verlag, 2006.

Westphal, Merold. "Commanded Love and Divine Transcendence in Levinas and Kierkegaard," in *The Face of the Other and the Trace of God: Essays on the Philosophy of Emmanuel Levinas*, edited by Jeffrey Bloechl, 200–233. New York: Fordham University Press, 2000.

———. "Intentionality and Transcendence," in *Subjectivity and Transcendence*, edited by Arne Grøn, Iben Damgaard, and Søren Overgaard, 71–93. Tübingen: Mohr Siebeck, 2007.

———. *Levinas and Kierkegaard in Dialogue*. Bloomington: Indiana University Press, 2008.

———. "Levinas, Kierkegaard, and the Theological Task," *Modern Theology* 8 (1992): 241–261.

————. *Overcoming Onto-Theology: Toward a Postmodern Christian Faith*. New York: Fordham University Press, 2001.

————. *Transcendence and Self-Transcendence: On God and the Soul*. Bloomington: Indiana University Press, 2004.

————. "Transcendence, Heteronomy, and the Birth of the Responsible Self," in *Calvin O. Schrag and the Task of Philosophy after Postmodernity*, edited by Martin J. Matuštík and William L. McBride, 201–225. Evanston: Northwestern University Press, 2002.

————. "The Transparent Shadow: Kierkegaard and Levinas in Dialogue," in *Kierkegaard in Post/Modernity*, edited by Martin J. Matuštík and Merold Westphal, 265–281. Bloomington: Indiana University Press, 1995.

————. "The Trauma of Transcendence as Heteronomous Intersubjectivity," in *Intersubjectivité et théologie philosophique*, edited by Marco M. Olivetti, 87–110. Padua: CEDAM, 2001.

White, David A. *Heidegger and the Language of Poetry*. Lincoln: University of Nebraska Press, 1978.

Wiedebach, Hartwig. *The National Element in Hermann Cohen's Philosophy and Religion*, translated by William Templer. Leiden: Brill, 2012.

————. "Rosenzweigs Konnektionismus: Der *Stern der Erlösung* als Tatsächlichkeits-System," in *Franz Rosenzweigs "neues Denken": Internationaler Kongreß-Kassel 2004*, edited by Wolfdietrich Schmied-Kowarzik, 2 vols., 371–392. Freiburg: Verlag Karl Alber, 2006.

————. "Wissenschaftslogik versus Schöpfungstheorie: Die Rolle der Vernichtung in Cohens Ursprungslogik," in *Verneinung, Andersheit und Unendlichkeit im Neukantianismus*, edited by Pierfrancesco Fiorato, 47–67. Würzburg: Königshausen & Neumann, 2009.

Wiehl, Reiner. "Das Prinzip des Ursprungs in Hermann Cohens 'Religion der Vernunft aus den Quellen des Judentums,'" in *„Religion der Vernunft aus den Quellen des Judentums": Tradition und Ursprungsdenken in Hermann Cohens Spätwerk: Internationale Konferenz in Zürich 1998*, edited by Helmut Holzhey, Gabriel Motzkin, and Hartwig Wiedebach, 63–75. Hildesheim: Georg Olms Verlag, 2000.

————. "Experience in Rosenzweig's New Thinking," in *The Philosophy of Franz Rosenzweig*, edited by Paul Mendes-Flohr, 42–68. Hanover: University Press of New England, 1988.

Wilder, Amos N. *Theopoetic: Theology and the Religious Imagination*. Philadelphia: Fortress Press, 1976.

Wittgenstein, Ludwig. *Tractatus Logico-Philosophicus*, translated by D. F. Pears and B. F. McGuinness, with an introduction by Bertrand Russell. London: Routledge & Kegan Paul, 1974.

Woessner, Martin. *Heidegger in America*. Cambridge: Cambridge University Press, 2011.

Wolfson, Elliot R. *Abraham Abulafia—Kabbalist and Prophet: Hermeneutics, Theosophy, Theurgy*. Los Angeles: Cherub Press, 2000.

———. *Alef, Mem, Tau: Kabbalistic Musings on Time, Truth, and Death*. Berkeley: University of California Press, 2005.

———. "Beyond Good and Evil: Hypernomianism, Transmorality and Kabbalistic Ethics," in *Crossing Boundaries: Essays on the Ethical Status of Mysticism*, edited by Jeffrey J. Kripal and G. William Barnard, 103–156. New York: Seven Bridges Press, 2002.

———. "Circumcision, Secrecy, and the Veiling of the Veil: Phallomorphic Exposure and Kabbalistic Esotericism," in *The Covenant of Circumcision: New Perspectives on an Ancient Jewish Rite*, edited by Elizabeth W. Mark, 58–70. Hanover: Brandeis University Press, 2003.

———. "Circumcision, Vision of God, and Textual Interpretation: From Midrashic Trope to Mystical Symbol," *History of Religions* 27 (1987): 189–215.

———. "Divine Suffering and the Hermeneutics of Reading: Philosophical Reflections on Lurianic Mythology," in *Suffering Religion*, edited by Robert Gibbs and Elliot R. Wolfson, 101–162. London: Routledge, 2002.

———. *A Dream Interpreted within a Dream: Oneiropoiesis and the Prism of Imagination*. New York: Zone Books, 2011.

———. "The Engenderment of Messianic Politics: Symbolic Significance of Sabbatai Ṣevi's Coronation," in *Toward the Millennium: Messianic Expectations from the Bible to Waco*, edited by Peter Schäfer and Mark Cohen, 203–258. Leiden: Brill, 1998.

———. "Facing the Effaced: Mystical Eschatology and the Idealistic Orientation in the Thought of Franz Rosenzweig," *Zeitschrift für Neuere Theologiegeschichte* 4 (1997): 39–81.

———. "From Sealed Book to Open Text: Time, Memory, and Narrativity in Kabbalistic Hermeneutics," in *Interpreting Judaism in a Postmodern Age*, edited by Steven Kepnes, 145–178. New York: New York University Press, 1996.

———. "Givenness and the Disappearance of the Gift: Ethics and the Invisible in Marion's Christocentric Phenomenology," in *Ethics of In-Visibility: Imago Dei, Memory, and Human Dignity,*, edited by Claudia Welz. Tübingen: Mohr Siebeck, 2014.

———. "Hebraic and Hellenic Conceptions of Wisdom in *Sefer ha-Bahir*," *Poetics Today* 19 (1998): 147–176.

———. "*Imago Templi* and the Meeting of the Two Seas: Liturgical Time-Space and the Feminine Imaginary in Zoharic Kabbalah," *RES: Anthropology and Aesthetics* 51 (2007): 121–135.

———. "Kenotic Overflow and Temporal Transcendence: Angelic Embodiment and the Alterity of Time in Abraham Abulafia," in *Saintly Influence: Edith Wyschogrod and the Possibilities of Philosophy of Religion*, edited by Eric Boynton and Martin Kavka, 113–149. New York: Fordham University Press, 2009.

————. *Language, Eros, Being: Kabbalistic Hermeneutics and Poetic Imagination.* New York: Fordham University Press, 2005.

————. *Luminal Darkness: Imaginal Gleanings from Zoharic Literature.* Oxford: Oneworld Publications, 2007.

————. "Negative Theology and Positive Assertion in the Early Kabbalah," *Da'at* 32–33 (1994): v–xxii.

————. "Nihilating Nonground and the Temporal Sway of Becoming: Kabbalistically Envisioning Nothing Beyond Nothing," *Angelaki* 17 (2012): 31–45.

————. "Occultation of the Feminine and the Body of Secrecy in Medieval Kabbalah," in *Rending the Veil: Concealment and Secrecy in the History of Religions*, edited by Elliot R. Wolfson, 113–154. New York: Seven Bridges Press, 1999.

————. *Open Secret: Postmessianic Messianism and the Mystical Revision of Menaḥem Mendel Schneerson.* New York: Columbia University Press, 2009.

————. "Revealing and Re/veiling Menaḥem Mendel Schneerson's Messianic Secret," *Kabbalah: Journal for the Study of Jewish Mystical Texts* 26 (2012): 25–96.

————. "Secrecy, Modesty, and the Feminine: Kabbalistic Traces in the Thought of Levinas," in *The Exorbitant: Emmanuel Levinas Between Jews and Christians*, edited by Kevin Hart and Michael A. Signer, 52–73. New York: Fordham University Press, 2010.

————. "Structure, Innovation, and Diremptive Temporality: The Use of Models to Study Continuity and Discontinuity in Kabbalistic Tradition," *Journal for the Study of Religions and Ideologies* 6 (2007): 143–167.

————. "Suffering Eros and Textual Incarnation: A Kristevan Reading of Kabbalistic Poetics," in *Toward a Theology of Eros: Transfiguring Passion at the Limits of Discipline*, edited by Virginia Burrus and Catherine Keller, 341–365. New York: Fordham University Press, 2006.

————. *Through a Speculum That Shines: Vision and Imagination in Medieval Jewish Mysticism.* Princeton: Princeton University Press, 1994.

————. *Venturing Beyond: Law and Morality in Kabbalistic Mysticism.* Oxford: Oxford University Press, 2006.

————. "*Via Negativa* in Maimonides and Its Impact on Thirteenth-Century Kabbalah," *Maimonidean Studies* 5 (2008): 393–442.

Wolosky, Shira. "Derrida, Jabès, Levinas: Sign-Theory as Ethical Discourse," *Prooftexts* 2 (1982): 283–302.

————. "An 'Other' Negative Theology: On Derrida's 'How to Avoid Speaking: Denials,'" *Poetics Today* 19 (1998): 261–280.

Wolzogen, Christoph von. *Emmanuel Levinas: Denken bis zum Äußersten.* Freiburg: Verlag Karl Alber, 2005.

————. "Negation und Alterität: Der 'Abgrund der Vernunft' bei Cohen, Heidegger und Levinas," in *Verneinung, Andersheit und Unendlichkeit im Neukantianismus*, edited by Pierfrancesco Fiorato, 93–106. Würzburg: Königshausen & Neumann, 2009.

Wood, David. *The Deconstruction of Time*. Evanston: Northwestern University Press, 2001.

———. *Thinking after Heidegger*. Cambridge: Polity Press, 2002.

Wrathall, Mark A. *Heidegger and Unconcealment: Truth, Language, and History*. Cambridge: Cambridge University Press, 2011.

———. "Heidegger on Plato, Truth, and Unconcealment: The 1931–32 Lecture on *The Essence of Truth*," *Inquiry* 47 (2004): 443–463.

———. "Heidegger, Truth, and Reference," *Inquiry* 45 (2002): 217–228.

Wright, Tamra. *The Twilight of Jewish Philosophy: Emmanuel Levinas' Ethical Hermeneutics*. Amsterdam: Harwood Academic Publishers, 1999.

Wright, Terence R. "Midrash and Intertextuality: Ancient Rabbinic Exegesis and Postmodern Reading of the Bible," in *Divine Aporia: Postmodern Conversations about the Other*, edited by John C. Hawley, 97–119. Lewisburg: Bucknell University Press, 2000.

Wurgaft, Benjamin Aldes. "How to Read Maimonides after Heidegger: The Cases of Strauss and Levinas," in *The Cultures of Maimonideanism: New Approaches to the History of Jewish Thought*, edited by James T. Robinson, 353–383. Leiden: Brill, 2009.

Wurzer, Wilhelm S. "Heidegger's Turn to *Germanien*—A Sigetic Venture," in *Heidegger toward the Turn: Essays on the Work of the 1930s*, edited by James Risser, 187–207. Albany: State University of New York Press, 1999.

Wyschogrod, Edith. "Autochthony and Welcome: Discourses of Exile in Lévinas and Derrida," in *Derrida and Religion: Other Testaments*, edited by Yvonne Sherwood and Kevin Hart, 53–61. New York: Routledge, 2005.

———. "Crossover Dreams," *Journal of the American Academy of Religion* 54 (1986): 543–547.

———. *Crossover Queries: Dwelling with Negatives, Embodying Philosophy's Others*. New York: Fordham University Press, 2006.

———. "Crucifixion and Alterity: Pathways to Glory on the Thought of Altizer and Levinas," in *Thinking Through the Death of God: A Critical Companion to Thomas J. J. Altizer*, edited by Lissa McCullough and Brian Schroeder, 89–103. Albany: State University of New York Press, 2004.

———. "Doing before Hearing: On the Primacy of Touch," in *Textes pour Emmanuel Lévinas*, edited by François Laruelle, 179–203. Paris: Collections Surfaces, 1980.

———. *Emmanuel Levinas: The Problem of Ethical Metaphysics*, second edition. New York: Fordham University Press, 2000.

———. *An Ethics of Remembering: History, Heterology, and the Nameless Others*. Chicago: University of Chicago Press, 1998.

———. "Hasidism, Hellenism, Holocaust: A Postmodern View," in *Interpreting Judaism in a Postmodern Age*, edited by Steven Kepnes, 301–321. New York: New York University Press, 1996.

———. "How to Say No in French: Derrida and Negation in Recent French Philosophy," in *Negation and Theology*, edited by Robert P. Scharlemann, 39–55. Charlottesville: University Press of Virginia, 1992.

———. "Language and Alterity in the Thought of Levinas," in *The Cambridge Companion to Levinas*, edited by Simon Critchley and Robert Bernasconi, 188–205. Cambridge: Cambridge University Press, 2002.

———. "Religion as Life and Text: Postmodern Re-figurations," in *The Craft of Religious Studies*, edited by Jon R. Stone, 240–257. New York: St. Martin's Press, 1998.

———. "Repentance and Forgiveness: The Undoing of Time," *International Journal for Philosophy of Religion* 60 (2006): 157–168.

———. *Saints and Postmodernism: Revisioning Moral Philosophy.* Chicago: University of Chicago Press, 1990.

———. *Spirit in Ashes: Hegel, Heidegger, and Man-Made Mass Death.* New Haven: Yale University Press, 1985.

———. "Trends in Postmodern Jewish Philosophy: Contexts of a Conversation," in Steven Kepnes, Peter Ochs, and Robert Gibbs, *Reasoning After Revelation: Dialogues in Postmodern Jewish Philosophy*, 123–136. Boulder: Westview Press, 1998.

Yan, Yunxiang. *The Flow of Gifts: Reciprocity and Social Networks in a Chinese Village.* Stanford: Stanford University Press, 1996.

Zabala, Santiago. *The Hermeneutic Nature of Analytic Philosophy: A Study of Ernst Tugendhat*, foreword by Gianni Vattimo. New York: Columbia University Press, 2008.

———. "Introduction: A Religion Without Theists or Atheists," in Richard Rorty and Gianni Vattimo, *The Future of Religion*, edited by Santiago Zabala, 1–27. New York: Columbia University Press, 2005.

———. *The Remnants of Being: Hermeneutic Ontology After Metaphysics.* New York: Columbia University Press, 2009.

Zaccagnini, Marta. *Christentum der Endlichkeit: Heideggers Vorlesungen "Einleitung in die Phänomenologie der Religion."* Münster: LIT Verlag, 2003.

Zahavi, Dan. *Husserl and Transcendental Intersubjectivity: A Response to the Linguistic-Pragmatic Critique*, translated by Elizabeth A. Behnke. Athens: Ohio State University Press, 2001.

———. *Husserl's Phenomenology.* Stanford: Stanford University Press, 2003.

———. "Michel Henry and the Phenomenology of the Invisible," *Continental Philosophy Review* 32 (1999): 223–240.

———. *Self-Awareness and Alterity: A Phenomenological Investigation.* Evanston: Northwestern University Press, 1999.

———. "Subjectivity and Immanence in Michel Henry," in *Subjectivity and Transcendence*, edited by Arne Grøn, Iben Damgaard, and Søren Overgaard, 133–147. Tübingen: Mohr Siebeck, 2007.

Zank, Michael. *The Idea of Atonement in the Philosophy of Hermann Cohen*. Providence: Brown Judaic Studies, 2000.

Zarader, Marlène. *The Unthought Debt: Heidegger and the Hebraic Heritage*, translated by Bettina Bergo. Stanford: Stanford University Press, 2006.

Ziarek, Krzysztof. *Inflected Language: Toward a Hermeneutics of Nearness: Heidegger, Levinas, Stevens, Celan*. Albany: State University of New York Press, 1994.

Zuckert, Catherine H. "Leo Strauss: Jewish, Yes, but Heideggerian?" in *Heidegger's Jewish Followers: Essays on Hannah Arendt, Leo Strauss, Hans Jonas, and Emmanuel Levinas*, edited by Samuel Fleischacker, 83–105. Pittsburgh: Duquesne University Press, 2008.

———. *The Truth about Leo Strauss: Political Philosophy and American Democracy.* Chicago: University of Chicago Press, 2006.

INDEX

Abraham, 139, 191–92, 204, 424n242, 435n152
absence
    in Buddhism, xxvi–xxvii
    in Derrida, 193, 195
    in Heidegger, 98, 124, 128–29, 130–31, 238, 244
    imagination and, 2
    kabbalah and, 193
    in Levinas, 98–99, 112
    metaphor and, 145–46, 147
    of the gift, 189–90, 237
    of God, xx, xxvi, 53, 140, 193
    of Godot, 118
    of ground, 68, 336n265
    of sensible form, 181
    of the other, 10, 107, 148
    of transcendence, 212, 222
    presence and, xvii, xxii, xxiv–xxv, xxvi, 2, 45, 51–52, 74, 95, 98–99, 111, 112–13, 119, 128, 130–31, 136, 137, 167, 171, 174, 178, 183, 193, 194, 195, 198, 208, 221, 225, 234, 235, 238, 244, 258, 374n174
    revelation and, 51–52
    theology of, in Marion, xxi
abstraction, 141–46
Abulafia, Abraham, 169, 275n26
adam, 4, 5
Adam, 22
adamah, 4
Adorno, Theodor, xviii, 147, 206–7, 264n29, 366n109, 404n10
affirmation, 76–77, 80
    negation of, 231

Alchemy of Discourse, The (Kugler), 374n174
al-Fārābī, 5
Altarity (Taylor), 360n72
alterity, xiv, xvi, xviii, xxii, 10, 12, 15, 18, 60, 91, 93, 98, 107, 114, 120, 123, 132, 141, 142, 143, 144, 149, 150, 152, 162, 187, 193, 205, 207, 210, 211, 214, 215, 220, 221, 222, 227, 258, 259, 414n115, 435n152
    diachrony and, 324n205
    ethics of, 222
    face and, 123, 402n520
    ipseity and, 148
    singularity and, 193, 419n188
    space of, 218
    temporality and, 324n205, 383n248, 384n267
    transcendence and, 123, 138, 144, 324n205, 354n17
Altered Reading (Robbins), 397n456
Altizer, Thomas, xxii–xxvii, 177, 211, 214–15, 270n62, 271n77, 277n83, 277n88–89, 380n212
Altmann, Alexander, 22, 23, 30, 290n37, 312n85
    Heidegger and, 290n37
altruism, 214, 218, 220, 221
"America and the Future of Theology" (Altizer), xxii
anatheism, 230
aniconism, 150
anthropomorphism, 19, 20, 22, 25, 31–32, 87, 136, 262, 297n120, 298n125, 298–99n131, 352n389

Dickinson, Emily, 90
Dionysius the Areopagite, xxi, 171, 178,
    393n386, 414n118
différance, 155, 166, 169–71, 177, 179, 182, 185,
    191, 196, 200, 206, 209, 261n2, 360n72,
    413n100, 420n193, 425–26n271, 430n25
Difficult Freedom (Levinas), 117
Discipline of Philosophy, The (Goetschel),
    307n39
disclosure, 27, 29, 48, 49, 53, 54, 71, 84, 94, 95,
    98, 101, 123, 128–29, 130, 131, 142, 170,
    183, 189, 191, 192, 193, 198, 236, 245,
    309n57, 314n106
disincarnation, xix, 136, 144, 210
dissemination, 169, 179, 182, 207
Dissemination (Derrida), 168, 175
distance, time and, 114
"Distance and Relation" (Buber), 297n112
dream, 63, 65, 111–12, 201, 374n174,
    374–75n177, 415n134
Dream Interpreted within a Dream,
    A (Wolfson), 277n52, 313n91, 326n221,
    327n223, 361n72, 374n174, 411n86,
    427n284, 436n4, 438n42, 439n56
Dream, Death, and the Self (Valberg), 374n174

Earth is the Lord's, The (Heschel), 322n184
Eckhart, Meister, xx, 13, 26, 79, 138, 171, 178,
    236, 267n40, 393n386
    Derrida's relation to, 413n110
    Heidegger's indebtedness to, 283n101,
    440n75
eddammeh le-elyon, 4, 5
"Edmond Jabès Today" (Levinas), 110
Ehrenberg, Rudolf, 38–39
ehyeh asher ehyeh, 19–20, 21, 27, 296n102. *See*
    also "I am that I am"
Ein Sof, 78, 79, 171–72, 173, 197, 198, 341n295,
    395n324, 412n94, 415n129
Either/Or (Kierkegaard), 305–6n26
Elucidations of Hölderlin's Poetry (Heidegger),
    300n2
embodiment, 33, 109, 184, 200, 235, 255,
    262n9. *See also* incarnation
emptiness, xxiii, xxv, xxvii, 78, 81, 136, 197,
    198, 208, 242, 245, 258, 272n89

End of Philosophy, The (Heidegger), 361n77
"Enigma and Phenomenon" (Levinas), 94
Ereignis, 51, 62, 101, 124, 125, 127, 232, 241,
    245, 246, 326n212, 386n292, 443n135
es gibt, 99, 125, 127, 129, 136, 237, 239, 240–41,
    244, 246, 360–61n72
Essence of Truth, The (Heidegger), 50–51
essentialism, 45, 198, 219, 312n86
eternity
    in Buber, 28, 295n96
    of God, 114
    in Heschel, 322n184, 323n192
    of the Jewish people, 74
    Judaism and, 319n173
    in Levinas, 61, 97, 114, 122, 381n217,
        383n244
    and the messianic, 117, 217
    and the return of the same, 217, 243,
        295n296, 442n108, 442n113
    in Rosenzweig, 44, 58–59, 61–62, 68, 85,
        317n136, 319–20n173, 321n176,
        323n192–93, 324n207, 325n209,
        337n270
    Sabbath and, 324n207
    time and, 40, 44, 46, 57, 58–59, 61, 68,
        70–71, 114, 117, 122, 217, 323n192,
        384n267
    of Torah, 56
ethics
    of alterity, 222
    in Altizer, 214
    being of God and, 21, 22–23, 24, 150
    cognition and, 15
    in Derrida, 137–38
    desire and, 211
    first philosophy, 93, 215
    Heidegger and, 130, 132
    hope and, 212
    in Levinas, 105, 131, 134, 137–38, 141, 143,
        150, 203, 210–11, 215, 394–95n407
    in Maimonides, 15, 342n311
    monotheism and, 14
    ontology and, 259
    other and, 215
    postmodern, 222
    religion and, 15, 22, 141

"I am that I am," 19–20, 27, 296n102. *See also*
   ehyeh asher ehyeh
I and Thou (Buber), 26
Ibn Laṭif, Isaac, 45
idealism
   Cohen and, 24
   ethical, 24
   in Hegel, 7
   in Heidegger, 99
   Kantian, 9
   Levinas's critique of, 134
   nothingness and, 37
   pantheism and, 14
   Rosenzweig and, 36, 38, 46, 85, 88
   Spinoza and, 285n4
   totality and, 34
   transcendental, 11
   truth in, 46–47, 85
idolatry
   Adorno's critique of, 264n29
   apophasis and, xviii, xxii, 228, 229,
      337n274
   ban on, xiv
   blasphemy and, 147
   divine configuration and, 29–33
   faith and, xix–xx, 21
   fear of, 216
   in Freud, 33, 228
   and the idol of Christ, 251
   image and, 29–33, 123, 132–33
   intolerance for, 21
   kabbalah and, 299n132
   Levinas and, 138, 384n273
   Maimonides's understanding, 132–33
   in Marion, 251
   metaphysical, 228, 252, 256
   monotheism and, xiv–xv, 21, 27
   negative theology and, 337n274
   paganism and, 348n356
   religion as codependent with, xviii–xxii
   representation and, xv, 25, 30–31,
      144
   theological, 228
   transcendence of, 258
   Weil and, 265n33
   worship of graven images, xiv, 261n3

il y a, 99, 110, 111–13, 120, 131, 136–37, 140, 211,
      360n72, 373n158, 373n169, 389n334,
      393n375
   es gibt and, 99, 136, 356n32, 360–61n72
image
   anthropomorphism and, 32
   idolatry and, 132–33
   representation and, 30–31
imagination
   absence and, 2
   anthropomorphism and, 25
   in Aristotle, 1
   in Blake, 3
   in Buber, 297n112
   in Coleridge, 3
   in Derrida, 2
   faith and, 25
   in Fichte, 2–3, 4, 274n21–22
   God and, 4–5
   in Heschel, 5–8
   infinity and, 3–4
   in Jewish lore, 4–5
   in kabbalah, 4–5
   in Kant, 1–2, 273n10
   in Kierkegaard, 3–4
   in Maimonides, 5, 274n26
   in philosophy, 1
   in Plato, 1
   presence and, 2
   reality and, 2–3
   reason and, 2
   in Romanticism, 2–3
   self and, 3–4
   symbolism and, 6–7
   synthetic function of, 2
immanence
   being and, 21
   in Judaism *vs.* Christianity, 9
   in Levinas, 134, 210
   monotheism and, 18
   in Muffs, xv
   pantheism and, 18
   time and, 223–24
   transcendence and, 151–52, 210
   transcendence *vs.*, xv, xvi, 9
   in Wyschogrod, 223–24